The Nature and Treatment of Depression

The Nature and Treatment of Depression

Frederic F. Flach, M.D.
Suzanne C. Draghi, M.D.

A Wiley Biomedical-Health Publication

John Wiley & Sons
New York • London • Sydney • Toronto

Library of Congress Cataloging in Publication Data:

Flach, Frederic F
The nature and treatment of depression.

(A Wiley biomedical-health publication)
Includes bibliographical references and index.
1. Depression, Mental. 2. Manic-depressive psychoses
I. Draghi, Suzanne C., joint author. II. Title.
[DNLM: 1. Depression. WM207 F571n]
RC537.F55 616.8'528 74-28265
ISBN 0-471-26271-4

Printed in the United States of America

10 9 8 7 6 5 4 3 2

Authors

Baldessarini, Ross J., M.D., Chief, Neuropharmacology Laboratory, Psychiatric Research Laboratories and Associate Psychiatrist, Massachusetts General Hospital, Boston, Massachusetts; Associate Professor of Psychiatry, Harvard Medical School, Cambridge, Massachusetts

Cadoret, Remi, M.D., Professor of Psychiatry, Department of Psychiatry, University of Iowa College of Medicine, Iowa City, Iowa

Chernik, Doris A., Ph.D., Clinical Research Scientist, Hoffman-LaRoch, Inc., Nutley, New Jersey

Diethelm, Oskar, M.D., Professor Emeritus of Psychiatry, Cornell University Medical College, New York, New York

Draghi, Suzanne C., M.D., Clinical Instructor in Psychiatry, Cornell University Medical College, New York, New York; Psychiatrist to Out Patients, Payne Whitney Clinic, New York Hospital, New York, New York

Dunner, David L., M.D., Psychiatrist, Department of Internal Medicine, New York State Psychiatric Institute, New York, New York; Assistant Professor of Clinical Psychiatry, College of Physicians and Surgeons, Columbia University, New York, New York

Faragalla, Farouk, D.Sc., Department of Mental Health, Division of Research, Raleigh, North Carolina

Fieve, Ronald R., M.D., Chief of Psychiatric Research, Lithium Clinic and Metabolic Unit, New York State Psychiatric Institute, New York, New York; Professor of Clinical Psychiatry, College of Physicians and Surgeons, Columbia University, New York, New York

Flach, Frederic F., M.D., Associate Clinical Professor of Psychiatry, Cornell University Medical College, New York, New York; Attending Psychiatrist, Payne Whitney Clinic, New York Hospital, New York, New York

Goldfarb, Alvin I., M.D., Associate Clinical Professor of Psychiatry, Mount Sinai School of Medicine of the City University of New York, New York, New York; Associate Attending Psychiatrist in Charge of Geriatric Services, Mount Sinai Hospital, New York, New York

Hogan, Barbara K., Ph.D., Assistant Director, Sex Treatment and Education Program, Cornell University Medical College, Payne Whitney Clinic, New York Hospital, New York, New York

Hogan, Peter, M.D., Associate Professor of Psychiatry, Cornell University

Medical College, New York, New York; Associate Attending Psychiatrist, Payne Whitney Clinic, New York Hospital, New York, New York

Ilaria, Robert, M.D., Clinical Director, Maryview Community Mental Health Center, Portsmouth, Virginia

Malmquist, Carl P., M.D., M.S., Professor of Law, Criminal Justice and Child Development, University of Minnesota, Minneapolis, Minnesota

Mendels, Joseph, M.D., Professor of Psychiatry and Chief, Affective Diseases Research Unit, Department of Psychiatry, University of Pennsylvania, Philadelphia, Pennsylvania; Veteran's Administration Hospital, Philadelphia, Pennsylvania

Mendelson, Myer, M.D., Professor of Clinical Psychiatry, University of Pennsylvania School of Medicine, Philadelphia, Pennsylvania; Senior Attending Psychiatrist, Institute of the Pennsylvania Hospital, Philadelphia, Pennsylvania

Motto, Jerome A., M.D., Chief, Psychiatric Service, San Francisco General Hospital, San Francisco, California; Professor of Psychiatry, University of California School of Medicine, San Francisco, California

Paykel, Eugene S., M.D., Consultant Psychiatrist, St. George's Hospital and Medical School, London, England

Prange, Arthur J., Jr., M.D., Professor of Psychiatry, Department of Psychiatry, Medical School, University of North Carolina at Chapel Hill, Chapel Hill, North Carolina

Sachar, Edward J., M.D., Professor of Psychiatry and Neuroscience, Albert Einstein College of Medicine, Bronx, New York

Salzman, Leon, M.D., Clinical Professor of Psychiatry, Albert Einstein College of Medicine, Bronx, New York; Deputy Director, Bronx Psychiatric Center, Bronx State Hospital, Bronx, New York

Stein, Aaron, M.D., Clinical Professor of Psychiatry, Mount Sinai School of Medicine of the City University of New York, New York, New York; Attending Psychiatrist and Chief, Group Therapy Division, Mount Sinai Hospital, New York, New York

Weiner, Irving B., Ph.D., Professor and Chairman, Department of Psychology, Case Western Reserve University, Cleveland, Ohio

West, Louis Jolyon, M.D., Professor and Chairman, Department of Psychiatry, School of Medicine, Center for the Health Sciences, University of California, Los Angeles, California

Winokur, George, M.D., Professor and Head, Department of Psychiatry, University of Iowa College of Medicine, Iowa City, Iowa

TO OUR PARENTS

Preface

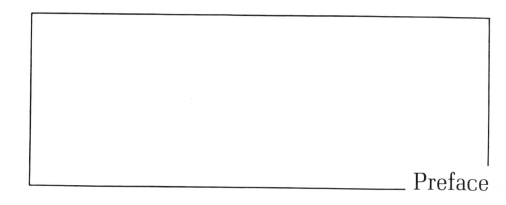

The most widely observed phenomena are often the least comprehended. Depression, a condition long recognized in its most limited aspects, and poorly understood, has come to reveal itself to investigators as multiple in etiology and presentation. Initial analytical theories postulated intrapersonal reactions to external factors as the precipitant of depression. From this grew inquiries posing the age old mind-body dilemma—how do such variations in mood affect the body's internal homeostatic mechanism, and conversely, do changes in physiologic functioning precipitate the mood changes observed. No individual is immune to his environment, either past or present, so any inquiry must take into consideration interpersonal relationships in all their aspects—from the relationship of man with man to the broader confrontation of man with society.

It was recognized that man appears subject to depression at almost any age of his life, and that although certain parameters of recognition are frequently present, depression may exist under numerous disguises, impairing individual functioning and disturbing personal environment, until the depression is recognized and treated. For example, the depression of adolescence may present itself in a far different manner than the depression of old age, and both may easily go undetected unless carefully understood.

Recognizing the varied and often confusing theories as to the etiology, identification, and treatment of depression, it is the aim of this book to bring together experts who have worked extensively in the area of depression, so as to present a comprehensive, integrated review of the subject. We hope that an increased understanding of the theories of the etiology of depression, both psychological and physiological, and the varying presentations of depression will make the treatment of depression more meaningful, easier to facilitate, and more widely practiced. Finally, it is our sincere hope that an increased awareness and understanding of depression will lead to the exploration and adoption of preventive measures, so that man may be more fully free to engage in life.

FREDERIC F. FLACH, M.D.

SUZANNE C. DRAGHI, M.D.

New York, New York
October 1974

Contents

index summary

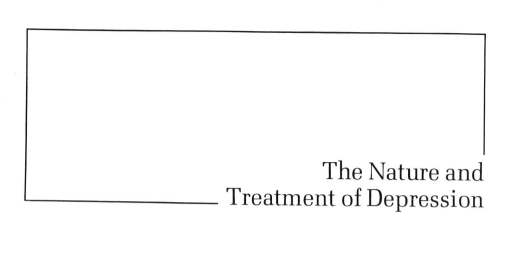

The Nature and Treatment of Depression

One

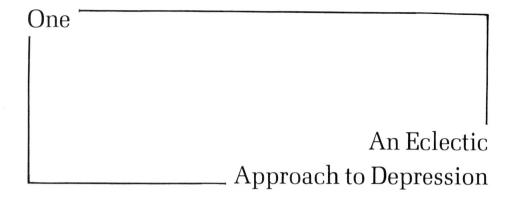

An Eclectic Approach to Depression

Frederic F. Flach, M.D.
Suzanne C. Draghi, M.D.

During the last 15 years, interest in the problem of depression has risen sharply. There are several apparent reasons for this trend. The introduction of tricyclic antidepressant drugs provided a new treatment approach to depression, one which could be employed not only by the psychiatrist but also by the primary physician. The effectiveness of the antidepressants, as well as that of electric convulsive treatments, underscored the probability of significant biochemical and physiological contributants to certain types of depressed states and promoted active research into the role of biogenic amines, mineral metabolism, and endocrine metabolism in depression.

A second major impetus came from popular media, which inevitably influence the direction of professional thinking. The coverage given to new developments in treatment, ranging from lithium for the control of manic-depressive states to fresh psychotherapeutic approaches such as transactional analysis, family therapy, and encounter groups, focused attention on the fact that depression is a condition which affects millions of people (1)—a condition which is definable, recognizable, treatable, and, in a real sense, preventable.

The major contribution to the treatment of depression in the 1930s was the introduction of electric convulsive therapy (2). During the next two decades, traditional psychoanalysis was shown to be of limited usefulness in modifying the course of a depressed mood, although it was doubtless of value for certain patients in reshaping attitudes and character traits that made the individual more prone to a recurrence of depression. The studies of Mabel Blake Cohen (3), for example, clarified some of the intrapersonal dynamics relevant to the manic-depressive patient.

With the introduction of chlorpromazine in the mid-1950s, it was possible to control fear, agitation, insomnia, and paranoid features as they might occur in the setting of depression, to carry out intensive dynamic psychotherapy while the patient was still depressed and still motivated to participate in treatment (4). With the advent of effective antidepressant drugs in the late 1950s, the rate of hospitalization for depression began to fall. Newer psychotherapeutic techniques were employed—specifically, short-term psychotherapy, crisis intervention approaches, group therapy, and family therapy. The patient was no longer seen as being depressed all by himself, but rather as part of a system of people living within a particular environment. His recovery and continued well-being depended not only on biological therapy and psychotherapy, but also on a constructive modification of his environment.

In the late 1960s another new perspective was introduced. A patient's depression was not seen just as an illness. It was, in fact, an important opportunity for the depressed individual to become motivated toward gaining insight into himself and toward improving his ability to cope with his personal world after recovery. This concept was reinforced strongly by the contributions of R. D. Laing (5) to the conceptualization and management of the schizophrenic patient. Many professionals raised the question: Is depression an illness, or is it often an appropriate mood experienced by people faced with certain kinds of stresses? Can the failure to become depressed be as much a problem as being depressed? Are the categories into which depression has been divided for decades—the exogenous as opposed to the endogenous, the agitated or retarded or paranoid, the postpartem, middle-life, or aging period, the psychoneurotic as opposed to the psychotic—tenable and valid? How does the depressed phase of the manic-depressive reaction differ qualitatively from the depression which is a direct response to many life stresses occurring in a short period of time, as demonstrated by Paykel (6) and others?

There is a very real need at the present time for a careful review of what is known about depression, and a reconsideration of its complex nature to set the groundwork for future research into etiology and treatment. To the extent that a depressed mood often seriously immobilizes the individual and is accompanied by an extensive loss of perspective, distortions in reality testing, and at times a high risk of suicide, it must be considered a disorder in coping that requires professional attention. Certain forms of depression, such as the depressed phase of the manic-depressive reaction, or, as it is now termed, bipolar mood disorder, suggest an important genetic factor with specific biologic changes, needing special treatment approaches such as the use of lithium to terminate manic excitements and possibly prevent recurrences of the mood swings.

On the other hand, there are many individuals who think themselves depressed or who may be described as being depressed who are, in fact, going through episodes of grief, discouragement, and disappointment. Some recover rapidly from the depressed mood with brief psychotherapeutic support alone. Others slowly enter a prolonged state of chronic depression that sometimes disappears "spontaneously" over a period of time, at other times is relieved by the administration of antidepressant medication in conjunction with psychotherapy, and at other times only by a major environmental change. Among such patients, the difference between a depressed mood that is normal and one that is a disorder of some type may lie not in the mood of depression itself, but in the lack of resilience to recover from the depression in a reasonable period of time. The biological changes that have been noted in certain patients recovering from states of depression, such as a decrease in the urinary and fecal excretion of calcium and the increase in calcium deposition in bone, may reflect the activation of such "resilience mechanisms" rather than a direct correlation with the mood itself (7, 8).

The variety of ways in which depression manifests itself and the settings in which it can occur raise the question of whether certain central changes in the psychological and behavioral aspects of the individual seem to be consistently associated with depression. Transcultural studies of depression offer some insight into this problem (9). Certain signs of depression, for example, have been found to be common to all cultures (10); these include insomnia with early morning awakening, social withdrawal, and a loss of interest in one's usual pursuits. However, there appears to be a marked difference between the way in which the mood is experienced in certain parts of Africa and its form in western Europe and the United States. In the former cultures, the element of guilt is singularly lacking, and there is a greater tendency to project the reasons for suffering onto the environment; consequently, anger and hostility are externalized and directed outwardly. In western cultures, on the other hand, the subjective feelings of guilt and personal responsibility are prominent. The individual often feels that he alone is responsible for his distress or failure, and his anger is directed inwardly, against himself. This difference between the two cultures, it is postulated, is rooted in the contrast in child-rearing practices, the nature of tribal and family life, and the value systems of the cultures.

It is apparent that any approach to depression, theoretical or practical, must be eclectic and take into account biological, psychological, environmental, intrapersonal, and interpersonal factors in an integrated way (11). With such an approach, the therapist can avoid not only the limitations of diagnostic rigidity, but also the tyranny of therapeutic exclusiveness, wherein the patient is treated only according to the lines to which the particular physician adheres. There are numerous therapeutic modalities available; the approach to be taken in an individual instance depends on the evaluation of the total picture which the patient presents. Although the therapist cannot expect to be skilled in every treatment process, it is essential that he be aware of the various possibilities and that he know when and how to apply them or that he refer the patient to someone else who is better trained to use a particular technique. If a patient enters into a major depressive reaction following a death in the family, for example, he may require antidepressant medication, or, if severely depressed and acutely suicidal, electric convulsive treatments. He may also require active intensive psychotherapy to enable him to settle the conflictual feelings involved in his relationship with the person who has died. In the course of psychotherapy, it may become apparent that the patient also has serious marital difficulties and that he will not be able to recover and remain effective unless these are also resolved. The therapist may be able at the right moment to engage the patient and his spouse in joint therapy. It may well be that to facilitate a resolution of interpersonal difficulties, special techniques—an encounter group experience or videotape playback sessions—will be indicated, and he may refer the patient for such additional therapy to someone skilled in these methods. While it is true that many depressed individuals respond well to brief psychotherapy and biological treatment, it is equally true that others present much more complex clinical pictures and require a more encompassing approach to their care.

In reconceptualizing the treatment of depression, it is important that the therapist recognize that a depressed mood may be, in itself, a normal phenomenon. After an experience of loss or an experience that hurts an individual's self-esteem, a sense of futility and lowered self-worth is to be expected. With this attitude toward the patient's experience, the therapist not only can more quickly enlist the cooperation of the patient in therapy, but also, from the very beginning, can eliminate or modify two important resistances: the tendency of the patient to incorporate the treatment experience into his depression in such a way as to see it as further confirmation of his weakness or inadequacy, and secondly, his conscious or unconscious tendency to build unreal assumptions about what can be expected from therapy—to assume, for instance, that he will remain free forever after of feelings of sadness and discouragement. The depressed person is already suffering with a lowered self-esteem, and in this culture he often feels guilty about being depressed. Entry into therapy may be seen by him as confirmation of his lack of self-worth and as further evidence of defeat. The more quickly the therapist convinces him that admitting to his need is not grounds for a sense of failure, but rather an opportunity for recovery and growth, the more quickly the patient can engage the therapist in a constructive rapport which will serve as the basis for future therapy. At the same time, the therapist should retain the authority of his medical role. Being aware of the suffering and immobilization which the patient experiences, he must communicate to the patient that he both understands and can treat the depression in an effective way.

The basis for the selection of a treatment strategy is the initial consultation—whether it takes an hour or several sessions, whether it involves only the patient or includes visits with the patient's family or other relevant figures in his life. Futhermore, setting the goals for treatment is an evolving process. The therapist must be prepared to modify his plans and expectations and techniques as he learns more and more from dealing directly with the patient and with the patient's situation. At first, it may be difficult to determine whether the patient is actually suffering with a depression or is reactively discouraged because of a state of profound anxiety and tension. The response to the first therapeutic session or two is significant diagnostically. There is an important difference between the patient who, after two or three sessions, notes a genuine improvement in his mood and outlook, and the one whose depression persists regardless of psychotherapeutic efforts. On the other hand, depression may be masked by anxiety and tension. The patient may initially appear to be suffering with various psychoneurotic symptoms. Only over a period of weeks, as the therapist becomes aware of the chronicity and tenacity of the tension, may he recognize that he is dealing with a fundamental depression and be guided accordingly in his treatment. It is commonplace to see a patient in consultation who has been treated over a period of several years with various forms of psychotherapy—with minimal relief—obtain a striking response to tricyclic antidepressant drugs, even though he would not have described himself as being "depressed."

Even in the setting of severe depression—when the patient may be deeply depressed, retarded or agitated, or even delusional—an eclectic approach to therapy should be employed, based on an integrated knowledge of the psychological, biological, and environmental aspects of depression. A serious loss can trigger a depression of psychotic proportions in vulnerable individuals. Such a patient may be seriously suicidal and unable to function, and may require brief hospitalization for protection, evaluation, and treatment. The therapist will then have to select an approach from among a variety of treatment modalities. Electric convulsive treatments will usually clear away the depressive symptoms rapidly and effectively, but the confusion and memory changes that accompany these treatments may interfere with active psychotherapy. He may prefer, in selected patients, to use antidepressant drugs instead, either alone or in combination with antianxiety drugs or phenothiazines. If, for instance, the depression is accompanied by paranoid ideation and fear, he will find it necessary to add phenothiazines to the regime of antidepressant medication to obtain an adequate response. In certain patients, he may note a rapid settling of the fear and depression with hospitalization; this should alert him to the probability that important environmental factors contribute to the patient's acute reactions. He may therefore withhold biological treatments until he is better able to identify the nature of the situational factors, and, in the end, may find that neither electric convulsive treatments nor antidepressants are required at all.

It is of considerable importance that the therapist recognize the many complications that the depression, long-standing and often unrecognized, may have caused for the individual. A 36-year-old lawyer, for example, entered therapy with a very severe depression characterized by marked insomnia, agitation, suicidal preoccupations, and strong feelings of hopelessness. This reaction was set off by his wife's decision to divorce him after a long period of marital strife. An analysis of his background revealed that he had experienced a mild depression during his second year in law school after his father's death. While suffering with a lowered sense of self-esteem, he married a young woman who had pursued him actively, and who subtly but deftly controlled him and made him feel increasingly dependent on her. The relationship remained in equilibrium for some time, but in subsequent years he began to suffer with recurrent depressive episodes which his wife regarded as evidence of weakness in his character. In an effort to escape her control and restore some degree of self-esteem, he began an extramarital affair, over which he felt considerable guilt. When his wife learned of the affair, she moved to divorce him; this event precipitated the acute depressive episode. In essence, he had attempted to resolve the initial depression, occurring after his father's death, by marrying—thereby complicating his life through poor selection and setting himself up for chronic and recurrent episodes of depression, culminating in a depression of psychotic proportions when his wife rejected him.

The importance of the complications which depression, unrecognized and untreated, can produce is relevant not only to treatment but also to the theoretical basis of the etiology of recurrent or chronic depressed states. It has been postulated, for example, that patients with recurrent depressive episodes may be suffering from a disorder that is fundamentally physiological in nature and that this accounts for the rhythmic quality of the condition—the tendency of the depressed mood to recur at somewhat regular intervals. At the same time, what may appear to be a biologically determined phenomenon may, in fact, involve a combination of unresolved conflicts within the individual—a failure to handle hostility adequately, for instance, as well as an ongoing or recurrent environmental situation, such as sexual problems or employment conditions which reinforce his low regard for himself.

Clinical experience points up the importance of understanding thoroughly the circumstances of the very first depressive episode in a series of such episodes to understand the dynamic basis and common threads running throughout the course of the condition. In the case of the young lawyer cited above, the death of the father triggered a depressive response because it involved the loss of a key person on whom the patient had been strongly dependent. In his marriage to an insensitive and controlling woman, his dependency needs were encouraged and rejected simultaneously, and his major depression, occurring at the time of her separation from him, involved the same psychodynamics as his first episode and other recurrences in between.

Complications of depression can take other routes as well. Alcoholism is one route. Men and women who become overtly alcoholic after the age of 40 or 50 frequently demonstrate an unrecognized period of depression prior to the emergence of the alcoholism that is often concealed by the use of alcohol. By fostering denial, self-deception, and ambivalence, and by facilitating a pattern of self-destructive behavior that may demolish family life or destroy economic security, the use of alcohol seriously delays the patient's coming to terms with the depression. That this pattern characterizes a special group of patients is documented by the clinical observation that, although treatment is more complicated and prolonged than for the average middle-life depression, the prognosis for recovery among patients with alcoholism and depression in combination is better than for many other forms of alcoholism.

Even as depression may occur in association with alcoholism, so too may such a mood change be seen in other diagnostic settings—schizophrenia, for example. While it is correct to interpret the unhappiness and feelings of futility of many patients in various types of schizophrenic states as resulting from their psychopathologic impairment and the difficult life situations that result, it is also correct that such patients, faced with loss, guilt, unexpressed anger, or other dynamic factors ordinarily associated with depression, can experience the same change in mood with the same lack of biological resilience as that demonstrated by patients with primary mood disorders. There is no reason why an individual cannot experience more than one kind of psychopathologic change, and this fact, in turn, should guide the therapist in selecting appropriate methods of treatment. A 20-year-old schizophrenic girl had been hospitalized for nearly 2 years with irregular evidence of improvement on a regime of psychotherapy, phenothiazines, milieu therapy, and group therapy. The persistence of self-destructive behavior patterns and suicidal impulses suggested the presence of an important depressive element, but because the current rationale for the treatment of schizophrenia, especially in private institutional settings, calls for drug therapy, she was not given electric convulsive treatments. Finally, almost in "desperation," electric convulsive therapy was instituted and led to a substantial clinical improvement. Evidence of a schizophrenic thinking disorder persisted, but the patient was dramatically less self-destructive and withdrawn, slept better, socialized more, and was able to be discharged to a half-way house for further rehabilitation. In short, one diagnosis should not preclude the possibility of another, particularly in the case of a significant mood involvement.

A recent study reported that psychopathic or sociopathic individuals demonstrated a significant improvement when given antidepressant drugs—a finding that again indicates that depression may be present in a variety of diagnostic settings, and perhaps even more importantly, the possibility that depression may be masked by antisocial behavior. It has been shown that the direct manifestation of depression is more common in highly structured societies. In more loosely structured societies, individuals have a greater tendency to translate conflicts into aberrant behavior patterns such as compulsive promiscuity, unethical business practices, violence, family disruption. Among adolescents, in particular, depression may be hidden by a pattern of behavioral disturbance—failure in school, withdrawal from social contacts, destructive actions, drug abuse. An important aspect of therapy is to combine the interruption of the behavior defense with treatment for the underlying depression. Attempting to do one without the other usually leads to poor treatment outcome.

The challenge to the psychiatrist and other therapists is the need for versatility and flexibility in the treatment of depression as it may occur in various settings. Moreover, the management of depression presents the clinician with a special set of countertransference problems. One of the most commonly encountered problems is the conflict within the therapist about employing biological and psychological methods of treatment with the same individual (12). In the biological research unit of a psychiatric hospital during the 1960s, it was demonstrated that the transfer of a patient to this unit for investigation of mineral and endocrine metabolism in association with biological treatment for depression usually led to a striking decrease in the interest of the patient's psychotherapist in the pursuit of psychological and environmental factors in the patient's condition. This phenomenon was partly due to the therapist's difficulty in envisioning and working with depression as a psychobiological entity, and partly due to his need for total control of the patient; when he was confronted with the need to share responsibility for the patient with other psychiatrists assigned to the research unit, his interest in the patient diminished considerably.

Two other countertransference problems deserve special mention. The first involves the feelings of anger and hostility which the depressed patient may stir up in the physician. Failure to anticipate and cope directly with these feelings may provoke the therapist to unwittingly, but hurtfully, reject the patient in one way or another. The second, and perhaps more significant, problem is the sense of futility and hopelessness which the patient may produce in the therapist. The patient communicates his own mood and, by so doing, may affect the therapist's mood. This is a particularly important problem for psychiatrists who, it has been reported, demonstrate the highest rate of suicide of any professional group. These findings suggest that a certain number of psychiatrists may be depression-prone themselves and curiously vulnerable to the impact of their depressed patients. This tendency has undoubtedly been reinforced by the traditional and often detrimental lack of involvement of the therapist in the therapeutic process. Passivity and the listening role have been so overemphasized that the therapist often has no outlet for his own feelings as they occur in the course of treatment.

Treatment of the depressed individual calls for active participation by the psychiatrist for several other specific reasons—among them the tendency of the depressed patient to interpret the therapist's silence as a reaffirmation of his feelings of hopelessness and guilt. Also, an active therapist can stimulate energy in the patient, and help him learn healthier ways of experiencing emotions by seeing them appropriately managed by the therapist. A more involved participation on the part of the therapist will not only serve the patient well, but also will relieve the therapist of some of his countertransference difficulties. Limiting the number of hours spent in direct patient care will also benefit the psychiatrist, especially when confronted with depressed patients. And finally, equally beneficial would be a better balance between individual therapy and more active pursuits, professional or social, in which the physician can take greater initiative and be more active.

A reconsideration of depression from an eclectic perspective not only will improve the approach to the treatment of depressed patients, but also will stimulate research into the etiology of depression. Envisioning the depressed individual in terms of his intrapsychic dynamics does not preclude seeing him as part of a system of interpersonal relationships—as an inhabitant of an environment that may be ego-bolstering or depressogenic. And this viewpoint does not preclude the recognition of the importance of biologic contributants to the depressed state or to the persistence of the depressed state. Moreover, changes in biogenic amines do not eliminate the possible importance of changes in mineral metabolism or endocrine function. There is no reason to adhere exclusively to any one school of thought—biological or psychological.

An eclectic vantage point will also permit the development of effective programs of prevention. Prevention in medicine can be conceived of in three stages—primary, secondary, and tertiary. Primary prevention involves the alteration of those factors that contribute to an illness so that the condition cannot develop in the first place. Secondary prevention involves earlier diagnosis and more effective treatment for the condition. Tertiary prevention involves proper aftercare to reduce the likelihood of a recurrence of the problem.

Preventive efforts with regard to depression have emphasized secondary and tertiary prevention—assisting the patient in recognizing the condition earlier, in seeking appropriate help for it, and in staying well afterward. Lesse (13) in his important study demonstrated that a 2- to 5-year time lapse usually separated the onset of depression and the point at which the individual or his family made an effort to reach out for help. During this period of time, innumerable complications resulted from the presence of the mood, in particular family and employment disruptions. A vital element in secondary prevention is sharpening the diagnostic skills of those most likely to first encounter the depressed person—the primary physician (particularly when the depression presents itself as sleep difficulty or a physical disorder) (14), the clergyman (especially when the depression is associated with strong elements of guilt or is enmeshed with marital and family difficulties), the school teacher (particularly when the depression shows itself as academic failure, interpersonal difficulties, or acting out on the part of children and teenagers), and the business executive (as when depression is associated with a falling off in work productivity and motivation). Closely related to the goal of earlier diagnosis and treatment is the establishment of a climate in which the individual can recognize depression in its myriad forms, know where to seek the help he needs, and be able to reach out for such help intelligently and without embarrassment (15).

Tertiary prevention, by and large, depends on the judicious use of antidepressant agents and, in manic-depressive or bipolar states, the continued use of lithium; active psychotherapy, short-term and long-term, to modify those psychodynamic factors within the personality that constitute a special vulnerability to depression; and suitable alterations of the environment, through family therapy, marital therapy, and changes in living and in occupational conditions, to diminish those forces in the life situation of the patient that work against his continued adjustment.

Programs of primary prevention must still be considered in their infancy. Eventually it may be possible to use information regarding the genetic factors in mood disorders, particularly of the bipolar type, in an effectively preventive manner, but these guidelines are not yet sufficiently clear. To the extent that certain psychological and environmental factors have been shown to be pertinent to depression, however, it is possible to create and activate educational programs designed to improve the individual's ability to cope with loss, anger, guilt, dependency needs, multiple stresses occurring over a limited period of time, and similar relevant factors. Such programs could be incorporated within the framework of health education in schools, and designed for family use by means of workshops and media presentations. Also, on an experimental basis, it may be feasible to identify depressogenic environments within organizations and institutions and modify these constructively, not only benefiting the individual in these groups but also improving the overall effectiveness of the groups themselves.

The keynote to an intelligent and useful comprehension of depression is an eclectic approach to research as well as to treatment. It is the purpose of this volume to present the problem of depression in a broad and encompassing manner and to avoid the hazards of absolutism, which, although appealing as a way of seizing attention and quieting the scientist's own insecurities, serve well neither the patient nor the search for truth.

References

1. Sørenson A, Strömgren E: Frequency of depressive states within geographically delimited population groups. *Acta Psychiatr Scand (Suppl)* **162:**62, 1961.

2. Kalinowsky L, Hippius H: *Pharmacological, Convulsive and Other Somatic Treatments in Psychiatry.* New York and London, Grune & Stratton, 1969, 4th ed.
3. Cohen MB, Baker G, Cohen RA, Fromm-Reichman F, Weigert EV: An intensive study of 12 cases of manic-depressive psychoses. *Psychiatry* **17:** 103–137, 1954.
4. Flach FF: The use of chlorpromazine to facilitate intensive dynamic psychotherapy in depression. *Psychiatr Neurol* **134**(5):289–297, 1957.
5. Laing RD: *The Divided Self.* London, Tavistock, 1959.
6. Paykel ES, Myers JK, Dienelt MN, Kierman GL, Lindenthal JJ, Pepper MP: Life events and depression. *Arch Gen Psychiatr* **21**(6):753, December 1969.
7. Flach FF: Calcium metabolism in states of depression. *Br J Psychiatr* **110**(467):588–593, 1964.
8. Faragalla FF, Flach FF: Studies of mineral metabolism in mental depression. *J Nerv Ment Dis* **151**(2):120–129, 1970.
9. Kiev A: *Transcultural Psychiatry.* New York, The Free Press, London, Collier-MacMillan, 1972.
10. Murphy HBM, Wittkower ED, Chance NA: Cross cultural inquiry into the symptomatology of depression: A preliminary report. *Int J Psychiatr* **3**(1):6–22, 1967.
11. Flach FF, Regan PF: *Chemotherapy in Emotional Disorders: The Psychotherapeutic Use of Somatic Treatments.* New York, McGraw-Hill, 1960.
12. Sheard MH: The influence of doctor's attitude on patient's response to antidepressant medication. *J Nerv Ment Dis* **136:**555, 1963.
13. Lesse S: The multivariant masks of depression. *Am J Psychiatr (Suppl)* **124**(11):35, May 1968.
14. Flach, FF: *Depression: Key Factors in Diagnosis and Management.* New York, audio cassette developed by The Life Sciences Advisory Group, 1973.
15. Flach, FF: *The Secret Strength of Depression.* New York, JB Lippincott Co, 1974.

Two

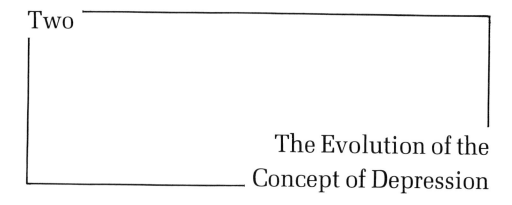

The Evolution of the Concept of Depression

Oskar Diethelm, M.D.

The present concept of depression, taken broadly, includes a group of illnesses having in common a depressed mood that is a subjective psychological experience. Objectively demonstrable symptoms support the patient's description. The etiology remains unknown. Many hypotheses have been proposed in ancient and modern times, but they can no longer be supported. However, careful clinical observations permit a physician to understand the patient's present condition and its development, and to carry out a plan of treatment.

Although a diagnostic classification does not fit readily a patient's pathological condition, a diagnostic formulation is essential. It forces the physician to carefully evaluate the available clinical data and the relationship of the psychopathology to somatic, psychological, genetic, social, and environmental factors. The result will permit him to be guided by the vast knowledge of these conditions found in medical literature as well as by his personal experience. The important point to keep in mind is that the patient who fits into a diagnostic framework must be studied and treated as an individual.

Depressive illnesses offer a well-chosen example of the complexities of psychiatric disorders. Psychologic and somatic functions are involved, and recovery may be affected through psychotherapy, somatic treatment, or modifications of environmental influences. A brief historical review may offer the background for a critical evaluation of current clinical knowledge, of proposed explanations, and of diagnosis and treatment.

Historical Review (1–3)

Many good clinical observations of mental illness are found in the books of modern medicine, but until the 19th and 20th centuries these were rarely well-described. Diagnosis and treatment followed accepted medical theories, and changes in the field of psychiatric disorders came slowly. Humoral pathology and Hippocratic teaching dominated medicine until the 16th century when changes came about through demand for accurate observations and the development of chemistry and later physics.

Even when the concept of melancholia was based on the theoretical black bile, psychological and constitutional influences were emphasized. In the briefly mentioned but often clearly described observations of Hippocrates and Galen, and of Greek, Roman, and Arabian physicians, the depressive mood and anxiety were stressed. Slowness of thinking and actions were considered important symptoms, as well as withdrawal from social contact, and suspiciousness. Melancholia included both depressive and schizophrenic disorders (catalepsy was considered a separate disease). The opposite of melancholia were excitements, designated by the term mania, and explained by the influence of yellow bile. (In this group were included manic and schizophrenic conditions and excitements of not-yet recognizable exogenic nature). The Greek writer Aretaeus (150–200 A.D.) mentioned that melancholia might be followed by mania. The treatment attempted the elimination of the noxious humor through bleeding, purgation, and sweating, to reestablish a harmony of the humors. In addition, a healthy regime was stressed that included nutritious food, satisfactory fluid intake, regular bowel movements, sufficient sleep, and a balance of rest and exercise. Disturbing influences, including emotional strain, were to be avoided. The same therapeutic rules, with modifications, were followed by the Arabs and the physicians of the 16th and 17th centuries. With a few exceptions, as in 15th century Spain, psychiatric hospitals did not exist but patients were generally treated with kindness.

With progress in chemistry, new theories were applied. A disturbance of the acidity in the body fluids was offered as an explanation of melancholia and treatment through dietary means attempted to reestablish a balance of acidity in the blood. The theoretical black bile was considered an additional factor and had to be eliminated. [Hermann Boerhaave (1668–1738), the famous leader of the school of Leyden, was most effective in presenting these theories through his own teaching and that of his former students which included Cullen in Edinburgh and the leading professors of the reorganized Vienna medical school (4)].

At the end of the 17th century the leading German internist, Friedrich Hoffmann (1660–1747), rejected the existence of black bile and offered a mechanical concept of change in the dura mater. Through him the therapeutic importance of mineral spring water, whose therapeutic value had been mentioned in previous centuries, was emphasized. It led to the development of spas in Europe and later in America, and was found to be especially helpful for mild depressions.

The humanist Juan Vives (1492–1540) (5) had directed attention to the role of emotions. The outgrowth of his influence in medicine is difficult to recognize but might be illustrated by the dissertation of Johann Hofer (1688) (6). He and others following him described a depression which he called nostalgia and presented psychodynamic factors involved—strong emotional dependence on the family and the home environment, leading to inability to adapt to the life and the people in a strange university city; sadness; hopelessness; and suicidal urge. The main therapy was encouragement of the patient and return to his family where he improved rapidly. (A hundred years later a leading Swiss scientist explained the illness by differences in the air of the Alps and the lowlands, and the patient's inability to adjust to it. In 1914 Karl Jaspers wrote his dissertation on homesickness and murder, illustrating the great progress made in psychological understanding and treatment of depressions).

Clinical progress in the observation of depressive illnesses became noticeable in the 17th century. The Dutch schools of medicine were effective in studying hypochondriasis and separated hypochondriacal depression from hypochondriasis. The English neuroanatomist and physician, Thomas Willis (1621–1675), gave considerable impetus to the study of hysteria and hypochondriasis (6).

A new approach was offered by Georg Ernst Stahl's theory of the body-soul unity which in French medicine led to the school of vitalism (7). The direct effect of Stahl (1660–1734) was increased attention to the psychological aspect in illness, stress on the patient-physician relationship, and the beginning of psychotherapy. Vitalism became accepted by the leading professors in Montpellier and later in Paris. To this group belonged Philippe Pinel (1745–1826), the professor of medicine who later became the reformer of hospital psychiatry.

The physiological contributions of Albrecht Haller (1708–1777) became the basis of the understanding of the nervous system and stimulated William Cullen (1712–1790), who proposed a lengthy systematization of all diseases. Mental illnesses including melancholia belonged to neuroses. His student, John Brown (1735-1788), divided all illnesses into sthenic and asthenic diseases. The latter included depressions. His theory was accepted in Italy, Germany, and the United States. Blood letting, based on Haller's mechanistic theory of blood stoppage in disease, was now considered scientific. The therapeutic effort was to strengthen the asthenic body by large amounts of alcohol and opium.

In the early 19th century F. J. V. Broussais (1772–1838), professor in Paris, postulated that the main pathological condition was gastroenteritis and recommended soft diet and excessive bleeding with leeches. The distinction between depression and hypochondriasis had become blurred toward the end of the 18th century, and physicians considered gastrointestinal disorders of great importance therapeutically. Broussais' theory and treatment were widely accepted.

A relationship of emotions and somatic symptoms was increasingly recognized in the 18th century and helped to clarify mild recurrent depressions and hypochondriasis. However, enthusiastic and dogmatic physicians put an exaggerated emphasis on psychological symptoms. In the period of enlightenment, critical reasoning and uncritical suggestibility and gullibility were both present, the latter resulting in a large number of "vapors" which were psychoneurotic or depressive reactions (8). *Taedium vitae* became fashionable and suicides increased. Prominent writers, through their sentimental presentations, had a destructive influence, especially on youth. The mode of suicide was dramatic and attention-craving. Another method of suicide was well described by Leopold Auenbrugger (9), who had introduced percussion into medicine. His patients attempted or succeeded in killing themselves in a state of excessive depressive anxiety, rushing with their heads against a wall or by other violent means.

The scientific thinking of Newton, Leibniz, and Kant exerted an increasing influence on medicine, including psychiatry. The cellular pathology of Virchow was the final end of humoral pathology. In the 19th century, marked progress in neuroanatomy and neurophysiology was made, and related psychopathology, but the clinical observations in depressions and their treatment were not productive. The contributions of English psychiatry of the late 18th and 19th century as well as those of French authors decreased rapidly, except for the clarification of essential deterioration in psychiatric diseases. The result was clearer definition of depressions, and the singling out of dementia praecox, catatonia, and, in the present century, schizophrenia. In the treatment of depressions, the psychiatrists depended on opium for agitated depressions, hydrotherapy, rest cures, and protection against suicide. The individual received less attention than in previous periods. English physicians still considered gastrointestinal disorders and their treatment of fundamental importance. In hospitals increased attention was paid to proper diet but death from starvation could not always be prevented in the chronic state of involutional melancholia.

In the middle of the 19th century, J. P. Falret (10) emphasized that a depression may occur as an isolated illness or as a periodic variety, with or without a manic excitement. The clinical entity of manic-depressive illness became generally accepted.

Kraepelin's attempt (11) to present a classification of all psychiatric illnesses proved to be most successful. His groups were based on etiology, course, physical, and postmortem findings. Well-recognizable clinical entities were generally accepted, including depression, manic-depressive illness, and schizophrenia.

In the beginning of this century, several important changes developed that forced a reconsideration of the diagnostic rigidities. The interest in the individual patient became increasingly accepted. The concept of a psychobiological unit replaced Cartesian psychology. Interest in the development of the personality was strengthened by the theoretical and practical contributions of psychoanalysis. Social and cultural aspects became increasingly evaluated (12, 13). All these manifold theories and findings led to a psychodynamic psychopathology that has remained elastic enough to permit contributions from new concepts and approaches to exert an influence on diagnostic formulations and on treatment.

Psychopathology of Depression

Modern psychopathology might be said to have started at the end of the 19th century when careful clinical observations were expected, and when Kraepelin and his school, based on Wundt's psychophysical parallelism, introduced experimental studies. Their use of drugs demonstrated the effect on thinking and actions, but there was little focus on emotions. Neurological-psychological studies (13) clarified memory functions but contributed less to the understanding of affective disorders. Psychosomatic disorders were studied in general hospitals, and hypnosis was used by O. Vogt and the psychiatrist A. Forel and their students to clarify further the effect of emotions on physiological functions.

In this century, the psychoanalytic school of Freud and his co-workers emphasized the significance of psychodynamics in personality development and in the expression of psychopathological symptoms. The tendency to become interested in emotions to the neglect of other aspects of psychodynamics became adjusted with further advances in psychoanalytic theories and studies.

The concept of the psychobiological unit, in German universities under the influence of monism and in English and American psychiatry through the neurophysiological concept of integration, became increasingly accepted. Under the leadership of A. Meyer, environmental and cultural influences in psychopathology gained recognition (14). Psychologists and sociologists, among them the behaviorist Watson, were able to make their contribution to broadening the study of psychopathology. This psychodynamic emphasis may have resulted in American psychiatry in insufficient interest in furthering the study of symptoms, an approach which has become more advanced in German and French psychiatry under the critical influence of Karl Jaspers and Henri Ey (15).

Modern psychopathology endeavors to understand the patient's personality from a psychological, physiological, social, and cultural point of view, combining careful observation of every symptom, and to investigate the psychodynamic factors involved. Clinicians are under the constant obligation to evaluate how investigative procedure will affect the patient and to avoid any damage which questioning or examination may cause. They have to decide whether a sensitive topic should be avoided because it would be unnecessarily painful or disturbing to the patient. The patient's behavior as well as his verbal communications offer information to the trained observer, whether obtained directly or through persons in the environment. Members of the family, friends, employer and co-workers, nurses, and professionals and employees may contribute to obtaining the needed understanding of the constantly changing psychopathological picture.

Many contributions in the psychopathology of depression have come from psychiatrists connected with psychiatric hospitals or in office practice. Considerable advances have come from the study of milder depressive states and psychoneurotic reactions by skilled therapists outside a psychiatric institute who were interested in keeping careful notes and analyzing them.

In the course of psychopathologic study, any findings have to be evaluated in the setting of the total psychopathologic picture as well as in regard to the patient's personality. In every depressed patient, one must study his behavior and actions, his emotional display as well as his subjective description, and his thinking and intellectual functions. It is not sufficient to obtain the statement of feeling depressed without knowing what other emotions are involved, such as hopelessness, anxiety, and feeling ill-at-ease, and determining what these mean to the patient. A good description of emotions, including their meaning to the patient, will give the physician leads to important underlying psychodynamic factors.

The important emotions include depression and sadness, usually focused on something which the patient believes is related to some life situation or personal experience. Hopelessness means it is useless to struggle against this feeling, a submitting to the situation causing it; anxiety may indicate some concern, guilt, or actual fear of something. Another common emotion is tension, an inability to relax. Tension indicates an unsolvable struggle, a continuous effort that may result in anxiety, fear, or sadness. Body overconcern, whether justified or not, contains anxiety, and may be expressed in gastrointestinal or mild cardiovascular symptoms, breathing difficulties, or general fatigue. Irritability or aggressiveness may be related to underlying anxiety or fear, or to resentment, hate, or anger. In some depressed patients these emotions may be hidden by dependent behavior with an appeal for sympathy or attention, or by repetitious self-blame, resulting in domination over persons or situations. Anger reactions are frequently the expression of fear which will be increased by critical attacks of others or be suppressed by the patient and then deepen a depressed mood because he feels guilty or rejected.

Depressive emotions may be recognized from a sad or tense facial expression, crying, and, when associated with anxiety, sobbing. The voice may become low, hesitant, or staccato, the speech slow. In some patients their motility is slowed, and their activity less spontaneous. The latter is especially noticeable in a group. This behavior led to the concept of retarded depression and may be related to indecision or procrastination because of feeling insecure or being unwilling to respond. Other depressed patients are restless, often to the degree of agitation, because of anxiety and fear. These agitated depressions may also have features of retardation.

In social behavior and especially behavior in groups where spontaneity or prompt response to others is expected, the depressive difficulties become obvious. The patients are unusually quiet and talk little. They avoid contact with others whenever possible. This behavior may be caused by depressive emotions. If their effort to carry out normal activities becomes a strain, they may become afraid of getting worse and may feel guilty for not fulfilling their obligations.

In some patients the thinking disorder, reflected in a slowness in responding to questions, is to some extent related to retardation, but it may also often be caused by tension or anxiety. In other patients the attention is diverted by unhappy or resentful preoccupations. The impairment in attention often becomes obvious in reading, one reason why the patient's selection of reading material should sometimes be guided by the physician's judgment. In aged patients mild disorders of attention, retention, and memory become worse with a depression, but improve again when this illness improves or clears up. The improvement of these symptoms may be striking when the depressive mood abates for a few hours or days.

Delusions may commonly be hypochondriacal, related to guilt or to imagined economic disasters. In other patients, suspiciousness and paranoid delusions may become more fixed for a period of months or longer. These symptoms are considered part of the depression if the content is self-depreciatory. If in such patients the depressive affect becomes absorbed in the formation of the delusion, the strength of the pathological conviction increases. In such cases the nature of the illness can only be recognized from the preceding depressive phase. With improvement these patients begin to express depressive emotions. In others a paranoid chronicity may develop.

Visual hallucinations are rare. They may occur under the influence of marked fear or in a panic state and are often related to illusions. In deep depressions auditory hallucinations accuse the patient of actual or imagined misdeeds and mention punishment.

Somatic changes are common. Loss of weight with intensification of the depression or gain of weight as an early indication of improvement may be explained by poor or increased proper food intake. Unsatisfactory diet or refusal of food was the explanation for death in deeply depressed chronic patients (histopathological changes of "central neuritis" were demonstrated by A. Meyer). Spastic and atonic constipation are common. The typical sleep disorder is early awakening or broken sleep while difficulty in falling asleep is caused by anxiety or tension. Satisfactory and continuous sleep seems to occur in psychoneurotic settings, in immature persons or in the aging period. The menstrual flow may be diminished or cease, accompanied by various degrees of frigidity or impotence. Sexual dreams are absent. The reappearance of sexual desires is often an early sign of improvement.

In most depressive illnesses the emotions and accompanying symptoms are marked in the morning, starting with awakening, and are less intense in the evening. In the depth of the depression, these daily variations may not be recognizable but may occur early with improvement. Gradually the depth of the morning depression lessens, and the depressive mood shortens but can still be noticed in convalescence. Difficulties in making an effort to be active or reach decisions, and lack of interest, concentration, attention, and grasping problems are demonstrable signs that change during the day. In convalescence a mild elation may hide still existing depressive symptoms. Underlying anxiety, related to having to face the demands of life, is often increased by the optimistic pressure of relatives or friends.

Suicidal urges, preoccupations, and attempts may occur in any phase of the illness. The evaluation of the strength of such urges and the prevention of suicide attempts are serious and difficult management considerations. The subjective description of the emotions may offer valuable leads. Hopelessness and despair reflect a diminished resistance to self-destruction. Guilt and shame may be unforgiveable to a depressed person of high and rigid ethical standards. Fear, and its extreme degree, panic, may drive a person to acts that he cannot evaluate. Death by violence may seem to be the only way open. The meaning of death varies greatly and may prevent or facilitate suicide. Investigations into the dynamic factors will often not be possible in the acutely suicidal patient, and the physician must be guided by an interpretation of what the patient's total picture represents. Direct confrontation should be made with great caution. In a hospital where strict supervision is available, more active dynamic psychotherapy may be possible (16). Sudden release of intense emotions—for example, guilt, anger to self, and shame—may be followed by suicidal attempts. The patient's dreams should attract the physician's attention, not for analysis but rather for guidance. Improvement in the depression may not occur rapidly, and the risk of suicide and the life situation of the patient must be evaluated carefully to determine if there are factors with which he cannot deal, or if the physician expects too much too soon. Dissimulation of his self-destructive intentions is often difficult to detect behind a smiling front. Periods of apparent calmness without improvement in the total picture should always put the physician on guard.

A long-lasting influence on the psychodynamic studies of depression resulted from psychoanalytic publication. Freud (17) presented a novel formulation in his "Mourning and Melancholia" which applied the results of the studies of Abraham (18) on infantile sexual activities to depression. Freud's introductory remarks state that melancholia takes on various clinical forms "that do not warrant reduction to a unity." Mourning is the reaction "to the loss of a loved person" or an abstraction which has taken its place, for example, fatherland, liberty, or an ideal. The symptoms may be grave but limited in time. Depression in grief lacks the decrease in self-esteem, while in a depressive illness conscience is affected and self-reproaches are against his ego. These observations led to the conclusion that the illness was a regression to the narcissistic oral phase of the libido, and the grief related to the loss of a particular loved object, oneself. Abraham developed these theories further and formulated the importance of the sadistic anal phase and considered the relationship between depression and compulsion neuroses. A strongly stimulating influence based on these concepts persisted but never resulted in the effect which psychoanalysis had on the clinical understanding of schizophrenia and psychoneuroses. The anal-sadistic and the narcissistic theory may readily be applied to many different symptoms, as may the studies of the formation of character (in the sense of personality). In more recent years emphasis has been directed to the nature of the period of free intervals between depression and an understanding of related hypomanic reactions. The outgrowth of these studies is especially recognizable in present-day psychopathology in the formulation of anxiety, of depression ending in a chronic rut-formation with anger, defeat, and an inability to adjust to unchangeable life situations, of an understanding of guilt feelings, and of the exaggerations in some delusional formation of sinning, physical illness, and poverty.

The main point for the practitioner of psychotherapy constantly to keep in mind is that theories should guide our thinking and be critically applied to technical procedures. Although overlapping, the psychotherapy of psychoneurotic reactions and depressive illness is not the same.

In panic reaction, the culmination of prolonged intense states of tension or anxiety, the underlying psychodynamic factors cannot be studied by direct investigation until the panic state has passed and the depression improved. Confrontation with dynamic factors in the midst of panic may be intolerably threatening to the patient. The careful observation and interpretation of symptoms will offer us dynamic leads to be used at a future stage of psychotherapy. In a panic, homosexual factors are not rare, but these may not be clinically important unless accompanied by other nonsexual emotional factors. The same careful approach to therapy is needed in the management of guilt, shame, or revenge.

The stress on the usual course of illness—limited in duration and terminating in apparent recovery—has resulted in a tendency to neglect dynamic psychotherapy and at best the use of cautious supportive psychotherapy. If such a procedure is to be that of choice, the therapist should note the psychopathologic symptoms in detail and use these clinical observations in the later phases of treatment.

The following case illustrates the necessity to adjust treatment according to changing psychopathology. A 70-year-old woman who had been a widow for 10 years developed a depression, characterized by fatigue, irritability, and sadness. These symptoms increased over a 2-month period. When seen for the first time, she complained of sadness, emptiness of life, lack of self-confidence, increasing tension and slowness in thinking, poor sleep and fearful dreams, loss of appetite and weight, and constipation. Under imipramine medication (150 mg/day) she became less restless and slept better. After 4 weeks she became conscious of desire for sexual intercourse with men she saw on the street, and somewhat later for sexual contact with young nurses. She was fearful and agitated, at times shrieking. Because of its demonstrated effect on sexual unrest, chlorpromazine (50 mg/day) was added to the imipramine and the sexual panic phase was soon controlled. She remained irritable and depressed, with self-accusatory thoughts. Her sexual preoccupations were completely gone after 2 months. Under the effect of imipramine, the depressive symptoms lessened and in the afternoon she was able to resume her normal social activities. When chlorpromazine was discontinued (after 2 months) sexual restlessness and anxiety reappeared and were again controlled by chlorpromazine which was continued for another 6 weeks. Her depression improved steadily, but morning sadness, mild retardation of thinking, and a feeling of futility persisted for several more months. Her daily routine of activities was adjusted accordingly. (The whole illness lasted 15 months). From the psychotherapeutic interviews which were conducted twice a week, it became clear that she had a long-standing severe psychoneurosis (hysterical in nature, with sexual frigidity, occasional phobias, and self-centered behavior). She was ordinarily easily discouraged, having had three previous depressions; a protracted phase of sexual panic accompanied her second depression at age 32. Her mother and a sister had also experienced severe depressions. A diagnostic formulation would state that the patient suffered from a "recurrent depression in the setting of a psychoneurosis [hysteria]." There were no indications of early senile psychopathology.

The period of recovery offers opportunities for active procedures, but the free intervals between depressions offer even more. Although the results of prolonged analytic therapy have not been encouraging, and in fact discouraging, one should recognize that the lack of definitive indications for intensive analysis may be more important than the procedure chosen. Careful studies directed at the causes of failure could give us valuable guidance for the future.

Important situational factors which influence the patient's condition are often treated too cursorily. The effect of the hospital environment has lately received much needed attention. Suicidal risk is usually carefully considered in evaluating a patient for discharge, but insufficient attention may be paid to the psychological and physical environment awaiting the patient, including lack of sympathetic interest or overconcern by friends and family members, the pressure placed on a still insecure person to make even minor decisions, or the meaning of occasional depressive episodes during convalescence. The comfort of feeling protected in the hospital or later at home and some freedom from the pressure to have to fit into a group with their expectations are often needed. The therapist has the responsibility to help the patient to make decisions and offer guidelines, based on changing psychopathology. Assured privacy of conversation with the patient and of sensitive material which relatives may have given is essential. It is always possible to give a co-worker relevant information without bending the privacy rules. There is also a desirable mean between placing a patient in a ward for chronic or highly excited patients or in a therapeutic group where too much is expected of him considering his mild retardation or severe anxiety. One should not expect group participation to a degree which a reserved patient would decline in his healthy life. Nor is it progress in hospital treatment if in the management of a highly disturbed patient one returns to the long-abandoned seclusion rooms or other forms of restraint, even on a temporary basis.

Diagnosis

The diagnosis of an illness is essential for many reasons. It presents the briefest expression of the kind of condition which we deal with and is important as a guide to treatment and to finding relevant references in literature. The danger is that one may not know clearly what the term means and what its limitations are when applied to the individual patient. Furthermore, it may take only a few years to change the meaning of the concept of an illness, and the diagnostic term may no longer fit the expanded medical knowledge.

For half a century, many psychiatrists accepted A. Meyer's proposal to use a diagnostic formulation which would do justice to the individual experiencing the condition. A shortcoming soon became obvious. Considerable knowledge was needed to formulate the essential aspects in a brief statement of one to two lines. Many psychiatrists insisted on including theoretical aspects. Others stated frankly that they accepted only broad terms, for example, psychoses or neuroses; or claimed that there existed no border between normal and pathological conditions or preferred "borderline" diagnosis.

The classification of diseases has been attractive and useful for epidemiological and public health studies. In using the acquired knowledge of other countries or studies published in other languages, restrictions in diagnosis are essential, but they will always be considered an undesired handicap by the practicing psychiatrist and by scientific workers. With the progress of medicine some physicians asked for an abolishment of classification. This proposal was a reaction to the uncritical and extremist development of classification of the 19th century. In psychiatry, and medicine in general, the need for diagnostic statements soon became obvious. In psychiatry it found its best expression in Kraepelin's classification. The progress of dynamic and individualistic psychopathology of the present century, and with it a wide broadening in clinical experience, demanded a reconsideration of diagnostic terms. The present international classification has great advantages over previous attempts, because it implies the necessity to clarify diagnostic formulations without impinging on the right for differing theories. It also accepts that a classification of diseases cannot remain fixed for a restlessly advancing psychiatry and medicine.

"Disease" implies a definable or hypothesized causal explanation, a clinically recognizable course, and, in most cases, positive postmortem findings. In psychiatry this is possible in only a limited number of disorders. In speaking of a psychiatric illness or disease one has to be aware of the limitations for proof. The advances of physics and chemistry have helped little to obtain demonstrable signs. Tests, including psychological procedures, have remained interpretative. They are valuable for a skilled investigator but are often as misleading as chemical or Roentgenological results are to a physician who does not evaluate them in relationship to the total clinical findings. The distinction between (objective) signs and (subjective) symptoms is questioned in medicine and in years past has been rejected by psychiatrists. It is preferable to distinguish between subjective and objective demonstrable symptoms, both of equal importance in reaching a psychiatric diagnosis.

In reaching a full understanding of a patient's illness we must understand the evolution of his complaints and subjective observations, his personality development and present status, his life history and the influences of his family, and his physical and social environment, including the culture in which he has lived. A psychiatric study is presented in a well-organized form which includes the presenting complaints, present illness, past history, personality, and family history. Based on such detailed information the psychiatric examination will be comprehensive, and at the same time, emphasis can be directed to aspects special to this person. This implies that a statement with regard to his physical health is available. The experienced examiner may obtain his facts in a more conversational procedure than does the methodical beginner, but in either case the facts must be recorded and short-cuts in examination avoided. Such an examination may be brief and a tentative diagnosis reached which permits the physician to outline his immediate advice, whether it be further visits to amplify the facts which have been obtained, immediate study and treatment in a hospital, referral to a specialist for special tests, or interviews with members of the family.

Every examination includes therapeutic aspects; for example, reassurance to the patient that the physician tries sincerely to understand him and his problems, and advice, tentative as it may be, about the immediate future. The beginning of a constructive patient-physician relationship is established. Too long an interview should be avoided to prevent undue fatigue or emotional turmoil by having touched on too many problems. It is a good custom to avoid interviews of more than 50 to 60 minutes, the last 10 minutes to be reserved for discussion of conclusions and advice. Additional time may be needed to interview accompanying relatives or friends.

To clarify the diagnosis of a depressive illness some points should be kept in mind. It is not only necessary to obtain a detailed description of the emotional experience but also the patient's reaction to it. These subjective descriptions should be more or less confirmed by the examination in the latter part of the interview and during succeeding therapy. Valuable corroboration may be obtained from the observations of others. The understanding of any preceding similar illness is important. Each illness presents some different aspects that may be quite significant. Any recurrence is disturbing to a patient, often leading to more marked discouragement or helplessness. The suicidal risk may increase. The attitude to increasing age since the preceding depression, added responsibilities, and disturbing life experiences may be meaningful. Some recurrent illnesses may be similar, although never alike. In literature one finds reference to an illness being a photographic copy of a previous one. This statement could be a correct description of a depressive episode but may not include the psychodynamic factors involved and their significance a few years later. Knowledge of the onset of the previous depression, its course, and the phase of convalescence may have a bearing on prognosis and treatment of the current episode.

The review of the life history needs to consider the emotional reactions to stressful situations and the adjustment to them. Stress may be present in school, in work, and in the family. Its significance changes in different life periods, and it is important to ascertain whether the patient has learned to balance emotional strain with suitable diversion or recreation. In recent years a dynamic formulation has been accepted that states that a sufficient degree of impaired reality testing or functional adequacy is to be considered a psychosis. Again, it is a quantitative distinction and does not define "psychosis."

Depressions in daily life may be of short duration and not very intense. Even so, they are significant to the patient and should not be dismissed under the term moody personality. They may represent a range from depressive reactions of a limited time span to specific life situations that can be studied psychotherapeutically. The goal of therapy is to help the patient understand the factors involved and learn to avoid certain situations and, if unavoidable, to tolerate the unpleasant or painful mood.

Depressive features in an incapacitating physical illness deserve constant psychotherapeutic attention and an awareness that minor symptoms may hide the development of a deepening depression that demands a change in the psychotherapeutic approach and often the aid of suitable drugs. Feelings of hopelessness about the physical condition, dread of being a burden to the family and of the family's reaction to it whether hidden from the patient or expressed to him, resentment, or guilt on the part of the patient are commonly seen. Suicidal thoughts are not rare. Any incapacitating illness without the physician being able to offer a satisfactory physical explanation or the knowledge of a self-determining course is a heavy emotional burden which must be evaluated.

Various types of depression are well recognized in psychiatry and grouped according to symptoms, course, and recurrence. Other types are proposed when psychodynamic factors are predominantly involved, for example, reactive, psychogenic, and psychoneurotic depressions. Other illnesses appear to be related to selected life situations—menarche or menopause, pregnancy, childbirth, puberty, and involutional period.

The distinction between psychotic and nonpsychotic depression is as difficult to define as that between psychotic and other psychopathological disorders. Psychosis is often used to describe a major psychiatric illness as opposed to a minor disorder. To the first group belong patients suffering from organic brain syndromes of more than a mild degree—schizophrenia, involutional melancholia, manic-depressive, and paranoid and paranoic illnesses. In all psychotic states the diagnosis is based on the intensity of the psychopathological condition and not on a special psychopathological disorder. (The clearest picture is offered in schizophrenia but even then different opinions exist when one deals with milder degrees of symptoms). For many clinicians this point may not seem important until he is confronted with the question of whether a patient can be certified for commitment, or to what extent a patient's reputation and opportunity are biased by having recovered from what has been termed a psychosis.

The term retarded depression signifies a depressive illness in which sadness and marked mental and motor retardation are outstanding. The patients have difficulty in understanding questions that may have to be repeated, and they are slow in responding. They may appear perplexed. Indecisiveness and inactivity interfer with social activities; even eating becomes an effort. In older literature the term melancholia attonita was applied, and stuporous phases were called benign stupors. The patient usually recovered from this phase which may last several weeks. It is obviously difficult to differentiate this condition from catatonia, especially because many catatonic illnesses are preceded by a depressive phase.

Another depressive reaction that has to be differentiated is characterized by aversion to the environment (e.g., hospital), or to specific persons or situations. The patients are usually self-assertive persons who are unable to yield and may react to treatment, especially therapeutic interference, with resentment and open antagonism. This behavior may be mistaken for schizophrenic negativism. With persistent unacceptable environmental pressure or other dynamic factors, a depressive stupor may result. Aversion may also be accompanied by suspiciousness and fear and lead to a paranoid picture. If persistent individualized psychotherapy can reach the patient, the depression may become displaced and recovery hastened with suitable drug administration. Retardation may become a factor in this symptom formation. However, the presence and effect of intellectual retardation is frequently used too readily to explain severe behavior disorders which are related to hate, suspiciousness, resentment, and fear. Mild retardation, adversely affecting thinking and decisions, is often not recognized in patients who are improving and should accordingly not be urged into activities for which they are not yet ready.

An agitated depression—a descriptive statement that is no longer considered a diagnostic term—is characterized by marked restlessness, which reaches a degree of overactivity that interferes with planned goal-directed activity. In contrast to overactivity in elated states where the patient is too readily distracted, in the agitation of a depressed person there is considerable repetitiousness, monotony, and lack of distractability. The driving emotion is marked anxiety, the expression of underlying or openly expressed guilt or hopelessness and despair. In this depressed state the patient can be reached only with great difficulty, but drug administration may decrease the excessive anxiety and speed up treatment. Sometimes agitated behavior may appear theatrical and instead of evoking sympathetic understanding in other persons may lead to the patient being avoided or openly rejected or criticized. This behavior occurs more often in the age group over 70 (20 years ago in the group over 60) but is largely culturally determined, related to environments where the exaggerated display of suffering is expected.

Tension depressions are characterized by tension being the outstanding emotion observed, concealing to some extent underlying depression. Somatic complaints may bring the patient to the physician. This depression occurs in patients who throughout adult life displayed marked conscientiousness and a need for self-reliance combined with feelings of inadequacy. They have developed an exaggerated tendency to anticipate difficulties and possible failure. Insufficient emancipation from parental or other early identifications is one of the key dynamic factors involved, and this is often expressed in immature habits. In the course of the illness an attitude of aversion to receiving help may become obvious. The patient may appear arrogant, sarcastic, often uncooperative, and evasive to questions. Confrontation with this behavior may increase the symptoms. The suicidal danger is not easily recognized. With an increase of tension, a developing panic reaction may be recognized by suspiciousness, misinterpretations, and fear. In the full panic the intense fear overwhelms the patient's thinking and actions; paranoid delusions may be self-depreciatory; and agitated behavior may reach the intensity of excitement with impulsive acts occurring.

Depressions of the manic-depressive type have been assumed to occur more frequently than a nonbiased observer could corroborate. The combination of melancholia and excitement (mania) has been mentioned in early medical literature, but under melancholia were included depressive reactions as well as chronic schizophrenia and under mania exogenic, schizophrenic, and manic excitements. When Kraepelin presented the manic-depressive disease entity, he brought diagnostic order into the clinical picture. In succeeding years critical observations and progressive psychopathological understanding led to a narrower application of the diagnosis. At present one can state that any depression that was preceded or followed by a well-marked period of elation, in close or distant relationship of time, belongs to the manic-depressive group. The physician must keep in mind that in direct time relationship a hypomanic picture may be the expression of underlying anxiety or depression and could involve a suicidal danger. The prognosis of these depressions is good for recovery but uncertain about future recurrences. The so-called mixed manic-depressive illnesses are not a separate type but represent a transitional stage in which symptoms of depression and manic excitement occur simultaneously. The resulting thinking disorder, including perplexity, confusion, and distractability with retardation, makes therapeutic contact difficult and often conceals potential suicidal dangers.

Involutional depressive reactions occur in the involutional period which includes roughly the period after 50. They must be differentiated from cerebral arteriosclerotic and senile depressions. It is the first well-defined depression in the patient's life, has a long duration (1 to 3 years), and ends in recovery. The depressed mood with surliness and irritability, distorted hypochondriacal and guilt delusions with need for punishment, and untidiness and incontinence of stool and urine has in the past made psychotherapy and general treatment difficult. Retardation, anxiety, and thinking disorders are usually marked. Fortunately, these disturbing disorders react well to convulsive therapy, and the duration of the illness may be shortened to a few months. The dynamic therapeutic investigations may take a considerable period of time during which a mild depression persists but interferes little with most daily activities. There is no evidence that particular physiological factors are primarily responsible. It is emphasized in literature that before their illness these patients were rigid and overly conscientious. When the patient is able to cooperate fully it usually becomes obvious that the depression started several weeks before it became recognized. The early onset was hidden by hypochondriacal complaints, unsatisfactory sleep, lack of usual interest, irritability, and indecision. The psychological factors may relate to the insecurities of the life period, such as economic and work insecurity, decrease of sexual activities and satisfactions, change in physical appearance and strength, approaching retirement, and realization of the limitation of hope for achievements.

In all depressions there are situational factors that demand attention and adjustment to them or correction. Sometimes they have precipitated the illness; sometimes, in fact, they seem to have been so important that one speaks of a situational depression. The historically best-known situational depression is nostalgia.

A similar situation is presented by separation from person or persons who have been important, on whom one has leaned too strongly, or who have been an important love object. These factors play a significant role in every person's life. The separation causes sadness or even anxiety, but this reaction is not a depressive illness. This diagnosis can only be justified by an unusual depth or duration of this mood and by the appearance of other signs of depression. Situational depressions may occur with a change of occupation or leaving one's living quarters and moving to a new place or neighborhood. Seasonal reactions are not significant from the point of changes in nature but rather what life changes are connected with it. Depression during pregnancy, childbirth, puerperium, and the involutional period belong to this group. (In all these depressive reactions, toxic and other physical factors should also be investigated.) The meaning of these situations varies individually and culturally. Other examples of important events include those of sentimental value, such as Christmas in the life of a lonely person, or patriotic events such as loss of a war or other important debacles.

Reactive depressions are fundamentally not different from reaction to life situations. They are usually of shorter duration than the previously described depression and lack marked signs of retardation. Freud's analysis of mourning and melancholia offered the first deep insight into the psychodynamics involved. Both aspects may be important in a reactive depression to bereavement.

Psychoneurotic depression must be distinguished from a depressive reaction in the setting of a psychoneurosis. In the latter case the psychoneurotic symptoms may color the symptomatology of the depression as previously illustrated. Compulsion neurosis may become aggravated in a depressed state and return to its predepressive condition after the depression has terminated. The term psychoneurotic depression implies that the depressive reaction is part of the patient's psychoneurosis. If that can be demonstrated, the treatment might have to be guided along different lines. There is little on this topic found in literature. Hypochondriacal reactions and depressive symptoms without feelings of depression which are of a well-defined duration have been termed depressive equivalents. The same term has been applied to well-circumscribed sleep disorders. The significance of periods of phobia or compulsions and of paranoid reactions has remained disputed.

Depressive symptomatology may change in different life periods. Their occurrence in children under 12 is recognizable from their behavior. Statements of unhappiness, accompanied by increased shyness, day-dreaming, forgetfulness, and inability to concentrate in school, might indicate a depressive reaction and possible suicidal danger. A similar clinical picture may occur in adolescents as well as an unmistakable depressive illness colored by the characteristics of the still immature personality. The usual symptoms are sadness, homesickness, loneliness, sulky behavior, and, with a deepening of the illness, confusion, misidentification, feelings of unreality and familiarity experiences. Many such patients feel drowsy, especially in the morning. Elaborate and fantastic hypochondriac concern may occur. In the early stages the differential diagnosis from a schizophrenic illness may be difficult. Most of these depressions are of short duration. (When such a patient has a recurrent depression in adult life, confusion, unreality, and familiarity feelings are missing).

Depressions in immature and dependent persons frequently resemble the adolescent psychopathology. In psychopathic personalities, inadequacy feelings and social insecurity may color the depression. Sulkiness, irritability, suspiciousness, anger, aversion, and paranoid features may appear. The feebleminded depressed patient may show marked thinking disorders, similar to the adolescent. In epileptic patients slowness and retardation seem to be marked as well as familiarity and unreality experiences.

In early cerebral arteriosclerosis the depressive reaction may not be influenced by the organic changes, while in well-developed brain-disease, including senility and brain tumor, the motor and intellectual retardation may become marked, and a serious lack of interest aggravate the picture. Hypochondriacal complaints and to a lesser extent delusions are frequent, as well as aversion reactions (critical and suspicious attitudes). In some patients anxiety, restlessness and agitation are prominent. The sleep disorders may be accompanied by fearful dreams, illusions, and brief confusional states. Various authors stress the similarity to symptoms of involutional depressions. The history of the development of the illness clarifies to some extent the significance of the organic changes. Frequently one gives too severe a prognosis because the depression can aggravate mild disorders of memory, attention, and judgment. However, during a prolonged illness cerebrovascular lesions may develop, and a chronic depressive state, with increasing apathy and deterioration of habits, may result.

In all patients who suffer from a marked depression, a thorough physical study is indicated to exclude physical illnesses. Exogenic possibilities should always be considered, including alcohol and other drug problems. Minor depressive reactions occur in many physical illnesses. A study of the meaning of the illness to the patient may clarify the factors that lead to or aggravate the depression. Such an approach will strengthen the patient-physician relationship and establish trust which permits the patient to confide worries and concerns.

In the present century the role of the patient has changed. He has now the recognized right to receive help from the society in which he lives. An increasingly large nonmedical group has become educated to understand minor as well as marked depressive illnesses and to analyze and modify factors involved. Physicians as well as specially trained psychiatrists are needed, but in addition, social workers, and psychologists who have studied the psychopathology of depressions can make a valuable contribution. In patients with a complicated psychopathological picture or when doubts occur whether psychotherapy alone is sufficient, a psychiatric consultation is indicated to clarify the diagnosis or the need for physical treatment.

References

1. Ackerknecht EH: *A Short History of Psychiatry.* New York, 1968.
2. Ackerknecht EH: *Therapie von den Primitiven bis zum 20. Jahrhundert.* Stuttgart, 1970 (*A Review of Theory and Practice of Treatment in Medicine*).
3. Lewis A: Melancholia: A historical review. *J Ment Sci* **80:**1–42, 1934.
4. Boerhaave H: *Boerhaave's Aphorism.* London, 1742.
5. Diethelm O: *Medical Dissertations of Psychiatric Interest,* printed before 1750, Basel, 1971, Chap. 2 ("Psychiatric Knowledge in the History of Medicine").
6. Diethelm O: *Medical Dissertations of Psychiatric Interest,* printed before 1750, Basel, 1971, Chap. 3 ("Melancholia").
7. Diethelm O: *Medical Dissertations of Psychiatric Interest,* printed before 1750, Basel, 1971, Chap. 8 ("Psychopathology and Cultural Factors").
8. Cheyne G: *The English Malady.* London, 1733.
9. Auenbrugger L: *Von der stillen wuth oder dem Trieb zum Selbstmorde.* Dessau, 1783.
10. Falret FP: *Des Maladies Mentales.* Paris, 1864.
11. Kraepelin E: *Lectures on Clinical Psychiatry.* New York, 1968.
12. Stainbrook E: *A Cross-Cultural Evaluation of Depressive Reactions in Depression.* Edited by Hoch P, Zubin J, Grune & Stratton, New York, 1954.
13. Diethelm O: *Medical Dissertations of Psychiatric Interest,* printed before 1750, Basel, 1971, Chap. 10 ("Psychiatry and Social-Cultural Factors").
14. Meyer A: *Collected Papers,* Vol. 2 (*Psychiatry*). Baltimore, 1950.
15. Ey H: *Etudes Psychiatriques* 1, 1948 and 4, 1951, Paris.
16. Diethelm O: *Treatment of Psychiatry.* Springfield, 1955, Charles C Thomas, 3rd ed.
17. Freud S: *Mourning and Melancholia.* Collected papers, London, 1953, Vol. IV.
18. Abraham K: *Selected Papers on Psychoanalysis.* London, 1929.

Three

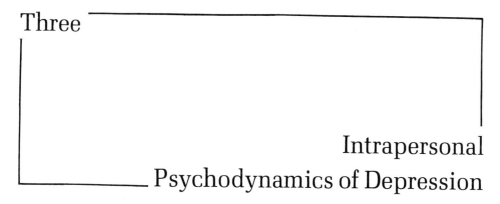

Intrapersonal Psychodynamics of Depression

Myer Mendelson, M.D.

Freud's (1) classic paper *Mourning and Melancholia* played an extraordinarily significant role in the psychodynamic understanding of depression. It considered depressive illness not only from the point of view of a reaction to life situations but also from the standpoint of the intrapersonal or intrapsychic events that constituted this reaction. It would, however, be a mistake to regard it as the last word on the subject. It should realistically be viewed as the beginning of an evolutionary process in the psychoanalytic conceptualization of the depressive reactions. It is this paper and the understanding of the intrapersonal aspects of depression that evolved from it that is the subject of this chapter.

Mourning and Melancholia represents one of the few papers that Freud devoted to psychotic disorders. In the development of Freud's thinking, it appeared at a point when he was interested in the phenomena of narcissism, identification, and aggression. It was written prior to his structural model of the human psyche which postulates the existence of the id, the ego, and the superego as the three important structures of the psychic apparatus. But it nevertheless contained the germ of the concept of the superego in its reference to the ego's "critical agency."

Since therapists have tended to apply Freud's ideas in this paper so indiscriminately to the treatment of so many kinds of depression, it is necessary to note his definition of melancholia:

> The distinguishing mental features of melancholia are a profoundly painful dejection, cessation of interest in the outside world, loss of the capacity to live, inhibition of all activity, and a lowering of the self-regarding feelings to a degree that finds utterance in self-reproaches and self-revilings, and culminates in a delusional expectation of punishment.

This is obviously the description of a psychotic depression, a fact which should clearly cause one to be very cautious about applying the findings in *Mourning and Melancholia* too widely. And, in fact, Freud warned that "melancholia takes on various clinical forms; the grouping together of which into a single unity does not seem to be established with certainty, and some of these forms suggest somatic rather than psychogenic affection."

Freud observed that melancholia, like mourning, developed after a loss of some kind. The loss might have been that "of a loved person" or "the loss of some abstraction which has taken the place of one, such as one's country, liberty, an ideal, and so on." The loss may even have occurred intrapsychically rather than in reality. In other words, the melancholic may have broken off his emotional attachment to his loved object unconsciously because of a hurt or a disappointment. He may not even have been aware that a loss had occurred or what it was that he no longer possessed in his lost object.

The "self-reproaches and self-revilings" of the melancholic interested and puzzled Freud, since it might have been expected that the lost or disappointing object might have been the target of the patient's angry laments and complaints.

Freud's explanation of this paradox was the one that later became so uncritically applied to depressions of all kinds even though he had explicitly disowned "all claim to general validity for our conclusions."

Freud's solution to the perplexing phenomenon that he had observed was characteristically perceptive. He noted:

> If one listens patiently to a melancholic's many various self-accusations, one cannot in the end avoid the impression that often the most violent of them are hardly at all applicable to the patient himself, but that with insignificant modifications they do fit someone else, someone whom the patient loves or has loved or should love. . . . We perceive that the self-reproaches are reproaches against a loved object which have been shifted away from it on the patient's own ego.

Thus Freud brought to our attention that the patient, rather than complaining, was actually accusing—and not himself but rather the disappointing or rejecting love-object.

Freud regarded "this substitution of identification for object-love as a regression from one type of object-choice to original narcissism . . . regression from object-cathexis to the still narcissistic oral phase of the libido." By this, Freud was referring to a developmental phase in which the infant was presumed to experience no differentiation between himself and the world—a lack of differentiation which Freud referred to as "identification." This phase was designated by Freud as "narcissistic," since he considered this to be a time when the libido was still entirely invested in the ego and was not yet directed out to the object world. This phase was also referred to as "oral" because of the infant's presumed manner of relating to objects during this period, and by the "introjection" or "incorporation" of these objects into his mouth, thus enhancing his presumed sense of identification with his infantile object world.

In other words, Freud postulated that melancholia represented a regression from object choice to this primitive mode of relating to objects, namely, narcissistic identification by means of oral incorporation of the object. It was because of this poor differentiation between the patient's objects and his ego that his hostility to the disappointing love-object became indistinguishable from his anger toward himself.

Freud theorized that this regressive identification and the resulting confusion in the patient's mind about the target of his hostility followed the loss of an object in a susceptible individual. This susceptibility was defined by the narcissistic type of object-choice such a person was likely to make. By this Freud meant that such a person was likely to fall in love with individuals very much like himself. That melancholia occurred only or most frequently in such instances he cautiously and prophetically acknowledged was still unconfirmed by investigation.

When Freud warned that "any claim to general validity for our conclusions shall be foregone at the outset," he was influenced in part by his uncertainty about the degree of constitutional or somatic elements in melancholia. He noted that some forms of this disorder appeared somatic rather than psychological in origin. He thought of the diurnal variation of mood that he noted in melancholics as "probably due to a somatic factor." In his caution concerning premature generalizations he even wondered "whether a loss in the ego irrespectively of the object (a purely narcissistic blow to the ego) may not suffice to produce the picture of melancholia." Here he was presciently commenting on the probability that a loss of self-esteem—an intrapersonal event—not occasioned by the loss of any object might trigger off a depressive reaction, a theme that was to be considered so extensively by later writers. It is worth noting that his thoughts about the constitutional factors in melancholia were echoed by psychoanalysts like Abraham (2) and Jacobson (3).

Abraham's speculations about constitutional elements derived from numerous clinical observations that he made in melancholics of symptoms, fantasies, and perversions centering around the mouth. From these observations he drew his conclusions not only about the patients' regression to the oral level but also about an assumed constitutional overaccentuation of oral erotism in certain individuals which led them to become fixated at this level of psychosexual development and to become potential melancholics. He believed that this fixation resulted in excessive oral needs and subsequent intense frustrations associated with acts of kissing, sucking, eating, and drinking.

He thought that the increased probability of such frustrations made these patients vulnerable to disappointments in their love-objects. And he drew attention to the presence in melancholics of an early emotional atmosphere of repeated disappointments in parental affection, presumably associated with these patients' exaggerated needs, and consequent susceptibility to disappointments.

He believed that the melancholic becomes ill when he experiences a repetition of these early disappointments. And since his "subsequent disappointments derive their importance from being representations of his original one, the whole sum of his anger is ultimately directed against one single person—against the person, that is, whom he had been most fond of as a child and who had then ceased to occupy this position in his life."

Thus Abraham, in addition to his other observations (4, 5), amplified Freud's hypothesis about the roles of anger and regression in melancholia. He especially focused on certain intrapersonal characteristics, namely the oral elements in this disorder, elements which he regarded as pointing to a constitutional accentuation of oral erotism, and also to the significance of the early emotional climate of the melancholic.

In 1923 Freud (6) published *The Ego and the Id* and laid the framework for what is generally referred to as the structural model in psychoanalysis, the theory in which the mental apparatus is conceptualized as being made up of three psychic "structures," the id, the ego, and the superego. It was in the context of this advance in metapsychology that Rado (7) made the next important contribution to the theory of depression.

In some ways this contribution was an elaboration of Abraham's stress on the melancholic's intensified oral erotism. Rado broadened this concept and in a sense translated it into psychological rather than semivisceral language by framing his observations in terms of the depressive's "intensely strong craving for narcissistic gratification" and of his extreme "narcissistic intolerance."

Rado visualized the depressive as being like a small child whose self-esteem is dependent on external approval, appreciation, affection, and love. A healthy individual derives self-esteem from his own accomplishments and effectiveness—from internal sources, as it were. Rado emphasized that the depressive still derives his self-esteem from external sources, still requires what he refers to as "external narcissistic supplies." These supplies consist of love, affection, and approval from his love-objects and from those around him; thus his self-esteem is particularly vulnerable to a reduction or a disappearance of these supplies.

Thus Rado expanded both Freud's concept of melancholia occurring after the loss of a love-object and Abraham's observations about the importance of oral erotism and the implications of "disappointments" in the life of the depressive.

Rado saw the "narcissistic regression" to the phase of identification that Freud observed and the self-derogation that was the clinical manifestation of this as a device or weapon to win back the love that was lost. Rado conceived of this aspect of melancholia as "a great despairing cry for love" in which the ego remorsefully castigates itself and cries for forgiveness.

Rado took cognizance of the difference between neurotic and psychotic depressions. He thought of a depression as neurotic when the external object was not given up and when this external object was the love-object who was being propitiated by the patient's self-reproaches. He thought of a depression as psychotic when the remorseful drama took place essentially in the psychic or intrapersonal sphere, which meant that the object whose forgiveness the patient was beseeching was the superego into which the external object had been partially incorporated. In such a case, like Abraham, he saw the disappointing object as merely the latest representative of the disappointing parental figures long since introjected as the superego.

Thus, in review, Rado, in partial contrast to Abraham, emphasized the psychological predisposition to depression. He elaborated the concept of narcissistic supplies and drew explicit attention to the tenuous self-esteem of the potentially depressed patient whom he saw as being so dependent on external narcissistic supplies. In line with what Waelder (8) was later to call the principle of multiple function, Rado read into the self-depreciation of the depressive the function of expiation designed to win back the lost love-object—whether it be the current or the original object. And as indicated, Rado cast his formulations in the language of Freud's structural concept, elaborated just previously in 1923.

In 1936 Gero (9) made a notable contribution to the literature on depression by an extensive outline of the therapeutic course in two depressed patients. In this paper he expanded the concept of "orality" in a direction that represents the current usage of this term. With a more sophisticated grasp of the importance of object relationships, he was able to view this concept not only as having to do with the sensual gratification of the mucous membrane of the mouth and alimentary canal but also as referring to the satisfactions implicit in the whole mother-child relationship: "The essentially oral pleasure is only one factor in the experience satisfying the infant's need for warmth, touch, love and care." Thus "orality" assumed the modern symbolic meaning of this term which now refers to the yearning for "shelter and love and for the warmth of the mother's protecting body" as well as the literal meaning that refers to the libidinal stimulation of the oral zone. It was in this more general sense of the need for dependency, gratification, love, and warmth that Gero agreed with Abraham and Rado in declaring that "oral erotism is the favorite fixation point in the depressive."

In the meantime and subsequently, a number of writers tended to question the universality and the implications of Freud's formula for melancholia and to elaborate the role of self-esteem in depressed patients.

Helene Deutsch (10) expressed uncertainty about the invariable presence of introjection in melancholia. She questioned "whether this is true for all cases of melancholic depression," and noted that "there are without a doubt cases of melancholic depression, in which an unusual severity on the part of the superego is alone enough to cause it to rage sporadically and even periodically against its ego."

Rado (11) too, in 1951, seriously questioned "whether or not significant psychodynamic differences exist between depressive spells that occur in different pathogenic contexts."

And in 1953 Gero (12) warned that not all depressions were similar to the ones Freud and Abraham had described. He even felt that "in the same type of depression different aspects of the` symptomatology necessitate different explanations."

Fenichel (13), from the perspective of the evolution of psychoanalytic theory, dissected out the two regressive processes in melancholia that Freud had telescoped into the concept of "oral narcissistic regression." He pointed out that in depression two distinct intrapersonal or intrapsychic regressive processes occurred, an "instinctual regression and a regression in the sphere of the ego." By "instinctual" regression, he referred, of course, to regression to the oral phase of psychosexual development which Freud, Abraham, Rado, and Gero had successively elaborated. This he felt to be common to both neurotic and psychotic depressions. But in a psychotic depression or "melancholia," as Freud termed it, there was in addition an ego regression as a result of which the individual could not distinguish himself from the love-object and which led to the substitution of self-vilification for reproaches more appropriately directed to the disappointing love-object. He visualized this as regression to a stage of ego development before there was an awareness of objects as distinct from the self. Thus, accepting Freud's disclaimer to general validity for his formulation, he revised Freud's theory as indicated and restricted his revised version of Freud's formula to psychotic depression.

Furthermore, Fenichel stressed the role of self-esteem in depression by defining a depressive as a "person who is fixated on the state where his self-esteem is regulated by external supplies."

He went so far as to state that the precipitating factors in depression "represent either a loss of self-esteem or a loss of supplies which the patient had hoped would secure or even enhance his self-esteem." Among these experiences he listed failures, monetary losses, remorse, drop in prestige, or the loss by rejection or death of a love partner.

Mention should be made here of Melanie Klein (14) who, although outside the mainstream of American psychoanalytic development, contributed a very important insight into the predisposition to depression. Freud, Abraham, Rado, and Gero had focused primarily on the psychodynamics of the depressive process. They viewed melancholia essentially as a reparative process designed in one way or another to repair the psychological damage subsequent to the loss of a love-object. For Freud and for Abraham, melancholia was a painful period of suffering during which the introjected object, now identified with the ego, was exposed to tormenting devaluation and punishment until the psychic trauma became somehow resolved. Rado added the concept of propitiation on an intrapsychic plane as one of the functions of this self-derogatory process.

To the extent that these writers thought of predisposition, they invoked hypotheses of constitutional predisposition, either of a general nature or related to the degree of oral erotism. And they also explained this predisposition on the basis of early disappointments experienced because of the patients' excessive need for external narcissistic supplies, for which in turn constitutional factors were also sometimes invoked.

Melanie Klein by contrast conceptualized the predisposition to depression as resulting, not from one or a series of disappointments or traumatic incidents, but from the very quality of the mother-child relationship in the first years of life.

Unless this relationship was of such a nature as to engender and consolidate in the child the feeling that he is accepted, loved, and worthwhile, he is unable to resolve the ambivalence that Melanie Klein believed each infant felt toward his mother, and the infant is therefore subsequently vulnerable to depressive episodes.

Thus she visualized the susceptibility to depression as based not on specific traumata or disappointment but rather on the child's inability to master his early depressive fears and anxieties and to establish a satisfactory level of self-esteem. She called this developmental phase, in which the child is faced with the resolution of this ambivalence and its accompanying fears, "the depressive position"—the position in which the depression-prone person is fixated and which consolidates his vulnerability.

Despite the interpersonal aspects of this process, she conceptualized this development and the quality of the mother-child relationship in terms of what was going on intrapsychically as a result of the infant's "uncontrollable, greedy and destructive phantasies and impulses against his mother's breasts," rather than emphasizing the actual behavior of the parents. However conceptualized, her focus on the resolution of developmental problems in the mother-child relationship rather than on specific traumata or disappointments remains a definite contribution.

Two writers, Bibring (15) and Edith Jacobson (3, 16), have been of special importance in the evolution of psychoanalytic concepts of depression. Rado and Fenichel had particularly stressed the importance of self-esteem in depression. But Bibring and Jacobson expanded this insight in very significant ways. They both visualized depressive reactions as affective states characterized by a loss of self-esteem.

Bibring, however, in breaking away from previous formulations, saw many depressed patients' lack of self-esteem as caused by fixations at other than those at the oral level. He fully acknowledged the great frequency of depressions related to the frustration of "the need to get affection, to be loved, to be taken care of, to get 'supplies' or by the opposite defensive need; to be independent, self-supporting."

However, he appealed to everyday clinical experience to support his thesis that many depressed patients experienced their loss of self-esteem because of the frustration of aspirations other than those associated with the oral level. He pointed out that self-esteem can be lowered and a depression precipitated by frustrations associated with either the anal or the phallic levels of development.

In the former case these frustrated aspirations consisted of "the wish to be good, not to be resentful, hostile, defiant, but to be loving, not to be dirty, but to be clean, etc." Depressions due to the failure to attain these goals will be characterized by feelings of being too weak and helpless to control one's impulses or by guilt about this lack of control.

Frustrations due to the failure to attain aspirations associated with the phallic level, namely, "the wish to be strong, superior, great, secure, not to be weak and insecure," will be characterized by feelings of inadequacy, inferiority, and ineffectiveness.

While acknowledging that the content of these three types of depression often overlapped, Bibring maintained that most depressions represented a loss of self-esteem and a feeling of helplessness related to the frustrations associated with one or another of these levels of psychosexual development, characterized clinically either by feelings of dependency, loneliness, and need for love or by feelings of guilt and "badness," or in still other cases by feelings of ineffectiveness and inadequacy.

While remaining in the general tradition of Rado and Fenichel in emphasizing the central importance of the loss of self-esteem in depression, Bibring departed from their and from Freud's formulations in denying that depression was related to the vicissitudes of aggression. Instead of seeing depression as the consequence of aggressive feelings deflected from a disappointing love-object back onto the self, Bibring visualized depression as an ego phenomenon not involving intersystemic tensions between the ego and the superego. There has been considerable controversy over this point (17), and more reference will be made to the role of aggression in depressive reactions after considering the next contributor to the evolution of the psychoanalytic concepts of depression.

Edith Jacobson (3) considered the subject of depression from the perspective of Hartmann's (18, 19) uniquely important contributions to ego psychology. Hartmann had introduced a number of pertinent and useful refinements in psychoanalytic thinking and terminology. He had, for example, made a distinction between the terms "self" and "ego." As he saw it—and his view has been assimilated into the main corpus of analytic theory—the "self" refers to one's own person as distinguished from others. The "ego," on the other hand, refers to a structure of the psychic apparatus which represents an integrated organization of psychic functions referred to as "ego functions." He did not think of the ego, as there is undoubtedly a tendency to do, as a reified part of the brain or as a homunculus directing operations.

He also adopted the terms self-representation or self-image by which he meant "the endopsychic representations of our bodily and mental self." In addition, he introduced the analogous concepts of "object-representation" or "object-image" to stand for the endopsychic representations of person- or thing-objects.

In his conceptualization, the self- and object-representations of what Sandler and Rosenblatt (20) later refer to as the inner "representational world" become cathected with either libidinal or aggressive cathexes depending on the individual's developmental fate. To say that a person's self-image is basically libidinally cathected is a perhaps clumsy metapsychological way of stating that his self-esteem is high. If his self-image is, on the contrary, largely aggressively cathected, his self-esteem is low and he may be depressed.

Jacobson adopted and expanded this terminology. She, too, as with Rado, Fenichel, Bibring, and others, found that lowered self-esteem represented the core of depression. She explored the determinants of this self-esteem that was of such central importance in depression and the great variety of depressive reactions that derived from these different determinants.

Her work on this subject represents the most comprehensive and sophisticated psychoanalytic model of depression currently in the literature. It is therefore worth examining in some detail.

She conceptualizes one's self-image as not being at first a firm unit but as representing early in life an everchanging series of transient self-representations derived from the infant's early fluctuating perceptions of himself and of those objects, or part-objects, such as the breast, to which he is exposed. Under optimal circumstances, the self-image gradually becomes integrated into a relatively enduring, consistent endopsychic or intrapersonal representation of his self and becomes clearly distinguishable from the internal representations of objects.

In other words, the child begins to acquire a clear sense of his identity and becomes able to distinguish himself from other people. Furthermore, under ideal developmental circumstances, his self-image becomes optimally libidinally cathected. In the context of loving parents and of tolerable frustrations adequately managed, he develops a high level of self-esteem and self-confidence and a decreased predisposition to depression.

This concept bears some resemblance to Melanie Klein's observations about the importance of the mother-child relationship in the development of the child's ability to retain his self-esteem in the face of the intermittent loss of the "good mother." Jacobson, however, places considerably more emphasis on the actual behavior of the parent and the experience of the child than Melanie Klein did. Furthermore, she has adopted the terminology of self- and object-representations for the "introjects" and the incorporated "good" and "bad" mother that are so familiar to readers of Melanie Klein.

When the desirable outcome described above does not occur, the child is burdened with a poorly integrated, aggressively cathected, and inadequately differentiated self-image. Expressed clinically, he is destined to experience problems of identity ("who am I?") and of low self-esteem (with a predisposition to depression) or difficulties in distinguishing himself from others (with possible psychotic troubles of a depressive, paranoid, or schizophrenic type) depending on the vicissitudes of his development.

One common type of patient with a negatively colored self-image is the lonely, "empty," "hungry" type of chronically depressed person who may present himself with just these symptoms and who has been variously referred to in the literature as a depressive fixated at the oral level or as a schizoid-depressive (21, 22) or as having a depression with an ego defect (23), the defect, of course, representing the maldevelopment of his self-image.

However, such patients may also present with a wide spectrum of seemingly unrelated complaints, for example, eating problems, alcoholism, drug addiction, promiscuity, kleptomania, and even "underachieving." This last symptom is a consequence of these patients' restless inability to concentrate and their constant search for companionship.

Jacobson also examines other determinants of self-esteem than this pathological development of the self-image which essentially represents the reflected appraisal of the patient by his earliest love-objects. His actual talents, capacity, and achievements also inevitably affect an individual's self-esteem. Problems in this area may give rise to depressions corresponding to Bibring's classification of depressions associated with the phallic level of development and characterized by feelings of inadequacy and ineffectiveness.

Another determinant of self-esteem is the character of the superego that the individual has developed. If developmental circumstances have endowed the person with a harshly critical, or even worse, a so-called archaic or primitive superego retaining the unmodulated, exaggerated, fantasy-related version of parental expectations associated with the early years of childhood, then, of course, his self-esteem is proportionately vulnerable and his predisposition to depression increased. The type of depression resulting from such a superego might correspond to Bibring's concept of the depression that is fixated at the anal level of development and characterized by feelings of guilt and "badness."

Jacobson also considers the ego-ideal an important determinant of self-esteem, since, of course, the more grandiose and unrealistic the individual's expectations of himself are, the more likely it is that his performance will not match this ego-ideal (24) and the more probable it is that he will suffer a loss of self-esteem and depression. Depending on the specific characteristics of this ego-ideal and of the patient's expectations of himself, the depression may be characterized by either feelings of inadequacy and inferiority or by feelings of guilt and weakness.

Thus Jacobson makes room in her conceptual framework for a great variety of depressive reactions and does so primarily in the language of ego psychology rather than in the more simplistic terminology of Bibring, who, while speaking of depression as an ego phenomenon, nevertheless used psychosexual fixation points as his major explanatory device.

But what of Freud's formulation of the regressive identification in melancholia? Jacobson takes account of this in the manner of Fenichel but with the refinement of conceptualization characteristic of ego psychology. She, too, differentiates instinctual regression from ego regression. She conceives of regressive identification occurring when the boundaries between the self-image and the object-representations dissolve away and result in a fusion of self- and object-images. The target of the patient's hostility—the disappointing object-representation—thus becomes indistinguishable from the self-image; hence the self-reproaches and self-vilification occur. But this kind of dissolution of boundaries between self- and object-representations is by definition a psychotic process. The depression resulting from this is therefore a psychotic depression, as indeed was the case in the patients that Freud described. And in accordance with his own prescient denial of "any claim of general validity" for his formulations, this process does not occur in neurotic depressions as Rado and Fenichel also pointed out. The regressive identification that Freud described represented the essence of a psychotic process but by a strange fate mistakenly became the model for all depressive reactions.

Freud considered that the patient who could not distinguish himself from the object was experiencing a regressive identification. "Identification," as we have seen, was used in *Mourning and Melancholia* to refer to a pathological regression. However, as we know, identification has come to be looked upon in current theory as part of the normal process of development, a process that Jacobson (16) reviews in considerable detail.

What about the role of aggression that Freud so emphasized in depressions? Bibring, as we have seen, thought of depression as an ego phenomenon not involving aggression or intersystemic tensions. Jacobson showed that Freud's formulation with respect to aggression applied only to certain psychotic depressions. There are some types of psychotic depression that do not conform to his formula. She nevertheless sees aggression as an integral feature of every depression in the sense that an aggressive cathexis of the self-image is the metapsychological counterpart of the low self-esteem that is characteristic of depression.

The manner in which the term aggression is used by various writers derives from a semantic confusion. The word is used, first of all, to refer to an affect, as, for example, in the phrase aggressive feelings. Thus in Freud's formulation of melancholia, the patient's "aggressive" or hostile feelings become directed toward the fused self-object. The term is also used, however, in a quite different sense. It applies also to a much more abstract entity, one of the two forms of psychic energy in the economic model of psychoanalysis, the other form being, of course, "libido." It should be pointed out that the very concept of psychic energy and the point of view represented by the economic model is currently under extensive and searching criticism in the literature (17, 25, 26–28).

But by making use of this disputed economic model, Jacobson is consistent when she states that "aggression" plays a role both when the angry feelings meant for a disappointing love-object are experienced as being directed against the self and when the depression is a result of an aggressively cathected self-image stemming from poor early object relations.

Clinically, however, the former case has to do with actual angry feelings whereas the latter case may have to do with feelings of loneliness, lovelessness, and emptiness.

These theoretical considerations are not mere academic exercises but have important therapeutic implications. Because of the theme of *Mourning and Melancholia*, a therapeutic tradition has persisted, especially among inexperienced therapists, that the appropriate psychotherapy for depression is to make the patient aware of his hostile feelings and to help him direct them toward their appropriate target.

But as we have seen, Freud's formulation applies primarily to certain types of psychotic depression in which psychotherapy in any form has not distinguished itself as an effective mode of treatment. But there are many kinds of depression—whether they are called neurotic or schizoid, associated with ego defects or simply described as lonely, pessimistic, narcissistic, or whatever—in which the pathology has more to do with low self-respect, loneliness, intense needs for affection, acceptance and intimacy, or with feelings of inadequacy and ineffectiveness, in which the element of hostility is either absent or secondary in nature.

In these patients, therapeutic emphasis on hostility and aggression rather than on the patient's poor self-esteem and on the ways to improve this self-esteem may produce a deepening of the depression, because, in addition to feeling lonely, unhappy, and inadequate, the patient is made to feel that he is also basically hostile, aggressive, and, as he experiences it, unlikeable and bad.

Finally, mention should be made of Beck's (29) cognitive model of depression that emphasizes yet another intrapersonal component of depression. This considers the vicissitudes of self-esteem in depressive illness from a perspective which conceptualizes depression in a new and provocative way, and which is consistent with the view expressed in the previous paragraph. Beck moves away from the traditional pattern of viewing depression as primarily a mood disorder. He draws attention to the cognitive distortions (e.g., "I am no good," "I am unlovable," "It's all my fault") that are so almost universally present in depression. He challenges the view that the depressed affect results in disturbances of thought and behavior. He proposes instead "that the typical depressive affects are evoked by the erroneous conceptualizations." He thus sees these intrapersonal distorted cognitions as playing an etiological role in what has been generally thought of as an affective disorder.

Even though his view that disturbed cognitions have etiological primacy in depressive states has not yet met with general acceptance, Beck has nevertheless made a significant contribution in underlining the importance of the presence of thought disorders in depression.

Summary

In summary, then, I have attempted to extract the essence of *Mourning and Melancholia* and have reviewed the evolution of psychoanalytic thinking about the intrapersonal aspects of depression that was initiated by this classic paper of Freud's. I have tried to indicate how this evolution kept pace with the developments in the general body of psychoanalytic thought beginning with Freud's interest in aggression, identification, and narcissism, moving on to his development of the structural model and ending with the post-Freudian conceptual refinements of ego psychology.

More specifically I have traced the theoretical fate of Freud's observation of the regressive processes that occur in melancholia. I referred to Fenichel's breakdown of the two regressive processes telescoped by Freud into one; and I sketched Jacobson's elaboration of this in the framework of Hartmann's and her own refinement and expansion of ego psychology. Also I described Abraham's, Rado's, Gero's, and Fenichel's elaboration of the depressed patient's excessive needs for dependency gratification, love, security, and other aspects of "orality." I reviewed Bibring's and Jacobson's views of the determinants of self-esteem other than orality. And finally I have directed attention to Beck's original views on the importance of still other intrapersonal factors in depression, namely, the cognitive distortions.

References

1. Freud S (1917): *Mourning and Melancholia.* Standard edition, London, Hogarth Press, 1957, Vol. 14, pp. 237–260.
2. Abraham K (1924): A short study of the development of the libido, in *Selected Papers on Psychoanalysis.* London, Hogarth Press, and The Institute of Psychoanalysis, 1942, pp.418–501.
3. Jacobson E: *Depression.* New York, International Universities Press, 1971.
4. Abraham K (1911): Notes on the psychoanalytic investigation and treatment of manic-depressive insanity and allied conditions, in *Selected Papers on Psychoanalysis.* London, Hogarth Press, and the Institute of Psychoanalysis, 1942, pp. 137–156.
5. Abraham K (1916): The first pregenital stage of the libido, in *Selected Papers on Psychoanalysis.* London, Hogarth Press, and the Institute of Psychoanalysis, 1942, pp. 248–279.
6. Freud S (1923): *The Ego and the Id.* Standard edition, London, Hogarth Press, 1957, Vol. 19, pp. 3–66.
7. Rado S: The problem of melancholia. *Int J Psa* **9**:420–438, 1928.
8. Waelder R: The principle of multiple function. *Psychoanal Quart* **5**:45–62, 1936.
9. Gero G: The construction of depression. *Int J Psa* **17**:423–461, 1936.

10. Deutsch H: *Psychoanalysis of the Neuroses.* London, Hogarth Press, and the Institute of Psychoanalysis, 1932.
11. Rado S: Psychodynamics of depression from the etiological point of view. *Psychosom Med* **13**:51–55, 1951.
12. Gero G: An equivalent of depression: Anorexia, in *Affective Disorders.* Edited by Greenacre P, New York, International Universities Press, 1953.
13. Fenichel O: *The Psychoanalytic Theory of Neurosis.* New York, Norton, 1945.
14. Klein M: *Contributions to Psychoanalysis, 1921–1945.* London, Hogarth Press, and the Institute of Psychoanalysis, 1948.
15. Bibring E: The mechanism of depression, in *Affective Disorders.* Edited by Greenacre P, New York, International Universities Press, 1953.
16. Jacobson E: *The Self and the Object World.* New York, International Universities Press, 1964.
17. Mendelson M: *Psychoanalytic Concepts of Depression.* 2nd ed., revised, New York, Spectrum Publications (in prep).
18. Hartmann H: The development of the ego concept in Freud's work. *Int J Psa* **37**:1956. Also in *Essays on Ego Psychology.* New York, International Universities Press, 1964, pp. 268–296.
19. Hartmann H: *Ego Psychology and the Problem of Adaption.* New York, International Universities Press, 1958.
20. Sandler J, Rosenblatt B: The concept of the representational world. *Psa Study Child* **17**:128–148, 1962.
21. Fairbairn W: *Psychoanalytic Studies of the Personality.* London, Tavistock Publications, 1952.
22. Guntrip H: A study of Fairbairn's theory of schizoid reactions. *Br J Med Psychol* **25**:86–103, 1952.
23. Hammerman S: Ego defect and depression. *Psa Quart* **32**:155–165, 1963.
24. Reich A: Early identifications as archaic elements in the superego. *J Am Psa Assoc* **2**:218–238, 1954.
25. Apfelbaum B: Ego psychology, psychic energy and the hazards of quantitative explanation in psychoanalytic theory. *Int J Psa* **46**:168–182, 1965.
26. Grossman WJ, Bennet S: Anthropomorphism: Motive, meaning and causality in psychoanalytic theory. *Psa Study Child* **24**:78–111, 1969.
27. Kubie LS: The fallacious use of quantitative concepts in dynamic psychology. *Psa Quart* **16**:507–518, 1947.
28. Pumpian-Mindlin E: Propositions concerning energetic-economic aspects of libido theory: Conceptual models of psychic energy and structure in psychoanalysis. *Annals NY Acad Sci* **76**:1038–1052, 1959.
29. Beck AT: *Depression.* New York, Hoeber, 1967.

Four

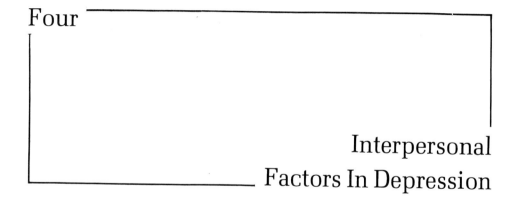

Interpersonal Factors In Depression

Leon Salzman, M.D.

Is depression a disease or a reaction in response to certain life experiences that can occur to anyone at any time? If it is a disease, then we can search for a definitive etiology, whether it be genetic, biochemical, or bacteriologic. There are many data that suggest that genetic and biochemical factors play a role in this disorder, but whether they are etiologic, contributory, or predisposing is yet to be clarified.

Until very recently, the concept of depression as a disease has occupied the forefront of psychiatric interest, and the search for a definitive etiology has been pursued ardently. This concept of depression as a disease, as with other psychiatric syndromes, was related to the development of psychiatric theory out of the medical discipline using the medical model of describing separate entities and disease categories with its distinctive etiology, pathology, and therapeutic program. While this procedure was entirely rational for disorders in which the pathology was demonstrable and the causative agents identifiable, the attempt to deal with mental disorders in this manner was both inaccurate and misleading. While mental disorders are clearly alterations in man's physiology as well as psychology, the concept of disease as defined in Koch's postulates may not apply. In the neuroses and psychoses we may be dealing with responses or defensive reactions designed to ward off threatening stimuli. These reactions constitute the symptomatology of the disorder. At times they may cluster and behave as syndromes. They may be transitory, but if they continue over a long period of time, they may produce somatic changes that may be irreversible. These physiological changes ultimately accompany the psychological responses. As advocated by many behavioral scientists in recent years, this phenomenon eliminates the necessity for extensive nosological categories that are only descriptive yet that mislead one into thinking that they are separate diseases. This situation is reflected in the tendency to describe the varieties of depressive disorders as if they were separate disease entities as well. Some psychiatrists make a distinction between exogenous and endogenous depression, implying that in these categories the major causative agent may be intrinsic and related to some genetic or physiological predisposition. Here the external events are minimal, while in the exogenous depressions the external precipitating agent is the essential factor. They go so far as to indicate that these categories represent different diseases. On the other hand, it is more likely that we are dealing with a total reaction due to multiple causes that interrelate to produce similar somatic and psychologic responses. A particular element may vary in its role and intensity but in view of the marked concordance of symptoms and behavioral manifestations, we must assume, like Occam's razor, the most economical explanation. In fact, such distinctions and the tendency to describe involutional melancholia, neurotic, or psychotic depression or the manic-depressive reactions as separate disease categories are subject to the same criticism. There is good reason to believe that these are not distinct disorders but rather varieties of a reaction which we call depression because it manifests itself at different times in the life cycle of the individual under different circumstances. The variety of symptomatology depends on the individual's premorbid personality. This fact would suggest that the dynamics or etiology may be similar in all the instances; however, the underlying personality in which such a depressive breakdown occurs may be the key issue.

In considering the psychological or interpersonal factors which are related to the depressive process, the notion of a predisposition in terms of some personality pattern is of relevance. Many impressive studies indicate that there is a collection of personality patterns that lend themselves to depressive reactions. However, every variety has been described ranging from the obsessional to the hysterical, particularly the oral type of personality, to account for the predisposition to depression. Therefore, there is reason to believe that a depressive is not a specific personality type, but that there may be a collection of personality factors that are operative in depression specific to depression. The premorbid personality may give special flavoring and coloring to the depression rather than being a predisposing issue or specific to its onset. These contradictions and dilemmas can be largely resolved if one gets away from viewing depression as a disease, and views it instead as a reaction to certain conditions of stress or tension. This would suggest that in the process of human development certain experiences may be predisposing to the development of depression in later life and that these factors might be present in any kind of personality structure where the particular defenses define the ways of dealing with these anxieties.

Dr. Melanie Klein has postulated that the predisposition to depression is present in all individuals in the inevitable frustration of the infant in relation to mother. She suggests that the infant reacts with anger and feelings of helplessness and guilt. Until the infant is assured of mother's love, these feelings may continue and be enhanced. This is called the depressive position, and in adult depressions there is a regression to this period of infantile dependency (1).

While Klein's views are almost entirely intrapsychic and based on the libido theory, they involve the notions of interaction and highlight the possibility of early experiencing being the source of later reactions of loss and deprivation. This view is shared by others even though they do not assume that the depressive position is inevitable and invariable.

However, the developmental notion of predisposition involves both motivational and adaptational concepts in regard to man's development and behavior. It focuses on the needs of an individual and on the processes and activities that are set into motion to fulfill these needs. When the needs are excessive, extreme, or distorted for various reasons, the behavior that is organized to fill them may be maladaptive and may fail to satisfy the individual's productive requirements. We call such responses neurotic or psychotic, and they constitute a wide range of reaction types. It is inevitable that since the needs of all men are identical biologically and essentially similar psychologically, their reactions to life experiences will be more or less the same. H. S. Sullivan suggested this when he said, "Man is more simply human than otherwise." It is only in the details that they may differ, and these depend on each individual's idiosyncratic experiences (2, 3).

The understanding of depression has been retarded because of this historical development in spite of Freud's contributions, particularly since it has been viewed as a disorder based on physiological or biochemical causes. Because it frequently had definable physical concomitants, it tended to be fixed even more strongly in the medical model.

In spite of the consistent biochemical changes in amino- and ketosteroids as well as in potassium distribution in the depressions, the disorder cannot be viewed wholly as a disorder of metabolism. There are many objections to the disease model ranging from the extensive, disparate views on its etiology to the almost chaotic state of therapy in which no particular approach is universally effective. However, the main objection to the medical model lies in the nature of the disorder, in which the symptoms are highly dependent on the individual's own background and experience. We can never hope to fulfill the requirements of a disease category in that we cannot consistently produce or predict depressive reactions, since under similar traumatic situations or physiological changes a wide spectrum of responses is possible. In addition, the universality of the reaction implies that, rather than being an intrusive, alien, and destructive element in human affairs, it may have adaptive purposes, which may go wrong under various circumstances.

Since a depression is a widespread phenomenon, it is more likely to be a response of the organism to some external stimulus which registers in a biochemical fashion in the cells. Depression is not something one has; it is something that is happening in a person in relation to others. This notion is supported by many depression studies (Freud, Gaylin, Beck, and Arieti) which indicate that psychological factors clearly play a role in the development of depressions (4, 5). However, the relationship lies in the context of some predisposing tendencies which react to certain experiences on the basis of prior sensitivities or immaturities. These do not necessarily represent particular personality constellations, but they do represent the byplay of unconscious, psychodynamic, or conflictual activities, which in the face of certain traumas may respond with feelings of despair, depression, and hopelessness.

The evidence for the role of psychological factors is extensive even though they cannot be identified as the sole causes or precipitants for the depressive process. However, the point is demonstrated most dramatically in the massive reaction in Voodoo Death, such that the "word" can produce lethal adrenal insufficiency, or forgiveness from the chief cause an immediate and striking change in the dying person. This reaction is a psychological one with marked physiological accompaniments and represents the response of disapproval or total rejection in a social setting where such beliefs are held. It is incidentally a dramatic representation of the power of the word and provides a major clue to the efficacy of psychotherapy in the depressive disorder.

If depression is not a disease, what is it? Does an individual react consistently in this way or does his reaction depend on his previous personality structure, the nature of the situation, and a host of other significantly related matters? Can we predict the reaction under certain conditions? What accounts for the differing severity of response? How do we account for the fact that certain therapeutic maneuvers, such as ECT, drugs, psychotherapy, or doing nothing at all, can be effective in altering the manifestations of the depressive reaction? Or putting it another way, can the notion of depression as a reaction account for all the diverse data that have accumulated over the past 500 years?

Psychological Theories of Depression

The early psychodynamic theories of depression as developed by Abraham, Freud in "Mourning and Melancholia," Rado, Klein, Bibring and Jacobson have been discussed in the previous chapter (1, 6–11). Initially, the etiological focus was on establishing the psychosexual phase of development that seemed most involved in the depressive reaction. The frequency with which depression was identified with starvation or denial of oral fulfillments tended to implicate the oral phase of psychosexual development. However, the tendency toward obsessionalism in the premorbid depressive personality suggested a relationship to the anal period of psychosexual development. Other clinical studies, particularly the work of M. Klein, stressed the crucial role of early object relationships. Because all the psychosexual periods were implicated, it was suggested that we were not dealing with a particular trauma at a particular phase of development, which alters the intrapsychic forces, but rather a more generalized reaction to life's experiences involving an inability to fulfill one's needs, desires, or neurotic goals in a world that is denying or frustrating. The earliest occasions for such a reaction were probably in the pregenital eras of psychosexual development. This is the direction of the ego psychological theories which stress the universality of the grief reaction and which visualize depression as a misfired and inappropriate response to a loss. These reactions can become totally disorganizing in a physiological as well as psychological sense.

Horney viewed the depressive process as an accompanying mood to all neurotic states and not a specific syndrome, since the fear of loss of love was present in all neuroses (12). Most of the symptomatology from the ultimate of despair with suicidal activity to the self-accusations of worthlessness and self-derogation and denunciation are the results of the individual's failure to fulfill his overly idealized expectations. These derive from the structure of his neurosis and are present throughout the range of the characterological disorders and the neuroses and psychoses. When the depressive elements are most pronounced, the reaction is labeled depression. However, the underlying hysterical, obsessional, or schizoid features may be present and participate in the symptomatology of the response. At times a manic excitement temporarily covers up the underlying anxiety and despair. In every instance the anxiety that results from a feeling of loss involves interpersonal elements which have been emphasized by some theorists, namely Bonime (13), who focused on the competitive elements in the depressive maneuver.

The psychological significance of the interpersonal features of a depression was noted by Sullivan, who viewed grief as a process of detaching oneself from a significant person and thought of it as a constructive process; however, depression is essentially a destructive process and is binding instead of liberating. It is only superficially related to grief. He said:

> While the true depressive is preoccupied with thoughts of the enormity of disaster, of punishment, hopelessness, and the like, the incipient schizophrenic is not the host of any simple content, but is burdened with pressing distresses and becomes more and more wrapped up in fantastic explanation and efforts at remedy. The distinction is one fundamentally dynamic: pure depression is practically a standstill of adjustment; the schizophrenic depression is a most unhappy struggle. Instead of literally or figuratively sitting still, these people are striving to cut themselves off from painful stimuli, escape the situation by mystic and more or less extraordinary efforts, and justify themselves by heroic measures. While the pure depression may end in suicide of a practical sort, the schizophrenic depression leads to fantastic methods of self-destruction often preceded by fear of being killed.

Essentially he saw a depression as an obscure way of dealing with anxiety and that the depression or the mania were more tolerable than the anxiety itself, since, for Sullivan, anxiety was a response to a feeling of disapproval from a significant "other" person. The concept of depression revolved about dealing with low self-esteem.

In 1954 Mabel B. Cohen and others (14) obtained findings similar to the above in an intensive study of the life history and the character structure of the depressive patient. They discovered that the depressive reaction occurs in response to the patient's inability to live up to his parents' and his own expectation of himself. His inability to deal with others as a whole, separate individual perpetuates his tendency to deal with others in extremes as good or bad, black or white, and his response to frustration or loss is also in the extremes of depression or mania. His relationship with others is generally in terms of an exploitative dependency gratified by his manipulation of them. They noted that the hostile factors in depression were overstressed and were not the major element in the illness. The patient's hostile feelings are the result of his irritating and demanding behavior. They concluded that the depressed person does not suffer genuine feelings but expresses such feelings as an exploitative technique.

This study, by implication, described the illness as an attempt to repair, reinstate, or revive a relationship which by the very nature of the symptoms of the reaction prevents its possibility.

Oral and Aggressive Elements in Depression

Abraham's description of the hostile elements in depression has been widely accepted as an explanation for suicide as well. The anger-in-anger-out hypothesis regarding depression and suicide implies that the outward expression of hostility would be a therapeutic goal in these situations which would thereby undo the depression and obviate the desire for self-destructive activities. However, this issue has been challenged many times. Balint, Bibring, Cohen, and Salzman have viewed the hostility and bitterness of the depressed individual as a secondary phenomenon and a reaction of others to their behavior (10, 14–17). Consequently, the depressed person may become hostile in response to others who become increasingly hostile to the depressed person's efforts to restore his loss. The demands are insistent, insatiable, and impossible to fulfill so that ultimately one is pushed to irritation, anger, and ultimately some form of rejection. The demands are generally made on those closest to and most intimate with the depressed person. This applies to the family, friends, and ultimately the psychiatrist or other "helping" person. These demands are essentially a power operation and a struggle to control and influence others to restore what has been supposedly lost. Self-destructive threats are often the most powerful weapons in this effort.

Mendelson concurs that there is no consensus on the relationship of aggression to depression either primarily or secondarily (18).

With regard to oral factors in depression, Mendelson's finding has had a more lasting influence in comprehending this disorder. While the notion of oral eroticism was stressed by Abraham and Freud, succeeding theorists have viewed it not as a libidinal or zonal issue but symbolically, as an issue of dependency and excessive reliance on others for love and affection to sustain self-esteem. These individuals are called oral characters, and their relationship to depression, whether it is viewed as libidinal or as the need for narcissistic supplies from the external world or internal sources, appears to be definable.

Some of our earlier psychological theories emphasized the element of "loss" in depression. While the loss was characterized as an object toward which one had ambivalent feelings, others viewed it as the loss of love for an object, person, value, standard, or ideal. In other words, this reaction seems to occur following a loss or the apprehension of a possible loss, of something or someone that is viewed as necessary and irreplaceable for the continued functioning of the individual. The depression is then an attempt to overcome or "repair" the loss, involving items relating to the individual's excessive demands and expectations that are not fulfilled. Therefore the reaction may follow a failure to maintain the individual's own unreasonable expectations of himself as well as of others. If the concerns continue and the apprehension becomes a conviction, depression may supervene. This is often the situation when a student becomes depressed when he fails to maintain his demands for "A" grades in all his subjects. His presumed failure demonstrates his fallibility, and his depression is a response to the feeling of loss of his standards and values. This is also the case when a person receives a promotion and an increase in authority with a contradictory depressive response. At such times his neurotic expectation that he be loved by all may be shattered by the realization that his promotion requires him to be a disciplinarian and perhaps an unpopular figure.

With this in mind, we can then recognize other elements in the depressive reaction, such as the gluttonous urge for fulfillment (sometimes called orality); the dependency-independency struggle; the obsessive elements in the requirements for perfection and infallibility leading to grandiose and omniscient attitudes; the anger at being denied psychological and physiological support; and finally, hostile attacks against those nearest the individual and the world in general. We can also see that despair, often to the point of that hopelessness which leads to suicide, can occur if the response fails to achieve its purpose. Depression, therefore, occurs as a neurotic maladaptive response in which the individual attempts to force the return of the lost object of value.

The effect of a loss of a valid standard or highly esteemed value or person in an individual who is not deeply involved in a neurotic struggle is different from depression; it is more like the process of mourning. The individual quickly attempts to reorganize his personality structure without the lost value or person. While some grief normally accompanies this process, there is a reasonable effort to be reintegrated at a higher level of maturity, and the experience may ultimately be a productive one.

Depression results from the failure to maintain excessive standards and may be relieved when some evidence of acceptability or some success in an unrelated area temporarily restores the illusion of self-worth. Depressed persons tend to overlook their assets in moments of temporary difficulty and despair. Since such feelings are widespread and describe almost the entire population, we can see why the mild morning blues and "low feelings" are so commonplace. It is the rare, truly mature, individual with solid self-esteem who does not have periodic depressed reactions.

At times, the basic dynamics of the reaction are apparent. At other times they are vague, clouded in symbolism, or so involved in a neurotic structure that is already heavily defended with numerous other mental mechanisms that these dynamics are difficult to discover without a long dreary investigation.

At times minor events trigger the reaction, because they touch off major systems of defense, while major tragedies leave no impact, since they are not related to the individual's neurotic requirements. For example, if an extreme reaction takes place because one has gotten a lower grade than one expected, it cannot be fully explained by this event alone. It could be better understood if one could realize the severe condemnation and utter contempt which the person feels for himself because he failed to fulfill his demands. His response is so severe that he anticipates total rejection and severe censure from others. When success brings on a depression, the same factors are at work. The person who has a depressed reaction to success has aspired to higher standards and values that he must achieve in his new status. His underlying feelings of inadequacy and his demands for a perfect performance in his new status leave him with feelings of uncertainty and incapacity to achieve them. If the apprehension is great enough, it may bring on a depression. Success in such instances is not regarded simply as a mark of achievement, but as a test and a challenge toward further achievement. When success produces tension and uneasiness instead of a comfortable feeling of recognition and acknowledgement, it tends to produce a depression. This concept of depression demonstrates that depression is more than a faulty process of learning in the past, but is more related to what is happening in the present and in the anticipations of the future. This concept also provides a significant clue to the treatment of depression and the necessity for focusing on the here and now, and not becoming obsessively preoccupied with the past.

In viewing depression as a response, we are interested not only in the threat or danger, but also in what effect the manifestations have on the environment as well as on the individual himself. This implies a phenomenological description of depressive behavior and its effect on others. This is crucial not only to the understanding of the disorder but also to adequate therapeutic management. In this connection, it becomes vital to distinguish between the patient's behavior that is wish-fulfilling and behavior that is a response to others in their reaction to the patient's behavior. In other words, not all behavior produces the response the patient either wishes or pursues. Often it produces the opposite effect. We must distinguish between the intent of a segment of behavior and its consequences. For example, in the early stages of a depressive reaction, the demands and pressures of the patient are rewarded with reassurances and support. Since these supports do not satisfy the patient or are unacceptable because they are insufficient, he presses further. Ultimately he alienates these individuals who reject his advances. They may get angry, sharp, or inattentive. This in turn angers the depressed individual who at the onset may have been pleading because of a need and later becomes demanding and hostile because this need is not fulfilled. Similarly, those who at the outset were interested and considerate to the patient now are angry, impatient, and rejecting. This vicious circle is particularly evident in the depression, and therefore the focus on hostility in the depression must often be viewed as a secondary response rather than the focal issue. Moreover, the hostility is more notable in those who deal with the depressive person than in the depressive individual himself.

Thus the hostile, demanding, and clinging behavior is related to the individual's desperate attempt to regain the lost object from those whom he feels have taken it away or could restore it. He pleads, begs, demands, cajoles, and attempts to force the environment to replace the loss.

At first the tenacious and demanding behavior evokes sympathy and pity. But since this does not restore what has been lost, either because it is impossible or because the needs are insatiable, the demands increase and produce resentment and anger toward the depressed person. The end result is an annoyed and distressed individual who generally feels guilty, even though he has tried his best to please and appease the depressed person. The annoyance turns soon to noticeable irritation and finally to anger. At this point there may actually be rejection of the depressed individual, and this confirms the latter's grievances, which in turn produces hostility and justifies his accusations against the environment.

The self-accusations and self-derogation that characterize the depressive process can be viewed as an attempt to stimulate the good will of the community to restore the lost object. The exaggerated focus on one's misery and worthlessness may stimulate some charitable concern and reassurance. Up to a point, it may provoke reassuring gestures and promises. Very shortly, the focus on self-deriding and abnegating tendencies stirs up contempt rather than compassion, and annoyance rather than sympathy. One feels accused by the depressed person, and guilt is evoked because of the failure to satisfy his request. The patient hopes that by stimulating guilt in others he may promote and sustain activity in his behalf. This is most noticeable in the agitated type of depression.

The silent, retarded depressive achieves the same goal. By being immovable and uncommunicative, he conveys a silent rebuke and reproach to the environment. The passive, seemingly undemanding attitude is actually a most potent device in producing intensive guilt and activity in others. There is always a note of criticism and implication of rejection in his view of the limitations and inadequate help that he is receiving. However, while he feels helpless and dependent, he is loath to accept any help, since his standards require total independence and omnipotence. He frequently rejects or distorts any sympathetic reassurance or aid even while he needs and asks for it, insisting that it is insufficient or patronizing. It is apparent that he strongly resents being in a dependent role, and much of his hostility is the result of this awareness. For the person who has prided himself on his independence the necessity of accepting, yet alone pleading, for help is humiliating and degrading. It is for this reason that the depressed person is most angry toward formerly loved individuals who are most prone to respond to his pleas, or toward other persons who are either responsive to his demands or feel sympathetic to his plight. While he is grateful for the attention, he strongly resents the dependent role in which it places him, and therefore he cannot gracefully accept what is done for him. This makes the giver feel that the depressed person is ungrateful, and the giver is then reluctant to give more.

The relationship of depression to the obsessional dynamism has been noted by many theorists. The obsessional need for magical control which is frequently frustrated may result in brief or prolonged depressive episodes. The failure to achieve the impossible standards of the obsessional neurotic is often felt as a loss of an essential value. Depression may supervene in an attempt to recover these standards. When the power operation of the obsessional succeeds or the magical impotence is fulfilled, then the individual may become grandiose to the point of a manic response. Lewin and others have described the manic reaction as a defense against the depression through furious distractions and exaggerated feelings of worthlessness. However, it might also be regarded as an aspect of the same process of attempting to retain a value essential to the neurotic integration. When this attempt succeeds, mania results, and when it fails, depression results. Depression may precede or follow the mania, depending on the course of events in the experiences of these individuals who respond to their anxiety through a defense of depression.

A variety of defensive responses may occur in the wake of a failing obsessional defense—for example, schizophrenia, paranoid developments, and other grandiose states, as well as depression. At present it is extremely difficult to determine why one response occurs and not another. However, it is clear that the depressive reaction is commonplace because the obsessional mode of behavior is universal. The depressive reaction may be mild or severe, and it represents the failure of the obsessional defense to maintain the standards or values considered by the individual to be essential. Depression follows the conviction or apprehension that the value, person, or thing that is deemed necessary may actually be lost or is no longer available.

These values or persons are not necessarily realistic, nor are the demands reasonable. They are invariably extreme and excessive and form part of the obsessive neurotic value system in which the requirements for perfection and omniscience are essential ingredients. While the obsessional system is intact, the illusion of omniscience and perfection can be maintained. However, a crisis, a sudden disease, or some unexpected event may stir up the individual's apprehension about his ability to maintain these standards. If the concerns continue and the apprehension becomes a conviction, depression may supervene.

The relationship of the obsessional dynamism to depression is portrayed frequently in a dramatic form in the involutional depressions that arise in retired or incapacitated people. The precipitating factor is the forced recognition that one's previous productivity and capacity have become limited. This recognition exacerbates any prior obsessional or perfectionistic traits about not being able to live up to one's previous standards.

A prototype of this situation is represented by a 62-year-old lawyer who had been very successful in his profession, and who had to slow down his pace for the previous 5 years because of a heart attack. Although he had been the organizer of a very successful law firm, he had over the past few years become increasingly depressed, with feelings of worthlessness and despair. He was, in his own words, a perfectionist who was dedicated to his job and would not settle for anything but the best. He had few other interests, and tried to acquire all the knowledge about his particular specialty. He was inflexible in his demands on himself and simply had to keep up with the best. Though he had achieved a large measure of success and was happily married, he was a tense, anxious person.

In trying to slow down at work, he began to feel less adequate than his colleagues, and guilty about not earning his way. He needed extra assurances about his output and his usefulness to the firm, while his colleagues tried to relieve him of difficult problems. He began to notice that he tired more easily and could not keep up with the younger staff in long-winded conferences that involved extensive drinking. He could not accept the realities of the aging process and was humiliated when he felt tired. He was compelled to try to prove that his efficiency was as high as ever—even though he was aware of his physiological limitations.

As he slowly began to feel depressed, he began wondering whether the firm would drop him in spite of his having participated in its founding. He felt he was a failure and wondered if he had a right to burden others. He began to assume some paranoid ideas. His sex life was less active, and he wondered if his wife would also abandon him. At this point, his depression was still mild, but it was clear that it would not be long before he might be involved in suicidal preoccupations or even in possible attempts at suicide.

The picture he described was related directly to his inability to accept the inevitable consequences of physiological aging, with its psychological accompaniments. By activity, success, and continuous acknowledgement from others, he could avoid the full recognition of his failing capacities. The heart attack forced this recognition upon him, as well as a recognition of his dependence upon others. He was forced to admit that being 62 years of age was different from being 40. As the recognition of his increasing limitations was forced upon him, he became depressed, despaired of the future, and saw no reason for existence. He concluded that he would have to go out and get a new batch of clients to prove that he was as good as ever—but he realized that this was not possible. He could not recognize that aging is inevitable and must be dealt with as a fact of life.

It is abundantly clear that a heretofore successfully adapted, obsessional individual was, under forced circumstances of aging and disease, unable to accept his human predicament. He could only react with despair, hopelessness, and depression.

Depression is, of course, hardly confined to older people. The demand for perfection often causes a student to become depressed if he fails to maintain his demands for "A" grades in all subjects. His presumed failure convinces him of his fallibility, and his depression is a response to the feeling of loss of standards and values. This is also the case when a person receives a promotion and an increase in authority and reacts with a contradictory depressive response. At such times his neurotic expectation to be loved by all may be shattered by the realization that his promotion requires him to be a disciplinarian and perhaps an unpopular figure.

The object or value that is supposed to be lost is considered essential; it may be the cornerstone of the neurotic integration which is endangered if it is lost.

Depression occurs only in response to the neurotic elements in a person's personality and is often the key that allows us to see these elements. The loss of real things tends to produce a determined effort to replace what has been lost. Depression is the neurotic's maladaptive response which attempts to force the return of the lost object or value.

This situation was dramatically portrayed in an extremely bright and ambitious young man. His expectations far exceeded his realistic potentials, which led to several severe depressive reactions while at college. In the early part of his marriage he became depressed when he felt that his wife was losing interest in him, and this feeling caused him to seek psychoanalytic therapy. During the treatment process he went into another severe depression, which made it possible to study the development in detail. The depression began after he became the director of a national organization which was faltering until he began making a notable success of it. He inaugurated a large fund drive, was in excellent spirits, and he functioned most effectively—even though his standards were extremely high and he was overly dedicated and conscientious. As the fund drive grew more elaborate and the deadline for a major event in the drive was approaching, he became overwhelmed by the details. He tried to handle every phase of the venture himself and demanded that every activity be perfectly executed. He wanted guarantees that the gala evening that was planned would come off perfectly. As evidence began to accumulate that it would be successful and as more prominent persons became involved, he became more depressed instead of being reassured. The participation of all these important people made it even more imperative that it be successful, and he demanded further guarantees that all would go perfectly.

As the day approached, he became increasingly agitated and preoccupied. His restlessness and insomnia were stimulated by a constant reexamination of all the plans. All the minutiae became major issues and every phase had to be scrutinized anew to prevent some disaster from occurring. What had begun as a successful venture which he was handling effectively turned into a nightmare of fear and danger. He saw himself on trial—as if the event would determine his entire future standing. Its significance was enormously exaggerated. He saw himself in the spotlight, critically appraised by all, which justified his concerns and perfectionistic strivings. He became self-critical, self-derogatory, and had crying spells—with demands for reassurance about impossible matters. His physical processes slowed down, which aggravated his depression further, until he was no longer able to get to the office. Although he withdrew several weeks before the event, it still came off well. He felt guilty about his failure to complete the project, but received much acclaim for its success. His depression now quickly lifted. The whole incident was strikingly similar to a depression that he suffered several years earlier when he was learning to drive. His expectations about his driving skill after a few lessons made the driver's test so distressing that he abandoned it for fear he would look ridiculous. Since he did not feel completely in control of the car and anticipated a debacle, he gave up driving altogether.

On both these occasions his depression was directly in response to the increasing demands that he made upon himself. As he became aware of this, he was overwhelmed by feelings of failure and tragedy and his illusionary requirements of omnipotence and perfection began to be shattered. Despair and hopelessness were the result. The understanding and the resolution of the depressive process strengthened his feelings of esteem and lessened his obsessional requirements. This was facilitated by his recognition of the success of the venture which was the result of his own efforts and which succeeded without guarantees of perfection.

There is a similarity that has been noted by a great many personality theorists, beginning with Freud and Karl Abraham, and including Karen Horney, Harry Stack Sullivan, Franz Alexander, and Sandor Rado, between depression, obsession, and power of operations. Their descriptions of the depressive personality are almost identical to that of the obsessive-compulsive personality.

The depressive person is described by Franz Alexander and others as one who has exceptionally high standards and who cannot accept any compromises. He is egocentric and overreacts to frustration and denial. His relationship to others is characterized as one of exploitative dependency, in which he controls and manipulates others. He tends to deal in extremes of good and bad (black and white) and fails to see that the total person is a mixture of both. He is serious, dedicated, and determined to achieve perfection in all things. He feels that he has failed to fulfill his own expectations as well as those of his parents. However, he maintains his level of existence by an illusion that he is achieving a perfect performance. When he is forced by circumstances to acknowledge some deficiency or failure in his system of values, he feels humiliated by the notion that he has lost status and esteem in the eyes of others. This feeling is accompanied by feelings of hopeless despair and depression. This description is a precise parallel of the descriptions of obsessionals who react with despair to any awareness of imperfections. When the failure is extreme and presumed to be irreparable, a severe depression may ensue. If the obsessional feels that total rejection may follow some failure on his part to maintain absolute control at all times, depression may also follow. As the excessive and exaggerated standards of the obsessional defense can rarely be maintained, it is inevitable that frequent depressions will occur—ranging from the mild to the severe forms.

Depression is a reaction or response, not a diagnostic entity or a psychiatric syndrome. It is not a disease, and therefore one does not have a depression; rather one is being or acting depressed. It is something someone is doing rather than something that is happening to him. It is a behavioral interaction as well as a mood alteration. It occurs in response to an event in the outside world that can be expressed in terms of a loss of something or someone that is considered essential to the person's integration. Generally, it is a reaction to the loss or threatened loss of some value that leaves the person feeling powerless and hopeless.

The development of a depressive reaction is therefore potentially present in everyone and is not exclusively tied to past experiences. It is intimately related to present hardships and future expectations. It is accompanied by physiochemical changes in amino acids and ketosteroids, and by other chemical changes that are reflected in definable physiological and behavioral responses.

The content of the depression consists of a variety of coercive, demanding, pleading, and extorting devices which attempt to force the return of the lost object or value. When depression supervenes, the person feels he has lost the esteem and good will of others because he has failed to live up to his perfectionistic goals and ideals. The loss may be concretized in terms of a person or thing, and his behavior is an expression of despair and hopelessness. He attempts to repair the loss by persuasion and coercion, or by the appeal of threats of self-damage. The hostility may be present at the original loss, but it occurs primarily when the behavior of the depressed person alienates and antagonizes others so that he is ultimately rejected. This behavior, instead of formulations related to the death instinct and the rage against the introjected hated object, accounts for the intense hostility present.

Viewing depression as a transactional reaction permits the therapist to recognize the physiological as well as psychological factors involved. It also requires him to view the response in the context of the real and present world, rather than as an instinctual deformation or disorder initiated and directly related to early experiencing, except in a broad, etiological sense. It allows the therapist to base the therapeutic work on the recognition of the false value system and the underlying neurotic supports which have been lost, rather than on the issue of hostility and its expression.

References

1. Klein M: A contribution to the psychogenesis of manic depressive states, in *Contributions to Psychoanalysis—1921–1945.* London, Hogarth Press, 1948, pp. 282–310.
2. Sullivan HS: *Conceptions of Modern Psychiatry.* Washington, DC, William A White Psychiatric Foundation, 1947.
3. Sullivan HS: *Schizophrenia as a Human Process.* New York, Norton, 1962.
4. Beck AT: *Depression: Clinical, Experimental and Theoretical Aspects.* New York, Harper and Row, 1967.
5. Arieti S: Manic depressive psychoses, in *American handbook of Psychiatry.* Edited by Arieti S, New York, 1959, Vol 1, pp. 419–454.
6. Abraham K: Notes on the psychoanalytic investigation and treatment of manic-depressive insanity, in *Selected Papers on Psychoanalysis.* New York, Basic Books, 1960, pp. 137–156.
7. Abraham K: The first pregenital stage of the libido, in *Selected Papers on Psychoanalysis.* New York, Basic Books, 1960, pp. 248–279.
8. Abraham K: A short study on the development of the libido, in *Selected Papers on Psychoanalysis.* New York, Basic Books, 1960, pp. 418–501.
9. Rado S: The problem of melancholia. *Int J Psa* **9**:420–438, 1928.
10. Bibring E: *The Mechanism of Depression—Affective Disorders.* Edited by Greenacre P, New York, International Universities Press, 1953, pp. 13–48.
11. Jacobson E: Transference problems in the psychoanalytic treatment of severely depressed patients. *J Am Psa Assoc* **2**:595–606, 1954.
12. Horney K: *Our Inner Conflicts.* New York, Norton, 1945.
13. Bonime W: Psychotherapeutic approach to depression. *Contemp Psa* **2**:48–53, Fall 1965.
14. Cohen MB, Baker G, Cohen RA, and others: An intensive study of 12 cases of manic-depressive psychoses. *Psychiatry* **17**:103–137, 1954.
15. Balint M: New beginning and the paranoid and depressive syndromes. *Int J Psa* **33**:214–224, 1952.
16. Salzman L: *The Obsessive Personality.* New York, Science House, 1968.
17. Salzman L: Depression: A clinical review, in *Science and Psychiatry.* Edited by Masserman J, 1970, Vol. XVII, pp. 109–119.
18. Mendelson, M: *Psychoanalytic Concepts of Depression.* Springfield, Charles C Thomas Press, 1960.

Five

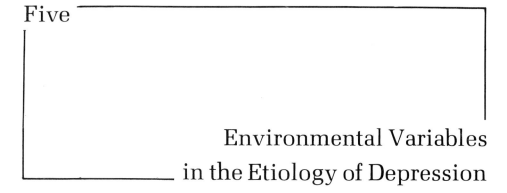

Environmental Variables in the Etiology of Depression

Eugene S. Paykel, M.D.

In the broadest sense environmental influences on the etiology of depression must be presumed to start shortly after conception, and to extend throughout prenatal, childhood, and adult environment to the moment of development of the depressive episode. Paradoxically, the most incontrovertible evidence for the importance of environmental factors in this general sense comes from genetic studies that show family risk rates, particularly for neurotic depressions, much below levels that would be expected if illnesses were entirely genetically determined.

This chapter is not concerned with the widest aspects of environmental influences. It focuses instead on the area of greatest clinical and research importance, that of recent life events immediately preceding the depressive episode. Prenatal environmental influences on depression have received little study. There is a plentiful literature regarding childhood environment, particularly childhood bereavement and other separations from parents, and birth order. For discussions, the reader is referred to reviews such as those by Heinicke (1) and Granville-Grossman (2).

Research Considerations

Much of the classical clinical literature on life events and depression has derived from the study of small numbers of cases, including intensive study by psychoanalytic methods. Intrapersonal and interpersonal psychodynamic theories having major implications for life events are dealt with in other chapters of this volume. In recent years this literature has been augmented by a growing number of studies employing more rigorous research methodology. This chapter focuses particularly on review of these newer studies.

The need for these studies arises from a number of problems which have led many psychiatrists, particularly in Europe and England, to question the degree to which life events are truly causative of depression. They point out that the events reported by depressed patients are mostly within the range of normal life experience and negotiated by most people, and even the depressed person at another time, without clinical depression developing. Moreover, apparently reactive depressives may show a high degree of genetic risk and of vulnerability to stress.

A major problem concerns event reporting. Both the clinical situation and most research studies depend on patients' retrospective reports of events which occurred some time in the past. Inaccuracies of recall of past material may be of major magnitude for anyone and have been well documented by psychologists. For the depressed patient there may be additional distortions. As with any ill person, the search for an explanation and meaning of the disturbances may induce him to seek hard for a cause in the past. Current depression, lowered self-esteem, guilt, hopelessness, and helplessness also may distort his view of the world to the point where he may overemphasize the significance of events that did occur.

Reliability of reporting has been studied. Hudgens and others (3) compared reports of events by psychiatric patients and their relatives. They reported concordances ranging from 44 to 71%, depending on the particular type of event. They questioned the value of retrospective studies in the light of these findings. However, Brown and others (4) obtained adequate reliabilities in a study of depressed patients, and described precautions to increase reliability. With detailed and careful research interviewing, accurate dating and description of the events can be achieved, particularly if the interview is postponed until the more severe mood disturbance has subsided.

Another set of difficulties concerns the origins of the events. Events do not occur in a vacuum, and all of us to some extent bring about the events from which we suffer. In particular, the depressed patient may experience new events as a result of his depression. For instance, he may leave his work because he cannot function in it. His spouse may misunderstand or be unable to tolerate his increased dependency, leading to increased marital friction. To eliminate such consequences of depression, studies should be confined to events that clearly preceded the onset of depression. This onset may, however, be gradual and difficult to define.

A further problem in research studies has been the absence of any effective methodology to measure stress in quantitative terms. Advances in most areas of scientific endeavour have depended on adequate tools for measurement. Until the last few years no attempts had been made to apply quantitative methods to life stress. Consensus scaling methods developed by Holmes and Rahe (5) have recently been successfully applied to depression in a few studies.

Two other research difficulties are not peculiar to life events. The first concerns control groups. The need for controls is obvious, since life events occur commonly and may precede depression coincidently. However, it is not always easy to find a suitable group and to hold constant all relevant factors. The second issue is that of representative sampling. Depressed patients are heterogeneous and may be admitted selectively to different treatment facilities.

One distinction emphasized recently is that between endogenous and reactive depressives. Selective sampling of only one type might seriously bias findings of studies.

These problems are not insurmountable, but they do explain the existence of some scepticism. However, the studies reported in recent years do provide convincing evidence of the importance of recent life stress.

Controlled Studies

The central research strategy in recent research studies has been that of the controlled comparison. Table 1 summarizes the findings of 12 studies published since 1964 in which depressives were compared with control groups, regarding experience of recent life events. Three different types of controls have been employed. The earliest studies used hospitalized patients with medical illness. Subsequently other groups of psychiatric patients were employed. Most recently, general population control groups have been studied. If we ignore for the time being the type of event, it is apparent that in almost all the studies at least some life events were reported significantly more by depressives than by control groups. Two studies showed no significant differences between life event experience of depressives and the experiences of another psychiatric patient group.

Matched general population subjects provide a particularly suitable control group. Paykel and others (6) compared events reported in the 6 months before the onset of depression by a varied sample of depressed patients, with those reported by matched subjects from a large general population survey. Overall depressives reported almost three times as many events as did controls. Thomson and Hendrie (7) compared depressed inpatients with staff controls, and using weighted stress scores found that depressives had experienced more stress. Brown and others (4) compared inpatient and outpatient depressed women with control subjects from the community. A considerable excess of events was reported by depressives, and these were spread over the entire period of one year before onset which was studied. Cadoret and others (8) compared depressives with their relatives. They recorded only deaths and other losses. Depressives reported at least twice as many of these prior to onset as did the controls, but the difference did not reach statistical significance.

Four studies have used other psychiatric patients as controls. This is a valuable form of controlled comparison; without it we cannot be sure that findings are specific to depression rather than pertinent to a variety of psychiatric disorders. Three of the studies showed at least some kinds of events reported more by depressives than by other groups. This would suggest that depression is particularly closely related to life stress. Sethi (9) studied recent and early separations. Recent separations were reported by 67% of depressives as compared to 30% of mixed psychiatric patients rated low on depression. Levi and others (10) studied suicide attempters. These represent only one segment of depressives, and are also likely to include other patients such as schizophrenics. Recent separations were reported by 60% of suicide attempters, compared with 50% of patients with suicidal urges, and 30% of nonsuicidal patients. Beck and Worthen (11) examined life situations

Table 1 Controlled Studies of Life Events at Onset of Depression

Nature of Controls	Author	Number of Depressives	Findings in Depressives: Excess Any Events	Excess Separations	Excess Other Types of Events
General Population	Paykel and others 1969	185	Yes	Yes	Various, especially undesirable events
	Thomson and others, 1972	74	Yes	Not reported	More stress overall
	Cadoret and others, 1972	100	Suggestive	Suggestive	Not reported
	Brown and others, 1973	114	Yes	Not reported	Markedly and moderately threatening events
Other Psychiatric Patients	Sethi, 1964[a]	45	Yes	Yes	Not reported
	Levi and others, 1966[a]	40	Yes	Yes	Not reported
	Malmquist, 1970[a]	94	No	No	No
	Beck and Worthen, 1972[b]	21	Yes	Suggestive	Events of higher rated hazard
	Uhlenhuth and Paykel, 1973[a]	15	No	No	No
	Jacobs and others, 1974[b]	50	Yes	Yes	Undesirable health, financial, interpersonal discord
Medical Patients	Forrest and others, 1965	158	Yes	No	Social factors
	Hudgens and others, 1967	40	Yes	No	Moves, interpersonal discord

[a]Controls were nondepressed mixed psychiatric patients.
[b]Controls were schizophrenics.

immediately prior to admission in neurotic depressives, schizophrenics, and patients with other mixed diagnoses. Clear precipitants were found in the majority of the depressives, but in only about half of the schizophrenics. Jacobs and others (12) studied depressives and schizophrenics. Overall the depressives reported 50% more events than did the schizophrenics.

Two studies, however, were negative. Malmquist (13) reported on psychiatric inpatients admitted to a community mental health center. Those receiving a diagnosis of depression showed no differences from the remainder regarding the occurrence in the year prior to admission of major or minor losses. Uhlenhuth and Paykel (14) found no difference in the event experience of 15 depressives and 22 anxious neurotics. Although this sample was small, analyses in a large mixed neurotic outpatient sample supported this negative finding. The type of psychiatric patient control is probably important here.

Two studies included in the table used medical patients as controls. Some investigators have regarded these as equivalent to general population subjects. However, in view of the accumulating evidence that medical illness may itself be preceded by a clustering of life events, medical controls are better regarded in the same light as are mixed psychiatric patients. Both studies found some events to be reported more by the depressives than the medical patients. Forrest and others (15) found more events reported by outpatient and inpatient depressives than by mixed medical patients. Hudgens and others (16) compared events in hospitalized depressives and medical controls. They found an excess of changes of dwelling and interpersonal discord in the year prior to admission but pointed out that some of these occurrences were probably consequences of depression which followed onset rather than preceded it. Thomson and Hendrie (7) used controls with polyarthritis as well as staff controls. They found that the depressives report more stress than do the polyarthritics.

Not all these studies were ideal in methodology. In a number of the reports it is not clear that patients were interviewed after recovery to avoid distortions due to current depression. Only five studies utilized events occuring before onset rather than those before hospital admission which might reflect illness behaviour subsequent to onset (4, 6, 7, 9, 12). Nevertheless, taken in combination these studies provide compelling evidence that life events are of importance in the genesis of many depressions. If we temporarily ignore the type of event concerned, depressed patients reliably experience more life events prior to onset than do general populations, medical patients, and among psychiatric patients, schizophrenics and mixed inpatients, although not mixed neurotic outpatients.

Types of Event

Clinical experience, however, indicates something more than just a general relationship between events and depression. It suggests that depression is particularly induced by some specific types of events. Most notable among these are losses, threatened or actual, real or imagined. The role of losses, in combination with predispositions based on early development, is central to much of the psychoanalytic literature on depression. The concept of loss has been broadened to include not only deaths and other separations from key interpersonal figures, but also losses of limbs and other bodily parts, losses of self-esteem, and narcissistic self-gratification. For research purposes the concept is better split into its components. Among these, deaths and other separations have received most attention, and provided the foundations for Freud's classic formulations.

What support does empirical research give to these views? The findings are also contained in Table 1. Ten studies reported specifically on recent separations. In six of these, depressives reported more separations than did the control groups. Two comparisons with mixed psychiatric patients and two with medical patients were negative, suggesting that separations may also play a part in the genesis of other psychiatric and medical disorders. One additional study focused on deaths. Birtchnell (17) in a study of psychiatric patients found recent death of a parent unrelated to diagnosis of depression, but it was commoner in the severely rather than the moderately depressed, and commoner in those who had attempted suicide. Clinically, the major interpersonal losses become increasingly important as age increases: they mostly occur in late middle age and the later phases of the life cycle.

In general these studies indicate that recent separations play an important role in the genesis of depressions. However, it is clear that the relationship is far from all-embracing. In most of the studies a substantial proportion of the depressives did not report recent separations. Moreover, it can be seen from Table 1 that seven of the nine studies which considered other types of events also found them reported more by depressives than control groups.

One class of events consistently related to depression in the controlled studies concerns the amount of implied stress or threat. Brown and others (4) rated the threatening implications of the event for the individual. Depressives were distinguished from general population controls in occurrence of markedly threatening events over a year prior to onset. Moderately threatening events were reported to excess only in the 3 weeks before onset, and events of little or no threat not at all. Beck and Worthen (11) obtained ratings by independent raters on the "hazard" in each stressful life situation. Depressives' life situations were found to be of significantly higher mean rated hazard than were those of schizophrenics. Paykel and others (6) used a different, but related, concept. This was the social desirability of the event in terms of generally shared values. Events categorized as undesirable strongly distinguished depressives from controls: desirable events did not do so.

Another group of events which appears closely related to depression in empirical studies comprises those reflecting interpersonal discord (12, 16). Some of these may involve the threat of separation. One such group of conflicts which received special attention are those between the depressed woman and her adult children in the "empty nest" situation at the end of childbearing (18).

A further important group of events is that of blows to the self-esteem. Bibring (19) had laid particular emphasis on these, and has regarded depression as a state of helplessness and powerlessness arising from situations where aspirations to be loved, strong, and good have not been fulfilled. Such threats to self-esteem, failures, and disappointments have not so far been specifically distinguished from other kinds of threatening events in the empirical studies, but many of the events reported in them wo into this group.

In a theoretical formulation which relates both to separation and to theories, Schmale and Engel have explored the role of depression mediating factor in somatic illness (20, 21). They have described "giving-up-given-up" complex in which they differentiate the affects of helplessness and hopelessness as two separate characteristic responses to the perception that a loss is irretrievable. With helplessness the subject feels powerless to overcome the loss but perceives the environment to be responsible and expects it to take over and provide the missing gratification. With hopelessness the subject assumes that he is responsible for the loss of gratification by personal inadequacies, for which he cannot be helped even if the environment takes action. They link these responses to those observed in separated human and animal infants.

One kind of event that does not emerge as important from these studies is the success event. The events related to depression appear largely to be those with negative connotations, threatening and undesirable. Nevertheless, it is clinical experience that depressions may in a small proportion of cases follow a promotion, an unexpected economic windfall, or the achievement of a long desired goal. Some of these events may contain a disguised threat such as greatly increased responsibilities. Major disruptions of established life routine may accompany some successes, and this element may be important in other events, such as moves, which may precede depression. Preexisting pathologies may be important in some successes. These include such elements as dependency that can no longer be gratified, inability to accept success as appropriate when esteem is low, or unconscious destruction of a love object to whom rivalry is felt.

There has been little empirical research into the effects of stressful situations that are persistent rather than new events and changes. The roles remain to be elucidated of such situations as a chronically bad marriage, physical invalidism, economic deprivation, and occupation of a disadvantaged role in society.

The general picture presented by the studies of life events is somewhat nonspecific. Certain types of events, most notably separations but also other events with threatening implications, including blows to the self-esteem, appear particularly related to depression. However, the range of events reported by depressives is too wide to be included in any single formulation. The concept of losses requires stretching beyond useful meaning if it is to comprehend them all. The more kinds of events that are inquired for in the depressed the more are reported to excess. Classical formulations of depressive psychodynamics usually imply a key triggering event. Not uncommonly, however, detailed inquiry of patients reveals several events suggesting a cumulative model of stress, without primacy of any single event. This accumulation of recent stress is consonant with descriptions in the psychosomatic literature of life crises as clusters of events. Depression appears to form a final outcome for a variety of stresses.

A truly specific relationship between certain events and depression would only result if these events did not precede other disorders. It is clear that such a

...st. It is beyond the scope of this chapter to ... conditions. However, there is good evidence ... precede schizophrenia and other psychiatric ...ness.

...s have been studied by means other than the ...roach. There have been a number of prospective ... including the classic work of Lindemann (22). In a ...on and others (23) followed up 40 bereaved subjects. ...d depressed mood, sleep disturbances, and crying, but ...uicidal thoughts were uncommon, suggesting some di... ...ical depression. Although 25% consulted a physician for sympto... ... grief, few saw psychiatrists. In a subsequent study of a new sample, 3... showed symptoms of depression after one month, 17% after one year (24). In general these studies suggest that normal grief shades imperceptibly into abnormal grief and depression. The rough rule of thumb that mourning lasting longer than 6 months may be pathological would still appear to have some validity.

Other events have received less study. There have been a few prospective studies of retirement. Childbirth is a special case that has received a good deal of attention, but here biological and hormonal changes are inextricably intertwined with psychological adaptations. There have also been some studies of moves, particularly those associated with relocation from deteriorated urban areas with strongly knit cultures (25, 26). Although these studies did not adopt a clinical framework, feelings of grief were commonly reported. A series of English studies using epidemiologic methods has explored transfer to newer housing in more impersonal communities. Two reports found increased rates of psychiatric disorder (27, 28); one carefully controlled study did not (29).

Predisposing Factors

It has often been pointed out by those sceptical of the role of life events that the events reported by depressives are common ones which are frequently experienced without depression occurring, so that their true contribution to the genesis of the episode is open to question. Detailed scrutiny of the events reported in research studies and in clinical practice shows that most of them are common personal and interpersonal crises which lack catastrophic qualities and might be expected to produce only fairly transient disappointment, sadness, or distress. Such major events as recent deaths of spouse, parent, or child are reported by only small proportions of clinical depressives.

It is easy in retrospective situations to lose sight of the base rates for the population. Whenever the incidence of a disease state is relatively low, the usefulness of single events in explaining the disease is quite limited if these events occur with even moderate frequency in the general population. Since the disease state occurs infrequently, most of the event occurrences will not be followed by onset of illness, even if a high proportion of ill subjects report the event.

There have been some attempts to estimate the magnitude of the contribution of events to depressive onset. In one such study it was estimated that, although occurrence of an interpersonal separation increased the risk of developing depression sixfold, less than 10% of subjects in the general population would become depressed: the large majority did not do so. Brown and others (4) devised a concept that they called the "brought-forward" time, corresponding to the amount of time by which the events might be considered on average to have advanced expectation of a spontaneous onset. They obtained a figure of about 2 years for depression, which was considered to be an important effect, and was substantially larger than that for schizophrenia. Although the exact figures are probably very unreliable, the general thrust of these calculations appears similar. The effect of life events is an important one. However, when viewed in the total context, a very large part in determining whether the event is followed by depression must be attributed to other factors.

These additional elements can be subsumed under the general rubric of predisposition or vulnerability. There are many elements to it; they may be genetic or environmental, psychological, or biological. Some personality types tend to be vulnerable to certain kinds of events. Obsessional personalities tolerate badly major changes in life routine: dependent personalities may be particularly threatened by events involving increase in responsibilities and withdrawal of support. English authors have emphasized the concept of the neurotic or inadequate personality with low ego strength, which may be vulnerable to stresses of many kinds (30). In both kinds of personality vulnerability, genetic inheritance clearly plays an important part. So too do early experiences. Thus childhood loss of a parent may sensitize to actual or threatened loss in adult life by reactivation of unresolved childhood mourning. Incorporation of a low self-image from hostile parental figures in childhood may render the adult vulnerable to criticism. Children who develop marked upward striving behaviour based on parental aspiration as described by Mabel Blake Cohen and others (31) may be particularly threatened by events involving downward change of status. Experiences after childhood may modify event reactions. Thus previous experience of the threatening event may have provided an adaptive repertoire for coping, or maladaptive responses leading to failure. There may in addition be various protective or aggravating elements in the current environment such as the support available from key figures in the interpersonal milieu.

In these circumstances it is not just the event that is important, but the way in which it interacts with predisposing factors. An event is followed by depression when it falls on fertile soil. It is likely that any single episode of depression in a particular person will be the outcome of multiple causes in a complex multifactorial etiology.

In this respect, evidence of predisposing factors such as genetic loading does not negate the influence of recent life events, but complements it. Although both events and predisposing factors have been studied in detail, there have not been many empirical research studies of the ways in which the two interact to produce depression. The controlled study by Levi and others (10) of separation in suicide attempters, cited in Table 1, included one relevant analysis. In addition to studying recent separations these workers obtained a history of childhood separations. The suicidal patients reported more recent separations and more childhood separations than did controls. The authors went on to test for the interaction between separation in early childhood and recent separations and found it significant; the suicidal patients tended to show a combination of both early childhood separation and separation prior to the suicidal attempt. These findings provide one of the most direct pieces of research evidence in the literature that childhood separation may sensitize to adult loss. However, a similar analysis in mixed depressives has shown negative results (9). Another study failed to find an expected inverse relationship between the amount of stress experienced and the amount of genetic predisposition reflected in family history (7). Several prospective studies of groups undergoing the same threatening event have shown that a variety of reactions may ensue, depending on coping styles.

Endogenous Depressions

In clinical practice, depressions are encountered which, even on detailed probing, appear unrelated to any life events or stressful situations. Estimates of the proportion of depressions which are unprecipitated vary widely from almost none to almost all. They depend heavily on the orientation of the psychiatrist and his willingness to search for events and to accept their relationship to depression. They also depend on the kind of treatment facility under consideration. Endogenous depressions, which tend to be more severe, are found more commonly among hospitalized patients, while reactive depressions predominate in office practice. In one study of a representative sample, 15% of episodes were judged endogenous (32). In most depressions there are some psychological elements, although these are often incomplete as full causes.

As it is usually employed, the concept of endogenous depression is a complex one. It involves the fusion of two distinctions: that between endogenous and reactive depression on one hand, and psychotic and neurotic depression on the other. The elements of the fused concept have been reviewed by Klerman (33). The first is etiologic, based on the presence or absence of precipitant events. The second involves symptom pattern. Endogenous depressions tend to show certain specific symptoms including severe depression, psychomotor retardation, more psychologic disturbances such as anorexia, constipation, and insomnia, a pattern of diurnal variation with morning worsening and of insomnia with early morning wakening, and absence of fluctuations with concurrent environmental change. The third element concerns personality prior to the episode, which is variously characterized in endogenous depressives as nonneurotic, obsessional, or stable.

In recent years a number of studies have employed factor analysis to demonstrate the relationship between these three elements (34).

Although full discussion of the complexities of depressive classification is beyond the scope of this chapter, one relevant problem in these studies concerns the relationship of precipitant stress to the other elements. Often in the research studies the presence or absence of life stress is recorded in a simple yes-no judgement. This judgement is a difficult one to make in practice, since the situation is usually one of partial and ambiguous precipitation in which the few events are not sufficiently overwhelming to be a sole cause of the depression.

Some recent studies have approached this problem more critically, using quantitative approaches to the measurement of stress based on the work of Holmes and Rahe (5). In one such study, in which the added precaution was taken of using separate raters for symptoms and life events to avoid bias, absence of life stress correlated with presence of an endogenous symptom pattern, but the relationship was quite weak (35). Patients diagnosed as psychotic depressives have been found to report as much life stress as those diagnosed as neurotic (7). The majority of severely ill psychotic depressives were found in one study to report environmental precipitants on detailed probing (36). Overall it appears that unprecipitated depressives tend only weakly to have any particular symptom pattern.

There has been a vigorous debate, particularly in the British literature, as to whether endogenous and reactive depressions are distinct entities or form opposite poles of a continuous distribution without bimodality. This debate has usually been applied to the full concept of endogenous depression, rather than that based on stress alone. The separation between endogenous and reactive depression appears at best a very indistinct one (37). Two recent studies have explored this separation based on precipitant stress alone, with similar findings (7, 32). Both studies examined the frequency distributions of quantitative scores reflecting amount of precipitant stress, and found a continuous distribution from predominantly unprecipitated to precipitated depressions, without any clear cut-off point or bimodality.

The distinction between unipolar and bipolar depressions has recently been of considerable interest. The relationship of precipitant stress to this distinction has not been sufficiently examined. Earlier reports often referred to precipitating factors in manic-depressive psychosis, but diagnostic criteria were not always clear. Perris (38) found no difference between recurrent bipolar and unipolar affective psychoses in incidence of precipitating factors. In another study there was no significant difference between bipolar and unipolar depressives on quantified stress scores, but bipolar depressives tended to score lower (7).

The consensus of these recent studies is that, while predominantly unprecipitated depressions do occur, they are related only weakly to any particular symptom pattern or clinical classification. Moreover, the separation between unprecipitated and precipitated depressions is not clear cut. One grades into the other without any clear cut-off point, as might be expected from the difficulty of sharply distinguishing the two in clinical practice. Current theories would suggest a neuropharmacological basis for endogenous depression in amine neurotransmitters. The ultimate mechanism for all depressions lies presumably in the neurophysiological mechanisms underlying mood. Here, psychological inputs and primarily biological disturbances such as enzyme defects, cyclical changes in function, and variations in metabolic pools of transmitter substance must come together. At that point any separation between endogenous and reactive depressions is artificial. It is easy to see how precipitant stress might combine with an endogenous disturbance to cross some sort of threshold, so that elements of both endogenous and reactive depression were combined.

Animal Models

Some fruitful experimental attempts have been made to derive animal models for the psychological precipitants of depression. The most common model has been that of separation, and most researchers have used monkeys as the experimental animal. In a series of studies Harlow and others have demonstrated the effects of separating infant rhesus monkeys from their mothers (39). The reaction occurs in two stages, an initial stage of protest, followed by a stage of despair and withdrawal. Return to the mother is characterized by increased mother directed behaviour and clinging. Kaufman and others have extended these findings and have demonstrated differences between pigtail monkeys and bonnet monkeys, who show much less of a reaction to separation (40). Bonnet monkey infants are able to obtain substitute mothering from other bonnet mothers, but pigtails will not mother other infants.

These patterns show close resemblance to those of anaclitic depression described by Spitz (41) and Bowlby (42) in human infants separated from their mothers. However, the majority of human depressions are in middle-aged adults; full blown clinical depressions are uncommon in childhood. Effects of separation in adult monkeys have not been described, but the effects of separating juvenile rhesus monkeys from their peers have been reported (43). These juveniles show hyperactivity, but do not go through the phase of despair.

Some studies have also been carried out in dogs (44). In one study, six German shepherd pups were allowed to form affectional bonds with a research psychiatrist and then separated from him. Changes were demonstrated in their behaviour. These were not uniform, but depended on the previous temperament of the dogs.

All these studies were based on the model of separation. Using a different model, other workers have confined monkeys in vertical pit-like chambers in an attempt to parallel human situations producing hopelessness and helplessness. Severe behaviour disturbances resembling depression were found (45).

The validity of these animal models for clinical depression in the human adult is not yet fully established, but they appear promising. They open wider possibilities for future study of many aspects, including the effects of environmental stress on neuropharmacological systems mediating affect. They also raise inevitable questions as to the biological function of depression. Kaufman (40) has suggested that the protest stage of agitation observed after separation is subserved by a system related to anxiety and aimed at restoring the infant to the mother, while the phase of despair and withdrawal subserves a conservation function if the mother cannot be regained. His formulation derives from the earlier work by Schmale (20) and Engel (21) on the affects of helplessness and hopelessness. They suggest that when the flight-fight response to an environmental threat is fruitless, a conservation-withdrawal system comes into play aimed at conserving energy, reducing contact with the environment, and minimizing the risk of detection by predators. These formulations are consistent with, but extend, earlier classical views on the function of mourning. They would explain the evolutionary persistence of mild depression as a normal and universal human mood.

Life Events in Outcome and Therapy

The role of life events does not end with onset of the episode. Depression profoundly impairs the individual's capacity to function and to relate to others. The depressive works poorly, may be obliged to stop work on account of incapacity, becomes markedly dependent on family members, and experiences considerable arguments and friction with family members as they fail to recognize the origins of these problems in depression (46). The new events induced by the depressive dysfunction and other spontaneous later events contribute cumulatively to clinical worsening until finally help is sought.

Continuing and earlier life events also have important effects on the recovery process, and there have been a few research studies of these. Havens (47) followed up patients 6 months after they had received ECT. Among patients with affective disorders, but not those with other diagnoses, loss of an immediate relative in the 18 months before admission predicted a poor rather than a good outcome. In patients with affective disorders, relief of the precipitating factors during the follow-up period was found to be associated with a much better outcome.

Events at onset are also related to response to somatic therapies in that immediate outcome of treatment with tricyclic antidepressants and with ECT is better in endogenous depressives. Whether this is a consequence of event precipitation or a reflection of a biologic mechanism remains uncertain. Effects of concurrent events on response to antidepressant medication have received little study. However, two drug trials of tranquilizers have examined effects of life events in mixed neurotics who were predominantly anxious rather than depressed (48, 49). Both studies found patients reporting negative events during treatment to respond less well than those with positive events. In one of these studies more positive events were reported by patients on active drug, suggesting a reporting effect (48). In the second study patients on active drug reported fewer positive events, and the drug effect was most marked in patients reporting no external events.

In clinical practice environmental precipitants and patterns of reaction to them are often central issues for therapy, both in resolution of the acute episode and in avoidance of recurrence. Irreplaceable losses may require working through. Many stresses involve relationships with spouse and family; marital and family therapies may be important here. Crisis intervention techniques designed to mobilize resources toward early resolution may be of help, particularly where stressful situations can be modified before the depressive episode is fully developed. Some stresses are best handled by environmental manipulation; for instance, substitution of outside paid or voluntary work for a maternal role when the last child has left home. In ongoing therapy aimed at prevention of further episodes, identification of maladaptive patterns of reaction to particular kinds of threat, exploration of their origins, and attempts to modify them are of obvious importance.

Conclusions

The extensive clinical and theoretical literature on the relationship between recent events and depression has been augmented by empirical research studies at an accelerating pace in the last decade. The consensus of these studies is to confirm clinically accepted views. Life events bear a causal relationship to the onset of most depressions and probably to a greater extent than with most other psychiatric disorders. A variety of types of event are implicated. Most prominent among these are separations and interpersonal losses. It is clear, however, that depression is a response to a wide range of events with threatening implications, including blows to the self-esteem, interpersonal discord, events that are socially undesirable, and major disruptions of life pattern. Animal models based on separation provide a promising avenue of research. These events and subsequent ones occurring after onset also influence the outcome of the episode and provide important foci for therapy.

A relatively small proportion of depressions appear to be endogenous and unprecipitated by life events. These depressions are not sharply distinguished from more clearly reactive episodes, either with respect to degree of precipitation or to a characteristic symptom picture, although a small number of typical cases occur. Most commonly, depressed patients do report some events at onset, but they are insufficient to fully explain the depression. The events reported are in the range of normal human experience, and more often their occurrence is not followed by depression. Predisposing factors are important, and the way in which they interact with the precipitating event is crucial in determining whether clinical depression results. The evidence suggests a Meyerian model in which many factors converge to produce depression. Life events comprise perhaps the most important single group of these.

References

1. Heinicke CM: Parental deprivation in early childhood: A predisposition to later depression? in *Separation and Depression: Clinical and Research Aspects.* Edited by Scott JP and Senay E, American Association for the Advancement of Science, 1973.
2. Granville-Grossman KL: The early environment in affective disorder, in *Recent Developments in Affective Disorder: A Symposium.* Edited by Coppen A and Walk A, *British Journal of Psychiatry.* Special Publication No. 2., London, Royal Medical Psychological Association, Chap. VI, pp. 65–79.
3. Hudgens RW, Robins E, Delong WB: The reporting of recent stress in the lives of psychiatric patients. *Br J Psychiatr* **117**:635–643, 1970.

4. Brown GW, Sklair F, Harris TO, Birley JLT: Life events and psychiatric disorders. Part I: Some methodological issues. *Psychol Med* **3**:74–87, 1973.
5. Holmes TH and Rahe RH: The social readjustment rating scale. *J Psychosom Res* **11**:213–218, 1967.
6. Paykel ES, Myers JK, Dienelt MN, Klerman GL, Lindenthal JJ, Pepper MP: Life events and depression: A controlled study. *Arch Gen Psychiatr* **21**:753–760, 1969.
7. Thomson KC, Hendrie HC: Environmental stress in primary depressive illness. *Arch Gen Psychiatr* **26**:130–132, 1972.
8. Cadoret RJ, Winokur G, Dorzab J, Baker M: Depressive disease: Life events and onset of illness. *Arch Gen Psychiatr* **26**:133–136, 1972.
9. Sethi BB: Relationship of separation to depression. *Arch Gen Psychiatr* **10**:486–495, 1964.
10. Levi LD, Fales CH, Stein M, Sharp VH: Separation and attempted suicide. *Arch Gen Psychiatr* **15**:158–165, 1966.
11. Beck JC, Worthen JC: Precipitating stress, crisis theory and hospitalization in schizophrenia and depression. *Arch Gen Psychiatr* **26**:123–129, 1972.
12. Jacobs SC, Prusoff BA, Paykel ES: Recent life events in schizophrenia and depression. *Psychol Med* **4**:444–453, 1974.
13. Malmquist CP: Depression and object loss in psychiatric admissions. *Am J Psychiatr* **26**:1782–1787, 1970.
14. Uhlenhuth EH, Paykel ES: Symptom configuration and life events. *Arch Gen Psychiatr* **28**:743–748, 1973.
15. Forrest AD, Fraser RH, Priest RG: Environmental factors in depressive illness. *Br J Psychiatr* **111**:243–253, 1965.
16. Hudgens RW, Morrison JR, Barchha R: Life events and onset of primary affective disorders: A study of 40 hospitalized patients and 40 controls. *Arch Gen Psychiatr* **16**:134–145, 1967.
17. Birtchnell J: Depression in relation to early and recent parent death. *Br J Psychiatr* **116**:299–306, 1970.
18. Deykin EY, Jacobson S, Klerman GL, Solomon M: The empty nest: Psychosocial aspects of conflict between depressed women and their grown children. *Am J Psychiatr* **122**:1422–1426, 1966.
19. Bibring E: The mechanism of depression, in *Affective Disorders*. Edited by Greenacre P, New York, International Universities Press, 1953, pp. 13–48.
20. Schmale AH: Relationship of separation and depression to disease: I: A report on a hospitalized medical population. *Psychosom Med* **20**:259–275, 1958.
21. Engel GL: A psychological setting of somatic disease: The "giving-up-given-up" complex. *Proc Roy Soc Med* **60**:553–555, 1967.
22. Lindemann E: Symptomatology and management of acute grief. *Am J Psychiatr* **101**:141–148, 1944.
23. Clayton P, Desmarais L, Winokur G: A study of normal bereavement. *Am J Psychiatr* **125**:168–178, 1968.
24. Bornstein PE, Clayton PJ, Halikas JA, Maurice WL, Robins E: The depression of widowhood after thirteen months. *Br J Psychiatr* **122**:561–566, 1973.
25. Fried M: Grieving for a lost home, in *The Urban Condition*. Edited by Duhl LJ, Basic Books, New York, pp. 151–171.
26. Gans HJ: Effects of the move from city to suburb, in *The Urban Condition*, Duhl, LJ, New York, Basic Books, pp. 184–197.
27. Martin FM, Brotherston JFH, Chave SPW: Incidence of neurosis in a new housing estate. *Br J Prev Soc Med* **11**:196, 1957.
28. Taylor S, Chave S: *Mental Health and Environment*. London, Longmans Press, 1964.

29. Hare EH, Shaw GK: *Mental Health on a New Housing Estate.* Maudsley Monograph No. 12, London, Oxford University Press, 1965.
30. Slater E: The neurotic constitution. *J Neurol Neurosurg Psychiatr* **6:**1–16, 1943.
31. Cohen MB, Baker G, Cohen RA, Fromm-Reichmann F, Weigert EV: An intensive study of twelve cases of manic depressive psychosis. *Psychiatry* **17:**103–137, 1954.
32. Paykel ES: Recent life events and clinical depression, in *Life Stress and Illness.* Edited by Gunderson EK, Rahe RH, Springfield, Ill, Charles C Thomas, Chap. 5.
33. Klerman GL: Clinical research in depression. *Arch Gen Psychiatr* **24:**305–319, 1971.
34. Mendels J, Cochrane C: The nosology of depression: The endogenous-reactive concept. *Am J Psychiatr* **124** (May suppl.), 1–11, 1968.
35. Paykel ES, Prusoff BA, Klerman GL: The endogenous-neurotic continuum in depression: Rater independence and factor distributions. *J Psychiatr Res* **8:**73–90, 1971.
36. Leff MJ, Roatch JF, Bunney WE: Environmental factors preceding the onset of severe depressions. *Psychiatry* **33:**293–311, 1970.
37. Kendell RE: *The Classification of Depressive Illnesses.* Maudsley Monograph No. 18, London, Oxford University Press, 1968.
38. Perris C: A study of bi-polar (manic-depressive) and unipolar recurrent affective psychoses. *Acta Psychiatr Scand* **42:** Suppl. 194, 1966.
39. Seay B, Hansen E, Harlow HF: Mother-infant separation in monkeys. *J Child Psychol Psychiatr* **3:**123–132, 1962.
40. Kaufman IC: Mother-infant separation in monkeys: An experimental model, in *Separation and Depression.* Edited by Scott JP, Senay E, American Association for the Advancement of Science, 1973.
41. Spitz RA: Anaclitic depression, in *The Psychoanalytic Study of the Child.* Edited by Freud A and others, New York, International Universities Press, Vol. 2, 1946.
42. Bowlby J: *Mental Care and Mental Health.* W.H.O. Monograph No. 2, Geneva, 1951.
43. McKinney WT, Suomi SI, Harlow HF: Repetitive peer separations of juvenile rhesus monkeys. *Arch Gen Psychiatr* **27:**200–203, 1972.
44. Senay EC: Toward an animal model in depression: A study of separation behaviour in dogs. *J Psychiatr Res* **4:**65–71, 1966.
45. McKinney WT, Suomi SI, Harlow HF: Depression in primates. *Am J Psychiatr* **127:**1313–1320, 1971.
46. Weissman MM, Paykel ES, Seigel R, Klerman GL: The social role performance of depressed women: A comparison with a normal sample. *Am J Orthopsychiatr* **41:**390–405, 1971.
47. Havens LL: Losses and depression. The relationship of precipitative events to outcome. *J Nerv Ment Dis* **125:**627–637, 1957.
48. Lipman RS, Hammer HM, Bernardes J, Parker LC, Cole JO: Patient report of significant life situation events. *Dis Nerv Syst* **26:**586–591, 1965.
49. Rickels K, Cattell R, Macafee BA, Hesbacher P: Drug response and important external events in the patient's life. *Dis Nerv Syst* **26:**781–786, 1965.

Six

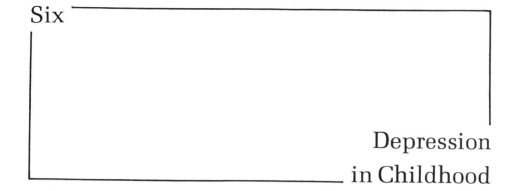

Depression in Childhood

Carl P. Malmquist, M.D.

The popularity of the diagnosis of childhood depressions is increasing. If their actual frequency has increased, we do not know. However, we are much more cognizant at the present time that children do experience depressive symptoms to a magnitude that can be classified as a clinical depression. This knowledge has come from more clinicians who work with children and who are attuned to the developmental significance of mood disturbances. Only a short time ago children were simply thought to get sad when they met disappointments but "not really get depressed." On the question of whether childhood depressions are in fact more prevalent than heretofore, we have no objective knowledge, since any adequate base line with which to make comparisons is lacking.

Just as with depressive phenomena in adults, mixed usages for the term "depression" are applied to children. One usage refers to an internalized mood which a child describes as feeling sad. A somewhat different meaning sees depression as a symptom referring to its external manifestations which are then ticketed as part of a depressive complex. Yet a third meaning introduces the dimension of neurophysiological concomitants with a sad mood or depressed symptom. When a cluster of signs and symptoms hang together with a certain regularity, a depressive syndrome is present—if not a diagnosis of a clinical depression. With children yet another meaning attaches to the presence of depressive mood states. These states may be a signal of a reactive pattern in the current life of the child, or reflect a deviation in the capacity of the child at a particular developmental period to modulate his moods. More enduring mood tones are distinguished from the immediate affective responses in a child, since they give a distinctive quality along this line to the personality.

While multiple descriptive diagnoses are available for adults with depressions as listed in the official *Diagnostic Manual* of the American Psychiatric Association, none are specifically available for depressed children

(1). An adult who is depressed may be considered a Cyclothymic personality, experiencing a Depressive neurosis, having a Psychotic depressive reaction or Involutional melancholic state, or he may be in the grips of a Manic-depressive illness, or he may be given a diagnosis of Schizophrenia, Schizoaffective type. Within the category of "Behavior Disorders of Childhood and Adolescence," there are specific categories for hyperactive, withdrawn, anxious, and unsocialized children, but there are none for depressed children. Of course, a diagnostician can borrow one of the adult diagnoses, such as a Depressive neurosis in childhood, but the omission signifies a continuing situation from the past when depression was not considered an entity encountered in children.

All of the arguments found in the literature about adult depressions remain debatable when encountered in children. These are distinctions between neurotic and psychotic depression or the exogenous or endogenous nature of depressions, and there are problems related to bias in diagnosis based on the socioeconomic class of the patient or clinician and the varied training the psychiatrist has received in different residency training programs which give him a particular orientation toward psychopathology (2). The reliability and usefulness of diagnoses are themselves sometimes challenged (3). More specifically, when dealing with depressions, interclinician diagnostic correlation is only somewhat better than 50% (4). When dealing with childhood depressions, such problems are all magnified due to a basic lack of familiarity with the clinical picture. The picture then may be not one of unreliability between clinicians as to types of depressions, but a situation of missing the diagnosis entirely most of the time.

The Anlage of Depression

Discussions of early manifestations of depression are often lumped together within some vague grouping called infantile depressions. The vagueness is attendant on the intrusion of many diverse syndromes. Another problem is the reliance on retrospective data from those children and adults who later begin to show depressive symptoms. More recently efforts have been made to extend directly the deprivation hypothesis to prospective follow-up studies of such children. Early reports had the further methodological difficulty of dealing with children of different ages in nurseries, foster homes, hospitals, and institutions where observations were made of disruptions in the capacity to form consistent human attachments based on affection. Another line of approach placed an emphasis on the associated deficits in cognitive-intellectual functioning. In attempts to treat these children hypotheses were extended to the earliest childhood as the vulnerable contributing period. Some of these approaches were based on clinical work while others were based on work with the mentally or emotionally retarded. The problems that arise in studying the developmental phenomenon of depressive-proneness are similar to those encountered in investigating many other areas of biopsychological development (5). This work began in the 1920s and 1930s, and some clinical examples are given for illustrative purposes. In 1937 Levy reported an 8-year-old girl who had been in a succession of foster homes before finally being adopted. She continued to manifest an incapacity to form attachments described as a lack of emotional responsiveness and having a "hunger" for affect (6). In 1943 Goldfarb studied 30 children, age 34 to 35 months, and concluded that 15 of the children brought up in institutions had lower IQs by 28 points than those raised in foster homes since the age of 4 months (7). Observations on children placed in the Hampstead nursery during the bombing of London in World War II revealed less serious maternal deprivation repercussions for the older child, but the effects were felt to be more serious when occurring at an earlier age (8). Still controversial and unsettled, either by observational research or by reconstructing the impact of earlier experiences in the course of therapy, is the question of whether greater emotional harm occurs from experiences that occur at a younger age. Clinical impressions based on the greater biological vulnerability of the young organism continue to favor this hypothesis. However, developmentally the younger organism possesses a greater adaptive capacity, such as being able to accept substitute objects, which can work in his favor. In this early work some of the confusion between emotional deprivation, lack of sufficient maternal care, possible organic cerebral impairment, and the syndrome of infantile depression can be seen.

The much-cited syndrome of "anaclitic depression" was elaborated by Spitz (9). Pediatricians had long been aware of such a condition and had referred to it as "marasmus." They classified it as one form of wasting disease of unknown etiology akin to some type of degenerative or dystrophic process. Separation from a maternal object after the period of a specific object recognition at about 6 months was held to lead to a grief reaction. It is now realized that various types of perceptual and attachment behaviors to objects occur from the period of earliest contact with a maternal object. Infants in such situations were described as sad, weepy, and apathetic, with immobile faces that had a distant expression. They reacted slowly to stimuli, exhibited slow movements, had a poor appetite and sleep pattern, and showed little of the motility that infants usually possess. Spitz believed these were symptoms of an "anaclitic depression," since the infants appeared similar observationally to adults who were depressed. The infants had been having a satisfactory relationship with their maternal object up to that time, but after 3 months of such a separation, a full emotional restoration was rare.

Similar symptoms and signs were observed in children institutionalized as infants who were kept permanently separated from their mothers without adequate stimulation and fondling. This had more serious overtones, since both mental and physical development lagged, repeated infections were common, and in some cachexia and even death occurred. This clinical picture was described as "hospitalism" from its frequent association with children maintained in hospitals or institutions. A similar clinical picture was seen in infants with gastric fistulas (10, 11). Engel and Reichsman hypothesized a "depression-withdrawal" reaction in their fistulic infant. In the presence of a stranger, descriptive features of inactivity, hypotonia, sad facial expression, decreased gastric secretion, and finally sleep occurred. Subsequent studies have attempted to expand and critically evaluate this earlier work on institutionalized children. Criticism has centered on methodological considerations and questions as to the adequacy of the organic evaluation procedures for inclusion or exclusion in this syndrome. Infants with nutritional deficiencies may appear overtly indistinguishable in some cases from those subject to prolonged institutionalization, as indeed the term marasmus indicated originally. Even more striking is the similarity in separation studies with nonhuman primates in which these primates show signs of distress similar to the anaclitic depression in human infants (12). Brief separation experiences produce symptoms in Rhesus monkey infants very similar to those in human infants (13). Such variables as the age at the time of separation, length of separation, and sex of the infant need consideration, since different behavioral consequences are associated with these variables (14). Most impressive are reports from animal work that the effects of experimental work with subhuman mammals last for months or years even in certain brief separations.

The 1951 monograph, *Maternal Care and Mental Health*, reviewed previous studies and presented new formulations (15). Updated reviews have appeared since then (16, 17). What is most impressive is that radically different conclusions have not emerged. There is the consistency of certain hypotheses on one hand, and on the other hand, the usual refining of hypotheses by criticism of methodology and the lack of conceptual clarity. One of the major difficulties when appraising these studies is to separate the impact of "maternal deprivation" which may be an independent variable relating to the genesis of depression from the syndrome of maternal deprivation *per se* among whose symptoms are many that appear like a depression—much like nutritional deficiency. Also different kinds of deprivation—psychological, social, cognitive, and organic—can each have components mixed in with depressive symptomatology. The need for specificity has been the greatest obstacle in unraveling the effects subsumed under maternal deprivation. Not until specific independent variables are tied up with components of an emerging depressive-proneness will higher correlations in outcome studies be achieved.

With this in mind let us take a brief look at some of the points originally made by Bowlby in 1951 when he summarized his impressions from the preceding 15-year work. We can now add more specifics and a shift in emphasis but not a rebuttal. For purposes of this discussion the focus is on selecting several of the factors frequently mentioned as related to an outcome of depressive-proneness. It was originally felt that prolonged disruptions during the first 3 years of life left a certain impact on the child's personality, such as appearing emotionally withdrawn and isolated, particularly with respect to children maintained in nurseries and residential settings with inadequate "mothering." "Inadequate mothering" is now considered only one of many variables. Not only do other members of the family have a significant impact, but also other individuals with whom the infants are in contact can play a crucial role. Particularly is this so if these other individuals are conflicted and have depressive problems of their own. In addition the various types of perceptual and cognizing experiences a child has will influence the way he begins to view the world. Early cognitive components are related to whether a child thinks of the world as a place where people are unhappy or a "vale of tears." Nor can the whole panoply of organic and genetic factors as antecedents toward certain lines of development be ignored (18).

In some of the early writings about maternal deprivations, almost an unlimited number of outcomes were possible, such as psychosis, neurosis, or delinquency. Does the deprivation concept have any specific etiologic role for the later emergence of depressions or depressive vulnerability in childhood, adolescence, or adulthood? Even though details of the specific mechanism as to why some children are fortunate enough to be excluded from later consequences are not certain, the hypothesis may yet be viable. Distinctions are now made between disruption of affectionate relationships that have already been established, which may be more conducive to a depressive outcome, and where such relationships have failed to form, which are then more related to psychopathy. A theoretical criticism pertains to the heavy emphasis in maternal deprivation formulations that later behaviors, such as depressions, are rigidly determined in the earliest months of a child's life. Without appraising deterministic philosophical arguments, there is a tacit assumption that early mother-child relationships will inevitably lead to certain personality manifestations. The position is that if we knew all the variables, such as a chance relationship with someone in an institution, we could predict the depressive or psychopathic outcome. Such a degree of specificity has not been established. The concept is weighted in the direction of an overemphasis on early infantile experiences leading to an unalterable outcome without sufficient cognizance of other significant variables in the child's life. Wooton has pointed out that subsequent broader influences in a child's life are also not sufficiently accounted for, such as school associations, vocation, and marriage, which can taper and modify early experiences. To that extent the seeming irreversibility may not actually be strictly true (19). Other specific experiences are known to contribute to depressive-proneness. Death of a friend, pet, or neighbor can contribute as well as death of a parent. Nor can deprivation be considered literally as losing an attachment to a person, since moving to a new neighborhood can elicit similar feelings.

Early Psychodynamic Formulations

Clinical knowledge concerning depressions in adults originated from a Kraepelinian descriptive model. Freud and Abraham extended this work by psychoanalytic theorizing. Although their work was with adults, they raise psychological hypotheses about what the childhoods of those later depressed were like. A selective extraction for what is now relevant to the problem of childhood depressions will be employed. The earliest formulations saw childhood as significant only to the extent that a "trauma" left a child vulnerable as an adult to depressive illness. These traumas were viewed primarily as retrospective curiosities. Concepts such as orality, introjection, turning against the self, narcissistic injury, loss of an object, anal-sadism, and ambivalence were used as explanatory constructs to account for the development and maintenance of depressed states. In a 1911 paper, Karl Abraham emphasized the repression of aggression leading to depressed states analogous to the postulation of "actual neuroses" in which repression of sexuality led to anxiety states (20).

Elaboration of psychosexual stages led to reconstructive efforts to account for the development of fixations and subsequent regressions. Freud stressed the importance of introjective processes with their attendant ambivalence, as well as successive regressions to anal-sadistic and oral cannibalistic stages. An early theory was that regression ensued subsequent to loss of a love object (21). Abraham expanded this intrapsychic explanation using the mechanism of a double introjection (22). The original love object is introjected as part of the ego-ideal and conscience, and such an introject can be the target for a hostile attack. Developmentally, the child treats the bonded object as something over which he exercises sovereignty similar to that he exercises over his other possessions, such as the parts and inner contents of his body. Loss of such objects is unconsciously equivalent to loss of these bodily possessions. A cognitive connection is made by children between "losing-destroying" and "retaining-controlling." Emergence of depressive-prone development in a child would reveal an emphasis on control and orderliness similar to that seen in obsessional personalities. This was one basis for the developmental connection between depressives and those with compulsive features.

An indication of the barren state of investigatory work is seen in the 50-year gap between the time Abraham drew attention to the possibility that childhood loss might have some connective to later depressive illness and attempts to seek empirical confirmation of the hypothesis to correlate with clinical work (23). Let us see what Abraham had in mind with respect to his idea of a "primal parathymia" in the context of later knowledge.

Abraham listed five antecedent factors whose presence in childhood predisposed a child to depressions. Inclusion of all five factors was seen as necessary. First was a constitutional element seen as a predisposing tendency toward oral erotism. In the course of evaluating past histories, excessive demands for gratification via the mouth and bodily surfaces would be indicators. Oral activities and close contact with the mother or mother surrogate's body could give such gratification. If the oral demands were powerful, or strongly frustrated, a regressive readiness was manifested by a constant clamor for gratification. From later therapeutic efforts, the presence of oral masochism as part of the depressive character was seen as tendencies to provoke suffering and humiliation in unwitting ways. Fixation from oral frustrations or excessive or inadequate handling (skin erotism) was stressed as a basic substratum of depression in this context. Distorted affectional relationships with other humans leave vital needs for love and formation of tender attachments ungratified. Behaviors and attitudes result that seek gratifications in a vicarious and strange manner, since frustration and nonlove are sought from the very people whose love is needed. Through demanding and incorporating activities and the need for bodily contact, the child absorbs—and later unconsciously seeks—displeasure, sadness, and suffering instead of love. As development progresses, highly sophisticated and unconscious mechanisms lead these children to seek approval and acceptance from individuals who do not and cannot meet their requests, and the child unwittingly involves himself in dependent relations with others who inflict pain and psychological suffering on him. Self-pity is an accompaniment of suffering, since such purification devices lead to a feeling that love has been earned and that if it is not forthcoming after suffering, one may justifiably be self-righteous. The resultant is a chronic feeling that one has never received what is rightfully his, which has ramifications for the child's narcissistic well-being.

A second factor proposed by Abraham as related to later depressive-proneness was the contribution of oral erotism. An antecedent of oral fixation led to an increase in demands for oral indulgence or a low frustration tolerance if demands were not met. Another predisposing influence listed was a blow to infantile narcissism due to repeated childhood disappointments from those toward whom the child is most affectionate, which leave a psychic "wound." The early examples cited were such things as the birth of a sibling, repeated humiliations, and a realization of the child that he was not a favorite or that his parents were actually not genuinely fond of him. The effect of these disappointments left the child feeling deserted, and he repetitively sought ways to gain the love of a person of the opposite sex. Contemporary formulations put this in terms of too rapid or severe a blow to a child's grandiose self, leading to a need to repair his wounded narcissism by endless efforts to reconstruct his grandiose image (24). Minor rebuffs, lack of interest by others in the child, and the need for constant approval are indicators.

A fourth cumulative factor originally held that the first major disappointment occurred prior to the resolution of oedipal strivings. Developmentally, at age 3 to 5 years the child is moving toward "object love." A rebuff then is seen as a "sensitizer" toward later disappointments. Toward the end of the phallic phase, objects acquire distinct recognition as separate. Cognitions revolve about these new objects mixed with sensual and tender feelings. Prior to this a mixture of love and hate has predominated which focused on part of objects or some erogenous zone in contrast to a wish to possess an entire object. Fusions of tenderness and oral-sadistic strivings occur as the mother is blamed for disappointments rather than a rivalrous paternal object. This is believed to be the basis for observations that depressive characters continue highly ambivalent relationships with maternal figures throughout their lives. This first disappointment is the "primal parathymia" whose occurrence is necessary but not sufficient for the occurrence of later depressions. A final necessary factor posited by Abraham was a repetition of the primary disappointment later in life. When this repetition occurred, it elicited the old depressive feelings with an accompanying upsurge of hate and other mechanisms of self-directed aggressions. Abandoned or abandoning objects cannot be psychologically dismissed without processes occurring that permit the internalized representation to be given up. This is not merely a matter of choosing to forget or giving up an object since the object is part of the self. The object representation has become part of the self-representation so that states of contentment depend on the harmonious relationship to the internalized objects.

Subsequent work continued to focus on intrapsychic alignments with the crucial goal of seeing how functions assigned to the superego aspects of the personality operated. Introjection and identification processes were perceived as psychologically equivalent to an object being destroyed (25). When children put themselves in place of one another, the "other" may be eliminated and also recreated. All types of magical creations and destructions in response to loves and hates become possible. One part of the personality was seen as being crucial for bestowing esteem—phrased as the superego giving to the ego. Rado elaborated this formulation as the precarious balance of self-esteem in the depressive being caused by the dependency of self-esteem on the approval of others (26). Depressive responses in the latency-age period are often triggered by minor disappointments and associated with the primitive rage of an infant from hunger caused by the failure to satiate from sucking ("alimentary orgasm").

The paradigm of self-esteem based on "feeding" experiences and their equivalents from others leads to a dependency on external narcissistic supplies. A series of intrapsychic maneuvers develops with respect to expiatory efforts of the ego toward the superego. Since part of the hostility and rage is directed against internalized representations from the past, as well as present objects, guilt is a concomitant development. Reparative efforts are made to atone. "Splitting of the incorporated object" permits anger against the object or anger received from it. These self-regulatory mechanisms do not operate effectively until the ego development of the child permits him to experience guilt. When that level of development is "achieved," the child has acquired a depressive character. Characterological maneuvers are observed in children of elementary school years. Interpersonal ingratiation and cautiousness with respect to expression of aggression are prominent. These efforts of the ego toward the superego as the controller of self-esteem attempt to reinstate a loving and beloved superego in place of one that is predominantly harsh and primitive (27). Gero felt that the perpetuation of pressing demands for approval and affection were associated with conflicts during the oedipal period which led to anxieties, aggression, and suffering (28). These conflicts introduced ambivalence into the pursuit of object relations.

Stimulated by psychotherapy with adult depressives, interest shifted to how the depressive character structure emerged. In the "individual psychology" of Alfred Adler, the stress was on the role of exploitative behavior (29): "The discouraged child who finds that he can tyrannize best by tears will be a cry-baby, and a direct line of development leads from the cry-baby to the adult depressed patient." Early infantile passive-aggressive activities such as pouty, whiny behavior, or feeding disturbances, were viewed as forerunners of how others could be manipulated. The childhood prototype of the potential suicide was saying in essence, "It serves my mother right if I break my leg." Similarly, the childhood prototype of the manic-depressive began everything with great enthusiasm only to give it up quickly with crying and protesting if brilliant success was not forthcoming. Such a child alternates between pessimistic ruminations about not having performed well and having no friends, and feelings of self-righteous superiority.

An expansion of this framework views the potentially depressed child as hostile and manipulative. He tries to outcompete others and resents personal demands since he feels he is being used unfairly by others for their own selfish interests. Consequently, such a child is unwilling to provide gratifications for others unless he is assured of receiving some himself. If he is not receiving, he seeks to extract from others or retaliate on them. During adolescence this type of sensitivity leads to antisocial tendencies. If these tendencies are acted on, they stem from a feeling that the acts are justified by past grievances. These traits are caused by childhood socialization experiences where the needs of a child for sincere, solicitous care were unfulfilled. Manipulative efforts toward peers and authorities are repeat patterns for dealing with extractive and manipulative parental figures: "He has been deprived, and he feels gyped and is angrily determined to get what is rightfully his. . . . In this defiant, stubborn, angry, begrudging battle of something-for-nothing, he loses the enjoyments of adolescence, of young adulthood, and of later adulthood" (30). What can be said about these astute observations? These character traits are observed as emerging in children, and they acquire increasing sophistication in their use. However, theorizing that makes manipulative aspects of personality development the crux of the depressive personality underemphasizes other key elements that are present as well. While those with a "depressive character" have elements of the "neurotic character" mixed in, they are not synonymous.

Attachment, Bonding, Dependency, and Object Relations

Hypotheses of how the development and maintenance of earliest interpersonal relationships are carried out have specific implications for studying depressions. One area of great relevance pertains to the composition of "high risk" categories for those who will later have disturbances in the depressive realm. Further opportunity for confirmation or disconfirmation of theories can take place via observations in the naturalistic setting in which children develop and begin to experience depressive disturbances. Confusions have emerged from different usages for the terms "object relations," "dependency," "bonding," and "attachment" (31). These are discussed primarily for their relationship to depressions. Workers from different disciplines and different theoretical backgrounds have accentuated the problem, since some have worked in nurseries, others in nursery schools, and others in experimental work with school children. None of these sources are derived from patient contact, which provides yet another major source based on clinical work.

Object relations is the term most customarily used by clinicians in referring to the agents who gratify or deprive an infant. This agent is also someone upon whom survival of the infant is dependent. This concept is an "instinct theory" where drives are discharged on a given object. The discriminatory and perceptual capacities are diffuse in the young infant with little cognitive appreciation of "objects." Rather, an awareness of tensions is present, experienced psychologically as a state of narcissistic disequilibrium. As more ego psychological functions develop, an increasing capacity to distinguish himself and his body from others permits the child distinctions between objects and their differing responses. This is not a passive registry but rather an active organization or seeking of stimulation (32).

When a stage of "object constancy" is reached, images, qualities, and affects associated with objects are maintained in their absence and are not just associated with satisfaction or deprivation. A correlative internal representation has then been accomplished. Separate objects are perceived as providers of food and bestowers of affection, and also as a source of feeling well about oneself which will later be cognized into such statements as, "I am worthwhile," or "I am no good," and such. It is via the internalization that the preobject child establishes the permanence of objects, but for this he pays a price. The major part of the price is related to how this continuing psychological representation, which is part of him, functions. It may be adverse or growth promoting. He also continuously experiences those in his environment who can reenforce the internalized images or stand as alternatives.

These formulations have kinship with early social learning theory which focused on "dependency" as an acquired or *secondary drive,* which held that need satisfaction was basic, and which held that incidental to this process was the developing awareness of an "object." In the process of satisfying his physiological needs, an infant was to learn about the source of gratification. Social needs were acquired by way of the object giving need-satisfaction. This drive-reduction theory has come under increasing criticism. One criticism holds that behavior attributable to "drives" can be accounted for in terms of "reinforcing stimuli" operating in the environment which control what behavior develops. The shift is then from the internal organism, as primary, to the environment. These stimuli are defined in terms of events occurring subsequent to behaviors which are operantly emitted and then controlled by instrumental conditioning. What has been called dependency is not viewed as a reflection of a drive or as a trait but as certain learned behaviors. The "object" is significant simply as a particular stimulus object. Dependency is linked to dependency objects, but is not restricted to the context of someone providing food or reducing tension. A shift may also occur from an emphasis on the "rewards" provided by an object in the service of drive reduction to an emphasis on importance of objects based on their salience. Cairns noted that salience attaches to a particular object's "attention-getting" characteristics, or by the greater frequency of exposure to it. Hence sheep become attached to television sets when kept in isolation from other animals but in constant propinquity to an operating set (33). However, there is an implication for a viewpoint on depressions hidden here. Separation from a salient object should have no more significance than setting in motion a process of relearning whatever new object currently is most salient (34). In time the strength of attachment should directly wane. This position is an example of applying experimental findings which seem incongruent not only with clinical work but also with the experience of continuity present in human psychological life. It cogently demonstrates a type of psychological theorizing divorced from a framework whereby account can be taken of internalized neurophysiological structures as well as cognitive and affective processes.

A third alternative for the development of object relations has more secure roots in biology and ethology. Developing an attachment in itself is seen as *primary.* The infant is viewed as having a built-in need for an object in his own right and independent of strict drive reduction. Attachment develops apart from feeding experiences and where "releasing" stimuli of many types activate the process. Internal neurophysiological and neurohumoral states are the "primers," operating on a genetic substrate which has the potential to activate attachments. Learning operates to reinforce or lessen certain attachment behaviors. The "attachment process" as originating in the organism must be distinguished from the various "attachment behaviors" which mediate it. Although the latter is overt and hence more easily measurable, it is not the same as the basis for these behaviors. The deceptiveness of attempting to quantify external behaviors can be seen in assessing a child who clings and weeps as necessarily more depressed than a child who sits forlornly with little demonstrativeness. Conversely, more demonstrative attachment behaviors need not imply greater attachment. Hidden in these formulations is material for a significantly altered emphasis than that which psychodynamic theory has relied on for many of its developmental hypotheses regarding depressions. Previously, stress has been on "oral mechanisms" going awry with either excessive indulgence or deprivation setting the stage for difficulties in the realm of self-esteem. The emphasis in this attachment theory stresses that the system underlying attachment, with its crucial significance for social relations, is independent of feeding and is its own discrete and endogenous system.

Bowlby originally posited five "instinctual response systems" in humans: sucking, clinging, following, crying, and smiling (35). These contributed to attachment, but are now subsumed as systems maintaining the proximity of children to their maternal objects. Attachment behavior occurs as certain behavioral systems are activated. These are present from evolutionary adaptedness and interact with the principal figure in the environment (36). The many unresolved arguments regarding the functions served by attachment behavior would take too much space to discuss. Prominent among these is the position that no reference to "drives" is needed and a reliance on control systems theory suffices. There is also the criticism that studying "attachment behaviors" in terms of manifest behaviors is not actually studying the internal psychological processes that are involved in attachment and object relations (37).

Many clinicians have utilized an object relations theory as basic to their theory of childhood depressions. Only the briefest condensation will be given of the Kleinian intrapsychic model (38). Melanie Klein postulated that introjective-projective processes were transacted psychologically from the beginning of extrauterine life—telescoping certain psychological processes into the first year which are ordinarily seen as spread out throughout childhood. The "depressive position" developed in association with the loss accompanying weaning between 3 and 12 months. This position is viewed as a normal and unavoidable developmental situation, succeeding an earlier "paranoid position" from which it is derived. Superego structuralization is posited during the first year and believed related to feelings of possessiveness and destructiveness toward a parental object rather than as incestuous wishes emerging several years later. The depressive position develops in moving from a "part" to a "whole" object relationship. In the predepressive position, only relations to parts of objects, such as a breast, were believed present.

During the depressive position the mother is perceived as a whole object, permitting ambivalence and accompanying anxiety about the loss of the entire love object. The infant then experiences a guilty anxiety with a need to preserve the good object, which he does by reliance on magical devices.

Reparative work is an effort to make amends or undo sadistic attacks on introjective objects, as well as from actual situations where the excited infant has achieved instinctual gratification, such as during feeding. The object "attacked" is the same one that provides security, and if reparative activities are unsuccessful, there is the despair that the provider is gone. The infantile depressive position is related to the possibility of later depressions from anxiety over loss of objects and the ongoing fear of abandonment and loss. In contrast is the security of one whose internalized objects are accepted as bestowing love and security. After a time an individual can build up memories of experiences felt to be good, so that the experience of the mother holding the situation becomes part of himself and assimilated into the ego. In this way the actual mother gradually becomes less and less necessary (39).

Grief and mourning in infancy have been discussed by Bowlby in many articles dealing with the activation of attachment behaviors when the maternal figure continues to be unavilable (40–44). This work is important in the nature of childhood bereavement, and for hypotheses of the pathogenic potential of mourning processes, and reaction to losses when they take a pathological turn. Removal of young children from their mothers initiates successive psychological phases: numbness, protest, despair, and detachment. Each has an accompanying parallel response of separation anxiety, grief and mourning, and defense, although they all operate as part of a unitary process. "Mourning" refers to a psychological process set in motion by loss of a loved object; "grief" is a parallel subjective state in such a loss. "Depression" is the affective state when mourning is occurring as distinguished from the clinical syndrome of melancholia. One of Bowlby's postulates is that the loss of a mother figure between 6 months and 3 to 4 years has a high degree of pathogenic potential for subsequent personality development due to the occurrence of mourning processes.

Protesting behavior manifests itself in crying, motoric restlessness, and angry efforts to regain the lost object by demands for its return. This behavior sows the seeds for later psychopathology. Subsequent disorganization with painful despair hopefully leads to a reorganization in relinquishing the image of the lost object in which new objects help. Anger is believed essential for efforts to recover the lost object, since yearning is mixed with repeated disappointments in not recovering the object that is lost. "Grief" is then associated with an irretrievable loss, while "separation anxiety" is a response to a situation where hope persists that the loss is not irretrievable.

Persistence of efforts to regain experienced losses has four possible types of pathological outcomes: The first are persistent and unconscious yearnings to recover lost objects which appear clinically surprising from an "absence of grief." The second consists of angry reproaches against the self and other objects to attain a reunion. Displacement of reproaches occurs in which inappropriate objects are used or "mourning at a distance" occurs. Development to the level where anger can be directed against the self as a psychological process is an index that guilt is experienced. Guilt can be generated via reality-based realizations that the child has played a role in the loss, or wished for the object to be destroyed. Psychopathological displacement is due to prolongation of anger without direct expression. An adverse effect of chronicity is the waning of affectionate components. The third is absorption in caring for others who are suffering rather than grieving oneself by way of projective identification and vicarious mourning. This is a possibility when a child is plagued by "bad luck" or where there is a compulsive pitying of others. The fourth is denial of the permanency of object loss operating on a conscious level that necessitates a "split in the ego." It is believed that acute losses have a greater tendency to result in such denial and that children are particularly prone to react to losses in this manner. Losses predispose the child to character changes which are believed to leave the child in a state of readiness to evoke similar reactions in subsequent developmental, psychological, or environmental loss analogous to being exposed to an allergen.

Theoretical controversy has arisen over Bowlby's theories. He once held that no qualitative differences between mourning in children and adults occurred because their behavior appeared similar. However, Bowlby's position was later clarified in that pathological mourning persists in children because of their failure to engage in normal mourning processes at the time of the loss of the object (45). A review of the literature concludes that children, in contrast to adults, do not go through a stage of mourning whereby they can gradually go through the painful detachment from the inner representation of the person who has died (46). A complex set of defensive phenomena to deny what has occurred may ensue which has a high pathogenic potential.

There is a need to consider differences in successive developmental stages and how they affect psychological reactions to object loss (47). Young children who grieve experience a "hurt" rather than undergo the same psychological processes as an adult. Some describe this as a lack of developmental readiness to mourn prior to adolescence: "Until he has undergone what we may call the trial mourning of adolescence, he is unable to mourn. Once he has lived through the painful, protracted decathecting of the first love objects, he can repeat the process when circumstances of external loss require a similar renunciation. When such loss occurs, we may picture the individual who has been initiated into mourning through adolescence confronting himself with the preconscious question: 'Can I bear to give up someone I love so much?' The answer follows: 'Yes, I can bear it—I have been through it once before.' Before the trial mourning of adolescence has been undergone, a child making the same tentative beginning of reality testing in regard to a major object loss is threatened with the prospect of overwhelming panic and retreats into defensive denial in the way we have observed" (48).

Object loss as a concept has been expanded far beyond that of a literal loss to include distortions in object relationships. Effects on the child can make him depressive-prone although they do not show up in the form of gross disturbance. Depressed moods in mothers during the first 2 years after birth create a tendency for similar moods in the children which later become manifest (49). Fusion with a depressed mother induces the mood disturbance in the child. This is especially true for children who live an "as if" existence where they perceive themselves as necessary for validation of parental needs. The liability is the threat of abandonment if they are not validating (50). Serious and chronic preoccupations in the parents leave little room for spontaneous curiosity and interaction with the child in his world. Pessimistic moods in the parents induce feelings of failure in children whereby the child feels he is somehow responsible for the predicament of the parents. Similarly, parents staving off their depressed moods by extreme and unpredictable activity and periodic overstimulating play with a child contribute to the depressive outlook of the child (51).

Clinical work reveals that not all children with "narcissistic vulnerabilities" have lost an external object. Relevant are the developmental lines striving to attain object constancy to achieve separation and individuation. Individuation gives rise to a period of increased psychomotor activity from 10 to 18 months in which the mood is believed to be one of infantile elation. For the infant in this activity, actively leaving and returning with a maternal readiness are steps toward acquiring an internal object constancy. "Giving up" the fusion promotes individuation and is a step toward lowering magical maneuverings (52). Depressive moods may be generated by relinquishment of the child's belief in his omnipotence and a feeling that the parents are withholding power from him. These moods manifest themselves by separation and grief reactions "marked by temper tantrums, continual attempts to woo or coerce the mother, and then giving up in despair for awhile; or it may be revealed in impotent resignation and surrender (in some cases with marked masochistic coloring). On the other hand, discontentment and anger may persist after a shorter period of grief and sadness" (53). The natural history of these early mood states in the preschool child reveals that many of them give way to a premature earnestness ("little adults") that appears as undue seriousness indicating precocious superego formation. Other signs of failing to attain object constancy with respect to mood are marked ambivalence, precocious overidentification, pseudo-self-sufficiency, and a flattened overt emotional spontaneity.

The evolution of a depreciated self-concept is a major predisposing influence in the formation of a depressive nucleus in a child. Emotional distantness on the part of family members puts the child into a nuclear conflict, since he is in no position to understand or appraise the whys and wherefores. Nor do parents comprehend the innumerable ways in which their reactions to the child are manifested. Early self-derogatory cognitions can be heard from children who describe themselves as "bad" or "I'm no good" after some trivial failing. In these elaborations of distorted childhood concepts the child evaluates himself as intrinsically defective or disappointing—a forerunner of what can develop to delusional proportions. Despair or detachment are accompaniments of feeling lonely and abandoned. A tearful 10-year-old girl, with feelings of not being as "valuable" as her two younger siblings, recalled a Christmas episode when all the gifts were brought in except hers. After everyone had opened theirs, her father noticed her sitting silently and attempted to "joke" as though the forgetting was merely a planned tease for which all the family laughed. When the gift was brought in, it was a huge doll house which was received with disappointment since the girl had never played with dolls. It continued to sit unused and conspicuous in her room.

The depressive child has an exaggerated fear of punishment for failure. It is as though the regulatory function for self-esteem has gone awry so that any failure is viewed as a cause for alarm—as though one will be externally attacked (54). This is far more punitiv completely intolerant. While parental conscience need not. Integrally related unattainable ideals with tendencies toward "he are a life-long quest for the hero on one hand wh for ways to escape from overstrict standards. regnant theme that emerges with these children, w overgeneralization where everything starts to look hypocritical (55). Psychotherapy is beneficial, since without the child needing to be good, clean, complian authoritarian manner.

Pathogenesis of the narcissistic character structure that is depressions is related to work on dependency and attachments. crucial variables in the developing disposition toward depres hypothesis ties pathogenesis in with the devalued self-image seen in n when they experience some early form of deprivation, neglect, o loss. Repeated rebuffs or losses are taken by the child as affirmation that a significant object did not value him and that he is discardable (56). His well-being is much more contingent on transient environmental approvals which leave him narcissistically vulnerable. Absence of expected interest in him or minor rebuffs give rise to a feeling of depletion with a heightening of narcissism (57). In some children this narcissism manifests itself as a deficiency in reality testing. This phenomenon is in accord with a principle that an increase in narcissism occurs as the importance of real objects diminishes. Yet this substitute gratification in itself is unsatisfactory to children and leads to "restitutive" attempts to restore a real relationship.

In the young child, "losses" are met not only by an increase in narcissism, but also by a greater flexibility due to their acceptance of substitute objects. Loss of self-esteem as a response to loss is not thought to appear until a structural division of mental activity has been accomplished. By then, object constancy has been attained so that mourning as a process of detachment from inner representations occurs. Only when an object has attained value does its loss lead to self-devaluation. Aggression may be directed against the self and witnessed in masochistic phenomena as part of a depressive picture. When an object becomes important the child becomes concerned with the question, "Who will love me when I am left?" and the answer, "No one may want you" (58). If a child feels depleted and devalued as an object, he is not worth much and may well be abandoned.

Accompanying these cognitive distortions in self-appraisal are variations in moodiness which emerge as prominent personality characteristics. Somatic manifestations appear to be the template for similar symptoms in later depressions which show up as hypochondriasis, motor restlessness, sleep upsets, and gastrointestinal complaints. Children's moods have three main characteristics (59): (1) affective manifestations are more intense than in adults because of insufficient ego-superego controls; (2) moods are of brief duration and change rapidly because of the instability of object relations and their greater readiness to accept substitute objects and gratifications; and (3) the affective range in children is more limited from the lack of ego differentiation.

...y toward pathological mood disturbance is developing, there ...ss variety and spontaneity of moods. A more exaggerated quality is ...t such as in persistent forlornness and sadness or exaggerated upward swings.

Family configurations offer another vantage point to study depressed children. There is a keen sensitivity in the family members to the norms of the wider group to which they aspire but from whom they feel alien. The child is used as a vehicle for family esteem by way of his accomplishments. Emphasis is placed on nonconformity and self-conscious dedication to duty. Industriousness becomes the price for self-acceptance, hence the compensated depressive as the budding obsessional. However, to be selected as a special object can give rise to the "Joseph Syndrome" based on the Biblical theme (60). Fear of arousing envy and jealousy in others leads to defensive efforts (61). One such defense is a pattern of chronically underselling coupled with a feeling of having to help or give to others. Being competitive and envious of others who are successful, these children quickly sense siblings and peers who have similar feelings toward them. If the fathers in these families are relatively unsuccessful—a not infrequent picture—there is a further narcissistic disappointment. Yet this parent is the one to whom the child becomes most attached. Many symptomatic disturbances not customarily associated with depression may ensue, such as learning disorders and patterns of chronic underachievement—the equivalent to the "success phobias" of adults. The unconscious goal is to have others like one at whatever personal cost. Yet, at the same time, the child has been selected to compete aggressively and bear the burden of maintaining family esteem.

The Picture of Depression in Midchildhood

Current work on adult depressions, apart from psychodynamic elaborations, centers around the problem of whether psychotic and neurotic depressions are two ends of a continuum, or if they divide qualitatively into two distinct entities (62). Discussion about the unitary or binary nature of depressions has gone on for some time. It presupposes a core of agreement about the symptomatic picture of depression. This agreement refers to the nature of the classification to be imposed by statistical techniques of intercorrelating items and by achieving "loadings" in the direction of a single general factor or in the opposite direction of bimodality (63). Contrast this situation with that present in the field of childhood depressions where the syndrome has not even obtained a general acceptance as to its occurrence. We are still at the stage of attempting to develop the clinical picture of a depressed child and proposing classifications based on whether a child who appears depressed came from a prior background of a good or marginal adjustment, or whether his depression is "masked" (64). While interest in the depressive responses of the young child has increased, along with interest in the more flamboyant behavior of the depressed adolescent, the child from 5 years of age to puberty may actually comprise the most hidden group in terms of incidence. Confusion is present as to how thwarted dependency needs, physical illnesses, and losses induce depressive reactions in this age group (65). Although internalized conflict creates possibilities for many types of neurotic conflicts, not all feel that the concepts elaborated about depression can be applied to children (66). Confusion is compounded by the "latent" manifestations of depression at this age in which there is often an absence of the overt symptoms associated with depressions. Hence crying, verbalized self-condemnations, and overt expressions of guilt are not the primary symptom picture. Parental use of denial regarding one of their children who appears sad or unhappy further masks true incidence.

Clinical and developmental studies have confirmed that latency is not quiescent. Coupled with this is the emergence of a perfected system of inner controls relative to the first few years of life. Superego functioning seems particularly prone to upset in view of the developmental status. It is not unusual to observe school-age children placing demands on themselves that are more severe than those of parental figures. This may be explained in terms of the immaturity of their superego, or a projection of aggression onto internalized objects which are then used against themselves to ensure that transgressions will not occur since the child is not "on his own."

Increasing numbers of articles describe children who are clinically depressed. These articles vary because of widely different initial problems and present difficulties in attempting the application of a systematic classificatory scheme. For most diagnostic purposes at present, perhaps nothing more is needed than a diagnosis of "Childhood Depression" indicating its presence. However, to increase our sophistication and research, a more elaborate system is needed to give an awareness of the protean possibilities for a child who presents with a depressive picture. Table 1 is a tentative classificatory scheme cutting across many boundaries. It relies in part on age but at least indicates other dimensions which contribute to the clinical picture.

How does the depressed child appear? As with depressions in different age groups, there are myriad possibilities. Although there is a confluence in some children, the signs of symptoms vary widely. Some of these observations have been made from children in intensive therapy while others are from children on inpatient units and yet others outpatient departments. Some of them stem from a retrospective awareness of a symptom picture in midchildhood by adolescents or adults who realize in the course of their own therapy how depressed they really were at that time (67–69). Drawn from these sources, the following is a composite picture of how a depressed child would appear if every conceivable possibility that we know were included.

1. A general picture of a sad, depressed, or unhappy-looking child may be present. The child does not complain of unhappiness, or even being aware of it, but rather conveys a psychomotor behavioral picture of sadness.
2. Withdrawal and inhibition with little interest in any activities may be most prominent. It is a listlessness which gives an impression of boredom, or physical illness, and often leads an observer to conclude that the child must have some concealed physical illness.

3. Somatizing takes the form of physical pain (headaches, abdominal complaints, dizziness), insomnia, sleeping or eating disturbances—"depressive equivalents."
4. A quality of discontent is prominent. An initial impression is that the child is dissatisfied and experiences little pleasure, and in time the clinician gets the added impression that somehow others—even an examiner who has barely met the child—are somehow responsible for his plight. In other cases there is a casting of blame on others in the sense of easily criticizing other children.
5. A sense of feeling rejected or unloved is present. There is a readiness to turn away from disappointing objects.
6. Negative self-concepts reflecting cognitive patterns of illogically drawing conclusions that they are worthless, and so on (70).
7. Reports are made of observations of low frustration-tolerance and irritability; this is coupled with self-punitive behavior when goals are not attained.
8. Although the child conveys a sense of need or wanting comfort, it is then accepted as his due, or he remains dissatisfied and discontent although he is often in ignorance as to why.
9. Reversal of affect is revealed in clowning and dealing with underlying depressive feelings by foolish or provocative behavior to detract from assets or achievements.
10. Blatant attempts to deny feelings of helplessness and hopelessness are seen in the "Charlie Brown syndrome," modeled after the cartoon character of a boy from 7 to 9 years who avoids confronting his despair and disillusionment by being self-deprecatory and then springing back with hope (71). These indicate a hope that self-depreciations, avoidance of rewards, dedicated effort, and other examples of being "good" will lead to rewards that are just—perhaps when one grows up or at least in the hereafter. In childhood, hope manages to avoid the more overt manifestations of depressive pessimism seen in the adult when disillusionment occurs.
11. Provocative behavior which stirs angry responses in others and leads to others utilizing this child as a focus for their own disappointments. Such scapegoating exhibits suffering which leads to descriptions of him as a "born loser." Difficulties in handling aggression may be a frequent initiator of referral.
12. Tendencies to passivity and expecting others to anticipate their needs. Since this is frequently impossible, they may express their anger by passive-aggressive techniques.
13. Sensitivity and high standards with a readiness to condemn themselves for failures. There is a preference to be harsh and self-critical. This appears as an attempt to avoid conflict associated with hostility by in effect saying, "I don't blame you—only myself." In some this extends to the point of feeling they are so bad they should be dead (72).
14. Obsessive-compulsive behavior in connection with other types of regressive, magical activities.

Table 1 Classification of Childhood Depressions

- I. Associated with organic diseases
  - A. Part of primary organic disease—Examples
    - 1. Leukemia
    - 2. Degenerative Diseases
    - 3. Infectious diseases—juvenile paresis
    - 4. Metabolic diseases—pituitary disease, juvenile diabetes, thyroid disease, etc.
    - 5. Nutritional or vitamin deficiency states
  - B. Secondary (reactive) to a physical disease process
- II. Deprivation syndromc—the reality-based reactions to an impoverished or nonrewarding environment
  - A. Anaclitic depressions
  - B. "Affectionless" character types
- III. Syndromes associated with difficulties in individuation
  - A. Problems of separation-individuation—symbiotic psychotic reactions
  - B. School phobias with depressive components
  - C. Masochistic character structures
- IV. Midchildhood types
  - A. Associated with object loss
  - B. Failure to meet unattainable ideals
  - C. "Depressive equivalents" (depression with depressive affect)
    - 1. Somatization (hypochondriacal patterns)
    - 2. Hyperkinesis
    - 3. Acting-out syndromes
    - 4. Delayed depressive reactions
      - a. Mourning at a distance
      - b. Overidealization processes postponing reaction
      - c. Denial patterns
    - 5. Eating disturbances (obesity syndromes)
  - D. Manic-depressive states
  - E. "Affectless" character types (generalized anhedonia)
  - F. Obsessional character (the "compensated depressive")
- V. Adolescent types
  - A. Mood lability as a developmental process
  - B. Reactive to current loss
  - C. Unresolved mourning from current losses
  - D. Reaction to earlier losses ("traumata")
  - E. Schizophrenias with prominent affective components
  - F. Continuation of earlier types (I–IV)

behaviors as a defensive maneuver to avoid
feelings associated with depression.

menological or pathological experience of the depressive-
is most likely sensitive and easily hurt because of his
ne narcissistic realm in which object ties are more easily
his gives a quality of inner hesitancy which is manifested as a
mmitment, whether in peer relationships or activities. It seems to
e with an uncertainty that others will remain reliable and steadfast.
icians sense a cautious seeking for attachments in the course of therapy
d in reports of his daily life. In contrast to a schizoid child who prefers his withdrawal, the depressed child hungers for a relationship but he is doubtful about its quality. Although the child is externally forlorn and sad, he is usually unaware of the reasons for his altered moods or why he periodically reacts this way.

Nostalgia and self-pity developmentally emerge at age 3 to 4. Children are then capable of verbalizing their feelings when someone leaves and they miss him. Sensitive observers sense mild depressive affect when a parent, pet, or friend is absent for more than a short period. Displays of narcissistic mortification may amuse adults. Thus a 4-year-old may refuse to participate in an activity which he enjoys a great deal when something is denied him or he is reprimanded. A miscarried attempt to hurt the frustrating and controlling object by not cooperating in some activity which is pleasing to the other party may ensue. This renunciation permits further self-pity. Families that utilize these mutual behavior patterns are basically pursuing retaliatory aims which permit the child to indulge his wounds in this manner. Conflicts centering on aggression, masochism, guilt over aggression or success, and expiation develop.

A frequent pattern is the presence in the home of an adult who is periodically depressed. The emotional tone of sadness and loneliness in the adult leaves a particular pessimistic imprint on the child. This could be based on the identification with a depressed parent, or use of depression as a defense to control rage which has not been handled effectively (73).

Some children with clinical depressions appear as pathetic, long-suffering individuals while others rely on somatizing processes or endless appearances at physicians' offices for problems which do not yield to an organic medical explanation. In many ways these are not dissimilar from those seen in adults as "masked depressions" and often subsumed under the endogenous category (74). The most frequent somatic symptoms are headaches, dizziness, cephalalgias, nausea, abdominal pain, or wandering pains in different parts of the body. In two successive series of 100 children investigated for recurrent abdominal pain ("little bellyachers"), only 8 and 6%, respectively, were found to have an organically explainable etiology (75). Not only abdominal complaints, but also anorexia, pruritus, and migraine headaches have been viewed as depressive equivalents in children (76). Severe encopresis has been considered a depressive equivalent in children where there is more open expression of aggression. Enuresis has similarly been seen as part of the symptom-complex in a depressed child when genitourinary evaluations and cystoscopy do not reveal organic pathology (77).

The depressed child can be a "loner," not in the sense of schizoidia, but because of his worries and preoccupation interfering with his involving himself with others. Profound pessimism may alternate with teasing and sadistic behavior when he feels lonely and not able to enjoy others. Vicarious pleasure in seeing others commit errors or get injured is part of lessening their own superego pressures for perfectionism. Abrupt shifts in behavior may indicate a depression. This can show up in a previously alert child who shows signs of withdrawal and apathy or inability to study and lack of interest. A previously outgoing and carefree child who grows quiet and preoccupied, or a conforming child with obsessional tendencies shows more mood variations with breakthroughs of "delinquent" behavior. A superior student whose achievement reflects high aspirations and ideals is more likely to react with depressive manifestations when rewards for his hard work are not forthcoming or maintenance of earlier overachievements becomes difficult. Their vulnerability lies in their overachievement and overconscientiousness. Obsessional activities in the depressed child represent efforts to compensate for feelings of helplessness. Jarvis noted an association between loneliness and compulsivity in children in which the compulsions served as a defense against sadness and loss (78). These feelings are evoked in response to a pattern of "withdrawn mothering" where the physical needs are adequately met but the absence of the mother emotionally makes her unable to gratify some of the psychological needs of the child.

Hyperactive and restless behavior in the depressed child seem paradoxical. It is interesting that these were depressive symptoms noted in a 1931 report by Kasanin (79). Hyperkinesis is seen in a variety of disturbances varying from cerebral dysfunction to reactive patterns. Hyperkinetic behavior in the depressive context may be equivalent to hypomanic activity in adults who are warding off depressive feelings. Hyperactive behavior, like antisocial behavior, brings parental condemnation and allows the parent to focus on such behavior while long-standing hostilities are ignored. An increasing amount of clinical work confirms a viewpoint that certain forms of antisocial behavior or acting-out in children are a response to a depressive core. In his original monograph Bowlby felt there was a specific connection between prolonged early deprivation and the development of a personality with shallow relationships with other people, poor impulse control, and the development of an "affectionless, psychopathic character" (80). There is a continued need for clinical documentation of the relationship between depressions and persistent criminality which is so often bypassed in the group statistics on crime (81).

Deficits in the area of object relations connected to some form of antisocial behavior need not necessarily reflect a depressive nucleus. Unmitigated hate toward an object and its introject can predominate with little ambivalence (82). Symptom formation as in a neurosis is then absent. Conscience deficits are ascribed to the absence of attachment to a maternal object, and to the concomitant lack of guilty affect as a regulator of behaviors. This type of deficit is described to delineate acting-out of this type from that associated with the presence of depression. Early losses are experienced as painful discomforts and as contributing to a depressive framework. Antisocial behavior is then related to the anxiety of object loss (separation). Attacking or taking from the environment expresses feelings of rage about losses. By mechanisms of acting-out, denial, and isolation, an attempt is made to ward off such an affect. Resistance to a treatment approach which sets limits to these mechanisms is obvious, since it requires them to confront the underlying depression. The emerging depression often makes its appearance in the form of somatic complaints. Self-destructive behavior often parallels strong self-hate. Provocative behavior toward other children and teachers which elicits punishment, or a pattern of repetitive self-injury during play, are suggestive of such trends. Aggressive behavior itself is used to avoid depressive feelings, especially in situations where there is a direct threat to the integrity of the child. Situations when a child cannot deny his cravings for affection or when past feelings of worthlessness become overwhelming pose such threats (83). Not only acting-out, and delinquent patterns, represent attempts at coping with a depressive nucleus, or a defense against experiencing depressive feelings, but also questions arise about the nature of distortions in ego development and to what extent they are reversible (84, 85). The question is when a "depressive character" becomes relatively fixed irrespective of the reversibility of overt depressive symptoms which will come and go throughout the remainder of the child's life.

Acting-out behavior has particular psychodynamic and social meaning. Some believe acting-out is a primary defense in a majority of depressive individuals. This belief does not exclude its presence with different diagnostic categories, such as impulse-ridden characters, defective socialization patterns, antisocial personalities, or as part of a schizophrenic process. The problem is partially a conceptual one, since the "primary theorists" view depressive affect as crucial to whatever overt diagnostic features are present. In the preschool year histories, these children are described as hyperactive, rebellious, and aggressive. When seen in latency, a progressive pattern of hatred and destructive behavior in fantasy, play, and overt behavior is present. The narcissistic basis and ambivalence in their object ties are striking. However, therapeutic work which deals with the personality structure beneath the external aggressive display sees a denigrated self-concept. The child and parent may both be mutually identifying with the "bad" part of each other, which reinforces a feeling of worthlessness. Repetitive play themes or fantasies relate to destroying bad things followed by magically reconstituting them.

The acting-out coupled with depressive moods gives rise to the possibility of "juvenile manic-depressive" diagnoses. Although the disorder has been questioned before puberty, occasional case reports appear (86–88). Consider the general symptoms of instability alternating with apathy, hyperactivity alternating with motor inhibition, bursts of creativity with learning problems, aggressiveness alternating with passivity, anxiety attacks, sleep upsets, swings in appetite, and the recurring nature of the symptomatology (89).

The formulations of Therese Benedek regarding the "depressive constellation" are relevant to the elaboration of depressive states (90). In situations where oral demands and frustrations of the infant reactivate similar conflicts in the mother, the transactions between them give rise to an ambivalent core.

Child and mother proceed to interact on a projective and introjective bipolar basis of aggression in an attempt to escape from feelings of being a "bad child" and "bad mother." The model is that of identification of the mother "backward" with her own child who is reenacting the provocative role of the mother as child. The hypothesis is that certain parents have had childhood experiences which heighten their "ambivalent core." A pattern of mutually reinforcing hostility is set in motion and gains momentum. The child's feelings of estrangement and anger are superimposed on the disappointment of the parent. In turn, the parent feels justified in condemning the angry, sullen child, who develops feelings of deep shame which lead to increasing distance. Repetitive acting-out then ensues with the original and now concealed depressive nucleus being the impelling motive to these patterns.

Summary

This chapter has reviewed the syndrome of depressions in childhood. The multifarious clinical manifestations presenting from infancy onward to adolescence have been presented from a critical perspective dealing with the methodological problems that are present in evolving a coherent clinical picture. A systematic set of signs and symptoms are needed so that an adequate assessment of a child who may be depressed can be made. We are now at the point of delineating a stage-related picture of depressions in children. At the present time it is considered an accomplishment when children who are depressed are recognized. Unless this recognition is possible, many treatment approaches will of necessity miss their mark.

References

1. Diagnostic and Statistical Manual of Mental Disorders, Second Edition, Washington, D.C.; American Psychiatric Association, 1968.
2. Silverman C: *The Epidemiology of Depression.* Baltimore, Johns Hopkins Press, 1968.
3. Zubin J: Classification of the behavior disorders. *Ann Rev Psychol* **18**:373–406, 1967.
4. Beck AT, Ward CH, Mendelson M, and others: Reliability of psychiatric diagnoses: A study of consistency of clinical judgments and ratings. *Am J Psychiatr* **119**:351–357, 1962.
5. Eisenberg L: Problems for the biopsychology of development, in *The Biopsychology of Development.* Edited by Tobach E, Aronson LR, Shaw E, New York, Academic Press, 1971, pp. 515–529.
6. Levy D: Primary affect hunger. *Am J Psychiatr* **94**:643–652, 1937.
7. Goldfarb W: Infant rearing and problem behavior. *Am J Orthopsychiatr* **13**:249–265, 1943.
8. Burlingham D, Freud A: *Infants Without Families.* London, Allen & Unwin, 1943.
9. Spitz R: Anaclitic depression. *Psa Study Child* **2**:113–117, 1946.
10. Engel G, Reichsman F: Spontaneous and experimentally induced depressions in an infant with a gastric fistula. *J Am Psa Assoc* **4**:428–456, 1956.
11. Coddington RD: Study of an infant with gastric fistula and her normal twin. *Psychosom Med* **30**:172–192, 1968.

12. Kaufman, IC, Rosenblum LA: The reaction to separation in infant monkeys: anaclitic depression and conservation-withdrawal. *Psychosom Med* **29**:648–675, 1967.
13. Hinde RA, Spencer-Booth Y: Effects of brief separation from mother on rhesus monkeys. *Science* **173**:111–118, 1971.
14. Young LD, Suomi SS, Harlow HF, McKinney WT: Early stress and later response to separation in Rhesus monkeys. *Am J Psychiatr* **130**:400–405, 1973.
15. Bowlby J: *Maternal Care and Mental Health.* Geneva, World Health Organization, 1951, 2nd ed.
16. *Perspective on Human Deprivation.* Washington, D.C., U.S. Department of Health Education and Welfare, 1968.
17. Rutter M: *Maternal Deprivation Reassessed.* Baltimore, Penguin Books, 1972.
18. Berger M, Passingham RE: Early experience and other environmental factors: An overview, in *Handbook of Abnormal Psychology.* Edited by Eysenck HJ, London, Pittman, 1973, 2nd ed.
19. Wooton B: *Social Science and Social Pathology.* London, Allen & Unwin, 1959.
20. Abraham K (1911): Notes on the psycho-analytical investigation and treatment of manic-depressive insanity and allied conditions, *On Character and Libido Development.* New York, Norton, 1966, pp. 15–34.
21. Freud S (1917): *Mourning and Melancholia.* Standard edition, London, Hogarth Press, 1957, pp. 237–260.
22. Abraham K: A short study of the development of the libido, viewed in the light of mental disorders (1924), *On Character and Libido Development.* New York, Norton, 1966, pp. 67–150.
23. Hill OW: Child bereavement and adult psychiatric disturbance. *J Psychosom Res:* 357–360, 1972.
24. Kohut H: *The Analysis of the Self.* New York, International Universities Press, 1971.
25. Weiss E: Regression and projection in the superego. *Int J Psa* **13**:449–478, 1932.
26. Rado S: The problem of melancholia. *Int J Psa* **9**:420–438, 1928.
27. Schafer R: The loving and beloved superego in Freud's structural theory. *Psa Study Child* **15**:163–188, 1960.
28. Gero G: The construction of depression. *Int J Psa* **17**:423–461, 1936.
29. Adler KA: Adler's individual psychology, in *Psychoanalytic Techniques.* Edited by Wolman BB, New York, Basic Books, 1967, pp. 299–337.
30. Bonime W: The psychodynamics of neurotic depression, in *American Handbook of Psychiatry.* Edited by Arieti S, New York, Basic Books, pp. 239–255, 1966, Vol. 3.
31. Ainsworth MDS: Object relations, dependency and attachment: A theoretical review of the infant-mother relationship. *Child Dev* **40**:969–1025, 1969.
32. Gewirtz JL: Attachment and dependence: Some strategies and tactics in the selection and use of indices for those concepts, in *Communication and Affect.* Edited by Alloway T, Krames L, Pliner P, New York, Academic Press, 1973.
33. Cairns RB: Development, maintenance, and extinction of social attachment behavior in sheep. *J Comp Physio Psychol* **62**:298–306, 1966.
34. Cairns RB: Attachment behavior of mammals. *Psychol Rev* **23**:409–426, 1966.
35. Bowlby J: The nature of the child's tie to the mother. *Int J Psa* **39**:350–373, 1958.
36. Bowlby J: *Attachment and Loss,* Vol. 1, *Attachment.* New York, Basic Books, 1969.
37. Engel G: Attachment behavior, object relations and the dynamic-economic points of view. *Int J Psa* **52**:183–196, 1971.
38. Klein M(1948): *Contributions to Psycho-Analysis 1921–1945.* New York, McGraw-Hill, 1964.

39. Winnicott DW (1954): The depressive position in normal emotional development, in *Collected Papers*. New York, Basic Books, 1958, pp. 262–277.
40. Bowlby J: Separation anxiety. *Int J Psa* **41**:89–113, 1960.
41. Bowlby J: Grief and mourning in infancy and early childhood. *Psa Study Child* **15**:9–52, 1960.
42. Bowlby J: Processes of mourning. *Int J Psa* **42**:317–340, 1961.
43. Bowlby J: Childhood mourning and its implication for psychiatry. *Am J Psychiatr* **118**:481–498, 1961.
44. Bowlby J: *Attachment and Loss*, Vol. II, *Separation, Anxiety and Anger*. New York, Basic Books, 1973.
45. Bowlby J: Pathological mourning and childhood mourning. *J Am Psa Assoc* **11**:500–541, 1963.
46. Miller J: Children's reactions to parent's death. *J Am Psa Assoc* **19**:697–719, 1971.
47. Freud A: Discussion of Dr. Bowlby's paper. *Psa Study Child* **15**:53–62, 1960.
48. Wolfenstein M: How is mourning possible? *Psa Study Child* **21**:93–126, 1966.
49. Freud A: *Normality and Pathology in Childhood*. New York, International Universities Press, 1965.
50. Brodey WM: On the dynamics of narcissism I. Externalization and early ego development. *Psa Study Child* **20**:165–193, 1965.
51. Davidson J: Infantile depression in a "normal" child. *J Am Acad Child Psychiatr* **7**:522–535, 1968.
52. Mahler MS: On sadness and grief in infancy and childhood. *Psa Study Child* **16**:332–354, 1961.
53. Mahler MS: Notes on the development of basic moods, in *Psychoanalysis—A General Psychology*. Edited by Loewenstein R, Newman L, Schur M, Solnit A, New York, International Universities Press, 1966, pp. 152–168.
54. Reich A: Pathologic forms of self-esteem regulation. *Psa Study Child* **15**:215–232, 1960.
55. Main AM: Idealisation and disillusion in adolescence, in *Sexuality and Aggression in Maturation: New Facets*. Edited by Klein HS, London, Bailliere, Tindall and Cassell, 1971, pp. 14–21.
56. Rochlin G: Loss and restitution, in *Grief and Its Discontents*. Boston, Little, Brown and Co, 1965, pp. 121–164.
57. Kohut: *op cit*, 1971, p. 17.
58. Rochlin G: The dread of abandonment. *Psa Study Child* **16**:451–470, 1961.
59. Jacobson E: On normal and pathological moods. *Psa Study Child* **12**:73–113, 1957.
60. Cohen MB and others: An intensive study of twelve cases on manic-depressive psychosis. *Psychiatry* **17**:103–137, 1954.
61. Joffe WG: A critical review of the status of the envy concept. *Int J Psa* **50**:533–545, 1969.
62. Kendell RE: *The Classification of Depressive Illnesses*. London, Oxford University Press, 1968.
63. Eysenck HJ: The classification of depressive illnesses. *Br J Psychiatr* **117**:241–250, 1970.
64. Cytryn L, McKnew DH: Proposed classification of childhood depression. *Am J Psychiatr* **129**:149–155, 1972.
65. Bierman JS, Silverstein PB, Finesinger JE: A depression in a six-year-old boy with acute poliomyelitis. *Psa Study Child* **13**:430–450, 1958.
66. Rie HE: Depression in childhood: A survey of some pertinent contributions. *J Am Acad Child Psychiatr* **5**:653–685, 1966.
67. Sandler J, Joffe WG: Notes on childhood depression. *Int J Psa* **46**:88–96, 1965.

68. Malmquist CP: Depressions in childhood and adolescence: I. *New Eng J Med* **284**:887–893, 1971.
69. Malmquist CP: Depressions in childhood and adolescence: II. *New Eng J Med* **284**:955–961, 1971.
70. Beck AT: *Depression Causes and Treatment.* Philadelphia, University of Penn Press, 1972.
71. Symonds M: The depressions in childhood and adolescence. *Am J Psa* **28**:189–195, 1968.
72. McConville BJ, Boag LC, Purohit AP: Three types of childhood depression. *Can Psychiatr Assoc J* **18**:133–138, 1973.
73. Poznaski E, Zrull JP: Childhood depression. *Arch Gen Psychiatr* **23**:8–15, 1970.
74. Lopez Ibor JJ: Masked depression. *Br J Psychiatr* **120**:245–258, 1972.
75. Apley J: *The Child with Abdominal Pain.* Springfield, Illinois, Charles C Thomas, 1959.
76. Sperling M: Equivalents of depression in children. *J Hillside Hosp* **8**:138–148, 1959.
77. Frommer EA: Depressive illness in childhood, in *Recent Developments in Affective Disorders.* Edited by Coppen A, Walk A, British Journal of Psychiatry Special Publication 2, 1968.
78. Jarvis V: Loneliness and compulsion. *J Am Psa Assoc* **13**:122–158, 1965.
79. Kasanin J: The affective psychoses in children. *Am J Psychiatr* **10**:897–924, 1931.
80. Bowlby: *op cit,* 1951, p. 34.
81. Cormier BM: Depression and persistent criminality. *Can Psychiatr Assoc J Suppl* **11**:208–220, 1966.
82. Berman S: Antisocial character disorder: Its etiology and relationship to delinquency. *Am J Orthopsychiatr* **29**:612–621, 1959.
83. Burks HL, Harrison SI: Aggressive behavior as a means of avoiding depression. *Am J Orthopsychiatr* **32**:416–422, 1962.
84. Kaufman I: Three basic sources for pre-delinquent character. *Nerv Child* **11**:12–15, 1955.
85. Kaufman I and others: Delineation of two diagnostic groups among juvenile delinquents: the schizophrenic and the impulse-ridden character disorder. *J Am Acad Child Psychiatr* **2**:292–318, 1963.
86. Anthony J, Scott P: Manic-depressive psychosis in childhood. *Child Psychol and Psychiatr* **1**:53–72, 1960.
87. Varsamis J, MacDonald SM: Manic depressive disease in childhood. *Can Psychiatr Assoc J* **17**:279–281, 1972.
88. Feinstein SC, Wolpert EA: Juvenile manic-depressive illness. *J Am Acad Child Psychiatr* **12**:123–136, 173.
89. Annell AL: *Depressive States in Childhood and Adolescence.* Stockholm, Almqvist and Wiksell, 1972.
90. Benedek T: Towards the biology of the depressive constellation. *J Am Psa Assoc* **4**:389–427, 1956.

Seven

Depression in Adolescence

Irving B. Weiner, Ph.D.

Clinicians who work with young people should always be alert to the role that depression may be playing in their problems. Such vigilance is justified on three counts: first, depressive reactions are relatively common during adolescence, probably more so than current diagnostic practices indicate; second, underlying depression contributes to a large number of maladaptive behavior patterns in adolescents, including some that are not always recognized as relating to depression; and third, depression is the form of psychopathology most frequently involved in suicidal behavior, which is the fifth leading cause of death among 15- to 19-year-olds in the United States. This chapter first reviews the epidemiology of diagnosed depression in adolescents and then considers in some detail the manifestations of adolescent depression, the etiology of adolescent depressive disorders, and the major considerations in psychotherapy with depressed adolescents.

Epidemiology of Adolescent Depression

The most informative and clinically relevant way to look at available epidemiological data on adolescent depression is to consider the incidence of diagnosed depressive disorder among adolescent patients. Such data are presented in Table 1, which indicates for three types of psychiatric services in the United States the percentage of discharged or terminated patients diagnosed psychoneurotic depressive reaction among three adolescent age groups (10 to 14, 15 to 17, 18 to 19) and among adults, age 25 to 44. Depressive disorder other than psychoneurotic depressive reaction (e.g., psychotic depressive reaction, manic-depressive psychosis) are not included because they are hardly ever diagnosed in youthful patients.

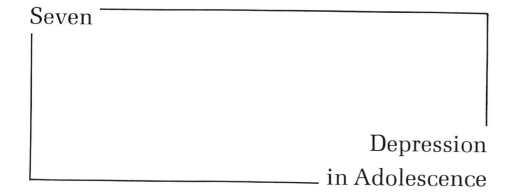

These data reveal some interesting age, sex, and setting differences in the

Table 1 Percentage of Psychiatric Patients Diagnosed Psychoneurotic Depressive Reaction, by Age and Sex

	Age			
	10–14	15–17	18–19	25–44
Outpatient Psychiatric Services[a]				
Total	1.7	3.3	7.6	14.8
Male	1.6	2.0	4.6	7.8
Female	2.1	4.8	10.4	19.7
General Hospitals[b]				
Total	5.8	11.6	15.8	15.9
Male	4.9	8.8	10.5	9.7
Female	7.2	13.8	19.8	19.6
Mental Hospitals[c]				
Total	2.3	3.5	6.6	10.0
Male	1.7	2.0	3.7	5.3
Female	3.6	5.6	11.0	16.8

[a]Derived from *Outpatient Psychiatric Services* (Public Health Service Publication #1982, 1969, Table 9), based on 466,102 terminated patients.
[b]Derived from *General Hospital Inpatient Psychiatric Services* (Public Health Service Publication #1997, 1969, Table 7), based on 380,922 discharged patients.
[c]Derived from *Patients in State and County Mental Hospitals* (Public Health Service Publication #1921, 1969, Table 2), based on 153,314 first admissions.

incidence of diagnosed depression. With respect to age, the percentage of depressed patients is negligible at age 10 to 14, almost doubles for age 15 to 17, and almost doubles again in 18- to 19-year-olds. Furthermore, with the exception of general hospital settings, 18- to 19-year-old patients are still only about half as likely to be diagnosed psychoneurotic depressive reaction as are 25- to 44-year-old patients. As viewed in the light of current diagnostic practices, then, depressive disorder is more an adult than an adolescent phenomenon and becomes gradually more likely to appear in disturbed individuals as they mature through the adolescent years toward adulthood.

With respect to sex, female patients at all ages and in all settings are more likely to be diagnosed depressed than are male patients. This sex difference becomes gradually more pronounced during the adolescent years and is most marked for the adult group, for whom depression is more than twice as likely to occur among female than among male patients.

With respect to setting, adolescents and adults alike are more likely to be diagnosed psychoneurotic depressive reaction in the psychiatric units of general hospitals than in either mental hospitals or outpatient clinics. These differences would seem related in part to the higher incidence in mental hospitals of serious disturbance, especially psychotic conditions, with a correspondingly lower incidence of neurotic conditions than is observed in general hospitals. In outpatient settings, where the general level of disturbance is still less serious than in general hospitals, there tend to be more frequent instances in which either no diagnosis or a diagnosis of transient situational personality disorder is made, with a corresponding decrease in the frequency of diagnosed psychotic, neurotic, and personality disorders relative to the general hospital psychiatric unit.

Focusing on the adolescent patient, there is good reason to believe that the data in Table 1, even though they indicate an appreciable incidence of depressive disorder in youthful patients, underestimate the frequency of depression in adolescents coming to psychiatric attention. Other sources of evidence suggest that adolescent patients are generally underdiagnosed in clinical settings and that some clinicians specifically avoid diagnosing depression in young people.

The Underdiagnosis of Adolescent Patients

Because of continuing confusion about the nature of normal and abnormal behavior in adolescents, the clinical diagnosis of teenage patients has been much less precise than it can and should be. Much of this confusion can be traced to the widespread belief that adolescents normally go through a period of turmoil resembling psychopathology. As elaborated by Deutsch (1), A. Freud (2, 3), Gardner (4), Geleerd (5), Josselyn (6), Spiegel (7), Winnicott (8), and numerous other influential clinicians, the notion of "adolescent turmoil" holds (*a*) that adolescent development involves considerable inner unrest and personality upheaval and (*b*) that the boundary between normality and psychopathology is consequently so blurred as to make clinical diagnosis inappropriate or impossible in most cases. With normal adolescence viewed as an unstable condition mimicking psychological disturbance, the task of the clinician is not to diagnose or treat apparent behavior problems in teenagers, but rather to urge forbearance in the face of turmoil. As Winnicott (8) states, "The cure for adolescence belongs to the passage of time and to the gradual maturation processes" (pp. 40–41).

Although this impressionistic view of adolescent development has achieved considerable popularity, abundant research data demonstrate that adolescents do *not* normally go through a period of turmoil resembling psychopathology (9–16). In reviewing these and other studies, Weiner (17, Chap. 2; 18; 19) clearly documents that there is no common picture of adolescent turmoil simulating psychopathology, that adolescents display no greater incidence of psychological disruption or instability than is normatively found among adults, and that there is no basis for blandly expecting a troubled adolescent to grow out of his adjustment difficulties.

This last point is particularly important to keep in mind, because follow-up studies of behaviorally disturbed adolescents reveal a striking persistence of their problems into adult life, rather than any gradual evaporation of turmoil with maturity. In comparing patient and nonpatient youngsters averaging age 16, Masterson (20, 21) and his co-workers at the Payne Whitney Clinic found not only that the two groups could be readily differentiated on the basis of symptom formation and degree of impaired functioning, but also that almost two-thirds of the patient group continued to demonstrate psychological impairment 5 years later, when they averaged age 21.

Similar results have emerged from follow-up studies of adolescent patients at Michael Reese Hospital and Medical Center (22, 23), the Massachusetts Mental Health Center (24), Washington University Medical Center (25), and the Menninger Foundation (26). The general import of these research reports is that, contrary to the adolescent turmoil notion, diagnostic categories are fairly stable in teenage patients and are predictive of recovery or chronicity, with neurotic youngsters having better prospects for a satisfactory adult adjustment than do youngsters diagnosed as schizophrenic or as having a personality disorder.

In short, then, the data indicate that an adolescent who appears disturbed is likely to *be* disturbed and to remain disturbed unless appropriate treatment measures are instituted. These findings, together with the availability of extensive guidelines for differentiating normal from abnormal behavior in adolescence (17, 20), provide the basis for arguing that the diagnosis of adolescents can and should be more precise than is advocated by clinicians subscribing to the notion of adolescent turmoil.

One additional datum testifies to the probable underdiagnosis of adolescent patients. Official statistics reveal that of all patients under age 18 terminated from psychiatric clinics with a diagnosis of "transient situational personality disorder," 51% have received treatment (27). The comparable figures for other major diagnostic categories are 60% receiving treatment among those with psychoneurotic disorder, 56% among psychotic disorder, and 45% among personality disorder. In other words, adolescents being given a situational diagnosis are just about as frequently taken into treatment as those with diagnosed disorder, even though "transient reaction" is usually intended to mean that existing symptoms will pass with time or with an improvement in the environmental situation, without psychological treatment being required.

Apparently, then, clinicians are applying the label of "transient situational personality disorder" to many young people whom they still regard as sufficiently disturbed to require treatment. Decisions about diagnostic labeling are of course complicated, especially with younger patients, by justifiable concerns about how official records will be used and who will have access to them. Whether clinicians are acting out of conviction or expedience, however, the data reported from outpatient clinics lend support to the conclusion that psychological disturbance is generally underdiagnosed in adolescent patients.

Reservations About Diagnosing Depression in Young Patients

Aside from whatever misgivings they may have about diagnosing young people in general, some clinicians are specifically reluctant to diagnose depression in children and adolescents. Such reservations are usually defended on both theoretical and clinical grounds. Theoretically, it is argued that depression is a compound affective response emerging in a conflictual context of orality, guilt, and aggression turned inward, and that not until late in the developmental years does an individual possess the psychic structures necessary to generate such a complex pattern of psychopathology (28–30). Clinically, it is stressed that children and adolescents rarely display the dysphoric affect, psychomotor retardation, feelings of hopelessness and helplessness, and constellation of guilt and self-depreciation that constitute the traditional identifying features of depressive disorder. It is presumably on these grounds that depression is given short shrift, if it is mentioned at all, in many textbooks on childhood psychopathology (31–36).

Yet there are other ways of viewing depression, both theoretically and clinically, that provide a comprehensive basis for acknowledging its existence in younger as well as in older patients. Whereas depression was originally conceptualized in dynamic personality theory as a reaction to the loss of internalized love objects (37), more recent developments in theory favor regarding it as a reaction to the real or fantasied loss of anything the individual holds dear—his loved ones, his self-esteem, his mental and physical capacities, his material possessions, or even the goals he fails to achieve (38–40). Viewed in this latter way, depressive reactions can occur as early in life as a person forms attachments to people, objects, or aspirations. Since children begin at 6 to 8 months of age to become attached to the important people in their lives and to display disturbed behavior when deprived of contact with these people (41–44), it is theoretically possible for depression to occur at virtually any point in the developmental years as well as following maturity.

With respect to clinical observations, it is important to distinguish between depression as an underlying disorder and depression as a cluster of symptoms (45). Many disorders produce different symptom patterns in patients of different ages. The symptoms of tertiary syphillis in older men bear little resemblance to the manifestations of primary syphillis in younger men, yet recognizing that both symptom patterns result from the same underlying disease process led to major advances in its diagnosis, treatment, and prevention. Closer to the subject of psychological problems in young people, the same point can be made with respect to minimal brain dysfunction, which is manifest primarily by hyperactivity in younger children and primarily by learning disabilities and acting-out in older children and adolescents (46).

Depression too can be understood as an underlying process that is manifest in different ways at different ages. Child clinicians who consider depression a reaction to loss accordingly tend to classify it in relation to developmental stage and to describe distinct symptom patterns for depression occuring in infancy, childhood, and early and late adolescence (47–50). When depression is conceived as an underlying disturbance with varying manifestations, the fact that children and adolescents seldom display "traditional" symptoms of depression no longer constitutes a reason for not diagnosing it in younger patients.

Manifestations of Depression in Adolescents

Although there is little consensus concerning the adolescent age range, it is reasonable to regard adolescence as beginning with pubescent physical changes between age 11 to 13 and extending to some point between graduation from secondary school at age 18 and the consolidation of some personal identity (17, pp. 5–12; 51, Chaps. 14–15). Major advances in physical and cognitive growth and in personality and social development take place during these years, making the adolescent period extremely diverse. Accordingly, manifestations of depression differ considerably during adolescence and especially with regard to the behavior patterns by which depression can be recognized in younger and older adolescents.

Depression in Younger Adolescents

There are two main reasons why adolescents prior to age 16 or 17 rarely display traditional adult symptoms of depression. First, youngsters at this age have strong needs to deny self-critical attitudes and to avoid admitting personal concerns to others. Hence they are relatively unlikely to experience or to exhibit the gloom, hopelessness, and self-depreciation that commonly characterize depression in adults. Second, early adolescents are at a developmental stage in which, like children, they are oriented more toward doing things than thinking about them. Consequently, younger people tend to express depression through various kinds of overt behavior, rather than through the introspective preoccupations that typify depressive symptomatology in adults.

Of the behaviors by which younger adolescents manifest depression, some represent the psychological toll of being depressed; some represent efforts to defend against or ward off depression; and others represent an appeal for help. Taking first the possible toll of depression on psychological functioning, adolescents suffering from a sense of loss frequently present a triumvirate of symptoms consisting of *fatigue, hypochondriasis,* and *concentration difficulty:*

Fatigue Although teenagers who are growing rapidly and leading active lives may often become tired, they typically exude energy and recuperate rapidly from fatigue. Physically healthy youngsters who complain of persistent fatigue, even after adequate rest, may well be worn out from struggling with a depressive disorder that they can neither resolve nor express directly.

Hypochondriasis It is not unusual for early adolescents to be concerned about the ongoing changes in their physical size, structure, and capacities. Inordinate body preoccupation, however, especially when accompanied by various psychophysiological reactions, often indicates depressing concerns about adequacy that a youngster has difficulty admitting to himself or expressing to others.

Concentration Difficulty Inability to concentrate, usually described in relation to declining school performance, is one of the most common complaints that bring adolescents for professional help. In some cases concentration difficulty can be traced to minimal brain dysfunction, and in other instances it may be associated with a schizophrenic impairment of the capacity to think clearly and logically. In the absence of supporting evidence for either of these disorders, inability to concentrate is likely to reflect the toll of underlying depression.

Although concentration difficulty is also a common symptom of depression in adults, older people usually recognize it as secondary to their pervasive apathy or preoccupation with depressing concerns. The depressed early adolescent, on the other hand, typically denies being apathetic or having anything on his mind that is troubling him. He may only be able to say that his grades are dropping and that no matter how hard he works on his studies he cannot seem to absorb and retain information. Whenever a young patient presents this type of complaint, underlying depression should be suspected as a source of the difficulty.

Turning next to efforts to defend against or ward off depression, the two most common symptoms of this kind in depressed adolescents are *boredom and restlessness* and *flight to or from people:*

Boredom and Restlessness It is well known that one way to avoid feeling depressed is to keep busy, to "keep your mind off things." Because younger adolescents are so intent on avoiding depressive feelings, they are particularly likely to display a high activity level as symptomatic of underlying depression. The activity of an adolescent attempting to ward off depression has a driven quality that makes him restless and easily bored. Stimulus seeking becomes a dominant feature of his behavior, and the youngster alternates between highly enthusiastic investment in new pursuits and a rapid loss of interest in them as soon as they have lost their initial glow. An adolescent who cannot tolerate any kind of routine in his life but instead has a constant craving for new and exciting activities is very likely to be defending against underlying depressive disorder.

Flight to or from People As one aspect of their need for stimulation, depressed adolescents frequently dread being alone and seek constant companionship. Having company may become so important to the adolescent that he spends most of his time moving among various circles of friends, always managing to find some who are not at the moment studying, sleeping, or engaged in some other private activity. For the depressed youngster, this may mean that little time is left for private activities of his own, and doing his school work, getting enough sleep, and taking on individual interests or hobbies all become secondary to finding people to do things with.

In some instances, however, a depressed youngster may prefer loneliness to company because being around other people exacerbates his underlying feelings of having been rejected or abandoned by others. Adolescents who avoid people for this reason often attempt to compensate for the lack of interpersonal stimulation in their lives by all the more intense stimulus seeking in solitary activities that are pursued with a vengeance. It is also not uncommon for teenagers who feel uncomfortable, inadequate, or rejected in interpersonal situations to ward off this source of depression by a heightened interest in animals, especially household pets with whom they can exchange affection with minimal risk of being scorned or abandoned.

Behavior by which depressed adolescents appeal for help consists primarily of *acting out* through temper tantrums, running away, stealing, and a variety of other defiant, rebellious, antisocial, and delinquent acts.

Acting Out By acting out in response to an underlying depressive disorder, an adolescent seeks to accomplish several purposes. First, the behaviors he engages in, to the extent that they are novel and exciting, serve his stimulus-seeking needs and help him avoid coming directly to grips with what is troubling him. Second, to the extent that his acting out involves public displays of strength, bravery, or cunning, it can impress his peers and bolster his own self-image. Most importantly, however, acting out by a young person who does not lack basic capacities for impulse control is usually an appeal for help, a mute statement to the important people in his world that he is in pain and desperately needs their attention and support.

To elaborate this differential diagnosis, acting out in adolescents is especially likely to reflect underlying depression when the problem behavior does not appear associated with sociopathic personality trends. Sociopathic youngsters typically have a childhood history of impulsiveness, poor frustration tolerance, and aggressive, antisocial behavior, and their adolescent acting out appears to be a continuation into the teenage years of a preexisting conduct disorder. In contrast, when acting out behavior emerges in an adolescent who is not characteristically prone to such behavior and has no history of conduct difficulties, the problem behavior is probably symptomatic of underlying depression.

Numerous case reports document the ways in which young people utilize aggressive behavior to ward off depression (52–54) and also the striking parallel that may exist between loss of a loved person, as through separation or divorce in the family or death of a parent, and the onset of uncharacteristic delinquent behavior (55, 56). Masterson (57), Weiner (17, pp. 300–314), and other writers have elaborated how such symptomatic delinquent behavior emerges when youngsters feel unnoticed, unappreciated, rejected, or deprived and resort to misconduct as a means of communicating their needs to be recognized and attended to. Consistent with the effort to communicate through acting out, rarely will the depressed adolescent misbehave secretively. Instead, his actions are as public as he can make them, and even if he makes a pretense of trying to get away with some transgression, he usually manages to be careless enough to get caught.

Depression in Older Adolescents

As they mature, adolescents become oriented toward ideational as well as expressive ways of dealing with their experience, and they become also more capable than before of thinking about themselves critically and sharing these thoughts with others. Hence they gradually become more likely to manifest depression in traditional adult symptoms. Yet older adolescents may still express depression indirectly, through maladaptive behavior. The most important behavioral indices of underlying depression that begin to emerge at age 15 or 16 are *drug abuse, sexual promiscuity, negative identity formation, suicidal behavior,* and, especially in late adolescence, *alienation and personality restriction:*

Drug Abuse In the face of rampant allegations of extensive drug use among young people, substantial evidence indicates that persistent regular use of psychoactive drugs is uncommon among teenagers and usually associated with maladjustment when it occurs (58–61). Of particular interest, it has been found that the more high school students use drugs, the more likely they are to do poorly in school, to be uninvolved in either academic or extracurricular school activities, and to lack any meaningful commitment to social, occupational, or athletic goals (62, 63).

While drug abuse has multiple causes, its association with the above signs of inhibited personality functioning identifies the role that underlying depression may play in it. In addition, persistent regular drug use may be serving in a number of ways to help a young person defend against feeling depressed: the intoxicating effects of the drugs can offer escape from depressing concerns; the process of illegally obtaining and using drugs can satisfy needs for excitement and stimulation; and the sharing of the drug experience with other youngsters can establish at least pseudocompanionship and provide a hedge against loneliness (64–67).

Sexual Promiscuity Sexual promiscuity, like abuse of drugs, is sometimes regarded as a common feature of contemporary adolescent behavior. However, abundant research findings demonstrate that there has been no "sexual revolution" in this country since the 1920s; that while young people are more open and sophisticated about sexual matters than in the past and more inclined to become physically intimate in the context of a close, trusting, and relatively enduring relationship, they are no more likely than in previous years to approve of or engage in promiscuous sexuality; and that sexual promiscuity—regularly engaging in physical intimacy without personal intimacy, maintaining concurrent sexual liaisons with multiple partners, and flitting with abandon from one sexual relationship to another—is relatively rare, especially among girls, and likely to be associated with psychological maladjustment when it occurs (18, 60, 61, 68–73).

Although adolescent girls are less active sexually than boys, they are more likely to use promiscuity as a defense against depression. Sexual encounters ordinarily place more demands on the male than on the female partner to be knowledgeable and proficient, and, since teenage boys are both inexperienced and uncertain of their capacity to perform, they tend to find sexual activity too threatening to serve as an adequate defense against depression. For girls, however, promiscuity requires only willingness, not performance, and it is therefore more effective than in boys as a symptomatic effort to compensate for an inner sense of loss.

The promiscuity of a depressed adolescent girl is seldom sexual, in the sense of providing her erotic gratification. Rather, it serves primarily to bring her into intimate physical contact with other people. The attention she receives from boys and young men seeking her favors, the experience of feeling needed and wanted, and the sensations of being held and caressed all help a depressed girl combat feelings of being unattractive, alone, and unloved.

Negative Identity Formation Erikson's (74) concept of negative identity formation suggests that adolescents who cannot successfully fill the roles and identities valued by the important people in their life may choose an identity "perversely based on all those identifications and roles which, at critical stages of development, had been presented to the individual as most undesirable or dangerous." Such a negative identity spares the adolescent from having to regard himself as a failure or a "nobody." Instead, he becomes a "somebody," even if somebody bad, and by doing a good job of being "bad," he achieves a sense of mastery and a degree of attention from others that would otherwise be lacking in his life.

Negative identity formation can participate in many specific kinds of problem behavior, including promiscuity and delinquency. Broadly speaking, however, it comprises any tendency of a young person to seize on and defend to the last breath a set of values diametrically opposed to the values espoused in his family, social class, ethnic group, religion, neighborhood, or school. It is not just that the adolescent is thinking for himself and embarking on a constructive approach to life different from the one in which he has been reared. Rather, it is an uncritical overemphasis on opposition for its own sake, accompanied by maladaptive and self-defeating behavior, that identifies negative identity formation and suggests an ongoing effort to ward off depressing feelings of failure and inadequacy.

Suicidal Behavior Although adolescents are less likely to kill themselves than are adults, suicide ranks 10th among causes of death in the total United States population but is the 5th leading cause of death among 15- to 19-year olds. Furthermore, while youngsters under age 20 account for 3 to 4 % of the yearly deaths by suicide in this country, they make an estimated 12% of the suicide attempts. Adolescent boys are more likely than girls to take their own lives, by a ratio of 4:1, but girls account for 80 to 90% of adolescent suicide attempts. These and other epidemiological data are presented by Seiden (75), Schrut (76), Stengel (77), and Weiner (17, pp. 176–180).

Suicidal behavior, especially when it is nonlethal, constitutes an active appeal for help (78, 79), and for the adolescent it is particularly likely to represent a desperate, last-ditch effort to get other people to recognize and help him with problems he feels helpless to resolve (80–86). Because it usually emerges in young people who have undergone cumulative psychological setbacks and have reached a point where they can no longer generate alternative solutions to their problems, *suicidal behavior must always be taken seriously.* If the appeal it represents falls on deaf ears, or if those who hear it respond not with sympathetic concern but with ridicule, scorn, or disinterest, there may be nothing left for the suicidal youngster to do except try again with a more dramatic and more dangerous attempt on his life.

Alienation and Personality Restriction Late adolescents who become depressed may in some instances develop a pattern of alienation and personality restriction. Such young people feel apathetic and out of touch with themselves and others, while at the same time they form pseudomutual relationships with each other that give them a pretense of intimacy and group belongingness. The alienated group is characterized by listlessness and cynicism, by lack of commitment to long-range goals, by dabbling in drugs and far-out causes, and by derision of anything conventional (87–91).

The main theme of such alienation and personality restriction is not doing anything, and herein lies its relationship to underlying depression. The alienated adolescent is avoiding any kind of effort that might end in failure and any kind of aspiration that might lead to disappointment. Thus it is that alienation develops when a youngster with underlying concerns about adequacy, who is afraid of not making a place for himself in the world, attempts to ward off failure and disappointment by not risking exposure to them.

Etiology of Adolescent Depression

The depressive disorders of adolescents, like those of adults, emerge primarily in response to the experience of loss. The loss may be loss of a personal relationship due to death, separation, or a broken friendship; it may consist of a loss of self-esteem subsequent to violating one's standards of conduct or failing to achieve some desired goal; it may consist of a loss of bodily integrity related to illness, incapacitation, disfigurement, or even normal bodily changes.

Whatever the particular sense of loss that evokes a depression, it may be either a *real* or a *fantasied* loss. A real loss is an actual event in the adolescent's life that deprives him of something important to him: for example, rejection by a boyfriend, finishing last in a race, or having to wear braces can respectively deprive a youngster of a valued personal relationship, of a highly desired success, or of a gratifying sense of bodily integrity. A fantasied loss is an unconscious or unrealistic concern that causes a youngster to feel deprived in the absence of any objective evidence to justify his concern. Feelings of being unloved, inadequate, or unattractive, arising without solid basis in fact, are among the common fantasied losses that contribute to adolescent depression.

The distinction between real and fantasied loss in the etiology of adolescent depression provides a basis for distinguishing between *reactive* and *endogenous* depressions in young people. Real losses tend to precipitate reactive depressions, in which the depressing circumstances are readily identifiable, whereas the outcome of fantasied loss is likely to be an endogenous depression, in which the origins of the distress are often not apparent to the depressed youngster or to an untrained observer. Reactive depression, like mourning, tends to be a self-limiting disorder that heals with the passage of time and the replacement of lost objects and goals with new ones. Endogenous depression, on the other hand, is a more chronic and lingering condition in which psychotherapy may be necessary to help the adolescent unravel and take a more realistic view of the concerns that are depressing him.

To understand why adolescents become depressed, it is important to recognize that the normal developmental process presents teenagers with a number of real losses and threats to their self-esteem. During the adolescent years young people are expected to loosen their ties to their parents, to direct their needs for affection and support increasingly to peers, and to take major responsibility for running their lives and planning their future. Although teenagers typically welcome the prerogatives that independence brings, few can escape some qualms about having to surrender the protected position of their childhood and undertake new social and interpersonal ventures that place their self-esteem in jeopardy. Furthermore, the various bodily changes of adolescence tend to disrupt a youngster's previous sense of knowing himself and to generate numerous concerns about adequacy (92).

The potentially depressing aspects of normal adolescent development, requiring as it does that young people give up previous attachments and risk self-esteem in the pursuit of new ones, have been discussed extensively in the psychoanalytic literature. Freud (93) described the detachment from parental authority as "one of the most significant, but also one of the most painful, psychical achievements of the pubertal period" (p. 227), and many other writers have observed that the period between the adolescent's disengagement from his parents and his initial successes in attaching to new objects may induce temporary states of apparent grief or mourning (2, 94–96).

Hence adolescence, like other transitional stages in the life cycle that involve learning to live without some previous sources of gratification, enhances temporarily the individual's susceptibility to becoming depressed. The better a youngster is prepared to meet the challenges of adolescence, to give up his earlier attachments, and to cope with real and fantasied loss, the more likely he is to avoid depressive disorder during the teenage years. Conversely, difficulty in making this teenage transition increases a youngster's vulnerability to depression in the face of real and fantasied losses he may encounter.

As one specific aspect of the predisposition to depressive disorder, some research studies have suggested that adolescents and adults who have experienced parental deprivation in childhood become particularly sensitized to loss and prone to depression in face of it (97–101). Although this proposed relationship between early deprivation and subsequent susceptibility to depression makes clinical sense, it has not yet been firmly established. Research in this area has been handicapped by the elusiveness of an objective criterion for early deprivation. Growing up in a broken home is the most widely used experimental index of deprivation, yet it is obvious that a child reared by a single parent who is loving and devoted experiences much less deprivation that one who lives with two parents who both ignore him. For the clinician who is attempting to assess whether an adolescent patient should be considered depression-prone in light of his earlier experiences, this type of distinction can be very useful: the more evidence he can find of *experienced* loss or deprivation in the youngster's earlier life, regardless of who and what were apparently available to him, the more reason he will have to suspect depressive disorder as a basis for current behavior problems.

Treatment

Psychological treatment of the depressed adolescent should always be guided by the general principles for conducting psychotherapy with this age group. Briefly, these principles include establishing treatment goals aimed at personality consolidation rather than personality reorganization; initiating treatment swiftly and incisively, with special attention to promoting the youngster's comfort, engagement, and self-motivation in the treatment relationship; and employing a high level of activity, directness, genuineness, and visible interest to sustain communication and foster positive identification with the therapist (17, Chap. 9; 102; 103). Beyond these general guidelines, successful psychological treatment of depression in young people depends largely on how clearly the therapist can recognize and respond to the messages implicit in the patient's symptoms.

Above all, the therapist needs to keep in mind that a depressed adolescent is responding to some real or fantasied loss with a sense of inner loss, and that it is the inner sense of being lacking or deprived that is producing the manifest symptoms of his depression. The origin of depression in experienced loss has two primary implications for psychotherapy. First, it means that the entry of the therapist into a depressed adolescent's life, as someone who respects him as a person and is genuinely interested in helping him with his problems, may provide a relationship that compensates in part for his previous object losses and by itself relieves his depression. Second, it means that the therapist can usefully direct his efforts toward helping a depressed youngster recognize and come to grips with the circumstances that are causing him to feel a sense of loss.

The manner in which the adolescent can best be helped to deal with depressing circumstances depends on whether they are real or fantasied. If he is experiencing loss in relation to a real event, such as a broken friendship or failure in school, it is often helpful through relatively superficial discussions to lead him to take a different perspective on the loss, to see it as less tragic, less permanent, and less irremedial than he has believed it to be. If the sense of loss stems from fantasied or unrealistic concerns, especially when the adolescent is not consciously aware of them, then a more intensive, interpretive approach may be necessary to aid him in identifying and working through what is troubling him.

Although the sense of loss holds the key to depressive disorder, and therefore needs to be foremost in the therapist's mind as he works with a depressed adolescent, attempting to trace the origins of depression does not necessarily obviate attention to its presenting symptoms. Failure to recognize and respond to what these symptoms mean can result in the adolescent's dropping out of treatment early or coasting along without becoming much engaged in the treatment effort. Furthermore, such behavioral manifestations of depression as acting out and alienation can become habitual and take on important secondary reward properties, which means that they will not automatically disappear as underlying depressive concerns are identified and resolved, but will instead require treatment in their own right. Hence psychotherapy with a depressed adolescent must usually include direct treatment of his symptoms as well as efforts to provide him a meaningful relationship and help him work through his underlying depressive concerns.

The specific symptom treatment approach called for varies with whether a youngster's depression is being manifest primarily through its toll, through attempts to ward it off, or through appeals for help. When apathy, fatigue, and personality restriction are the behavioral manifestations of underlying depression, the therapist needs to look resourcefully for ways of getting the youngster's life moving again. Every effort should be made to ferret out where his talents lie, what kinds of things he has enjoyed doing in the past and might continue to derive enjoyment from, and what aspirations he has had that might still stir some enthusiasm in him. Such information identifies activities and goals toward which the youngster can be encouraged to make at least some token effort; hopefully, in so doing he will receive enough pleasurable reward to motivate him to further effort and drive a wedge into his symptomatic pattern of personality restriction.

In pursuing this approach, the therapist should avoid encouraging the youngster to take up activities and goals because it is "the thing to do" or would be "good for him." He probably will have heard his fill of such exhortations from parents, teachers, and other well-meaning adults. Rather, the therapist must strive to instill intrinsic motivation in his depressed adolescent patient, beginning with efforts to help him realize what he is missing by not doing things he would be able to do well and get satisfaction from. Every step the youngster can be cajoled into taking toward engagement in rewarding pursuits replaces apathy with activity and alienation with commitment.

When efforts to ward off depression are prominent features of the complaints that bring an adolescent for professional help, the treatment approach resembles work with acting-out youngsters (17, pp. 332–338; 50; 57). The therapist avoids outright disapproval of the problematic behavior, to sustain a positive treatment relationship, yet he also avoids appearing to sanction the behavior or to have a permissive stance regarding what the adolescent should and should not do. Instead, the therapist makes every effort to help the youngster recognize that his behavior is self-defeating, that the personal price he is paying for his acting out is too great to justify any pleasure it gives him, and that the best thing he could do for himself would be to alter his behavior. This treatment approach, like work with acting-out adolescents in general, makes heavy demands on the therapist's patience and skill. If he can win the youngster's confidence, however, he will have a good foothold from which to offer firm, direct criticism of the problem behavior, phrased not in terms of any abstract or generalized set of values but specifically in terms of how the behavior is causing him more trouble than it is worth and preventing the youngster from getting more of what he really wants out of life.

When the manner in which an adolescent manifests depression represents primarily an appeal for help, the therapist's most important task is to make certain the youngster knows his message has been received and is being responded to. In many cases this task is accomplished simply by the therapist's becoming involved with the youngster and taking interest in his difficulties. Whether he is a younger adolescent whose parents have obtained professional help for him or an older adolescent who has been referred for help by someone close to him, he knows even before he sees the therapist that his problems are being recognized by other people who are concerned about him. When the therapist adds to these indications of interest and support his own readiness to meet with the youngster and try to be of help to him, the symptomatic appeal for help may be largely satisfied.

For this reason, adolescents who have only recently begun to display uncharacteristic acting-out behavior, and in whom such behavior has not become habitual or self-perpetuating, may abruptly stop misbehaving as soon as they become engaged in ongoing psychotherapy. Yet the propensity for resuming problem behavior may linger in the wings for an extended period, ready to take center stage at the slightest cue that people are again failing to appreciate his needs, and it may remain there until the youngster has been able to resolve or compensate constructively for his underlying sense of loss.

The importance of responding to a depressed adolescent's mute appeals for help through problem behavior is especially critical when the youngster has been suicidal. For the adolescent who has made a suicide attempt or gesture, every effort possible must be made to muster support and provide clear messages that other people care. In addition to what the therapist may do himself, it is essential that he involve other family members in the treatment, whether in family therapy or parent counseling, to encourage continuing awareness of and response to the adolescent's needs on their part. As noted earlier, suicidal behavior that does not elicit increased attention and support from the environment is highly likely to be followed by further, more serious suicidal behavior (104).

In summary, then, the clinician working with adolescent patients needs to keep in mind that they may be expressing underlying depressive disorder through a number of behavior patterns differing from traditional adult manifestations of depression; that some of these behavior patterns represent the toll of depression on personality functioning (e.g., apathy, fatigue, alienation), some represent efforts to ward off depression (e.g., restlessness, stimulus-seeking, sexual promiscuity), and some represent appeals for help (especially suicidal behavior); that adolescent depression arises out of real or fantasied losses that cause a young person to feel inadequate, incompetent, unattractive, or unloved; and that psychotherapy with depressed young people usually combines constructive use of the treatment relationship to compensate for the sense of loss, efforts to promote understanding of the concerns that have evoked and are perpetuating the depression, and specific focus on helping the youngster alter the maladaptive behavior patterns through which his depression is being expressed.

References

1. Deutsch H: *Selected Problems of Adolescence.* New York, International Universities Press, 1967.
2. Freud A: Adolescence. *Psa Study Child* **13**:255–278, 1958.
3. Freud A: Adolescence as a developmental disturbance, in *Adolescence: Psychosocial Perspectives.* Edited by Caplan G, Lebovici S, New York, Basic Books, 1969, pp. 5–10.
4. Gardner GE: Psychiatric problems of adolescents, in *American Handbook of Psychiatry.* Edited by Arieti S, New York, Basic Books, 1959, pp. 870–892.
5. Geleerd ER: Some aspects of ego vicissitudes in adolescence. *J Am Psa Assoc* **9**:394–405, 1961.
6. Josselyn IM: The ego in adolescence. *Am J Orthopsychiatr* **24**:223–227, 1954.
7. Spiegel LA: A review of contributions to a psychoanalytic theory of adolescence. *Psa Study Child* **6**:375–393, 1951.
8. Winnicott, DW: Adolescence: Struggling through the doldrums, in *Adolescent Psychiatry.* Edited by Feinstein SC, Giovacchini PL, Miller AA, New York, Basic Books, 1971, pp. 40–50.
9. Douvan E, Adelson J: *The Adolescent Experience.* New York, Wiley, 1966.
10. Grinker RR: "Mentally healthy" young males (homoclites). *Arch Gen Psychiatr* **6**:405–453, 1962.
11. Kysar JE, Zaks MS, Schuschman HP, and others: Range of psychological functioning in "normal" late adolescents. *Arch Gen Psychiatr* **21**:515–528, 1969.
12. Masterson JF: The psychiatric significance of adolescent turmoil. *Am J Psychiatr* **124**:1549–1554, 1968.

13. Offer D: *The Psychological World of the Teenager.* New York, Basic Books, 1969.
14. Offer D, Offer J: Four issues in the developmental psychology of adolescents, in *Modern Perspectives in Adolescent Psychiatry.* Edited by Howells JG, New York, Brunner/Mazel, 1971, pp. 28–44.
15. Silber E, Coelho GV, Murphey EB, and others: Competent adolescents coping with college decisions. *Arch Gen Psychiatr* **5**:517–527, 1961.
16. Weiss RJ, Segal BE, Sokol R: Epidemiology of emotional disturbance in a men's college. *J Nerv Ment Dis* **141**:240–250, 1965.
17. Weiner IB: *Psychological Disturbance in Adolescence.* New York, Wiley, 1970.
18. Weiner IB: The generation gap—Fact and fancy. *Adolescence* **6**:155–166, 1971.
19. Weiner IB: Disruption and stability in adolescence, in *Issues in Adolescent Psychology.* Edited by Rogers D, New York, Appleton-Century-Crofts, 1972, 2nd ed., pp. 98–101.
20. Masterson JF: *The Psychiatric Dilemma of Adolescence.* Boston, Little, Brown, 1967.
21. Masterson JF: The symptomatic adolescent five years later: He didn't grow out of it. *Am J Psychiatr* **123**:1338–1345, 1967.
22. Garber B: *Follow-Up Study of Hospitalized Adolescents.* New York, Brunner/Mazel, 1972.
23. Garber B, Polsky R: Follow-up study of hospitalized adolescents. *Arch Gen Psychiatr* **22**:179–187, 1970.
24. Hartmann E, Glaser BA, Greenblatt M, and others: *Adolescents in a Mental Hospital.* New York, Grune & Stratton, 1968.
25. King LJ: Depressive reactions of childhood and adolescence. *Psychosomatics* **11**:429–433, 1970.
26. Levy EZ: Long-term follow-up of former inpatients at the Children's Hospital of the Menninger Clinic. *Am J Psychiatr* **125**:47–53, 1969.
27. Outpatient Psychiatric Services, Public Health Service Publication 1982, Table 8, Washington, DC, 1969.
28. Mahler MS: On sadness and grief in infancy and childhood: loss and restoration of the symbiotic love object. *Psa Study Child* **16**:332–351, 1961.
29. Rie HE: Depression in childhood—A survey of some pertinent contributions. *J Am Acad Child Psychiatr* **5**:653–685, 1966.
30. Rochlin GR: The loss complex: A contribution to the etiology of depression. *J Am Psa Assoc* **7**:299–316, 1959.
31. Kanner L: *Child Psychiatry.* Springfield, Charles C Thomas, 1960.
32. Kessler JW: *Psychopathology of Childhood.* Englewood Cliffs, N.J., Prentice-Hall, 1966.
33. Quay HC, Werry JS (Eds.): *Psychopathological Disorders of Childhood.* New York, Wiley, 1972.
34. Rie HE (Ed.): *Perspectives in Child Psychopathology.* Chicago, Aldine-Altherton, 1971.
35. Shaw CR, Lucas A: *The Psychiatric Disorders of Childhood.* New York, Appleton-Century-Crofts, 1970, 2nd ed.
36. Verville E: *Behavior Problems in Children.* Philadelphia, Saunders, 1967.
37. Freud S (1917): *Three Essays on the Theory of Sexuality.* London, Hogarth Press, Standard Edition, Vol. VII, pp. 125–243.
38. Bibring E: The mechanism of depression, in *Affective Disorders.* Edited by Greenacre P, New York, International Universities Press, 1953, pp. 13–48.
39. Gaylin W (Ed.): *The Meaning of Despair: Psychoanalytic Contributions to the Understanding of Depression.* New York, Science House, 1968.

40. Mendelson M: *Psychoanalytic Concepts of Depression*. Springfield, Charles C Thomas, 1960.
41. Ainsworth MD: Object relations, dependency, and attachment: A theoretical review of the infant-mother relationship. *Child Develop* **40**:969–1025, 1969.
42. Ainsworth MD, Bell SM: Attachment, exploration and separation: Illustrated by the behavior of one-year olds in a strange situation. *Child Develop* **41**:81–95, 1970.
43. Bowlby J: *Attachment and Loss*. New York, Basic Books, 1969.
44. Maccoby EE, Masters EM: Attachment and dependency, in *Carmichael's Manual of Child Psychology*. Edited by Mussen PH, New York, Wiley, 1970, Vol. II, pp. 73–158.
45. Mendels J: Depression: The distinction between syndrome and symptom. *Br J Psychiatr* **114**:1549–1554, 1968.
46. Wender PH: *Minimal Brain Dysfunction in Children*. New York, Wiley, 1971, pp. 24–26.
47. Glasser K: Masked depression in children and adolescents. *Am J Psychotherap* **21**:565–574, 1967.
48. Krakowski AJ: Depressive reactions of childhood and adolescence. *Psychosomatics* **11**:429–433, 1970.
49. Toolan JM: Suicide and suicidal attempts in children and adolescents. *Am J Psychiatr* **118**:719–724, 1962.
50. Toolan JM: Depression in adolescents, in *Modern Perspectives in Adolescent Psychiatry*. Edited by Howells JG, New York, Brunner/Mazel, 1971.
51. Weiner IB, Elkind D: *Child Development: A Core Approach*. New York, Wiley, 1972.
52. Anthony HS: The association of violence and depression in a sample of young offenders. *Br J Crim* **8**:346–365, 1968.
53. Bonnard A: Truancy and pilfering associated with bereavement, in *Adolescents: Psychoanalytic Approaches to Problems and Therapy*. Edited by Lorand S, Schneer HI, New York, Hoeber, 1961, pp. 152–179.
54. Burks HL, Harrison SI: Aggressive behavior as a means of avoiding depression. *Am J Orthopsychiatr* **32**:416–422, 1962.
55. Keeler WR: Children's reactions to the death of a parent, in *Depression*. Edited by Hock P, Zubin J, New York, Grune & Stratton, 1954, pp. 109–120.
56. Shorr M, Speed MH: Delinquency as a manifestation of the mourning process. *Psychiatr Quart* **37**:540–558, 1963.
57. Masterson JF: Depression in the adolescent character disorder, in *The Psychopathology of Adolescence*. Edited by Zubin J, Freedman AM, New York, Grune & Stratton, 1970, pp. 242–254.
58. Gossett JT, Lewis JM, Phillips VA: Extent and prevalence of illicit drug use as reported by 56,745 students. *JAMA* **21**:1464–1470, 1971.
59. Hager DL, Veneer AM, Stewart CS: Patterns of adolescent drug use in middle America. *J Counsel Psychol* **18**:292–297, 1971.
60. Merit Publishing Co. *Merit's Who's Who Among American High School Students: Second Annual National Opinion Survey*, 1971.
61. Weiner IB: Perspectives on the modern adolescent. *Psychiatry* **5**:20–31, 1972.
62. Smart RG, Fejer D, White J: *The Extent of Drug Use in Metropolitan Toronto Schools: A Study of Changes from 1968 to 1970*. Addiction Research Foundation, Toronto, 1970.
63. Tec N: Some aspects of high school status and differential involvement with marijuana: A study of suburban teenagers. *Adolescence* **7**:1–28, 1972.
64. Bowers M, Chipman A, Schwartz A, and others: Dynamics of psychedelic drug

abuse. *Arch Gen Psychiatr* **16**:560–566, 1967.

65. Hartmann D: A study of drug-taking adolescents. *Psa Study Child* **24**:384–398, 1969.
66. Levy NJ: The use of drugs by teenagers for sanctuary and illusion. *Am J Psa* **28**:48–56, 1968.
67. Wiedner H, Kaplan EH: Drug use in adolescents: Psychodynamic meaning and pharmacogenic effect. *Psa Study Child* **24**:399–431, 1969.
68. Kaats GR, Davis KE: The dynamics of sexual behavior of college students. *J Marriage Family* **32**:390–399, 1970.
69. Luckey EB, Nass GD: A comparison of sexual attitudes and behavior in an international sample. *J Marriage Family* **31**:364–379, 1969.
70. Offer D: Attitudes towards sexuality in a group of 1500 middle class teen-agers. *J Youth Adoles* **1**:81–90, 1972.
71. Reiss IL: *The Social Context of Premarital Sexual Permissiveness.* New York, Holt, Rinehart & Winston, 1967.
72. Reiss IL: Premarital sexual standards, in *The Individual, Sex, and Society.* Edited by Broderick CB, Bernard J, Baltimore, Md, Johns Hopkins Press, 1969.
73. Simon W, Berger AS, Gagnon JH: Beyond anxiety and fantasy: The coital experiences of college youth. *J Youth Adoles* **1**:203–222. 1972.
74. Erikson EH: The problem of ego identity. *J Am Psa Assoc* **4**:56–121, 1956.
75. Seiden RJ: *Suicide Among Youth.* Public Health Service Publication 1971, Washington, DC, 1969.
76. Schrut A: Suicidal adolescents and children. *JAMA* **188**:1103–1107, 1964.
77. Stengel LA: *Suicide and Attempted Suicide.* Baltimore, Md, Penguin, 1964.
78. Darbonne AR: Study of psychological content in the communications of suicidal individuals. *J Consult Clin Psychol* **33**:590–596, 1969.
79. Farberow NL, Shneidman ES (Eds): *The Cry for Help.* New York, McGraw-Hill, 1961.
80. Jacobinzer H: Attempted suicides in adolescence. *JAMA* **191**:7–11, 1965.
81. Jacobs J: *Adolescent Suicide.* New York, Wiley, 1971.
82. Levenson M, Neuringer C: Problem-solving behavior in suicidal adolescents. *J Consult Clin Psychol* **37**:433–436, 1971.
83. Schrut A, Michels T: Adolescent girls who attempt suicide—Comments on treatment. *Am J Psychother* **32**:243–251, 1969.
84. Teicher JD, Jacobs J: Adolescents who attempt suicide: Preliminary findings. *Am J Psychiatr* **122**:1248–1257, 1966.
85. Toolan JM: Suicide and suicidal attempts in children and adolescents. *Am J Psychiatr* **118**:719–725, 1962.
86. Yusin AS: Attempted suicide in an adolescent: The resolution of an anxiety state. *Adolescence* **8**:17–28, 1973.
87. Halleck SL: Psychiatric treatment of the alienated college student. *Am J Psychiatr* **124**:642–650, 1967.
88. Shainberg D: Personality restriction in adolescents. *Psychiatr Quart* **40**:258–270, 1966.
89. Teicher JD: The alienated, older male adolescent. *Am J Psychother* **26**:401–407, 1972.
90. Unwin JR: Depression in alienated youth. *Can Psychiatr Assoc* **15**:83–86, 1970.
91. Walters PA: Student apathy, in *Emotional Problems of the Student.* Edited by Blaine GR, McArthur CC, New York, Appleton-Century-Crofts, 1971, 2nd ed., pp. 129–147.
92. Dwyer J, Mayer J: Psychological effects of variations in physical appearance during adolescence. *Adolescence* **3**:353–380, 1969.

93. Freud S (1905): *Three Essays on the Theory of Sexuality.* London, Hogarth Press, 1953, Standard Edition, Vol. VII, pp. 125–243.
94. Jacobson E: Adolescent moods and the remodeling of psychic structures in adolescence. *Psa Study Child* **16:**164–183, 1961.
95. Laufer M: Object loss and mourning during adolescence. *Psa Study Child* **21:**269–293, 1966.
96. Lorand S: Adolescent depression. *Int J Psa* **48:**53–60, 1967.
97. Bowlby J: Childhood mourning and its implications for psychiatry. *Am J Psychiatr* **118:**481–498, 1961.
98. Brown F: Depression and childhood bereavement. *J Ment Sci* **107:**754–777, 1961.
99. Caplan MG, Douglas VI: Incidence of parental loss in children with depressed mood. *J Child Psychol Psychiatr* **10:**225–232, 1969.
100. Gregory I: Anterospective data following childhood loss of a parent. *Arch Gen Psychiatr* **13:**99–103, 1965.
101. Masterson JF, Tucker K, Berk G: Psychopathology in adolescence: IV. Clinical and dynamic characteristics. *Am J Psychiatr* **120:**357–366, 1963.
102. Holmes DJ: *The Adolescent in Psychotherapy.* Boston, Little Brown, 1964.
103. Meeks JE: *The Fragile Alliance: An Orientation to the Outpatient Psychotherapy of the Adolescent.* Baltimore, Md, Williams & Wilkins, 1971.
104. Barter JT, Swaback DO, Todd D: Adolescent suicide attempts: A follow-up of hospitalized patients. *Arch Gen Psychiatr* **19:**523–527, 1968.

Eight

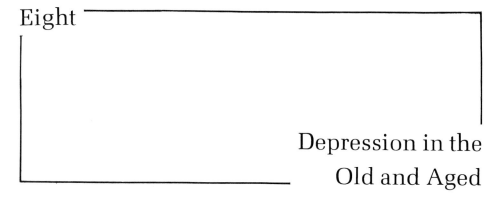

Depression in the Old and Aged

Alvin I. Goldfarb, M.D.

The aged are subject to the same mental and emotional disorders as are found in younger persons. When such disorders are present in youth, they often persist or recur in later life. The disorders may first emerge in old age with functional decline when circumstances change or when attractive appearance, opportunities, skills, or social position is lost. The disorders may complicate or be complicated by aging.

This chapter discusses the symptoms, evolution, and treatment of depressive disorders in the chronologically old and aged from an adaptational point of view. From this viewpoint, "depressed" ways of life may be one style of adjustment; depressive episodes may be due to intensification of such efforts or new adaptational trials; or depressive disorders may be complex adaptational efforts in the face of special stresses.

Chronologic Age, Aging, and the Aged State

The term *elderly* or *old* is used here to denote persons who are chronologically old. The age of 65 is arbitrarily taken to signify the end of middle age and beginning of old age. The term *aged* is reserved for those persons who have suffered a measurable decline in physical or mental functional status related to structural changes occurring with disease or the so-called aging process. Thus individuals may be old without being aged, and may be either physically or mentally aged, or both in varying degrees.

The aged state is not so much a matter of chronology as of functional status. *Aging* is characterized by the decline or loss of physical or mental capacities because of many factors, genetic and experiential, of early occurrence in infancy or childhood, or of late onset. Old problems or illnesses may be reinforced or modified, or new ones may be added. As noted above, with aging of the brain there is a measurable decline in mental agility, in the ability to remain oriented, in one's facility for remembering events in the past and the present, and in the capacity to recall and utilize general information and to make accurate calculations. These losses are a reflection of generalized cortical brain cell loss and of cellular loss in the hippocampal areas. The development of mental impairment is an important contribution to mental and emotional disorders in old people.

However, merely because the old have lived more than 65 years and because the aged have experienced a decline in functional capacity, they do not form a homogeneous group. The organs and systems of a human body may age at different rates, and these rates vary in different persons; therefore, as people grow older they become dissimilar rather than alike. Also, there are wide differences in ethnic, religious, occupational, educational, and experiential backgrounds. Moreover, aged persons differ functionally because of genetic factors, environmental influences, the diseases contracted in the course of a lifetime, and their unique styles—their well-established psychological and emotional habits of adjustment.

Depressive disorder means behavioral changes reflecting loss of interest, decreased attention and concentration, overt behavioral slowing or agitation, together with a subjectively experienced lowering of mood or affect—at times experienced as sadness, pain, or distress—and of loss of morale and of "desire to do." When this pattern is accompanied by specific, severe, persistent gastrointestinal, sleep, and psychomotor dysfunction, it is often referred to as "endogenous" or "psychotic"; it is this group that seems to present a family history of the disorder, and is more likely to have delusions and to show distortions, usually self-deprecatory and laden with guilt and anger, in retrospective reminiscence and in the evaluation of the present situation and expectations, as well as suicidal ideation. The classification of these troublesome and inefficient efforts to achieve personal or social adjustment as disorders of mood or affect is probably preferable to calling them "depressions." What this method emphasizes is that these mental illnesses have an "emotional quality" which influences thought-content and behavior. The changes in mood may be psychologically determined, or may be a response to thought-content determined by and traceable to the premorbid state. At times mood and content appear to be related to current real life experience. The mood change, however, may be a psychophysiologic state acquired early in the lifetime, because of its seeming value in obtaining desirable social response.

Depression and Organic Brain Syndrome

Depression in old age may complicate or be complicated by organic brain syndrome. Organic brain syndrome comprises disorientation for time, place, and person (confusion), memory loss both recent and remote, decreases in general information and the ability to calculate; it is the psychiatric reflection of diffuse cortical brain cell loss (chronic, irreversible) or dysfunction (acute, reversible). When organic brain syndrome is present there are frequently changes in mood, thought-content, or behavior. To recognize and understand the full scope of depressions in old age, the physician should be aware of the nature of these changes as well, for even as depression in patients with organic brain syndrome is responsive to treatment, depression may mimic brain syndrome, and organic brain syndrome may be mistaken for depression. The use of simple, rapid screening procedures such as the Mental Status Questionnaire and the Double Simultaneous Stimulation of the face and hand is advocated as an aid to differential diagnosis for correct treatment. These special tests are more dependable than are other tests of cognitive functioning because the decrease in attention, concentration, and motivation which is part of depressive disorders renders many tests of cognitive function invalid.

The Measure of Organic Brain Syndrome

By means of the Mental Status Questionnaire (Table 1) the severity of brain syndrome can be graded as mild, moderate, or severe (Table 2). The test consists of 10 questions which, in a condensed manner, elicit the components of the organic brain syndrome.

Usually the deficits in orientation, memory, information, and calculation, when more completely evaluated than is possible by the short screening test alone, are found to be rather uniformly affected by a chronic brain syndrome. When the syndrome is acute the defects may be less uniformly affected—they are "patchy" and may fluctuate in severity. Moreover, in acute brain syndrome the defects of cognition are complicated by confabulation. This is also true when the chronic brain syndrome is developing or growing worse, and can occur either episodically or stepwise.

A special type of confabulation occurs in persons who have good, well-automatized, and socially adaptive patterns and who, in their politeness,

Table 1 Mental Status Questionnaire—"Special 10"

Question	Presumed Test Area
1. Where are we now?	Place
2. Where is this place (located)?	Place
3. What is today's date-day of month?	Time
4. What month is it?	Time
5. What year is it?	Time
6. How old are you?	Memory—recent or remote
7. What is your birthday?	Memory—recent or remote
8. What year were you born?	Memory—remote
9. Who is president of the U.S.?	General information—memory
10. Who was president before him?	General information—memory

Reproduced by permission from Goldfarb, AI: The evaluation of geriatric patients following treatment, in *Evaluation of Psychiatric Treatment.* Edited by Hoch, PH, Zubin, J, New York, Grune & Stratton, 1964, pp. 271–308.

Table 2 Rating of Mental Functional Impairment by Mental Status Questionnaire

No. of M.S.Q. Errors	Presumed Degree of O.B.S.
0–2	Absent or mild
3–5	Moderate
6–8	Moderate to severe
9+	Severe
Nontestable[a]	Severe

Reproduced by permission from Goldfarb, AI: as modified from The evaluation of geriatric patients following treatment, in *Evaluation of Psychiatric Treatment.* Edited by Hoch PH, Zubin J, New York, Grune & Stratton, 1964, pp. 271–308.
[a]In the not uncooperative person without deafness or insuperable language barrier.

prefer to appear untroubled, so as not to be troubling or embarassing to persons around them. Acute brain syndrome may be complicated by hallucinatory phenomena or dream-like episodes such as are commonly seen with drug intoxication or drug withdrawal.

The face-hand test (double simultaneous stimulation) is also helpful in screening for brain syndrome and is of value in estimating the degree of the condition (see Table 3).

Table 3 Order of Stimulation Used in Face-Hand Test

1. Right cheek–left hand	6. Right hand–left hand
2. Left cheek–right hand	7. Right cheek—left hand
3. Right cheek–right hand	8. Left cheek–right hand
4. Left cheek–left hand	9. Right cheek–right hand
5. Right cheek–left cheek	10. Left cheek–left hand

Reproduced by permission from Goldfarb, AI: The evaluation of geriatric patients following treatment, in *Evaluation of Psychiatric Treatment.* Edited by Hoch PH, Zubin J, New York, Grune & Stratton, 1964 pp. 271–308.

If the seated patient places his palms on his knees and the examiner touches the back of the patient's hands and cheeks, the patient's constant failure to report the touch correctly is reliable evidence of cerebral damage of the senile or Alzheimer type, caused by organic brain syndrome in the chronologically old. The errors made include: extinction—failure to report touch at all; displacement of the touch to a part of the examiner's body; and exsomesthesia—reporting the touch as somewhere "out there" or "over there." The number of errors is first recorded for the test done with eyes closed and repeated with eyes open. Anxious, distressed, socially "unpoised" persons may make many more errors with eyes open than with eyes closed.

It is important to screen for organic brain syndrome lest signs of this impairment be mistaken for depression, and also because if these screening tests are not strongly "positive," other cognitive defects present can probably be attributed to the depressive disorder. Patients who have good scores on Mental Status Questionnaire and on Face-Hand Test probably do not have brain syndrome.

An Adaptational View of Depressive Disorders

From an adaptational view, depressive disorders can be regarded as communications or signals to obtain assurances of aid. They are complex behavioral maneuvers in a personal-environmental adjustment transaction. These are aimed at real or fancied persons, who are regarded as strong and potentially helpful by individuals who feel weak and helpless because of real or fantasied losses of assets for life adjustment. By "real persons" is meant individuals in the patient's social system; by "fancied persons" is meant those special aspects of self to which he may respond as though to other persons and also those persons he may "delusionally" believe can be conjured up by special action. The signal, communication, or appeal is patterned in ways determined by the individual's values, his perception of society's values, and his expectations.

These patterns, like the "hysterical neuroses," include symbolic, intra- and extrapunitive, self-justifying and appealing, or aid-justifying factors. The patterns have as a core what has been variously called dependency striving, transference, rapport, and regression, and similar terms including "search for love," "search for a significant other," or search for an understanding person. These concepts are here subsumed under the general term, "search for aid," by which is meant the search for the sense of promise of assistance—emotional support, reassurance—rather than an expectation of material or actual aid. This search for an emotionally supportive relationship has its psychological roots—was learned—in the period of infantile and childhood biological dependency when the child was in actual need of the parents' maintenance and protection. It becomes established in variable degree as a persistent characteristic dependent upon the enculturation process. This adaptational view of depressive disorder is shown in Figure 1. Depressive disorders which become medically identified appear to be attempts to circumvent defects or failures in the individual's culturally acceptable dependency-striving adapting mechanisms. They are attempts to repair organismal dysfunction or psychological ineptitude. As repair, such a disorder is, to use Rado's terms, miscarried. While motivationally correct, from the viewpoint of the individual's enculturation, it nevertheless becomes grossly inefficient, personally costly, and socially troublesome.

The adaptive patterns that emerge in these miscarried attempts at repair vary in type and in the complexity of their psychological elaboration. From the motivational viewpoint, they appear to be explicable as a subjectively painful searching for a protective figure. In this search there may be painful yearning as part of pain-dependent pleasure seeking. This consists of the belief that the desired parental response is contingent on the presence of sufficient distress: if it is not forthcoming then the suffering of additional pain may be required as

Figure 1

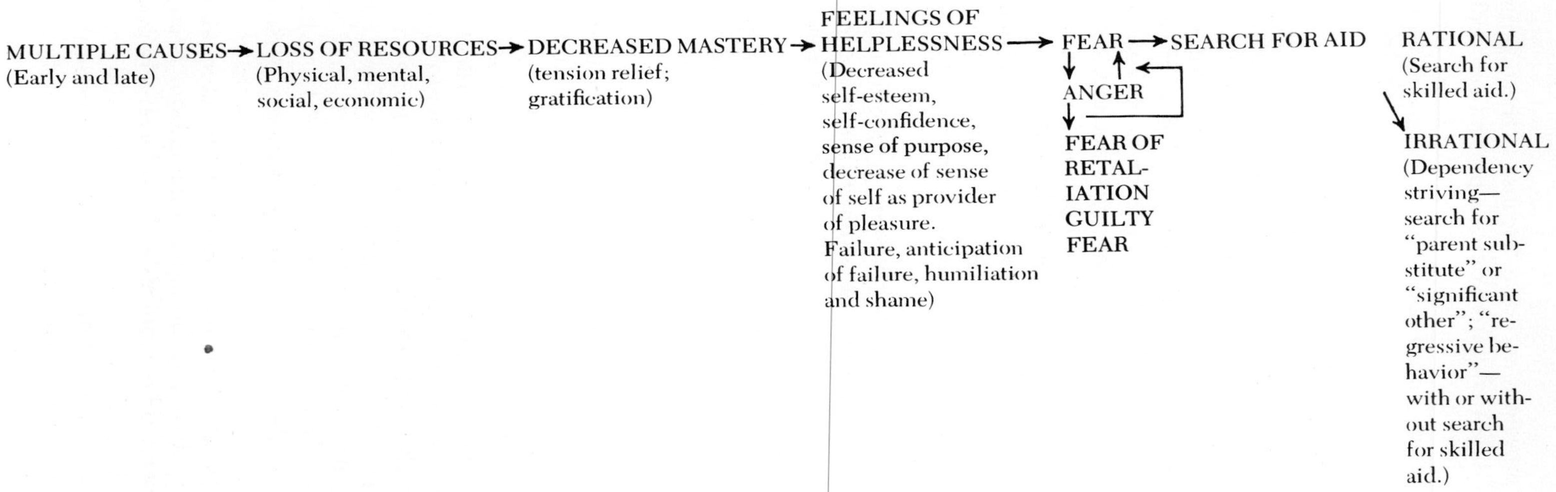

(1) Multiple causes or initiating factors which occur either early in life and are reinforced or modified with aging or occur late in life and are peculiar to old age, several of which may combine forces and some of which may be necessary but insufficient alone, result in

(2) an absence or loss of resources for minimal, adequate functioning, so that

(3) there is decreased mastery of problems, challenges, and adjustments posed by internal changes (biologically determined drives or acquired needs) and external changes and threats, with resulting

(4) feelings of helplessness or actual powerlessness, and consequent

(5) fear with accompanying or subsequent anger, with consequent

(6) "rationally" or "irrationally" aimed and elaborated search for aid which becomes patterned in terms acceptable to the individual in accord with his personality organization based upon his past, his present, and his expectations; and contingent on his perception of what is acceptable to and likely to work in "his world" as well as by the social response it receives. In this search there are observable constellations of motivated personal action which range from apathy through pseudoanhedonia, display of helplessness, somatization, hypochondriasis, depression, and paranoid states to the most open and manipulative behavior. In predisposed persons there may be a physiologic shift to a new and relatively inefficient homeostatic level with depressive states which are then revealed by altered appetite, bowel function, sleep, and other vegetative signs.

prepayment and a signal for the desired reward. Distress, in turn, leads to increased need for the supportive parental figure. This then becomes part of a vicious circle of increasingly intense and more complexly elaborated depressive disorder.

Also of interest is the fact that in the case of genetically determined depressive disorder, biochemical changes may appear first and lead to decreased flexibility of functioning. This then leads to, or is experienced as, a change of mood and is reacted to with feelings of helplessness, fear, and anger—which are then elaborated as motivated attempts to gain aid from others.

In the case of psychodynamically-determined depression, psychological inhibitions acquired in childhood have decreased the individual's ability to assert himself, with a resultant need for assistance from parental surrogates throughout his lifetime. When new physical, personal, or intrapersonal problems arise, the previously culturally acceptable search for assistance from persons viewed as potentially helpful emerges in a new, less efficient and more troublesome way—this "way" will later be described in terms of characteristic patterns.

The adaptational view of depression can be summarized in the heuristic schema (Figure 1) which subdivides its components into causes: the early and late loss of persons or resources; the functional decline; and the subsequent subjective, emotional, and behavioral effects. All or several of these components of the depressed state are usually simultaneously noted when a patient appears for treatment. The components of this schema are briefly defined as a basis for discussion of the goals, techniques, and efficacy of treatment.

Depressive Disorder as a Specific Adaptive Maneuver

Depressive disorders which become medically identified appear to be attempts to circumvent defects or failures in the individual's culturally acceptable dependency striving adapting mechanisms. They are attempts to repair organismal dysfunction or psychological ineptitude. As repair, such a disorder is, to use Rado's terms, miscarried. While motivationally correct, from the viewpoint of the individual enculturation, it nevertheless becomes grossly inefficient, personally costly, and socially troublesome.

The Central Position of Helplessness

The helpless state is that which is usually presented by the patient in terms such as, "I feel nervous . . . I can't cope . . . things are too much for me," or "I need help . . . they won't help me." The state is central to the subjective distress and the observable adaptive maneuvers. It may be defined as the one in which persons feel they have or will soon have no supportive or reparative resources and no way of obtaining them, and are therefore also without purpose and ability to gain pleasure. Nonhelplessness exists in the presence of self-confidence, self-esteem or a sense of worth, a conviction of goal or purpose, and the belief that one can be a self-provider of pleasure. It is a biosocial aspect of personality derived from the nurture of one's nature: enculturation molds the diffuse potential of the developing organism adaptively. Nonhelplessness rests in the personal belief in one's worth and ability as sufficient for the realization of one's constructive potential. Our culture encourages the development of personalities which measure their own worth and ability in terms of their actual or potential success in using other persons; this is variously described in terms of the ability to gain—and give—love, and the capacity to fulfill for, and inspire in others—duties and obligations. In essence, such enculturation constitutes the encouragement of the establishment of domination-submission types of personal behavior. In these there is relatively small capacity for true affectionate bonds derived from pleasurable interaction.

Helpless feelings arise under conditions that lead to a real or fancied loss of persons or special items which are regarded as essential elements in the achievement of successful adaptive maneuvers—"mastery" in usual life situations. Adaptive maneuvers or mastery of challenges posed by the individual's external or internal world are those that yield gratification and relief from tensions in everyday life. The sense of helplessness is diminished with tension relief and gratification or when there is expectation that such successes will be achieved. In addition to biologically elicited tensions, many expectations (needs for relief) are acquired; among these are the conviction that one must have a readily available "loving" or obligated individual. In the absence of such a person the individual may feel tense and ungratified.

Diminution of Resources

The loss or absence of resources in chronological old age that leads to failures in mastery or anticipation of such failures may be physical, mental, economic, or social. In our culture, as noted above, the loss or threat of loss of persons regarded as of special significance appears to be the most important in the evolution of serious depressive behavior. This is because the socialization of the individual is such that nonhelplessness rests on the conviction that personal adequacy consists of the ability to properly identify, obtain, and hold one or more protective persons simultaneously or separately in a supportive relationship.

Early Causes of Decreased Resources

Absence of resources of dynamic (nurturant) origin may emerge as a significant obstruction to adaptation. In the child-parent or equivalent relationship that socializes the person, the psychological inhibitory processes that are intended to mold an adaptive person may be overdone. The frightened person is then dependent on the presence of a parental surrogate for aid, or approval and support, if self-assertive, self-realizing, or fulfilling behavior is to be achieved. The decreased ability to be self-assertive constitutes an experientially determined absence of resources. Anger may help such persons "break through" the fear—that is, to act despite the fear. The absence of the ability to act in constructive problem-solving ways or decreased self-assertion due to psychological inhibition, like a genetically determined mood change, may be understood as a pathophysiologic state which decreases adaptive capacity; this contributes to feelings of helplessness and the elaboration of the depressive patterns as attempts at repair. A breakthrough of self-assertion with anger (aggression) usually increases the need for parental support because it leads to guilt and fear of retaliation, which increase the psychological inhibition. The mood changes of early experiential-developmental origin that were learned (believed) to be manipulative of the parent may precede the full elaboration and expression of depression. The inefficiency of these maneuvers constitutes a loss in behavioral flexibility which leads to full fledged, psychiatrically identifiable depressive disorder.

From this point of view there seem to be three general types of depressive etiologic factors of early life origin (See Table 4): (1) genetically determined mood swings which are elaborated subjectively and in social action contingent on the importance of the "defect" to the individual; (2) recurrent experientially determined subjective distress together with behavioral display which the person in infancy or childhood came to believe is, and therefore continues to use as, a signal or call for aid, from the actual or fantasied parentified persons; and (3) subjective distress as a reaction to loss—threatened, actual, or feared. This last, in Western culture, appears to be a normally enculturated way of life in which open or masked dependency on others is practiced as natural and healthy. It is almost universally present, takes various expressional forms, and as a basic personality characteristic appears to explain the high incidence and prevalence of depressive disorders. That is to say, because almost all persons are dependently acculturated, they behave throughout life as though they are chronically depressed in that they seek, find, hold, may lose, then resume the search for, delegate, and try to hold other persons who will function, as they experience it, as parental surrogates. Depression of any origin is symptomatically experienced in a number of ways which are influenced by the person's enculturation, his values, the current situation, and his expectations.

The reactions or patterns that appear to be "fragments" of depressive disorders can be listed on the basis of the apparent degree and ratio of fear to anger in each. In the first five, fear predominates; in the sixth—relatively pure depression—fear and anger seem to be equally admixed; in the remaining, anger exceeds fear in its importance. These patterns, then, as they may be discerned by the physician, can serve as guides to treatment. This list of reactions is also one that may serve to aid in the differential diagnosis. Organic brain syndrome, from mild to moderate degree, may be present with any of these patterns—but it is less likely that patterns 6 through 10 will be found with moderately severe organic brain syndrome. The patterns most frequently seen are as follows.

1. Apathy. A seeming indifference, lack of interest, lack of motivation for any action, inertia.
2. Pseudoanhedonia. An expressed inability to experience pain or pleasure, which appears designed to call attention to misery while denying that it can be felt. Experience in the treatment of aged persons has illuminated the propensity of the human organism to derive pleasure through problem-solv-

Table 4

	Origin	Clinical Emergence	Physical Changes[a]	Subjective Depression	Usual Classification	Response to Rx: Drug, etc.	Response to Rx: Psychotherapy	Course
1. Genetically determined mood changes	Heredity	Early or late life	Present	Variable	"Major disorders," "psychoses"	Excellent	Poor	Self-limited circular, relatively brief episodes
2. Experientially determined mood changes	Mother-child and familial interaction	Early years	Minimal or absent[b]	Present	"Major disorder," depressive reaction	Variable	Fair to good	Continuous or episodic relatively long
3. Reactive changes of mood[c]	Culturally determined social values	Early or late in life	Absent[b]	Present	Minor disorder, "Reactive Depression"	Poor	Good	Fluctuating in severity, continuous over years, recurrent

[a]Gastrointestinal, sleep, and psychomotor signs.
[b]Unless also genetic factors.
[c]These, of course, may be associated with 1 and 2.

ing. In aged, emotionally ill persons the persistence from early life, or the assumption or development in later years of an attitude of joylessness, or of physical suffering, is an active attempt to master the environment. As such, it is accompanied by a pleasurable feeling tone which increases sharply when the mastering is subjectively experienced as successful. The elderly person's joylessness, his attitude of welcoming death but not having "the courage to commit suicide" is not entirely or truly a turning of anger against himself; it is rather a state of pseudoanhedonia rooted in an illusion that helplessness is an effective means to power and an effective method of wielding it.

3. Display of helplessness. Expressed as nervousness and an "inability to cope."

4. Somatization. Emphasis on somatic impairment, aches, or pains; these may be the physiologic accompaniments of "emergency" emotion—as tachycardia, respiratory distress, or the effects of hyperventilation, aspects of specific illness or impairment, or without real foundation.

5. Hypochondriasis. Minor disorders or functionally determined symptoms are reacted to with fright and the conviction that disintegration and doom are imminent.

6. Depressive reaction. This is the combined subjective sense of distress, objectively discernible lowering of interest, spontaneity, and constructive activity which was described above. With depression there may be either a slowing of thought and action or a racing of thought and agitation. The latter may at times be, or resemble a hypomanic state with subjective depression. In all of these states, there is decreased motivation, attention, and concentration to the point of impairing cognition in variable degree.

7. Hypomanic and manic states. Here the individual feels and behaves in euphoric or elated, overactive, grandiose, and expansive ways.

8. Paranoid reactions. These may range from excessive irritability, anger, and fault-finding to delusions with ideas of reference and auditory, olfactory, and, rarely, visual hallucinations.

9. Exploitive-manipulative activities. In which clinging, ingratiating, and demanding behavior may alternate with punitive, coercive, commanding, and domineering behavior.

10. Coercive behavior. Here threatening, manipulative, dominating words and actions are prominent. Suicidal statements, attempts, or completed attempts are examples of coercive behavior as are threats, assaults, demands, and legal action.

11. Antisocial behavior. The socially "criminal," forceful and open, or hidden seizure of what is regarded as one's right but which has been withheld.

Suicidal thoughts and acts are here worthy of elaboration for their illustrative value. Suicide occurs most commonly in the ill, unemployed, kin-wrecked, often alcoholic, chronologically oldest persons; that is to say, in those who have suffered the greatest physical, economic, social, and emotional losses in resources for nondependent or dependent characteristic ways of adaptation, or for the gaining of potential assistance. The motivational background is overdetermined; many psychodynamic factors contribute to the act or attempt. The motives may be simultaneously present in variable degree contingent on circumstances, expectation, and the personal targets. Desire for freedom from physical or mental pain (tension relief) may play a part. Reproach leveled at those around is common.

A design to hurt the feelings and severely prick the conscience of the persons desired as protectors so as to gain them, even though dead, may lie behind the resentful, vengeful action. The desire to rejoin—to be reunited with—a lost protector or to gain—via expiation—restitution of an alliance is often clearly present. Thus the suicidal act may be a display of pain and helplessness, in which not only is the self attacked because of shame and guilt so as to signal for aid, but also the coercive, exploitive, subjectively depressed person who feels neglected—possibly persecuted—frightened, and angry is attacking the individuals from whom he desires assistance so as to signal his distress and gain their support. Suicide may also be compliance; it may be an expiatory type of sacrifice which appears to state, "you want to be rid of me, I am a burden or harmful, and will rid you of me." In such compliance the other aims also determine the behavior.

The patterns are not mutually exclusive nor usually well defined. In different cultures and at different times, one or another of these patterns may take precedence for display in depressive reactions. Which pattern is emphasized appears to be a product of the individual's enculturation: each person interprets—more or less correctly—what is most likely to succeed in gaining the desired response from parental surrogates or significant others in his social environment.

Also, each pattern is clearly "overdetermined." Like the symptoms of the "hysterical neurosis," the adaptational pattern serves to symbolize the subjectively experienced problem, while justifying failures, earning aid by way of its painful and disabling nature, punishing the self for being a failure and for behaving badly in response to the failure, and punishing others for their neglect or lack of sympathy while all the while pressing others into the delegated protective, nurturant, gratifying, implementary, effective parental role.

In psychotic reactions the appeal appears to be largely to "incorporated" or fantasied figures. The appeal is to parts of the individual's personality, or, more likely, is action to bring about the reappearance of a desired person by feeling, thinking, or behaving in the proper way by performing the correct rites. This is often called magical thinking. Personal suffering is frequently believed to be the signal that will call forth the desired help; this leads to behavior classified as "pain-dependent-pleasure mechanisms"; that is, pleasure is wooed by suffering; the individual behaves as though reward will follow if suffering is of the right type or sufficiently intense. Such suffering may precede, accompany, or follow actual pleasurable events as "payment," or as a self-punitive and apologetic expiatory behavior for having experienced the forbidden or "bad" (pleasure), and as self-punishment for having been self-assertive, because this is a seeming denial of the usefulness of, and the need for, the parental figure.

Depressions of the biochemical type at times appear to be "triggered" by feelings of humiliation, shame, or guilt because of loss of self-esteem or self-confidence experienced as failure and helplessness, and by the emergency emotion which may follow actual, anticipated, or belief of failure. These depressed states, as with those which "come out of the blue" as genetically determined recurrences, can also be shortened, and discomforts reduced by proper pharmacotherapy or psychotherapy.

In any individual the assistance-seeking behavior patterns that characterize his depression may change with time or as the situation changes—as the individual is more or less successful in decreasing fear, anger, and feelings of helplessness, or as biochemical changes occur. Many depressive reactions which begin with a display of helplessness or with pseudoanhedonic complaints go on to include somatization, and then become clearly hypochondriacal. All of these may occur before subjective depression is clearly displayed or experienced. Those who have a propensity for recurrent mood disorder, especially of the cyclic type, may experience sleep disturbance, anorexia, constipation, and decreased capacity to concentrate, to pay attention, or to display initiative well before subjective depression is noted and before any behavioral patterns which appear to be motivationally a "search for aid" are elaborated.

There are, then, many identifiable components of depressive disorders among older patients. There are the intrapunitive elements of self-deprecation, retrospective falsification of a self-derogatory nature, and retroflexed rage with guilt, shame, and feelings of humiliation. There is also suffering in payment for the expected returns, and there is suffering which the patient has inner conviction is a signal for aid. There are extrapunitive elements in that the patient's needs are troublesome: often there is open hostility in that there are paranoid accusations; also the attitudes of dejection, despair, desolation, and distress serve to castigate the family and other intimates. The patterns are apologetic and justifying; they account for the ineptitude of the individual and create a vicious circle which accounts for the subjective depression and then "accounts for" the disability. The patterns symbolize, without clear verbalization, what the patient feels has happened as well as what he wants: that he feels unloved and needs love, reassurance, support, and care. And, because they are patterned within the cultural values to gain the type of care and response he feels he deserves—or so the patient thinks by his enculturated conviction about the values of his society—the individual can maintain hope despite protestations of despair.

These patterns or constellations of behavior which serve as searches for aid may be seen in all depressive disorders, sequentially, or in a shifting, kaleidoscopic way. They are found in depression of the type which seems to be genetically determined as behavioral elaborations of mood and as a search for aid because of the helplessness engendered by the affect disorder. In the recurrent and in the entirely psychodynamically determined depressive reactions, they constitute, as signals and communications, the primary defect in functioning.

That these patterns rule out and deny pleasures of various kinds is ignored by the patient because of that pleasure which accrues to the illusory success achieved, or to the anticipation of success. The purposeful search for a parental figure by the helpless patient can be viewed as a partially pleasurable problem-solving maneuver, the enjoyment of which can be augmented when it is clearly delineated in the form of a patient-doctor relationship wherein the patient feels successful. The patient's pleasure, derived from making an end out of this means, is essentially an illusory fulfillment; this satisfaction yields increased self-esteem which may result in improved functioning and in the actual achievement of real goals. Further successes in interpersonal relationships may follow. With real success there may be a relinquishing of the pattern for a more realistic and more gratifying pattern of behavior.

General Concepts for Treatment

The patterns of depressive behavior are such as to tax the patience of family, community, and therapists. Depressed persons are indecisive, puzzled, and bewildered in their thinking and, despite protests to the contrary, appear to obstruct—because of their irrational efforts—all constructive efforts to provide care. In their frightened, angry state they plead for care yet fear to accept it, demonstrate open or covert hostility to the caretakers, and must be handled with an understanding of this "ambivalence." The therapist must follow the associational flow of the patient's conversation, and recognize and respond to its symbolic import while responding sensibly to its seeming real content. This may at times mean that the therapist must permit himself to be regarded as being disapproving or punitive—this should never be real and harmful but only token in fact. At all times the therapist should permit himself to be regarded as authoritative, but he should never be authoritarian or dominating. This does not mean that he cannot be helpfully informative or even democratically directive and rationally persuasive. At all times he must be aware of his special status as a delegated parental-surrogate who is viewed as possibly harmful in action but potentially—if properly approached—as powerfully helpful.

Because many of the aged are physically or mentally impaired or have limited socioeconomic opportunities, the therapist must be prepared to limit his treatment goals and yet be wary of personal predilection or social persuasion to give up too easily. Treatment of mental disorders in the aged requires that attention be paid to more than the patient. Not only the complaints of the patient but those of his family, the community, and the persons charged with his care must be attended to. The need for treatment is often recognized when the disorder creates a family or community disturbance.

The physician must be certain that any acute or chronic medical condition of the patient is diagnosed, that action is taken where indicated for the amelioration of physical pain, and that acute brain syndrome is reversed through specific and generally supportive medical care. Furthermore, the presence and degree of chronic brain syndrome must be ascertained in planning the type and goals of treatment.

Treatment Goals

In general, the goals of treatment are to decrease the patient's suffering so that he has a minimum of complaints; to improve his behavior and decrease interpersonal friction so that he is minimally complained about; to increase his capacity for making and sustaining friendships with persons of both sexes and for socially acceptable sexual behavior; to restore him to work or an equivalent avocational activity within the limits of his remaining resources and commensurate with his intelligence, training, skill, and customary social role; to motivate or remotivate him; and to evoke a desire to act so that he is maximally productive and creative. When a patient is motivated or remotivated and takes part in what he feels is meaningful and effective problem-solving, there is accompanying pleasure through successful action. He regains a sense of purpose and identity.

To reach these goals the physician can aim specifically to decrease the patient's actual or felt helplessness or his fear and anger. In some persons, the fear or anger that arises at the beginning of treatment may cause action that decreases the sense of helplessness. Subsequent feelings of guilt, fear of retaliation, and resentment may be useful in directing behavior along socially and personally acceptable lines. Although the warning and inhibitory actions of emergency emotion can often be utilized, emotional overreaction usually grossly disorganizes behavior; its unfavorable effects on self-confidence and self-esteem are particularly undesirable. Self-esteem and self-confidence must be fostered and restored; the patient's motivation to do and to succeed must be heightened; he must be encouraged to develop purpose and interest. When he acts and has a goal, his sense of who he is and what he is and where he is going—his sense of identity—is reinforced or restored.

These goals and aims can be achieved by a variety of techniques. Psychotherapy, occupational or avocational activity, group or individual therapy, and drugs or physical methods all have as their effective common denominator motivation and organization of behavior within the framework of a personal relationship.

Whatever the vehicle for psychotherapy, the psychiatrist starts by regarding the elderly depressed patient as having become bogged down in his own ineffective attempt to recoup losses and to compensate for weakness. He has become increasingly helpless, frightened, and angry because of continued failure. He is caught up in a search for aid or support. The psychiatrist responds to this search by permitting the patient to regard him as the sought-for surrogate parent. He refrains from discouraging the patient's tendency to delegate him as such and allows the patient to take pride in his ability to interest the physician. With patients who have socioeconomic and personal mobility, the physician can help the patient gain insight, learn new techniques, and make helpful major changes in patterns of action and life situations. In the care of the aged, however, especially the mentally or physically impaired, the gains must often be limited to what the patient derives from the reassuring and supportive relationship.

Treatment Methods

In the treatment of depressions, except for that aspect which is characterologic, or a way of life, time is on the side of the therapist. Depressive disorders tend to be episodic, self-limited, self-healing. They tend to "lift" if obstructions to the self-repair are removed. This includes assisting the patient toward regimes which favor physical well-being. He must be helped to make no practical moves which will damage him in the present or future or which he may look back upon with shame, guilt, remorse, or regret. A therapist must often "stall for time" while he helps the patient wait out the emotional storms. Medication is of help as is electro-stimulant treatment in decreasing the intensity of the suffering and in shortening the course of the disorder.

The depressive reactions that are largely or entirely psychological in origin, and are accompanied by no significant degree of biochemical change, are the ones most likely to be improved by psychotherapy—and are least helpfully influenced by medication. In depressions with biochemical changes, psychotherapy helps patients take and benefit from the drugs. Drugs help the patient accept and benefit from the controlled life experience called psychotherapy.

As suggested by Figure 1, treatment can be directed toward increasing resources or the improved use of remaining assets, decreasing the challenges to adjustment and adaptation, decreasing fear, anger, and their consequences—immobility, disorganization, and pathophysiologic disturbances—or reducing the subjective experience of helplessness. Usually treatment is aimed at several components simultaneously. For example, physiatric techniques to improve ambulation would be a vehicle for the delivery of psychotherapy by way of the relationship established. Usually, treatment is aimed at behavioral change without regard to etiology. The most expedient method and the most easily modifiable component of the disorder is chosen for melioration so as to interrupt the disorder's progress by way of vicious circles. In this way its course is shortened and its intensity decreased. Approach to etiological factors where a cyclic mood disorder is genetically determined or where there has been a shift in biochemical homeostasis is chiefly by way of medicines; where the etiology is chiefly psychologically determined and based upon socialization and its results, psychotherapy is the primary approach and medication is useful secondarily. This is shown, together with some of the special characteristics of the general types, in Table 5.

According to this view treatment plans for elderly depressed patients can be subdivided into two general types. One is for the state some call psychotic in which vegetative symptoms, chiefly gastrointestinal, sleep, and psychomotor, are present, and the second is for the "nonpsychotic" disorder in which such phenomena are minimally and inconsistently present or entirely absent. In the first, medication or electro-stimulant treatment is indicated as the primary

Table 5

Vegetative Symptoms	Modes of Treatment	
	Drugs or ECT	Psychotherapy
Present	Primary	Secondary
Absent	Secondary	Primary

technique to shorten the episode and to decrease the patient's suffering; here the patient-doctor relationship is fostered to enlist the patient's cooperation, help him to follow the prescribed regime, and to add psychological and emotional benefits that are derived from this psychotherapeutic situation. In the other type the personal relationship is the primary means by which an increase in self-esteem, self-confidence, a sense of purpose, and the belief in self as a provider of pleasure is achieved; here, medication may be a useful adjunct in facilitating the development of the relationship. In the first type the patient may accept medication and physical treatment as a favor to the doctor; in the second type the doctor may fulfill his expected role as strong, protective, helpful figure by first accepting delegation as a healer who can, and does, "magically" reduce anxiety, decrease agitation, decrease fatigue, and help induce sleep—whatever the needs may be—by way of his formulae.

Psychotherapy

When indicated, psychotherapy is adjunctive to pharmacologic treatment, electroshock, special regimens, and even hospitalization to aid the elderly patient toward optimal social use of his personal resources.

It would seem as though reducing the psychologically inhibiting state which decreases self-assertion would be helpful in decreasing the need for "parental care" and thus lead to less intensity in the search for aid. This is, however, a long task at best and often a hopeless one. What is required, then, is to answer the individual's need to decrease emergency emotion and to decrease his sense of helplessness. This is best achieved by proper response to the patient's appeal for aid by way of believing he has found the parent surrogate he wittingly or unwittingly searches for.

Psychotherapeutic effects are achieved by increasing self-esteem, self-confidence, sense of purpose, and the conviction that one can be a self-provider of pleasure. These, in turn, are achieved by way of favoring the establishment of a transference relationship, that is, by accepting the patient's delegation of oneself as parental surrogate. Once done, the therapist as parental surrogate accepts the patient's belief that he will be of help to the patient as he hoped the disillusioning actual parents or their later substitutes would be; once so ensconced the therapist can use his status to suggest to the patient constructive action which yields success in personal relations and which then establishes a beneficial circle of continuing successes. Finally, the approving supportive therapist is introjected and is maintained as a psychologically internalized and therapeutic force even though the therapist is revisited infrequently for reinforcement of the incorporated ideas.

Technique of Psychotherapy

Elderly depressed patients of all types require reassurance and support. Patients receive this reassurance and support by way of the personal relationship with the physician; this relationship serves to help the patient feel secure (decreases the sense of helplessness) through his belief that he has found the "significant other person" that he needs. All psychiatrically ill persons need reassurance and emotional support either to accept the implied suggestions for new ways of behaving or to be helped to follow the required drug or other helpful regimens. A discussion of technique must include how the therapist reassures and how one supports. Reassurance and support are given if the patient believes he is being understood. This is felt as being loved by and in the control of the therapist. The patient experiences a sense of dominance or, paradoxically, being controlled and submissive; the latter feeling may be helpful because if he feels misunderstood and resentful then by way of pain-dependent-pleasure he expects to achieve the basic goal of victory over or alliance with the strong figure he sees in the therapist; expectation of eventual victory over him leads the patient to function efficiently.

Within a so-called psychotherapeutic session the patient must be permitted to feel he is establishing the relationship he needs and desires. He must leave the session feeling somewhat better than when he came in; this may be because he feels that he has gained information, or impressed the therapist, or the therapist has smiled upon him. Within this framework it is also helpful if the patient has been able to pick up a practical, very indirectly placed suggestion which actually helps him toward more constructive and gratifying behavior. What the therapist does not do is sit, nod, and press the patient to feel that he must help himself. The therapist may say at times that he does not know how to specifically help, but the patient must be permitted to feel that the physician is engaged or involved. Some patients will not feel he is constructively involved unless the therapist is quiet: others need conversational aid. Usually it is essential for the depressed person to actually see the therapist. Many depressed patients need protective and material evidence of the therapist's concern, even to the point of being asked if they would like a cup of tea or some social equivalent.

If emotional dependency is recognized to be the depressed patient's way of life, and the therapist accepts the role of parental surrogate thrust on him, he can help to bring about effective change in the patient's feelings, attitudes, and behavior. Patients can be helped toward self-sufficiency and toward treatment or regimes of therapeutic value if they are permitted to be emotionally dependent and to feel secure in a relationship with a respected other.

Psychiatrists frequently fear that the patient will use a therapeutic dependency relationship as a "crutch" for continued pathologic behavior. Such fears fail to take into account the fact that the patients usually become self-sufficient within the security of a dependent relationship; once they feel emotionally secure and supported, they can be taught to "walk on their own two feet."

By recognizing the value and usefulness of helplessness, the field of the therapist expands. He can welcome and even encourage it in his patients because it is the chief determinant in the search for aid and support, in the desire to hold on to the therapist as a potentially helpful person. This is what enables the therapist to encourage some types of behavior, discourage others; this is what places him in the "driver's seat"; this is what heightens the suggestibility of the patient, facilitates the diminution of fear, anger, and other unpleasant or troublesome emotions. Anxiety need not be decreased slowly and its total elimination postponed; satisfaction of the patient's needs does not have to be judiciously discouraged lest he "stop working" or leave with a "transference cure." The psychiatrist's response to the search for aid leads to a relationship that can (1) be maintained for the patient's good; (2) be incorporated by the patient to his advantage; and (3) encourage the evolution of insight that will enable the patient to exploit his own resources. Last but not least, in many patients the relationship established is used beneficially to influence the patient toward constructive efforts and pleasurable activity. He is assisted to revise his behavior with respect to himself and his environment so as to be successful within the scope permitted by actual limitations in interpersonal (including sexual) relationships and at work and play.

Pharmacotherapy and Physical Therapy in the Elderly

The patterns of depressive reaction discernible to the therapist are often clues to what will work in treatment. As noted earlier, in patterns 1 through 5 fear appears to be present in a greater amount than anger; in pattern 6—depressive reaction—fear and anger (especially as reflected by paranoid trends) appear to be almost equally admixed with only a slight predominance of fear; in the hypomanic and manic states anger begins to predominate and is seen in increasing amounts, exceeding the proportion of fear, as one moves through patterns 9, 10, and 11. In the following discussion of treatment, therefore, this should be kept in mind: both psycho- and pharmacotherapy can be understood as having the common aim of decreasing the amount of disorganizing, immobilizing, or inefficiently and unconstructively mobilized emergency emotion, and where there is a choice of method or of drugs to deal primarily with fear or anger the choice can be suggested by the patterns elaborated. In all depressive disorders, anticholinergic drugs which help make noradrenaline more available at central nervous system synapses by increasing its production, decreasing its destruction, or blocking its reuptake into the manufacturing neurone may be helpful; but these drugs may be most helpful in the patterns 1 through 6 where fear is greater than anger and the mobilization of anger may be helpful to correct behavior. Conversely, cholinergic or similarly tranquilizing drugs which promote parasympathetomimetic action may be more helpful in patterns 6 through 11. When fear and anger are clearly coexisting, both types of medication may be combined. In the following discussion of the uses of drugs and ECT which is organized along classical nosologic lines, this concept is to be kept in mind.

For convenience of discussion, these treatments are discussed under the usual psychiatric headings which distinguish common constellations of generally experientially determined disorders as displayed in our culture. Not included is discussion of depressive episodes in so-called schizophrenia; it is likely that the so-called decompensation in schizophrenic persons is actually the occurrence of depression, and that if the depressive aspect is successfully handled, the "schizophrenic" individual may be less intrapersonally troubled and interpersonally troublesome.

Various depressive syndromes are difficult to classify. They are found either alone—or because depressive reactions can occur in schizoid, retarded, or otherwise mentally impaired or ill persons—in association with other mental disorders or as concomitants of physical illness. According to this scheme, the disorders or syndromes of the maladjusted aged are viewed as motivated goal-seeking appeals for aid within a social transaction, and depending on circumstances and environmental response, variations of a search for aid can be displayed by different persons or by the same persons at different times. The variations are patterned according to the values and beliefs of the individual, his view of his culture, and the social response to his behavior.

A patient may be openly frightened or brave, ingratiating, seductive, belligerent, coercive, withdrawn, or pseudoanhedonic—all with appropriate subjective dynamics as circumstances appear to require. Even late developing depressive reactions, manic-depressive, paranoid, and schizophrenic syndromes can be viewed as struggles between special types of persons and their social environments. In all, the patient appears to be attempting to manipulate others in a context of misunderstanding. Even when he appears to be withdrawn and apathetic or violently hostile, the patient may be attempting to gain assistance or emotional support from those about him or from a desired special other person of his fantasy.

Manic-Depressive Psychoses

These conditions appear to be genetic in basic origin though their manifestations may differ. In general, the manic, hectic behavior is accompanied by paranoid trends; domineering manipulation may be present; and depressive affect may frequently be discerned. A large number of persons with these affective disorders remain effective in the community despite intermittent depressive and hypomanic or relatively well periods.

Many persons with manic-depressive psychoses have been in hospitals from an early age; others, although ill from youth, have remained socially integrated. In some of them the disorder has escaped attention in youth but emerges as troublesome in old age. Treatment of the three groups does not differ from the pharmacotherapeutic aspect. With aging, the disorder may become more regular and predictable. Some persons have shorter or more rapidly alternating episodes; in others, the episodes become longer, and there is no true free period. A large number become chronically depressed. It is doubtful that age ever brings with it a relief from such symptoms. With the advent of organic brain syndrome, the thought-content which reveals depression and mania as subjective distress may not be clearly elaborated, and the disturbed and disturbing behavior may be mistaken for disorganization or "senile agitation." Careful evaluation may suggest a beneficial trial of special treatment.

Manic and hypomanic episodes, although less frequent than clear depression, of which they may be a variant, are common disorders in old age. The patient and his family frequently fail to recognize the hypomanic phase of mood-cyclic disorder. They may regard it as a period of well-being, despite the presence of aggressiveness, overactivity, and poor judgment. The afflicted persons are usually hostile or paranoid, often accusing a specific close person, such as the spouse or child. The family may regard this behavior as an exaggeration of previous characteristics and unpleasant disposition rather than as a phase of illness. Treatment or hospitalization may be sought only when the disorder threatens the family's physical, social, or economic welfare.

When excitement is prominent, these disorders may be mislabeled as agitated reactions or be mistaken for dementia. Their resolution sometimes results in their being called, in retrospect, states of pseudodementia. They usually follow a depressive reaction which may have been so brief as to escape attention. They may be mixed with depression and invariably include paranoid trends. They may occur in compulsive, relatively passive persons after a frightening illness or bereavement or in anticipation of loss, as by the marriage of a child. The response to treatment is good; phenothiazines or butyrophenones alone, followed by the addition of antidepressants as the manic behavior subsides, are usually effective. Electroshock therapy may be dramatically helpful but is of no greater long-term value than is medication. Lithium salts are now well established as the preferred method of treatment.

Persons in the depressed period of cyclic disorders generally respond fairly well to antidepressant drugs. These medications—amitriptyline, imipramine, and the monoamine oxidase inhibitors—must be carefully supervised medically. Electroshock therapy is probably of no greater value than are the antidepressant drugs. It is useful when antidepressant drugs are contraindicated by special medical conditions or the intolerance of the patient to side effects. As mentioned above, some patients with detectable organic brain syndrome may be given one, two, or three electro-stimulant treatments as a diagnostic aid; in some seemingly intellectually disorganized patients, a reduction in the level of depression or mania reveals improvement in their cognitive functioning along with melioration of a cognitively disturbing affective component of their disorder. Also, electroshock therapy may be used because of its usual speedier efficacy than drugs. This is valuable for persons in whom vegetative signs are intense, where agitated, belligerent or suicidal behavior is prominent, and where there are dangers of exhaustion, accident, self-harm, or harm to others. The use of prophylactic electroshock treatment is of doubtful value.

Lithium salts have proven to be of value in manic states. If begun in the manic or "well" intervals, regular daily oral administration of lithium carbonate (about 500 mg) may reduce the severity of the manic symptoms and both shorten and decrease the intensity of the depressive episodes, with eventual almost complete subsidence of the disorder. The blood level is not as important as clinical response. Many chronologically old persons show benefit when the level is from 0.4 to 0.8 mEq/l. Lithium carbonate may exercise a prophylactic effect: this salt may also be occasionally helpful in agitated depressions. Leukotomy has been recommended by some European authorities for intractable depression, but it appears unnecessarily drastic.

Pseudoneurotic Affective or Mood Cyclic Disorder

With the advent of old age or life-threatening physical disease, many persons begin to review their past with feelings of regret; they feel that they have failed to achieve cherished goals, to make adequate use of their assets, or to realize their potential. They are grieved and depressed by the loss of a potentially viable self, much as is a woman after an abortion, but less consolably so, for they feel that there is no second chance. Treatment is chiefly by way of psychotherapy.

Involutional Psychotic Reaction

The existence of involutional psychotic reaction as an entity has been legitimately questioned. Nevertheless, there does appear to be a special subgroup of mental disorders, probably culturally determined, worthy of this special classification. This subgroup is characterized by depression, hypochondriasis, low self-esteem, and guilt (especially about sexual behavior and desire) with self-deprecatory and self-accusatory trends (especially about sex and sinfulness), often associated with florid paranoid ideation and behavior. In women with considerable psychosexual fears who have had emotional reactions temporally related to their menstrual cycle, there is often an emergence with aging (but not necessarily related to sexual involution) of prolonged tension, depression, and paranoid trends similar to those that periodically occurred in the past. In both men and women in whom mental disorders become prominent in middle age or later life, the prognosis when paranoid ideation is present is not as good as when such ideas are absent or are very clearly secondary to depression or elation. In many persons of middle age or early old age such patterns are charged with the conscious statement or belief that this is fitting for the age reached—for example, about sex, "I am (or you are) too old for that now." For the treatment of these disorders, electro-stimulant treatment has generally been considered as the first choice. This may be because the "typical" involutional melancholic reaction has commonly been found in the relatively unlettered and unsophisticated persons in whom there is little motivation for a conversational relationship, who inspire a hostility-charged patient-doctor relationship, and in many of whom the disorder is primarily biochemical and a late emergence of mood cyclic disorder.

Affective disorders that closely resemble the involutional psychoses are often incorrectly categorized as organic mental syndromes when they occur in chronological old age rather than middle age. At first glance, they may appear to be first depressive episodes, but a careful history often reveals that they are actually exaggerations of prior symptoms. The previous episodes or symptoms had either gone unnoticed or had been considered an aspect of psychoneurotic behavior, periodic hypochondriasis, or recurrent exacerbation of such physical disorders as arthritis. In retrospect, many of these persons appear to have been suffering with pseudoneurotic mood-cyclic disorder. Some of these prior episodes may have been recognized as depressions and classified as involutional.

In the past, electroshock therapy was regarded as specific for depressions in the elderly. Now, there is disenchantment with respect to its efficacy as increasing experience attests to the recurrent nature of these depressive reactions of middle age and early old age. It may well be useless to attempt to differentiate between endogenous or reactive, mood-cyclic, involutional, and neurotic affective reactions. It is probably best to simply differentiate between affective disorders with prominent, typical vegetative signs and disorders of affect with few or no such signs in the choice of treatment, and to keep in mind that all depressions in old age, especially those which emerge in a "psychoneurotic way," are likely to be chronic, and benefit from a life-long supportive relationship.

Social Factors and Depression in the Elderly

The incidence and prevalence of mental disorder in old age are high. With advancing age, there is increasing likelihood of losses in familial, financial, physical, and mental resources. The prevention of medical crises and meticulous attention to supportive regimens are prophylactic against disabling mental diseases of the aged. Thus comprehensive medical care for this age group is of prime importance.

Families, community agencies, hospitals, clinics, and private physicians play important roles in providing for the many medical and psychiatric needs of the aged ill. Few families can provide, unassisted, the comprehensive care an aged ill person needs; consequently, he is usually undertreated at home. Families may ask for assistance later than is desirable for their good or the patient's welfare. Psychiatrists, physicians, and welfare agencies may mistakenly minimize the burden that the geriatric patient places on his family; worse, they may resist the admission of aged patients to their services and generate guilt by implying that families who appeal to them for aid want to avoid responsibility for their aged relatives' care. Many professionals share a popular misconception that families are eager to dump their aged kin; in actuality, the sick aged often have no families or have families who are themselves aged, ill, or struggling for survival, so that assistance must be provided by way of social organizations. Basic services, the provision of adequate board and lodging, good general medical care, intelligently pursued efforts toward encouraging interest and activity, and psychiatrically supervised pharmacotherapy are unquestionably helpful in decreasing the intensity of long-term reactions and in preventing the emergence of new depressive episodes.

Prevention of mental disorders in the aged is not yet possible, but the severity of prevalent disorders may be ameliorated and their incidence decreased. Vulnerability to affective disorder or brain damage leading to brain syndrome appears to be genetically determined in many persons. The importance of inherited constitutional type and of incidental illness is suggested by the frequent association of arterial hypertension, atherosclerosis, arteriosclerotic cardiovascular renal disease, diabetes, glaucoma, hyperthyroidism, and exaggerated adrenal cortical function with affective disorders. These conditions appear to accompany depressive reactions over and beyond the depressing effect of severe or long-term illness. Persons in whom these conditions develop appear to be especially prone to mood-cyclic or depressive reactions and may have displayed this propensity even before the appearance of the somatic disorder. Other conditions, such as peptic ulcers or asthma, are also seen in close association with depressive reactions, sometimes accompanying the disorder and at other times masking it and appearing to be depressive equivalents.

Laudable measures likely to help avert mental illness in old age for even the constitutionally susceptible include environmental advantages in early life conducive to optimal growth, development, education, choice of occupation, and economic security; minimal exposure to noxious substances, trauma, and disease; and maximal timely use of prophylactic and remedial medical services.

Education which aids in the constructive anticipation of failure and actual failures that accompany decline of functional capacity and the loss of resources can lead to rational rather than to irrational pleas and search for aid. Socially encouraged willingness to seek and accept socially organized and governmentally supervised assistance requires, as a necessary complement, the governmental provision of the ready availability of protective, supportive, and rehabilitative services.

Ideally, the individual should be so well integrated that socioeconomic reverses, changed personal relationships, and stressful experiences would be handled without a serious decrease in self-esteem, loss of self-confidence, or the emergence of serious doubts as to his purpose and sense of identity; he should feel challenged rather than defeated by adversity and should retain his desire to act and to do, within the limits of his capacity, despite loss of vigor and functional capacity. He should wish to maintain pleasurable personal relationships yet be able to tolerate the absence of congenial, companionable persons and not become desolate when he loses family members and friends. The sense of worth, dignity, and self-confidence should be preserved by social institutions and by the behavior of surrounding persons, which encourage feelings of personal control and of influence on others, and the belief that one has the capacity to contribute personally to the mastering of daily problems. Such social influences appear to favor the development of persons capable of social integration in old age who are also capable of tolerating isolation. However, most persons in our society do not achieve this ideal.

Although aging persons may fear death as an ultimate helplessness, they appear to be more afraid of humiliation, pain, mental suffering, and the loss of those for whom they feel affection or need. Most of all, they fear the loss of control over their own behavior or destiny. Consequently, in the very old and impaired, small victories that appear to win them a place in the sun, protective attention from a child, or the self-attained relief from tensions, as from bowel distress, may yield pleasures such as might be expected from a guarantee of everlasting fame. The belief that their will or wishes will be followed after death may elicit more joy than that which in the past might have followed on the attainment of riches. Because pleasure appears to accrue from a sense of effectiveness in personal action, whatever contributes to the aged person's belief that he is effective and efficient, as measured according to his own values, helps to preserve his emotional equilibrium and his psychological aplomb. It appears that the adaptive organism maintains its social poise, even in the face of obvious decline, when it feels its chance is governed by choice; he who feels in command may die with little pain and small grief—even with joy.

Psychiatrists who can contribute to the understanding of aged persons are needed to consult, supervise, and teach in old age homes, general hospitals, state hospitals, old age centers, and clubs, as well as to see and treat patients and their families in their offices, the homes of patients, and hospitals and clinics. They can exercise an important function by sustaining the morale of those who are concerned with the day-to-day care of the aged.

Summary

Depressive disorder is the most common mental illness of the elderly and aged. It may be carried over from youth or first emerge or develop in old age. It may be genetically or experientially determined and is also frequently related to and complicated by physical changes. Often it is seen as a reaction to losses of physical, social, or economic status and as a complication of intellectual deficit with organic brain damage or dysfunction. Depressive disorder tends to be patterned in ways related to the amount and type of emergency disorder—fear and anger—present, and the individual's physiologic capacity to deal with these emotions as well as his cultural background, circumstances, and expectations. Treatment can be as effective as in young persons provided that the person's concomitant losses—physical, mental, and social—are not ignored and do not prevent removal of the obstructions to healing. Relatively severe and severe chronic organic brain syndrome may be blocks to treatment but neither acute brain syndrome nor the cognitive defects which accompany depression should be mistaken for the chronic brain syndrome. The patterning of depressive reactions often yields clues to treatment which overlap nosologic categories. Psychotherapy, pharmacotherapy, and physical therapy are all of value: most often they are combined with pharmaco- and physical therapy as the primary correctives where genetic factors have predisposed to biochemical shifts which constitute the basic losses in function. Psychotherapy is of greatest value where experiential factors are etiologically most important. The basis of psychotherapy appears to be the establishment of a personal relationship in which the therapist accepts delegation to quasi-parental status and thus reassures and supports the sufferer who feels helpless, frightened, and angry; reassurance stems from the connotation of strength in the victory over or alliance with the person delegated to this special role. Assumption of this role simply requires care on the part of the therapist not to destroy the patient's illusion that he has found or will find in the therapist the personal assistance and strengths he requires. Recognition of these factors can limit the degree of suffering and interpersonal disturbances of elderly and aged depressed persons.

References

1. Goldfarb AI: Psychotherapy of aged persons: II. Utilization and effectiveness of "brief" therapy. *Am J Psychiatr* **109** (121):916–921, June 1953.
2. Goldfarb AI: Psychotherapy of the aged: III. Brief therapy of interrelated psychological and somatic disorders. *Psychosom Med* **16**(3):209–219, May–June 1954.
3. Goldfarb AI: Psychotherapy of the aged: I. The use and value of an adaptational frame of reference. *Psa Rev* **42**(2):180–197. April 1955.
4. Goldfarb AI: Psychotherapy of aged persons: IV. One aspect of the psychodynam-

...utic situation in the aged patients. *Psa Rev* **42**(2):18–87, April

...The rationale of psychotherapy with older persons. *Am J Med Sci* ...35, August 1956.

...I: Contributions of psychiatry to the institutional care of the aged and ...y ill persons. *J Chronic Dis* **6**(5):483–496, November 1957.

... AI: Minor maladjustments of the aged, in *American Handbook of ...atry.* Edited by Arieti S, New York, Basic Books, 1959, pp. 378–397.

...arb AI: Depression, brain damage and chronic illness of the aged: ...chiatric diagnosis and treatment. *J Chronic Dis* **9**(3):220–233, March 1959.

...ldfarb AI: Psychiatric disorders of the aged: Symptomatology, diagnosis and ...reatment. *J Am Ger Soc* **8**(9):698–707, September 1960.

10. Goldfarb AI: *The Psychotherapy of Elderly Patients.* The International Association of Gerontology, Proceedings of Fifth Congress 1960. Also in *Medical and Clinical Aspects of Aging.* Edited by Blumenthal HT, New York, Columbia University Press, 1962.
11. Goldfarb AI: Age and illness, in *The Psychological Basis of Medical Practice.* Edited by Lief H, New York, Hoeber, 1963, pp. 203–218.
12. Goldfarb AI: Patient-doctor relationship in treatment of aged persons. *Geriatrics* **19**(10):18–23, January 1964 (Abstract No. 1228).
13. Goldfarb AI: The evaluation of geriatric patients following treatment, in *Evaluation of Psychiatric Treatment.* Edited by Hoch PH and Zubin J, New York, Grune & Stratton, 1964, pp. 271–280.
14. Goldfarb AI: Responsibilities to our aged. *Am J Nursing* **64**(11):78–82, November 1964.
15. Goldfarb AI: Intimate relations of older people, in *Man and Civilization: The Family's Search for Survival.* Edited by Farber SM, Hustacchi P, Wilson RHL, New York, McGraw-Hill, 1965, pp. 183–195.
16. Goldfarb AI: Psychodynamics and the three generation family, in *Social Structure and the Family: Generational Relations.* Edited by Shanas E and Streib GF, Englewood, New Jersey, 1965, pp. 10–45.
17. Goldfarb AI: Geriatric psychiatry, in *Comprehensive Textbook.* Edited by Freedman AM, Kaplin HI, Baltimore, The Williams & Wilkins Co, 1967, pp. 1564–1587.
18. Goldfarb AI: Masked depression in the old. *Am J Psychother* **21**(4):791–796, October 1967.
19. Goldfarb AI: Psychiatry in geriatrics. *Med Clinics N Am* **51**(6):November 1967.
20. Goldfarb AI: The psychodynamics of dependency and the search for aid. The dependencies of old people, in *Occasional Papers in Gerontology.* Institute of Gerontology, University of Michigan, No. 6, pp. 1–15, August 1969.
21. Goldfarb AI: Integrated psychiatric services for the aged. *Bull N Y Acad Med* **49**(12):1070–1083, December 1973.
22. Kahn RL, Goldfarb AI, Pollack M, Peck A: Brief objective measures for the determination of mental status in the aged. *Am J Psychiatr* **117**(4):326–328, October 1960.
23. Kahn RL, Goldfarb AI, Pollack M, Peck A: Factors in selection of psychiatric treatment for institutionalized aged persons. *Am J Psychiatr* **118**(3):241–244, September 1961.

Nine

Unipolar and Bipolar Affective States

Ronald R. Fieve, M.D.
David L. Dunner, M.D.

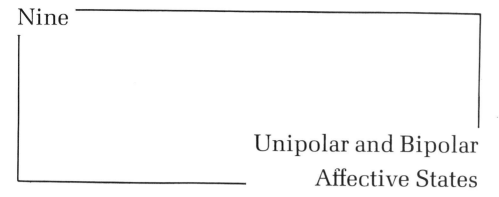

Although the classification of affective disorders into unipolar and bipolar types is of relatively recent origin, this classification system has been supported by studies of clinical, familial, pharmacological, and biological factors of depression. The recent dramatic demonstration that lithium carbonate is an effective therapeutic aid in the treatment of acute mania and, more importantly, that it benefits bipolar patients when used prophylactically has placed considerable value on the discernment of unipolar and bipolar affective states. The evidence for the unipolar-bipolar classification and its implications from both the research and clinical perspectives are reviewed here.

Definitions

In the simplest terms, patients with primary affective disorder are classified as unipolar if they experience depression only, and as bipolar if they have depressions with mania or hypomania. The bipolar group is somewhat clearer to delineate, as mania usually presents a striking contrast to other mood states. The use of the term bipolar to describe patients with mania is based on the opposite phases they exhibit of either being speeded up (mania) or being slowed down (depression). By mania is meant a psychiatric state defined by a mood that is characterized by euphoria or irritability, which often is labile with short bursts of depressive affect, accelerated physical activity (insomnia, increased sexual drive, greater physical movement), increased mental activity (distractibility, racing thoughts, push of speech, flight of ideas), and augmented social activity (grandiose schemes, increased spending). Criteria for this diagnosis have been summarized by Feighner (1) and include a change in mood for at least a 1 to 2-week period with a minimum of at least two of the following associated symptoms: hyperactivity, push of speech, flight of ideas, grandiosity, decreased sleep, and distractibility.

The manic condition may occur in a severe form which may require medical intervention or hospitalization, or in a milder form (hypomania) which may either be disruptive or socially rewarding. Psychotic states during severe mania are not uncommon; grandiose delusions are reported to be the most common psychotic manifestation, but paranoid delusions, delusions of passivity, and auditory and visual hallucinations have also been reported (2).

The other phase of bipolar illness is depression. The mood is one of sadness or discouragement; physical activity is diminished (psychomotor retardation, latency of verbal response, poverty of speech), yet at times increased physical activity is also observed (agitated depression). Mental activity is slowed (sluggishness of thought, difficulty concentrating), social activity is diminished (lack or interest in usual activity), and the outlook for the future is one of sheer pessimism. Suicidal thoughts, while uncommon during mania, are often encountered in the depressed phase, as are suicide attempts and accomplished suicide. Physical complaints, such as headache, constipation, anorexia, and weight loss (or hyperphagia and weight gain) are also typically observed. The mood may fluctuate and be improved in the evening (diurnal variation) and is most often not responsive to environmental changes. Sleep disturbance, usually trouble getting to sleep or early morning awakening (but at times hypersomnia), is also seen.

Criteria for the diagnosis of depression include a change in mood for at least 2 to 4 weeks with a minimum of four of the following associated symptoms: anorexia or weight loss, sleep difficulty, loss of energy, agitation or retardation, loss of interest in usual activities, self-reproach or guilt, diminished ability to think or concentrate, and recurrent thoughts of death or suicide (1). The depression may be severe and incapacitating to the patient, requiring medical intervention and hospitalization, electroshock therapy, and/or treatment with antidepressant medication. More commonly, the depression may be mild and characterized by a diminished interest in usual activities, a feeling of boredom, lack of initiative, difficulty in concentrating and an anhedonia with a pessimistic attitude toward the future.

Whereas bipolar patients experience both manic (or hypomanic) states and depression, unipolar patients suffer depression only. Their symptoms of depression are similar to those experienced by bipolar patients, although agitated depressions may be seen more commonly in unipolar patients.

Leonhard (3) first described patients separated in terms of bipolar and unipolar (monopolar). While the term bipolar is not especially controversial, Court (4) has suggested that it is a misnomer—that manic states represent a more severe form of depressive illness on a continuum, rather than a condition opposite to depression. Evidence to support Court's thesis can be found, for example, in the fact that certain treatments are effective for both mania and depression, particularly electroshock therapy.

Nevertheless, other studies tend to support a dichotomous (bipolar) model rather than a continuum model. For example, many manic-depressive patients experience a period of normal mood (euthymia) between depressive and manic states. Although the continuum model is of some interest, it has not been generally adopted.

Perris (5) used the term unipolar to describe a group of patients who had severe manias but were apparently never depressed. Such "unipolar manics" probably constitute a small percentage of manic-depressive patients, and Perris was able to isolate only 17 unipolar manics in his study of 1539 patients. In our clinic of about 200 manic-depressive patients, we have identified two patients who have mania without depressive episodes. The family history characteristics of Perris' unipolar manic patients were more like those of his bipolar than those of his unipolar depressives, suggesting that such patients be grouped with bipolar patients.

An additional prerequisite for the classification of unipolar-bipolar illness is that patients meet the criteria for a "primary affective disorder." This relatively recent diagnostic term was developed by the Washington University group to classify depressions without regard to presumptive etiology, symptomatology, or age of onset, and they defined several syndromes that have distinctive symptomatology and clinical outcomes on follow-up. Several of these syndromes, such as hysteria (6); antisocial personality (7); anxiety neurosis (8); drug abuse and alcoholism (9) occur in patients who also may have depression. Such depressions are termed secondary—that is, they occur during the course of (not necessarily "due to") another well-defined psychiatric syndrome. Thus a primary affective disorder is an affective illness which occurs in a patient who has no other specifically defined psychiatric illness predating the onset of the affective disorder. By the same token, a depression occurring during the course of a severe or life-threatening medical illness or associated with the administration of drugs that affect mood is not included as a primary affective disorder but is classified under secondary affective disorder.

Evidence suggesting that the primary-secondary affective disorder distinction has validity comes from studies demonstrating that the symptoms and courses of patients with anxiety neurosis, hysteria, sociopathy, and the like are separable from patients with primary affective disorder, and that suicidal behavior is somewhat different in primary and secondary depressions. While both groups of patients attempted suicide frequently, patients with primary affective disorder were disproportionately represented in a group of patients who died by suicide (10, 11). Of note is the fact that the only group of patients with secondary depression who were significantly represented among a group of suicides were alcoholics, and the distinction between a patient with a primary affective disorder who is drinking versus an alcoholic with a secondary depression is often difficult to make.

The designation of primary affective disorder operates more frequently to exclude patients from the unipolar group than from the bipolar group, since the unipolar group by its definition is a more heterogeneous population. Secondly, this distinction has been applied only relatively recently in the American studies but generally not in the European studies of affective disorder. Unipolar and bipolar patients who also meet the criteria for primary affective disorder are discussed here.

Bipolar patients can be further separated into four subtypes based on severity of and treatment received for manic and/or depressive symptoms:

Bipolar I, Bipolar II, Bipolar Other, and Cyclothymic Personality. Bipolar I patients are those who have been hospitalized for a manic episode or who have required medical management at home for severe manic behavior. (Bipolar I patients may additionally have been treated or hospitalized for depression.) Bipolar II patients are those bipolar patients who have been hospitalized for depression or have required medical management at home for depressive behavior. The severity of manic symptoms in such patients has never led to hospitalization, although outpatient treatment for these (hypo)manic symptoms may have been received.

Bipolar Other patients have been treated for depression or hypomania but never hospitalized; and Cyclothymic Personality describes patients with bipolar mood swings who have not sought help for or been treated for either depression or hypomania. The classification of Bipolar II patients includes patients whose hypomanic episodes may coincide with treatment and recovery from depression. Thus a patient is considered Bipolar II and not unipolar if clear hypomanic periods are "induced" by drug or electroshock therapy of depression. (It is not clear whether such patients were excluded from the unipolar patients studied in European centers.)

A similar subclassification of unipolar patients, based mainly on Winokur's studies, would include Unipolar I, Unipolar II, Unipolar Other, and Depressive Personality. The Unipolar I group corresponds to Winokur's Depressive Disease group, and includes patients with at least one hospitalization for depression, no personal history of hypomania, and no family history of mania or hypomania (12). Unipolar II patients have been hospitalized for depression and have a family history of mania or hypomania. Unipolar Other have sought help for or been treated but not hospitalized for depression; and Depressive Personality includes patients who have periods of depression but have not been specifically treated for affective illness.

These classification concepts are summarized in Table 1. It should be noted that the subclassifications are largely hypothetical constructs based on several studies accomplished to date and are intended to provide a frame of reference for future research.

Rationale for the Unipolar-Bipolar Classification

Systems of classification are developed for the purpose of isolating populations of greater homogeneity. Previous classifications of affective disorder have been based on depressive symptoms (agitated-retarded; psychotic-neurotic), assumption of cause (reactive-endogenous), time or age of onset (involutional, postpartum), and course (chronic, episodic, cyclical).

The unipolar-bipolar classification was developed on a clinical basis (history of mania) and was initially supported by family history studies. European investigators noted a higher family loading of psychosis and suicide in families where the index case was bipolar. Further investigations (in Europe and the United States) revealed that relatives of bipolar patients had both bipolar and unipolar illness, whereas relatives of unipolar patients had unipolar but not bipolar illness. At the same time, other and more sophisticated studies of affective illness were being reported, and the data from family

Table 1 Subclassification of Unipolar and Bipolar Affective States

Primary Affective Disorder	
Bipolar	Unipolar
Bipolar I (Hospitalized[a] for mania)	Unipolar I (Hospitalized[a] for depression; negative family history of mania)
Bipolar II (Hospitalized for depression only)	Unipolar II (Hospitalized for depression; positive family history of mania)
Bipolar Other (Outpatient treatment for depression or hypomania)	Unipolar Other (Outpatient treatment for depression)
Cyclothymic Personality (Meets criteria for hypomania but never treated)	Depressive Personality (Meets criteria for depression but never treated)

[a]Equivalent to the term hospitalized is treatment received in the home requiring special observation and nursing care.

studies and linkage studies lent credence to the unipolar-bipolar dichotomy.

Other research units which have been studying biological correlates of depression then began applying the unipolar-bipolar system to classify their patients. Several biological factors associated with depression separated out when the patients were classified as unipolar or bipolar, and these studies lent further support to the potential value of this classification system in defining homogeneous populations for research (13).

As mentioned above, the unipolar-bipolar classification was first supported by evidence from family studies. Leonhard (3) found an increased incidence of psychosis and suicide in the families of bipolar (Types I and II) probands, as compared to families where the proband was unipolar. Winokur and Clayton (14) studied a group of affectively ill probands who had two generations of illness (which might be seen in single dominant gene transmission) and compared them to affectively ill patients with no family history of mental illness. A significantly greater number of probands in the former group had histories of mania. At about this time (1965 to 1969), lithium was emerging as an interesting and effective new treatment for mania. Perhaps the impact of the "discovery" of a new therapeutic agent set in motion several investigations into familial factors in affective illness, with a group of patients who had mania contrasted to a group of patients who did not. Thus Perris' monograph was published in 1966, Angst's study in 1966, and Winokur's studies of bipolar and unipolar illness in 1969.

Perris (5) studied 138 bipolar, 137 unipolar depressives, and 17 unipolar manic probands who had been hospitalized. The bipolar group included patients we would term Bipolar I and II. The unipolar patients had at least three episodes of depression apparently of sufficient severity to warrant hospitalization. (It is not clearly stated whether mild periods of hypomania not requiring treatment occurred in these patients.) Data regarding illness in the families were obtained by interviewing at least one relative of the patient. (Thus Perris did a partial family study; in a family history study none of the relatives are interviewed, and in a complete family study all available relatives are interviewed.) Perris found that 11% of first degree relatives of bipolar patients had bipolar illness and only 0.5% had unipolar illness; whereas for unipolar probands, unipolar hereditary occurred in 7% and bipolar hereditary in 0.4% of first degree relatives.

Angst's (15) findings were essentially identical to Perris' for unipolar probands, although he required only one episode of depression rather than the three called for by Perris. Whereas Perris found only a small percentage of relatives of bipolar patients having unipolar illness, Angst found that 11% of first degree relatives of bipolar patients had unipolar illness. This discrepancy may be in part due to the difference in definitions of bipolar illness. Angst defined it as when one or more episodes of depression were present, and Perris always required three episodes or more of depression.

Winokur studied 61 patients who were diagnosed as manic during an index admission. This study, which has become a basic reference text for students of bipolar illness, was a family study in that all available first degree relatives were interviewed (2). The morbid risk for primary affective disorder was 13% for fathers and 56% for mothers. Both bipolar and unipolar illness were demonstrated in these relatives, and male relatives also had an increased morbid risk for alcoholism. Attempts to demonstrate linkage of bipolar illness with the X chromosome by using two known X chromosome markers (color blindness and Xga blood types) were successful in a limited number of families studied by Winokur (16, 17). These studies have recently been confirmed in a larger sample of 20 families from our own lithium clinic (18, 19).

Winokur also studied a group of unipolar probands who had no family history of mania or hypomania (Depressive Disease), and he was able to separate this group further (using family history criteria) into two "prototypes"—a female with an early age of onset (depression spectrum disease) showing more female than male relatives with depression and a high familial load for alcoholism, and a male with a late age of onset ("pure depressive disease") in which male and female relatives are equally affected with depression and no increased alcoholism occurs in male relatives (12, 20).

The bipolar group studied by Winokur is the basis for the Bipolar I classification described in Table 1, and similarly, the depressive disease group of Winokur defines Unipolar I patients. These subclassifications represent a tentative attempt to provide a basis for current research, and as new data emerge they will require modification accordingly. Bipolar I patients and Unipolar I patients have been studied rather extensively. The Bipolar II classification is important in removing patients with hypomania from the unipolar group. Data regarding Bipolar II patients have been reported by Dunner (21); a family history and follow-up study of these patients suggested that they had relatives who had hypomania and suicide, and that this Bipolar

II group was disproportionately represented among patients who committed suicide in the follow-up period. While Unipolar II patients have not been studied extensively, they are of considerable interest inasmuch as they may carry a bipolar genotype.

Clinical Phenomenology

Several clinical differences have been reported between unipolar and bipolar depression, particularly between the Unipolar I and Bipolar I groups. As previously mentioned, an important clinical differentiating point, and the basis for the distinction, is that bipolar patients experience mania whereas unipolar patients do not. A number of studies have demonstrated that the mean age of onset of illness is later for unipolar patients than for bipolar patients. In Winokur's studies, the median age of onset for bipolar patients was 28 years, as compared to 36 years for unipolar patients. Bipolar patients have more affective episodes than do unipolar patients, who are more likely to have only a single episode of depression.

A regular or predictable cyclical pattern to the depression is seen more frequently in bipolar than in unipolar patients. In our own lithium prophylaxis study, 11 of 68 bipolar patients had a rapid cyclical pattern to their illness, and it is unusual for a patient with depression and no history of hypomania (unipolar) to have regularly recurrent depressions over a lifetime (22). The importance of this point is elaborated on in the discussion of lithium prophylactic studies.

Other clinical features which distinguish unipolar and bipolar depressions include an increased incidence of postpartum episodes in bipolar patients (23). In the Perris study, an increased mortality from causes other than suicide was noted in bipolar patients, with a concomitant shortening of life expectancy.

Beigel and Murphy (24) studied an age and sex matched group of unipolar and bipolar patients who had been admitted to the Clinical Center at the NIMH. Bipolar patients tended to have "retarded" depressions, whereas agitated as well as retarded depressions were noted among unipolar patients. Also, higher global ratings for anxiety, physical complaints, and anger were noted in unipolar patients. A larger series of 97 of these patients, reported by Dunner and coworkers (25), also demonstrated higher ratings for anxiety for the unipolar patients, although the degree of depression, as measured on a global rating scale, was similar for both groups.

Mortality due to suicide in patients with affective disorder is about 15%. In the Perris and Angst studies, the rates for unipolar and bipolar patients were similar and a slightly (but not significantly) higher familial risk for suicide was found in bipolar patients. In the study of the 163 NIMH patients, Dunner (21) noted that Bipolar II patients were disproportionally represented in the group of patients who had died by suicide 1 to 9 years after discharge, and also noted that a history of suicide attempts was seen most frequently in Bipolar II patients. Furthermore, the familial incidence of suicide was higher in Bipolar (particularly Bipolar II) patients as compared to unipolar patients.

A wide range of behavior is also observed in the manic symptomatology of Bipolar I and Bipolar II patients. Carlson and Goodwin (26) studied a group of patients with severe mania during hospitalization. Two clinically separable types emerged. One group had mania characterized by euphoria; delusions if present were grandiose; and ward management was fairly uncomplicated. The second group displayed irritability and anger rather than euphoria; delusions tended to be more of a persecutory type; and their clinical care was complicated by frequent use of chemical and physical restraints. Otherwise, both types were similar in terms of prior histories, family histories, and global severity of the manic condition.

Some Bipolar II patients have an episodic hypomania which is rather severe and perhaps have even received treatment (but not hospitalization) for their hypomania. Clinically, these patients tend to merge with some Bipolar I patients, since the Bipolar I-Bipolar II distinction is in no small part dependent on the many social and economic factors that related to psychiatric hospitalization in addition to the severity of mania itself.

A possible variant of Bipolar I illness may be those patients who function well between episodes but whose psychiatric illnesses are schizophreniform in nature—acute onset episodes of increased activity, decreased sleep, affective lability, perplexity, and hallucinations or delusions, often of a bizarre nature. These schizophreniform illnesses often remit, are often associated with a family history of more classical affective disorder, and, as with manic episodes, are often followed by depression (27). Episodes of schizophreniform illness have been observed in patients who previously had typical manic-depressive cycles and who, after the remission of the atypical episode, continued to have episodes of a more typical nature. Although further research in schizophreniform illness is necessary to clarify the classification of patients with recurrent atypical episodes, many similarities may be drawn between these episodes and more typical bipolar illness.

The clinical characteristics of hypomania in bipolar patients have not been systematically studied. However, many of these patients report a sustained productive and at times creative lifestyle (28). Frequently, they describe their general personalities as on the "up side" with a high drive and high energy level. It is often difficult in obtaining a psychiatric history from such patients to determine whether they have mild hypomania which meets the criteria described above, or if their high drive represents a skewed segment of normal personality variation. Often the history of these effective and constructive hypomanic periods in such patients can be obtained only from close friends or relatives and may consist solely of periods of unusual productivity and high energy. In fact, these individuals' high energy levels are often socially rewarded by others and may represent a positive driving force in the society, accounting for the productivity and creative accomplishments that sometimes characterize their lives.

It has been observed that creativity and financial success may be associated with some forms of bipolar illness. Although no systematic evidence bears on this point, Woodruff (29) studied the social and educational status of relatives of bipolar and unipolar patients who were matched for age, sex, and socioeconomic level. A higher social and economic status and educational achievement level were found for relatives of bipolar patients, irrespective of illness in these relatives.

Moreover, lithium treatment of manic-depressive patients who are, in addition, highly productive and/or creative individuals has recently been reported to increase the overall creativity and sustain productiveness while simultaneously dampening the abnormal mood swings (28). These creative manic-depressive patients report that previous treatment of their illness with electroshock therapy, major tranquilizers, and antidepressants has resulted in severe disruption of their creative process and lifestyle, with at times severe memory impairment and drowsiness and chemical straight-jacketing. In contrast, lithium therapy of these individuals is well tolerated without side effects and without apparent impairment of mental functioning or the creative process.

Biological and Pharmacological Differentiation of Unipolar and Bipolar Patients

If the unipolar-bipolar dichotomy does isolate subgroups of greater homogeneity and if, as has long been assumed, biological factors are of importance in the genesis of some affective states, then metabolic differences should be demonstrable. To date, several biological and pharmacological differences between unipolar and bipolar patients have been reported, although the role of these differences in any possible etiologic mechanisms of affective disorders has not been delineated.

The initial demonstration of biological differences between unipolar and bipolar patients came from Perris' study. Whereas the routine EEG did not demonstrate differences, after photic stimulation bipolar patients had a greater amplitude of response to lower frequencies than did unipolar patients. The flicker threshhold to visual stimuli was lower in bipolar patients than in unipolar patients in remission. Subsequently, other investigators have demonstrated that bipolar patients increase their amplitude of cortically evoked response with increasing stimulation (augmentors), whereas unipolar patients have a reduced amplitude of response (reducers) under the same experimental conditions (30).

The urinary excretion of 17-hydroxycorticosteroids (17 OHCS) in these subgroups was studied in patients at the NIMH. The mean 17 OHCS excretion was significantly reduced for Bipolar I patients. Data for the unipolar patients were analyzed separately for Unipolar I and Unipolar II patients, and no significant differences in 17 OHCS excretion were demonstrated for these two groups (25).

The activity of three enzymes involved in biogenic amine metabolism has been studied in blood from affectively ill patients. Catechol-*0*-methyltransferase (COMT) is an enzyme which is involved in the metabolism of norepinephrine and dopamine. The activity of this enzyme can be determined from preparation of erythrocytes, and Cohn (31) and Dunner (32) have reported that the mean erythrocyte COMT activity is reduced in women with primary affective disorder, and further reduced in women with unipolar rather than bipolar illness. However, there was considerable overlap in the activities of COMT for affectively ill women and normal controls. Women with chronic schizophrenia had normal mean COMT activity.

Monoamine oxidase (MAO) is an enzyme involved in the metabolism of both catecholamines and indoleamines. The activity of MAO can be determined in plasma and platelets. Murphy and Weiss (33) have reported that platelet MAO activity is reduced in male and female patients with Bipolar I illness, whereas normal mean MAO activity is found for patients with unipolar and Bipolar II illness. In patients with schizophrenia, mean MAO activity was below that found for bipolar patients.

Dopamine-Beta-Hydroxylase (DBH) is the enzyme involved in the synthesis of norepinephrine from dopamine. This enzyme is present in plasma and is thought to be released into the circulation with catecholamines during times of increased sympathetic nervous system activity. Studies of DBH activity in affective states have failed to reveal differences in mean DBH activity for patients who are bipolar versus unipolar, affectively ill versus controls, or manic versus euthymic or depressed (34,35). Similarly, no significant difference from normal could be determined for DBH activity in schizophrenics (36).

Although it has not been determined that these enzymes in blood are identical to the enzymes in brain, the blood enzymes have kinetics and cofactor requirements similar to the brain enzymes. Further studies with these enzymes, and particularly their development as potential genetic markers, are in progress.

Recently, biogenic amine metabolites in cerebrospinal fluid (CSF) have been assayed in patients after the administration of large doses of probenecid. The rationale for these studies is that probenecid blocks the active transport process for the removal of the acidic metabolites of dopamine and serotonin from CSF to blood. The probenecid-induced accumulation of these metabolites in CSF is thought to reflect brain amine turnover. Preliminary data from the NIMH probenecid study suggest that higher turnover of dopamine is found in Bipolar I as compared to Bipolar II and unipolar patients (37).

Pharmacological differences between unipolar and bipolar patients have also been reported. A mild antidepressant effect has been noted to occur more frequently during administration of lithium carbonate to depressed bipolar than unipolar patients (38). Similar results were noted by Mendels (39), who reported that this antidepressant effect of lithium was equivalent to the antidepressant effect of tricyclic antidepressant medication. An elevation of plasma magnesium has been reported to occur during lithium administration of bipolar but not unipolar patients.

Several other pharmacological differences have been reported. L-dopa, a precursor of biogenic amines, appeared to induce hypomanic-like episodes when given to depressed Bipolar I patients (40). Bipolar II patients tended to respond with some antidepressant effect from L-dopa, whereas unipolar patients had little clinical change (41). The administration of L-Tryptophan, a precursor of serotonin, to depressed patients has resulted in antidepressant responses in bipolar but not unipolar patients (42). An antidepressant response to tricyclic antidepressants was easier to demonstrate in unipolar patients than in bipolar patients.

Perhaps the most impressive pharmacologic differences have been in the prophylactic uses of lithium and tricyclic antidepressants. During lithium administration to Bipolar I patients who are euthymic, clear reduction in future manic and future depressive episodes occurs, as compared to placebo (43–45). This prophylactic effect becomes more evident as lithium is given over longer time periods, since most of the prophylactic failures during lithium treatment occur in the first year (22). Similar prophylaxis of depression can be demonstrated for Bipolar II patients.

According to several studies, unipolar patients also have a prophylactic lithium effect as compared to placebo (43, 46, 47). Since Bipolar II patients have not been carefully screened from most of these studies, lithium's prophylactic value in unipolar illness is not generally agreed upon.

Prien (43, 48) reported the results of the VA NIMH cooperative study of lithium prophylaxis. Part of this study involved prophylactic trials of tricyclic antidepressants. It appears that bipolar patients (particularly Bipolar I) are especially sensitive to the chronic administration of tricyclics in that they will frequently develop manic episodes. A slight depressive prophylactic effect of chronic administration of imipramine or amitriptyline has been reported in unipolar patients (48, 49).

In summary, the unipolar-bipolar classification is supported by evidence from several biological and pharmacological studies of depression. However, in all of these studies, data from unipolars and bipolars tended to overlap; that is, none of the biological or pharmacological criteria could be employed as a laboratory basis for the diagnosis. It may be that these biological and pharmacological differences reflect a basic biological alteration of metabolism which itself has not been directly studied.

Treatment of Unipolar and Bipolar Affective States

Since the approaches to treatment of depression are covered elsewhere in this text, the discussion here is limited to the prophylactic use of lithium in mania and bipolar manic-depression (50). In general, the same principles are used in treating the affective episodes of both unipolar and bipolar patients.

Of particular importance in the management of the bipolar patient is an awareness of the natural history of bipolar illness, which is of a recurrent episodic condition. Although lithium carbonate treatment is quite effective in many bipolar patients as a prophylactic agent for the prevention of recurrent depressions and particularly manias, it is not completely effective. The fact that a significant percentage of patients will have relapses during lithium treatment should be conveyed to the patient. Of equal importance, lithium therapy should not be terminated in the face of a relapse within the first year of treatment, as many patients apparently do not achieve a prophylactic effect until after a year or so (22).

Treatment with lithium carbonate has to be monitored with scrupulous care to avoid toxic levels. Contraindications are renal conditions, decompensated heart disease, and pathology of the central nervous system. The patient should maintain a normal diet, including salt and adequate fluids. Diuretics should not be given with chronic lithium therapy.

Patients in acute mania can tolerate high doses, but the dosage should be rapidly reduced to maintenance levels when the acute attack is over, and twice weekly lithium levels should be taken the first few weeks to avoid excessive serum concentration and toxic reactions. For the moderately severe manic state, the initial daily dose ranges from 1500 to 2100 mg (a 70-kg patient). After 5 to 10 days, when the mania usually abates, daily dosage should be reduced to 900 to 1200 mg. Individual patient dosage is determined by continuous periodic clinical observation and achievement of a serum lithium level of 0.8 to 1.5 mEq/l. Monthly lithium levels are essential to obtain to prevent toxicity and to ensure that the patient is taking his medicine.

Side Effects

Possible side effects include hand tremor, abdominal cramps, nausea, vomiting, and diarrhea; also seen are thirst and polyuria, fatigue or sleepiness, and weight gain (from 5 to 10 lbs in several weeks). These symptoms may occur during the first 2 to 4 weeks of lithium stabilization, but they disappear either spontaneously or when the dosage is lowered.

A diagnosis of lithium poisoning is determined by the clinical condition of the patient and a serum lithium value exceeding 2.0 to 3.0 mEq/l. Treatment consists of stopping the drug immediately and applying those supportive measures usually employed with patients in coma. In the case of lithium, this includes replacement of extracellular fluid depletion, along with the administration of aminophylline and mannitol to induce a lithium diuresis. Reinstitution of normal electrolyte balance is essential, and periodic electrocardiograms and serum hematocrit, as well as serial measurements of body weight, allow the physician to restore normal fluid and electrolyte balance. Antiepileptic agents should be used during severe lithium poisoning because of the high incidence of seizure phenomena.

A critical precondition for treatment is the ability to correctly diagnose affective disorders in general and bipolar states in particular. In one study of diagnostic styles, only 14% of patients given a diagnosis of affective disorders based on research criteria were diagnosed as being affectively ill by their treating physicians (51). No doubt the increased interest in the use of lithium will be a factor in correcting this situation.

Supportive psychotherapy may be of particular benefit to some patients during the depressed phase of their illness. Most bipolar patients, who will respond well to prophylactic lithium therapy, do not require or want psychotherapy during their remissions. Few studies have been conducted regarding the role of psychotherapy during the depressive episode or during the interim period. In the study by Klerman (49), the effect of psychotherapy was evaluated in comparison to prophylactic administration of tricyclic medication. Little advantage of intensive psychotherapy was found in that study.

A high rate of marital failure is found among bipolar patients, and couple therapy may be of assistance in stabilizing the marriages of such patients. This seems to be of particular benefit for the patients who have recently been manic.

Selected Areas for Future Research

Although many studies have supported the unipolar-bipolar classification, several important questions remain to be answered. The validity of the Bipolar

I-Bipolar II division needs to be evaluated. Likewise, the relationship between Bipolar I illness and schizophreniform psychosis should be more clearly defined. Whether Bipolar II patients whose only hypomanic periods occur during administration of tricyclic medication should be included as bipolar is also in need of investigation. Carefully performed biological and family studies may help to clarify these issues.

The Unipolar II group, which accounts for a small (about 6%) percentage of unipolar patients, is of great interest. These patients, whose relatives are bipolar, may carry a bipolar genotype. It would seem of interest to determine if biological and pharmacological data from Unipolar I patients are more similar to bipolar or unipolar patients.

The relationship of secondary depressions to unipolar illness requires study. A few family studies of these conditions suggest that familial illness in certain secondary depressions is not similar to that found for primary affective disorders.

Attempts to subclassify the Unipolar I group on the basis of clinical data, such as late age of onset males versus early age of onset women, provide a basis for further corroboration by biological studies. By its very nature, the unipolar group is less homogeneous than the bipolar groups, and such problems as the number of depressions required to obtain more homogeneous unipolar subgroups are of interest.

Although several biological studies support the unipolar-biopolar classification, none has been without overlap in the data between controls or patients with other psychiatric disorders. Many of these studies were undertaken to test the catecholamine hypothesis of affective disorder, a hypothesis which has provided a useful framework for the propagation of research studies. However, it is not certain that this hypothesis will continue to be of as much value in the future as it has been in the past.

What is needed from the "biological" side of the psychiatry of depressions is some kind of laboratory test on which clinical data (impressions, symptoms, diagnoses, etc.) can be validated. This assumes that such data will be forthcoming—that affective disorders have some biological etiology or consequence which is distinctive. By using the unipolar-bipolar classification, one hopes to provide populations of greater genetic, biological, and behavioral homogeneity for future research.

Acknowledgments

The authors are most appreciative of the editorial assistance provided by Henrietta Gilden of Dr. Fieve's staff.

References

1. Feighner J and others: Diagnostic criteria for use in psychiatric research. *Arch Gen Psychiatr* **26**:57–63, 1972.
2. Winokur G, Clayton P, Reich T: *Manic Depressive Illness.* St. Louis, CV Mosby Co, 1969.
3. Leonhard K, Korff I, Shulz H: Die Temperamente in den famillien der monopolaren und bipolaren phasischen psychosen. *Psychiatr Neurol* **143**:416–434, 1962.

4. Court JH: The continuum model as a resolution of paradoxes in manic-depressive psychosis. *Br J Psychiatr* **120:**133–141, 1972.
5. Perris C: A study of bipolar (manic-depressive) and unipolar recurrent depressive psychoses. *Acta Psychiatr Scand* **42** (Suppl 194): 1966.
6. Perley MJ, Guze SB: Hysteria—The stability and usefulness of clinical criteria: A quantitative study based on a follow-up period of 6-8 years in 39 patients. *New Eng J Med* **266:**421–426, 1962.
7. Robins LN: *Deviant Children Grown Up: A Sociological and Psychiatric Study of Sociopathic Personality.* Baltimore, Williams & Wilkins Co, 1966.
8. Wheeler EO, White PD, Reed EW and others: Neurocirculatory asthenia (anxiety neurosis, effort syndrome, neurasthenia). *JAMA* **142:**878–888, 1950.
9. Barchha R, Stewart MA, Guze SB: The prevalence of alcoholism among general hospital ward patients. *Am J Psychiatr* **125:**681–684, 1968.
10. Robins E, Schmidt EH, O'Neal P: Some inter-relations of social factors and clinical diagnosis in attempted suicide: A study of 109 patients. *Am J Psychiatr* **114:**221–231, September 1957.
11. Robins E and others: Some clinical considerations in the prevention of suicide based on a study of 134 successful suicides. *Am J Public Health* **49:**888–899, 1959.
12. Baker M, Dorzab J, Winokur G and others: Depressive disease: Classification and clinical characteristics. *Compr Psychiatr* **12:**354–365, 1971.
13. Gershon ES, Dunner DL, Goodwin FK: Toward a biology of affective disorders: Genetic contributions. *Arch Gen Psychiatr* **25:**1–15, 1971.
14. Winokur G, Clayton P: Family history studies: 1. Two types of affective disorder separated according to clinical and genetic factors, in *Recent Advances in Biological Psychiatry.* Edited by Wortis J, New York, Plenum Publishing, 1967.
15. Angst J: Zur atiologie und nosologie endogoner depressiver psychosen, in *Monographien aus dem Gesamtgebiete der neurologie und Psychiatrie.* Berlin Springer-Verlag, 1966, No. 112.
16. Reich T, Clayton PJ, Winokur G: Family history studies: V. The genetics of mania. *Am J Psychiatr* **125:**1358–1369, 1969.
17. Winokur G, Tanna VL: Possible role of x-linked dominant factor in manic-depressive disease. *Dis Nerv Syst* **30:**89, 1969.
18. Mendlewicz J, Fleiss JL, Fieve RR: Evidence for x-linkage in the transmission of manic-depressive illness. *JAMA* **222:**1624–1627, 1972.
19. Fieve RR, Mendlewicz J: *Linkage studies in affective disorders 11: The XGa blood group and manic depressive illness.* Presented at the VIII CINP Congress, Copenhagen, Denmark, 1972.
20. Winokur G, Cadoret R, Dorzab J and others: Depressive disease, a genetic study. *Arch Gen Psychiatr* **24:**135–144, 1971.
21. Dunner DL, Gershon ES, Goodwin FK: Heritable factors in the severity of affective illness. Read before the annual meeting of the APA, San Francisco, May 1970.
22. Dunner DL, Fieve RR: Clinical factors in lithium prophylaxis failure. *Arch Gen Psychiatr* **30:**229–233, 1974.
23. Baker M, Dorzab J, Winokur G and others: Depressive disease: The effect of the postpartum state. *Biol Psychiatr* **3:**357–365, 1971.
24. Beigel A, Murphy DL: Unipolar and bipolar affective illness: Differences in clinical characteristics accompanying depression. *Arch Gen Psychiatr* **24:**215–229, 1971.
25. Dunner DL and others: Excretion of 17-hydroxycorticosteroids in unipolar and bipolar depressed patients. *Arch Gen Psychiatr* **26:**360–363, 1972.
26. Carlson GA, Goodwin FK: The stages of mania. *Arch Gen Psychiatr* **28:**221–228, 1973.

27. Fowler RC, McCabe MS, Cadoret RJ and others: The validity of good prognosis schizophrenia. *Arch Gen Psychiatr* **26:**182–185, 1972.
28. Fieve RR: Clinical use of lithium in manic depression, recurrent depression, and the creative personality. Presented at the annual meeting, AMA, New York, 1973.
29. Woodruff RA Jr, Robins LN, Winokur G and others: Manic depressive illness and social achievement. *Acta Psychiatr Scand* **47:**237–249, 1971.
30. Buchsbaum M, Goodwin FK, Murphy DL and others: Average evoked response in affective disorders. *Am J Psychiatr* **128:**19–25, 1971.
31. Cohn CK, Dunner DL, Axelrod J: Reduced catechol-*0*-methyltransferase activity in red blood cells of women with primary affective disorder. *Science* **170:**1323–1324, 1970.
32. Dunner DL, Cohn CK, Gershon ES and others: Differential catechol-*0*-methyltransferase activity in unipolar and bipolar affective illness. *Arch Gen Psychiatr* **25:**348–353, 1971.
33. Murphy DL, Weiss R: Reduced monoamine oxidase activity in blood platelets from bipolar depressed patients. *Am J Psychiatr* **128:**1351–1357, 1972.
34. Shopsin B and others: Serum dopamine-B-hydroxylase activity and affective states. *Psychopharmacologia (Berl)* **27:**11–16, 1972.
35. Levitt M and others: *Plasma Dopamine-Beta-Hydroxylase Activity in Affective Illness.* In preparation, 1974.
36. Dunner DL, Cohn CK, Weinshilboum RM and others: The activity of dopamine-beta-hydroxylase and methionine-activating enzyme in blood of schizophrenic patients. *Biolog Psychiatr* **6:**215–220, 1973.
37. Goodwin FK and others: Cerebrospinal fluid amine metabolites in affective illness: The probenecid technique. *Am J Psychiatr* **130:**73–79, 1973.
38. Goodwin FK, Murphy DL, Dunner DL and others: Lithium response in unipolar vs. bipolar depression. *Am J Psychiatr* **129:**44–47, 1972.
39. Mendels J, Secunda SK, Dyson WL: A controlled study of the anti-depressant effect of lithium carbonate. *Arch Gen Psychiatr* **26:**154–157, 1972.
40. Murphy DL, Brodie HKH, Goodwin FK and others: Regular induction of hypomania by L-dopa in "bipolar" manic-depressive patients. *Nature* **229:**135–136, 1971.
41. Gershon E and others: Catecholamines and affective illness: Studies with L-dopa and alpha-methyl-para-tyrosine, in *Brain Chemistry and Mental Disease.* Edited by Ho BT, McIsaac W, Plenum Press, New York, 1971.
42. Murphy DL and others: Behavioral and metabolic effects of L-tryptophan in unipolar depressed patients, in *Serotonin and Behavior.* Edited by Barchas J, Usdin E, New York, Academic Press, 1972.
43. Prien RF, Caffey EM Jr, Klett CJ: Prophylactic effect of lithium carbonate in manic-depressive illness. *Arch Gen Psychiatr* **28:**337–341, 1973.
44. Stallone F, Shelley E, Mendlewicz and others: The use of lithium in affective disorders: 111. A double blind study of prophylaxis in bipolar illness. *Am J Psychiatr* **130:**9:1006–1010, 1973.
45. Fieve RR, Mendlewicz J: Lithium prophylaxis of bipolar manic depressive illness. *Psychopharmacologia (Berl)* **26:**1972.
46. Coppen A, Noguera R, Bailey J and others: Prophylactic lithium in affective disorders. *Lancet* **2:**275, 1971.
47. Baastrup PC, Poulsen JC, Schou M and others: Prophylactic lithium: Double-blind discontinuation in manic depressive and recurrent depressive disorders. *Lancet* **2:**326, 1970.
48. Prien RJ, Caffey EM, Klett CJ: Lithium prophylaxis in affective disorders. *Sci Proc Am Psychiatr Assoc* **126:**55, 1973.
49. Klerman GL and others: Treatment of depression by drugs and psychotherapy. *Sci*

Proc Am Psychiatr Assoc **126:**57–58, 1973.

50. Fieve RR: Lithium for manic depressive disorders. *New York State J Med* **71:**2219–2222, 1971.
51. Cooper JE and others: *Psychiatric Diagnosis in New York and London.* London, Oxford University Press, 1972, p. 105.

Ten

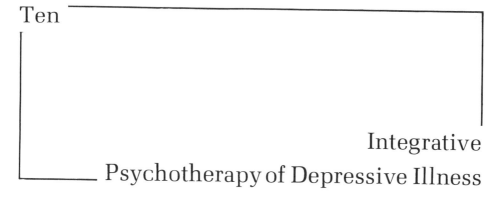

Integrative Psychotherapy of Depressive Illness

Louis Jolyon West, M.D.

I'll change my state with any wretch
Thou canst from gaol or dunghill fetch.
My pain's past cure, another Hell,
I may not in this torment dwell!
Now desperate I hate my life,
Lend me a halter or a knife. [1, p. 10].

In the now famous study where he lived at Christ Church College, Oxford, Robert Burton laid aside his pen on December 5, 1620, after writing the last lines of his masterpiece, *The Anatomy of Melancholy* (1). The first comprehensive treatise on depression, it had occupied him intermittently for many years. In many ways it remains unrivaled to this day.

From personal experience, Burton was an expert on melancholy. Although his symptoms were never overwhelming, they were painful enough; he experienced episodes of total gloom against a background state of genteel sadness, a scholar's *Weltschmerz,* an appreciation of the existential impasse of his own life and time. But every imaginable type of depression was grist for the mill of his leisurely scholarship, his endless curiosity, and his microscopic eye for detail.

Burton well knew how difficult it was to remedy a depressive episode. "For this particular disease, him that shall take upon him to cure it . . . will have to be a Magician, a Chemist, a Philosopher, an Astrologer . . ." (1, p. 390).

Nevertheless, no matter how difficult treatment might be, Burton realized the importance and the inevitability of attempting it. Furthermore, he appreciated the central necessity for a psychotherapeutic approach. "Whosoever he is that shall hope to cure this malady . . . must first rectify these passions and perturbations of the mind; the chiefest cure consists in them" (1, p. 467).

While psychotherapy was seen by Burton to be essential, he did not consider it to be the sole or specific treatment for melancholy. Rather, he recommended an integration of various methods and approaches, depending on the patient and also on the nature, intensity, and course of the depression together with its response to various aspects of therapy. Burton described numerous adjuncts to psychotherapy, including diet, rest, exercise and other physical activity, ventilation, correction of bowel functions, provision of ample sleep, "rectification of terrible dreams," help from friends, music, environmental manipulations of various kinds, sexual intercourse, religious counseling, symptomatic treatment of concomitant physical complaints (which he called "hypochondriacal"), various recreations including chess and the visiting of museums, intellectual distraction through reading and study, working at mathematical puzzles and verbal acrostics, other recreational therapies, occupational therapies, physiological therapies (including blood-letting, clysters, and purges), and an endless assortment of medications.

Depression is a symptom and not a disease, even though some diseases may be named after it; one is reminded of the typologies of fever before specific pathogenesis was defined. The indications and contraindications for treatment of depression should, of course, be based as far as possible on an understanding of cause and effect relationships in pathogenesis. This holds true even when the treatment itself is empirical, as in the use of such techniques as hypnotherapy, behavior therapy, or chemotherapy for the relief of symptoms. It also holds true even if symptomatic relief is the patient's only stated desire.

There are dozens of contemporary psychotherapies defined by different names; they all have characteristics in common. Sometimes the differences between them are minor to the point of apparent irrelevance; sometimes the differences are profound. There is virtually no brand of psychotherapy that has not been used for treatment of depression. Therefore, a brief look at the classification of psychotherapies may be in order. At least seven criteria for classifying psychotherapies are in common use.

Classification of Psychotherapies

1. Psychotherapies may be classified according to the conceptual orientation of the therapist. This may incorporate his theoretical view of psychiatric illness, of personality structure and function, or of the therapeutic process itself. Such conceptualizations, and the names of the related treatments, usually derive from the teachings of their originators. Thus we find psychotherapies called Freudian, Jungian, Kleinian, Myerian, Sullivanian, even Skinnerian, and such. Psychoanalysis and the various psychoanalytically oriented modifications of it, now usually called *dynamic* psychotherapies, are good examples of conceptual classification. The *eclectic* approach, on the other hand, suggests a willingness to pick and choose among theories and accept what seems to be useful in each, but without commitment to a single major theoretical position. The term dynamic suggests the importance given by the therapist to understanding—and working with—the forces interacting within

the patient's personality to produce the illness. These forces are additionally seen as having an important influence (both intrapersonally and interpersonally) on the therapeutic process. As long as the therapist is dynamically oriented he is allowed considerable leeway in what he actually does without changing its classification (2).

2. Psychotherapies may also be named by their phenomenological and quantitative signs, symptoms, and behavioral manifestations of psychopathology, together with the direct process of changing them. Various behavior therapies and behavior modification techniques suggest themselves in this connection.

3. A third approach to classification of psychotherapy emphasizes the interpersonal circumstances of treatment, especially (but not necessarily) if it is other than one-to-one. Thus we find references to group therapy, family therapy, conjoint marital therapy, and so forth.

4. Another way of classifying psychotherapies places emphasis on a particular technique used in the treatment. Examples would include hypnotherapy, psychodrama, narcosynthesis, various specific environmental manipulations, transactional analysis, and such.

5. A fifth criterion is one that places emphasis on some presumably crucial events or experiences that are expected or produced in the course of treatment. Catharsis, gestalt, and primal scream are a few labels that come to mind.

6. Still another approach stresses the circumstances or constraints under which treatment takes place: emergency psychotherapy, brief psychotherapy, crisis intervention, and the like.

7. A seventh way of classifying psychotherapies gives a central place to the goals of treatment. Supportive therapy, insight therapy, and reality therapy might be examples. The sector psychotherapy of Felix Deutch is often placed somewhere between psychoanalysis and supportive therapy in its goals. Goal-oriented psychotherapy is, of course, very close to the medical model for treatment of disease.

Selection of Cases

There is much variation in the willingness of advocates of one or another of the psychotherapies to limit their employment of the method according to the nature of the illness. For example, nonprofessional psychotherapists are notoriously global in their approach. They place no limits on their method of choice, and often seem to feel that this particular method (dianetics, transcendental meditation, Christian Science, etc.) would benefit anyone regardless of his condition. Such nonprofessional methods are not infrequently attempted in treatment of depressions regardless of the type or intensity of illness.

On the other hand, psychoanalysis perhaps defines its conditions and applications with the greatest precision of all the psychotherapies. The orthodox psychoanalyst consulted by a depressed patient is unlikely to undertake psychoanalysis unless he has made a diagnosis of neurotic depressive reaction (as contrasted with senile, involutional, manic-depressive, organic, postpartum, and other varieties of depression generally held to be less suitable for classical analysis). The analyst is also likely to look for a number of characteristics in the patient that suggest suitability for treatment by psychoanalysis. For example, an appropriate case would be young, intelligent, well-motivated (i.e., in considerable emotional discomfort), free of major environmental turmoil, capable of enduring the stresses and strains of the procedure but also capable of experiencing and describing strong emotions, able to meet the conditions of treatment (i.e., to appear in the office at the appointed time regularly, reliably, and frequently), psychologically minded, and capable of good object relations and thus of an analyzable transference.

Needless to say, many therapists who do not limit themselves to psychoanalysis but who engage in long-term dynamically oriented psychotherapy are likely to be somewhat less rigorous in defining indications for treatment. Those doing brief, dynamic psychotherapy with more limited goals or foci of treatment [e.g., the "psychoanalytic therapy" of French and Alexander (3)] may be even more inclusive in their scope.

My concern here, however, is to describe an approach to the psychotherapy of depression that will be generally applicable in all—or nearly all—cases. It is an approach based on the twin concepts that there is no such thing as a depressed patient who cannot be treated, and that a well-trained general psychiatrist can treat any depressed patient if he must. This is not to suggest that every patient can be cured, or even significantly improved by treatment at a given time, but rather that in undertaking treatment, no matter what the circumstances, the physician fulfills a basic function that is better for the patient than neglect. Furthermore, while there may always be someone somewhere better qualified or more highly skilled than oneself, that does not relieve each psychiatrist of the necessity to function in a competent way when the responsibility is his.

Integrative Psychotherapy

For some years I have been utilizing and teaching an approach that might best be called integrative psychotherapy. It is difficult to define, but would probably be classified in the goal-oriented group (the last) of those listed above. Many colleagues engaged in the modern general practice of psychiatry are in fact employing such an approach, regardless of what it might be called. Wolberg has been teaching it for years (4).

Integrative psychotherapy, in the sense that I am using it here, lays a heavy burden on the verb, "to integrate," and its derivatives. The approach is integrative in two orientations (*goals* of treatment and *processes* of treatment), and in three senses within each of those orientations. My conceptualization of it is outlined below.

1. *The integrative goal.* The goal of integrative psychotherapy is to restore and promote the patient's integrity in three senses: functional wholeness, existential continuity, and adaptational relevance.

a. *Functional wholeness.* Integration here means successful utilization, and coordinated interaction, of the several components of the self, which permits maximal fulfillment of the potentialities of the whole. Integrative psychotherapy in this sense is a healing process; it restores and promotes healthy personality function in mood, thought, and behavior.

b. *Existential continuity.* Integration here means the constant and fruitful extraction of the personal lessons of the past—of historical reality—for comprehension of the present, and for utilization in the future. Integrative psychotherapy in this sense is an educational, maturational, growth-provoking process; it restores and promotes integration of the evolving self through time.

c. *Adaptational relevance.* Integration here means a balanced or harmonious relationship with the physical, social, and moral environment, which engenders wisdom to appreciate and preserve biosocially sound value systems, courage to effect changes in the environment in keeping with such values, and tolerance meanwhile for the inevitable ambiguities, frustrations, and suffering of life in the real world—what might be called the innate stresses of the human condition. Integrative psychotherapy in this sense is a philosophically and ethically enriching process; it restores and promotes humane sensibilities.

2. *The integrative process.* The integrative process in psychotherapy connotes the coordinated utilization of methods that are scientifically derived, patient-centered, and professionally committed.

a. *Scientifically derived.* Integration here means drawing on and judiciously applying knowledge from the various biomedical and psychosocial sciences (including knowledge of personality development, structure, and functional dynamics). Integrative psychotherapy in this sense is applied science; it brings together and integrates a variety of information, focusing it upon specific human problems.

b. *Patient-centered.* Integration here means analysis and consideration of the patient's needs, wishes, assets, liabilities, strengths, and weaknesses, and the formulation of indications and contraindications for specific therapeutic modalities based on clinical experience. Integrative psychotherapy in this sense is a healing art; it integrates and utilizes various appropriate treatment techniques, singly or in combination, and constantly revalidates or modifies them according to their actual effectiveness in each individual case.

c. *Professionally committed.* Integration here means the incorporation of various requirements for ethical safeguards (e.g., confidentiality, informed consent) during treatment, interpersonal responsibilities in the doctor-patient relationship, and the simultaneous social responsibilities of a licensed professional person. Integrative psychotherapy in this sense is morally legitimate, and subsumes the professional integrity of the therapist in his commitments to the patient and to society.

Thus the integrative psychotherapy of depressive illness must deliberately integrate various knowledge, methodologies, techniques, and values into a consistent whole. It is not the purpose of this discussion to define integrative psychotherapy in every possible application. For example, I do not try to specify how it might relate to the particular use of psychoanalytic therapy for certain cases of reactive depression, pharmacological therapies for unipolar periodic depression, electroconvulsive therapy for involutional melancholia, environmental manipulation for adolescent situational depression, pastoral counseling for the depression of bereavement, stimulation and cuddling for the depressed neglected infant, a highly structured milieu for the senile depression, and the like. As indicated previously, an element of depression may enter into every known psychiatric syndrome, even mania.

If the primary thrust of treatment can be directed toward the basic disorder rather than the symptomatology of any illness, well and good. Unfortunately much treatment of depressive illness is still empirical and symptomatic, even when theory suggests, for example, psychogenesis, or excessive monoamine oxidase, or both. There is much to be said for the formulation of general psychotherapeutic guidelines in approaching patients with depression, whether depression is the primary problem or merely one of several significant issues in the creation of an overall treatment strategy. It is to the formulation and integration of such overall guidelines to the psychotherapy that this discussion is addressed.

The idea of "success" in treatment of depression is that the patient be restored to what would be for him a normal mood state, without serious mishap, and that his subsequent adjustment at least be in some measure stabilized, improved, or enhanced. In greater detail, successful treatment could be defined as full achievement of the goals set forth in item 1 of the description of integrative psychotherapy (above). It should be noted, however, that success does not imply either immediate symptomatic relief or a guarantee against recurrence.

Utilizing traditional criteria it might be stated that psychoanalytically oriented individual psychotherapy would be most appropriate for the patient with a neurotic illness having depressive symptomatology (2); that group methods are most likely to be effective with depressive patients classified as character or behavior disorders (including alcoholics and addicts) (5); and that brief supportive psychotherapy and milieu therapy are the most appropriate adjuncts for patients whose depressive symptoms are manifestations of a psychosis for which physiological or pharmacological methods are indicated as the primary forms of treatment (6). However, extensive clinical experience inevitably demonstrates the limitations of such guidelines. Each case must be evaluated in terms of a great many variables, and the overall treatment strategy must be comprehensive, flexible, and subject to modification or change. Thus I have seen a patient with involutional melancholia respond to psychotherapy alone; I have seen a neurotic depressive patient, quite resistant to a psychoanalytic approach, experience an apparent cure through a Synanon type of residential therapy even though drugs were not a problem in the case; I have seen a chronically depressed alcoholic, for whom AA had failed, pastoral counseling foundered, and supportive psychobiological therapies by physicians proved useless, finally obtain complete and apparently permanent achievement of normal mood and abstemious behavior through classical psychoanalysis by a lay analyst. Every experienced student of depressive illness has made similar observations. Some cases to illustrate the fundamental need for flexibility in integrative psychotherapy are described below.

Illustrative Case 1

John Doe was a 67-year-old accountant; he was divorced with two children, and had no prior history of major psychiatric disorder. He was employed by a large company with a secure position for many years. Recently the question of retirement had come up, which produced moderate anxiety and mild depression and resulted in some impairment of performance on the job.

Mr. Doe's employers reassured him that he would be retained indefinitely (even though he could retire comfortably) if he wished to work, but insisted that he have a thorough physical check-up, his first in several years. It was found that the patient had lost considerable vision in both eyes as the result of a condition that was, fortunately, correctable by surgery.

Following the surgical procedures there was a period of hospitalization during which Mr. Doe was without vision, and a longer period during which his sight gradually returned. Meanwhile the nurses noticed that he had become morose, withdrawn, and frequently tearful. He was eating poorly and became constipated. Insomnia became a severe problem. Intermittently agitated for no apparent reason, the patient gradually grew almost mute. Psychiatric consultation revealed a depression of major proportions with somatic manifestations, suicidal thoughts, feelings of worthlessness and hopelessness, psychomotor retardation, and depressive delusions, including one that he was being poisoned by the hospital to rid society of him because he was an evil and worthless man.

The patient was transferred to the psychiatry service. A fairly busy, highly structured routine was organized for him. Two brief (20-minute) visits daily by the therapist were scheduled for the first month of his psychiatric hospitalization. Medications that had been prescribed on the surgical service variously for agitation, for insomnia, and for depression were discontinued. A vigorous, integrative approach to psychotherapy began to yield some improvement by the end of a month.

The patient's delusional ideas were ignored except for reassuring statements by the therapist whenever the patient mentioned them—which became less and less. Considerable attention was paid to Mr. Doe's life situation, the meaning for him of continuing to work, and his relations with his two brothers (one older, one younger) and his children. After the first month psychotherapy was rescheduled to comprise three 45-minute sessions weekly. The patient was queried about his suicidal preoccupations, which were revealed to have preceded the eye surgery by at least 6 months. The meaning of death to him was repeatedly discussed in therapy, and found to be equated with uselessness, which in turn was related to retirement. The paucity of outside interests in the patient's life was reviewed. Old hobbies and long-neglected recreations were resurrected. Contact was made with his employer. The idea of Mr. Doe's gradually cutting down his time on the job—at a rate he himself could set—rather than either abrupt retirement or continued full-time employment (which he feared he could not handle) was approved.

Meanwhile his whole life was reviewed in psychotherapy. He was repeatedly reassured about his usefulness in the past and his continued value as a person. The meaning of the eye surgery was discussed. The patient spontaneously referred to the procedure as equivalent to a castration. "Without my vision I'm totally impotent; you might as well cut off my balls." This was then related to his attitude toward work as the manifestation of masculinity, and retirement as the loss of it: "Retire and I would just turn into an old woman."

For a man who apparently had never been very psychologically minded, Mr. Doe was able to make surprising use of the psychotherapeutic process. The relationship with the therapist was initially quite dependent, but gradually changed to one capable of supporting challenge and assertion of autonomy. By the third month of psychiatric treatment the patient was on partial hospitalization status, with progressively more time spent at home. He was then discharged and seen as an outpatient for two more months twice weekly, and three subsequent months once a week. Three years later this patient is still well, and still working, although taking more time off for recreation and travel. This has been abetted by the influence of his new wife, a widow he had known for some years, but decided to marry only after psychotherapy and his recovery from the depressive illness.

The decision to attempt integrative psychotherapy alone, rather than to combine it with chemotherapy or electroconvulsive therapy in this case of psychotic depressive illness, was based on rather definite criteria (fairly acute onset, obvious precipitating factors of great psychosocial significance, previous mental stability, etc.). The discontinuation of medication at the onset was an important step. I sometimes think that one of the most important advantages to a psychotherapist in being a physician is not so much the authority to prescribe medication as it is the authority to discontinue it. Of course, if there had been an urgent need to provide this patient with specific medication as an adjunct to psychotherapy, it would have been done at least for a limited time. As it was, no drugs were necessary.

The role of environmental stress in the genesis of depression has been much discussed, recently by Thomson and Hendrie (7). But regardless of the effect of particular stressful events, the meaning of those events to the patient must be included in the integrative psychotherapy of each case.

Illustrative Case 2

Mrs. Mary Roe was a 42-year-old housewife with a history of several depressive episodes in the past. The first one, when she was 18, was occasioned by starting college, which was also her first time away from home. She had been hospitalized briefly at that time and received six electroconvulsive treatments. She dropped out of college but returned the next year and was graduated in due course. Her second depression took place shortly after Mrs. Roe's husband was called into military service, leaving her home alone with their first child, then an infant. The patient was seen by a psychiatrist who suggested that she return with her daughter to her mother's home. This she did, and the depression gradually abated. A third depression was diagnosed after the birth of her second child, when she was unable to resume household responsibilities for many months. Various medications were administered to her during this illness. Some were discontinued because of side effects.

The present illness had no obvious precipitating factor. It was a depression of gradual onset, with loss of ability to cope with the problems of homemaking and everyday life. The patient would sit for long periods of time staring out the window at the passing traffic. She complained of insomnia, apathy, loss of interest "in everything," and admitted suicidal thoughts. She had been saving up a supply of sleeping capsules, "in case it gets intolerable." Marital sexual intercourse, usually satisfactory, had become repugnant. The oldest child, now in her first year of college, had, she was sure, "no more use for me." The younger (male) child, a high school sophomore, was "too much for me to handle; he deserves better." Her death would be a relief to the family; her husband could remarry a far better wife (and mother for the children) than she was.

The decision was made to treat this patient in the office and to avoid hospitalization if possible. A tricyclic antidepressant was used for a time as an adjunct to psychotherapy, but the dosage was gradually reduced and the drug was soon discontinued as good rapport was established and the patient became well involved in psychotherapy. This consisted of 1-hour sessions, three times a week for 3 months, then twice a week for 3 more, then once weekly (with some interruptions) for about 8 more months. Mrs. Roe recovered and has remained well for several years without further treatment and without medication.

Of great importance in this case were family dynamics, too complex to discuss here in detail, but clearly significant to the patient as Mrs. Roe came to understand them. Great dependency on—and ambivalence toward—her mother was a central issue. The separation from her mother at the time of college matriculation was experienced as a great loss of security, with accompanying death wishes toward the mother for having "sent her away," and also fears of acting out sexually promiscuous fantasies as a punishment for the mother. Each of the three subsequent depressions had, in a different way, followed a regression related to life stress, and a recapitulation of the earlier depression. The basic precipitating factor in the most recent depression had in fact been the daughter's departure for college; this daughter was named after the patient's mother, resembled her, and indeed had grown to relate to the patient more like a mother than a daughter.

Integrative psychotherapy in this case utilized a variety of resources and techniques. At first the therapist was quite active, but later became more nondirective. Some role playing was eventually employed in psychotherapeutic sessions, with the therapist cast first as the mother, then as the patient, and finally as the departed daughter. On two occasions, during periods of apparent stalemate, and at the patient's request, hypnosis was employed to foster recollection and abreaction. Several sessions included the patient's husband, in what amounted to a period of conjoint marital therapy.

This patient gained considerable insight through psychotherapy. Rearrangements were made in her life. The intense focus on family relationships was diminished by her new-found willingness to participate in community activities of genuine value to her. The League of Women Voters became particularly important to this patient, and has provided a continuing source of real satisfaction long after psychotherapy became a thing of the past.

Illustrative Case 3

Betsy Coe was a 19 year-old college student who, following a freshman year of creditable work, had become immensely discouraged, depressed, and "bored with it all." After neglecting sophomore classes for many weeks she withdrew from school to the dismay of her parents, who insisted that she seek psychiatric help.

The patient appeared listless and sad. She repeatedly expressed boredom, disinterest not only in school but also in everything, and a sense of great emptiness in herself. While lacking in appetite she nevertheless had been stuffing herself with food for months; as a result her previously petite figure was now swollen with 20 lbs. of extra flesh. She described herself as sleeping "constantly"; in fact she often lay in bed doing nothing for hours, although not asleep. Efforts to ascertain the circumstances that had produced this illness were met with great resistance. It appeared at first that some romantic disappointment might have played a role. The patient also admitted (grudgingly, a bit at a time) a sense of great disillusionment and melancholy at the state of the world, including the (then) war in southeast Asia, the prospect of thermonuclear holocaust, the ecological deterioration of the planet, the population explosion, and such. The patient became extremely opaque whenever the subject of drug use was introduced. However, it gradually became evident that she had experimented with LSD on several occasions. She smoked marijuana intermittently but not in large amounts.

Because of this patient's resistance to communication with adults (including parents, teachers, and the therapist), it was decided to involve her with an ongoing therapy group of college-age individuals (mostly students or former students), all of whom had been in serious trouble with drugs. For several months the patient met with the group once a week, and also individually with the therapist once a week.

The group had a swift and substantial impact on this patient. She was soon expressing strong feelings. Her depressed mood, apathy, and boredom rapidly disappeared. Instead there was an outpouring of scorn and disgust toward her parents, particularly her father, a protestant minister. It soon became evident that a combination of influences at college (including both classwork and peer group social learning situations) had caused her to lose her religious faith, and with it her confidence in the entire "establishment" which her father represented.

Rapport with the therapist began to improve as soon as the one-to-one relationship was modified by the group therapy sessions. Seeing her peers make use of the therapist's willingness to help enabled the patient to do so as well. A variety of topics were explored with increasing candor, feeling, and trust. These feelings reached a climax when the therapist supported the patient in a showdown with her family, in which she refused to return to college. Instead the patient—with the therapist's help and the family's reluctant concurrence—undertook a placement with VISTA as a volunteer teacher's assistant in the rural South.

This patient has maintained a relationship with the therapist "as a friend" by telephone and letter ever since. Following a period of volunteer service she returned to college and has since been graduated and married. She has begun work on a master's degree in education. Her symptoms have not recurred.

There are many types of depressed adolescents, and differential approaches to treatment have been well described by specialists in this area, such as Anthony (8). My purpose here is to show the necessity for adapting to the individual patient's particular needs, integrating both the patient's characteristics and the available therapeutic resources into the most promising possible strategy of treatment.

General Elements in Psychotherapy of Depression

As the foregoing suggests, integrative psychotherapy of depressive illness is predicated on the proposition that psychotherapy will be of significant value in the treatment of every case of depression, regardless of the basic diagnosis, regardless of other psychopathology, regardless of coexisting physical disease (even including brain damage), and regardless of other treatment modalities (e.g., medication and physiological therapies) that may also be employed. It charges the physician to foster integration of the patient in every possible way, and to draw on all resources available to him (the therapist) in the fulfillment of that responsibility.

There are four "Rs" in the general strategy of integrative psychotherapy of depression: rapport, reassurance, revelation, and reorganization.

1. *Rapport.* Most experienced clinicians realize that the psychopathology

of depression poses unusual problems in the doctor-patient relationship. While the depressed patient may feel very dependent on the therapist, he may not feel at all close to him. Often he feels unworthy of receiving help from the therapist, or incapable of responding to the therapist's efforts. The element of anxiety that may foster relief through an early positive transference ("transference cure") in some neurotic disorders is much less likely to produce such a result when depression is present to any significant degree. Thus the therapist must make a greater effort to establish sufficient rapport with his depressed patient than is usually called for in other illnesses. This may necessitate frequent short visits between regular longer ones.

In developing good rapport it is important to utilize every possible point of contact with the depressed patient. This may require considerable study of his family, his business, his hobbies, and his personal history. Sometimes a virtually mute patient will look up with surprise and begin at least a halting conversation on some subject like a long-neglected childhood interest, a college sport of decades before, an exciting political event of yesteryear, or an old friend.

A quiet approach, warm and accepting, but also firm and objective, is generally the most useful in initiating a therapeutic relationship with a depressed patient. The noncommittal, detached, or "blank screen" image is not likely to promote rapport, and often serves merely to prolong the initiation of significant psychotherapeutic work in cases of depression. On the other hand, an overvigorous, assertive, aggressive approach may drive the patient away from the therapist and create a sense of distance between them. Boisterous *bonhomie*, complete with jokes and slaps on the back, adopted in an effort to cheer up the patient, is one of the most contraindicated of all approaches. While it may seem to work temporarily for friends and relatives to behave this way toward a depressed person, his answering smile is likely to be a false one, and behind it his sense of alienation from other people will be exacerbated. Certainly a professional therapist should not properly begin a treatment relationship with the induction of pretense, or the promotion of distancing behavior, in the patient he is supposedly trying to help.

2. *Reassurance.* The depressed patient often seems to experience an insatiable hunger for verbal reassurance, but a lack of capacity to derive any satisfaction or relief from it. It is a mistake to believe that because reassurance fails to produce an obvious response, it is useless or even antitherapeutic. On the contrary, the depressed patient has a genuine need for reassurance, and the therapist should be prepared to express it, calmly but warmly and without irritation, over and over again. It is like the use of cooling compresses in cases of prolonged fever—symptomatic treatment that is beneficial, not only for its transient comfort, but also for the care and concern it represents.

At the same time it is important to let the patient know that the therapist is aware of a depressed person's inability to take much comfort from reassurance. Depressed patients who have been told hundreds of times that their mood will return to normal eventually may agree that it is possible for recovery to come, but still feel no real emotional comfort from the prospect of relief. Even the recollection of former happiness is often clouded by the immediate gloom.

Past days of joy are often seen in depressive retrospect as a time of self-deception. Only the present depression is real; happiness—past or future—is merely an illusion.

Nevertheless, after recovery from depression, often the patient will express appreciation for the reassurances that were given during the depths of despair. To be most effective, reassurance should be more than verbal. Many procedures arranged for the hospitalized depressed patient—routine group activities, occupational and recreational therapies, and even the administration of medication—can exert a valuable reassuring effect far beyond any therapeutic specificities they may possess.

Every effort should be made to keep the depressed patient physically active. This of course is difficult because of the sense of apathy and listlessness that accompanies depression. However, group pressures, personal encouragement, and even physical assistance to keep the patient moving should be undertaken. Physical exercise has a positive benefit, not only because it has salubrious psychophysiological effects, but also because it exerts a constant reassurance to the patient that he can expect what his caretakers obviously must be expecting: that he will once again be capable of vigorous and constructive action. Monotonous solo exercises (e.g., walking, jogging, or swimming laps), less appealing to most patients (who are likely to prefer games involving other people), are often surprisingly acceptable to the depressed individual. Numerous other reassuring maneuvers will suggest themselves in each individual case, and can often be developed from natural opportunities that arise in the course of individual or group psychotherapy.

3. *Revelation.* The process of self-discovery is basic to all the dynamic psychotherapies. However, it should play an important part in every psychotherapeutic relationship. This holds true even for the most symptomatic approaches such as behavior therapy and hypnotherapy; often the patient is learning far more about himself than either he or the therapist realizes. Frequently, the mental content of the depressed person includes ruminations over putative discoveries that are ego-dystonic ("I've discovered that I'm just a hypocrite." "I've learned to despise myself for what I really am." "All these years I've been so destructive, so selfish, so inadequate; now I can see it.")

The therapist must deal with these depressive revelations, or pseudorevelations, and incorporate them into an overall strategy of improved self-understanding for the patient. This may range from increased but fairly limited awareness of self in some cases to profound emotional insight in others. To be consistent with the concepts of integrative psychotherapy, the therapist should attempt to accomplish as much as possible for the patient and be guided by his awareness of both potentialities and limiting factors. He should be prepared to expand or modify treatment goals as therapy progresses, and as new variables intervene or stand revealed.

4. *Reorganization.* This refers both to the personality of the patient, and to his life style. It is often necessary to spend considerable time in assembling, synthesizing, and integrating the total experience of the patient after his mood has lifted, but before he is ready to resume full normal living. Discussions must include a review of the illness, its precursors, precipitants, and course.

The relationship with the therapist should receive attention, whether it be a straightforward conscious look at the doctor-patient relationship at the end of a relatively brief period of mostly supportive psychotherapy, or a profound analysis of the transference prior to termination of a classical psychoanalysis.

For the patient to integrate all that he has learned about himself into his functional personality structure as it is emerging from a depression will usually require a considerable amount of deliberate work in psychotherapy. An important component of this will often prove to be the formulating of specific plans for a healthier organization of the patient's post-illness life. This can include anything from rearrangement of schedules (e.g., providing for frequent short vacations rather than for one long one that somehow never gets taken) to profound revision of some major interpersonal relationships (e.g., conjoint sexual counseling together with the marital partner to resolve some long-standing frustrations of erotic needs).

Whatever the strategies of reorganization on all levels may be, they should take into account the risk of future depressions, and should include review of preventive measures, early warning signs, and procedures for instituting early intervention if needed in event of a recurrence.

The need to integrate what has been learned, and to put that knowledge to use, can be found in all types of depressive reactions, even including depression in a dying patient.

Managing the Suicidal Risk

To a greater or lesser degree every depressed patient poses some risk of self-destruction. This issue must be made explicit from the very beginning of the therapeutic relationship (9). The matter should be discussed often, and in detail, to ensure a good open channel of communication about it. An inexperienced therapist sometimes will avoid discussing suicide with a depressed patient, as though fearing to give him the idea of killing himself, as though discussing it might appear to sanction it, or as though the mention of suicide would suggest to the patient a lack of confidence in the patient or mistrust on the therapist's part. Such avoidance can only work to the patient's disadvantage and obtund rapport and actually increase the suicidal risk.

Another common misconception about suicide risk holds that those who threaten suicide never commit it. Actually it has long been known that those who commit suicide do, in fact, communicate their intention in advance—often to a physician (10). To be sure, most of those who contemplate suicide, or even openly discuss their desire for death, in fact do not take their own lives. Furthermore, most suicidal gestures are not fatal. However, even those attempts that are not consciously intended to succeed may represent a more profound death wish than the perpetrator realizes. Because of this wish sometimes an accident may be fatal, when it is patently an avoidable accident.

Shneidman (11) has emphasized the importance of recognizing and quantitatively evaluating both *perturbation* and *lethality* in assessing suicidal risk. It is important to continue this evaluation during the course of psychotherapy, and to be wary of sudden changes in either characteristic. An abrupt decrease in perturbation may be accompanied by a profound increase in lethality. This circumstance can lead to a profoundly misleading external appearance.

Such a patient may present a surprisingly cheerful facade to give the therapist the impression that there has been a sharp turn for the better. Actually this patient has crystallized a firm intention to commit suicide, sees it as a solution—the only solution—to all his problems, and is relieved at the resolution of his prolonged conflict over whether to live or die. At this juncture the alert therapist will often discern some type of farewell message. If he has been maintaining good rapport, and open communication on the subject of suicide, he may still save the patient by seriously challenging him to reveal the cause of his peculiar cheerfulness. At a time of separation (e.g., a vacation—especially if the patient comes up with an unexpected plan for one) the therapist should be particularly alert.

When the topic of suicide is rendered explicit, it may well become the center of much struggle between therapist and patient in psychotherapy. The essence of such a struggle is the patient's reiterated statement of desire for death, or even his declaration of intention to take his own life, and the therapist's attempts to keep the patient alive. In this struggle the best rule for the therapist is simply to persevere, and never to accept the patient's proposition that death would be the best solution to his problem.

There are some psychotherapists who maintain a hands-off attitude regarding suicide. "If you really want to kill yourself I can't stop you, so let's discuss something else." There are even those therapists who, on occasion, take a bolder course, challenging the patient's real determination to die, or even offering him the wherewithal to do away with himself. Such maneuvers may on occasion produce the desired effect; they may force the patient to shift to a more constructive line of discourse; they may even mobilize some healthy anger by the patient toward the therapist and away from himself. (For more on "anger in" and "anger out," see below.)

However, I am generally opposed to the use of such tactics. They are altogether too risky. If death is on the patient's mind, it is best to deal with it—and to keep dealing with it as long as necessary—in the psychotherapeutic relationship. Deliberately angering the patient may lead to a serious—or successful—suicidal attempt as a means of hurting the therapist. Challenging the seriousness of the patient's suicidal intentions may lead to a dangerous suicidal act out of pride, to prove sincerity or even to retain the therapist's respect. And to shrug off the patient's suicidal talk may close a door of communication that should be kept open at all costs.

A Note on the Right to Die

Sooner or later the psychotherapist working with depressed patients will be challenged on his right to interfere with someone else's right to die. In fact, at the present time this question has become quite politicized. There are civil libertarians who seriously contend that the right to take one's own life is precious, and that psychiatrists have no prerogative to intervene. Needless to say, depressed patients will sometimes present the same argument.

The medical profession itself is not of one mind on this matter. However, my own view is quite clear, and I offer it here for whatever it may be worth to others. It is that the physician is sworn to preserve life. He should do so whenever dealing with a sentient being, regardless of stated preferences to the contrary, to the limit of his ability, using all resources—including both medical and legal—available to him. (I use the term sentient to differentiate suicidal patients from cases in which an attitude—or change of attitude—regarding death is biologically impossible: for example, newborn monstrosities with no functional tissue above the brain stem, or victims of accident or disease who have already suffered brain death and are being maintained mechanically in hospitals as heart-lung-kidney specimens.)

The experienced psychiatrist through the years is likely to see dozens—perhaps hundreds—of patients who have made serious suicidal attempts, but who somehow survived or were saved by heroic medical, surgical, and psychiatric intervention. With striking regularity such persons are glad to find themselves alive, and sooner or later will thank those who saved them, even though at the time rescue may have seemed to be against the patient's wish.

A rational person who firmly decides to bring his life to an end, and is not handicapped by major psychopathology, is very likely to succeed. In fact, many rational people secretly preserve for themselves the prospect of suicide as an emergency escape hatch if life becomes intolerable. Some such people are likely to react with anger at the idea of psychiatrists being given the power by society to intervene in the final extremity, and to frustrate the outcome of such an ultimately personal decision.

Yet it has been my experience that even such seemingly rational individuals, when saved by the merest chance from death at their own hands, have been grateful that life was still vouchsafed them after all. In my view, the responsible psychiatrist is fully justified in exercising his responsibility to preserve life in every case where it is possible to do so. Occasions when the psychiatrist is subsequently rebuked by a patient for having saved his life will prove in practice to be exceedingly rare.

A Note on Depression and Aggression

It has long been accepted as a general rule, in the psychotherapy of depression, that the depressed patient suffers from hostility that he has somehow turned against himself instead of directing it against its appropriate object. Certainly many suicides have revenge as a motive (although probably no more than are motivated by hopelessness, desire for escape, or desire for reunion with the departed). Karl Menninger once noted that every suicide is half a murder. More recently, West (12) has provided data to show the frequency of the reverse: in England one third of all murderers eventually commit suicide; in Denmark the figure is approximately 40%.

Many acts of violent aggression are in fact acts of despair (13). Some 10% of those who call the Los Angeles Suicide Prevention Center are seeking help for impulses to commit, not suicide, but murder. Many others are not sure whether they want to kill themselves, others, or both.

The implications of all this for the psychotherapy of depression are considerable. A simple, hydraulic approach to aggression in the depressed patient—that it should be mobilized and directed outward—may have tragic consequences. While it is true that deeply depressed patients are often self-condemnatory and excessively uncritical of others, it is not necessarily true that they will be otherwise even when they have recovered (14). Sometimes the restoration of competitiveness, aggressiveness toward others, and the capacity to express anger are simply manifestations of a return to previous personality functioning in a recovering patient, whose energy, vitality, and self-confidence are restored.

The psychotherapist will be well advised to include work on both passivity and aggressiveness in his transactions with the depressed patient, but to avoid the basic assumption that it is necessarily beneficial to encourage the patient to express hostility other than that which comes naturally as integration proceeds. Artificial maneuvers to humiliate or outrage a depressed patient in the hope of inducing an outburst of hostility—presumably for his own benefit—have been employed by certain psychiatrists and institutions in the past. I recommend against such maneuvers. At best they are unnecessary; at worst, inhumane.

Psychotherapy of Bereavement, Mourning, and Grief

Freud classically delineated the differences between mourning and melancholia. Most of the literature on treatment of depression concentrates on the latter. However, it would be a mistake to exclude painful depressive reactions to life's real losses from a discussion of therapeutic approaches to depression.

Every symptom of depressive illness, from the mildest to the most severe, can be manifested in certain cases of bereavement. Persons of nearly all ages may be affected. It is not necessary that the lost one be a spouse, a parent, a sibling, or a child; it is the nature and strength of the emotional bond that counts. In occasional instances, even the loss of a highly cathected pet may cause a deep and meaningful grief reaction; on rare occasions such a reaction maybe of life-threatening intensity.

Several studies, such as those by Rahe (15) and by Parkes (16), reveal the profound psychophysiological impact of grief. Illness, accident, suicide, or death from any cause are far more likely to occur during the year following bereavement than would be statistically expected in a less stressful year in the life of that person at that age.

Clear data are not yet available to correlate the *circumstances* of bereavement with the severity of the consequent grief reaction. However, clinical impressions suggest that abrupt loss, especially by violence, is particularly traumatic for the survivors. With the numbers of violent deaths steadily rising in American cities, post-traumatic grief reactions among their survivors are becoming more and more frequent.

Other real losses in specific life situations may precipitate acute depressions nearly indistinguishable from the grief of bereavement. The loss of a highly valued position, of one's business, or of one's money can lead to a suicidal depressive reaction. The approach to therapy in such cases is not dissimilar from that for treatment of grief reactions in bereaved adults.

Many grief reactions go untreated because the patient, friends, and family consider the syndrome "natural." Often amateur assistance is rendered. Sometimes this can be quite effective. However, on occasion such efforts may be counterproductive, because of the relationships involved, or because simple procedural blunders make matters worse instead of better. Much psychotherapy of grief reactions is done by ministers and by family physicians. Some of these helpers are exceedingly wise and helpful; others are less so. The former are more likely to make an appropriate psychiatric referral than the latter.

Psychotherapy of grief reactions, while usually brief, is not always as brief as one might expect. Many of these depressions last a full year. A few persist for an even longer period of time. Treatment is based on the principles described previously, but with certain special considerations and areas of emphasis.

Acceptance of Mourning

From the outset it is important to establish and make clear that the therapist accepts the depressive grief reaction as being *natural,* but still justifying professional help. The patient should be made to understand that it is perfectly appropriate to seek and receive medical care for a naturally occurring health crisis which need not be considered a disease. An example that some patients find understandable is that of professional care during childbirth and the postnatal period for both mother and child.

Frequently, it will be found that a significant component of the patient's problem stems from the family's intolerance for his grief, or his own efforts to conceal it to protect others from discomfort or inconvenience. It is important for the therapist to give the patient permission to continue to grieve, and personal support while the sadness runs its course. The patient may need help in dealing with other people who are interfering with his need to experience the pain and sorrow which his bereavement requires of him.

The fact that an illness has a natural history, or course, does not obviate the desirability or need for treatment. Suffering can be modified, the course abbreviated, complications prevented, and the aftermath made healthier through proper care during any health crisis, even one such as natural mourning that is self-limited. Reassurance that it is natural to suffer through mourning should include reassurance that in time the suffering will pass.

Acceptance of the Cessation of Mourning

A counterpart to the therapist's giving permission to grieve is giving permission to improve. The patient should be made to understand that the therapist expects him to recover sooner or later, and that to recover sooner does not signify lack of a true sense of loss or of a genuine devotion to the lost person. Swift improvement does not dishonor the dead, nor does prolonged depression honor them more, and the patient should be helped to see this.

Other Aspects of Psychotherapy of Grief Reactions

As is often the case with other depressive illnesses, the psychiatrist may be referred a patient suffering from an acute situational depressive illness only after others have seen him—and tried to treat him—first. The picture may have been confused by various medications since the very day of bereavement. It is not uncommon for physicians to administer heavy sedation to a person who has just experienced an unexpected, shocking loss. On rare occasions this may be justified. However, medication can also create complication rather than simplification in the total treatment of grief. One of the most useful things the psychiatrist can do when such a patient finally reaches him is to discontinue the psychotropic medications (frequently of several varieties) that have been prescribed by well-meaning previous helpers. I have found it quite helpful to explain to the patient that it is important for him to experience his loss fully, to live and suffer through a clearly perceived and fully conscious grief, before he can recover properly and finally. This advice is usually received with gratitude, and the patient willingly gives up his assorted pills.

The actual work of psychotherapy in grief reactions must explore and analyze in considerable detail the relationship of the bereaved to the lost person, and how that relationship fits in with the rest of his life. Discussion of ambivalence toward the loved one, and guilt related to death wishes, is inevitable in such therapy. To be dealt with effectively these points need not necessarily be labored. Nor must they usually be forced, through the interpretation of a dream, slip of the tongue, or some other discovery. Usually the mixed feelings will be expressed in the fullness of time, depending on the patient's trust in the therapist and the effectiveness of their relationship. If they do not emerge spontaneously, it may be best to let well enough alone, especially if a good recovery is underway.

There is an almost universal sense of guilt by the living toward their dead. This seems to stem in part from the sense of relief at finding oneself still alive, regardless of how the loved one died. There is also frequently relief at the termination of an illness that was expensive, inconvenient, and painful for the watchers as well as for the dying person. Guilt may be increased by this sense of relief, and depression deepened thereby. Gentle, nonjudgmental guidance by the therapist into these areas of feeling, together with the therapist's acceptance and even his stated expectation that such conflicting emotions would naturally be present, often suffices to provide some relief. However, it will often prove necessary to go over this ground again and again.

Illustrative Case 4

Mr. Richard Rob was a 71-year-old, self-employed business man whose wife of nearly 50 years had died of cancer after a prolonged decline and a futile exploratory operation. Following her death he was inconsolable for many weeks, weeping often, avoiding the company of others, and rejecting attempts by friends and family to comfort him. Gradually he resumed something resembling his usual way of life, but with considerable persistence of depressive symptoms. He often appeared mournful, preoccupied, and remote. Crying spells were frequent. Always a moderate imbiber before, he began drinking heavily even in social settings, becoming maudlin and childish to the disgust of his companions (mostly relatives and their families). He complained of poor appetite (although weight loss was not great), constipation, insomnia, and an unshakable feeling of sadness and futility. His overall adjustment, at home and at work, was barely marginal.

Mr. Rob's two younger brothers spoke to him frequently about the necessity to pull himself together. They appreciated his loss; they missed their late sister-in-law too. But his endless weeping and seeming self-pity were becoming a nuisance to them. They repeatedly declared that life must go on. "Why?" he would reply. "To what purpose?" He was an agnostic who rejected the advances of clergymen.

The patient had no previous history of psychiatric disorder, and had always been considered a calm, rather passive, but good-natured individual who was relatively successful in business (despite lack of aggressiveness) through a combination of honesty, reliability, and family connections. Medical help was finally sought for his depression, first from the family physician, then from an internist who had also cared for Mr. Rob in the past. Each physician in turn prescribed various medications without success for several weeks. Then a psychiatric referral was made.

The mental status examination was consistent with a reactive depression in an aging patient. Mood was one of sorrow. There was an occasional sad apologetic smile, perhaps following a self-critical remark. Hopelessness and self-abnegation were prominent. Concentration was only fair. Reasoning and judgment were not severely impaired. Recent memory was fair for his age. The patient stated that he frequently longed for death, but felt he lacked the will to kill himself. There was much rumination about his wife and their life together, now lost forever. An assortment of minor physical complaints was described.

Integrative psychotherapy in 1-hour sessions on a twice-weekly basis was initiated. This was soon diminished to weekly, then fortnightly, then monthly, then on an open basis at his request (three more sessions during the next 5 months). Treatment altogether comprised 28 sessions over a period of nearly a year.

The patient was taking 11 different medications, some of recent prescription, others of long standing. In consultation with his internist I discontinued these one by one, until he was using none of them. Interestingly, one medicament was supposedly for high blood pressure. The patient had been using it for years; yet his hypertension did not return until many months after the drug was discontinued and the depression was gone. The hypertension, when it did return, was of a degree so mild that less than half the previous dose of medication now sufficed to control it. B-12 injections, testosterone injections, and several other procedures were also discontinued. The patient was placed on a single multivitamin capsule (with minerals) daily as his only dietary supplement.

From the onset of psychotherapy I told Mr. Rob to use no alcoholic beverages until further notice, with the understanding that he would be permitted a gradual return to moderate drinking in time. This instruction was accepted without difficulty, although he would occasionally forget and accept a drink before recalling his agreement to abstain. By the end of 6 months he was able to resume his premorbid drinking pattern (an evening cocktail, dinner wine, or sometimes a nightcap at bedtime) without ill effects.

Psychotherapy was active from the start. A strong rapport was established. The patient was allowed to ventilate extensively about his wife. Ambivalence, and guilt over death wishes toward her, were discussed first tentatively, then freely. Mr. Rob was advised that his brothers were mistaken in their reiterated belief that he had grieved long enough. Instead, reassurance was given that he was perfectly justified in continuing to mourn—it was natural, he need not be ashamed of it. By avoiding alcohol (and other drugs such as sedatives) he would be better able to control the social circumstances and outward behaviors previously related to his grieving. From the outset, frequent reassurance was also given about his acceptability and value as a person, and about the ultimate disappearance of the depression.

Carefully reviewed was the history of this patient's gradual decline of sexual feelings, both with age and in connection with his wife's illness and incapacity. Mr. Rob had not had intercourse with his wife (or anyone else) for more than 2 years before her death. Since losing her, he had experienced no sexual feelings whatsoever. He assumed and accepted the idea that he was "over the hill" sexually (i.e., permanently impotent).

The patient expressed surprise and disbelief at my suggestion that, as his depression lifted, there might well be a return of sexual desire. This proved to be the case. He began to make dates with younger (i.e., middle-aged) women after 3 months of psychotherapy. When his relatives protested ("Such women can only be after your money!") I advised him to ignore their objections; what did it matter, as long as he was enjoying—and not deceiving—himself? Less than a year later Mr. Rob married an attractive divorcee in her 50s. She was no fortune hunter; she was, in fact, more affluent than he. The marriage is proving to be quite happy in every way; including sexually, with mutually satisfactory intercourse every week or two. There has been no return of depressive symptomatology in this case for 2 years. The patient is now nearly 75.

In closing let me state again that there is nothing unique in the psychotherapy of the four cases described in this chapter. Many contemporary psychotherapists trained in general psychiatry use essentially the same flexible, integrative approach.

In each of the four cases discussed, the overall strategy of treatment was governed by the patient's needs, personality resources, and potentialities. However, it would have been possible to describe work with other depressed patients in whose treatment the use of medication played a greater part; or who were seen in more prolonged intensive psychotherapy; or whose families were involved throughout; or who were referred elsewhere after a brief period of evaluation (which always includes psychotherapy as well); or who were seen only a few times in an acute crisis intervention; or who fled treatment; or who committed suicide. I have tried simply to provide a reminder of the ubiquity of depressive symptomatology, a definition of the integrative approach being employed by many psychiatrists today, and an expression of confidence that such an approach can continue to develop, evolve, and become increasingly useful.

References

1. Burton R: *The Anatomy of Melancholy.* New York, Dutton, 1961.
2. Alexander F: Individual psychotherapy. *Psycholog Med* 8(2):110–115, March-April 1946.
3. Alexander F, French T: *Psychoanalytic Therapy.* New York, Ronald Press, 1946.
4. Wolberg LR: *The Technique of Psychotherapy (Parts One and Two).* New York, Grune & Stratton, 1967, 2nd ed.
5. Mowrer OH: New directions in the understanding and management of depression, in *The Future of Psychotherapy.* Edited by Frederick CJ, Boston, Little, Brown, 1969, pp. 317–360.
6. Castelnuovo-Tedesco P: Brief psychotherapeutic treatment of the depressive reactions. *Int Psych Clinics* 3(4):197–210, Winter 1967.
7. Thomson KC, Hendrie HC: Environmental stress in primary depressive illness. *Arch Gen Psychiatr* **26:**130–132, 1972.
8. Anthony EJ: Two contrasting types of adolescent depression and their treatment. *J Am Psa Assoc* **18**(4):841–859, October 1970.
9. Friedman P: Some considerations on the treatment of suicidal depressive patients. *Am J Psychiatr* **16:**379–386, 1962.

10. Shneidman ES, Ortega MJ (ed.): *Aspects of Depression.* Boston, Little, Brown, 1969.
11. Shneidman ES, Farberow N, Litman R: *The Psychology of Suicide.* New York, Science House, 1970.
12. West DJ: *Murder Followed by Suicide.* London, Heinemann, 1965.
13. Lion JR: The role of depression in the treatment of aggressive personality disorders. *Am J Psychiatr* **129**(3):347–349, 1972.
14. Friedman AS: Hostility factors and clinical improvement in depressed patients. *Arch Gen Psychiatr* **23**:524–537, 1970.
15. Rahe RH: Subjects' recent life changes and their near-future illness reports. *Ann Clin Res* **4**:250–265, 1972.
16. Parkes CM: The first year of bereavement: A long study of the reaction of London widows to the death of their husbands. *Psychiatry* **33**:444–467, 1970.

Eleven

Group Psychotherapy in the Treatment of Depression

Aaron Stein, M.D.

This chapter describes the utilization of group psychotherapy in the treatment of certain kinds of depression. The dynamics of certain types of depression make their treatment by means of group psychotherapy especially effective. The theoretical considerations are outlined and clinical illustrations are given.

Indications for the Use of Group Psychotherapy in the Treatment of Depression

It is well known that group psychotherapy is contraindicated for certain types of depression. Many workers have stated this: Foulkes (1); Slavson (2); Johnson (3); Wender (4); Day and Semrad (5); and Stein (6). Acute and severe depressions with marked withdrawal and particularly psychotic depressions including the depressed phase of manic-depressive psychoses and the involutional melancholias are *not* suitable for treatment with group psychotherapy and require other forms of treatment.

On the other hand, other types of depression have been considered suitable for treatment with group psychotherapy. As early as 1936, Wender stated that depressions without marked retardation could be treated with group psychotherapy. Johnson (3) felt that neurotic patients with depressive reactions were suitable for group psychotherapy. Day and Semrad (5) felt that both neurotic and psychotic types of depression could be tolerated in therapeutic groups and could be treated with group psychotherapy.

Of special interest is the fact that all of the writers above, especially Foulkes (1) and Slavson (2), state that character disorders are most suitable for treatment with group psychotherapy. This was said to be true of even relatively severe character disorders, particularly of the masochistic type.

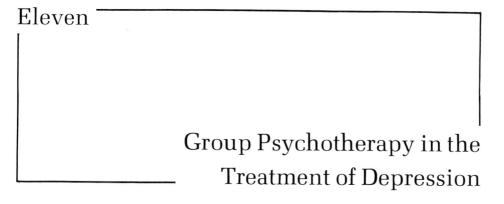

Many patients with character disorders tend to have more or less chronic underlying depressive reactions, and the exacerbations of this underlying depression frequently bring these patients to treatment. While the acute phase of depressive reactions associated with characterological disturbances may respond to antidepressants, the more chronic aspects of the depression in these patients do not respond to antidepressant medication. Also, treatment with ECT is largely unsuccessful in this type of depression.

Accordingly, the type of chronic depression associated with character disorders is helped most effectively by treatment of the basic pathology—the characterological disturbance. Here group psychotherapy is most useful. As the tensions and frustrations associated with the character disturbances are exposed and dealt with, the accompanying depression also subsides. This is particularly true of masochistic characterological disturbances.

The dynamic factors involved in the development of the depression associated with character disorders are described, particularly in relation to their treatment with group psychotherapy. Clinical illustrations are cited.

Psychodynamic Factors in Depression

Elsewhere in this volume, many of the etiologic factors thought to contribute to the development of depression are discussed. However, from the standpoint of describing the utilization of group psychotherapy in the treatment of depression, it is useful to discuss the dynamic factors involved in the development of depressive reactions. This is done from the psychoanalytic point of view, which for this writer has been found to be most useful in formulating the most effective form of treatment for certain types of depression. Obviously, others may find other viewpoints of the dynamics of depression equally or even more useful in understanding the condition and in planning treatment.

The psychoanalytic view of the psychodynamics of depression, including a review of the important literature, has been very thoroughly described by Fenichel (7) and Wisdom (8). The following summary is largely taken from their accounts.

The person with a predisposition to depression has in his development tended to remain more or less fixated at the oral stage. In his very early childhood, he sustains a "narcissistic injury"—a traumatic disappointment in the love of his parents, especially the mother, at a time when he especially needed external parental attention, love, and appreciation to sustain his self-esteem. This narcissistic injury may be in the nature of a major abandonment or the usual type of humiliation and frustration. This leads to a violent rage against the cruel parental image—the bad mother, the bad object—and the psychological image of the bad object is violently expelled (by anal expulsion, according to Abraham) in that the emotional ties to the image of the bad object are disrupted, representing a loss of the object, by hate and rage. In these predisposed persons, at this early stage in life, the original love for the parental image is replaced by strongly ambivalent feelings, representing a regression to an earlier stage of development.

The pain of the loss of the object (and the narcissistic supplies from the object) and the resulting loss of self-esteem lead to an attempt at restitution. This constitutes the depressive reaction: an attempt at restitution following a narcissistic injury in a predisposed person who has been partially orally fixated.

In fantasy, the image of the object is introjected in the sense that the patient turns back to the disappointing parent and seeks again to obtain forgiveness and love, to obtain narcissistic supplies and to restore this lost self-esteem. However, this introjection is a strongly ambivalent one, full of hate and of violent rage, and one that leads to a fantasied oral incorporation and symbolic destruction of the image of the hated parent (a cannibalistic-love-murder of the hated image of the parent, in analytic terms). This phenomenon leads to a narcissistic regression in that the image of the parent is not seen as a separate object but is ambivalently identified within the patient's ego. In analytic terms, object choice has regressed to identification.

The stage is now set for the narcissistic struggle that constitutes the depression. The fantasied ambivalent incorporation of the object, with its attendant hate and rage, leads to strong feelings of guilt. The superego (always rigid and strict in these patients) harshly condemns the patient whose ego has now identified with the psychological image of the hated introjected object.

This leads to a masochistic need to placate and submit to self-punishment at the hands of the harsh superego. The superego uses the sadism of the ambivalence to turn this against that part of the ego which has identified with the object. This leads to the violent self-reproaches of the depressed patient. This internalized narcissistic struggle characterizes the depressive reaction.

Once this type of reaction has occurred in early childhood, it sets the pattern for repetition of this type of depressive reaction in later life, when similar narcissistic injuries are sustained. The repetition of this type of depressive reaction in these persons also stems from the fact that the original narcissistic injury and depressive reaction tend to leave them with what Freud calls a narcissistic predisposition—enhanced need for external supplies to bolster this self-esteem, narcissistic object choices and relationships, and a harsh superego, whose demands increase the need for external supplies to build up self-esteem.

This summary only conveys a small part of the mechanisms involved in susceptible individuals who have developed the pattern of depressive reactions to narcissistic injury—a loss of self-esteem. The important elements are the loss of self-esteem, the introjection and the ambivalence, the narcissistic regression from object choice to identification, the guilt, and the masochistic reaction of self-punishment of the ego by the superego. These are the elements most effectively dealt with by the relationships and interactions that occur in group psychotherapy.

The Dynamics of Group Psychotherapy in Relation to the Treatment of Depression

In psychoanalytic group psychotherapy, the therapist utilizes a group (which affects the relationships in the group and hence the transference) and the group method (which influences the communication in the group and hence the resistance) in performing psychotherapy. He sets up conditions to foster the interactions and the "free-floating" discussions which constitute the group psychotherapy.

The emotional ties which lead to the formation of a small unstructured group like a psychotherapy group consist largely of a series of identifications between the leader and the members and between the members themselves [Freud (9); Slavson (2); Stein (6)]. The most important of these is an identification with a narcissistically idealized figure of the leader. As Freud puts it: "The formula for the libidinal constitution of groups that have a leader and not too much secondary characteristics is: a number of individuals who have substituted the same object for their ego ideal and have consequently identified themselves with one another in their ego." This phenomenon involves an "inhibition"—a blocking of the intensity and "aims" of the transference drives directed toward the leader or the therapist.

According to this formula, the next most important relationship in the group is the identification of the members (in their ego, as Freud puts it) with each other on the basis of their common identification with the leader. Other kinds of identifications also occur in a group; that is, having the same symptoms and feelings, having similar conscious guilt feelings and unconscious conflicts and fears and resistance to treatment, and such. However, the identification with the leader and with each other on the basis of this shared identification constitutes the most important relationship in the group.

The similarity of these dynamic factors to those previously described as specifically occurring in depression is immediately apparent. In the group there is also, as Freud (9) pointed out, a regression from "object choice to identification" but this is, one might say, "regression in the service of the ego." This regression is for constructive purposes and it occurs for the purpose of treatment; while the relationship to one object—the leader—is inhibited, a series of new relationships is set up as a result. This is very different from the painful loss of the object in depression and immediately provides identifications to the leader and the others, which helps the member loosen the infantile relationship to the leader and find substitutes [Fenichel (7)]. Another way of putting this is that the relationships in the group enable the members to relinquish the infantile transference relationship to the leader and to begin working through a process similar to mourning.

The specific identification with the leader, involving an introjection of a narcissistically idealized image of him in place of the ego-ideal—the protective part of the superego—is similar to what occurs in depression but is much less ambivalent and almost immediately serves constructive therapeutic purposes. Instead of a violently ambivalent introjection and then an identification in the ego with the hated object and a subsequent punitive condemnation by the primitive harsh superego, the kind, tolerant, protective figure of the leader is incorporated and set up in place of the punitive superego of the members. This almost immediately lessens the punitive condemnation by the superego which now helps the patient to find ways, through his identification with the therapist, to overcome painful loss of self-esteem. The positive identification with the idealized figure of the therapist who is set up in the patient's ego-ideal begins to replace the bitter internalized conflict between the depressed patient's superego and altered ego. The ambivalence and rage lessen, and the subsequent guilt and masochistic self-punishment begin to subside.

In addition to the dynamic changes produced by the series of identifications occurring in a group, alterations in the way transference manifestations occur in the group also result in changes in the group interactions. Because of the presence of several members of the group and the realistic fact that the attention of the therapist must be shared, the intensity and "aims" of the transference to the leader are blocked or inhibited. A diminution in the intensity of the transference drives directed toward the leader is a necessary condition for the therapeutic work of the group. This is facilitated by the therapist's limiting his own interaction with the members of the group.

As a result of the inhibition of the transference directed toward the leader, these transference drives are deflected or diverted or displaced onto the other members of the group, thus increasing the opportunity for transference manifestations in the group.

Because of this inhibition and deflection of the transference from the leader to the members of the group, an increase in *intragroup* tension occurs. Thus despite its diminished intensity and altered manifestations, the transference to the leader continues to operate as one of the essential dynamic factors in the group and determines to a considerable extent the nature of the intermember transference manifestations.

The intermember transference manifestations are intensified by the increased intragroup tension. Based on unconscious fantasies, patients utilize roles in the group to act out and try to involve other patients in acting out transference roles and conflicts. The group members are available for each other as multiple transference objects who are realistically present and who will actually respond to transfer-manifestations. This results in group member interactions which constitute a therapeutic type of "acting out" in the group, since this acting out is, initially, an unconscious and uninterpreted response of one member to another's transference manifestations. This occurs in a very real fashion in the group, and one of the functions of the therapist is to ensure that it occurs in the group session, not outside of it, so that it is available for the therapy. Because of this type of interaction among the group members, pathological character traits and attitudes are much more quickly evident in group psychotherapy than in individual psychotherapy and are more readily available for therapeutic scrutiny.

Again, these changes in the transference manifestations and the nature of the interaction that take place in a therapy group have direct beneficial effects on certain types of depression. The inhibition of the transference wishes directed toward the leader or therapist, together with the previously described positive type of introjection and subsequent identification with him as an idealized figure, immediately lessen the strong ambivalent transference feelings usually directed toward the therapist. Consequently, there is much less rage and guilt about the unconscious feelings focusing on the therapist, and the internalized relationship to him through the identification is more positive and less threatening. This relationship, together with the fact that he is actually there and is seen in a more realistic fashion as a figure who continues to function as a helpful person, lessens the narcissistic deprivation and provides support to bolster the patient's self-esteem. (In depressed patients, some individual therapy is required prior to and perhaps after the patient enters a group to lessen the impact of the loss of the gratification because of the impossibility of having the therapist's exclusive attention in the group.)

All of this is aided by the deflection onto the other members of the group of the transference wishes directed toward the therapist. In depressed patients, this means that their strong ambivalence is displaced onto the other members. As noted above, this permits the therapist to remain to some extent as a supportive figure for the patients, externally and internally. Similarly, the ambivalence can be directed toward some patients (or even certain aspects of some patients) while others are seen and reacted to less ambivalently, remaining as positive and supportive objects for the depressed patient. In the group discussion, the knowledge that other members also have felt frustrated and enraged toward disappointing figures in their lives helps the depressed share their guilt over their ambivalence and view it more tolerantly. The actual realistic support voiced by the patients also lessens the guilt and provides narcissistic supplies to increase the patient's self-esteem. However, the initial uninterpreted interaction of two patients reaching out to each other in transference roles may be very troublesome for the depressed patient, and the therapist must be prepared to intervene, by interpretation or by generalizing the interaction, to prevent effects that are too disturbing.

The most important aspect of the interaction stemming from the patients in the group using each other as multiple transference objects is that it quickly and clearly makes evident pathological character traits. For this reason, the therapist encourages and permits interaction while making sure it is not too disturbing. [As noted elsewhere, interaction is also most useful and necessary in bringing out the transference manifestations (10).] By means of these interactions, the characteristic attitudes that the patients display toward each other and the specific ways that they relate and react to each other are clearly evident and can actually be seen occurring in the group sessions. Obviously, the important traits that are revealed are the unconscious characterological ones. Sadistic and masochistic patterns, passive and aggressive ones, demanding and submissive ones, paranoid and compulsive attitudes, and such all are displayed clearly and quickly and are available for therapeutic scrutiny.

In the depressed patients, their ambivalence and masochism are thus clearly and quickly evident. The same is true of their arrogant insistence that others supply their demands immediately and that others be the kind of persons that fulfill all their narcissistic needs and expectations. Depressed patients, when confronted with a consensus by the group that they display such attitudes and reactions, are initially angered but accept the evidence much more quickly and readily than in individual therapy.

This is particularly helpful for depressed patients whose depressive reactions are the result of narcissistic disappointments stemming from unrealistic attitudes, expectations, and reactions specifically related to character traits of which they have been unaware. A patient who has not been aware of indicating excessive demands or of showing inflexible arrogance and rage if his demands are not met is quickly able to see this and adopt a more flexible and considerate attitude. With this, there occurs [illegible] ambivalence and a decrease in his guilt and depression. Many [illegible] especially those occurring in masochistic patients, can be cited to sh[illegible] awareness of and even a slight change in characterological attitu[illegible] reactions can lessen painful guilty and depressive feelings. An attempt is m[illegible] later on to illustrate these dynamic effects and interactions by clinical example.

Group Psychotherapy in the Treatment of Depression: Review of the Literature, Effectiveness, and Clinical Examples

As noted previously, many group therapists, including the authors of standard works on group psychotherapy, state that group psychotherapy is *not* indicated for the treatment of certain types of depression, particularly the acute and severe types. Several of these workers do indicate, however, that other types of depressions are suitable for treatment with group psychotherapy. A fairly thorough review of the literature reveals only a few articles dealing with the use of group psychotherapy in depression. None of these cite any objective data or figures to show its effectiveness, although favorable results are indicated.

This literature can be summarized as follows: Wender (4) feels that the results obtained with group psychotherapy are good, although he does not mention the improvement of specific symptoms, except improved social adjustment. Schilder (11), one of the pioneers in the field of group psychotherapy, reports good results with various types of social and other neuroses, but failure with two cases of depression. Johnson (3) reports good results with group therapy with neurotic and borderline patients, including neurotic patients with depressive reactions. Slavson (2) mentions that character disorders and certain kinds of depressed and withdrawn patients benefitted from the guilt lessening, the reality reinforcing, and the consistent supportive atmosphere of group psychotherapy. Foulkes and Anthony (12) describe good results with some types of depression. Mullan and Rosenbaum (13) find group therapy useful in depressed patients and indicate that it helped them bring out their despair and provided hope and support, while building up self-esteem. As noted above, many authors, for example Foulkes (1) and Slavson (2), have reported good results in the treatment of character disorders, including those with depressive reactions, by means of group psychotherapy.

There are some other reports in the literature of the use of group psychotherapy in depression. Miller and Ferone (14) obtained good results in the treatment of 14 depressed middle-aged women with outpatient group psychotherapy. They felt the interaction in the group lessened the clinging demands on the therapist and since members of the group demonstrated similar character structures, this helped patients to see how they affected others and thus to change. Wolk and Goldfarb (15) obtained good results with group psychotherapy in the treatment of depressed long-term hospitalized patients.

Livingston (16), in a most interesting article, describes the dynamic effects of analytic group psychotherapy that make it specifically useful in the treatment of depression. He points out that the loss of a "heavily cathected object"

…bidinal strivings," which needs to be …of the emotional ties to the object and its …eading to an identification. This two-part …nd needs to precede slowly and bit by bit so …vingston feels this is exactly the same process …ence resistance in therapy and cites Rado and … this: "The carrying out of this second part of …mbivalent introjection of the loved object], the …introjects and the dissolution of their projection in …tance of the working through process." In addition, …sm is related to the working through process and …endency to resist working through. . . . Masochism …ubborn refusal to separate from parental figures or …sistence on maintaining fantasies of security and o… refusal to complete the second portion of the mourning process, …ng of ties to the introject. . . . Working through is the repetitive an… …ious process of completing the mourning process by confronting the patient with progressively less distorted derivatives . . . until the ties to the introject are loosened sufficiently to allow growth and separation."

Livingston points out that the group setting offers many advantages to help the patient complete the mourning and working through; it confronts the patient with his refusal to mourn and his characteristic masochistic struggle to hold on to the infantile object. He sees this more quickly and accepts it more readily from his peers and projects it less onto the therapist. At the same time, the group members help share his guilt and grief and are there to help him do the work of the mourning as he gives up his neurotic ties and defenses.

Glatzer (17) is another author who describes the specific way that the depressive reaction of the masochist can be treated more effectively in the group. The sharing of the guilt, the support of the other members, the lessening of the ambivalent dependence on the therapist, the confrontation with self-punitive and masochistic demands all help in a less traumatic fashion than in individual therapy to lessen the ties to the bad introject and substitute healthy identification. This experience assists in the working through of the transference, as Livingston pointed out, and helps complete the work of mourning—the gradual loosening of ties to the introjected infantile image of the parental figure.

Foulkes and Anthony (12) give one of the few descriptions of the dynamics of how a depressive reaction was handled in group therapy. After offering support and understanding and the sharing of guilt to a member in anticipation of the death of her very sick father, the other members reacted with denial and rejection when the bereaved patient first expressed her grief. She made an initial improvement, and then the others became guilty and depressed and criticized her for not mourning sufficiently. These reactions alternated for a considerable time: first, the patient was depressed while the others denied this and then the situation was reversed. It was felt these alternating reactions were "complementary" and a way in which the patient and the others alternated in the work of the mourning for the death of the father and the sharing of the guilt over this. Some of these reactions included the therapist. The authors felt these reactions show the way the group helped the bereaved one to carry out the work of mourning and cite the Greek play, Iphegenia, as an example of how important it is not to interfere with the work of mourning.

Some clinical examples are now described:

R. C., a 26-year-old single financial analyst, joined the group after a year of individual therapy with another therapist. She had long-standing symptoms of anxiety and depression, going back to her adolescence even before the suicide of her depressed mother when the patient was 15. These became worse when she graduated from college and returned home. Her father was an alcoholic, who had repeatedly caressed her in a very seductive fashion and also was very critical of her. She claimed he blamed her for her mother's death, although she herself felt very guilty about this. She felt that she had inherited her mother's depression and her father's alcoholism. She had fears that her angry and vengeful thoughts might harm others and she would be punished for these. She often thought of her mother saying critical things to her, although she did not hear her mother's voice.

In the group, the patient participated well from the first. Gradually, she began to have a more realistic view of herself and her anxiety and depression improved considerably. She showed two contrasting attitudes in the group. At times, she would speak in a clear logical way, often in a rather dominating manner, making statements and giving advice in a definitely paternalistic fashion. At other times, she would speak in a highpitched, whining, little girl voice, telling of difficulties she had gotten into and saying she couldn't help it, and so on. She often expressed rebellious and defiant attitudes in this little girl fashion, clearly verbalizing that she felt the group and the therapist had forbidden her to do certain things. This was, of course, not so and when challenged, she would admit her distortions but continued to express defiance. She used the little girl attitude to compete with the others and to monopolize the group, and continued to do so although this was repeatedly pointed out to her.

She had always been extremely devoted to horseback riding and 6 months before the present incident had purchased a horse. The group had helped her to do this; she had inherited money and had funds. They helped her approach this in a realistic fashion and had encouraged her to tell her father and her step-mother, despite her great guilt and fear. Things had gone relatively well with the horse, and she had made plans to move him to another stable where there would be more opportunities for riding.

She made the move and the owner of the stable, in checking out the horse, found he was suffering from a chronic condition which lessened both his value and soundness. This meant she had been cheated when she bought the horse. She became furious and extremely guilty and depressed. At first, she was fearful and embarrassed to discuss it in the group, but finally she did, in the little girl fashion. The group pointed out she had to confront the owner of the last stable, a woman who had sold her the horse, and ask for a refund or an adjustment. R. C. said she realized this, but she felt guilty and was afraid to hurt the woman; she might get sick and die, and so on. Besides, she was fond of the woman and she couldn't believe the woman would cheat her.

This type of discussion went on for several weeks. The group, guided by the therapist, helped her face the disappointment, rage, and depression underlying her guilt and fear and to move on realistically in acknowledging the woman had cheated her. Her childish way of thinking and speaking was pointed up to her, as was her masochistic way of holding on to the old relationship, instead of facing her disappointment and hurt at being taken advantage of and being let down. Finally, she did call the woman and confronted her and then, with the help of her lawyer, was able to get a considerable refund.

As she worked through her rage and disappointment with the help of the group, her depression subsided. Subsequently, the group helped her make a realistic decision about getting another horse and establishing more mature relationships with the new stable owners, a man and his wife. This coincided with establishing a more mature relationship with her parents.

This patient had set up the group and the therapist as parental figures to whom she reacted with unrealistic expectations and guilt and fear, as she did with others, for example, the woman stable owner who cheated her. When she learned that the woman had betrayed her, she reverted to an old pattern of childish rage, depression, guilt, and fear and handled this in her former masochistic way. By pointing this out to her and by helping her express her feelings and supporting her in a realistic approach to these, she was enabled to give up the old masochistic relationship, accept a realistic frustration with a consequent improvement of her depression, and the establishment of new, more adult relationships. This summary cannot adequately describe the nature of the interaction in the group—R. C. clinging defiantly to her childish masochistic attitude while the others expressed anger and criticism and then support and encouragement.

The following is a second clinical example:

In a group of four men and four women, in the 25-to-30-year-old range, one of the women had been depressed for several weeks. She was a small, pretty, married woman, who looked much younger than her 28 years. She sat quietly most of the time in the group, looking moderately depressed and sighing heavily and frequently. A single, young man of 28, who had joined the group after the young woman, also was depressed and silent at times but he had slowly begun to participate more actively in the group, while the young woman spoke only briefly and infrequently and continued to sigh and look depressed. B. (the young man) began to ask J. (the young woman) how she felt; she would reply, "I feel nervous and depressed." This continued for a few weeks with B. becoming clearly more and more irritable when he asked J. how she felt, saying such things as "What's the matter with you?" and "Are you still depressed?" On one occasion, after J. had given one of her heavy, depressed sighs, B. burst out irritably and said, "There you go again! You sigh all the time." A little later in the session, J. sighed again and B. said angrily, "I can't stand it when you keep sighing. It makes me uncomfortable to see you depressed."

During the next session, B. intently watched J., who still looked depressed. She gave a heavy sigh and B. said, half in anger and half in distress: "There's that sigh. Oh, Mommy, what did I do to hurt you?" The rest of the group reacted with surprise, and asked B. if his mother sighed like J. did and looked depressed. B. said "Yes—she always looks sad and depressed and gives me those heavy Jewish mother sighs. It makes me feel so guilty. I can't stand it! Whenever J. would sigh like that, it would make me feel depressed and guilty and angry like I used to with my mother. I'd have to go to her and ask, 'What did I do?'."

Others in the group cited similar feelings, as did J., who acknowledged that she too felt guilty when her mother looked sad and depressed. Following this, B. began, during the sessions, to talk about difficulties with his family, something he had not discussed before. Also, he began to interact with and react to J. more in the group sessions, which he had not done before.

At times, in subsequent sessions, B. would comment again on J.'s sighing and how it reminded him of his mother. Several weeks after the incident described above, J. complained of having some difficulty with gassiness and mild diarrhea, symptoms similar to the colitis symptoms she had had a year ago. B. again became depressed and irritable on hearing this and questioned her rather sharply about her colitis. He commented that she always looked sickly and depressed.

J. reacted to this with shock and anger. She said she resented B.'s critical attitude and thought that he was exaggerating. B., again in an irritable fashion, said he was not exaggerating; she almost always looked sickly and depressed—just like his mother. That and the sighing really got to him.

J. said he was accusing her of looking sickly and depressed because he was confusing her with his mother. She turned to the others in the group and asked if they thought she looked sickly and depressed. To her dismay, they agreed with B., although they spoke in a much more sympathetic fashion. One man, M., who had frequently been critical of the way J. spoke in the sessions, said she reminded him very much of his mother who was always sick and depressed.

J. verbalized her dismay and said she hadn't realized she came across that way. It hurt, but now that she knew, she was going to try to change this. She did not want to appear sickly and depressed. Then, turning to B., she said she was glad he brought it up, but she was very angry at his critical and irritable manner. He was just like her father, who couldn't stand it when she was ill with asthma and told her to go away so he wouldn't have to listen to her labored breathing.

At the next session, J. informed the group that she had asked her husband and some friends if she looked sickly and depressed and had again been shocked and dismayed when they said she did appear this way often. She realized she was often tense and angry and apparently when she felt this way, she looked sickly and depressed. Maybe it was a way of getting attention; her mother used to fuss over her when she was sick.

Gradually, after this J. did change. First she became more outspoken and reacted more with the others. In addition, she was less concerned with being placating and making a good impression, and her preoccupied look, her sighing, and her depressed manner in the group slowly improved.

Here the intermember transference manifestations are quite clear. (The transference to the therapist is implied in J.'s fear of complaining and annoying him, as she had been afraid of annoying her father.) Again, the reaction to J. was, to some extent, a reaction to a past object—the sighing, the sickly look, and the depressed look reminding the others of their sick and depressed mothers. On the other hand, B.'s irritability—and that of the others—reminded J. of her father's dislike and fear of her being sick. The confrontation in the group enabled J., despite her hurt and anger, to test the validity of the group's impression of her. When this was validated, with the help of their accepting and sympathetic attitudes, she began to change the nature of her relationships in the group and move on to a more mature and realistic presentation of herself and a more mature relationship with the others. As she worked out her depressed, ambivalent relationships in the group, her attitude changed, and her depression lessened. Hence the presence of the other group members as transference objects and the acceptance and support they gave her enabled her to give up her depressed and masochistic reaction to the parental introject and move on to more realistic and less depressed and masochistic relationships.

The third clinical example follows:

I. S., a 60-year-old lawyer, had had several episodes of depression prior to the present one. This had begun 3 years previously, about the time his wife became severely and chronically ill and about the same time new partners in his firm criticized his actions as the senior partner. He developed classic symptoms of depression. He withdrew from work at the office and isolated himself when at home. His wife, who had formerly supported and encouraged him, now added to his burdens by complaining he didn't care for her, and so on.

He was placed on antidepressant medication in large doses and seen in individual psychotherapy. After several months with no improvement, despite increases and changes in antidepressant medication, he was hospitalized and given a series of ECT with considerable improvement. However, while the acute severe depression had subsided, a moderate degree of chronic depression remained, manifested by complaints of feeling useless, inability to work or accomplish anything, discouragement, and such.

He had been seen in individual psychotherapy throughout this time. Here he displayed an unchanging and characteristic attitude as follows: He would say he felt bad and he didn't know what to do. He would then say he had been unable to do any work and hadn't been able to help out at home. All this was said in a somewhat whining, reproachful fashion. When his complaints were gone into, it was readily apparent he had been able to accomplish a considerable amount of work and a lesser amount at home. Attempts to interpret his childish attitude and complaints were accepted, but this ambivalent clinging and reproachful attitude persisted.

He joined a new group with one other man and three women, all with borderline conditions with characterological defects, several of whom had had depressive episodes. The group, led by two of the women, was active and somewhat confronting from the first. I. S. immediately began to participate. When something of his complaining attitude was pointed out to him, he readily accepted this and discussed this as something that went back to his relationship with his mother and had continued with his wife. His ambivalent and unsympathetic attitude to his wife was discussed and was related to anger at his feeling of loss at not being taken care of by her as in the past. While this had been pointed out to him in individual therapy, he accepted it more readily in group and began to act more helpful to his wife. His childish attitudes became evident and his need for constant praise and attention were discussed. Again, he accepted this much more readily in the group and became more active and realistic in his relations at work. As these changes occurred, over a period of several months, his chronic depression gradually subsided, as did the need for antidepressant medication.

This passive-aggressive, childishly dependent, and ambivalent man with a chronic depression was helped much more quickly and effectively in group therapy than in individual therapy. The deflection of the demanding and ambivalent transference onto the other members of the group and the development of relationships with the other members of the group helped him give up the old relationships. He wanted to be well thought of and liked by them and accepted the need to change more readily because of this, and thus obtained narcissistic supplies from the approval of the group. The more realistic attitude of the group, the support and sympathy of the others, and the sharing of the guilt over vengeful disappointments all helped him to give up some of his narcissistic rage and disappointment and led to improvement in his chronic depression.

These clinical examples illustrate the manner in which group psychotherapy is specifically useful in the treatment of a depressed and masochistic attitude in one patient, the treatment of a depressive reaction in a second patient, and improvement in a third patient of a chronic depression related to character traits.

In summary, the examples above, from the literature and from clinical practice, demonstrate that group psychotherapy is specifically useful in treating certain kinds of depression, particularly those related to pathological character traits. The positive identification with the therapist as an idealized figure who is incorporated and replaces a part of the harsh superego of the group members lessens the ambivalent and punitive conflict between the superego and ego in depressed patients. The identification with the other group members replaces the identification with the image of the introjected bad mother, which can now be relinquished and replaced by new and more adult and realistic relationships in the group. The inhibition of the transference to the therapist also serves to diminish and loosen the ambivalent transference ties to him and lessens the intensity of the rage and guilt. The deflection of the transference to the other members of the group diffuses the ambivalence, and the transference interactions with the other group members enables the depressed patient to clearly have demonstrated to him the nature of his demanding and masochistic self-punitive attitudes and other character traits. The knowledge that others have ambivalence and the sharing of the guilt concerning this, as well as the realistic sympathy and support of the group members, enable the depressed patient to lessen his guilt, give up his pathological identification, and obtain more realistic narcissistic supplies from the relationships to the others in the group. These processes facilitate mourning and working through for the depressed patient when he is treated with group psychotherapy.

References

1. Foulkes SH: *Therapeutic Group Analysis.* New York, International Universities Press, 1965, pp. 45–48.
2. Slavson SR: *A Textbook in Analytic Group Psychotherapy.* New York, International Universities Press, 1964, pp. 189–191.
3. Johnson JA: *Group Therapy: A Practical Approach.* New York, McGraw-Hill, 1963, pp. 87–89.
4. Wender L: The psychodynamics of group psychotherapy and its application. *J Nerv Ment Dis* **84**:54–60, 1936.
5. Day M, Semrad E: Group therapy with neurotics and psychotics, in *Comprehensive Group Psychotherapy.* Edited by Kaplan H, Sadock BJ, Baltimore, Williams & Wilkins, 1971, pp. 575–576.
6. Stein A: Indications for group psychotherapy and the selection of patients. *J Hillside Hos* **12**:145–155, 1963.
7. Fenichel O: *The Psychoanalytic Theory of Neuroses.* New York, Norton, 1945, pp. 387–414.
8. Wisdom JO: Comparison and development of the psycho-analytical theories of melancholia. *Int J Psa* **43**:113–132, 1962.
9. Freud S: *Group Psychology and the Analysis of the Ego (1921).* Standard Edition, London, Hogarth Press, 1955, Vol. 18, pp. 67–145.
10. Stein A: The nature and significance of interaction in group psychotherapy. *Int J Group Psychother* **20**:153–162, 1970.

11. Schilder P: Results and problems of group psychotherapy in severe neuroses. *Ment Hyg* **23**:87–98, 1939.
12. Foulkes SH, Anthony EJ: *Group Psychotherapy: The Psychoanalytic Approach.* Baltimore, Penguin Books, 1965, pp. 177–185, 2nd ed.
13. Mullan H, Rosenbaum M: *Group Psychotherapy: Theory and Practice.* New York, Free Press of Glencoe, The Crowell-Collier Publishing Co, 1962.
14. Miller PR, Ferone L: Group psychotherapy with depressed women. *Am J Psychiatr* **23**:701–703, 1966.
15. Wolk RL, Goldfarb AI: The response to group psychotherapy of aged recent admissions compared with long term mental hospital patients. *Am J Psychiatr* **23**:1251–1257, 1967.
16. Livingston MS: Working through in analytic group psychotherapy in relation to masochism as a refusal to mourn. *Int J Group Psychother* **21**:339–344, 1971.
17. Glatzer H: Analysis of masochism in group therapy. *Int J Group Psychother* **9**:158–165, 1959.

Twelve

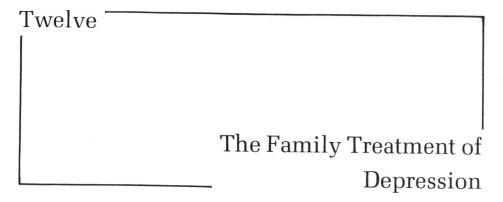

The Family Treatment of Depression

Peter Hogan, M.D.
Barbara K. Hogan, Ph.D.

Families in difficulty come into therapy with problems in identifying and communicating their feelings and demands. Typically, they place the central motivation for their feelings and behavior onto other family members. ("He made me do it." "Her behavior forced us to bring her into therapy.") Families with one or more depressed members have, of course, particular difficulty in identifying and expressing anger. In addition, as with the depressed person generally, the family member who is currently depressed experiences a sense of powerlessness or lack of impact in his personal life, feels trapped in the sense of not seeing alternatives, and in addition has grandiose expectations of himself. These are usually expressed indirectly in terms of feelings of worthlessness, minimization of real achievements, or conviction that he has made mistakes that cannot be repaired. He measures his effectiveness only by the results he gets without regard to the nature and quality of the effort he puts forth. Furthermore, he shows magical responsibility for the feelings of others.

Before discussing these factors in detail, we give a case illustration from a family in therapy at a point where some of these factors are in the process of change.

At the time of the episode, the family had been seen together for two sessions. Immediately prior to these sessions, the father, Harry, chronically depressed, had been in group therapy for about 9 months. He was about 40 years old. The daughter, Sue, 16, had been in individual therapy for 6 months, with the presenting complaint of a sexual dysfunction. This dysfunction rapidly cleared in therapy and revealed an underlying depression and difficulty in her relationship with her father. The mother, Martha, approximately the same age as the father, had been in therapy previously, but not for several years. Before undertaking regular sessions, the whole family had been seen at scattered intervals in the past at points of crises. During these previous sessions, the mother had taken on the major guilt for family difficulties.

The incident occurred following a family session in which Harry realized that he expressed his anger depressively by saying, "Oh, God, I feel like killing myself," instead of directing it outward with, "I am so angry I feel like killing you." At the same session, Sue realized that she was using anger to hide her hurt feelings. The incident to be recounted was reported by the daughter, Sue, in a subsequent individual session as follows:

Sue walked in on her parents in the kitchen as they were apparently arguing about a can of tuna fish. Martha and Harry were each holding onto the same can of white tuna. As soon as he saw her, Harry turned to Sue and attacked her for all of her demands, especially criticizing her latest demand for the more expensive white tuna fish rather than chunk tuna.

Clearly, Martha had claimed that Sue had asked for white tuna. Now Martha added (weakly) that she also liked white tuna fish, and perhaps she said things to stir Harry up and get him mad. Harry turned to her (by this time quite angry) and told her to "keep out of it!"

Sue began to counterattack but realized "This is ridiculous," and that her anger hid her real feelings of hurt. She then cried and shouted, "I am hurt" and ran into her room. Martha followed Sue and tried to calm and comfort her by rubbing her back. Sue reacted with anger and was about to push her mother away when she realized that it was easier for her to express her anger toward Martha rather than toward Harry and was thus able to accept her mother's comforting. Next Martha went to Harry and tried to calm him. However, far from calming down, Harry maintained his anger toward Sue, finally saying, "I hate that kid." This was in sharp contrast to his usual depressive response to an argument ("I feel like killing myself"); furthermore, he was able to feel good about this change in his behavior, rather than guilty.

Some time lapsed before Harry and Sue had a talk where Harry, wanting to share his change in behavior with her, said, "I was angry with you and mother tried to calm me, but I said 'I hate that kid' and I don't regret it—I didn't say 'I am going to kill myself.' "

Sue felt very hurt, thinking: "But I said I was hurt." However, she did not share this hurt feeling with Harry, nor did she respond to his good feeling about his change in behavior. Instead, she began a depressive internal dialogue. "Why does Harry hate me? What have I done? I'm afraid he doesn't love me or want me around." On the other hand, if Sue did not respond to Harry overtly, neither did she grow further depressed and withdrawn, as she would usually have done in such a situation.

While aspects of this episode were unresolved when reported by Sue, each member involved in the episode was able to take more responsibility for himself than was usually the case.

1. Martha was unable to take responsibility for buying the can of white tuna and implied that she had purchased it for Sue. However, she did recognize that she had played a role in the antagonism of Sue and Harry, and attempted to clarify this with Harry by saying, "I didn't mean to imply that I bought the white tuna because Sue was the *only* one who likes it"—as well as, "I think I say things to stir you up and get you mad." When this was unsuccessful, she attempted to help both Sue and Harry individually with their feelings of isolation and anger, "to calm them."

2. Harry was also ready to give Sue the responsibility for Martha's acts and attacked her for other demands, thereby implying that he and Martha were powerless to resist them. However, though reacting hastily and being unable to stop the attack on Sue once

he began, he was able to direct his anger outward at Sue ("I hate that kid!") rather than inwardly as usual ("I'm going to kill myself!"). He was able to express this anger without guilt, and was further able to share his relief with Sue, although he was unable to spontaneously respond to her hurt. In the past, his response to Sue's pain would have been to feel solely responsible for it, followed by a depressive self-attack. To respond directly to her pain by an empathic response would have made him too vulnerable to her.

3. Sue, while counterattacking Harry, was able to realize during the episode itself that she was more hurt than angry and was able to express her hurt, although she then had to isolate herself from the family by going to her room. When Martha comforted her, she was able to recognize that she could express anger more easily to her mother than to her father, and chose not to attack her mother. Later, when she talked with Harry, she was again hurt and angry, was unable to express these feelings, and began to react depressively. However, Sue was distinctly not as afraid of Harry's rejection as she had been in the past, and did not counter at the end of the episode with sulking and further withdrawal as she had previously. After her individual session, she was ready to confront Harry directly with her hurt and anger about his lack of response to her pain when she originally left the kitchen, and was ready also to confront Martha with her "setting up" the argument with Harry.

The foregoing clinical excerpt illustrates the kind of behavior characteristic of a family with one or more members who act depressively. We approach such a family from the framework of systems theory with a special emphasis on dependency as we define it. We see dependency as a culturally induced, self-perpetuating prolongation of the infantile polarity of powerlessness to act directly on the environment on the one hand, and omnipotence on the other. We discuss the systems approach to family therapy, and then the development of depression from the standpoint of systems theory and dependency, before returning to the treatment of depression by family therapy.

The Systems Approach to Family Therapy

Family therapists approach symptoms, including depression, from the standpoint of intervening into an ongoing system. As Jay Haley (1) has indicated, whatever the beginning orientation of a therapist, after a certain amount of exposure to families, he tends to view therapeutic intervention from a standpoint similar to other family therapists, even though the nature of his intervention might be quite different. For example, instead of discussing the advantages of individual versus family therapy in a particular case, he would consider individual therapy as one method of intervening into a family system. The whole family is taken into consideration even though the whole family may not be in treatment. Freud anticipated this approach, when, in the case of little Hans, he advised the father instead of directly treating little Hans. From the standpoint of family therapy this may be seen as the most effective method of intervening into the family system which showed its disturbance through Hans' phobia.

Symptoms, from the standpoint of systems theory, are not simply a product of internal or even interpersonal dynamics, but an outgrowth of the workings of the family system. From this standpoint, biological aspects, intrapsychic aspects, and intrapersonal aspects of depression are subsystems that operate subject to the influence of the larger family system. Again, while the family system is considered the primary system for the development of symptoms, it in turn is a subsystem of even larger systems: the local community, the school, the religious community, and such. Auerswald (2), as well as Hoffman and Long (3), has written on the contribution of these larger systems to the treatment and disposition of family members. Rashkis (4) has particularly considered these larger systems as they are relevant to the family system in the development of depression in the parents of disturbed adolescents.

While Bertalanffy (5) has written on the application of general systems theory to psychiatry, the systems approach to family therapy seems to have developed more from experience with families, than from an *a priori* attempt to apply general systems theory. Jackson (6), in his writings on "family homeostasis," codified what other family therapists were experiencing: when one member of a family improved, another member of the family developed symptoms. From this experience, in turn, it is a short step to conceptualize, as Jackson did, that a family is a system whose members influence and are influenced by each other in a way that cannot be explained by an evaluation of the individual dynamics alone; and furthermore, that each family member operates to maintain the "steady state" of the family as he experiences it.

Haley (7) defines the first law of human relationships as: "When one person indicates a change in relation to another, the other will act upon the first so as to diminish and modify that change." Satir (8), in discussing symptom production within the family, states that the rules of the dysfunctional family system interfere with the growth needs of the family members or ignore these needs altogether. These rules do not seem to allow negotiation, or clear, open, direct communication within dysfunctional families. Neither do they allow for the family members to interact with the world outside the family, to grow personally, or to modify the family experiences. She states, "The behavior of any family member is entirely appropriate and understandable in terms of the rules of his family system. That is, the behavior of an individual may not fit his own growth needs or the expectations in the awareness of other family members, but it does fit the rules of the family system—and the context in which he is behaving. To understand a symptom, then, one must understand the family system of which the symptom-bearer, or identified patient, is a member." She goes on to suggest that symptoms are a result of a pattern of relationships that require dysfunction in one or more members for the family to continue operating as unit.

The writers mentioned so far have been looking at symptoms from the viewpoint of error-correcting feedback which tends to inhibit deviation from the family pattern. This is the so-called negative feedback loop. (A loop consists of a series of elements, each of which acts upon the other and is in turn acted upon by them. Given an initial stimulus, the negative feedback loop would, in general, act in a manner to reduce or nullify the effect of that stimulus. In biology, the temperature-regulating mechanism in mammals is a good example of error-correcting feedback.)

On the other hand, these writers, as well as others writing from the systems standpoint, also discuss vicious cycles, escalating arguments, and other events that do not fit easily into the error-correcting patterns so far described.

Hoffman (9), as well as Speer (10) and Wender (11), describes these patterns more formally by using the work of Maruyama (12), who described these events as a "mutually causative deviation *amplifying* system" (emphasis added). In such systems (previously called positive feedback loops in systems terminology) events tend to remain operating in the direction that was initially triggered. While previous scientific writers generally gave examples of the destructive or pathological effects of such processes, Maruyama has pointed out that amplifying systems are necessary to explain normal biological and economic processes, such as the growth of a young animal, or an industry. He further stated that complicated systems, such as biological systems, were governed by a series of both deviation-reducing and deviation-amplifying feedback loops, the balance between which determined the outcome of the process at any one time.

Hoffman (9), in particular, has applied these ideas to family theory and therapy. She noted that, in a family system, an event could be viewed or experienced as being both deviation-amplifying and deviation-reducing, depending on the observation point or the level. For example, she hypothesizes the child who develops deviant (deviation-amplifying) behavior to heal a marital split (deviation-reducing on the second level). However, on the next level, the community, the effect may once again be deviation-amplifying for the entire family. This concept is an important one for understanding some aspects of depression in the family system, and is returned to when depression as a symptom is being specifically discussed.

Therapists who have had extensive training and experience with internal dynamics, while well aware of the system implications, are loath to consign their training and experience to the trash bin. One of the foremost writers to tackle this problem has been Framo (13), who has written extensively on the incorporation of the object-relations theory of Fairbairn (14) into the family systems approach. The "bad internal object subsystem" results in "life situations in reality which are not only unconsciously interpreted in the light of the inner object world, resulting in distorted expectations of other people, but *active, unconscious attempts are made to force and change close relationships into fitting the internal role models*" (Italics in the original). In this way, the family member is saved from having to deal with disassociated aspects of the self, and can instead preserve that aspect while ostensibly attempting to change the other. We illustrate this concept by a treatment case in the clinical section of this paper. Now, however, we proceed to a discussion of the specific symptom, depression, in the light of the systems approach just summarized.

The Development of Depression

The fundamental question we address is: how does a child move from early infancy into the clinically depressed state? Such a state has been described by Bonime (15), for example, as "an exaggeratedly lowered mood precipitated by a definable loss, frustration or disappointment. The patient shows diminution of incentive, retardation of activity, and decline in enjoyment or anticipation of his customary physical, social, affective or intellectual sources of pleasure. He tends toward a sense of helplessness, hopelessness and incontrollability. He may respond favorably to encouragement, but usually does so only briefly; initially, or soon, he responds irritably or by withdrawing further. His mental processes remain intact, though tending to manifest mild or moderate degrees of sluggishness, which he may tentatively overcome by effort. He is likely to feel overburdened by ordinary tasks, to find difficulty in concentrating, or soon tire from it, and he tends to digress or divert himself from responsible activity. In addition to feeling excessively the weight of responsibility, the patient may be frustrated, angered, even made anxious, by an unaccustomed disorganization, lack of persistence and in his approach to tasks. *Whatever his achieved level of productivity, it is reduced*" (Italics in the original).

We respond to this question from three different aspects related to a systems approach—the need for impact in the early mother-child system, the development of dependency and its implications for depression, and deviation-amplifying systems.

The infant must be integrated into the ongoing system of the family as well as the larger systems of society. As Birdwhistell (16) states, "The child is born into a society already keyed for his coming. A system exists into which he must be assimilated if the society is to sustain itself. If his behavior cannot, after a period of time, become predictable to a degree expected in that society, he must be specially treated. In some societies the nonassimilator will be allowed to die; in others he may be given special institutional treatment. This special treatment can range from deification to incarceration. But ultimately the goal is the same: to make *that child's* behavior sufficiently predictable that the society can go about the rest of its business" (Italics in the original).

It is our belief that this integration takes place in our culture in a manner that prolongs the infantile polarity of powerlessness to act directly on the environment, on the one hand, and the magical power to have one's needs fulfilled without apparent activity on the other hand. Powerlessness takes the form of feelings of ineffectiveness or inadequacy. It is manifested not only by significant problems in work or social areas, but also by the inability to know and express one's perceptions, emotions, or needs directly, and the inability to act effectively or to plan and/or implement plans effectively in everyday life. The pole of infantile omnipotence can take many forms, among them the expectation of being considered unique or "special" without activity, the expectation of obtaining results without effort, the minimization of efforts that are not crowned with perfect success, and the idea that mistakes cannot be repaired. The result is an impairment of realistic evaluation of one's self and others.

Dependency, then, as we define it can be seen to underlie a number of the manifestations of depression. We also consider the depressed person's inability to deal with loss, the inability to experience or express anger directly, and the sense of being trapped to be manifestations of dependency. In particular, the sense of having little or no impact on his world, characteristic of dependency, is centrally true for the depressive patient. It is this factor that we address first.

To become a separate, autonomously functioning adult, the infant must negotiate the transition from the original biological system of mother and fetus. In the first step of the process, this original biological unit must become a psychobiological unit through "the mutual stimulation and adaptation between the infant and his mother" (17).

This process of adaptation begins in the first hours of life. Call (17), observing infant-mother interactions around breast and bottle feeding, found definite adaptations of the infant to the mother's feeding style within the first 2 days of life. In several cases specific adaptations on the part of the infant developed and were maintained. For example:

"A third infant (M) . . . consistently turn(ed) away from the mother at 5½ weeks. The mother held this infant fairly close in the first few days of bottle feeding while in the hospital, but when she got home, she consistently held the infant in her left arm away from her body with inconsistent head support, seldom looking at its face. The father, who fed the infant about one third of the time, held the infant close to his body well supported in his right arm, and consistently looked in the infant's face. The mother also engaged in a teasing game which consisted of brushing the nipple across the infant's mouth, having him reach for it with his mouth, only then to take it out of reach. From 5½ weeks to eight months of age, Baby M continued turning away from the mother when she fed him and towards the father when he fed him."

The nature of the developing mother-child system, then, depends first of all on how the reactive tendencies of mother and child mesh with each other. For example, a quick-reacting infant and a slow-reacting mother, if outside the limits of tolerance for both, begin a mutually causative deviation-amplifying system (MCDAS) of an unpleasant nature from their earliest encounter. As Bettleheim (18) points out, children are prepared by nature only for an average environment and so the major adaptation, if one is to be made, must come from the mother. That is, the infant's initial impact on his world must be revealed primarily in his mother's adaptation to him. However, this adaptation becomes complicated if the mother responds to distress cues from the child, not from the standpoint of simple information that something has gone wrong, but from the standpoint that any distress on the part of the child indicates a deficiency on the part of the mother. For example, a woman in individual therapy recounted an extremely difficult relationship with her first child. The mother's grandiose attitude was that a child would not cry if perfectly taken care of. When the child developed colic with almost constant crying, the mother became furious because of her idea that every cry was an accusation that she was a bad mother. On several occasions, she almost swung the baby into a wall in her rage.

At the other extreme from an intensive response to the infant from the mother (or mothering figure) is an ignoring of the child's cues. When this happens, the child may react by increased activity temporarily, distress symptoms such as feeding difficulties (19), withdrawal or giving up (20), or finally by such serious withdrawal that malnutrition leading to emotional dwarfism (21) or marasmus (22) may result. Aside from the necessity of continuity of physical and emotional contact for survival, which seems adequately documented by the authors above as well as others (23), the continuity of a matrix in which the child has a feeling of interpersonal effectiveness seems necessary for normal emotional and social development.

The work of Leitch and Escalona (24) observing tension in infants and young children seems illustrative of this point. They report many instances of "tension" responses in children when the mother or mothering person is not sensitive or reactive to the child's cues but behaves with the child according to some internal program of her own: "For example, a 2-months-old infant received abundant loving care from a mother who was tolerant and flexible with one exception; she insisted on forcibly administering spoon feedings of semi-solids despite the baby's lack of willingness to accept this. Forced feedings always precipitated rigidity of the whole body, apparently in an attempt to resist the procedure, and were invariably followed by rapid, nervous burping, spitting up and at times vomiting. In all other situations except feeding this infant was relaxed and normally responsive."

Either extreme of response on the part of the mother or mothering person may say in effect to the child "you don't exist" or "I don't want you to exist." In the less extreme instances, the message may be "I don't want you to exist as you are."

In any event, difficulties of adaptation between mother and child in the early months of infancy must necessarily lead to an impairment of any sense of effectiveness or value that the child is developing. His sense of effectiveness and value must depend on evoking a "taking care of" or nurturing response on the part of the mother, as, indeed, his very survival depends on it. Thus the child's first means of being effective and having an impact on his environment is through the "behavioral manifestations of affect . . . as a means of communication to and with others to indicate needs, distress or degree of comfort" (20).

It must be remembered, however, that these affective communications are not specific. Crying, for example, is primarily a communication about the mother-child relationship, while the specific need or distress involved has to be translated by the mother. This first level of communication is similar to all mammalian communication as described by Bateson (25). As an example, he states:

"When your cat is trying to tell you to give her food, how does she do it? She has no word for food or for milk. What she does is to make movements and sounds that are characteristically those a kitten makes to a mother cat. If we were to translate the cat's message into words, it would not be correct to say that she is crying 'Milk!' Rather, she is saying something like 'Mama!' Or perhaps still more correctly, we should say that she is asserting 'Dependency! Dependency!' The cat talks in terms of patterns and contingencies of relationship, and from this talk it is up to you to take a *deductive* step, guessing that it is milk that the cat wants. It is the necessity for this deductive step which marks the difference between preverbal mammalian communication and *both* the communications of bees and the languages of men [Italics in the original]."

In summary, at this point of the child's development he is dependent on others for his survival, and his impact on his environment is limited to his impact on the mother. His needs must be identified and responded to by another, and power to act directly on the environment remains outside of himself.

While most people survive this period quite well, most people also leave it with residuals. Common residuals are a feeling of personal ineffectiveness or inability to act, the requirement for one's needs to be translated and responded to by another, the sense that the power in a relationship resides in the other person, the continued need to evoke a "taking care of" response from others to feel loved or to have a sense of value, and the need to have "power over" others to have value.

With the development of muscular control, the infant takes the first steps toward recognizing and taking care of his own needs. He moves from the power merely to evoke a nurturing response from others to the ability to act on his own behalf (effective action toward the environment). The major source of his self-esteem shifts from having power over people to having a direct impact on his environment.

Parallel to the development of muscular control is the beginning of speech. Engel (20) states that the development of speech changes the means of communication in a unique way; thus, "once speech is possible, affect expression is no longer the only medium of communication of need, distress, desire or reassurance of the other." With speech, the psychobiological unit can develop into a psychosocial unit and can expand beyond the mother and natal family.

However, in our culture, although speech and motor activity allow the possibility of more precise identification and satisfaction of one's needs, very often the original infantile mother-child or family-child relationship is maintained. By this we mean that affect expression (very often, now, taking the form of "body language") and translation remain the rule. Direct requests, not requiring translation, are discouraged by the parents because they are seen as mandates that must be obeyed if the parents are to remain "good" parents. They are also seen as inherent criticisms of the parents' translating ability—which is taken to be a sign of love. The result is that, in many families, open requests are punished subtly. The effect is to foster and perpetuate the feeling that "real love" is expressed by understanding and responding to the needs of another family member *in the absence* of clear verbal communication. One makes requests of a stranger, not of a loved one. In addition, the response to a clear request is "worthless" because one *has* to respond to such a request, whereas the spontaneous awareness of and response to nonverbal messages is "voluntary" and a sign of caring. These family pressures (although not consciously directed to this end) result in the child giving up his ability to perceive and act independently and effectively. Some of these processes have been detailed elsewhere (26).

While there are many ways of directly impairing the sense of independent effective behavior in children and thus reinforcing the idea of powerlessness, we here describe some more subtle incidents that are particularly relevant to depression. An 8-year-old boy wanted to fly model airplanes. His father promised him one for his birthday and planned to buy a special model that could be put back together after crashing, since he, the father, did not know how to fly planes either. The boy did not want to wait, saved his allowance, and bought his own plane. The father, angered by the son's independent activity, at first refused to help him fly the plane and suggested that he get an experienced friend to help. The boy was unable to arrange this and persisted in asking his father for help. Finally the father reluctantly agreed. However, once they got the plane off the ground, the father turned the flying over to his son—who immediately crashed the plane. Since the plane was not the special crash-resistant model, it was destroyed except for the engine. The boy immediately grew depressed, saying that he should never have bought the plane, and would not get another one.

The father in this instance not only discouraged his son's step toward independence by refusing to help him fly the plane originally, but also set the son up for a depressive response when he did agree to help. In reviewing the incident later, the father realized that he himself was likely to crash the plane, since he had no experience. He was unable to tolerate being the source of his son's disappointment and so arranged for his son to be the agent of his own disappointment. By allowing the child, in effect, to hang himself, he unwittingly but strongly reinforced the message that independent activity leads to ineffectiveness and disappointment.

That this kind of attitude is learned quite early is seen in the earliest memory reported by Sue, the 16-year-old mentioned previously. At the age of 4 she wanted some water, which her mother gave to her in a glass cup, telling her to stay on the front steps. A friend came by and Sue ran to her, falling and cutting her hand. Her immediately response was, "I should listen to Mother." She reported feelings of mild depression subsequently when she would go against her mother's wishes. Of course, for this incident to have the consequences described, the groundwork of discouraging independent activity must have already been done. Along similar lines, a 30-year-old woman reported wanting to buy herself a $25.00 skirt when she was a teenager. She asked her father for the money but was refused. She then secretly took money out of her savings account (which she had opened in kindergarten) and bought the skirt. Her father had always matched her deposits, and it was infrequent that a week would go by without a deposit. When her father learned what she had done, he never again put money into her account. Her independent activity had done "irreparable damage" and no restitution was possible.

The following example was reported by the mother of a depressed teenager, when we were exploring what might have triggered the depression. The girl had learned to cook spaghetti in a home economics course, and asked permission to cook it for the family, who had never had spaghetti. The mother agreed and the subsequent meal was a great success—so much so that the other members wanted it as part of the regular menu. The mother did not realize it consciously at the time, but was later able to become aware, that she felt threatened in her role of homemaker by the family's delighted response to the change of menu. However, at the table she ostensibly joined in the family's enthusiasm. When she checked the kitchen, however, she found utensils and ingredients still on the counter. Instead of helping her daughter realize that part of cooking is cleaning up, so that the girl could take pleasure in the preparation of the next meal in a clean kitchen, she ripped into her angrily with statements such as, "How dare you leave my kitchen in such a filthy mess?"

After a repetition of this incident, the daughter gave up interest in cooking for the family and became generally depressed. One aspect of the depression was a reduction of spontaneous activity; the daughter often asked the mother for suggestions for what she could do, which were followed by little enthusiasm or pleasure in doing them. This mother had given her daughter the covert message that her successful independent activity and her development of homemaking skills were destructive to the mother. While the mother *was* angry with the daughter's success, she did not consciously intend such a drastic reduction of the daughter's area of effective behavior, with a consequent increase in her sense of powerlessness.

Grandiose attitudes are also inculcated by a variety of means within the family. These also have been given in more detail elsewhere (26). Aside from direct indications that the child or family is special and unique, a variety of incidents give that message to the child obliquely. For example, a young girl carried a package home for a neighbor for the first time in her life. At the walkway to the neighbor's house she handed the package to the neighbor. When they arrived home, her mother turned to her and said, "How dare you humiliate me by not carrying that package all the way to the door for our neighbor!" When the daughter protested that she had not realized that this was expected of her, her mother replied that she should have known. She thereby suggested that to know correct rules of polite behavior without learning or experience was a reasonable rather than a grandiose expectation.

Another way in which grandiose expectations are taught or perpetuated occurs when realistic limits are not set by the parents or allowed for the child. For example, when a depressed man in therapy was exploring his inability to set realistic work goals for himself, he remembered a job that he had of mowing the lawn for his family. It was a large lawn and the mowing was done by hand. Although he was allowed the choice not to mow the lawn on a particular day, he was never allowed the choice of doing less than the full job at one time. His parents had an all or nothing-at-all attitude toward work, which became a part of his self-evaluation.

However, the most powerful means of maintaining the powerless/grandiose polarity while simultaneously impairing a sense of effective action is guilt-evoking blame. A childhood incident reported by a depressed man in therapy illustrates this point. While shopping with his mother, at about the age of 4, he saw some blocks that he wanted. He pestered his mother until eventually she bought them. However, as he walked happily home with the blocks in his hand, his mother informed him that to buy the blocks for him she had spent money that was to be used to buy meat for dinner. Because of his selfishness and inconsiderateness of other family members, there would be no meat for supper. The mother's conscious aim, of course, was to teach the boy consideration for others. What she was also teaching him inadvertently was that his desire for pleasure was destructive to others, an idea that he still believed as an adult. She was also saying that her 4-year-old son had the power to force her to do something against her wishes, and to deprive the family of their evening meal through his persistent requests. That is, he had the magical, evil, grandiose power to injure others and "make" them suffer. Furthermore, on the level of direct activity, he was powerless to repair the "damage" he had done. It was "too late"; the evening meal was "ruined." The alternative of returning the blocks for a refund was never suggested, contributing to the "irreversibility" of the incident and undermining his ability to evaluate consequences, consider alternatives, and learn how to repair or make restitution for errors.

This apparent inability to find alternatives or to make repairs is a characteristic of depressive behavior, and is an important component of the feeling of being trapped. The depressed person not only has these attitudes toward his own behavior, but also applies them to the behavior of others toward him. The ultimate message, in this incident and other incidents involving guilt-evoking blame, is that the child's first responsibility is not to his own feelings and needs but to the feelings and needs of others. Their feelings and welfare must take precedence over his out of his own "spontaneous" behavior, and not out of an interactive process between people. Furthermore, he must suppress and deny his own feelings for the sake of theirs. An important consequence of this kind of experience, then, is that both responsibility for oneself and clear communication are interfered with so that one's needs must be translated and met by others. Thus the child remains relatively powerless in relationships. The power to act remains with others, not with the self; the infantile condition is repeated.

The child in our society not only is taught to place his feelings secondary to others even to the point of suppressing or denying them, but also he is taught that any strong feelings are offensive to others. To express certain feelings, such as tenderness or hurt, is considered an indication of weakness. Other feelings, such as strong anger, are considered "bad" or destructive to others; the expression of such feelings is an indication that one may be losing "control" or going crazy. One woman, when her mother died, felt that her grief was an unfair burden to place on her family, so she left her house to sit in the car and cry. Children and adults are encouraged to be "rational," not "emotional" or "hysterical."

This discouragement has several consequences. We noted previously, in dealing with the early child-mother system, that the expression of affects is the first kind of communication, the communication of needs, pleasures, and displeasures in relationship terms. But it is more than this: it is also the first means of impact on the environment. Suppression of the expression of affects, then, is both isolating in relationship terms and a contributing factor to the sense of powerlessness. Furthermore, since the expression of affects is so important for clarifying and maintaining relationships, interference with the open expression of emotion results in their indirect expression through somatization, acting-out behavior, or symbolic symptoms. Clear communication about relationships is then hindered.

For example, an adolescent youth saved his money and bought his father an electric razor for a special occasion. The father, on opening the present, taunted the son and ridiculed him for buying such a present. The son took the razor, returned it to its box, and put in a drawer in his room, feeling rejected and hurt. One morning later in the week, he heard the sound of a razor coming from the bathroom. He said nothing, but checked the razor box and found it empty. Later in the day he found the razor back in its box. The next day the same thing occurred. Neither father nor son mentioned these happenings even though they continued for some months before the razor stayed in the bathroom. Not having information from the father, we can only speculate on his involvement. However, we can see the effect. The effect of the taunting was that the son felt foolish in his choice of gift and in his ability to make decisions about spending money. The taunting also gave the more subtle message that expressions of appreciation or warmth on the part of a man are a sign of weakness. (This may, indeed, have been a large part of the father's motivation.) The subsequent secret use of the razor was apparently an attempt to repair the hurt, but the secrecy meant that the father was not taking responsibility for the repair, nor for any feelings of regret that he might have had concerning his son's hurt. The secrecy also gave the message that the son should not officially know or comment on his father's action—a further impairment of clear communication.

The difficulty experienced by the depressed person in identifying and expressing anger directly has played a prominent part in most dynamic formulations concerning depression. Guntrip (27) states that the depressive has the central idea that anger is destructive. The depressed person believes that anger is stronger than love. It is our contention that the depressive's difficulty with anger not only is due to this belief in the destructive power of anger—the grandiose pole of the infantile polarity—but also is due to the depressive's sense of powerlessness in human relationships.

The nature of the grandiose pole has been suggested in the clinical anecdote illustrating guilt-evoking blame. A further example from the same man illustrates this point further. When he was 10, his mother asked him to chop some firewood for the kitchen. Since he was involved in an activity of his own at the time, he irritatedly said that he would do it later. His mother wanted the firewood then, so proceeded to chop the wood herself. In the process she cut her finger with the axe. Although she said nothing directly to her son, she fixed her finger ostentatiously in front of him. In fact, she never said anything directly to her son, but held her finger stiffly extended for several months after her accident—a constant reminder of the destructive effect of his lack of consideration and the anger behind it.

At the same time that the depressed person fears that his expression of anger will destroy others, he also fears that a direct expression of anger will have no effect, no impact on others. Taken to an extreme, the fear is that he has no value, that he does not exist in a meaningful way for others. This is first seen clinically when the depressed person is encouraged to feel and express anger; "What good will it do?" and "Nothing will change" are common responses.

This fear of lack of value to others related to a lack of impact on them is not restricted to the expression of anger, however. It is very important to the depressed person's readiness to "give up," to his difficulty in finding alternative courses of action, and to his need to manipulate others (to exercise power "over" others rather than exercise open communication). However, the need for impact is particularly relevant to the expression of anger in depression. This need is one factor in the depressive's turning of anger inward rather than outward toward the environment. When anger is turned inward, one is assured of having an impact on the target of anger. Furthermore, to the degree that a person suffers, anyone emotionally involved with that person also suffers, though perhaps not to the same extent.

For example, a young boy had just learned to tie his shoes. Since he took great pleasure in independent activity, this step was an important one for him. The next day, his mother said something to him that aroused his anger. The need for his anger to have an impact was so strong that he gave up his pleasure in his independent activity. With transparent anger in his voice he said to his mother, "I've forgotten how to tie my shoes, you have to tie them for me." Here, although the immediate target was himself, the real target was his mother. Insofar as she had an investment in his independent growth and development, she was affected by the child's withdrawal from his new skill. However, while this depressive tactic is successful in having an impact on others, in having power "over" people, it is at the expense of effective behavior and thus at the expense of a sense of value or self-esteem that is related to one's own activity rather than primarily to the responses of other people. The child's development into an autonomous individual is interfered with, and the infantile polarity is reinforced.

A more complex example illustrates further. This episode occurred between the father and son involved in the electric razor gift described previously. While the young adolescent was building a model airplane, his father came in and mocked him about being a baby. The young man crushed the plane in anger, saying to his father, "See what you made me do?" In this incident, the young man not only acted self-destructively to have an impact on his father to equalize the impact of his father's words on him, but he also gave the responsibility for this action to his father. Again, this maneuver achieved an equalizing power "over" his father at the expense of destroying the product of his own pleasurable and productive activity.

The incident did not end at this point. The young man left the house for a while, and when he returned to his room, there was a new plane on the bed. As in the previous incident, the father did not say anything to his son, leaving unclear whatever message he was trying to convey. The son reacted with confusion, anger, and depression. Again, the effect was not only the promotion of unclear communication and lack of responsibility for confronting the relationship, but also the young man's manipulative attempt to have an impact with his anger was neutralized in a way that did not lead to constructive alternatives.

In the examples given, the anger behind the acts of the child and young man was clear to themselves and transparent to the other. With the progression of disassociation from emotions, particularly anger, that is characteristic of depression, the behavior remains, but is experienced and described differently. Now, instead of transparent anger, there is a sense of disinterest or loss. For example, once disassociated from his anger, the man in the second example would typically respond to the same incident by a sudden sense of worthlessness or loss of self-esteem accompanied by disinterest in model planes, and a taking over of the father's belittling attitude toward the activity.

In summary, our view of the difficulty in identifying or expressing anger in depression is that the depressed person is caught in a situation in which, no matter what he does, he risks deprivation. (This contributes, incidentally, to the trapped feeling that is characteristic of depression.) At the grandiose pole, the expression of anger risks the "destruction" of others, with consequent guilt and the feeling that one is worthless though possessed of evil power. At the powerless pole, the depressed person risks having no impact on the other, again leading to a feeling of powerlessness, worthlessness, and lack of value to others.

Previously, we stated that the depressed person cannot handle loss. Several aspects of this are related to dependency. First of all, loss triggers both poles of the infantile polarity: it indicates that the person does not have "power over" in the grandiose sense and is therefore worthless or has no value; and it indicates that the person is ineffective in acting in such a way as to prevent loss, thereby evolving feelings of powerlessness and lack of value. Secondly, that aspect of dependency which is connected with the suppression of or disassociation from emotions interferes with feeling and with expressing both the anger and grief which are appropriate to loss, whether minor or major. The disruptive effects of the inability to mourn the loss of a person have been documented by a number of authors, among them Whittis (28) and Jensen and Wallace (29). Paul and Grosser (30) have developed a specific technique to help a family to learn and experience an appropriate mourning process for major loss.

An additional aspect of the inability to deal with loss does not derive from dependency but contributes to it. This factor is the inability of the infant to tolerate a lack of response from the mothering person. In this chapter we have dealt with this factor from the standpoint of lack of impact. Previously, lack of contact and the anxiety underlying it have been the focus of discussion (26). We believe that this factor is responsible for the development of the Child/Parent ego states, to use the terminology of Berne. That is, the threat of loss of or abandonment by the mothering person leads to two results. The first is a denial of and going underground of disapproved-of aspects of the personality which are expressed in the Child ego state. The second result is the identification with the aggressor aspect of the development of the Parent ego state. The mechanism of identification with the aggressor has at least two functions.

The first function is to protect the child from the loss of a relationship by incorporating the disappointing person. This function has been amplified by the object-relations theorists (27). A consequence of this mechanism is that the relationship is preserved symbolically while individuation is interfered with—an important consequence for the family system. The second function of this mechanism is to protect the child from injury from a threatening or disappointing person. The greatest threat comes from, in terms of the early mother-child relationship, abandonment or the threat of nonexistence. This function has been detailed extensively by classical psychoanalysts.

Once this division has occurred, the infantile polarity is self-perpetuating. The sense of powerlessness is centered in the Child ego state. The sense of grandiose expectations is centered in the Parent ego state. Any incident that triggers a sense of powerlessness not only evokes the Child ego state, but also triggers the Parent. Similarly, any event that first triggers grandiose expectations also triggers a subsequent sense of powerlessness when the expectations cannot be fulfilled. An additional consequence of this division occurs with the evocation of anger. In addition to the formulations presented earlier in this paper, we now wish to add that a factor in the depressive's turning of anger back on himself comes from the feeling of powerlessness in the Child when a person does not seem to have an impact on the external environment. The pain of feeling powerless can be somewhat mitigated by the mechanism of identifying with the aggressor, by shifting the anger and center of power to the parent. It is more comfortable to be attacked than to be ignored. The anger can then be directed toward the Child aspect of the person, a suitably reactive target, with a secondary impact on anyone who is emotionally involved with the depressed person, as noted above. A further consequence of this division is the "family projection process" which Framo has detailed.

Closely related to the depressive's difficulty in dealing with loss is his tendency to equate his value on the basis of results alone rather than on the nature and quality of his activity and effort. Results are important from the reality standpoint. Not to achieve certain results after putting in effort is disappointing, and it would be appropriate to feel and express disappointment. As we have noted, this is difficult for the depressive to do. Furthermore, measuring a person by results is a characteristic of the culture of the United States, so that there is considerable cultural support for this tendency. However, in this view a person is only as good as his last result, and his value can rise and fall like a stock in the market depending on many factors beyond his control in addition to his perception, planning, effort, and activity. The person's sense of self and self-respect are not tied into effective action, but into visible results for display to others. The center of one's behavior then resides in the opinion of others rather than in the person's pleasure and satisfaction in using himself well. The person who does well participating in the classroom but who cannot perform well on exams, and subsequently has a poor opinion of himself, is an example of this attitude. The underlying fear is that one's basic self is unacceptable, even unlovable, and therefore one will be abandoned. A variation of this fear is that one's existence has no meaning for others, that one is basically worthless.

To conclude this section on dependency, we note that Seligman (31), reporting on the work of Seligman and others (32, 33) as well as other experimental psychologists, independently confirms our ideas about the connection between the powerless aspect of dependency and depression. Experiments with both animals and humans that result in their being exposed to situations where their behavior has no effect develop "learned helplessness." These animals and humans, once having learned that their behavior was useless in one experimental situation, gave up without exploring alternatives in a new experimental situation where their behavior could have had an effect. After drawing a number of parallels between the characteristics of "learned helplessness" and depression, Seligman suggests that "successful therapy occurs when the patient believes that his responses produce gratification, that he is an effective human being." Forms of therapy that he reports as being helpful to depression are "graded task assignments," "self assertion," and "expressing strong emotions," particularly anger. We agree both on theoretical grounds and clinical experience that these therapeutic approaches are useful in depression.

The final topic we cover in this section is that of depression as a mutually causative deviation-amplifying system (MCDAS). Beck (34), while not using the specific terminology of MCDAS, suggested a "circular feedback model" for depression. "The discussion so far has viewed the connection between cognitive structure and affect as a kind of one-way street; that is, the direction has been from cognition to emotion. But it is conceivable that there is an interaction between these, and that feelings may also influence thought content. The lack of concrete clinical data to support the concept of a reverse flow makes such theorizing highly speculative. Nevertheless, the formulation of a mutually reinforcing system (35) can provide a more complete explanation for the phenomena observed in depression. The operation of this system can be presented as follows: Let us assume that an unpleasant life situation triggers schemata relevant to loss, self-blame, and negative expectancies. As they become activated, these schemata produce a stimulation of the affective structures connected to them. The activation of the affective structures is responsible for the subjective feeling of depression. These affective structures, in turn, further reinforce the activity of these schemata. The interaction thus consists of schemata ↔ affective structures. This model could explain the downward spiral in depression: The more negatively the patient thinks, the worse he feels; the worse he feels, the more negatively he thinks." Wender (11), on the other hand, diagrams a deviation-amplifying feedback (DAF) model based on the hypothesis that "depression is due to anger unexpressed or turned inward; consider the fate of an individual who is angry at another and unable to express that anger and whose values do not permit him to perceive himself as weak or succorant. As may be seen in Figure 2 [not reproduced in the present chapter], several loops operate to increase the probability that unexpressed anger and concurrent depression will increase.

1. Depression leads to decreased coping ability, which leads to negative self-evaluation. The latter may lead to increased anger, increased depression, or both.
2. Decreased coping ability 'forces' others in the environment to provide assistance. The patient's perception of himself as one who requires aid may generate anger and/or a decreased self-evaluation, both of which will probably lead to increased depression."

These authors have applied a systems viewpoint to the intrapsychic process primarily, although Wender has included "aid from others" in his factors leading to depression. We believe that mutually causative deviation-amplifying processes begin in the earliest mother-child interactions as we have suggested earlier in this chapter.

Under ordinary circumstances, however, the DAF cycles are countered by deviation-reducing feedback (DRF) cycles so that homeostasis within the person and the family follows the pattern first recorded by Jackson. Once the triggering event for depression occurs, events that may have been deviation-reducing can become deviation-amplifying. For example, effective behavior ordinarily enhances self-esteem. However, once the depressive system has been activated, effective behavior may be experienced by the depressed person as "selling out" to get the approval of other family members. It then has the DAF effect of lowering self-esteem and increasing the depression. A full detailing of DAF effects relating to the aspects of dependency that we have discussed is beyond the scope of this chapter. Some effects have been suggested during the previous discussion. As an illustration of DAF within the family that helps to perpetuate depression, we relate briefly some implications of the need to evoke approval as the source of self-esteem, rather than effective behavior as the source of self-esteem. The need to evoke approval leads to the manipulation of others that is one of the characteristics of the depressed person. The tendency to manipulate is increased by the attitude, prevalent among families, that the expression of a caring or loving feeling is a sign of weakness that renders the initiator of such a feeling vulnerable to other family members. Once depression is triggered, with an increase in the infantile polarity, the failure of a manipulation immediately leads to a sense of powerlessness, a loss of self-esteem, and an increase in depression. The failure of a manipulation also triggers anger. However, anger cannot effectively be directed to other family members because of the dual fear of lack of impact on the one hand, and destructive magical impact on the other hand. The only effective target, as described earlier, is the Child aspect of the self, and so depression is again increased. The success of a manipulation fares little better once depression has started. When the depressed person deprecates himself, he experiences the response from others as coming not from their genuine caring but from his manipulation. Once again, self-esteem is diminished, and increased depression results. At this point, even a spontaneous reaching out by another family member is experienced as the result of a manipulation and is rejected. Even effective behavior to which other family members respond is now experienced as a manipulation to get that response, with the consequences just described. The depressed person experiences himself as a fraud who cannot live up to the expectations of others, expectations that are now projections of the Parent aspect of himself. Finally, the depressed person is reduced to feeling effective by rendering others as impotent as he feels, rejecting their efforts to help, and reacting to their frustration by further self-deprecation, feelings of worthlessness, and depression.

This process leads to a progessive polarization of the depressed person and other family members in such a manner that each pole is reinforced by the behavior of the other pole. That is, not only the depression is reinforced, but also the behavior of other family members which in turn stimulates a depressive response, is reinforced by depressive behavior. In a unilateral depression, this polarization is of a complementary nature as described by Bateson (36). Bateson referred to the progressive differentiation of two cultures that came in contact with each other as schizmogenesis. In addition to the complementary variety, he also described symmetrical schizmogenesis. In this variety, the behavior involved is of the same nature on the part of both cultures, such as boasting. In depression, symmetrical schizmogenesis would occur when depressive behavior on the part of one family member was met by reactive depressive behavior on the part of another family member, and where each person's depression increased the depression of the other.

Treatment

We now come to the actual treatment of depression within the framework of family therapy and the theoretical principles outlined above. We discuss treatment under the topics of diagnosis and general principles of treatment.

The diagnosis of depression, when overt, presents no problem when dealing with an individual alone. However, although only one member of a family may complain of depression, or be brought into therapy for depressive complaints, it is helpful to interview the whole family in a diagnostic session. As we have discussed in the section on systems theory, and as Tabachnick (37) has specifically written about, the symptom of depression can be seen as an indirect method of communication about needs and relationships. While this symptom might be inferred in interviewing an individual alone, it can be seen directly when interviewing the family together. The method of intervening into the family system, whether it be conjoint family therapy, therapy of the individual, or of a significant subgrouping within the family, is best determined by the family interview. In addition to the family interview, we have been using a structured task, the Ravich Interpersonal Game/Test (RIG/T) in conjunction with videotape, for the past several years to evaluate the family system. The RIG/T itself, through a system of coding developed by Ravich (38), is a quick method of determining the relationship rules under which the family operates. The videotape of the family interaction while performing this task is especially valuable for determining the communication patterns within the family system. The advantages of using videotape playback with a structured task have been presented elsewhere (39). Specifically for depression, the depressive facies and behavior are available for all family members, including the depressed person, to see and react to directly.

The RIG/T is a clinical version of the Deutsch-Krause Acme-Bolt trucking game, which in turn had been developed to explore conflict and bargaining situations. Ravich has described the RIG/T and its use in a number of articles (38, 40, 41). Briefly, it consists of two identical but reversed model train layouts with a short (direct) or long (alternate) route to an end point. The family is tested in dyads beginning with the parents. Ravich (38) describes the procedure as follows:

"Over a series of trips, each person must maneuver a vehicle from separate starting points located at opposite ends of a small table. A panel divides the two sides of the table so that each person can see his own vehicle and the track system along which it can travel, but cannot see the other person's vehicle or track system.

On successive trips, each person must decide whether to move his vehicle to its destination by way of the short Direct route or the long Alternate route. Collisions may occur along a section (electrically) common to both Direct routes. In addition, each person controls a barrier that can be closed to stop the other person's vehicle when it is on the Direct route. If the longer Alternate route is taken by one or both individuals no collisions can occur. Also, a vehicle on the Alternate route cannot be stopped by closing the barrier. Scoring on each trip is determined by the time required for the vehicles which travel at fixed velocity to reach the destination against a standard time (o). A vehicle that travels unimpeded on the Direct route can reach the destination in $T=+1$, while a vehicle on the Alternate route can do so in $T=-1$.

A wide range of options on any single trip exists and the series of twenty or more trips that constitute a test allows an almost infinite array of possibilities."

In addition to the coding developed by Ravich, the choices of Direct route, Alternate route, and Barrier can be seen in the terms suggested by Horney (42) for behavior, and Davitz (43) for emotion: toward, away, and against. When one or several family members consistently choose the Alternate route (away) or a combination of Barrier and Alternate route (against-away), our clinical experience indicates that a depressive process is going on within the family. These families have a sense of hopelessness about encounters, about negotiating, and about seeing and developing alternatives. They have no constructive way to express anger and tend toward acting-out behavior both with anger and any discouragement. When both members of any family dyad being tested settle into a pattern of using the Barrier and Alternate route on each trip, the prognosis is quite poor. Intensive individual therapy as well as conjoint therapy appears necessary to combat the tendencies to "give up" or to escalate a mutual tendency to act out in a manner that is destructive to the relationship. These dyads also tend to develop a "rotating depression" pattern as described by MacGregor and others (44). That is, when a depressed member of a family works through the loss of a sphere of influence, another family member risks the loss of his, and develops depression in turn.

The behavior of a separated couple that had this pattern during a segment of the test is illustrative. On the basis of an initial interview with the wife alone, a joint interview and test was suggested. Even before the first conjoint session, the husband called to cancel his participation because of discouragement. Although he had originally been enthusiastic since he wanted a reconciliation, he was at this point ready to give up. "She wants me to crawl," he said, "and I just can't do it." However, he was able to accept the possibility that he misunderstood his wife's expectations; the interview and testing took place, and conjoint therapy began. Within a few sessions the husband was able to express his anger, and began asserting himself in an angry way during one session. He was so determined to assert his anger that he would not pause or allow any interaction.

The wife's response to this session was to become discouraged about any change in the relationship. She decided to continue conjoint sessions and, even though she had made the original therapeutic contact, decided to permit her husband to remain in individual therapy with the conjoint therapist while she found another therapist. It later turned out that this behavior was only the manifest level. Secretly, she hoped that her behavior would be translated as meaning that she was frightened and concerned for the future of the relationship. She further hoped that the therapist and her husband would reach out to her reassuringly so that she could risk further participation. In actuality, this was done by telephone after one conjoint session was missed. However, this was done not because of a correct "translation," but because of evidence of a positive nature from previous conjoint sessions that the relationship could be worked out. The correlation of the RIG/T pattern and the behavior of both husband and wife was helpful to the course of therapy.

Almost any complaint other than depression can be used as a presenting complaint. Improvement of the presenting complaint then reveals the underlying depression. This is illustrated by Sue, the daughter in the clinical excerpt with which this chapter began. When her initial complaint of a sexual dysfunction cleared in a rapid treatment approach, her underlying depression about her relationship to her father surfaced.

Kohl (45), writing about the pathological reaction of marital partners to clinical improvement on the part of their spouses who were hospital inpatients, observed that 21 of 39 partners had a depressive response. Forrest (46) reports on a number of cases where both partners in a marriage were seen in addition to individual therapy for the partner initially entering therapy for depression. Her observations were that both partners shared depressive tendencies that required therapy. In her cases, when the identified depressed patient improved, the asymptomatic partner developed a reactive depression.

Another form of disguised depression is manifested after conjoint treatment has been initiated with some subsequent success. The first return to a pretherapy kind of incident is followed by discouragement, the feeling that nothing has changed or will change, and the impulse to stop therapy. The depression may be in one or more family members and requires quite active intervention on the part of the therapist. The ability to predict such an eventuality by means of the depressive pattern on the RIG/T is helpful in many cases. In families with "rotating depression" or where several members are simultaneously depressed, this pattern may recur a number of times during the treatment process. These families forget that they have successfully resolved their discouragement in the past.

At times a period of individual treatment is necessary before the conjoint treatment can continue. For example, a couple in their 30s sought conjoint treatment as a final effort to salvage the marriage before getting a divorce. The wife, depressed but with anger quite close to the surface, came reluctantly, since she experienced the marriage as over for her. Her depression was related to two areas. Three years previously they had learned that they were unable to have a child because of a physical dysfunction on the part of the husband. Without a child, the wife felt unfulfilled as a woman. Her depression was aggravated when they moved to New York from a rural state. In New York, because of licensing differences, she could not work in her area of professional competence. To keep busy she worked as a secretary, which she again felt was unfulfilling and even degrading. After 3 months of conjoint treatment, with improved communication, the wife entered individual treatment in addition to conjoint therapy to deal with her work problem. Improvement in the work area resulted in a lifting of her depression to the degree that conjoint therapy was terminated. At this point she was able to take responsibility for and make arrangements for adoption. This was something the couple had tried to arrange together in the past, but which the wife had been too depressed to follow through on. This movement on the part of the wife threatened the husband's area of influence in the marriage. He responded by initiating arguments about responsibility for the adopted child, talking about divorce, telephoning the therapist about his wife's assertive behavior, and beginning an affair. He refused further conjoint meetings, stated that the marriage was worse than ever, and expressed pessimism about their future. Fortunately, the gains made in previous conjoint therapy were sufficient to enable the couple to work through the husband's acting-out reaction. The adoption was carried through and the wife terminated therapy. At the time of termination she was able to spot the triggers for her depressive responses and change her behavior effectively.

General Principles

In our opinion, family therapy is not limited to conjoint family therapy. The nature of the intervention into the family system depends on the evaluation of that system. A shift may occur from one therapeutic modality to another depending on whether the whole system or a subsystem (limited to one individual at times) needs attention at any particular time.

Our main theme in attempting to alter the depressive, mutually causative, deviation-amplifying system is dealing with the infantile polarity within and between the various family members. As noted in our introduction, family members place the motivation for their behavior onto other family members. Instead of "owning" or taking responsibility for their thoughts, behavior, and feelings, family members describe each other as well as assigning motivation to each other. Naturally, since the other is considered the powerful one, the other is expected to initiate change. In some families, change in the other is seen as the only possible source of hope for change. A further difficulty is seen in depressive families. Since the powerful others have not listened or responded, or if they have, they have responded with "too little, too late," the depressive person renders them as powerless as himself by obstructing any efforts to help him.

The first step in altering the infantile polarity consists of helping family members take responsibility for their thoughts, actions, demands, and feelings by focusing on clear communication. It is suggested, for example, that family members talk to each other rather than about each other. It is also suggested that they take responsibility for asking directly for what they want rather than expecting the wish to be translated. Frequently, in the early phases of work with a family, extensive clarification and translating of family members to one another is necessary. Particularly helpful is supporting the positive connections between family members, and translating the positive aspects of negative communications. For example, behind much parental criticism is a positive concern which cannot be directly risked. We have found videotape replay of ongoing family interactions to be quite useful in this phase of therapy (47–49). In addition, we have found specific verbal and nonverbal exercises to clarify communication to be helpful. We have detailed these elsewhere (50). An example of such an exercise is the gestalt exercise called "hear and imagine."

This exercise is given to dyads within the family. One person is asked to make a brief statement to another family member. The second member is then asked to repeat the first member's statement word for word to demonstrate that it has been heard correctly. The second person is then asked to state what he "imagines" the first person to mean by his original statement. Then the second person is asked to "check out" his translation with the first person. This exercise serves two functions. First, it slows down the rapid, coded, escalating interchanges that frequently happen when a family is trying to discuss a problem area. Second, it helps the responder in the interchange to take responsibility for the translating process which goes on automatically within him, usually without conscious awareness. Most people confuse the hearing and the translation and so make attributions to other family members which are often incorrect.

In addition to learning to communicate directly and clearly, families with one or more depressed members need to learn that emotional repair is both possible and necessary to a satisfying ongoing relationship. Making repair or restitution enhances the feeling of effectiveness and self-esteem in the person making the repair. The person allowing the repair develops enhanced self-esteem and a feeling of effectiveness from expressing directly the feelings of hurt and anger that usually underlie the refusal to allow another person to repair an emotional injury. The person allowing repair also shifts from a sense of value based on the "power over" manipulation of defining the other as destructively evil to a sense of value based on the ability to work out a give-and-take relationship. In addition, that person discovers that exposing his vulnerability to another family member can lead to a closer relationship once the mutually destructive patterns are changed. The capacity to make and allow repair enhances the process of centering the sense of effective power and value within the self.

An example of repair comes from an incident that happened between Sue and Harry. Harry and Martha had a rule that homework had priority over other activities. Since the den was always the study room, either daughter wanting to do homework could ask anyone else in the family to turn off the TV or to leave the room. At the time of this incident, Sue had been living with a friend in New York where she went to school. Previously, she had commuted daily from her suburban home. Sue was home one weekend and asked her younger sister to turn off the TV as she wanted to study. Harry overheard this and yelled to Sue, "You don't have any rights here because you don't live here." Sue was upset and ran up to her room angry and hurt. Following Sue's reaction, Harry realized that he had basically felt hurt that Sue had chosen to live with a friend in New York rather than continuing to live at home. He realized that he missed her and loved her. He went upstairs, apologized to Sue, and shared his underlying feelings of hurt and love. He shared a memory of buying her first Easter bonnet with her and how beautiful he had thought she was. They had a long talk sharing their positive feelings for each other and came downstairs together as Sue returned to finish her homework. Both Harry's initiation of the repair and Sue's willingness to respond had a positive effect on the other family members. Martha had overheard the incident in the den. Seeing the positive outcome stirred up feelings about unresolved aspects of her relationship with her parents. She decided that she wanted to return to therapy to deal with those feelings. Jane, the younger sister, responded by asking how old she had to be to be able to see the therapist.

The experience of effectiveness or impact is experienced in terms of one's effect on other family members primarily. We have suggested that direct, clear communication and emotional repair are important healthy means to achieve this effect. Family therapists who have been trained or influenced by Bowen, such as Guerin (51) or Fogarty (52), help family members achieve a sense of effective participation by changing their usual role within the family through assignments. An assignment for an adult family member might be to take a family history from his parents. This assignment changes the interaction from Parent-Child to Adult-Adult, allows emotional distance, and enhances changed relationships based on new understanding of the parent's struggles and difficulties. One of us (BH) uses assignments within the family based on principles of assertive training from a behavioral standpoint. These assignments directly enhance self-esteem based on effective behavior. In addition, effective behavior outside of the family setting not only enhances general self-esteem, but also helps the family member experience himself as less vulnerable to the criticism or approval of other family members.

A sense of effectiveness can also develop from the expression of intense emotions. The ability to identify and communicate emotions directly, particularly anger, has a number of effects within the family. In families where one or more members are depressed, the idea that emotions may have either no impact or magical destructive impact is a shared one that is reinforced by the behavior of family members with one another. The direct expression of anger in a therapeutic session may initially be reacted to at either pole, or at both poles simultaneously on different levels of communication. For example, an angry protest by a child may be ignored by both parents as though nothing happened. Or the anger may be acknowledged but disqualified by a response of "I know you really didn't mean it." Frequently, because of competitive feelings ("I won't give them the satisfaction of knowing they hurt me" or "I won't let them know I'm vulnerable to them") one member will not acknowledge the impact of another's emotions on him. At the other extreme, the expression of anger may be met by indications that the person to whom the anger is directed has been "totally destroyed." Even more powerful is a situation where the responding family member states on the verbal level that the expression of anger has made no impact, while simultaneously indicating on a nonverbal level that serious injury has been done. With the help of the therapist, family members can learn to identify these ideas and change their reactions to the expression of anger. They can learn to admit that anger does have an impact, that it is painful to the receiving person, but that the emotion is not in itself destructive. However, hurtful behavior which is done out of a need to have a visible impact on another can be destructive. The end result of this learning process is to increase the sense of effectiveness within the family, and to increase the sense of value of the members to one another.

The expression of intense emotions also helps to decrease the isolation of family members from each other. The suppression of emotions not only reduces the sense of interpersonal effectiveness, but also has the effect of isolating family members in a number of ways. First, family members do not know in a clear way how others react to them or experience them. They literally do not know each other. Second, the powerless/grandiosely powerful polarity leads to a belief that one is basically unlovable, which in turn leads to masking behavior within the family. [This aspect has been further developed elsewhere (26).] The free expression of emotions, then, corrects these distortions and helps the family connect positively to each other. Third, since affect expression is the earliest form of relationship communication and is associated with the earliest contact experiences, suppression of emotions creates emotional distance which reinforces isolation between family members. The expression of emotions closes emotional distance and leads to a sense of connection and value within the family. The helpful effects of expressing emotion are not limited to anger, although that emotion is perhaps the most important to express. The direct expression of grief over loss is also very important. Paul and Grosser (30) have demonstrated the ameliorating effects of such direct expression on isolation in a three-generation family.

One further result of the expression of basic emotions is relevant to the family therapy of depression. Expression of basic emotions in a safe setting leads to a memory of and working through of early childhood incidents that are associated with the "family projection process" discussed by Framo (13).

We approach this "family projection process" in two ways. The first way is applicable to any form of therapy and consists of using a transactional (TA) theoretical approach combined with gestalt role-play technique. The Parent aspect of the personality is particularly harsh in depressive families and the Child aspect particularly powerless.

When a depressed member deprecates himself, a gestalt role between the "critic" (Parent) and the "doer" (Child) is suggested. As Perls (53) developed this technique, he suggested a dialogue between "top-dog" and "bottom-dog" and helped the patient to integrate the two poles by modifying the extremes toward each other. In our work with patients, we found that the Adult aspect of the personality, which is usually available in a compassionate way for others, is forgotten by the person when he is in the Parent/Child polarity. We therefore introduce the Adult into the dialogue between Parent and Child to act as a compassionate friend of the Child, and as an assertive rational equal to the Parent. One of us (BH) has developed this dialogue in conjunction with videotape playback as a particular therapeutic aid in depression (54). When a crossed transaction (P–C) occurs between family members, we use a modification of this technique as well as identifying the nature of the transaction for the family. We ask each family member to role-play the dialogue between himself and the other person in the transaction, beginning with the transaction as it occurred until the point of therapeutic intervention, but continuing on with the dialogue as the role-player anticipates that it would develop. It soon becomes quite clear to the observing family member, that the other as played by the role-player is not that person as experienced by himself and the observing family members, but is a fantasy of that person held by the role-player. More precisely, the other is a projected aspect of the self—Parent or Child.

The "family projection process" also becomes apparent through the confusion between intent and effect in family communications. The family member receiving a communication is quite aware of the effect of that communication on him. He then assumes, without checking it out with the sender, that the effect on him is intended and reacts accordingly. Distortions, of course, can occur in either sender or receiver. The sender can be blind to certain aspects of his communication that are clear to others. The receiver can emphasize certain aspects of the communication to the exclusion of other aspects. While both types of distortion are important to examine, the receiver's distortion is the type that is most seen in the projective process. While a certain amount of this distortion is inevitable in any family, families in difficulty operate this way during a large part of their communication. In families where depression is the predominant symptom, the distortion takes the form of translating most communications as indications that the receiver has little value to the sender. For example, when Sue chose to live in New York for convenience rather than commuting to school, Harry translated this behavior as meaning that the family, and Harry in particular, had little emotional value for Sue. Videotape, exercises such as the hear and imagine, and role-plays are helpful in correcting such distortions.

However, self-deprecation, crossed transactions, and confusion between intent and effect are all ways to avoid either a sense of loss about past relationships or anxiety about the possibility of future loss in a present relationship. When these underlying feelings can be identified and expressed, then the loss or fear of loss can be worked through directly with consequent mitigation of the projective process within the family. The expression of intense basic emotions, as mentioned previously, is an important part of the working through process and is the second approach we use to change family projections. While this approach is also applicable to other forms of therapy, it has unique difficulties and values in family therapy. Among the difficulties of expressing basic emotions is the problem of too little/too much impact mentioned previously. In addition, most families cannot tolerate overt pain in one of the members. The beginning expression of such pain is met by a variety of "cooling" responses such as premature comforting, or explanations which have the effect of removing justification for the expression. Both the expressing and observing family members need considerable support from the therapist to allow the expression of pain and its consequent working through. The result, a diminishing of the projective process, allows greater individualization of family members and a greater genuine intimacy. Greater intimacy, however, renews fear of a relationship loss in the present or future and can reinforce a tendency to a depressive response to a setback, or to a premature ending of therapy by a "flight into health."

A couple in the ending phase of treatment illustrates some of the points made in this section of the chapter. They had previously been in conjoint treatment for a number of years with the wife's individual therapist. The emphasis in conjoint treatment had been their sadomasochistic relationship. The emphasis in individual treatment had been the wife's depression. Treatment had been terminated on the husband's initiative. Although he personally felt helped and considerably improved through the conjoint therapy, he saw no changes either in his wife or in their ongoing relationship.

Characteristic of their relationship were periodic episodes precipitated by discussion of the "Joe story" (to be identified below). These discussions invariably ended in irrational screaming and fugue behavior on the part of the wife, Judith, and in intense fury and assaultive behavior on the part of the husband, David. In recent years, these episodes were followed by increasing depression on the part of Judith. She entered individual therapy with one of us for her depression after one of these episodes. David refused to be interviewed at that time, since he believed the problem to be entirely Judith's.

Within a brief period Judith entered group therapy where she was able to report these episodes, but was able to do little in the way of expressing her emotions regarding them, other than reporting her pervasive depression. Within a short time, Judith's depression deepened and she developed several episodes of suicidal preoccupation. At that time, conjoint therapy was thought necessary for any improvement to occur, and David was asked to come in for an interview. He did so reluctantly, feeling that he had no role to play in Judith's therapy other than to describe her behavior more accurately than she usually did. However, since he was concerned about her suicidal thoughts, he did agree to do that much.

In the initial interview, David was somewhat belligerent to both Judith and the therapist. Judith appeared terrified but made no statements expressing fear. David reacted to her fearful appearance by getting quite angry and at one point began to leave the room to avoid hitting Judith when she "refused" to stop looking frightened. However, he was quite responsive to the therapist's suggestion to return to his chair and examine what was going on between Judith and himself. The therapist saw David as being angry primarily because he felt accused by Judith's frightened appearance, and because he felt powerless to find a solution to their difficulties. David saw Judith's attitudes and behavior as being responsible for his own behavior and could not see how to change unless she changed first. However, their history did not seem sufficient to account for the degree of anger that David experienced and expressed. Judith's fear, while ostensibly explained by the history of the beatings by David, seemed out of proportion to David's actual behavior. The therapist did not experience David as being either assaultive or out of control to any degree during the session. Judith also seemed to be reacting to her sense of powerlessness in the relationship. She experienced her fear as being caused by David's anger alone and saw no way to change unless David was no longer angry. However, she did feel somewhat reassured and safer when David was responsive to the therapist's suggestion to return to his chair. Both Judith and David agreed to conjoint therapy after this interview.

The positive aspects of their relationship were stressed: for example, that in spite of many years of painful turmoil, they were still together and were willing to work together to find a solution. The positive feelings and intent behind ambiguous communications were stressed, as was the necessity for Judith and David to take responsibility for themselves through clear communication of their needs and feelings, expecially positive feelings initially. The theme of giving the power in the relationship to the other was consistently focused on. The "Joe story" was not dealt with directly initially. Consideration of the "facts" of the "Joe story" was postponed until later in therapy, although incidents in their relationship which led up to the "Joe story" were discussed. The idea was suggested that the "Joe story" represented a recurrent problem in their relationship that they could not identify or deal with in any other manner. Briefly, the "Joe story" was a pattern of several suspicious incidents which indicated to David that Judith may have been unfaithful to him with Joe at one time in the past. He was constantly looking for the "truth" from Judith and stated that he was willing to forgive her if she had been unfaithful, although because of the type of person Joe was, he would have been very humiliated. At one time in the past, Judith had "confessed" that she had an affair with Joe to placate David and stop the repetitive cycle. However, David wanted more details and further "proof," and thus Judith withdrew her "confession" and ever since had been protesting her innocence. The sequence of questioning and denial, anger and fear, escalated inevitably to the beatings and fugue behavior noted earlier.

An important turning point in therapy came several months after conjoint treatment began when the RIG/T with videotape playback was given. As a result of the playback several aspects of the relationship became clarified. David reacted from a competitive frame of reference and was out to win. However, it was quite clear to Judith watching the tape that he was genuinely encouraging her to take care of herself in an equally competitive manner. Judith, on the other hand, saw the cooperative possibilities of the game quite early but was unable to state them clearly because of her distrust of David's encouragement. Both David and Judith were able to see the loss to their relationship that came from Judith's reaction. After this experience, Judith was able to believe that David was basically "for" the relationship even when he was angry and was also able to believe the therapist's positive translations of David's assertive behavior.

They both came to understand that their confusion about the difference between intent and effect was a clue to their different approaches to anger. David was hyperalert to the possibility of danger coming from the environment. All antennae were constantly extended, and the slightest indication of danger was followed by evasive or protective behavior on his part. Judith reacted in an opposite way. She had learned from her early family experiences that the best way to cope with danger was to deny its existence. Then she was less likely to act in a way that would trigger an attack from her parents, particularly from her father. Each person's style then acted as a mutually causative deviation-amplifying feedback to the other to produce a complementary schizmogenesis that continued to exaggerate their already polarized styles. David would become frightened and angry that he could not completely protect himself from danger because his love for Judith rendered him vulnerable through her blindness. Judith became frightened and secretly resentful that David's constant search for the "truth" would expose her to further danger through his confronting tendencies. David, in turn, would react to Judith's appearance of fear with anger that his attempts to protect them both were so misunderstood. He was angered that Judith experienced him as threatening to hurt her when he wanted to protect them both. He would finally get to the point that he believed that Judith must want to be beaten, so he justified his assaultive behavior by her "provocation." Judith, on the other hand, would translate David's initial frustration as the first step on the road to an inevitable beating, and from fear would avoid dealing with issues that David raised. She did this in a way that excited David's suspicions that he was vulnerable through her. She in turn justified her behavior as being "provoked" by David.

In the course of therapy, each person began to take responsibility for his or her share of this continuing pattern, and in the process began to be aware that each was dealing through the other with a disassociated aspect of himself or herself. With this realization, they were able to do the additional work of tracing their projections to the original source in their families of origin. David was able to realize that there was a frightened Child aspect of himself that, like Judith, just wanted to hide and hope that everything would go away. He was then able to realize that his mother not only withheld information from him that made life in the family more difficult for him, but also often lied to him so that he was confused. Judith was able to realize that there was an angry Child part of her, similar to David, that wanted to strike out against the world and particularly her family. She was fearful that exposing this Child would result in retaliations. To the contrary, David felt safer when this aspect of Judith was revealed. She was also able to recover memories of being beaten by her father for "lies" about her activities, although to the best of her memory she had been telling the truth.

There have been several results of taking these steps. With the clarity of communication, taking responsibility for their own behavior, and the identification of the projective process, David and Judith have been able to develop a cooperative effort to deal with their internal enemies, and to change the repetitive pattern of their interactions. They are able to use the reappearance of the "Joe story" as a clue that they have developed anxiety about their different coping styles. They are increasingly able to abort the full MCDAF sequence that had been previously introduced. Judith's suicidal episodes ended within several months of treatment and currently, when she does have a depressive response, it takes the form of ideas of a separate life or getting a divorce. Since termination was agreed on, David and Judith have taken primary responsibility for using the ideas and skills that they have learned in therapy, both between sessions and during sessions.

Other Approaches

There are a number of studies concerning the effects of suicide on family survivors [Beukenkamp (55), Goldberg and Mudd (56), Herzog and Resnik (57), Whittis (28)], and a number of reports on the family treatment of suicidal family members [Morrison and Collier (58), Resnik et al (59), Speck (60)], but a dearth of articles on the family treatment of depression. At the time of this writing, we have found only the article by Forrest on combined individual and conjoint marital treatment that specifically deals with the treatment of depression. Forrest's theoretical approach is an interpersonal one that stresses the sharing of certain characteristic depressive attitudes on the part of both marital partners although only one may demonstrate overt symptomatology at the time of entering treatment. Combined treatment has several advantages in her experience. This approach allows direct examination of and therapeutic intervention into the disturbed relationship. In addition, it reduces the burden on the therapist of the negative approach of the depressed spouse, helps maintain motivation for therapy, and provides immediate access to the spouse who is not the designated patient when he or she reacts depressively to the designated patient's improvement.

Conclusion

We have described our approach to the family therapy of depression, which is based on a systems approach with particular reference to dependency. Dependency, as we describe it, is a maintenance of the infantile polarity of powerlessness and omnipotence into adult life. Our techniques in the family therapy of depression are directed toward changing the family system in the direction of effective behavior and communication, as well as realistic expectations of the self and other family members.

References

1. Haley J: Approaches to family therapy. *Int J Psychiatr* **9**:233–242, 1970.
2. Auerswald EH: Interdisciplinary vs. ecological approach. *Fam Proc* **7**:202–215, 1968.
3. Hoffman L, Long L: A systems dilemma. *Fam Proc* **8**:211–234, 1969.
4. Rashkis H: Depression as a manifestation of the family as an open system. *Arch Gen Psychiatr* **19**:57–63, 1968.
5. Bertalanffy Von: General systems theory & psychiatry, in *American Handbook of Psychiatry.* Edited by Arieti S, New York, Basic Books, 1966, Vol. 3
6. Jackson DD: Family interaction, family homeostasis, and some implications for conjoint family psychotherapy, in *Individual and Familial Dynamics.* Edited by Masserman J, New York, Grune & Stratton, 1959.
7. Haley J: *Strategies of Psychotherapy.* New York, Grune & Stratton, 1963, p. 189.
8. Satir VM: Symptomatology: A family production, in *Theory and Practice of Family Psychiatry.* Edited by Howells JG, New York, Brunner/Mazel, 1971, pp. 663–670.
9. Hoffman L: Deviation-amplifying processes in natural groups, in *Changing Families.* Edited by Haley J, New York, Grune & Stratton, 1971, pp. 285–311.
10. Speer DC: Family systems: Morphostasis and morphogenesis, or is homeostasis enough? *Fam Proc* **9**:259–278, 1970.
11. Wender P: The role of deviation amplifying feedback in the origin and perpetuation of behavior. *Psychiatry* **31**:309–311, 1968.
12. Maruyama M: The second cybernetics: deviation amplifying mutual causative processes. *Am Sci* **51**:164–179, 1963.
13. Framo JL: Symptoms from a family transactional viewpoint, in *Family Therapy in Transition.* Edited by Ackerman NW, Boston, Little, Brown, 1970.
14. Fairbairn WRD: *Psychoanalytic Studies of the Personality.* London, Tavistock Publications, 1952.
15. Bonime W: The psychodynamics of neurotic depression, in *American Handbook of Psychiatry.* Edited by Arieti S, New York, Basic Books, 1966, Vol. 3, pp. 239–255.
16. Birdwhistell RL: *Kinesics and Context.* New York, Ballantine Books, 1972, p. 7.

17. Call JD: Newborn approach behavior and early ego development. *Int J Psa* **45**:286–295, 1964.
18. Bettelheim B: *The Empty Fortress.* New York, The Free Press, 1967.
19. Escalona S: Feeding disturbances in very young children. *Am J Orthopsychiatr* **15**:76–80, 1945.
20. Engel GL: Anxiety and depression—withdrawal: The primary affects of unpleasure. *Int J Psa* **43**:89–97, 1962.
21. Patton RG, Gardner LI: *Growth Failure In Maternal Deprivation.* Springfield, Charles C Thomas, 1963.
22. Spitz RA: Hospitalism, in *The Psychoanalytic Study of the Child.* New York, International Universities Press, 1945, Vol. 1, pp. 53–74.
23. Bowlby J: *Attachment and Loss.* New York, Basic Books, 1973, Vol. 2.
24. Leitch M, Escalona S: The reaction of infants to stress, in *The Psychoanalytic Study of the Child.* New York, International Universities Press, 1949, Vol. 4, pp. 121–140.
25. Bateson G: Problems in Cetacean and other mammalian communication, in *Steps to an Ecology of Mind.* New York, Ballantine Books, 1972, p. 367.
26. Hogan P: Some aspects of my theory and practice of therapy, in *Group Process Today.* Edited by Goldman GD, Milman DS, Springfield, Charles C Thomas, 1974, pp. 250–272.
27. Guntrip H: *Schizoid Phenomena, Object Relations and the Self.* New York, International Universities Press, 1969.
28. Whittis PR: The legacy of a child's suicide. *Fam Proc* **7**:159–169, 1968.
29. Jensen D, Wallace JG: Family mourning process. *Fam Proc* **6**:56–66, 1967.
30. Paul NL, Grosser G: Operational mourning and its role in conjoint family therapy. *Comm Ment Health J* **1**:339–345, 1965.
31. Seligman MEP: Fall into helplessness. *Psychol Today,* 43–48, June 1973.
32. Seligman MEP, Maier SF: Failure to escape traumatic shock. *J Exp Psychol* **74**:1–9, 1967.
33. Seligman MEP, Maier SF, Geer JH: Alleviation of learned helplessness in the dog. *J Abn Psychol* **73**:256–262, 1968.
34. Beck AT: *Depression: Clinical, Experimental and Therapeutic Aspects.* New York, Harper & Row, 1967.
35. Feshback S: Personal communication to Beck AT in 1965.
36. Bateson G: Culture contact and schizmogenesis, in *Steps to an Ecology of Mind.* New York, Ballantine Books, 1972, pp. 61–72.
37. Tabachnick N: Interpersonal relations in suicidal attempts. *Arch Gen Psychiatr* **4**:42–47, 1961.
38. Ravich RA: A system of notation of dyadic interaction. *Fam Proc* **9**:292–300, 1970.
39. Hogan P: Studies in marital interaction: Video and train game techniques. Presented at the second annual Fordham-Einstein Symposium, Family Psychotherapy—Theory and Practice, New York, June 1971.
40. Ravich RA: The use of an interpersonal game-test in conjoint marital psychotherapy. *Am J Psychiatr* **23**:217–229, 1969.
41. Ravich RA: The marriage/divorce paradox, in *Progress in Group and Family Therapy.* New York, Brunner/Mazel, 1972, pp. 531–536.
42. Horney K: *Collected Works of Karen Horney.* New York, WW Norton, 1937, Vol. 1.
43. Davitz JR: *The Language of Emotion.* New York, Academic Press, 1969.
44. MacGregor R and others: *Multiple Impact Therapy with Families.* New York, McGraw-Hill, 1964.
45. Kohl RN: Pathologic reactions of marital partners to improvement of patients. *Am J Psychiatr* **118**:1036–1041, 1962.

46. Forrest T: The combined use of marital and individual therapy in depressions. *Cont Psa* **6**:76–83, 1969.
47. Alger I, Hogan P: The use of videotape recordings in conjoint marital therapy. *Am J Psychiatr* **123**:1425–1430, 1967.
48. Alger I, Hogan P: Enduring effects of videotape playback experience in family and marital relationships. *Am J Orthopsychiatr* **39**:86–98, 1969.
49. Hogan P, Alger I: The use of videotape recording in family therapy. Read at the annual meeting of the American Orthopsychiatric Association, San Francisco, Calif, April 1966.
50. Hogan P, Hogan BK: Group treatment by co-therapists. Presented at the third annual regional institute and conference of the Eastern Group Psychotherapy Society, New York, December 1971.
51. Guerin P: Study your own family, in *The Book of Family Therapy.* Edited by Farber, Mendelsohn, Napier, New York, Science House, 1972, pp. 445–458.
52. Fogarty T: Study your own family, in *The Book of Family Therapy.* Edited by Farber, Mendelsohn, Napier, New York, Science House, 1972, pp. 459–479.
53. Perls F: *Gestalt Therapy Verbatim.* Lafayette, Calif, Real People Press, 1969.
54. Hogan BK: The use of videotape for confrontation in the treatment of depression. Unpublished manuscript.
55. Beukenkamp C: Parental suicide as a source of resistance to marriage. *Int J Group Psychother* **11**:204–208, 1961.
56. Goldberg M, Mudd EH: The effects of suicidal behavior upon marriage and the family, in *Suicidal Behaviors: Diagnosis and Management.* Edited by Resnik HLP, Boston, Little, Brown, 1968, pp. 348–356.
57. Herzog A, Resnik HLP: A clinical study of parental response to adolescent death by suicide, with recommendations for approaching survivors. *Br J Soc Psychiatr* **3**:144–152, winter 1969.
58. Morrison G, Collier J: Family treatment approaches to suicidal children and adolescents. *J Am Acad Child Psychiatr* **8**:140–154, 1969.
59. Resnik HLP and others: Videotape confrontation after attempted suicide. *Am J Psychiatr* **130**:460–463, 1973.
60. Speck RV: Family therapy of the suicidal patient, in *Suicidal Behaviors: Diagnosis and Management.* Edited by Resnik HLP, Boston, Little, Brown, 1968, pp. 341–347.

Thirteen

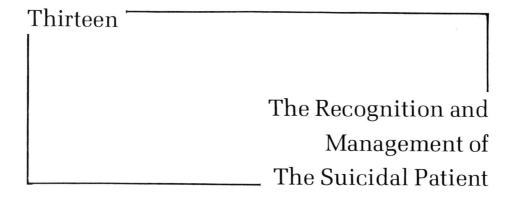

The Recognition and Management of The Suicidal Patient

Jerome A. Motto, M.D.

The study of depressive states can scarcely be pursued in a clinical setting without considering the problem of suicide. This connection reflects the numerous observations throughout man's history of so strong an association between depression and suicide that suicide has been suggested as representing, epidemiologically, "the mortality of depressive disorders" (1). Available data indicate that about 15% of persons with primary affective disorders ultimately suicide (2), and that at least half the certified suicides in the United States are the result of primary affective disorders (3).

Such epidemiological data clearly identify persons who are in a depressive state as constituting a high risk population for suicide. In individual cases, however, the very terms depression and suicide can be highly ambiguous. "Depression" must be differentiated from "despondency" and from "grief," and "suicide" must be delineated from a broad spectrum of self-destructive behaviors that reflect activity on all levels of consciousness. The data above consider depression as it is defined in the current diagnostic and statistical sense, which is primarily on a descriptive level. A dynamic definition of depression as related to suicide is given below under "etiology." Suicide is defined in this discussion as "the act of self-inflicted, self-intentioned death."

Many persons with a depressive disorder see a physician or other health related resource to complain of various somatic problems, such as sleep or appetite disturbance, weight loss, "nervousness," headache, or back pain. Unless the underlying emotional state is recognized and treated, the likelihood of a suicidal outcome is certainly increased. Recent data indicate that about 70% of depressed persons who commit suicide are in touch with a physician within 30 days of their death, nearly half during the preceding week (4). Though much can be said about the recent development of programs in suicide prevention, it is clear that physicians remain a first line of defense against preventable suicides, especially those related to depressive states (5–8).

Aside from its observed relationship to depression, the problem of suicide commands attention as a public health issue in its own right. Though consistently underreported it ranks among the first ten causes of death in the United States, among the first five in the 15–24 age group, and second only to accidents among college students. Although about 25,000 deaths a year are officially certified as suicide, estimates of the true figure start at twice that number. The national suicide rate remains in the range of 10–12 per 100,000 per year, though in the past two decades the rates under age 45 have been rising and those over age 45 have been decreasing.

About 200,000 suicide attempts are estimated to occur annually, indicating a growing high risk population from which many subsequent completed suicides are drawn (9). If estimates are extended to suicidal threats and to personally concerned collaterals, the prevalence of involvement with the problem exceeds four million people yearly (10).

Etiology of Suicidal States

The impulse to bring about one's own death stems from an infinite variety of life circumstances which have been expressed in behavioral, social, and theological terms (11). For clinical purposes they are considered here under four basic etiological patterns, which are not mutually exclusive.

1. *Depressive Suicide* refers to circumstances generating an overwhelming homicidal level of rage which the organism effectively keeps out of consciousness by repression but experiences as impulses toward self-destruction, usually observed as a manifestation of a depressive state. About 45 to 50% of all suicides can be considered to be in this group, although suicides in office practice have a much higher proportion of depressive etiology than other populations. Patients may view their suicidal impulse as appropriate ("I don't deserve to live") or inappropriate ("I can't understand it—I know I have everything to live for but all I can think about is what's the use of living").

Depressive suicide focuses on the dynamic concept of unacceptable rage, generated in susceptible persons by life events over which they have little or no control. Such persons often have a "predepressive personality," characterized by an array of socially approved attributes, including an unusually even temper. This reflects the unconscious cortical inhibition (repression) of rage which they have learned as a condition of worthiness of love. Unacceptable rage refers primarily to rage generated toward those on whom the person is emotionally dependent (e.g., spouse or parent figures) or toward the innocent (e.g., a congenitally blind child, or cared-for mother dying of cancer), or precipitated by such uncontrollable forces as accidents, fate, or acts of God (e.g., a disabling illness, the process of aging, or death of a meaningful person). These personality characteristics are widely represented among the professions and highly responsible persons of all occupations. Such persons may be quite capable of experiencing and expressing rage directed toward elements generally recognized as "evil" and which generate righteous indignation. Only when the source of pain is uncriticizeable, such as the circumstances mentioned, is the rage kept out of awareness.

Freud's early exposition (12) and Menninger's later elaboration (13) of this type of concept have generally stood the test of time. In practice, Freud's statement that "any blow to the ego," rather than simply loss of a significant person, can precipitate the anger that generates the depressive process is most pertinent to the issue of suicide. Thus rejection or threat of rejection by a spouse would be more conducive to suicide than would an accidental or natural death, as would being fired from a long-held position rather than its loss through a required reorganization.

Another important element in the depressed suicidal state is a painful sense of isolation, of unconnectedness and aloneness that is extremely difficult to influence. The person may be quite aware of this and even express it as a source of dismay; "I know my family all love me, but no matter what they do I just can't feel it."

The fact that many depressed persons have the need to repress or otherwise defend against not only their rage but also their depressive symptoms ("hidden depression," "smiling depression") sometimes explains why a suicide can come as a complete surprise to family and friends. Persons long known for competence, toughness, and independence often characterize this sequence. Edwin Arlington Robinson's well-known short poem, "Richard Cory," presents a quiet overdramatization of such a suicide pattern (14).

2. *Suicide for relief of pain* refers to life circumstances generating levels of physical or emotional pain which exceed the organism's tolerance, producing an irresistible need for relief from pain rather than a primary desire for one's existence to come to an end. About 35 to 40% of suicides are accounted for in this category, many of whom have the diagnostic label of depression but clinically do not reveal the dynamic pattern described above. Patients often express their suicidal ideas as, "I don't want to die but I don't know any other way out—I just can't stand it any more."

Suicide to relieve pain reflects the interplay between the intensity of pain to which a person is subjected and the level of the person's pain threshold. A useful clinical concept is that when one's ultimate threshold is exceeded, so that the experience of continued living is unbearable in spite of available psychological defenses, three alternatives are available: (1) psychotic distortion of reality which reduces the pain, (2) use of drugs, including alcohol, which raises the pain threshold, or (3) suicide. If a given organism is resistant to psychotic defenses (by virtue of a stable nervous system and sound early life experience), it is apparent that encountering unbearable pain will push the person toward either pharmacological relief or suicide. If the former is denied, or is impossible for the person to accept, suicide becomes essentially predictable unless some alteration of the life situation can be accomplished. The same can be said if the protective function of the psychosis or the pharmacological agent is insufficient for the task, thus anticipating the observed vulnerability to suicide of persons who experience psychotic states or develop dependence on alcohol or other drugs.

Persons with a low pain threshold constitute a chronic risk for suicidal behavior because so many common life experiences can cause the threshold to be exceeded. Though a number of such crises may be survived by virtue of nonpsychotic defenses protecting that threshold, the long term risk remains high unless a stabilizing external support system can be developed.

Even persons with a high threshold may experience acute and overwhelming pain levels that push them to precipitous and tragic suicide. This phenomenon has been referred to as a "panic reaction" (15). For example, a radiologist reads his own X-ray film as revealing a renal carcinoma, but the autopsy following this abrupt suicide reveals a benign cyst; a young man showing a handgun to a visiting relative accidentally shoots her and immediately turns the gun on himself; a teenager has an auto accident in which a friend is killed, following which he quickly runs to an overpass and jumps to his death; a man who accidently kills a neighbor in a hunting accident shoots himself as soon as he realizes what has happened. Such suicides can best be explained by unbearable emotional pain in the form of overwhelming guilt, fear, and grief, especially in persons known to be relatively free of psychological handicaps.

Similarly, in a less acute sense, the impending or actual loss of a loved person or the emergence of an emotionally charged life situation can precipitate suicide without evidence of depression or other diagnostic entity. Schneidman's use of the word perturbation to characterize the emotional state of increasing vulnerability to this form of suicide is probably more useful than any other term (16).

An etiological element that can be mentioned here, though to a certain extent it cuts across clinical patterns, is the "appeal function" of suicidal behavior. This concept emphasizes the view that such behavior is a social act, and as such the impact that it makes on other people always plays a part in its motivation, even if a fatal outcome is felt to be certain (17). Clinical study has indicated that the importance of this motivation is inversely related to the severity of the attempt and the presence of psychosis in the person (18). This can be interpreted to mean that the depressed person who is most likely to suicide is the one who is least able to fulfill his dependent needs through relationships with others (19), and emphasizes the importance of symbiotic patterns (20).

3. ***Symbolic suicide*** refers to circumstances giving the suicidal act a specific and highly valued meaning not directly related to the desire for death per se. About 5 to 10% of suicides are in this group, most of whom represent psychotic disorders. The suicidal act often has a bizarre quality to it that reflects the presence of the thought disturbance.

Symbolic suicides frequently suggest some idealized, albeit distorted, goal; for example, offering the self as a sacrifice to redeem mankind; the idea that some magical benefit will be obtained; that death will be a means of achieving rebirth; that a loved person will be joined; that persecutors will finally be satisfied and peace will be achieved. Though such ideas are usually the manifestation of a pyschotic disorder, they may also reflect intense belief in a philosophical or religious system. A number of instances of such suicides accompanied the recent emergence of widespread use of psychedelic drugs.

The symbolic goal may also be a rational and realistic one such as sacrificing oneself for a patriotic cause, as a condition for benefitting others or to further a highly valued goal or tradition. An example would be the four chaplains who sacrificed their lives in the sinking of the U.S.S. *Dorchester* by giving up their life jackets to save other's lives. Durkheim refers to such circumstances as "altruistic" suicide (21).

4. *Suicide resulting from organic dysfunction* refers to various organic conditions affecting brain function, especially toxic and delirious states. This is a poorly defined group in which the suicidal mechanism is unclear, and the frequency unreported. The self-destructive impulse apparently represents a primitive pattern which emerges when the usual controlling devices of the body, primarily at the cortical level of brain function, are interfered with. A suicide attempt may occur in the course of a delirious state with no recall whatsoever after the sensorium is clear. In some instances suicide from organic dysfunction appears to be a reaction to persecutory fears or ideas during the dysfunctional period only, and simply represents an effort to escape, even though the escape route, for example, a sixth floor window, gives the appearance of a self-destructive effort.

Virus infections have received too little attention as one organic source of suicidal states, possibly due to the fact that the self-destructive issue does not always appear during the acute phase but may comprise a residual problem persisting for months or even years. One could postulate a subclinical encephalitis that requires a very long healing period. Depressive symptoms with suicidal elements which emerge with no plausible dynamic explanation can sometimes be accounted for by the postviral syndrome. It has been observed in all age groups from adolescence on, and may be involved in some perplexing and tragic suicides among college students. No systematic studies substantiating this have been reported but some excellent case reports are available, especially in the British literature (22, 23).

Recognition of Suicidal States

The recognition of a suicidal state starts with the awareness that any degree of perturbation can generate self-destructive ideas and impulses. These are so often unexpressed that routine inquiry about them is essential in every thorough assessment of a person's physical or emotional state. This would be one step toward minimizing the unexpected suicide which so often occurs to the consternation of friends, colleagues, and physician.

Because of the traditional association of depression with suicide it is customary to approach the recognition of suicidal risk with a systematic review of the symptoms of depressive illness. It must be the rare clinician, or even the layman, who is not well acquainted with the thoughts, feelings, and behavior associated with depression. It is certainly one of the most widespread of human experiences, and aside from one's personal acquaintance with it both the professional and lay literature have accurately recounted its many manifestations essentially unchanged for centuries.

The first step in recognition is rather for the clinician to resolve his own anxiety about the issue of suicide sufficiently to readily elicit the pertinent information and translate it into degree of risk. The vast majority of persons are well aware of the significance of despondency, sleeplessness, loss of appetite, crying spells, self-criticism, listlessness and apathy, feelings of guilt, or a sense of hopelessness. The more experienced will inquire about tension, weight loss, exaggerated fears of cancer or other physical preoccupation, loss of prior interests, social withdrawal, indecisiveness, a sense of helplessness, feelings of failure and of being a burden to others, preoccupation with unpleasant thoughts such as death or dying, ideas of self-punishment, and self-destructive thoughts, fantasies, or dreams. They are aware that opposites can have a similar significance, such as excessive crying or inability to cry, excessive sleep or insomnia, overeating or anorexia, agitation or psychomotor retardation, and despondency or euphoria

Perceptive persons will recognize the implications of termination behavior: quietly putting affairs in order, making out a will, checking insurance, or giving away sentimentally valued objects. They will also pick up verbal clues, such as that commonly used items "won't be needed anymore," or "I won't be around to trouble you," and "no one will have to worry about me any more."

A major problem is that these clues to depressive and suicidal states tend to generate a high level of anxiety in the person hearing them, and the anxiety is frequently dealt with by various forms of denial and rationalization: "If I ask about suicidal ideas it may upset him more than he already is—I don't want to push him into it"; "I might put the idea into his mind"; "He won't admit it to me anyway"; "There's nothing I could do about it—I'm not a psychiatrist—emotional disorders are not my field." The result is too often a breakdown in communication such that suicidal feelings are not openly examined, and subsequent suicidal behavior therefore comes as a surprise. Only by taking a direct approach to this issue will the clinician's role in suicide prevention begin to develop its potential force. Of the many difficulties that exist in the field of prevention, anxiety about full and open inquiry seems most widespread and to influence many astute and informed practitioners.

Once this problem is resolved, reviewing the signs and symptoms of depression should be a routine first step in recognizing the potentially suicidal person, followed by an inquiry about suicidal thoughts or impulses. The wording of questions is best dictated by the language style of the interviewer, with emphasis on matter-of-factness, clarity, and freedom from implied criticism. Candid, straightforward concern on the clinician's part will generally evoke the same qualities in the response, permitting a rapid and accurate assessment.

One can begin by asking if the person ever has any periods of feeling low or despondent, and if so, how long they last, and how severe they get. Do they produce crying spells or interfere with daily activities, concentration, work, sleep, or appetite? Are feelings of hopelessness, discouragement, or self-criticism present? Are these periods sometimes so severe that life does not seem worthwhile, that thoughts of suicide occur? How persistent are such thoughts; how strong have they been; was much effort required to resist the idea? Have there been any impulses to carry them out? Have any plans been made? How detailed have they been? Have any tentative or preliminary actions been taken, such as collecting pills or obtaining a gun? What deterred the person? Does he think he can manage such feelings if they recur? Is there anyone he can turn to for help at such times? Would he be able to call the interviewer if he feels he cannot control the suicidal impulse? The use of expressions such as "harm yourself" or "do something foolish" should be avoided as indicative of anxiety on the interviewer's part, which tends to reduce candor in the response.

The key questions are those about episodes of despondency and about suicidal thoughts, which, if the response is in any degree positive, lead into the detailed information on which decisions are based. If the response to both is negative, and other sources of information do not contradict, it can be assumed that at least for the present a potential suicidal crisis is not being overlooked. It is possible for a person to mislead the interviewer, of course, but we have to accept that there is no way to avoid that risk. It can be minimized by establishing a firm, trusting relationship with the person, based on mutual respect.

Assessment of Suicide Risk

It is possible to subjectively estimate the degree of suicidal risk solely on the basis of the clinical information outlined in the foregoing discussion. However, this estimate can be sharpened by consideration of additional variables, even though numerous efforts to translate these into measuring devices or "predictive scales" have not yet provided a generally accepted instrument. Nor are there yet valid psychological tests to serve this purpose (24). Intuitive judgements combined with the person's responses to direct questions such as "Can you stand it?" or "How do you feel now about killing yourself?" still deserve more weight than any other specific consideration. The clinician's task is to estimate both the likelihood of suicide and how immediate the risk is. In any given instance the outcome is not the sole criterion for validity of the assessment, as a person evaluated as a "high risk" may not suicide, or a "low risk" may do so, without necessarily indicating that the evaluation was inaccurate. The prediction of suicide as such is not possible, but the *chances* of this outcome can be determined with sufficient confidence to provide a basis for management.

It is also necessary to differentiate between the risk of "suicide" and of "suicidal behavior," for example, suicide threats or attempts, as the risk of one can be very different from the risk of the other. Investigative efforts have focused primarily on completed suicide as the major concern for predictive and preventive measures, and the term "risk" as used here refers to the completed act.

Before considering specific predictors, it is desirable to present some clinical observations about which there are common misconceptions, as follows (25):

1. About 80% of suicides have given definite warning of their intent, including verbal statements. The misconception: "People who talk about suicide don't commit suicide."
2. Most suicidal people are ambivalent about seeking death, and respond to therapeutic efforts. The misconception: "If someone wants to kill himself there's nothing you can do to stop him."
3. Most suicidal states are definitely time-limited. The misconception:

"Once a person is suicidal the risk is always there."

4. Most suicides occur within 90 days following the beginning of improvement in the clinical picture. The misconception: "When improvement occurs the crisis is over."

5. Suicide occurs at about the same rate in all socioeconomic groups. The misconception: "Suicide is more frequent in the rich [poor]."

6. Suicide has no specific genetic determinants. The misconception: "Suicide runs in the family."

7. Most persons who suicide are not psychotic. Many are not psychiatrically ill. The misconception: "A person must be mentally ill to want to kill himself."

Numerous studies have produced a bewildering array of variables to consider in assessing the suicidal risk in a person recognized as experiencing a suicidal state (26–31). This reflects the fact that there is no generally recognized "suicidal syndrome" or "suicidal personality," but rather a broad spectrum of behavioral elements identified as contributing to suicidal potential. These have been derived primarily by determining statistically what characteristics differentiate suicides from nonsuicides in a known high risk population and secondarily by clinical observations that have led experienced clinicians to an impressionistic typology, or set of "clinical models" for suicide.

General Indicators

Though it is clear that no single characteristic is very strongly predictive, a few observations have been so consistently identified statistically with increased risk that they deserve special attention on their own. The following items have been most frequently reported and should be seriously considered when a suicidal state has been recognized, regardless of other circumstances. The following are demographic data.

1. *Age over 45.* Some experiences are felt more keenly by the young, but many painful experiences are psychologically more devastating to those in middle and later life. These are such traumatic events as the loss of close and meaningful persons, the onset of disabling physical disorders, or the threat of physical or economic dependence (32, 33). Suicidal manifestations must be regarded with increasing seriousness after the teens and 20s, even though the person may reassure us about them. This may be less so at present than in past years, especially considering the high suicide rate among young women and young Blacks and American Indians (34–36), but still deserves special emphasis.

In general, the older the person the greater the suicide risk (37), an observation complicated by the fact that older persons tend not to make their needs known, and case-finding programs are not usually directed to them. Even in the Soviet Union, where suicide is not often discussed in the psychiatric literature, special interest is shown in the tendency of older persons to become suicidal, especially in the presence of depressive states (38).

2. *Sex—male.* A consistent statistical observation has been the predominance of males among completed suicides and of females in the suicide-

attempt population. The ratio of male–female suicide rates has generally been about 3–1, but has gradually narrowed, especially in the younger and middle age groups. This pattern may reflect the greater lethality of methods used by males which preclude intervention, less willingness to accept help on the part of males, and a recent marked increase in suicide among women, most strikingly in the Black population (36, 39–44).

3. *Race—white.* As suggested above, this traditional predictor is weakening in the younger age groups and in women, but can still be useful in persons over 45 years old. As socioeconomic and educational opportunities continue to equalize, it can be expected to diminish in importance. In areas with a large Oriental population this culture group gives evidence that it may replace the Caucasian as the highest risk (27).

The following are clinical data.

1. *History of prior suicide attempt.* Inherent life-preserving responses of the organism seem to be weakened by the experience of a suicide attempt, and such an act subsequently becomes psychologically more readily available under stress. Empirically, persons with a history of suicidal behavior have been widely recognized as a high risk population. Though inconsistent reports have appeared, it becomes increasingly evident that the degree of seriousness of a prior attempt is positively related to subsequent risk. This holds whether the estimate of seriousness is based on "intent" or on the degree of physical injury that was involved (6, 45, 46).

2. *Chronic self-destructive pattern.* Persons whose life history reveals a long-standing pattern of suicidal fantasy, preoccupation, or behavior constitute a high long-term risk regardless of other considerations. Such persons often appear as a low risk because at a given time they may not be in the kind of severe stress situation usually associated with crisis. Yet they tend to remain in a near-suicidal state which can be very quickly activated, in contrast to the traditional sequence of suffering an acute crisis which gradually reduces in intensity till the person is again in a stable state.

3. *Recent severe loss or threat of loss.* This is, of course, the classic circumstance for an acute suicidal state, and can generate self-destructive behavior through an intervening depressive reaction or by the intensity of emotional pain produced, as discussed above. Essentially, every major theoretical system includes this concept as a key issue in suicide, whether it be expressed specifically as "recent loss of a loved person" (37) or in broad terms involving diminished self-esteem or existential satisfaction. Sociologically, the relationship of loss to the problem of suicide can be developed systematically as one aspect of interaction theory (47) as well as a facet of "egoistic" suicide as formulated by Durkheim (21).

Murphy and Robins (48) point out that the loss of an important person is of special importance in the precipitation of suicide in persons suffering from alcoholism. Rorsman (49) found this to be a sex-related issue, in that recent object loss by death was strongly associated with suicide in males but not in females. A particular life style has been identified as generating special vulnerability specifically to the loss of a significant person, discussed below under the clinical typologies of "satisfied symbiotic" (50) and "I can't live without you" (30).

Practically, the effect of loss is important insofar as it involves specifically those elements that serve to stabilize the person's emotional life. Thus the apparent paradox that one may easily survive the loss of a parent or spouse but not that of a job or a pet. Again, the older age groups are generally more vulnerable than the young.

4. *Poor health or fear of poor health.* This is a different element to define, depending as it does on the subjective view of the suicidal person. Thus the presence of a chronic, progressive disorder or a condition requiring a basic change in the life style of a person who is not of a very flexible temperament can indicate special risk. It has been observed that diseases which impair respiration, for example, emphysema or lymphoma of the neck and chest, are more often associated with suicide than are other chronic illnesses (15). Severe depressive states sometimes involve unfounded fears of cancer or other disabling illnesses with a poor prognosis. These fears often lead to repeated visits to the doctor's office without relief in spite of the physician's reassurances and negative diagnostic tests. The somatic manifestations of depression alone, for example, sleep and appetite disturbance, weight loss and apathy, can generate fear of some exotic disease that defies medical diagnosis. Statistically this is found to be most applicable to males over 40 (26, 29, 51, 52) but is observed clinically to be widely applicable (53).

5. *Presence of a detailed suicide plan.* This has been characterized as the most important single element in evaluating an immediate suicide emergency, referring to the person's proposed method, place, and time. Lethality of the proposed method, availability of the means, and specificity of the details must be considered (15, 54, 55). Both clinical and statistical evidence, as well as common sense, indicate that if the contemplated method is at hand the risk is very serious (28).

6. *Inability to accept help.* Resistance to help, especially in persons susceptible to depressive illness, is socially and dynamically clearly understandable. A person whose self-esteem rests on meeting high standards of performance, in a society which reveres rugged individualism, tends to avoid any situation that can be interpreted as reflecting weakness, dependence, or inability to cope with the stresses of living. Especially threatening is any suggestion of a "mental" disorder, with its implication of diminished control over one's behavior and intellectual functions.

Professional persons and others who are characteristically highly responsible and dependable can pose a special problem, in that their need to maintain an image of invulnerable stability may push them to resist depending on someone else regardless of how serious their situation, manifested clinically by their rejecting or quickly discontinuing therapeutic efforts. The expression, "Thank you, but I can manage OK," too often presages a premature death. As Litman emphasizes, a person must be able to accept help, as well as locate it and elicit it from his environment (37).

Our cultural stereotypes seem to have made this a greater problem for men than for women. Rorsman found the tendency of suicidal male psychiatric patients to remain out of treatment to be the most interesting difference between this group and a control population (49), and Lettieri reports the item, "accepts help now," as a predictor of lower risk in men aged 40 and over who called the Los Angeles Suicide Prevention Center (51). Wold makes the same observation for depressed persons aged 40 to 60 (30) while Fawcett found "help negation" to be one of four characteristics of interpersonal behavior which significantly differentiated a high risk suicidal group from a moderate and low risk group (19). Motto (56) reported that 14 of the 15 suicides in a cohort of prior suicide attempters had tended to remain out of any treatment setting.

It seems apparent that such persons might benefit by heeding the I Ching: "To accept help in a difficult situation is not a disgrace but a sign of inner clarity" (57).

7. *Resources.* A tendency for clinicians to focus primarily on pathological processes may lead to insufficient awareness and evaluation of a person's resources. Minimum pathology in a suicidal person bereft of strengths may be lethal, while severe pathology in a person with unusual strengths may constitute only a moderate risk. Subjective judgements are required here. Examples of the kind of strengths referred to are:

a. Capacity to control behavior. That is, the person can stand the pain or impulse. This appears to be more assessable in women than in men (53).

b. Capacity to relate readily and in a meaningful way to someone else. Thus it is possible to reach the suicidal person emotionally to provide a supportive and therapeutic influence. One helping person may suffice for this relationship, and health personnel are often in this role. The presence of family members and friends who are supportive also can be invaluable assets which literally make the difference between life and death. This too is more often seen to operate in women than in men, perhaps as a cultural bias regarding social patterns, in that it is more acceptable for women to assume a dependent role (51, 53).

c. Motivation for help and willingness to work actively on the problem. This is a powerful determinant of outcome, and applies to both men and women, statistically as well as clinically (53).

d. A variety of resources which facilitate the therapeutic process and the transition back to a stable life pattern, for example, job skills, intelligence, physical health, communication skills, a capacity to trust, close ties to a church, or freedom from severe personality disturbance or addictive problems.

The following are diagnostic data.

1. *Depressive disorder.* The statistical association of depression and suicide was mentioned above in epidemiological terms, and their dynamic relationship in psychological terms. It has been demonstrated further that the more severe a depressive state, the more serious is the intent of an accompanying suicide attempt (58), and that the seriousness of intent is more closely correlated with one manifestation of depression—a feeling of hopelessness—than with the global depressive state itself (59–61). The latter observation is clinically crucial in that the most commonly used depressive scales (62–64) are not useful as short-term predictive instruments as regards suicide (53), and Pokorny's follow-up studies suggest an inverse long-term relationship between severity of depression and degree of suicide risk (65). It

has been observed, however, that the suicide attempts of depressed persons tend to be more serious than those of nondepressed attempters when an overdose of sedatives is involved (66), and that the subsequent suicide rate in persons hospitalized for a suicidal state with a primary diagnosis of depression is high (65).

The issue of repressed rage is a primary consideration in the etiology of depressive suicide; hence the clinical observation of externalized hostility can be interpreted as diminishing the risk as long as it is in evidence (27, 53). This can be overdone to the point that homicidal impulses must be dealt with. If a homicide ensues, suicide may then be resorted to as a final resolution. Though not a common occurrence in the United States, it is frequently observed in England, where about one third of the homicides are followed by suicides, and of these about one third involve a depressive state (67). Various sociological and psychological aspects of this issue have been reported by Henry and Short (68) and Pokorny (69).

Persons with depression tend to demonstrate the resistance to accepting help described above to an extreme degree. Often highly competent persons who are extremely sensitive about their image in the community, they frequently manage to continue functioning for a remarkable period in spite of a crushing burden of depressive pathology. With the current emphasis on avoiding inpatient care, recent data indicate a surprising agreement between patients and hospital staff members regarding the need for hospitalization with the sole exception of "affective psychotics" who grossly overestimated the avoidability of hospital care (70).

Manic states deserve mention as constituting a high risk factor though it is rarely mentioned in statistical studies. Recent data, however, indicate that in a large population of depressed and suicidal persons, "euphoria" in the suicidal male was one of the major characteristics of those who subsequently completed the act (53). Efforts to compare unipolar with bipolar disorders in regard to suicide suggest that suicide attempts are most common in bipolar females, but no clear pattern is discernible for completed suicides (71,72).

2. *Thought disorders (psychoses).* The psychoses are receiving progressively more attention as indicators of increased risk, as emergency rooms become more involved in mental health care and more follow-up studies are reported. Suicidal patients with a diagnosis of schizophrenia in Pokorny's long-term study showed an even higher subsequent suicide rate than did those diagnosed as depressed (65). Schizophrenic suicides tend to have a somewhat bizarre quality, such as multiple methods or numerous bodywide lacerations, but this is not constant.

Persecutory ideas are a special concern, and demand first priority attention as indicators of high risk *even if there has been no indication of suicidal thinking or behavior.* It is possible for any of the major psychiatric disorders to manifest persecutory ideas, especially in the more severe forms—mania, depression, schizophrenia, and organic psychoses of all kinds—as well as primary paranoid states. In a recent large scale study of depressed and suicidal persons, the item "ideas of persecution" was the most discriminating depressive symptom indicating subsequent completed suicide for both men and women (53).

Efforts to improve obsolete involuntary procedures, to which persons with suicidal and persecutory ideas have sometimes been subjected, have at times led attorneys to make questionable statements regarding the risk of harm to self or others in this population. It is especially misleading when observations valid for psychiatric patients as a whole are applied to this particular subgroup (73).

3. *Alcoholism.* Persons suffering from alcoholism are recognized as a high intermediate or long-term risk for suicide in spite of some variation in the definition of alcoholism. Intense remorse after a drinking episode, a psychotic state during withdrawal, a closely associated depressive state, "accidental" ingestion or aspiration during severe intoxication, limited ability to cope with a serious loss, and diminution of psychological defenses due to the pharmacological effects of alcohol have all been observed to contribute to a suicidal outcome in this population (48, 74).

Assessment of various drinking patterns provides evidence that a sporadic drinker is more vulnerable to suicidal outcome than is a chronic heavy drinker (53). Tuckman and Youngman found that current drinking at the time of a suicide attempt was an indication of lower risk for subsequent completed suicide (29), though the rate was still quite high in this group. Blachly's observation that 39% of 80 physicians who suicided were considered to drink heavily, and that half of these were drinking at the time of their death, tends to blur distinctions between drinking patterns (75). Thus a past history of alcoholism or the presence of sobriety in a pattern of periodic heavy drinking should not be considered less significant than current drinking as indicators of increased suicide risk.

The special problem is that alcohol serves both as a defense against pain and a source of new pain. Hence in the active drinker if the defensive value is outweighed by the progressive increase in social stresses generated by the drinking, its protective function does not suffice, and a suicidal crisis may be precipitated. In the "dry" alcoholic, with regard to the low pain threshold seen in alcoholism, if these same stresses (threats of divorce, jail, etc.) are not bearable in the sober state, the person may find psychosis unavailable to him and have little choice regarding suicide, as discussed earlier.

That alcohol can serve as a defense against depression has been widely observed, preparing us for the onset of depressive symptoms during periods of sobriety and focusing therapeutic efforts on this underlying and more treatable form of pathology (76). It is often in such persons—known to be depressed and using alcohol and often other medications—that the most troublesome "equivocal" suicides occur. Specifically, the person is found with lethal blood levels of combined alcohol and barbiturates or other medications, and no clear indication of whether the person had intended to end his life or had ingested a lethal combination of these synergistic agents during a period of alcohol-induced confusion. It is especially in such instances that the "psychological autopsy" can serve a very useful purpose (77–79).

4. *Drug abuse.* Alcohol is only one of a number of drugs that serve to reduce painful feelings and hence serve as protection from suicide, its most unique features being its ready availability, low cost, and legality. The chronic overuse of other agents such as tranquilizers, stimulants, barbiturates,

psychedelics, or narcotics follows the same psychological and dynamic principles as does the misuse of alcohol. Whether by persons whose value system does not seriously consider legality, or by responsible persons in the health field (doctors, pharmacists, nurses, and dentists) who have them too readily at hand, the abuse of drugs is a sign of increased vulnerability to suicide. Blachly reports 19% of his sample of physicians had shown drug dependence or severe abuse, and another 48% had used drugs to some extent (75).

Statistical Models

Though all the preceding general indicators can serve to supplement one's clinical judgement of suicide risk, experience has led some clinicians to lean more heavily on specific items. For example, Litman (15) refers to the suicide plan as the most important single element in evaluating the immediate emergency, and Minkoff and others (61) emphasize that a sense of hopelessness is the most crucial of the depressive symptoms. Discriminant function analysis permits a statistical ordering of importance (27), a technique for developing predictive scales which, as with other combinations of items, is still hampered by the inherent complexity of the problem leading to inclusion of an excessive number of false positives (80, 81).

The suggestion (82) that "situation specific" items be used indicates the most promising direction for generating predictive scales, the first example of which is the set of eight scales developed by Lettieri (51), now undergoing clinical testing. These scales are applicable to four age and sex specific groups, "younger females," "older females," "younger males," and "older males," with the age division at 40 years. A short form and a long form is available for each group, providing a score indicating low, moderate, or high risk of death by suicide within 1 to 2 years after the suicidal episode. The theoretical basis for this approach is that the choice of suicide for an older male would involve different dynamics than, for example, for a younger female. Hence a different set of variables is needed to assess the risk in each.

Another statistical approach to "situation specific" evaluation of risk was reported by Wold (30), who used clustering techniques to generate sets of items along three dimensions: age, sex, and acute versus chronic suicidal state. Although not in quantifiable form, this approach indicates, for example, that the high risk *younger* age groups are characterized as tending to be impulsive, unstable, living with their family, and having a history of a low lethality suicide attempt; the high risk *older* age groups are more frequently not impulsive, with stable life styles, living alone, and having no history of a suicide attempt. High risk *men* are more often single and on a downhill life course; high risk *women* tend to have repeated marriages and good resources. High risk *acutely* suicidal persons usually have a stable character and life style, disrupted by the loss of a close relationship, while high risk *chronic* suicidal persons show an unstable background, with no specific stressful circumstances at the time of assessment.

The usefulness of these statistical methods for assisting the clinician is still in the process of evaluation. In the meantime, experience forces our attention to certain frequently encountered patterns which can supplement intuitive judgements in addition to the individual considerations discussed above.

Clinical Models

The identification of descriptive "suicide types" is not a new approach (30, 50, 83) but is yet to be put on a systematic, clinically useful basis. These characterizations provide a means of classifying known suicidal people with a view toward refinement of both prediction and treatment. They can aid in the recognition of risk as well as its magnitude. Such recognition can serve an invaluable purpose, in that some of those who are in need of assistance but are unwilling to seek it may accept help if a perceptive person in their environment takes the initiative. Though these models are generally regarded as variants of depression, they may be placed in a number of diagnostic categories depending on the bias of the observer. The number of models is limited only by the extent of the clinician's experience and one's willingness to accept the innumerable variations that exist. Three typical examples of this approach are the following:

1. *Stable prior pattern with forced change.* This is seen more often in women in their 30s or later, and is characterized by a stable life pattern which is built around a symbiotic relationship that is seriously disrupted. The stabilizing element usually involves personal relationships, but may be an issue such as a geographical location and life style or a specific job situation which provides form and meaning to the person's life. In such instances there is usually no history of prior suicide attempts, alcohol, psychosis, or socially disruptive behavior, but rather a consistent stability in schooling, residence, work, and marital and social relationships. This pattern has been referred to elsewhere as the "Satisfied Symbiotic" (50) or "I Can't Live Without You" (30).

Serious alteration of the stable core of such a person's life pattern may reveal an otherwise invisible vulnerability in the form of "brittleness," or lack of adaptability when life circumstances change. As long as the structure is intact it may reflect impressive strength, but when a crack appears the lack of flexibility leads to disintegration rather than reshaping into a new pattern of stability.

2. *Progressive constriction.* This is seen more often in males who display considerable strength and ability in many aspects of their life, only to experience a gradual but relentless diminution in their sources of emotional support. For example, a parent may die, a child grow up and leave the home, occupational limitations encountered, economic losses incurred, social or church activities relinquished, sexual capacity diminished, alcohol resorted to, friends drift away, and a separation or divorce threatened. Any one of these issues alone might be dealt with effectively, but in such cumulative circumstances the onset of a new issue such as a handicapping medical problem may be unendurable, though it seems a minor problem by itself.

3. *Adolescent transition.* The basic issues producing emotional stress in the teens and early 20s are the same as at any other age; that is, needs for a feeling of worthiness of love and a sense of relatedness to other significant figures in one's life. The means of satisfying these needs, which have

depended largely on parental figures earlier in life, become rapidly dependent on peer relationships as well during the adolescent transition from childhood to young adulthood. Difficulties may exist at any point along this bridge. However, the stability of the family structure and parental relationships are the most crucial elements in providing a sound preparation for both relating to the rest of the world and for developing a unique identity distinct from either family or peer figures.

One pattern of suicidal vulnerability in the adolescent, therefore, includes a family background of disruption or chronically unsatisfactory relationships, difficulty establishing close ties with peers, a "loner" pattern or excessive dependence on peer approval, and use of alcohol or drugs as a means of bringing about those feelings which are optimally generated by healthy relationships with others. Wold characterizes this pattern as "Adolescent-Family Crisis" (30, 84–89).

The current social trend toward shifting the adolescent transition to a younger age span leads to the normal stresses of this period being premature for some young persons even though their family relationships are good. They are often unprepared for the extreme emotional pain that can be generated by their idealized world, and can be so devastated by it that the ties to family members are insufficient to sustain them. The rapid pace of the trend toward adolescents' assuming increasing responsibilities at an earlier age has probably contributed to the dramatic and tragic increase in suicide in younger people over the past two decades.

These clinical patterns have been extended to include the "Dependent-Dissatisfied" and "Unaccepting" person (50), as well as the "Violent Man," "Middle-Age Depression," "Old and Alone," and other characterizations (30). Further work is also being done on specific occupational groups such as physicians (75) and college students (82, 90). Current efforts are to develop, for each of these clinical models, a set of statistically derived variables that will serve as "situation specific" predictors applicable only to persons who fit the particular model.

Management and Treatment of Suicidal States

Identifying, assessing, managing, and treating suicidal persons are intertwining parts of comprehensive clinical care, with the emphasis shifting from one to the other but often with more than one proceeding simultaneously. The treatment phase is crucial yet is most often given insufficient emphasis, especially in clinic and emergency room settings. The National Institute of Mental Health Task Force on Suicide Prevention in the Seventies emphasized that the therapist should maintain an "active relatedness" to the person as opposed to a more reflective approach, that he be should be willing to take more initiative with poorly motivated persons than might be appropriate in other situations, and that methods for long-term follow-up are needed to provide optimal care (91).

The initial patient contact is critical. The careful process of thoroughly and systematically clarifying the emotional state of the patient is in itself the first step in management and treatment, as it is conducive to a sense of sharing, of "relatedness," of being both understood and accepted—all of which are emotional lifelines to a desire for continued existence. It is essential that this be maintained and nurtured. Any sense of rejection, belittlement, or unworthiness intensified during a suicidal state is the most common precipitant for further suicidal behavior. Even one dependable source of esteem can suffice to sustain the person through a crisis, and that source is often the therapist. Various considerations involved in this have been discussed in detail in several excellent reports by experienced clinicians (15, 92—96).

The treatment of a suicidal person varies considerably with the unique circumstances involved and with the therapist's interest, experience, training, inclination, and time available to work with such problems. Though opinions may differ as to what the best treatment would be in a given case, relief from the underlying state which gives rise to the suicidal impulse must be a primary consideration. Since the optimal therapeutic approach varies with the therapist as well as the suicidal person, the statement that each therapist has the responsibility "to treat his patient as best he knows how" (80) is probably the only generalization that can be made. In the suicidally depressed person, helping to permit awareness of rage and developing means of externalizing it in a nondestructive way would be primary goals. Reducing the level of pain would also be attempted, especially by the reduction of the sense of isolation, striving to develop what Kaiser so aptly refers to as the "delusion of fusion" that is necessary for the maintenance of meaningful living (97).

Whatever the therapist's skill or therapeutic modality, a number of principles that can provide a sound basis on which to make decisions deserve mention. Exceptions do exist, but as general guidelines the following should be considered:

1. The therapist must remind himself that he is not omnipotent, that the person's life is not on his shoulders, and that his role is to offer what assistance he can and that is all. Litman (15) refers to this as maintaining a "medical attitude," which makes it easier for the therapist to relax and deliberately work out a feasible plan (treatment, consultation, referral, hospitalization, etc.). Such an attitude is not contrived, but is in accord with the realities of the situation.

2. In a serious situation, do not handle the matter alone. Responsible family members, minister, family physician, or other persons in the patient's life should be included in management plans. Consultation with a psychiatrist or a nonpsychiatric colleague is indicated if the circumstances are especially complex or plans are difficult to formulate. The inclusion of others should be discussed candidly. Wold emphasizes the importance of including the family of adolescents in the therapy itself (30), and Litman points out the value of sharing responsibility with colleagues through consultation (98).

3. Be sure communication is kept open. The telephone can be used to great advantage for frequent brief contact, to stay in touch with the person. In a high risk situation such contact should be at least daily. The person should be *instructed* to call the therapist if at any time he feels unable to cope with the situation. It is often necessary to be very firm about this, as many suicidal

persons are sensitive about "imposing on the therapist's valuable time." Mayer (94) emphasizes the need to inform the person when the therapist is most likely to be available, when he is going to be away longer than a day, and even how to reach him when he is on a holiday. That such an arrangement is not abused is attributed to the fact that the person's need is not so much to have the therapist immediately available as to know the therapist's concern extends well beyond the ordinary conditions of treatment.

4. Do not underestimate the critical importance of sleep and of maintaining a sense of productivity. A frantic effort to obtain relief from insomnia often triggers a drug overdose. Barbiturates are valuable for sleep in spite of the obvious risk, which can be reduced by giving the person enough for only two or three nights at one time. It is preferable to have the person handle his own medication, but in some circumstances a responsible family member may be asked to do so. The possibility of the person saving the medication to accumulate a lethal dose is a matter of concern, but is often a risk worth taking in view of the increased effectiveness. In a hospital, of course, this is not as much an issue, but even here some clinicians avoid barbiturates and other sleeping medications in favor of milder tranquilizers such as chlordiazepoxide or meprobamate (99). If in doubt, especially if the person is impulsive, undependable, or tends to misuse drugs or alcohol, chloral hydrate or other nonbarbiturate sedative-hypnotics are preferable. For outpatients many clinicians use antidepressants or diazepam as sleep medication to avoid the risk of barbiturate toxicity, tolerance, or addiction, reserving the more potent agents for limited periods during extreme states of panic or agitation.

The relationship of sleep to productivity is well known, and is exaggerated in depressed persons whose self-esteem rests largely on their ability to continue functioning at a high level of productivity. Because loss of sleep interferes with such functioning, further lowering of self-esteem and an increased sense of hopelessness, with the attendant increase in suicide risk can be brought about by insufficient attention to the problem of insomnia.

5. Do not rely on drugs alone. Some psychotherapeutic effort must be maintained during active treatment, whatever the underlying circumstances producing the suicidal state. Regardless of approach or style, persistent expression of concern and firm optimistic determination to find some solution tend to create a relationship that can have more sustaining force than any other element. Later disengagement from this relationship must be done very gradually, and the door left unequivocally open for further assistance if needed.

Aside from the value of psychotherapy, the efficacy of what are called antidepressant drugs is still in some dispute (100–105), though there seems to be a growing consensus that certain symptom patterns may respond to the use—singly or in specific combinations—of tricyclic agents, monoamine oxidase inhibitors, antianxiety agents, amphetamines, phenothiazines, and electroconvulsive therapy. An approach to the pharmacotherapy of depressed and suicidal persons has been provided by Kline (106). It is unfortunate that the toxicity of the commonest tricyclics is fairly high, which necessitates caution in view of their frequent use for suicide attempts. Mayer (94) allows that antidepressives or tranquilizers may be useful adjuncts but are "greatly overrated as a means of preventing suicide." Though lithium shows considerable promise in the treatment of mood disorders, its effect on the incidence of suicide is not yet demonstrated.

6. The therapist must have a high tolerance for dependent behavior in others to avoid a growing resentment toward the demands imposed by some suicidal persons. Emergency room and medical/surgical wards are notorious for the outspoken hostility that is often expressed toward the suicidal patient, more by physicians than by nurses (107). Even in a mental health setting, suicidal persons are not usually sought out nor particularly welcomed, especially if the risk or attempt is not demonstrably serious. Expressions such as "manipulative," "encouraging dependent needs," and "crisis approach" are often heard as a rationale for minimizing the services offered.

In the nonprivate area of mental health care, at least, it is desirable that depressed and suicidal persons have access to therapists who have special interest, training, and experience in dealing with this problem. Such resources are now emerging in the form of group therapy specifically for these persons (108–111). A group approach provides a means of diffusing the many needs experienced by suicidal persons in a setting which is receptive, understanding, and responsive, not only during the group sessions but between them as well. Especially when a crisis arises, the resources of the group tend to mobilize in a way that provides both support and therapeutic experience for the member whose special needs would be difficult for a therapist to handle alone. A remarkable esprit thus develops which in open-ended groups can have a longstanding stabilizing influence. Traditional professional training is generally not required for the group therapist, because the quality of genuinely caring for another person is the single most important condition in working with suicidal patients. Though not sufficient by itself, this quality can contribute more to therapeutic efficacy than years of formal training.

7. In depressed persons it is important to caution them explicitly that the process of recovery involves some ups and downs. Nothing is more shattering during a depressive illness than to experience a ray of hope, only to have it disappear in a subsequent fluctuation that is interpreted as meaning that all the progress is lost, that the hopelessness perceived earlier was the correct perception all the time, the ray of hope an illusion. This sequence accounts for many instances of suicide during a period of improvement, which have marked such periods as being fraught with special risk.

8. It is important to maintain an attitude of quiet confidence that the person's problems can be resolved, even though the means of doing this are not immediately evident. Many experienced clinicians can attest to the value of such optimism, which is based on the realistic observation that very few human conflicts are immutable. The effects of time alone often modify what persistent effort and spontaneous developments do not. Helping a person simply to endure a period of severe crisis can thus be a lifesaving procedure for what began as a hopeless-looking situation.

9. Hospitalization must be considered imperative if in the opinion of the therapist the person is not likely to survive without it. Mayer considers either fear on the patient's part that he will suicide or the presence of a frank psychosis as indicators for inpatient care (94). Tabachnick suggests the

presence of a psychotic state, a history of repeated impulsive suicide attempts while depressed, or a feeling of hopelessness which is not improved during the initial interview as criteria for hospitalization (96).

Often these are not clear-cut issues, and one has to come to a decision on somewhat arbitrary grounds. Conservatism is the preferred choice, but which course is the conservative one may also be unclear, especially if the person is resistant to entering a hospital and involuntary measures would have to be used. In the presence of psychosis or delirium, hospitalization is definitely indicated. With a clear sensorium, a patient who is imminently suicidal and refuses voluntary hospitalization poses a question not of health care but of social philosophy, for which definitive answers do not exist but clear opinions have been expressed (112, 113).

At times it is best for the therapist to settle for less than the ideal, inform the person of his serious concern, offer whatever help the person will accept, assure him of his availability and desire to be of continued assistance, and ask that if the person changes his mind about hospitalization to let the therapist know. That has often helped sustain a patient through the crisis and at times has been responded to by a request for hospitalization without further delay (96, 99, 114). Further considerations pertinent to hospital management have been reported in some detail (99, 114).

10. For patients who are hospitalized it is crucial that all pertinent information be clearly communicated to the staff of the clinical unit, and that the treatment plan be carefully monitored. In this situation the responsibility for patient care is shared by a number of people, and preventable mishaps can result from the communication problems entailed. The critical issues are *documented* evidence of the following:

a. A careful assessment of the degree of suicide risk, with due regard for the reports of family members, prior hospitals, or other outside agencies. The risk should be explicit; for example, "low," "moderate," or "high."

b. A statement of the measures to be taken to deal with the defined risk in clear, specific terms. For example "visual contact with patient at least every 15 minutes," or "accompany at all times when off the ward." Do not use ambiguous terms such as "suicide observation" unless it refers to a specified set of procedures, nor indicate a near-impossible task like "constant observation." If the orders change, be sure that is indicated clearly in the record.

c. Assurance that the measures indicated are carried out. This should be explicitly indicated in nurse's notes and follow-up notes, as well as checked verbally with key ward personnel to assure that there are no misunderstandings.

If these three steps are followed carefully the patient will be receiving optimal care as regards suicide, and both the staff and the hospital can feel confident that in the event that the patient does manage a self-destructive act in spite of their efforts, the threat of subsequent legal problems is minimized. Errors in judgement occur in any human endeavor, but legal liability is more a product of insufficient meticulousness in carrying out what available judgement dictates (114–118).

That confused, delirious states constitute a significant risk, as well as mood and thought disorders, bears repeating, especially for general hospitals where concentration on organic ills can preoccupy the staff, and such patients are often on upper floors with unprotected windows. There is legal precedence for general hospitals not being held to the same standard of care for emotionally disturbed patients as a specialized institution would be (119), but responsible staff can only be satisfied with the best possible care their resources permit.

Responsibilities in Suicide Prevention

When a health professional recognizes that a person is in a suicidal state, there has been little question but that he should assume responsibility for coping with the possibility of suicide. This stems from the basic premise in the health field that preservation of life is a primary goal. With recent developments in health care delivery and social philosophy the assumption of responsibility for dealing with the risk of suicide cannot be as readily taken for granted. The question is repeatedly raised whether intervening in a person's self-destructive actions—that is, suicide prevention—is an unwarranted violation of that person's right to choose the time and manner of his own death. A person's birth, it is maintained, is beyond his control, but his death is his own to do with as he will. This view tends to come from strong, independent thinkers who speak forcefully for autonomy but give no guidelines for helping the less strong, who constitute so large a part of those with mental health needs (113). Perhaps this has been provided by Gibran (120), another speaker-for-the-strong:

> *Najeeb*: Not all of us are enabled to see with our inner eyes the great depths of life, and it is cruel to demand that the weak-sighted see the dim and the far.
>
> *Zain*: You are correct, but is it not also cruel to press wine from the green grape?

Such sentiments have a certain limited appeal but get little support from those working with suicidal persons on a day-to-day basis, who recognize how frequently suicidal states are transient, fraught with extreme ambivalence, impinge on other vulnerable persons, and respond to a clear demonstration of humanistic concern. These workers also tend to perceive other persons not as clusters to consider *en masse* but as individuals, each deserving respect and concern for his unique needs.

To consider the issue as primarily a conflict between personal liberty and the value of life is to oversimplify what is an intensely personal and individual matter, both for the suicidal person and the potential intervener. Each clinician must come to his own philosophical position derived from his own experience and temperament (83, 112, 113, 121, 122).

Our goal is to reduce unnecessary and preventable suicide to a minimum. This does not imply attempting to control others' lives or to impose our values on them. The primary effort is to exert a beneficial influence on fellow human beings who are in pain and who struggle with a sense of hopelessness and isolation. If these efforts in a given situation are in vain, we must accept our shortcomings and in spite of our dismay take some satisfaction from having done what we were able to do, whether it was sufficient for the other's needs. Most important, we should not abandon the task because it is often difficult and long, nor abandon hope ourselves because we fail to foresee a favorable outcome.

The basis for our persistence can be the underlying awareness that, as James Baldwin so clearly expresses it, "nothing is fixed, forever and forever and forever, it is not fixed; the earth is always shifting, the light is always changing, the sea does not cease to grind down rock. Generations do not cease to be born, and we are responsible to them because we are the only witnesses they have. The sea rises, the light fails, lovers cling to each other, and children cling to us. The moment we cease to hold each other, the moment we break faith with one another, the sea engulfs us and the light goes out" (123).

References

1. Silverman C: The epidemiology of depression. *Am J Psychiatr* **124:**833–891, January 1968.
2. Guze S, Robins E: Suicide and primary affective disorders. *Br J Psychiatr* **117:**437–438, 1970.
3. Robins E, Murphy G, Wilkinson R, and others: Some clinical considerations in the prevention of suicide. *Am J Pub Health* **49:**888–899, 1959.
4. Barraclough B: The diagnostic classification and psychiatric treatment of 100 suicides, in *Proceedings Fifth International Conference for Suicide Prevention.* Edited by Fox R, International Association of Suicide Prevention, 1970, pp. 129–132.
5. Dorpat T, Ripley H: A study of suicide in the Seattle area. *Comp Psychiatr* **1:**349–359, 1960.
6. Motto J, Greene C: Suicide and the medical community. *Arch Neurol Psychiatr* **80:**776–781, December 1958.
7. Tuckman J, Lavell M: A study of suicides in Philadelphia. *Pub Health Rep* **73:**547–553, 1958.
8. Vail D: Suicide and medical responsibility. *Am J Psychiatr* **115:**1006–1010, 1959.
9. Dublin L: Suicide: An overview of a health and social problem. *Bull Suicidol,* 25–30, December 1967.
10. Farberow N: *Quoted in Suicide—The Will to Die.* National Association Blue Shield Plans, 1973.
11. Farberow N, Shneidman E: *The Cry for Help.* New York, McGraw-Hill, 1961, Part II.
12. Freud S: Mourning and melancholia, in *Collected Papers.* London, Hogarth Press, 1949, Vol. 4.
13. Menninger K: *Man Against Himself.* New York, Harcourt, Brace and World, 1938.
14. Robinson EA: *Collected Poems.* New York, MacMillan, 1937.
15. Litman R: Acutely suicidal patients: Management in general medical practice. *Calif Med* **104:**168–174, March 1966.
16. Shneidman E: Perturbation and lethality as precursors of suicide in a gifted group. *Life-Threatening Behav* **1** (1):23–45, Spring 1971.
17. Stengel E: *Suicide and Attempted Suicide.* Baltimore, Penguin Books, 1964.

18. Rubenstein R, Moses R, Lidz T: On attempted suicide. *Arch Neurol Psychiatr* **79**:103–112, January 1958.
19. Fawcett J, Leff M, Bunney W: Suicide: Clues from interpersonal communication. *Arch Gen Psychiatr* **21**:129–137, 1969.
20. Tabachnick N: Interpersonal relations in suicide attempts. *Arch Gen Psychiatr* **4**:16–21, 1961.
21. Durkheim E: *Suicide.* Glencoe, Ill, The Free Press, 1951.
22. O'Neill D: The post viral state. *Med World* **90**:233–236, 1959.
23. Steinberg D and others: Influenza infection causing manic psychosis. *Br J Psychiatr* **120**:531–535, 1972.
24. Piotrowski Z: Psychological test prediction of suicide, in *Suicidal Behaviors.* Edited by Resnik H, Boston, Little, Brown, 1968.
25. *Facts About Suicide: Causes and Prevention.* US Public Health Service Publ 852, Health Information Series 101, 1961.
26. Cohen E, Motto J, Seiden R: An instrument for evaluating suicide potential. *Am J Psychiatr* **122**:886–891, 1966.
27. Litman R, Farberow N, Wold C, and others: Prediction models of suicidal behaviors, in *The Prediction of Suicide.* Edited by Beck A, Resnik H, Lettieri E, Bowie, Md, Charles Press, 1974.
28. Motto J: Refinement of variables in assessing suicide risk, in *The Prediction of Suicide.* Edited by Resnik H, Beck A, Lettieri D, Bowie, Md, Charles Press, 1974.
29. Tuckman J, Youngman W: A scale for assessing suicide risk of attempted suicides. *J Clin Psychol* **24**:17–19, 1968.
30. Wold C: Sub-groupings of suicidal people. *Omega* **2**:19–29, 1971.
31. Zung W: Index of potential suicide: A rating scale for suicide prevention, in *The Prediction of Suicide.* Edited by Beck A, Resnik H, Lettieri D, Bowie, Md, Charles Press, 1974.
32. Rachlis D: Suicide and loss adjustment in the aging. *Bull Suicidol* **7**:23–26, Fall 1970.
33. Resnik H, Cantor J: Suicide and aging. *J Am Geriat Soc* **18**:152–158, 1970.
34. *Suicide, Homicide and Alcoholism Among American Indians.* DHEW Publication (HSM): 73-9123, 1973.
35. Havighurst R: The extent and significance of suicide among American Indians today. *Ment Hyg* **55** (2):174–177, 1971.
36. Hendin H: *Black Suicide.* New York, Basic Books, 1969.
37. Litman R, Farberow N: Emergency evaluation of self-destructive potentiality, in *The Cry for Help.* Edited by Farberow N, Shneidman E, New York, McGraw-Hill, 1961.
38. Elozo E: Suicidal tendencies in depressive psychoses of late age. *Zhurnal Nevropatologii Psikhiatrii* **73** (1):431–434, 1973.
39. Allen N: *Suicide in California.* State of California Department of Public Health, 1973.
40. Aponte R: Epidemiological aspects of suicide and attempted suicide in Venezuela, in *Proceedings Fifth International Conference for Suicide Prevention.* Edited by Fox R, International Association of Suicide Prevention, 1970, pp. 52–57.
41. Headley L: Suicide in Israel, in *Proceedings Sixth International Conference for Suicide Prevention.* Edited by Litman R, International Association of Suicide Prevention, 1972, pp. 72–77.
42. McCulloch J, Philip A, Carstairs G: The ecology of suicidal behavior. *Br J Psychiatr* **113**:313–319, 1967.

43. Pederson A, Awad G, Kindler A: Epidemiological differences between white and non-white suicide attempters. *Am J Psychiatr* **130:**1071–1076, 1973.
44. *Prevention of Suicide.* PHS 35. Geneva, World Health Organization, 1968, p. 9.
45. Heyse H, Kockett G, Feuerlein W: The serious suicide attempt, in *Proceedings Fifth International Conference of Suicide Prevention.* Edited by Fox R, International Association of Suicide Prevention, 1970, pp. 42–45.
46. Rosen D: The serious suicide attempt. *Am J Psychiatr* **127:**764–770, 1970.
47. Breed W: Suicide and loss in social interaction, in *Essays in Self-Destruction.* Edited by Shneidman E, New York, Science House, 1967, pp. 118–202.
48. Murphy G, Robins E: Social factors in suicide. *JAMA* **199:**303–308, 1967.
49. Rorsman B: Suicide in psychiatric patients. *Soc Psychiatr* **8:**55–66, 1973.
50. Leonard C: *Understanding and Preventing Suicide.* Springfield, Charles C Thomas, 1967.
51. Lettieri D: Suicidal death prediction scales, in *The Prediction of Suicide.* Edited by Beck A, Resnik H, Lettieri D, Bowie, Md, Charles Press, 1974.
52. Tuckman J, Youngman W: Assessment of suicidal risk in attempted suicides, in *Suicidal Behaviors.* Edited by Resnik H, Boston, Little, Brown, 1968, p. 196.
53. Motto J: Depressive States and Suicide Prevention. Unpublished data from work in progress.
54. Farberow N, Heilig S, Litman R: Evaluation and management of suicidal persons, in *The Psychology of Suicide.* Edited by Shneidman E, Farberow N, Litman R, New York, Science House, 1970, p. 278.
55. Litman R: Suicide as acting out, in *The Psychology of Suicide.* Edited by Shneidman E, Farberow N, Litman R, New York, Science House, 1970, pp. 303–304.
56. Motto J: Suicide attempts: A longitudinal view. *Arch Gen Psychiatr* **13:**516–520, 1965.
57. *I Ching.* Wilhelm Baynes translation, Pantheon Books, 1961, p. 19.
58. Silver M and others: Relation of depression to attempted suicide and seriousness of intent. *Arch Gen Psychiatr* **25:**573–576, 1971.
59. Diggory J: The components of personal despair, in *Essays in Self-Destruction.* Edited by Shneidman E, New York, Science House, 1967.
60. Kobler A, Stotland E: *The End of Hope.* Glencoe, The Free Press, 1964.
61. Minkoff K and others: Hopelessness, depression and attempted suicide. *Am J Psychiatr* **130:**455–459, 1973.
62. Beck A and others: An inventory for measuring depression. *Arch Gen Psychiatr* **4:**561–571, 1961.
63. Hamilton M: A rating for depression. *J Neurol Neurosurg Psychiatr* **23:**56–61, 1960.
64. Zung W: A self-rating depression scale. *Arch Gen Psychiatr* **12:**63–70, 1965.
65. Pokorny A: A followup study of 618 suicidal patients. *Am J Psychiatr* **122:**1109–1116, 1966.
66. McHugh P, Goodell H: Suicidal behavior. *Arch Gen Psychiatr* **25:**456–464, 1971.
67. West D: *Murder Followed by Suicide.* Cambridge, Mass, Harvard University Press, 1966.
68. Henry A, Short J: *Suicide and Homicide.* Glencoe, The Free Press, 1954.
69. Pokorny A: Human violence: Homicide, aggravated assault, suicide and attempted suicide. *J Crim Law, Crim Police Sci* **56:**488–497, 1965.
70. Lipsius S: Judgements of alternatives to hospitalization. *Am J Psychiatr* **130:**892–896, 1973.
71. Perris C: The separation of bipolar from unipolar recurrent depressive psychoses. *Behav Neuropsychiatr* **1** (8):17–24, 1969.

72. Winokur G, Clayton P, Reich T: *Manic-Depressive Illness.* St. Louis, Mosby, 1969.
73. Shaffer T: Introduction to symposium on mental illness, the law and civil liberties. *Santa Clara Lawyer* **13**:369–378, 1973.
74. Murphy G, Robins E: The communication of suicidal ideas, in *Suicidal Behaviors.* Edited by Resnik H, Boston, Little, Brown, 1968, pp. 168–170.
75. Blachly P, Disher W, Roduner G: Suicide by physicians. *Bull Suicidol,* 1–18, 1968.
76. Curlee J: Depression and alcoholism. *Bull Menninger Clin* **36**(4):451–455, 1972.
77. Curphey T: The forensic pathologist and the multidisciplinary approach to death, in *Essays in Self-Destruction.* Edited by Shneidman E, New York, Science House, 1967.
78. Litman R and others: The psychological autopsy of equivocal deaths. *JAMA* **184**:924–929, 1963.
79. Shneidman E, Farberow N: Sample investigations of equivocal suicidal deaths, in *The Cry for Help.* Edited by Farberow N, Shneidman E, New York, McGraw-Hill, 1961, pp. 118–128.
80. Murphy G: Clinical identification of suicidal risk. *Arch Gen Psychiatr* **27**:356–359, 1972.
81. Rosen A: Detection of suicidal patients. *J Consult Clin Psychol* **18**:397–403, 1954.
82. Brown T, Sheran T: Suicide prevention: A review. *Life-Threatening Behav* **2**(2):67–98, 1972.
83. Sprott S: *The English Debate on Suicide.* La Salle, Ill: Open Court, 1961.
84. Frederick C, Lague L: *Dealing with the Crisis of Suicide.* Public Affairs Pamphlet 406A, New York, 1972, p. 10.
85. Glaser K: Attempted suicide in children and adolescents: Psychodynamic observations. *Am J Psychother* **19** (2):220–227, 1965.
86. Jacobziner H: Attempted suicide in adolescence. *JAMA* **191**:7–11, 1965.
87. Seiden R: Campus tragedy: A study of student suicide. *J Abnor Psychol* **71**(6):389–399, 1966.
88. Seiden R: Suicide among youth. *Bull Suicidol (Suppl),* p. 33, 1969.
89. Wesselius L: Notes on adolescent suicide. *J Nat Assoc Private Psychiatr Hosp* **4**(4):5–9, 1972–1973.
90. Braaten L, Darling C: Suicidal tendencies among college students. *Psychiatr Quart* **36**(4):665–692, 1962.
91. Fawcett J and others: Priorities for improved treatment approaches, in *Suicide Prevention in the Seventies.* Edited by Resnik H, Hathorne B. DHEW Publication (HSM), 72-9054, 1973, p. 92.
92. Litman R: Some aspects of the treatment of the potentially suicidal patient, in *Clues to Suicide.* Edited by Shneidman E, Farberow N, New York, McGraw-Hill, 1957.
93. Litman R: Emergency response to potential suicide. *J Michigan Med Soc* **62**:68–72, 1963.
94. Mayer D: A psychotherapeutic approach to the suicidal patient. *Br J Psychiatr* **119**:629–633, 1971.
95. Mintz R: Some practical procedures in the management of suicidal persons. *Am J Orthopsychiatr* **36**:896–903, 1966.
96. Tabachnick N: The crisis treatment of suicide. *Calif Med* **112**(6):1–8, 1970.
97. Kaiser H: *Effective Psychotherapy.* New York, The Free Press, 1965.
98. Litman R: Psychotherapists' orientations toward suicide, in *Suicidal Behaviors.* Edited by Resnik H, Boston, Little Brown, 1968, p. 363.

99. Harris J, Myers J: Hospital management of the suicidal patient, in *Suicidal Behaviors.* Edited by Resnik H, Boston, Little, Brown, 1968.
100. Hollister L: *Clinical Use of Psychotherapeutic Drugs.* Springfield, Charles C Thomas, 1973, pp. 91–93.
101. Hollister L: Uses of psychotherapeutic drugs. *Ann Int Med* **79**:88–98, 1973.
102. Kline N: *Depression: Its Diagnosis and Treatment.* New York, Brunner/Mazel, 1969, p. 15.
103. Pöldinger W: The activity spectra of antidepressives and their indications, with particular reference to suicide prevention, in *Proceedings Sixth International Conference for Suicide Prevention.* Edited by Litman R, International Association of Suicide Prevention, 1972.
104. Smith A and others: Studies on the effectiveness of antidepressant drugs. *Psychopharmacol Bull (Special Issue),* March 1969.
105. Wheatley D: Drowsiness and antidepressant drugs in mild depressive illness. *Br J Psychiatr* **120**:517–519, 1972.
106. Kline N: Pharmacotherapy of the depressed and suicidal patient, in *Suicidal Behaviors.* Edited by Resnik H, Boston, Little, Brown, 1968.
107. Welu C: Psychological reactions of emergency room staff to suicide attempters, in *Proceedings Sixth International Conference for Suicide Prevention.* Edited by Litman R, International Association of Suicide Prevention, 1972, pp. 309–318.
108. Farberow N: Group psychotherapy with suicidal persons, in *Suicidal Behaviors.* Edited by Resnik H, Boston, Little, Brown, 1968.
109. Farberow N: Vital process in suicide prevention: Group psychotherapy as a community of concern. *Life-Threatening Behav* **2** (4):239–251, 1972.
110. Hadlick J: Group psychotherapy for adolescents following a suicide attempt, in *Proceedings Fifth International Conference for Suicide Prevention.* Edited by Fox R, International Association of Suicide Prevention, 1970, pp. 57–59.
111. Motto J, Stein E: A group approach to guilt in depressive and suicidal patients. *J Rel Health* **12**(4):378–385, 1973.
112. Motto J: The right to suicide: A psychiatrist's view. *Life-Threatening Behav* **2**(3):184–188, 1972.
113. Szasz T: The ethics of suicide. *Antioch Rev* **31**(1):7–17, Spring 1971.
114. Shneidman E: Suicide prevention: The hospital's role. *Hospital Prac,* 56–61, September 1968.
115. Davidson H: Suicide in the hospital. *Hospitals, J Am Hosp Assoc* **43**:55–59, November 1969.
116. Elopement and suicide. Malpractice Prevention Workshops, Section 1. *Calif Med* **112**(3):89–90, March 1970.
117. Krieger G: Suicides, drugs and the open hospital. *Hosp Commun Psychiatr* **17**:196–199, July 1966.
118. Litman R, Farberow N: The hospital's obligation toward suicide-prone patients. *Hospitals, J Am Hosp Assoc* **40**:64–68, December 1966.
119. Holder A: Does the patient have a case? *Prism* **1**(7):45–46, 1973.
120. Gibran K: *Secrets of the Heart.* (Transl Ferris A) New York, Citadel Press, 1971, p. 257.
121. Murphy G: Suicide and the right to die. *Am J Psychiatr* **130**:472–473, 1973.
122. Noyes R: Shall we prevent suicide? *Comp Psychiatr* **2**(4):361–370, 1970.
123. Baldwin J, Avedon R: *Nothing Personal.* New York, Atheneum Press, 1964.

Fourteen

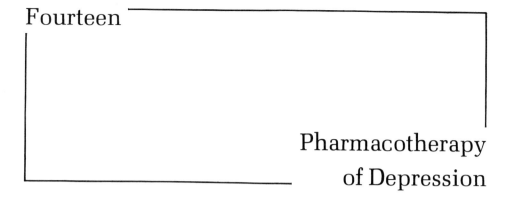

Pharmacotherapy of Depression

Arthur J. Prange, Jr., M.D.

If a patient with frank depression seeks medical advice, the chances are better than even that he will be given an antidepressant drug. Since depression is a common complaint (1), it follows that antidepressant drugs are among the most frequently prescribed medications. These considerations provide the rationale for still another review (2–7) of the use of these substances.

An Orientation to Drug Treatment

I write about antidepressant drugs from the point of view of a psychiatrist rather than that of a pharmacologist. A psychiatrist starts with a patient, not with drugs. If his patient is depressed, the psychiatrist's first decision is whether to recommend hospitalization. This decision—based on a number of factors, most prominently an estimation of suicide potential—will in turn influence treatment, including drug selection if, in fact, a drug is to be used. If the patient is hospitalized, all treatments are potentially available; if he is to be treated as an outpatient, this fact may militate against the use of electric shock treatment (ECT) and monoamine oxidase inhibitors, in my opinion.

After the decision concerning hospitalization has been made, the next question is the selection of treatment. With hospitalized patients one may start by considering ECT. The main advantage of this modality is its speed of action, and its main indication is the need for a rapid response. Its use will usually be dictated by severe suicidal risk, as, for example, in an agitated middle-aged man with stated suicidal intentions or a history of serious attempts. There is little justification, apart from medical contraindications, for withholding ECT from such a patient. Occasionally, the patient's public or private responsibilities will demand the briefest possible hospitalization and the most rapid possible remission, and these considerations may override others. A final indication for beginning treatment with ECT is a history of poor response to drugs during a previous attack of depression.

If ECT is not chosen for a patient who has been hospitalized, then usually a drug should be used. I do not mean to gainsay the value of psychotherapy. I think psychotherapy is useful between depressive attacks to bring about psychodynamic and environmental changes that may render the patient less vulnerable. During attacks it may amplify the benefits initiated by drugs and, for that matter, ECT. In fact, I regard it as a "side effect" of ECT that patients given this treatment tend to be sequestered by hospital personnel and thus relatively deprived of supportive psychotherapy (8). Some simple counseling maneuvers should always be included with drug treatment. For example, patients should be cautioned that drugs are slow to act and they should not be further disheartened by the absence of apparent effect even into the third week. Meanwhile, nuisance side effects can be cited as evidence that the drug is "starting to work," and there is no reason not to exploit this opportunity to employ suggestion for the patient's benefit. On the other hand, I believe that exclusive reliance on psychotherapy during a depressive attack is unwarranted. The psychodynamics of the condition, I think, more or less specifically oppose such efforts. I see no incompatibility between a psychopharmacologic and a psychotherapeutic approach.

The considerations outlined above are diagrammed in Figure 1. It suggests that ECT, though it may sometimes be the initial treatment of choice, is often used to treat drug failures. It shows that while ECT usually succeeds, it

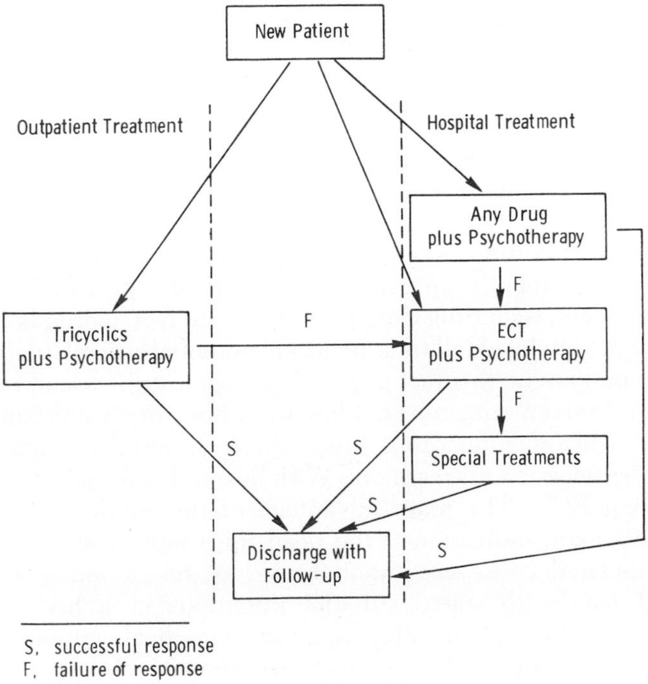

Figure 1. Treatment options for the depressed patient.

sometimes fails, and when it does, "special" means of treatment are available. These are discussed in the succeeding chapter. Figure 1 also implies that remission is almost always obtainable. This is the case, providing suicide can be prevented. Since follow-up is recommended on discharge, one is reminded that depression is almost as likely to recur as it is to remit.

A Theoretical Position

A perusal of Baldessarini's contribution to this volume will convince the reader that the regulation of affect and the symptoms of affective disorders are importantly related to the metabolism in strategic areas of the brain of the so-called biogenic amines. These amines are chemically characterized as the catecholamines, principally norepinephrine (NE) and dopamine, and the indoleamines, serotonin and tryptamine. Much is known about the synthesis, storage, release, and inactivation of these substances (9), and much is known about how they are affected by drugs (10, 11). It is also known that, for the most part, drugs that affect these substances one way or another tend to affect depression or mania in some fashion. However, as Baldessarini points out, investigators have tended to focus on either catecholamines (12–14) or indoleamines (15–17). Since they are intimately related geographically and pharmacologically and, presumably, functionally, the need arose as to how to relate them in a biochemical theory of affective disorders. Following a suggestion by Kety (18), my colleagues and I have stated what we have termed a permissive biogenic amine hypothesis of affective disorders: A deficit in central indoleaminergic transmission permits affective disorder but is insufficient for its cause; changes in central catecholaminergic transmission, when they occur in the context of a deficit in indoleaminergic transmission, act as a proximate cause for affective disorders and determine their quality—catecholaminergic transmission being elevated in mania and diminished in depression.

In other places (7, 9, 20) we have cited the evidence that favors this notion, and we have contributed some findings to support it. At the same time we have acknowledged its incompletion. Most neurons depend on acetylcholine, and cholinergic fibers as well as aminergic fibers appear to play a role in the regulation of affect (21). Thus any biochemical theory of affective disorders must be acknowledged as premature until cholinergic functions are integrated within it. Other systems, of course, not presently recognized, may also be involved. The clinician, however, while eagerly anticipating a more enlightened day, is accustomed to making do with the best tools presently at hand.

A Compendium of Drugs

Table 1 lists most of the substances that in modern times have been represented as possessing antidepressant properties. Lithium is used mainly as an antimanic agent (22, 23) but may have value in certain depressed patients (24) when they are of the bipolar (as opposed to unipolar) variety (25). It is useful in the prophylaxis of mania (22, 23) and perhaps in the prophylaxis of

Table 1 Mood-Active Substances

A. MAO inhibitors
  1. Hydrazines
     e.g., phenelzine (Nardil)
  2. Nonhydrazines
     e.g., tranylcypromine (Parnate)
B. Tricyclics
  1. Nonsedating
     a. Methylated
        e.g., imipramine (Tofranil)
     b. Demethylated
        e.g., desipramine (Pertofran, Norpramin)
  2. Sedating
     a. C = C, ring to side chain
        e.g., amitriptyline (Elavil)
     b. C = C, ring to side chain; oxygen in ring
        e.g., doxepin (Sinequan)
C. Stimulants
  1. Potent but addicting
     e.g., *d*-amphetamine (Dexedrine)
  2. Nonaddicting but impotent
     e.g., methylphenidate (Ritalin)
D. Lithium salts
E. Amino acids
     e.g., L-dopa, L-tryptophan
F. Phenothiazines
     e.g., chlorpromazine (Thorazine)

depression, unipolar and bipolar types about equally (26). Lithium is discussed elsewhere in this volume.

The amino acid, L-dopa, is the precursor of catecholamines. It is useful in Parkinson's disease (27), but its relative inefficacy in depression can be cited as a criticism of the concept that catecholamines are preeminently important in this condition (28). L-dopa often precipitates mania in bipolar depressed patients (29), and this supports the importance of catecholamines. However, other antidepressant treatments appear to share the liability to produce mania in bipolar depressed patients (30). L-dopa cannot be recommended in depression except for experimental purposes.

L-tryptophan is the amino acid precursor of indoleamines. Given with pyridoxine, a co-factor for its transition from acid to amine, it has sometimes (30, 31) but not always (32, 33) been found to act as an antidepressant. It is commercially available for this purpose in the United Kingdom. Recent studies suggest that L-tryptophan may have antimanic properties (20, 34). According to the permissive hypothesis, an increase in available indoleamines would diminish permission for affective disorder, both mania and depression. One wonders if this substance might not rationally be given with other more standard antidepressant and antimanic treatments. Indeed, systematic studies have shown that monoamine oxidase (MAO) inhibitors are more effective in depression when combined with L-tryptophan than when combined with placebo (35–37).

Phenothiazines, of course, find their greatest use in schizophrenia. In mania they have largely been supplanted by lithium. They may be useful in agitated depressions (38) or in depression accompanied by anxiety. In a popular commercial preparation a phenothiazine, perphenazine, and a tricyclic, amitriptyline, are combined. Wonder is justified at the attempt to block catecholamine activity even while trying to promote it. One must recall, however, that phenothiazines perform more than the former action (39), and tricyclics more than the latter (11, 40–42). Moreover, the test of whether a substance or a combination of substances is antidepressant is empirical; the test is not whether their known actions are congenial to current theories.

Stimulants are also easily dispatched from a list of practical antidepressants. Amphetamine and its congeners elevate mood in nondepressed persons, and they are popular drugs of abuse. In depressed patients they often produce a tense dysphoria, and even when they produce a brief mood elevation, it tends to be followed by a postamphetamine worsening of depression. It may be of theoretical import that chronic amphetamine administration may produce a state not easily distinguished from paranoid schizophrenia (43). Presumably, this is the result of catecholamine depletion. Methylphenidate is also a stimulant. Unlike amphetamine, it has little if any addiction potential, but it is rather impotent as an antidepressant. It probably has some value in the treatment of mildly depressed outpatients (44).

Standard antidepressant drugs consist of the MAO inhibitors and the tricyclics. The MAO inhibitors were the first to be introduced in clinical practice. They inhibit the enzyme, monoamine-oxidase, which accounts for the intraneuronal destruction of biogenic amines. Thus when one of these drugs is used, more amine is available for release into the synaptic cleft, and synaptic transmission is promoted. Chemically these drugs may be classified as hydrazine derivatives or nonhydrazine derivatives. A nonhydrazine, tranylcypromine, resembles amphetamine in molecular structure and like amphetamine has direct stimulating properties. Both chemical types of MAO inhibitors share several liabilities. Monoamine oxidase enzymes are widely distributed. Their substrate specificity and drug specificity may vary from tissue to tissue (45, 46), but if an MAO is inhibited in one place, brain being the psychopharmacologist's target, other MAOs are likely to be inhibited as well, at least to some extent. A patient treated in this manner stands in jeopardy. Otherwise innocuous foodstuffs (47, 48) and amine-active drugs (47–50), including other antidepressants (51), may cause serious and even fatal toxicity. In addition, the drugs as a class are inherently toxic, especially to the liver. MAO inhibitors potentiate alcohol. They are, of course, specifically contraindicated in patients with pheochromocytoma. Many MAO inhibitors have been removed from the United States market (52).

I mentioned my belief that the use of MAO should be limited to hospitalized patients. The only reason to begin pharmacotherapy with an MAO inhibitor, in my opinion, is the existence of a history of poor responses to tricyclics during a previous depression coupled with a history of a good response to an MAO inhibitor. After a drug-free interval, an MAO inhibitor may reasonably be used in patients in whom tricyclics have failed.

The tricyclics are the most useful members of the antidepressant class. One possible mode of action was suggested when Hertting and his colleagues (53) showed that imipramine, the prototypical tricyclic, blocks the reuptake of NE into nerve end following its release. This action amplifies the activity of NE, and the fact that it is performed by a substance empirically known to be an antidepressant gave strong support to the belief that catecholamine insufficiency plays a role in depression. However, the actions of imipramine are more complicated than first appeared, and chronic actions must be distinguished from acute ones (54). Moreover, not only NE but serotonin as well appears to depend on reuptake as a major means of physiological inactivation.

Table 2 characterizes the chemical differences among the tricyclics presently available. Tricyclics are either secondary or tertiary amines. These drugs resemble phenothiazines in molecular structure, but tricyclics have an additional atom in the central ring. The connection between the central ring and the side chain may be single bonded or double bonded. Doxepin, a relatively new drug, is unique in having an oxygen atom in the central ring. However, neither molecular structure nor other basic pharmacologic considerations are precise guides to clinical activity. Detailed accounts of the pharmacology of imipramine are available (40, 41).

At one time it was believed that for imipramine to become active one of its two terminal methyl groups had to be metabolically removed. Its demethylated congener, desipramine, was advocated on the grounds that its use would spare the body the trouble of demethylation, as it were, and would thus be a faster acting drug. However, there is little clinical support for the belief that

Table 2

	IMP	AMI	DOX	DMI	NOR	PRO
Tertiary amine	X	X	X			
Secondary amine				X	X	X
Ring to side chain bond						
Nitrogen to carbon						
Single bond	X			X		
Carbon to carbon						
Single bond						X
Double bond		X	X		X	
Oxygen in central ring			X			

IMP, imipramine
AMI, amitriptyline
DOX, doxepin
DMI, desipramine
NOR, nortriptyline
PRO, protriptyline.

desipramine acts faster than imipramine or that nortriptyline, a secondary amine, acts faster than amitriptyline, its corresponding tertiary amine (2). Tertiary amine tricyclics are probably active in themselves. Recently Maas (55) has reminded us that if we administer a tertiary amine our patient experiences the effects of this drug and the corresponding secondary amine, due to *in vivo* demethylation, while the converse does not appreciably occur.

The synthesis of amitriptyline established an important difference between tricyclics. This drug and its congeners, nortriptyline and doxepin, are more sedating than are imipramine and desipramine. They have also been represented as having greater anxiolytic properties. The difference is not remarkable, in my opinion, and in any case antianxiety potential and sedative potential are not easily distinguished. Doxepin may deserve special comment as its tranquilizing effect compares favorably with that of chlordiazepoxide (56). Protriptyline is a stimulating drug and is more potent on a milligram basis than the others. It may find special use in the treatment of grossly retarded depressed patients.

Since tricyclics differ so little one from the other, depressive typology is often used to choose between them. A neurotic-psychotic dichotomy depends in part on the presence of anxiety in the former group. It follows that neurotic patients are more apt to benefit from a sedating drug, but one would be far advanced to choose a tricyclic on the basis of the need for sedation. If depressed patients are regarded as agitated or retarded, then one thinks of a sedating tricyclic, perhaps with a phenothiazine, in the former group, and a nonsedating tricyclic, perhaps even protriptyline, in the latter. Wilson and I, however, have found imipramine an effective remedy for both groups (57, 58). Patients can be separated not only by description of current symptoms but also by a consideration of history. Thus depressed patients who have never displayed mania are termed unipolar while those who have displayed mania are regarded as bipolar (59). As stated above, bipolar patients have a proclivity for developing hypomania in response to L-dopa and imipramine, and they derive some benefit from lithium though even in this relatively small group standard antidepressants are probably more effective. The reactive-endogenous dichotomy is not particularly useful in choosing a drug although it may be of some value in deciding whether to use a drug at all. Klein (60) believes that reactive patients recover about as promptly without a drug as with one, while endogenous patients clearly benefit from pharmacotherapy. However, assignment of a patient to one or the other group is not easy prospectively. Reactive features may only unfold as communication increases *pari passu* with recovery.

I do not dispute the validity of psychodynamics, but in my view choosing a drug according to psychodynamic considerations is somewhat less reliable than leaving the matter to chance. If a patient has experienced object loss and is manifestly anxious, psychopharmacologic measures should be directed toward the latter, not the former. If such a patient needs a drug at all, it is an anxiolytic, not an antidepressant.

Just as there are no chemical means of diagnosing depression, there are at the present time no practical chemical means of selecting the best drug for a given depressed patient. Nevertheless, recent evidence suggests that amitriptyline may be more effective than imipramine in patients who show high excretion rates of 3-methoxy-4-hydroxy phenylglycol (MHPG) (61), and conversely (62). Since much of this substance occurring in urine comes from brain, where it is a major metabolite of NE, a high excretion rate probably indicates relatively high central noradrenergic activity. This in turn might correlate with anxiety or agitation which are in themselves, as suggested above, indications for the selection of amitriptyline. Amitriptyline may also be more effective than imipramine in elderly patients. Klein and Davis (2) believe that this assumption may rationalize the discrepancy between findings by Sandifer and others (63) and by Hordern and others (64). However, in neither normals nor depressed patients does MHPG excretion appear to increase with age (65).

A Consideration of Side Effects

The desired effects of tricyclics are similar, and so are their unwanted effects. I hesitate to call them side effects, for they may be as intrinsic as the wanted effects and no less regular. Furthermore, some side effects, for example, dry mouth, may be a particular expression of a general effect, in this case an anticholinergic effect that may be important to the desired action. In any case, a consideration of what are conventionally called side effects may assist in drug selection.

The most important side effects of tricyclics are due to their anticholinergic properties. Dry mouth occurs more often than not but is usually a tolerable nuisance. Palpitations, tachycardia, and orthostatic hypotension are among the cardiovascular events that may occur. Toxic confusion, urinary retention, and the aggravation of glaucoma are more serious. Tricyclics should be avoided in patients with glaucoma, prostatic enlargement, or recent myocardial infarction. Side effects are most apt to occur and most apt to be serious in the elderly. Thus a drug that seems to have a somewhat reduced anticholinergic potential, such as doxepin (66), may be of special value in the elderly when other considerations do not countervail. For similar reasons, elderly patients should be given full doses of tricyclics only by gradual increments while one watches for side effects. It is probably unwise to give an elderly patient his entire daily dosage at bedtime, as has been recommended for younger patients (2).

Tricyclics may cause not only orthostatic hypotension but also, less commonly, hypertensive phenomena (67). Whether blood pressure is affected at all, and, if so, in what direction, probably depends on the balancing out of the drugs' effects on cholinergic, noradrenergic, and serotoninergic systems. Blood pressure is also a concern when a depressed patient is discovered to suffer concomitantly from hypertension. In this situation the MAO inhibitor pargyline would appear a rational choice, since it is often used in the medical clinic as an antihypertensive agent and since it might have been introduced commercially as an antidepressant had not MAO inhibitors fallen into disfavor. In fact, hypertensive patients are often taking a medley of drugs and a hazard may arise from the introduction of still another. ECT should be evaluated as an alternative to drugs in this situation.

The interaction between the antihypertensive drug guanethidine and tricyclics is a matter of equal interest to the practitioner and researcher. Briefly, tricyclics block the access of guanethidine into nerve ends, thus increasing the dose needed to lower blood pressure. Guanethidine blocking is a nice test of tricyclic potency. By the same token, discontinuation of a tricyclic may result in nerve ends being flooded with guanethidine. Fann and others (68) have reviewed this subject.

Finally, it should be remembered that tricyclics can cause a Parkinsonian syndrome but that tricyclics have also been used with some success to treat Parkinson's disease. This is a matter that should interest theorists as well as those who treat the elderly (69).

Technique of Administration

Having decided that his patient requires an antidepressant, having decided that a tricyclic is preferable to an MAO inhibitor, and having selected a drug on the basis of the fit between its special potentials, desired and undesired, and the special characteristics of the patient, the physician must next decide on dosage. A few patients benefit from a starting dose of 100 mg/day or even less, but the majority need more, and I believe 150 mg/day is a reasonable starting dose except, of course, in the case of protriptyline. There are many styles of administration. One acceptable style is to start with full dosage on the first day but to divide it into three or four units. If this is tolerated, the entire dosage can then be given at one time, most conveniently at bedtime. I believe, however, that some patients benefit from taking medication more frequently. It reinforces their sense of taking active measures against their illness.

It is astonishing that some pharmacotherapists who show great flexibility in dosing with phenothiazines confine themselves to prescribing tricyclics at almost a fixed level. With tricyclics the most common cause of inadequate response is inadequate dosage. If the patient fails to respond to beginning levels, the dose should be increased gradually to as much as 300 mg/day in the case of imipramine. Of course, the patient should be carefully watched for the appearance of side effects.

Giving too little is a common error in using tricyclics, but so is giving too much. Here I refer to the total size of the first prescription given to an outpatient. The potentially fatal dose is only in the order of 10 multiples of the average daily dose. To send home a patient who is statistically at risk for suicide with this much medication is an error. Pharmacotherapists should consult Brophy's data on this point (70).

Finally, the question arises as to how long to continue tricyclic therapy. There is little systematic information at this point. I suggest a trial of dose reduction 1 month after remission seems complete, reinstating full doses if symptoms recur. It is accepted practice to give half doses for 6 months after remission (2).

Special Problems

A number of problems remain pertaining to depression that can reasonably be discussed in a treatise on drug therapy. Drugs are an aspect of management, but management depends in the first instance on diagnosis. While diagnosis is often easy, it sometimes can be difficult. This is the case in a population of patients who have been described as showing depressive equivalents (71, 72). These patients tend to manifest vague but persistent somatic complaints, gloomy outlooks, impoverished descriptions of their situations, and sometimes a stoical attitude that is contradicted by their complaining. While their response to antidepressants is not notably good, a trial of one of these drugs is often justified. Patients of this kind may become acutely suicidal when, after a series of referrals, they have been studied at a medical center that they regard as a court of last appeal and are told that "nothing is wrong." It should also be remembered that depression even of suicidal severity may accompany any illness (73).

All antidepressants, MAO inhibitors and tricyclics alike, share the drawback of being slow to act. Although I think the problem has been somewhat overstated, most authorities maintain that little benefit may be seen for as long as 3 weeks. Whether latency is as brief as 7 days or as long as 21, the point must be obvious that the prolongation of morbidity and of mortal risk is serious. In a series of studies Wilson and I and our colleagues found that in both retarded and nonretarded depression the beneficial action of imipramine could be significantly accelerated by the addition of a small amount of the thyroid hormone, L-triiodothyronine (T3) (57, 58). We confirmed this in a collaborative study with Coppen's group (30). Wheatley (74) extended the principle to include amitriptyline. Feighner and others (75) were unable to confirm our findings, but we have offered a differing interpretation of their data (76). A compilation of our studies showed that the acceleration of imipramine by T3 was limited to women (77). Methylphenidate has also been used to accelerate the antidepressant effect of imipramine (78). The former drug interferes with the enzymatic destruction of the latter (79). Thus after methylphenidate, one might expect both greater benefits and more side effects from imipramine. Contrariwise, T3 appears to *reduce* the side effects of imipramine (30). The salient point is that T3 clearly does not increase side effects; the apparent reduction may only indicate enhanced antidepressant effect, since any side effect inventory will share items in common with any depression inventory.

Latency of action and failure of action may be related matters. It may be that time is required for imipramine to do whatever it does that is antidepressant and that T3 simply accelerates the onset of chronic effects. Animal data support this notion (54). As regards definitive failures, it may be that a certain subgroup of depressed patients simply do not profit from the effects of imipramine. However this may be, the size of the imipramine failure group can be substantially reduced by increasing the dose. Concerning the residual patients one thinks of ECT or the use of an MAO inhibitor. These are standard measures to pursue.

In England an MAO inhibitor and a tricyclic are sometimes combined in the treatment of patients who have failed to respond to either drug alone (80). This practice is generally shunned in the United States, but Schuckit and his colleagues (51) have reexamined this problem and found that the two classes of drugs combined in usual doses are not excessively toxic. While this may be, a tricyclic can hardly reduce the *inherent* toxicity of an MAO inhibitor. Reserpine or tetrabenazine can also be added to imipramine. This can convert an imipramine failure to an imipramine success, but cardiovascular toxicity is notable (81). In animals, of course, imipramine pretreatment reverses the lethargy induced by reserpine (82).

Our group has not claimed that T3 will convert imipramine failures to successes—only that T3 will accelerate the action of imipramine in women who would otherwise probably respond. Nevertheless, informal experience suggests that about half of imipramine failures can be converted by the addition to their treatment of 25μg T3/day. A number of clinicians have informed us of similar results. Earle (83) found somewhat better results in a single-blind trial, and the phenomenon seems to pertain to men as well as to women.

Elderly depressed patients also present special problems (69). Since they often suffer from illnesses not related to depression and since they tend to develop side effects more readily, smaller doses of tricyclics are usually recommended. I think that one should commence treatment with small doses, but if they prove ineffective one should not be limited to small doses. Dosage may be increased gradually with constant attention to the appearance of side effects and with special attention to the liabilities of the individual patient. Since MAO activity in brain appears to increase with age, with concomitant reduction of biogenic amines (84), the use of an MAO inhibitor may appear especially indicated. However, it remains to be shown that MAO inhibitor toxicity is reduced in old people.

Conclusions

Modern drugs have produced a substantial change in the management of depression. They have reduced the need for hospitalization and the need for ECT. Information concerning drugs has formed the backbone of chemical theories about affective disorders which promise to lead to further improvement in treatment.

Nevertheless, exclusive reliance on drugs is unreasonable. ECT is still sometimes the modality with which treatment should be started. It is occasionally needed when drugs have failed.

The tricyclics are the most important antidepressants. A drug can be chosen from among this group by a consideration of the beneficial effects and potential side effects of the various members and by fitting these to the characteristics of each patient. Latency of action and inefficacy are problems for which measures are available. The drug treatment of the elderly depressed patient must be undertaken with special consideration in mind.

Acknowledgment

Support provided in part by U.S. Public Health Career Scientist Award MH-22536 (A.J.P.).

References

1. Silverman C: *The Epidemiology of Depression.* Baltimore, Johns Hopkins University Press, 1968.

2. Klein DF, Davis JM: *Diagnosis and Drug Treatment of Psychiatric Disorders.* Baltimore, Williams & Wilkins Co, 1969.
3. Cole JO, Davis JM: Antidepressant drugs, in *Comprehensive Textbook of Psychiatry.* Edited by Freedman A, Kaplan H, Baltimore, Williams & Wilkins Co, 1967, pp. 1263–1275.
4. Cole JO: Therapeutic efficacy of antidepressant drugs. *JAMA* **190**:448–455, 1964.
5. Hordern A, Burt CG, Holt NF: *Depressive States.* Springfield, Charles C Thomas, 1965.
6. Davis JM: Efficacy of tranquilizing and antidepressant drugs. *Arch Gen Psychiatr* **13**:552–572, 1965.
7. Prange AJ Jr: The use of drugs in depression: Its theoretical and practical basis. *Psychiatr Ann* **3**:56–75, 1973.
8. Abse DW, Ewing JS: Transference and countertransference in somatic therapies. *J Nerv Ment Dis* **123**:32–40, 1956.
9. Glowinski J: Some new facts about synthesis, storage, and release processes of monoamines in the central nervous system, in *Perspectives in Neuropharmacology.* Edited by Snyder SS, New York Oxford University Press, 1972, pp. 349–404.
10. Axelrod J: The fate of catecholamines and the effect of psychoactive drugs, in *Enzymes in Mental Health.* Edited by Martin GJ, Kisch B, Philadelphia, JB Lippincott Co, 1966.
11. Schildkraut JJ: Neuropharmacology of the affective disorders. *Ann Rev Pharmacol* **13**:427–454, 1973.
12. Prange AJ Jr: The pharmacology and biochemistry of depression. *Dis Nerv Syst* **25**:217–221, 1964.
13. Schildkraut JJ: The catecholamine hypothesis of affective disorders: A review of supporting evidence. *Am J Psychiatr* **122**:509–522, 1965.
14. Bunney WE Jr, Davis JM: Norepinephrine in depressive reactions. *Arch Gen Psychiatr* **13**:483–494, 1965.
15. Coppen A: The biochemistry of affective disorders. *Br J Psychiatr* **113**:1237–1264, 1967.
16. Glassman A: Indoleamines and affective disorders. *Psychosom Med* **31**:107–114, 1969.
17. Lapin IP, Oxenkrug GF: Intensification of the central serotoninergic processes as a possible determinant of the thymoleptic effect. *Lancet* **1**:132–136, 1969.
18. Kety S: Brain amines and affective disorders, in *Brain Chemistry and Mental Disease.* Edited by Ho BT, McIsaac WM, New York, Plenum Press, 1971, pp. 237–244.
19. Prange AJ Jr, Sisk JL, Wilson IC, and others: Balance, permission, and discrimination among amines: A theoretical consideration of the actions of L-tryptophan in disorders of movement and affect, in *Serotonin and Behavior.* Edited by Barchas J, Usdin E, New York, Academic Press, 1973, pp. 539–548.
20. Prange AJ Jr, Wilson IC, Lynn CW, and others: L-Tryptophan in mania: Contribution to a permissive hypothesis of affective disorders. *Arch Gen Psychiatr* **30**:56–62, 1974.
21. Janowsky DS, El-Yousef MK, Davis JM, and others: A cholinergic-adrenergic hypothesis of mania and depression. *Lancet* **2**:632–634, 1972.
22. Davis JM, Janowsky DS, El-Yousef MK: The use of lithium in clinical psychiatry. *Psychiatr Ann* **3**:78-99, 1973.
23. Goodwin FK, Ebert MH: Lithium in mania: Clinical trials and controlled studies, in *Lithium: Its Role in Psychiatric Research and Treatment.* Edited by Gershon S, Shopsin B, New York, Plenum Publishing Corp, 1973, pp. 237–252.
24. Dyson WL, Mendels J: Lithium and depression. *Curr Ther Res* **10**:601-609, 1968.

25. Dunner DL, Cohn CK, Gershon ES, and others: Differential catecholo-methyltransferase activity in unipolar and bipolar affective illness. *Arch Gen Psychiatr* **25**:348–353, 1971.
26. Coppen A, Noguera R, Bailey J: Prophylactic lithium in affective disorders. *Lancet* **2**:275–279, 1971.
27. Keenan RE: The Eaton collaborative study of levodopa therapy in parkinsonism: A summary. *Neurology (Minneap)* **20**:46–59, 1970.
28. Prange AJ Jr: Discussion of Dr. Schildkraut's paper (Neuropharmacological studies of mood disorders, pp. 65–84), in *Disorders of Mood.* Edited by Zubin J, Freyhan FA, Baltimore, Johns Hopkins Press, 1972, pp. 85–92.
29. Murphy DL, Brodie HKH, Goodwin FK: Regular induction of hypomania by L-dopa in "bipolar" manic-depressive patients. *Nature* **229**:135–136, 1971.
30. Coppen A, Whybrow PC, Noguera R, and others: The comparative antidepressant value of L-tryptophan and imipramine with and without attempted potentiation by liothyronine. *Arch Gen Psychiatr* **26**:234–241, 1972.
31. Broadhurst AD: Tryptophan versus ECT. *Lancet* **1**:1392–1393, 1970.
32. Bunney WE Jr, Brodie HKH, Murphy D, and others: Studies of alpha-CH_3-*p*-tyrosine, L-dopa, and L-tryptophan in depression and mania. *Am J Psychiatr* **127**:872–881, 1971.
33. Carrol BJ, Mowbray RM, Davis B: Sequential comparison of L-TP with ECT in severe depression. *Lancet* **1**:967–969, 1970.
34. Murphy DL, Baker M, Goodwin FK, and others: Large-dosage L-tryptophan treatment: Minimal antidepressant and antimanic effects despite marked changes in indoleamine metabolism. *Psychopharmacologia,* in press 1974.
35. Coppen A, Shaw DM, Farrell MB: Potentiation of the antidepressive effect of a monoamine-oxidase inhibitor by tryptophan. *Lancet* **1**:79–81, 1963.
36. Pare CMB: Potentiation of monoamine-oxidase inhibitors by tryptophan. *Lancet* **2**:527–528, 1973.
37. Glassman A, Platman SR: Potentiation of a monoamine oxidase inhibitor by tryptophan. *J Psychiatr Res* :83–88, 1969.
38. Hollister LE, Overall JE: Reflections on the specificity of action of antidepressants. *Psychosomatics* **6**:361–365, 1965.
39. Domino EF: Human pharmacology of tranquilizing drugs. *Clin Pharmacol Ther* **3**:599–664, 1962.
40. Klerman GI, Cole JO: Clinical pharmacology of imipramine and related antidepressant compounds. *Pharmacol Rev* **17**:101–141, 1965.
41. Gyermek L: The pharmacology of imipramine and related antidepressants. *Int Rev Neurobiol* **9**:95–143, 1966.
42. Lidbrink P, Jonsson G, Fuxe K: The effect of imipramine-like drug and antihistamine drugs on uptake mechanisms in the central noradrenaline and 5-hydroxytryptamine neurons. *Neuropharmacology* **10**:521–536, 1971.
43. Angrist BM, Gershon S: Psychiatric sequelae of amphetamine use, in *Psychiatric Complications of Medical Drugs.* Edited by Shader RI, New York, Raven Press, 1972, pp. 175–199.
44. Rickels K, Gordon PE, Gansman DH, and others: Pemoline and methylphenidate in mildly depressed outpatients. *Clin Pharmacol Ther* **11**:698–710, 1970.
45. Shih J-HC, Eiduson S: Multiple forms of monoamine oxidase in developing tissues: The implications for mental disorders, in *Brain Chemistry and Mental Disease.* Edited by Ho BT, McIsaac WM, New York, Plenum Press, 1971, pp. 3–20.
46. Fuller RW, Warren BJ, Molloy BB: Selective inhibition of monoamine oxidase in rat brain mitochondria. *Biochem Pharmacol* **19**:2934–2936, 1970.

47. Goldberg LI: Monoamine oxidase inhibitors. *JAMA* **190:**132–138, 1964.
48. Stockley IH: Interactions of monoamine oxidase inhibitors with foods and drugs. *Pharm J* **203:**174–179, 1969.
49. Mason J: Fatal reaction with parnate and methylamphetamine. *Lancet* **1:**1073, 1962.
50. Tonks CM, Lloyd AT: Hazards with monoamine-oxidase inhibitors. *Br Med J* **1:**589, 1965.
51. Schuckit M, Robins E, Feighner J: Tricyclic antidepressants and monoamine oxidase inhibitors. *Arch Gen Psychiatr* **24:**509–514, 1971.
52. Lifshitz K, Kline N: Psychopharmacology of the aged, in *Clinical Principles and Drugs in the Aging.* Edited by Freeman JT, Springfield, Charles C Thomas, 1963.
53. Hertting G, Axelrod J, Whitby LG: Effect of drugs on the uptake and metabolism of H^3-norepinephrine. *J Pharmacol Exp Ther* **134:**146–153, 1961.
54. Schildkraut JJ: Neuropharmacological studies of mood disorders, in *Disorders of Mood.* Edited by Zubin J, Freyhan FA, Baltimore, Johns Hopkins Press, 1972, pp. 65-84.
55. Maas JW: Urinary MHPG in primary affective disorders. Presented at the 12th Annual Meeting of the American College of Neuropsychopharmacology, Palm Springs, December 4–7, 1973.
56. Sterlin C, Ban TA, Lehmann HE, and others: A comparative evaluation of doxepin and chlordiazepoxide in the treatment of psychoneurotic outpatients. *Curr Ther Res* **12:**195–200, 1970.
57. Prange AJ Jr, Wilson IC, Rabon AM, and others: Enhancement of imipramine antidepressant activity by thyroid hormone. *Am J Psychiatr* **126:**457–469, 1969.
58. Wilson IC, Prange AJ Jr, McClane TK, and others: Thyroid hormone enhancement of imipramine in non-retarded depressions. *N Engl J Med* **282:**1063–1067, 1970.
59. Winokur G, Clayton PJ, Reich T: *Manic Depressive Illness.* St. Louis, CV Mosby Co, 1969.
60. Klein DF: Pharmacological response as a basis for syndrome identification. Presented by the 12th Annual Meeting of the American College of Neuropsychopharmacology, Palm Springs, December 4–7, 1973.
61. Schildkraut JJ, Draskoczy PR, Gershon ES, and others: Effects of tricyclic antidepressants on norepinephrine metabolism: Basic and clinical studies, in *Brain Chemistry and Mental Disease.* Edited by Ho BT, McIsaac WM, New York, Plenum Press, 1971, pp. 215–236.
62. Maas JW, Fawcett JA, Dekirmenjian H: Catecholamine metabolism, depressive illness, and drug response. *Arch Gen Psychiatr* **26:**252–262, 1972.
63. Sandifer MG, Wilson IC, Gambill JM: The influence of case selection and dosage in antidepressant drug trial. *Br J Psychiatr* **111:**142–148, 1965.
64. Hordern A, Holt NF, Burt CG, and others: Amitriptyline in depressive states: Phenomenology and prognostic considerations. *Br J Psychiatr* **109:**815–825, 1963.
65. Dekirmenjian H, Maas JW: Urinary excretion of norepinephrine and its metabolites in human control subjects and depressed patients. Presented at the 126th Annual Meeting of the American Psychiatric Association, Honolulu, May 7–11, 1973.
66. Ayd FJ: Recognizing and treating depressed patients. *Mod Med:* 80–86. November 29, 1971.
67. Hessov IB: Hypertension during imipramine treatment. *Lancet* **1:**84–85, 1970.
68. Fann WE, Cavanaugh JH, Kaufman JS, and others: Doxepin: Effects on transport of biogenic amines in man. *Psychopharmacologia* **22:**111–125, 1971.
69. Prange AJ Jr: The use of antidepressant drugs in the elderly patient, in

Psychopharmacology and Aging. Edited by Eisdorfer C, Fann WE, New York, pp. 225–237.

70. Brophy JJ: Suicide attempts with psychotropic drugs. *Arch Gen Psychiatr* **17**:652–657, 1967.
71. Earley LW: The clinical signs and early recognition of depressions as they are met with in general practice. *Pa Med J* **59**:1355–1358, 1956.
72. Mendels J: *Concepts of Depression.* New York, John Wiley and Sons, Inc, 1970.
73. Fawcett J: Suicidal depression and physical illness. *JAMA* **219**:1303–1306, 1972.
74. Wheatley D: Potentiation of amitriptyline by thyroid hormone. *Arch Gen Psychiatr* **26**:229–233, 1972.
75. Feighner JP, King LJ, Schuckit MA, and others: Hormonal potentiation of imipramine and ECT in primary depression. *Am J Psychiatr* **128**:1230–1238, 1972.
76. Prange AJ Jr: Discussion of Feighner JP, King LJ, Schuckit MA, and others (Hormonal potentiation of imipramine and ECT in primary depression, pp. 1230–1235). *Am J Psychiatr* **128**:1235–1238, 1972.
77. Wilson IC, Prange AJ Jr, Lara PP: L-Triiodothyronine alone and with imipramine in the treatment of depressed women, in *The Thyroid Axis, Drugs, and Behavior.* Edited by Prange AJ Jr, New York, Raven Press, 1974.
78. Wharton RN, Perel JM, Dayton PG, and others: A potential clinical use for methylphenidate with tricyclic antidepressants. *Am J Psychiatr* **127**:1619–1625, 1971.
79. Perel JM, Black N: In vitro metabolism studies with methylphenidate. *Fed Proc* **29**:345, 1970.
80. Gander DR: The clinical value of monoamine oxidase inhibitors and tricyclic antidepressants in combination, in *Proceedings of the First International Symposium on Antidepressant Drugs.* Edited by Garattini S, Dukes MNG, Amsterdam, Excerpta Medica Foundation, 1966, pp. 336–343.
81. Dick P, Roch P: The interaction of tricyclic antidepressants and tetrabenazine. Its clinical use and therapeutic results, in *Proceedings of the First International Symposium on Antidepressant Drugs, ibid.*, pp. 311–315.
82. Sulser F, Watts J, Brodie BB: Antagonistic actions of imipramine and reserpine on central nervous system. *Fed Proc* **19**:268, 1960.
83. Earle BV: Thyroid hormone and tricyclic antidepressants in resistant depressions. *Am J Psychiatr* **126**:1667–1669, 1970.
84. Robison DS, Nies A, Davis JM, and others: Aging, monoamines, and monoamine-oxidase levels. *Lancet* **1**:290–291, 1972.

Fifteen

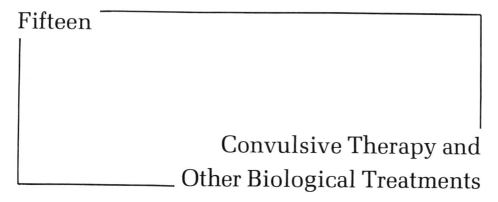

Convulsive Therapy and Other Biological Treatments

Robert Ilaria, M.D.
Arthur J. Prange, Jr., M.D.

In contemporary practice, the common modality for administering convulsive therapy (CT) is ECT. The electrical aspect of the treatment, while important, is not fundamental. Electrical induction is preferred because it is a safe, simple, and reliable method for the induction of a therapeutic seizure. Any general discussion of CT deals almost exclusively with ECT for these reasons, but this should not obscure the fact that the therapeutic efficacy in depression derives from the seizure event itself rather than the method of induction (1).

Unfortunately, the all too frequently used misnomer "electroshock therapy" further misfocuses attention. Delivering an electrical "shock" is not the purpose and to that extent, not accurate; shock is a minor and inconsequential aspect of the treatment, certainly with a preceding anesthetic. The term is not only misleading but also unnecessarily frightening. Probably deriving from a careless association with insulin shock therapy (2), it deserves to be expunged on the grounds of concern for its effect on patients and their families, if not for reasons of accuracy. Regrettably, reference to ECT as "electroshock" is all too frequently perpetuated by psychiatrists themselves in conversation and publication.

Historical Background

Convulsive therapy began as pharmacoconvulsive therapy. Camphor was used to induce a therapeutic seizure by Oliver in 1785. This early date is a reliable indication that the favorable influence a spontaneous convulsion might temporarily exert in certain mental illnesses had been observed long before Von Meduna began his attempts to more systematically exploit the implication. Von Meduna used camphor in his initial trials, as had Oliver, but camphor proved clinically unreliable as a convulsant agent; this gave impetus to a search for one more predictable. Pentylenetetrazol (Metrazol), a synthetic, soluble camphor preparation suitable for intravenous administration, was found to be more reliable. However, a consistent feature associated with the use of Metrazol was a sense of impending doom, often with precordial discomfort, during the few seconds prior to the convulsion. Consequently, patients feared the treatment excessively and frequently refused it, which resulted in a brief vogue for Metrazol. This outcome was further hastened by the demonstration that convulsions could be induced easily, safely, and with precision by electrical means without sacrifice in therapeutic effect (3). These features of the then new technique, which became known as electroconvulsive therapy (ECT), plus its greater acceptance by patients, rendered pharmacologically induced convulsive therapy (PCT) of historical interest only, until 1957 when Krantz and his co-workers discovered flurothyl (Indoklon) and showed it had some utility in CT. Despite enthusiastic early reports and claims, Indoklon has remained an ancillary method of CT in contemporary practice. A superior efficacy has been claimed for the Metrazol-induced convulsion over that of ECT, but objective verification of this claim has not been established (70).

Once the knowledge of the ease and practicality of electrically induced seizures became widespread, its use disseminated rapidly, and since the early 1940s it has represented the primary method of induction in convulsive therapy.

Initially, ECT was believed to be of greatest value in the schizophrenias and was extensively used for these disorders. Such early successes as occurred prompted its use in a wide variety of other psychiatric conditions, often with little or no sound rationale, as seems ineluctable with new therapies. One favorable consequence of this indiscriminate approach did result, however. It became evident that the most consistent benefits were achieved in the affective disorders, especially the depressions (4). In fact, up until that time, no somatic therapy had produced such generally gratifying results, save possibly the use of malarial therapy in general paresis (2).

For the first few years, ECT was administered without benefit of premedication, except for the unusually apprehensive patient for whom a barbiturate would be given. In this "unmodified" form, hundreds of thousands of treatments were given with a quite low incidence of serious side effects and a virtual absence of fatalities (5); although fractures did occur in almost half of the cases, usually compression fractures of the dorsal vertebrae, only occasionally did they prove clinically significant. In fact, their existence and frequency were not appreciated until several years after the introduction of the technique (6). However, fractures of the femur, especially when complicated by related pelvic fractures, and other orthopedic problems were another matter. They dictated a search for agents that could modify or eliminate the muscular component of the seizure. Curare was used initially, but its long duration of action with the rather frequent occurrence of fatalities led to its abandonment. Succinylcholine (Anectine) proved to be an extremely effective "softening" agent and had the paramount advantage of very short action, usually 1 to 2 minutes. It soon became the standard agent for this purpose. Unfortunately, it produced an extremely unpleasant, painful sensation associated with the onset of respiratory paralysis. This so adversely influenced continuation of therapy that this modification required the addition of another—anesthesia. The short-acting barbiturates, suitable for intravenous administration, proved most compatible with the procedure. While they effectively eliminated the problem associated with succinylcholine and contributed to a greater overall acceptance of ECT, they also added the usual problems attendant upon general anesthesia.

ECT: Efficacy and Indications

Electroconvulsive therapy is an effective treatment for most depressions when compared to placebo (7, 8) and conservative measures or psychotherapy alone (9, 10). However, its absolute efficacy has been questioned (11). In comparisons of efficacy with antidepressant agents ECT has proven superior (7, 8, 12–21), although results can depend on when the assessment is made (22). Methodological differences in the comparative trials render any general conclusions tentative. However, two studies are of especial interest, those of Greenblat and others (7) and Shepard (8); both are large scale and rather well controlled. Greenblat and others (7) compared ECT to imipramine, two monamine oxidase inhibitors, and placebo in 281 depressed patients. ECT proved clearly superior to all other methods; 75% of patients markedly improved after 8 weeks compared to the 52% in the imipramine group. The dosage of imipramine was limited to a maximum of 200 mg/day during the initial phase of comparison; later an optional increase of 50 mg was allowed. It is probable that at least some patients received a dosage less than optimal which may have resulted in a bias in favor of ECT. Wilson and others (17) have shown that imipramine in a daily dosage of 240–275 mg/day produces comparable efficacy to ECT, at least in women. Shepard's (8) study, with 270 depressed patients investigated, found ECT superior to imipramine, but the margin was not commanding. In their study, over half of the patients unresponsive to antidepressants were subsequently successfully treated with ECT.

In the past the issue of choice between ECT and drugs apparently was more vocal and acrimonious (23) than at present, although there still is an insufficiently objective basis for selection. The decision largely is based on clinical experience and judgment. One of the most pressing needs for research in this area is the establishment of a sounder rationale both for choice of modality and patient selection.

Generally, most of the relatively pure depressions respond predictably to ECT, and excellent results are obtained in some 75 to 90% of cases. Classical endogenous depression has been considered almost a specific indication for ECT, the benefit approaching 100% (24, 25). Involutional melancholia, most psychotic depressions, and depressions associated with and complicating some forms of organic brain disease usually prove predictable responders to ECT. Involutional depressions with marked paranoid features may prove a prominent exception (6). Manic-depressive illness in the depressed phase responds well to ECT (26), although the treatment of the cyclic type is perhaps more variable, and the danger of precipitating hypomania or mania is a real possibility (6). In a recent study, no difference in response to ECT was found between 28 unipolar and 15 bipolar depressives (27).

The antidepressant activity of ECT generally proves more rapid in onset than drugs, but this has been disputed; to the extent accurate, this feature favors the selection of ECT over drugs in severe depressions, especially in those highly suicidal.

Neurotic depressions, particularly those with conspicuous reactive, hysterical, or hypochondriacal features, prove less satisfactory in response to ECT. Some patients with this diagnosis do respond well, but the basis for selection is empirical and one must be cautious. Neurotically depressed patients who fail to respond to antidepressants or who worsen, especially with the appearance of weight loss and characteristic sleep disturbance, probably deserve a trial of ECT. Unilateral ECT (U/ECT) may well be the method of choice for patients with neurotic depression, since as a group they react more adversely to the memory disturbance and confusion frequent with the bilateral technique.

The combination of antidepressant medications with ECT is prevalent; although enhanced results are claimed, there is little in the way of reliable documentation. This form of therapy seems to have been derived empirically and certainly is applicable on this basis. The concern that the addition of drugs may increase the incidence and severity of side effects, as well as make them more difficult to treat and obscure the responsible cause, is legitimate. The cardiac effects of the tricyclics used alone are well known. The wisdom of their addition to a procedure which has the potential for similar effects, without clear demonstration of a significant increase in efficacy, is problematical. On the other hand, they are widely employed (16, 28) without much obvious harm, though it is difficult to determine objectively if with much good (29).

Perhaps the best documented use of antidepressants with ECT is to reduce the incidence of relapse. Seager and Bird (30) showed that in a parallel study of two treatment groups, ECT followed by imipramine and ECT followed by placebo, the relapse rate at 6 months was 17 versus 69% respectively. A later study found that the relapse rate at 6 months in patients treated with ECT approximated 50%, a rate that could be halved by the use of phenelzine or imipramine (20). An excellent recent study (31) combining either amitriptyline or diazepam introduced during or after ECT found that when evaluated 1 month after the last ECT, both of the drug groups fared significantly better in regard to suicide rate, the need of further ECT, or failure of improvement. The best results were obtained with amitriptyline; however, when used together with ECT it seemed to favor the development of hypomania in some patients, which led to the conclusion that its use should be reserved for the post-ECT period.

Clinical Aspects

Unmodified ECT is probably seldom routinely used now, but a brief description of the unmodified convulsion is worthwhile because certain variations produce less modified convulsions than the usual technique and they do have a place in current practice. Even with experienced clinicians, fully modified techniques do not always result in the degree of softening expected. Unrecognized perivascular infiltration of succinylcholine or failure to deliver the stimulus at the peak time of muscular depolarization are two reasons for this possibility. Furthermore, with the amounts of succinylcholine commonly used, it is usually more difficult to determine if a full seizure has occurred than the contrary (32). Knowledge of the basic "anatomy" of the unmodified convulsion should facilitate this determination and is a convenient reference from which to discuss variations.

When a supramaximal stimulus is applied to an unpremedicated patient, he immediately starts to convulse. Clinically, the seizure is similar to the spontaneous grand mal of epilepsy, except the onset is more brisk and the tonic response more forceful; these are results of the instantaneous effectiveness of the convulsive stimulus characteristic of electrical induction. The initial tonic phase lasts only about 10 seconds, and then is supervened by a clonic phase of 30 to 40 seconds. Signs of cyanosis become prominent during the period of apnea associated with the seizure. At termination, a deep, noisy breathing resumes. Profuse sweating, salivation, and upper respiratory secretions are to be expected more often than not. Post-ictally the patient will be confused and somewhat disoriented but will recover in a few minutes, and then may sleep for some period. A slower build-up of current, planned or inadvertent, will induce a petit mal response and a variable period of unconsciousness followed by a mild tonic phase without a succeeding full convulsion.

Conventional Modified ECT

The usual apparatus for supplying and delivering the stimulus current in essence varies little from that originally used. Probably because of its simplicity, the prevalent instrument supplies a sine wave stimulating current at 60 cps derived from the usual electrical socket. Before applying the electrodes, the skin should be cleaned with alcohol to remove sebum. If present in excess, it may form a resistance to the current, and this occasionally results in skin burns (29). Saline soaking of the electrode pads or the use of a conductive jelly will facilitate the passage of current. A forceps type electrode device is fitted bitemporally, well anterior relative to the occipital lobes to reduce the incidence or degree of side effects. The stimulus current is delivered at a voltage between 70 and 150 V, applied for a varying duration between 0.1 to 1 seconds. On average, most patients will convulse at a setting of 70 to 130 V applied for 0.35 seconds. The machines may differ in details but essentially allow one to set a given voltage to be applied for a variable time, or some equivalent electrical combination in settings.

The early literature abounds with descriptions of variations in the type and method of delivery of the electrical stimulus, often with claims of greater efficacy attributed to them. There seems little objective evidence to support such claims (2). However, a reduction in adverse effects with certain alterations in electrical wave form may rest on a sounder basis (33). Liberson (34) introduced a "brief stimuli" technique in which square pulses of 2-msec duration, utilizing a peak voltage of between 200 and 600 V at a frequency of 100 to 2000 cps, are used. This is an extremely effective mode of stimulation and results in a reduction in the amount of electrical current by a factor of 20

(35). Another useful variation is the unidirectional wave form method of Friedman and Wilcox (36), which eliminates the common alternating current source and may result in a considerable reduction in the amount of electrical energy and apparently is associated with less memory disturbance (37). While there is a theoretical basis for keeping the electrical energy as low as possible, while ensuring the reliable production of a seizure, from a clinical viewpoint with the usual equipment and technique there seems no realistic basis for concern that damaging amounts of current will be administered (38). Applying current insufficient to ensure a full seizure is a more realistic concern, since the seizure is the *sine qua non* of the therapy. Having facilities on the equipment to provide pulse forms which lower the amount of electrical energy may be useful in reducing the possibility of adverse effects, but electrode placement and frequency of treatment are considerably more pertinent in this respect.

A modification found on some ECT machines is a device for allowing a gradual build-up of current intensity. It originated in the days of unmodified ECT. By this method, the "glissando" technique, it was hoped that the convulsion would more closely resemble that of epilepsy. The gradual peaking of the stimulus current was hoped to favor muscular relaxation, reducing the chance of fractures. This technique seems to lead to fewer skeletal complications (39); therefore, it is of value when one desires to keep the dosage of succinylcholine low.

The effective convulsive stimulus cannot be predicted in advance for any given patient although it usually falls within the range of the settings specified. Once an individual's threshold is established it remains fairly constant except that during a course of ECT it increases with the number of seizures. It is higher in females, increases with age, and is, of course, higher with barbiturate anesthesia (2, 40, 41). These observations are not usually of practical value, except when the petit mal-grand mal technique (PM-GM) is used (42), in which case they may serve as a guide to the setting of the PM stimulus. In this procedure an initial subconvulsive stimulus induces unconsciousness and then a GM stimulus is applied. This technique has been recommended in situations where it is desired to exclude barbiturate anesthesia and/or keep the dosage of succinylcholine low. It has two potential disadvantages: Should the PM stimulus prove too low, it is painful; if too high, a GM seizure is immediately induced.

The usual regimen of premedication in modified ECT employs atropine, barbiturate, and succinylcholine. The atropine is given either intramuscularly, a half hour to one hour before treatment, or intravenously along with the barbiturate. After the desired level of anesthesia is effected, the succinylcholine is quickly injected.

Atropine is customarily used to reduce the danger of aspiration by decreasing bronchial secretion and salivation, and to diminish vagal tone. Given intramuscularly 30 to 60 minutes before treatment, it probably exerts these actions. However, although its administration intravenously directly before the convulsion exerts a vagal blocking action, little time is available for an antisecretory effect (43). Kalinowsky questions its use at all, stating that he has not found it necessary in his extensive experience and cites an animal study in which a high percentage of fatalities resulted in electrically induced seizures in atropinized mice (2; p. 175). He further states that the evidence is doubtful in support of its contribution to the safety of ECT. The cardiovascular changes after a convulsion may be quite variable, and the addition of atropine can further cloud the picture. A point both theoretical and empirical can be made against the use of atropine, especially directly before the seizure, since evidence indicates that anticholinergic substances may be antagonistic to the therapeutic effects of a seizure (44).

Whatever the controversy concerning atropine, the use of succinylcholine is well defined in modern ECT. Properly used, it virtually eliminates the occurrence of orthopedic difficulties with little or no added risk. For routine purposes, a dosage not in excess of 0.6 mg/kg should be employed. Up to this dose, it does not seem to produce adverse cardiac effects of consequence; above this dose apnea is prolonged; an adequate attenuation of the motor component of a seizure can be obtained at or below this dosage (45).

Although comparatively rare (1 in 3000), the presence of undetected pseudocholinesterase deficiency probably represents the greatest potential for complications with the use of succinylcholine. In the usual dosages employed, postconvulsive apnea may be prolonged for over 40 minutes. Even a dose as small as 5 mg can result in a 10-minute period of apnea (46). It has been recommended that the plasma level of butyrylcholinesterase (BChE), the enzyme that inactivates succinylcholine, be routinely determined. This has been criticized on the grounds of being impractical (47) and unreliable by Impastato (46). An alternative clinical test has been proposed to detect this deficiency (46). A 3-mg test dose of succinylcholine is given intravenously. During the first minute, signs of apnea, paralysis, or loss of the knee jerk are taken as presumptive evidence that the ChE is deficient. At this time the seizure can be induced, for muscle relaxation will be sufficient and apnea should not last over 2 to 3 minutes. It does not seem that in actual practice this test is much used. Since the condition is both reversible and rare, the value of the test has been questioned (2).

Shortly after succinylcholine is administered, fasciculations about the neck and chest should be detectable. Their appearance is a reliable sign of effective depolarization, and at this time the stimulus should be applied. Determining if a seizure has occurred is often difficult with the dosages of succinylcholine commonly used. However, even in heavily modified ECT, some degree of bilateral toe movement towards plantar flexion lasting for at least 30 seconds should be evident if a proper seizure has been induced. A less used method for evaluating success is that of excluding one of the extremities, usually a forearm, from equivalent exposure to the succinylcholine by means of a tourniquet (48). Its routine use is probably unnecessary, although it certainly should remove any doubts. It is worth considering with certain patients; for example, amputees or those showing marked flaccidity. Another stimulus should be quickly administered if there is any doubt that a full bilateral seizure has resulted, for anything less is inadequate therapeutically and wastes an anesthetic exposure.

The use of barbiturate anesthesia represents the greatest hazard associated with ECT. Selection of the safest of these compounds is obviously of importance. Thiopental has been extensively used, especially during the earlier days of modified ECT. However, evidence now indicates that methohexital is the agent of choice. Patients are sooner alert after treatment (49), and in a well-designed study, it was shown to produce fewer irregularities on the EKG than thiopental (50). A recent study by the same group indicated that the use of methohexital, in a dose range of 0.6 to 0.9 mg/kg, probably resulted in little or no increased cardiac risk over unmodified ECT as determined by controlled observations of its effect on vital signs, pretreatment EKG, and posttreatment apnea (51). Alternate anesthetic agents for ECT have been studied and may at times be usefully employed when there is a known allergy or idiosyncratic reaction to barbiturates. Diazepam is probably the most familiar alternative agent (52). In a comparison with thiopental it seemed to offer no significant benefit; its anesthetic effect was judged less reliable and it produced more drowsiness and ataxia (52). Propanidid, a short-acting nonbarbiturate, has been compared to thiopental (53) and methohexital (54). In relation to thiopental, it was associated with a faster rate of physical arousal and recovery of mental functions with less post-ECT confusion. Compared to methohexital it caused the same number of cardiac arrhythmias but a longer period of postconvulsive apnea. Based on this evidence methohexital still seems to remain the preferred anesthetic agent.

Without evidence or indication of major physical disease, any pretreatment studies are excessive beyond those usually required of hospitalized patients scheduled to undergo general anesthesia. Although many special screening procedures and examinations have been and are still performed, in fact their basis derives more from misconceptions and ignorance rather than from the actual likelihood of risks with ECT. Clinical judgment based on adequate knowledge of the patient and his medical history dictates the extent to which this generality is exempted. Unnecessary laboratory examinations and diagnostic evaluations not only waste time and money, but they also often add to the patient's apprehension. The fact is that ECT has proven to be a remarkably safe procedure. This is not to advocate throwing caution to the winds but to stress that overly elaborate, ostensibly thorough pre-ECT work-ups, without bona fide indications of potentially complicating conditions, merely add false confidence and foster inattention to basic clinical acumen. Routine X rays of the spine do not prevent or even reliably predict the probability of vertebral fractures (2), while skill and knowledge in the use of succinylcholine do. Age may be a factor that in itself justifies a different approach, since statistically, death is some 10 times as frequent in patients over 45 years of age (29), no doubt because of concomitant disease, recognized or not.

Whether the routine presence of an anesthesiologist is justified is questionable. Certainly, his services will usually be unnecessary, and the additional cost is not insubstantial. However, for the occasional complication his immediate presence may substantially contribute to a reduction in the consequences. In large centers a "stand-by" arrangement is probably a practical compromise. Alternatively, the responsible psychiatrist can profit from the brief training courses in cardiopulmonary resuscitation techniques increasingly available in many locations.

Every effort should be made to ensure that the patient is dealt with in a calm, confident, informing manner to facilitate his comprehension of what is being done and appropriately minimize his concerns. Although an "organic" therapy, ECT must be planned, prepared, and administered with a constant regard for both psychological and physical untoward results. Despite the best efforts, some patients will remain unduly anxious or agitated. An antianxiety drug given on the morning of treatment, or at bedtime the night before, should suffice.

In regard to the details of patient preparation and the use of sensible precautions, we only state that it is wise to use and be familiar with those safeguards which clinical experience has dictated for the administration of general anesthesia and ECT in its basic, unmodified form. Any treatment session may bring surprises, and any convulsion may be less modified than desired, for a complex of reasons not always preventable or predictable. For further details, the reader is referred to the standard texts (2, 6, 29, 55).

After termination of the seizure, most patients will be reasonably alert in about 10 minutes, but this may vary as a function of patient idiosyncrasies and the amount and types of premedicant agents used. Until fully awake and lucid, the patient should be kept in a designated recovery area in full attendance.

Infrequently, a patient will awaken in a highly agitated state for which active pharmacotherapy or physical restraint is necessary. This is unusual in patients with "pure" depressive disorders (6). If there is a history of such a response, an alternative method of dealing with it is to administer higher doses of barbiturates before treatment or maintain an intravenous infusion of such an agent throughout.

Some confusion and memory disturbance can be expected in most patients, but not in all. Generally it is not a major factor until after the first few treatments, and is transient or minor in degree early on. This aspect will be dealt with in greater detail in the section on dysmnesia. Commonly, during the posttreatment intervals, the patient tends to appear affectively blunted and seemingly unconcerned about his surroundings. He is usually easily occupied with simple activities. With successive treatments and clinical improvement, this state gives way to a more responsive mood pattern more in keeping with the premorbid personality. Other patients may respond with a fairly consistent euphoria. Such patients may become more self-assertive and able to make decisions, one of which may be that he is "well," influencing him to prematurely refuse further therapy and leave the hospital (56). This reaction may be reinforced by memory disturbances and confusion, which can contribute to making him less aware of his previous degree of depression and unreceptive to advice.

A distressing and too common feature that appears during a course of ECT is the formation of an ill-defined, although strongly held, dread of subsequent treatments. This is quite distinct from the fear and apprehension that may exist prior to the initial treatments, which usually dissipate after they prove much less frightening and painful than anticipated. The basis of this apprehension is not clear. It seems to derive from the experiences, progressively more subject to recall, associated with the immediate recovery period when the patient feels a total bewildering disorientation. This fear generally will not prevent completion of treatment, as the patient responds to verbal persuasion before each successive treatment. Despite the patient's awareness of its illogicality and his memory that previous therapy was painless and beneficial, this dread may resurface, constituting a resistance to the acceptance of future recommendations of ECT (2).

Complications

The extent and nature of side effects with ECT are primarily a function of whether the procedure is modified—the sole exception being the memory disturbance and confusion that is common to both. Orthopedic problems were common, though not often clinically important, with the unmodified treatment (2, 6). In modern therapy these problems are virtually absent. Aside from mishaps or serious misjudgments in the use of succinylcholine, such complications are not to be anticipated. Their incidence can be further reduced by deploying sufficiently trained aides around the treatment table to moderate and control—rather than rigidly contain—unexpectedly vigorous clonic movements. The use of a special restraining sheet is an alternative means that has been recommended (6).

The chance of fatal outcome is, of course, the greatest concern, but, on the evidence, one overly emphasized and feared. Before the routine use of modified ECT, fatalities were rare, on the order of 1 per 30,000 patients (57, 58). It is generally agreed that with the advent of modified ECT the incidence became higher. Nonetheless, the death rate is probably the residual one associated with general anesthesia, approximately 1 in 2-3000 patients (6). Establishing the true incidence is probably impossible, because the available surveys vary in the population studied, the method of ECT, the time span covered, and such. However, one should not view the reports with a highly pessimistic slant, as one can only conclude that the risk of death is negligible (59). Certainly in the otherwise healthy psychiatric patient, the chance of death need scarcely be a worry. Even in the older age groups or in those with major medical disease, present or suspected, current techniques and medical support enable ECT to be administered with a morbid risk scarcely differing from that of general anesthesia (6). Although a commonplace observation, the potential adverse effects of ECT must be weighed against the risks of the alternatives available.

Deaths that occur close to the actual seizure are probably cardiovascular in origin, although any important clinical application of this inference is in patients with existing heart disease (6, 60). Transient arrhythmias are common with either form of ECT (61, 62). They are probably more frequent in those with heart disease (63). It is reasonable to assume on the evidence available that in most cases death results from myocardial infarction or coronary artery insufficiency (58, 64). These events or their pathophysiological equivalents, for example, coronary artery spasm, are probably in part brought on by arrhythmias or the intense sympathetic discharge (60). Hypoxia resulting from the seizure or its sequalae probably predisposes to arrhythmias. This hypoxia can be eliminated or markedly reduced by positive pressure ventilation before or during the procedure (65–67). Intravenous barbiturates are the best documented source of cardiac arrhythmias with ECT. Therefore, the petit mal-grand mal procedure previously described may be the method of choice when significant myocardial irritability is of concern. While appropriate care and precautions need to be exerted for patients with heart disease, a certain balance, if not a degree of assurance, comes from the fact that ECT has been given to many patients with angina, recent myocardial infarction, and active heart failure without incident (2; p. 224) (6; p. 77).

Clinically, the most likely major complications are post-ECT memory loss and confusion. These are considered in detail in the section on memory and ECT.

A variety of other complications following ECT are essentially minor in nature, usually transient and rather easily remedied—headache, nausea, and less frequently vomiting, ataxia, and dizziness. Of these, headache is probably the most frequent complaint.

Contraindications

Only two contraindications are absolute: the presence of brain tumor or increased intracranial pressure from other sources (2, 29). The adverse potential of both conditions is likely to be accentuated by the substantial increase in CSF pressure occurring during a seizure. This may readily lead to severe or fatal consequences from compression or herniation of brain tissue. Beyond these, contraindications are more relative in nature (68). With the availability of an expert ECT team, competent medical support from anesthesiology and cardiology, and the sophisticated variations in options available with modern techniques, it is difficult to rationalize any additional conditions that in their own right preclude this treatment.

Memory and ECT

Disturbances in memory function are the most consistent and generally distressing complication resulting from modified ECT (6, 69, 70). Almost invariably, some degree of confusion is produced as well, although in the usual treatment course for the typical depressive, dysmnesia tends to be the more prominent and often is the source of bitter complaint (71). However, both disturbances in mental status can be pronounced, fusing into an organic, dysmnesic confusional state. Merely for convenience they are considered as discrete entities, but they obviously mutually influence the clinical expression of each other; an absolute delineation is probably not tenable clinically (33).

Dysmnesia can produce a degree of disability that requires delaying treatment, and it may prove psychologically so disturbing for the patient or his relatives that pressures to prematurely abandon the treatment prevail. After the first treatment or so, dysmnesia may not be particularly noticeable or may ameliorate after a few hours. With successive treatments it becomes more persistent and extensive. It can reach a degree and intensity that may require an extended period of hospitalization for its management after the ECT is completed. Typically, it will not reach this level, but some impairment after discharge may persist up to a month or so and delay the resumption of normal work and responsibilities. Generally, past this time significant impairment is unusual, although some deficit may either be demonstrable or the source of complaint for a year or more. It may prove such a distressful, unpleasant experience that in the future ECT will be rejected by the patient. Older patients (2), especially those with complicating cerebral vascular disease or hypertension, seem more susceptible to both memory impairment and confusion (6). There is evidence that the premedication regimen of conventional ECT may adversely influence memory function (72).

Without minimizing the difficulties that ECT-induced organicity can produce, a clinically balanced view requires some qualification. Not uncommonly, memory dysfunction is quite minimal or insufficient in degree to be of clinical concern. Patients show a striking variability in susceptibility to dysmnesia, and it is rather easy to find reports of a patient undergoing a complete course of ECT with virtually no sign of memory loss (73). Unfortunately, no reliable way to predict such cases is in evidence. It has been shown that patients suffering from depression, particularly of the endogenous type, often experience considerable overall improvement in memory function compared to their pretreatment performance, an occurrence more consistently observed when a concurrent improvement in affect occurs (74). Even if some dysmnesia is present, it results in little critical functional impairment and few complaints. In contrast, clinical experience has repeatedly indicated that the most bitter and long-standing complaints of memory loss—certainly the ones that seem to receive or result in the most notoriety—derive from that neurotic group of depressives in whom one finds a large admixture of features and symptoms other than depressive affect, especially hysteria and anxiety (6). Patients in this admittedly heterogeneous and rather ill-defined class usually are poor prospects for ECT in any case, and their selection for ECT has no doubt largely contributed to the concern about memory loss (4, 6).

The degree and extent of memory disturbance and confusion resulting from conventional ECT are directly proportional to the frequency and number of treatments administered, although there are other important variables as well. Increasing the rate and number of treatments rapidly induces a severe organic confusional state. Administering treatments less than 48 hours apart significantly increases the degree of organicity without any increase in efficacy (75). There is no basis in fact for attributing clinical improvement with ECT to the degree of amnesia and confusion produced (32). An obvious corollary is that a clinically useful way of minimizing the degree of memory loss and confusion is by selectively spacing the treatments, based on the patient's condition and responses. Judicious spacing of treatments will not sacrifice the therapy effect, and by striking a sensible balance between the two, the overall experience for the patient is likely to be more beneficial. In a sense, there is no "routine" course of ECT. In the severely suicidal patient, a somewhat more rapid rate in the application of ECT may prove useful. The greater degree of organicity resulting may render such patients less able to carry out their intent.

Whether the organic syndrome associated with ECT is truly temporary is without doubt the most nagging fear concerning ECT on the part of many, if not all, psychiatrists. There are few objective animal or human studies to support this concern (2). However, it is not uncommon to find references to clinical experiences that mention certain patients in whom memory or intellectual functions remain permanently or indefinitely impaired to some degree (29, 76). Unfortunately, specifics as to diagnosis, number and method of treatments, or evidence for relating the impairment to ECT are not usually given. Klein and Davis state they have "personally observed several patients with I.Q.'s in the 70's after multiple courses of ECT who had histories of excellent educational attainments" (76; p. 300). Based on data from the experimental and postmortem studies that are available (77–79), it is difficult to conceive of morphological brain damage sufficient to induce such a gross change in intelligence deriving from any sort of properly administered ECT. Patently, properly designed, long-term studies to conclusively settle the issue have not been concluded. Nonetheless, an extensive body of studies and a wealth of clinical experience fail to indicate that permanent brain damage results from modern techniques of ECT employed in the treatment of depression (80).

A more comprehensive understanding of the nature and type of memory loss resulting from ECT requires certain distinctions. The faculty of memory can be conceptualized as consisting of four functional elements: (1) registration, (2) retention, (3) recall, and (4) recognition (81). Defects induced in one element may not be accompanied by defects in the others. These functions have temporal relationships so that memory for past events may be differentially affected as compared to that for events subsequent to the treatment. Another important parameter is the somewhat indefinite aspect of remembering characterized as short-term and long-term memory. An extensive series of investigations have shown that memory impairment suffered from ECT is both of the RA (retrograde amnesia) and AA (anterograde amnesia) type (32, 69, 82–84). The functional element that seems most disturbed is that of retention, with perhaps recall the next most seriously affected (85). A not untypical example of the interaction of these variables can be demonstrated by the following: Testing a recently treated ECT patient with simple visual items may indicate no evidence of defect if the response (request for recall) is elicited in immediate proximity to the test; that is, short-term memory of recognition would indicate intact function (33). If the period is lengthened between exposure and recall even slightly, a total amnesia may be evidenced. In general, memory loss is most deficient for events in close proximity to the treatment (83, 86). As the number of treatments increases, the extent of dysmnesia extends further back in time, and there is increasing inability to retain information (83). The basis for the retention defect seems to derive from disruption in the consolidation phase of memory function (87).

The extent and type of memory defects are determined by a host of factors, two of which have been mentioned: the number and frequency of treatments. The amount and type of current are important (37), but within any sensible limits, not to the same extent as the site of electrode placement (88). The seizure itself contributes something but not to the same degree as amount of current or method of electrode placement (33). The importance of electrode placement on memory function had been noted for some time before systematic attempts were made to exploit the possibilities (2). Combining the implications of these early investigations with the extensive, consistent body of findings derived from postoperative observations of neurosurgical patients and the results of direct stimulation of specific brain areas indicates that the disruption in the function of the temporal lobes and their hippocampal connections produced by conventional bilateral ECT (B/ECT) constitutes the major source for the associated memory disturbances (88, 89).

Once it was demonstrated that the therapeutic effect derived from the seizure and not from the occurrence of disturbed memory and confusion, the ability to separate the antidepressant activity of ECT from its disruptive organic effects became a possibility. The technique of unilateral ECT (U/ECT) seems to provide this clinically desirable feature without an appreciable loss in efficacy.

Unilateral ECT

The first published work in English which systematically explored the clinical use of U/ECT and B/ECT was that of Lancaster and others (90). Less memory disturbance with U/ECT was found with little statistically significant difference in efficacy, but clinically B/ECT seemed slightly more effective. Their procedure of unilateral electrode placement seems to have become fairly standard. Using a line drawn between the external auditory meatus and the lateral angle of the orbit as a reference, the lower electrode is placed just above this line and the upper one 7.5 cm higher. Minor deviations in the points of placement have usually been considered unimportant. As can be seen, the description fixes the vertical relationship but is not too precise in regard to deviations in the anterior-posterior axis. There is good evidence that variations from the standard technique are not unusual and that positional variations may significantly alter the therapeutic effect and profile of side effects. (32, 89, 91).

Cannicott (92) reported results of several studies, one of which was a controlled study of 50 depressed patients, including neurotic and endogenous types. No important differences were noted therapeutically, while U/ECT was strikingly better in regard to amnesia and confusion. He indicated that U/ECT seemed especially suitable for outpatients because of its reduction in such effects.

Successive studies during this early period of comparisons generally tended to find approximate equivalent efficacy, with a notable decline in memory disturbance and disorientation (72, 91, 93–97). However, derived from clinical impressions or fairly small differences in data, qualifications to the main result were frequently cited which gave the therapeutic edge to B/ECT because it was either quicker in effect (94–96), more effective in certain patients (93), or more efficient (95, 97). Such qualifiers probably helped form the opinion that U/ECT was less effective, although the objective results are not in fact much different.

Until the work of Zamora and Kaelbling (98), it was not unequivocally clear if the lessened memory disturbance associated with U/ECT was a function of the unilateral aspect of the treatment or the hemisphere stimulated. Their study conclusively demonstrated that the reduction in dysmnesia was obtained only when the nondominant (ND) hemisphere was treated. A subsequent, very well-designed study confirmed their finding and showed that the differential functions of memory affected depended on which hemisphere was treated. In the nondominant group greater impairment resulted in nonverbal, visually presented material, while in the dominant group the greatest defect was in auditory, verbal material (99). Generally, these findings have been replicated in subsequent studies, and there seems general agreement that U/ECT-ND is reliably associated with less dysmnesia and disorientation (11, 32, 72, 73, 84, 100–102). However, certain studies cast some doubt on the clinical importance of this result. Bidder and others (73) concluded that although U/ECT is likely to result in less memory dysfunction initially, by the tenth day after treatment no significant difference was present. Levy's study (72), while finding better memory function for general events in the U/ECT group, could not demonstrate differences in performance on the Wechsler or the Paired Association memory tests. This seemed to influence his conclusion that the evidence of benefit for U/ECT was insufficient to universally recommend it. McAndrew and others (103) found little clinically significant differences in memory function between U/ECT and B/ECT.

The issue of whether U/ECT substantially retains the efficacy of B/ECT is more difficult to resolve than that of its apparent benefit in regard to confusion and dysmnesia. In part, this derives from the difficulties of assessing efficacy in depression generally, regardless of the treatment modality. Additionally, methodological differences abound, and, particularly in the first reports, diagnoses other than depression were included; or the depressed patients were simply characterized as neurotic, psychotic, or having depressive symptomatology. Therefore, in treating this issue only the more recent, better controlled studies in which the treatment population is specified and limited to depressive syndromes are cited.

Halliday and others (95), in a very well controlled and designed study of 52 depressed patients evaluated blind, found no therapeutic differences between B/ECT or U/ECT; nondominant and dominant (ND and D). Their findings are especially significant from a clinical viewpoint, since the assessment of outcome was both short and long term (3 months).

Bidder and others (73) reported on 96 depressed patients studied double blind and included the longest term of follow-up, 1 year. This report incorporates data and further observations on patients studied earlier (97). In that study they had found B/ECT somewhat superior in clinical effect but with the extension of their observations, outcome between groups was virtually identical at 1 year. An interesting aspect of this study is that it included a group of patients who had relapsed after initial treatment and were retreated with the alternative method, serving as their own controls. In this group, no differences in their response to either treatment was found, either in regard to memory or efficacy. The one parameter in which a difference persisted for the overall group was in the number of treatments given: 7.5 for B/ECT and 8.4 for U/ECT. Although statistically significant (P<01), from a clinical view it does not seem to represent a practical difference. Costello and others (11) critically review the literature and conclude that the confusion over the possible benefits of U/ECT result because "to date all of the studies suffer from one or more serious errors of psychometrics or research design." Their investigation was formulated to avoid their own criticism. Although they found therapeutic equivalence for three treatment groups (B/ECT and U/ECT-ND and D), assessment was made after the fourth treatment, which limits the clinical pertinence of the study. Fleminger and others (102) conducted a double-blind trial on 36 very carefully selected patients and found that after six ECTs no difference therapeutically could be found between U/ECT and B/ECT. In view of this finding and that of marked reductions in memory disturbance and other side effects with U/ECT-ND, they concluded that it was the treatment of choice for depression. They made an important observation in their discussion—namely, that by neglecting the complaints of patients regarding their response to side effects, an important benefit of U/ECT was obscured in many studies. They found that complaints were more frequent and severe with B/ECT, the clinical consequence being that patients who received U/ECT were rarely reluctant to accept further treatment.

D'Elia (32) presents some of the most convincing data indicating equivalent efficacy between B/ECT and U/ECT. By a double-blind technique he studied 120 meticulously selected and precisely described endogenously depressed patients. Therapeutic results were completely comparable. As a major basis for the controversy over the issue of efficacy, he implicates the greater chance of failure in producing a generalized seizure with U/ECT, which is less therapeutic regardless of the type of induction. He notes that this contingency had not been adequately considered in previous studies, since the production of a full, bilateral seizure was made on the basis of clinical observation rather than by EEG. Therefore, with the amounts of premedications employed, the reliability of such determinations must be suspect even when made by experienced therapists. D'Elia employed continuous EEG monitoring throughout an entire treatment. The findings supported his contention, since the pattern after U/ECT consistently indicated slightly increased dominance of activity on the side stimulated; thus if electrode placement is not carefully controlled such dominance could be accentuated, resulting in a therapeutically submaximum seizure, predominantly unilateral in nature. Further analysis of the EEG data indicated that the amount of electricity needed to induce a seizure was the same with both B/ECT and U/ECT, and postseizure activity was essentially similar—the obvious inference being that one would be theoretically justified in inferring that properly administered U/ECT produced efficaciously equivalent seizures. The study included an equally elegant evaluation of side effects, which demonstrated superiority in this respect for U/ECT. He concluded that U/ECT-ND was the treatment of choice for endogenous depression and that the claim of a more rapid response with B/ECT, even if proved accurate, was insufficient reason not to employ U/ECT-ND routinely. He stated that when a quick effect was desired, U/ECT could be given daily with the same rapidity of benefit while retaining the significant reduction in adverse effects as had been shown by others. Here he cites Abrams' (104) experience with daily administered U/ECT; however, that study consisted primarily of schizophrenic patients. The study of Stinnett and Di Giacomo (105) perhaps lends more precise support to this view, since all 15 patients treated were endogenously depressed.

The most recent, comprehensive study concerning the issue of comparative efficacy between U/ECT and B/ECT is that of Strömgren (84). One hundred endogenously depressed patients were allocated to only two treatment groups: U/ECT-ND (52 %) and B/ECT (48%). The study was double blind throughout, with first-rate design, evaluation, and controls. As to the therapeutic results, there was no significant difference between groups. B/ECT seemed slightly better during the first six treatments, though any difference disappeared before a course of treatment was completed. This similarity in response extended to patients described as being "severe," and those categorized as unipolar or bipolar depressives. This result, coupled with the markedly lower incidence of side effects associated with U/ECT, led to what seems to be the obvious conclusion: "when ECT is applied to patients with endogenous depression the unilateral technique should be the method of choice" (84; p. 60).

The recent studies generally agree that U/ECT produces clinically equivalent efficacy. A major exception is the study of Abrams, Fink, and others (101). Assessing response after only an average of four treatments, they report a significant difference in depressive scores favoring B/ECT. However, assessment at this stage may be more influenced by and indicative of the trend to earlier response, frequently observed in other studies, rather than a reflection of an absolute superiority in antidepressant activity.

The final role of U/ECT in the treatment of depression probably remains to be fixed, although it will very likely be strongly influenced by the favorable decrease in adverse effects. While it may be claimed that a difference in efficacy exists, almost every study indicates that it is of minor degree at most. The reduction in side effects is without question of major degree. Virtually without exception this has been demonstrated. Not only are dysmnesia and confusion frequently reduced to the point of virtual absence, but so too are other usual side effects—headache, nausea, vomiting, ataxia, dizziness (32, 84, 102). Post-ECT recovery is strikingly quicker and has been cited as possibly the most notable differential effect (102). All indications suggest a greater patient acceptance of the procedure (92, 102, 105). Not only patients are negatively affected by the organic syndrome of B/ECT. A prominent criticism by certain psychiatrists is that the treatment renders the patient so organically impaired that little else can be done with him during his treatment. Perhaps the therapy is unnecessarily avoided or delayed because of this concern. U/ECT markedly changes the picture. In Stinnett and Di Giacomo's study, patients who underwent daily U/ECT were described as being able to participate in all ward activities, including group and individual psychotherapy, and able to remember the events of the day prior to treatment. The average hospital stay was 19 days, and all patients were able to be discharged 48 hours after the last treatment.

Anterior Bifrontal ECT (ABF/ECT)

This technique was suggested by Inglis (88) in his excellent discussion on the effects of electrode placement on memory and confusion. To avoid the disruptive effects on temporal lobe function, he postulated that frontally placed electrodes might retain the improvement in mood while significantly reducing the effect on learning and memory.

Abrams and Taylor (106) employed this technique in an open clinical trial with 17 patients. Their clinical impression was that the method was intermediate in efficacy between conventional B/ECT and U/ECT. Administering the treatment daily on weekdays, little or no post-ECT confusion resulted; the patients were fully alert and oriented in 5 to 10 minutes without post-ictal clouding. Clinically, no evidence of anterograde or retrograde amnesia was noted; in this respect their memory function was similar to that of post-U/ECT patients. In accounting for the reduced efficacy, it was postulated that B/ECT alters cerebral physiology differently because the amnestic syndrome does not occur with ABF/ECT or U/ECT. This amnestic syndrome reflects bilateral dysfunction of median brain structures involved in memory consolidation, because, as shown by the results of unilateral temporal lobectomy, a unilateral dysfunction in this system is insufficient to account for the general memory disorder of B/ECT. The authors believe that the full therapeutic effect of ECT depends on the bilateral stimulation of these median brain structures which subserve mood and memory, as occurs with conventional B/ECT.

Indoklon Convulsive Therapy (ICT)

While involved in a general investigation of the fluorinated ethers with the purpose of finding a nonflammable anesthetic, Krantz and his co-workers (107) discovered quite unexpectedly the convulsive properties of one member of this series, flurothyl (hexaflurodiethyl ether). It is best known as Indoklon, from inducere—to lead into—and klonos—motion or movement (82). Extensively studied in a variety of laboratory animals (dog, rat, mouse, frog, and monkey), it uniformly produced convulsions in extremely low concentrations—35 parts per million of inspired air. No evidence of any harmful effects was found in laboratory or postmortem examinations. This demonstration of potency and apparent safety suggested a role for Indoklon in convulsive therapy, prompting a trial in humans. Accordingly, several mentally ill patients for whom ECT was indicated were administered Indoklon (108). Each patient was exposed one time to the agent, experienced a grand mal seizure, and clinically seemed to suffer no ill effects (107).

Larger scale open clinical trials soon followed (109–112). There were many claims that ICT was superior to ECT either because it was more therapeutic (113, 114), produced fewer side effects (82, 110, 115), or because it enjoyed greater patient acceptance (113, 116). This last point was especially stressed in many of the earlier papers (82, 113, 117), but was not always noted (118). Whatever the basis for claims of superiority of this method, they largely derive from uncontrolled studies (70).

Properties and Administration

Indoklon is a colorless, mildly pleasant-smelling, water insoluble, rather volatile, nonflammable liquid (119). Its volatility was naturally suited to an inhalation technique. At first it was used without premedication, since the gradual onset of the seizure, usually preceded by unconsciousness, offered the advantage of a single drug exposure. However, in practice it proved unreliable in this respect; many patients experienced and remembered highly unpleasant sensations before the onset of the seizure. This feature dictated the employment of essentially the same premedication regimen as was common to ECT. Obviously, this substantially detracted from its alleged simplicity. Attempts were made to better coordinate and time its actions by developing an intravenous preparation. This proved difficult by virtue of its insolubility in water. Eventually a reasonably satisfactory solvent was found and employed. It proved more predictable in the production and timing of a seizure, but the frequent occurrence of venous thrombosis and a persistent uncertainty concerning the toxicity of the solvents caused the abandonment of this form of administration (120). Modified inhalation remains the accepted method in current practice. Aside from the IV form, Indoklon has proved remarkably nontoxic and seems to be free of incompatibilities with other drugs (82, 110).

The inhalation technique requires a face mask connected to a 5-liter breathing bag and through it to a vaporizor. Volatized Indoklon and oxygen are mixed in the breathing bag and introduced through a closely applied face mask by the simple act of squeezing. The mask is fitted after the anesthetic is given. Four to twelve inhalations usually suffice to induce a seizure in about 40 seconds (121). Indoklon is then excreted by the lungs, metabolically unchanged (82).

The Indoklon-induced seizure is different in certain aspects from that of an electrically induced one. The onset of the seizure is more gradual and is preceded by an initial myoclonic phase of 10 to 30 seconds in duration (110), a feature absent with ECT but characteristic of pharmacoconvulsive agents generally—for example, metrazol. This makes it difficult to determine precisely the onset of the tonic phase of the convulsion proper. Indeed, discerning the clonic phase may prove equally difficult, especially with the usual doses of succinylcholine employed. Without careful clinicial observation and accuracy in dosage determination, the patient may merely continue a prolonged initial myoclonic phase, easily misinterpreted as a full convulsion. A poorly fitted face mask, leaking connections, and patient variables in circulation time and pulmonary absorption predispose to this outcome. Even with proper care and equipment, the occurrence of a therapeutically inadequate convulsion remains a persistent, though occasional, possibility. Conversely, multiple or extremely prolonged seizures may result from too large a dosage or too quick a delivery. Clinically, the duration and force of a flurothyl-induced convulsion were noted to be greater than those obtained with ECT (82). EEG studies have confirmed the longer duration (69). This characteristic apparently has been an important basis for claims of greater efficacy.

The first study in which ECT and ICT were compared with reference to side effects and therapeutic outcome was by Kurland and others (122). Patients were randomly assigned to either treatment. Approximately two-thirds of the total patients were diagnosed as depressed; there were 90 in each group. Side effects were essentially similar in the two groups, with the striking exception of death: three fatalities in the ECT group; none in the ICT group. The authors concluded that the cause of death could not be reliably related to the therapy. An analysis of the conditions associated with the fatalities seems to support that view: thyrotoxicosis, "massive" diarrhea, glomerulonephritis. Fewer fractures with ICT were anticipated because the gradual onset of the convulsion was expected to afford a similar degree of muscular relaxation as that of an epileptic seizure, with which fractures are rare. Such was not the case. Fractures occurred equally, and this has proven to be the case generally (69). They concluded that "ICT had no definite advantage over ECT." In the main, subsequent comparative studies have sustained this conclusion, especially in regard to antidepressive effectiveness (69, 70, 123, 124). While many of them included a mixture of diagnoses, and methodologically are at variance, little evidence supports claims of enhanced efficacy for ICT in depression. This observation is substantiated by two well-designed studies in which only patients with precisely defined depressive diseases are included (70, 123).

Despite earlier claims, Indoklon does not seem to be associated with a clinically significant reduction in memory disturbance or confusion (69, 125, 126). Greater impairment was reported by Spreche (123) and Laurell (70), except for retrograde amnesia (RA) in the latter study. These two investigations are of special importance because their study population contained only depressed patients. Of the many variables related to memory changes after CT, perhaps one of the most significant is the diagnosis. There is no obvious reason to presume that the type or degree of memory loss found in schizophrenia is similar to that induced in depression after CT. This difference alone can be expected to yield contradictory findings, even if design and methodology are otherwise similar (70).

Spreche's (123) study included 24 psychotically depressed patients. His study is one of the few that employ the Bender-Gestalt test for determining organicity. A quantitative version of this test was used and indicated a significantly large degree of organic impairment in the ICT group.

Laurell's (70) study is the most extensive and comprehensive study to date; 119 endogenously depressed patients diagnosed according to well-defined and enumerated criteria were studied. Tests employed and components of memory evaluated were precisely defined. Apparently it is the first study in humans to specifically isolate and evaluate retrograde amnesia objectively. Significantly less RA was found in the ICT group. This had been anticipated on the basis of early investigations that established that the degree of loss in this function was directly proportional to the amount of electrical current used in ECT (74, 127). Anterograde amnesia (AA) was greater in the ICT group as compared to the ECT group, a finding related to the greater duration of the Indoklon seizure. This results in an increased degree of cerebral hypoxia in those systems upon which the retention function of anterograde memory is dependent. Laurell speculates that there is sufficient experimental data to fix the anatomical site subject to derangement in the hippocampal-mammillary system, since it is essential in the maintenance of anterograde memory, is more susceptible to hypoxia by virtue of its demonstrated higher oxygen requirements, and has a lower seizure threshold. Although there were no clinical signs of hypoxia in any of the patients during seizure, this would not rule out a focal hypoxia. In contrast to anterograde function, the benefit of less impairment in retrograde memory resulting from the absence of an electrical current is sustained because different subsystems, less susceptible to hypoxia, are therefore less disrupted. Corroborative evidence of these interpretations was provided by the results of the EEG studies. Previously, EEG patterns were judged essentially similar in both treatments (69, 125). However, in this study significant differences in EEG patterns were consistently found. With the Indoklon seizure, the pattern showed more fast activity and dysynchrony. There was a later onset of alpha waves. Overall, the Indoklon tracings were rated as demonstrating more "global abnormalities," and it was concluded that this consistent feature was indicative of a greater functional disturbance within the brain. The reports of an increased average duration of seizures with Indoklon were confirmed (120 seconds versus 71 seconds), and it was verified that the duration was directly proportional to the dosage, as had been reported (128).

Posttreatment confusion, headache, nausea, dizziness, restlessness, and agitation are as severe and frequent, or more so, with ICT as with ECT (70, 123, 128).

Although the therapeutic efficacy achieved with ICT seems to be essentially equivalent to that of ECT, several factors preclude its routine use. Perhaps the most important is the greater likelihood of failure in the induction of a full convulsion, 15% in one series (125). On balance, it does not offer a clinically useful reduction in side effects and is technically a more difficult procedure. Most psychiatrists find it "cumbersome" and more time consuming (70). Its use in pregnancy is contraindicated (70, 82), while ECT is relatively safe.

ICT is probably best viewed as an alternative procedure, occasionally useful in situations that preclude ECT; for example, when a patient will not accept convulsive therapy at all if delivered by "electric shock" and in patients with a cardiac pacemaker (129). Based on clinical experience alone, there is evidence that some patients unresponsive to ECT respond well to Indoklon (114); but this has not been subjected to rigorous evaluation, and a reliable basis for predicting how such patients may be identified is absent. The substantiation of reports that combining ICT and ECT yields a therapeutic response superior to that obtained with either method alone (130, 131) stands on similar grounds.

Biochemical Aspects of ECT

A wide variety of biochemical events follows ECT (132), and sorting out those fundamental to the antidepressant effect of the treatment is presently not possible. Many of the changes are nonspecific, deriving from stress, anesthesia, the motor component of the seizure (to the extent it exists), and other features of the overall procedure. Other changes more or less directly related to the extensive consequences caused by the current and the seizure upon the brain are more difficult to evaluate. Undoubtedly, many must be merely concurrent and nonspecific. Even to the extent that a reasonable basis exists for assuming important connections between biochemical changes and improvement, as with the biogenic amines, the evidence is insufficient to delineate the pertinent interactions or the manner in which they relate to mood and behavioral change. Aside from the fact that the overwhelming bulk of work has been done on healthy animals rather than on depressed humans, a host of reasons render any biochemical interpretations of ECT highly speculative and tentative; prime among these reasons is that the biochemical basis for depression is itself almost as fragile. Although presently tentative, theories about the role of brain chemistry in depression are nevertheless extensive. They are presented in Chapter 18 and are necessary to understanding the significance of what follows.

Catecholamines

The evidence in animals suggests an acute decrease in brain norepinephrine (NE) levels as the result of an electrically induced seizure (EIS) (133, 134) which seems to be the result of immediate neuronal release. This has not always been found, however (135). By use of radioactively labeled NE intracisternally injected, it was found that the outflow of the labeled NE was increased, as was its conversion to normetanephrine—a finding consistent with most of the earlier reports of a net decrease in endogenous NE levels (136). The manner of disappearance of intracisternally injected NE is not linear, and the possibility of alternate pathways makes conclusions about its fate somewhat tentative (136).

With progressively administered EIS, there is reasonable evidence of an increased turnover of NE (137, 138) with possibly a net increase in NE levels in brain and an increased synthesis (137, 139); but the differences often are not significant (138, 140, 141), or they are similar in degree and direction to those observed in a variety of stresses (142–145). Supportive evidence for an increase in synthesis and functionally available NE comes from the finding that EIS induces an increase in the activity of tyrosine hydroxylase, the rate-limiting enzyme in its formation (146).

The generally small degree of these changes, their nonspecificity to EIS, and their ubiquitous occurrence in other stressful situations make the clinical importance of such findings questionable (138, 142).

The few human studies do little to establish the pertinence of the animal work to depression. Usually, findings of increased NE turnover cannot be reliably attributed to central rather than peripheral events (147), and the fact that alterations in catecholamine metabolism are considerably reduced with the usual form of modified ECT suggests that they are largely due to nonspecific stresses (148).

Recently, changes in the urinary excretion of 3-methoxy 4-hydroxyphenylglycol (MHPG) in a depressed patient undergoing ECT have been reported (149). MHPG has been reputed to be the best peripheral metabolite for monitoring central NE metabolism (134, 150), perhaps some 20 to 30% of the 24-hour urinary excretion deriving from CNS sources. The urinary level of MHPG progressively rose with successive ECTs and reached the highest levels after the therapy had stopped and was associated with the development of hypomania.

Dopamine (DA) has been considered until recently to function primarily as a precursor for NE. Current investigations seem to clearly indicate that DA is important in its own right as a neurotransmitter and perhaps functionally important in normal and abnormal behavior (151). Increases in the levels of DA in the caudate portion of the rabbit brain have been reported with EIS and shown not to be merely a function of muscular contractions (152). In the rat brain, an increase in turnover rate is suggested by the finding of no change in DA levels with an increased accrual in homovanillic acid, the main metabolite of DA (153). The importance of relating time to the observation in amine levels is highlighted by the study of Cooper and others (154), who found no change in CSF HVA levels in the dog during a single EIS but a rise to small but significant levels throughout a course of seizures.

Indoleamines

Generally, levels of brain serotonin (5-HT) in animals have been found to be elevated acutely with a single EIS (133, 155, 156), but not always (154, 157, 158). Even if the absolute level of 5-HT seems unchanged acutely, there is evidence that the metabolism is affected by concurrent findings of increased levels of its precursor, tryptophan, and/or its metabolite 5-hydroxyindole-acetic acid, (5-HIAA) (159, 160). With a series of EIS, the evidence seems rather uniform that brain levels of 5-HT increase (135, 137, 140), and probably reflect an increase in turnover (138, 154). Even the 5-HT depleting effect of reserpine has been shown to be resisted by EIS (161). However, as with the catecholamines the findings are not always consistent (160), usually small (138), and not specific (143). Furthermore, the permeability of the blood-brain barrier is altered with EIS, allowing the influx of the various amines normally excluded (162), which makes any definite interpretation of the metabolic events rather tentative.

Serotonin metabolism was studied in 20 endogenously depressed patients by determinations of CSF 5-HIAA levels just before and at 2 to 6 days after a course of ECT. Despite considerable clinical improvement, no significant changes in 5-HIAA were detected. CSF HVA was also determined without changes noted (163). These findings are somewhat at variance with an earlier study in which abnormally low CSF levels of 5-HIAA in patients with endogenous depression rose to more normal levels with remission (164); not all of these patients were treated with ECT. Conclusions from studies of CSF metabolites are open to question because there is evidence that in affective disorders, monoamine levels may take weeks to months to change (165).

Monoamine oxidase (MAO) is an important enzyme in the breakdown of both 5-HT and NE, and it has been described as playing a major role in the regulation of the intracellular concentrations of these amines (166). Its activity is consistently increased during a series of EIS after at least seven daily seizures are administered (167–169) and seems to persist for some time after the completion of the last administration, up to 6 weeks in the dorsal cortex of the rat (170). A certain importance may be signified by this finding, since other enzymes related to amine metabolism (catechol-*0*-methyl-transferase) or in proximity to intracellular MAO (succinate dehydrogenase) do not seem much affected by EIS (171). An increase in MAO activity in brain, if not offset by other events, would diminish levels of monoamine. Thus this effect of EIS and the empirical observation that ECT has an antidepressant effect are inconsistent with current biochemical theories of depression.

Acetylcholine

The cholinergic system has been cited as perhaps central to the convulsive therapy process (44), and increasing attention has been focused on cholinergic mechanisms in the affective disorders generally (172–174). There seems to be clear evidence of an acute release of acetylcholine (ACh) generally throughout the brain as a result of ECT (44), and evidence deriving from studies of ACh and choline levels in spinal fluid following ICS suggests an increased activity of this system (175). However, changes in the enzymes cholinesterase and acetylcholinesterase have been found to be inconsistent or slight (167). Since the appearance of increased free acetylcholine occurs with cerebral trauma and convulsions generally, it is problematical as to what significance can be attached to these observations.

Endocrine Changes

Many changes in the depressed patient undergoing improvement with ECT are suggestive of hormonal influences. Among functions notable and common in this regard are weight gain, increased libido, and alterations in the menstrual cycle. However, studies relating these changes to demonstrated alterations in endocrine function as a result of ECT are virtually absent. ECT does seem to induce changes in hormone secretion, but an assessment of the importance of these changes or a reliable relation of them to its efficacy are lacking.

ACTH secretion is increased with the usual hormonal sequalae, but this influence seems to be primarily related to the preexisting level of function in the hypothalamic-pituitary-adrenal (H-P-Ad) axis. Many depressives, especially the more severe, tend to exhibit high plasma levels of cortisol, and the higher the level the less likely is ECT to further produce a rise. However, this has been shown to be a function of endogenous activity of the H-P-Ad system rather than related per se to the plasma 17-OH level (176). Feighner and others (161) noted that unsystematic clinical observations suggested that dexamethasone, a synthetic steroid, potentiated the action of ECT, and he conducted a controlled study to determine if this was the case. The study failed to confirm this effect and tended to show the reverse, but this finding did not reach statistical significance.

Urinary gonadotropins in the male have been reported to increase with ECT (177), and, in some males, increases in serum levels of FSH and LH have been observed (178). In this latter study, approximately half of the patients carried a primary depressive diagnosis. Most of the subjects were male and the only females (five) were postmenopausal. None of the females exhibited changes in serum gonadotropins. Significant effects on serum TSH and HGH levels were not observed in any of the subjects, regardless of sex.

A recent study does not indicate consistent changes in plasma TSH levels as the result of ECT (179). The patient sample of 15 included only depressives. The responsiveness of TSH secretion was established by the administration of exogenous thyrotropin releasing hormone (TRH), leading to the conclusion that ECT did not result in a release of TRH.

Animal studies demonstrate that the changes in cerebral protein metabolism as the result of electrically induced seizures are prominent and include alterations in RNA, nucleotides, and fatty acids (175). Alterations in protein synthesis seem more related to memory function than therapeutic efficacy, but a relationship between 5-HT turnover and protein changes as they relate to behavior has been suggested (180).

Mineral metabolism has received considerable attention in depression, especially since the advent of lithium. There is evidence that depression may be associated with increased intracellular sodium and water, and an intracellular deficiency of potassium (181). Russell (182) showed that initially ECT was associated with a retention of Na, followed by a diuresis. However, similar changes occurred in patients in whom the preliminaries were administered without the seizure, but he concluded that the changes, although small and not strikingly different between controls and treated subjects, might be of consequence with time. This is supported by the observation that endogenous depressed patients treated with ECT who improved did show a significant decrease in exchangeable Na (183). Changes in potassium have usually been shown to remain constant with recovery (183, 184), but a normalizing trend with successive ECT in some of the cases has been claimed (181, 185).

It has been demonstrated that depressed patients responding to ECT show a significant decrease in the urinary excretion of calcium and that this change seems to persist past the termination of treatment (186). In a subsequent study this effect was confirmed, and it was shown that there was a shift toward a positive calcium balance, generally the result of increased absorption from the gut and decreased urinary excretion. The authors suggested that this effect might be related to general neurohumoral changes associated with improvement in depression and speculated that studies of calcitonin metabolism were indicated (187).

Magnesium has been reported to be lower in depressives (23 neurotics, 56 endogenous) when compared to controls (188). After ECT the values were comparable, but therapeutic outcome did not correlate with the mean serum levels; the differences found may have been the result of seasonal variations found for Mg in both patients and controls.

ECT and Sleep

Sleep is often severely disturbed in depression, and with a clinical remission, an improvement in sleep often follows. Since ECT is an effective antidepressant, the effects on sleep are of special interest.

Based on studies in the cat, ECT administered after a period of REM deprivation results in less compensatory REM rebound than in controls (189), and if administered during the period of actual REM deprivation, exerts a similar effect (190). In the normal cat, REM is reduced by electrically induced seizures apparently as the result of the seizure and not merely current passage through the brain. After the cessation of ECT, the expected REM rebound duration was reduced (191). Interestingly, speculations were made by the authors of both studies that in some manner the effects of ECT could be considered as a substitute for REM sleep. Extrapolating these observations to the effect of ECT on the sleep of depressed patients was problematical for many obvious reasons, perhaps foremost being the observation that the cat may be an especially poor animal model because of the large percentage of time spent in sleep, some 16 to 18 hours per day. The chimpanzee would be a more suitable model (192), but we are not aware of any studies with ECT in this animal.

Zarcone and others (193) reported the effects of ECT on nine psychiatric patients and found a decrease in REM and the total REM percentage with a tendency to increased slow wave sleep and total sleep. None of these patients seemed to be primary depressives, although some apparently exhibited depressive symptomatology. All of the patients studied were taking psychoactive agents which themselves are known to affect sleep patterns (194).

Of the few studies relating to the effects of ECT in depression, Van de Castle and Hawkins (195) found, contrary to the animal studies and those of Zarcone and others, that REM sleep was increased. In a general discussion of sleep and depression, which included some of their findings (196), they described the severely disturbed sleep pattern (typical of that usually observed in psychotic depression) in one of their patients which abruptly changed after six ECTs, normalizing from then on in terms of total sleep and amount of wakefulness. His REM sleep showed a compensatory increase while stage four sleep only gradually returned to normal. Other vegetative signs and symptoms sharply improved with the change in sleep pattern.

The sleep of a single psychotically depressed patient was monitored, somewhat infrequently, over a 10-week period as he underwent a course of ECT. Early in the course of treatment an increase in REM sleep and REM latency was observed which tended to return to normal values for this patient by the end of treatment (197).

Depressive mood during the day was found to be inversely proportional to the amount of phasic REM the night before, regardless of treatment with ECT. A different releasing or triggering mechanism for Pontine-Geniculate-Occipital spikes was postulated in depression. Presumably, this "abnormal mechanism" persists until the therapeutic effect becomes sufficient to normalize the sleep-regulating centers (198).

Psychosurgery

The history, misconceptions, and theoretical bias against psychosurgery bear an interesting parallel to those against ECT. After initial successes, both were unwisely extended to disorders and patients for whom little benefit could be expected. The schizophrenias were an important focus in the early history of both therapies, and the therapeutic disasters that occurred at times with this population have lived on and obscure the very real benefits that could be obtained with the depressions. The mistakes, inevitable unexpected side effects, and false promises—part and parcel of new therapies—seemed to have remained in current memory more vividly than the value which was eventually established. Also, pharmacotherapy was viewed as a modality which would render ECT and psychosurgery obsolete (2, 199).

The standard prefrontal lobotomy was often connected with severe side effects, even when the overall result was an improvement. Without obtaining therapeutic benefit, the occurrence of such side effects seemed disastrous and inhumane. Superficial or casual exposure to lobotomized patients enhanced these conceptions. In fact, many features of the adverse effects passed off or ameliorated with time. It often took months to years for adaptation and stabilization to coalesce (199). Judgments or determinations made prior to that time resulted in biased assessments. Early theory and practice were based on animal observations, relatively crude, purely empirical, or unsure in application (200). Patients frequently were drawn from back wards, selected without careful attention to the state or duration of the disease; and sometimes lobotomy was employed primarily to produce a more tractable patient. Experience, good and bad, was necessary to work out some sort of practical basis for applying this approach.

Not long after its introduction, modified leucotomies were developed as increasing experience and knowledge in neuroanatomical and neurophysiological investigations were gained (201). In the case of the affective disorders, it became apparent that a full lobotomy was unnecessary for substantial therapeutic results. More limited surgery focusing on the inferior, medial portion of the frontal lobes and on the thalamic connections proved as beneficial, with a gratifying reduction in operative mortality and in the extent of personality change (6, 199, 200, 201). These findings were further extended and refined, as evidenced by the recent techniques of stereotactic tractotomy (202), which bears little resemblance to the old lobotomy, differing "in every possible respect in accuracy, location, and clinical effect" (203).

The greater precision in selection and ablation of the pertinent areas without the unnecessary destruction of tissue has not only enhanced the results but also to a marked degree has diminished the side effects of the old procedure (200). Operative mortality probably does not exceed 1% (199, 203), and major postsurgical bleeding or the development of a seizure disorder is extremely uncommon (204). The fear of significant personality change is groundless (6, 203). It is difficult indeed to clinically demonstrate any substantial impairment in intellectual function, ethical sensibility, or social functioning (6, 203, 205). Obviously this is not meant to exclude the possibility of some changes, usually in the sphere of creativity or imagination. However, they generally are subtle and of little practical import, if in evidence at all. Any comparisons made must be against some reference; clinically, this is the level of premorbid personality function. The level of function and achievement in most patients who have undergone psychosurgery appears to be generally far better as judged in these patients by the degree of reduction in symptoms and need for further psychiatric treatment, by their own evaluations, and by those of family and friends (205).

Patients must be carefully selected according to strict criteria to afford the best chance of obtaining a favorable response and to limit this treatment to its proper sphere. An intensive, comprehensive treatment period of at least 3 years prior to considering psychosurgery should first prove essentially valueless or at best transient in benefit (204, 206). All therapeutic modalities known to be of some value in depression should be employed singly, repeatedly, and in combination (205, 207). Potential patients for psychosurgery constitute an extremely difficult group to manage with techniques that generally are satisfactory otherwise. Often the services of other psychiatrists will be needed to employ treatments in which one may not be experienced. Since surgery is a therapeutic one-way street, the patient should have full advantage of more reversible methods. However, an excess of heroism is not required, for some nonsurgical measures are not without risk or substantial cost; and psychosurgery often, in balance, will prove the most beneficial treatment for patients in whom drugs, ECT, and psychotherapy have repeatedly failed. It has been recommended that before leucotomy, a final treatment course of modified narcosis, ECT, and MAOI-tricyclic combination therapy be tried (208).

Any of the depressions described in the standard diagnostic manuals, if they are unremitting or chronically recurring despite one's best efforts, are potentially suitable (203, 207). In addition there is a less easily categorized group of depressed patients who do well. In such patients, depressive symptomatology is admixed with prominent degrees of tension, anxiety, or obsessional tendencies which often mask the rather severe depressive component (2, 203, 206). Patients who demonstrate some improvement with ECT but concurrently display a heightening of tension and anxiety or the appearance of these symptoms for the first time often prove to be good candidates for leucotomy (6). Pronounced hysterical features, psychopathic tendencies, or gross immaturity should preclude this treatment (205). A patient in whom emotional deterioration has set in is a poor subject indeed (199), and there should be evidence of a basically sound personality structure which retains the potential for adaptation to his life situation providing that symptoms could be alleviated or at least attenuated (205). Symptoms should be predominantly in the affective sphere and show at least some response to the intensive therapy cited. Reactive depressions deriving from irremediable environmental situations or physical disease often will respond well (6). Manic-depressives, or those with fairly prominent cyclothymic moods swings, may have their depression relieved or their depressive swings attenuated, but the hypomanic or manic component may be less affected although usually easier to treat (6, 209).

A well-trained, experienced psychiatric team is important in speeding adaptation and recovery. A degree, at times marked, of lack of drive, affective blunting, and withdrawal is common but usually not severe or long lived. It is usually responsive to appropriate pharmacotherapy and supportive measures (199).

On the average, this difficult, chronic group of depressives who come to surgery do quite well; some 80% will show worthwhile improvement (207, 210). A result less than hoped for or a subsequent relapse will sometimes benefit from repeat surgery with excellent results. Improved patients may well be able to manage with little or no psychiatric treatment. For those requiring further treatment, the various modalities of therapy, drugs, ECT, and psychotherapy prove more effective and predictable than prior to leucotomy (203).

While not as true in the United Kingdom (6), in the United States this treatment is deferred excessively or not even considered. There is absolutely no place for haste in considering patients for psychosurgery, but deferring treatment beyond the bounds of proper clinical practice prolongs considerable misery pointlessly and endangers the chance for a good response. An affectively flat, chronically ill patient, severely deteriorated and fixated, is not the proper end point for employing this method.

References

1. Ottosson JO: Psychological or physiological theories of ECT. *Int J Psychiatr* **5**:170–174, 1968.
2. Kalinowsky LB, Hippius H: *Pharmacological, Convulsive and Other Somatic Treatments in Psychiatry.* New York, Grune & Stratton, 1969.
3. Cerletti U, Bini L: L'elettroshock. *Arch Gen Neurol Psychiatr* **19**:266–268, 1938.
4. Kalinowsky, LB: The Paul H. Hoch Award Lecture: Developments in the Treatment of Mood Disorders, in *Disorders of Mood.* Edited by Zubin J, Freyhan FA, Baltimore, Johns Hopkins Press, 1972.
5. Will OA, Duval AM: Use of electroshock therapy in psychiatric illness complicated by pulmonary tuberculosis. *J Nerv Ment Dis* **105**:637, 1947.
6. Sargant W, Slater E: *Introduction to Physical Methods of Treatment in Psychiatry.* Edinburgh and London, E. & S. Livingstone LTD, 1969.
7. Greenblatt M, Grosser GH, Wechsler H: Differential response of hospitalized depressed patients to somatic therapy. *Am J Psychiatr* **120**:935–943, 1964.
8. Shepherd M: Clinical trial of the treatment of depressive illness. *Br Med J* **1**:881, 1965.
9. Alexander L: *Objective Approaches to Treatment in Psychiatry.* Springfield, Charles C Thomas, 1958.
10. Appel KE, Myers JM, Scheflen AE: Prognosis in psychiatry. *Arch Neurol Psychiatr* **70**:459–468, 1953.
11. Costello CG, Belton GP, Abra JC, Dunn BE: The amnesic and therapeutic effects of bilateral and unilateral ECT. *Br J Psychiatr* **116**:69–78, 1970.
12. Robin AA, Harria JA: Controlled comparison of imipramine and electroplexy. *J Ment Sci Br J Psychiatr* **108**:217–219, 1962.
13. Hutchinson JT, Smedberg D: Treatment of depression: A comparative study of ECT and six drugs. *Br J Psychiatr* **109**:536, 1963.
14. Bruce EM, Crone N, Fitzpatrick G, Frewin SJ, Gillis A, Lascelles CF, Levene LJ, Mersky H: A comparative trial of ECT and Tofranil. *Am J Psychiatr* **117**:76, 1960.
15. Stanley WJ, Fleming H: A clinical comparison of phenelzine and ECT in the treatment of depressive illness. *J Ment Sci* **108**:708–710, 1962.
16. King PD: Phenelzine and ECT in the treatment of depression. *Am J Psychiatr* **116**:64–68, 1959.
17. Wilson IC, Vernon JT, Guin T, Sandifer MG Jr: A controlled study of treatments of depression. *J Neuropsychiatr* **4**:331–337, 1963.
18. McDonald IM, Perkins M, Merjerrison G, Podilsky M: A controlled comparison of amitriptyline and electroconvulsive therapy in the treatment of depression. *Am J Psychiatr* **122**:1427–1431, 1966.
19. Wittenborn JR, Plante M, Burgess F, Maurer H: A comparison of imipramine, electroconvulsive therapy and placebo in the treatment of depressions. *J Nerv Ment Dis* **135**:131–137, 1962.
20. Imlah NW, Ryan E, Harrington JA: The influence of antidepressant drugs on the response to ECT and on subsequent relapse rates. Edited by Bradley PB, Bente D, *Neuropsychopharm* **4**:438–442, 1965.
21. Fahy P, Imlah NW, Harrington JA: A controlled comparison of electroconvulsive therapy, imipramine and thiopentone sleep in depression. *J Neuropsychiatr* **4**:310–314, 1963.
22. Kiloh LG, Child JP, Latner G: Controlled trial of iproniazid in treatment of endogenous depression. *J Ment Sci* **106**:1139–1144, 1960.

23. Beck AT: *Depression: Clinical, Experimental, and Theoretical Aspects.* New York, Harper & Row, 1967.
24. Kalinowsky LB: Convulsive shock treatment, in *Amer Handbook Psychiatry.* Edited by Arieti S, New York, Basic Books, 1959, Vol. 2, Chap. 75.
25. Kalinowsky LB: Biological Psychiatric Treatments Preceding Pharmacotherapy, in *Discoveries in Biological Psychiatry.* Edited by Ayd FJ, Philadelphia, JB Lippincott Co, 1970, Chap. 4, pp. 59–67.
26. Winokur AB, Clayton PJ, Reich T: *Manic Depressive Illness.* St. Louis, CV Mosby Company, 1969.
27. Abrams R, Taylor MA: Unipolar and bipolar depressive illness. Phenomenology and response to electroconvulsive therapy. *Arch Gen Psychiatr* **30**:320–321, 1974.
28. Abrams R, Volavka J, Roubicek J, and others: Lateralized EEG changes after unilateral and bilateral electroconvulsive therapy. *Dis Nerv Syst (GWAN suppl)* **31**:28–33, 1970.
29. Detre TP, Jarecki HG: Modern psychiatric treatment, in *Convulsive Therapies.* Philadelphia, JB Lippincott Co, 1971, Chap. 15, p. 641.
30. Seager CP, Bird RL: Imipramine with electrical treatment in depression: Controlled trial. *J Ment Sci Br J Psychiatr* **108**:704–707, 1962.
31. Kay DW, Fahy T, Garside RF: A seven-month double-blind trial of amitriptyline and diazepam in ECT-treated depressed patients. *Br J Psychiatr* **117**:667–671, 1970.
32. d'Elia G: Unilateral electroconvulsive therapy. *Acta Psychiatr Scand, Suppl* **215**:5–98, 1970. For EEG study: Perris C is co-author.
33. Ottosson J: Experimental studies of memory impairment after electroconvulsive therapy. *Acta Psychiatr Neurologica Scand, Suppl* **145**:103–127, 1960.
34. Liberson WT: Brief stimulus therapy. *Am J Psychiatr* **105**:28–39, 1948.
35. Maxwell RE: Electrical factors in electroconvulsive therapy. *Acta Psychiatr Scand* **44**:436, 1968.
36. Friedman E, Wilcox PH: Electrostimulated convulsive doses in intact humans by means of unidirectional currents. *J Nerv Ment Dis* **96**:56, 1942.
37. Kendall BS, Mills WB, Thale T: Comparison of two methods of electroshock in their effect on cognitive functions. *J Cons Psychol* **20**:423–429, 1956.
38. Hemphill RE, Walter WG: The treatment of mental disorders by electrically induced convulsions. *J Ment Sci* **87**:256, 1941.
39. Goldman D: Historical aspects of electroshock therapy, electrical current modification, treatment techniques and some electroencephalographic observations. *J Neuropsychiatr* **3**:210–215, 1962.
40. Shankel LW, Dimassimo DA, Whittier JR: Changes with age in electric convulsive reactions in mental patients. *Psychiatr Quart* **34**:284, 1960.
41. Essig CF: Frequency of repeated electroconvulsions and the acquisition rate of a tolerance-like response. *Exp Neurol* **25**:571, 1969.
42. Impastato DJ: P.M.-G.M. Succinylcholine-modified electroshock therapy without barbiturates. *Am J Psychiatr* **114**:698–702, 1958.
43. Parry-Jones W: Oral atropine in premedication for electroconvulsive therapy. *Lancet* **1**:1067–1068, 1964.
44. Fink M: Cholinergic aspects of convulsive therapy. *J Nerv Ment Dis* **24**:475–484, 1966.
45. Pitts FN Jr and others: Drug modification of ECT: II. Succinylcholine dosage. *Arch Gen Psychiatr (Chicago)* **19**:595–598, 1968.
46. Impastato DJ: The safest possible clinical use of succinylcholine in electroshock therapy. *Acta Psychiatr Scand* **41**:294–302, 1965.

47. Porter IH: Genetic basis of drug metabolism in man. *Toxic Aptl Pharmacol* **6**:499, 1964.
48. Adderley DJ, Hamilton M: Use of succinylcholine in ECT, with particular reference to its effect on blood pressure. *Br Med J* **1**:195–197, 1953.
49. Osborne RG, Tunakan B, Barmore J: Anesthetic agent in electro-convulsive therapy: Controlled comparison. *J Nerv Ment Dis* **137**:297–300, 1963.
50. Pitts FN Jr and others: Induction of anesthesia with methohexital and thiopental in electroconvulsive therapy: Effect on the electrocardiogram and clinical observations in 500 consecutive treatments with each agent. *New Eng J Med* **273**:353–360, 1965.
51. Witztum J, Baker M, Woodruff RA Jr, Pitts FN Jr: Electrotherapy: The effects of methohexital on EKG. *Dis Nerv Syst* **31**:193, 1970.
52. Martin DJ, Kaelbling R: Diazepam-modified electroconvulsive therapy. *Biol Psychiatr* **3**:129, 1971.
53. Finlayson P, Burheim RB, Boots UJ: A comparison of propanidid (Epontol) and thiopentone anesthesia in ECT. *Br J Psychol* **116**:79–83, 1970.
54. Rollason WN, Sutherland MS, Hal DJ: An evaluation of the effect of methohexitone and propanidid on blood pressure, pulse rate, and cardiac arrhythmia during electroconvulsive therapy. *Br J Anaesth* **43**:160, 1970.
55. Freedman AM, Kaplan HI: *Comprehensive Textbook of Psychiatry.* Baltimore, Williams & Wilkins Co, 1967.
56. Karagulla S: Evaluation of electroconvulsive therapy as compared with conservative methods of treatment in depressive states. *J Ment Sci* **96**:1060–1091, 1950.
57. Gaitz CM, Pokorny AD, Mills M Jr: Death following electroconvulsive therapy: Report of three cases. *Arch Neurol Psychiatr* **75**:493–499, 1956.
58. Barker JC, Baker AA: Deaths associated with electroplexy. *J Ment Sci* **105**:339–348, 1959.
59. Matthew JR, Constan E: Complications following ECT of a three-year period in a state institution. *Am J Psychiatr* **120**:1119–1120, 1964.
60. Perrin GM: Cardiovascular aspects of electric shock therapy. *Acta Psychiatr Neurol Scand, Suppl* 152, 1962.
61. Woodruff RA Jr, Pitts FN Jr, McClure JN Jr: The drug modification of ECT. 1. Methohexital, thiopental, and preoxygenation. *Arch Gen Psychiatr (Chicago)* **18**:605–611, 1968.
62. McKenna G, Engle RP, Brooks H, Dalen J: Cardiac arrhythmias during electroshock therapy: Significance, prevention, and treatment. *Am J Psychiatr* **127**:4, 1970.
63. Lewis WH Jr, Richardson DJ, Gahagan LH: Cardiovascular disturbances and their management in modified electrotherapy for psychiatric illness. *New Eng J Med* **252**:1016–1020, 1955.
64. Hussar AE, Pachter M: Myocardial infarction and fatal coronary insufficiency during electroconvulsive therapy. *JAMA* **204**:146–149, 1968.
65. McAndrew J, Hauser G: Preventilation of oxygen in electroconvulsive treatment: Suggested modification of technique, give O_2 right after succinylcholine to prevent anoxia. *Am J Psychiatr* **124**:251–252, 1967.
66. Michael KD, Wunderman DC: Prevention of anoxia during succinylcholine—Electroshock therapy by the use of a new treatment technique. *J Nerv Ment Dis* **126**:535, 1958.
67. Blachly PH, Gowing D: Multiple monitored electroconvulsive treatment. *Comp Psychiatr* **7**:100, 1966.
68. Kalinowsky LB: Electro convulsive therapy within the framework of other

available treatments, in *Biological Treatment of Mental Illness.* New York, Farrar, Straus & Giroux, 1966.
69. Fink M and others: Inhalant-induced convulsions. Significance for the theory of the convulsive therapy process. *Arch Gen Psychiatr* **4**:259, 1961.
70. Laurell B: Flurothyl convulsive therapy. *Acta Psychiatr Scand, Suppl* **213**:5–79, 1970.
71. McGaugh JL, Williams TA: Neurophysiological and behavioral effects of convulsive phenomena. Presented at conference Psychobiology of Convulsive Therapy, April 1972, Puerto Rico.
72. Levy R: The clinical evaluation of unilateral electroconvulsive therapy. *Br J Psychiatr* **114**:459, 1968.
73. Bidder TG, Strain JJ, Brunschwig L: Bilateral and unilateral ECT: Follow-up study and critique. *Am J Psychiatr* **127**:737–745, 1970.
74. Cronholm B, Ottosson JO: The experience of memory function after electroconvulsive therapy. *Br J Psychiatr* **109**:251, 1963.
75. Fink M: Clinical progress in convulsive therapy. Presented at conference Psychobiology of Convulsive Therapy, April 1972, Puerto Rico.
76. Klein DF, Davis JM: *Diagnosis and Drug Treatment of Psychiatric Disorders.* Baltimore, Williams & Wilkins Co, 1969.
77. Ebaugh FG, Barnacle CH, Neuburger KT: Fatalities following electric convulsive therapy. *Arch Neurol Psychiatr* **49**:107, 1943.
78. Alexander L, Lowenbach H: Experimental studies on electroshock treatment. 1. The intracerebral vascular reaction as an indicator of the path of the current and the threshold of early changes within the brain tissue. *J Neuropath Exper Neurol* **2**:139, 1944.
79. Hartelius H: Cerebral changes following electrically induced convulsions. *Acta Psychiatr Scand, Suppl* 77, 1952.
80. Kalinowsky LB: The convulsive therapies, in *Comprehensive Textbook of Psychiatry.* Section 35.5, 1967, pp. 1279–1285.
81. Brain Lord: The meaning of memory, in *Modern Perspectives in World Psychiatry.* Edited by Howells JG, Chap. 5, pp. 109–129, New York, Brunner Mazel, 1972.
82. Dolenz BJ: Indoklon. A clinical review. *Psychosomat* **6**:200, 1965.
83. Cronholm B: Post-ECT amnesias, in *The Pathology of Memory.* New York, Academic Press, 1969.
84. Strömgren LS: Unilateral versus bilateral electroconvulsive therapy. Investigations into the therapeutic effect in endogenous depression. *Acta Psychiatr Scand, Suppl* **240**:8–65, 1973.
85. Stones MJ: Electroconvulsive treatment and short term memory. *Br J Psychiatr* **122**:591–594, 1973.
86. Dornbush R, Abrams R, Fink M: Memory changes after unilateral and bilateral convulsive therapy. *Br J Psychiatr* **119**:75–78, 1971.
87. McGaugh JL, Zornetzer SF, Gold PE, Landfield PW: Modification of memory systems: Some neurobiological aspects. *Quart Rev Biophys* **5**:163–186, 1972.
88. Inglis J: Shock, surgery and cerebral asymmetry. *Br J Psychiatr* **117**:143–148, 1970.
89. Inglis J: Electrode placement and the effect of ECT on mood and memory in depression. *Can Psychiatr Assoc J* **14**, 1969.
90. Lancaster N, Steinert R, Frost I: Unilateral electroconvulsive therapy. *J Ment Sci* **104**:221–227, 1958.
91. Martin WL and others: Clinical evaluation of unilateral E.S.T. *Am J Psychiatr* **121**:1087–1090, 1965.

92. Cannicott SM: Unilateral electroconvulsive therapy. *Postgrad Med J* **38**:451–459, 1962.
93. Impastato DJ, Karliner W: Control of memory impairment in EST by unilateral stimulation of the non-dominant hemisphere. *Dis Nerv Syst* **27**:182, 1966.
94. Zinkin S, Birtchnell J: Unilateral electroconvulsive therapy: Its effects on memory and its therapeutic efficacy. *Br J Psychiatr* **114**:973–988, 1968.
95. Halliday AM, Davidson K, Browne MW, Kreeger LC: A comparison of the effects on depression and memory of bilateral ECT and unilateral ECT to the dominant and non-dominant hemispheres. *Br J Psychiatr* **114**:997, 1968.
96. Valentine M, Keddie KMG, Dunne D: A comparison of techniques in electroconvulsive therapy. *Br J Psychiatr* **114**:989, 1968.
97. Strain JJ, Brunschwig L, Duffy JP, Agle DP, Rosenbaum AL, Bidder TG: Comparison of therapeutic effects and memory changes with bilateral and unilateral ECT. *Am J Psychiatr* **125**:294–304, 1968.
98. Zamora EN, Kaelbling R: Memory and electroconvulsive therapy. *Am J Psychiatr* **112**:545–554, 1965.
99. Cohen BD, Noblin CD, Silverman AJ: Functional asymmetry of the human brain. *Science* **162**:475–477, 1968.
100. Sutherland EM, Oliver JE, Knight DR: EEG, memory and confusion in dominant, non-dominant and bitemporal ECT. *Br J Psychiatr* **115**:1059–1064, 1969.
101. Abrams R, Fink M, Dornbush RL, Feldstein S, Volavka J, Roubicek J: Unilateral and bilateral electroconvulsive therapy. Effects on depression, memory, and the electroencephalogram. *Arch Gen Psychiatr* **27**, July 1972.
102. Fleminger JJ, Horne DJ, Nair NPV, Nott PN: Differential effect of unilateral and bilateral ECT. *Am J Psychiatr* **127**:4, October 1970.
103. McAndrew J, Berkey B, Matthews C: The effects of dominant and non-dominant unilateral ECT as compared to bilateral ECT. *Am J Psychiatr* **124**:483–490, 1967.
104. Abrams R: Daily administration of unilateral ECT. *Am J Psychiatr* **124**:384, 1967.
105. Stinnet JL, Di Giacomo JN: Daily administered unilateral ECT. *Biol Psychiatr* **2**:303–306, 1970.
106. Abrams R, Taylor MA: Anterior bifrontal ECT. A clinical trial. *Br J Psychiatr* **122**:587–590, 1973.
107. Krantz JC Jr, Truitt EC Jr, Speers L, and others: New pharmacoconvulsive agents. *Science* **126**:353, 1957.
108. Krantz JC: Indoklon—A Fluorinated Ether Convulsant, in *Discoveries in Biological Psychiatry.* Edited by Ayd FJ, Philadelphia, JB Lippincott Co, 1970, Chap. 8, pp. 107–114.
109. Krantz JC Jr, Esquibel A, Truitt EB Jr, Ling ASC, Kurland AA: Hexafluorodiethyl ether (Indoklon): An inhalant convulsant. Its use in psychiatric treatment. *JAMA* **166**:1555, 1958.
110. Esquibel AJ, Krantz JC Jr, Truitt EB Jr, Ling ASC, Kurland AA: Hexafluorodiethyl ether (Indoklon): Its use as a convulsant in psychiatric treatment. *J Nerv Ment Dis* **126**:530, 1958.
111. Karliner W, Padula L: Improved technique for Indoklon convulsive therapy. *Am J Psychiatr* **116**:358, 1959.
112. Karliner W, Padula L: The use of hexafluorodiethyl ether in psychiatric treatment. *J Neuropsychiatr* **2**:67, 1960.
113. Karliner W: Present status of Indoklon convulsive treatments. *Dis Nerv Syst* **27**:470, 1966.

114. Lapolla A, McBurney RE, Sutton CE, Nash LR: A clinical report on the use of Indoklon. *Dis Nerv Syst* **26:**735, 1965.
115. Freund JD, Warren FZ: A clinical impression of hexafluorodiethyl ether (Indoklon) following more than 800 treatments. *Dis Nerv Syst* **25:**56, 1965.
116. Karliner W: Further clinical experience with 10% intravenous Indoklon. *Am J Psychiatr* **120:**1007, 1964.
117. Kafi A, Dennis MS: Advantages of Indoklon convulsive therapy. *Hosp Commun Psychiatr* **17:**297, 1966.
118. Sandifer MG, Albert RF, Wilson IC: Patient preference: Indoklon vs electroshock therapy. *J Nerv Ment Dis* **134:**184, 1962.
119. Speers L, Neeley AH: The synthesis, chemical and physical properties of Indoklon. *J Neuropsychiatr* **4:**153–156, 1963.
120. Dolenz BJ: Further report on Indoklon. *Am J Psychiatr* **121:**510, 1964.
121. Impastato D: Electric and chemical convulsive therapy in psychiatry. *Dis Nerv Syst* **22:**91, 1961.
122. Kurland AA, Hanlon TE, Esquibel AJ, Krantz JC, Sheets CS: A comparative study of hexafluorodiethyl ether (Indoklon) and electroconvulsive therapy. *J Nerv Ment Dis* **129:**95, 1959.
123. Spreche D: A quantitative comparison of electroconvulsive therapy with hexafluorodiethyl ether. *J Neuropsychiatr* **5:**132, 1964.
124. Small JG, Small IF, Sharpley P, Moore DM: A double-blind comparative evaluation of fluorothyl and ECT. *Arch Gen Psychiatr* **19:**79–86, 1968.
125. Small JG, Small IF, Sharpley P, Moore DF: A double-blind comparative evaluation of fluorothyl and ECT. *Arch Gen Psychiatr* **19:**79, 1968.
126. Scanlon WG, Mathas J: Electroencephalographic and psychometric studies of Indoklon convulsive treatment and electroconvulsive treatment (a preliminary report). *Int J Neuropsychiatr* **3:**276, 1967.
127. Cronholm B, Ottosson J: Memory functions in endogenous depression before and after ECT. *Arch Gen Psychiatr* **5:**193, 1961.
128. Gander DR, Bennett PJ, Kelly DHW: Hexafluorodiethyl ether (Indoklon) convulsive therapy: A pilot study. *Br J Psychiatr* **113:**1413, 1967.
129. Rose L, Watson A: Fluorothyl (Indoklon) experience with an inhalational convulsant agent. *Anaesthesia* **22:**425–434, 1967.
130. Karliner W, Padula L: Further clinical studies of hexafluorodiethyl ether convulsive treatments. *J Neuropsychiatr* **3:**159, 1962.
131. Regestein OR, Roper P: The treatment of psychiatric patients by simultaneous use of electroconvulsive and pharmacoconvulsive therapy. *Can Med Assoc J* **95:**875, 1966.
132. Holmberg G: Biological aspects of electroconvulsive therapy. *Int Rev Neurobiol* **5:**389–412, 1963.
133. Breitner C, Picchioni C, Chin L: Neurohormone levels in brain after CNS stimulation including electrotherapy. *J Neuropsychiatr* **5:**153–158, 1964.
134. Schildkraut JJ, Schanberg SM, Breese GR, Kopin IJ: Norepinephrine metabolism and drugs used in the affective disorders: A possible mechanism of action. *Am J Psychiatr* **124:**600–608, 1967.
135. Kato L, Gozsy B, Roy PB, Groh V: Histamine, serotonin, epinephrine and norepinephrine in the rat brain following convulsions. *Int J Neuropsych* **3:**46–51, 1967.
136. Schildkraut JJ, Draskoczy PR, Lo PS: Norepinephrine pools in rat brain: Differences in turnover rates and pathways of metabolism. *Science* **172:**587–589, 1971.
137. Kety SS, Javoy I, Thierry A-AM, Julou L, Glowinski J: A sustained effect of elec-

troconvulsive shock on the turnover of norepinephrine in the central nervous system of the rat. *Proc Nat Acad Sci,* 1249–1254, 1967.

138. Ebert MH, Baldessarini RJ, Lipinski JF, Berv K: Effects of electroconvulsive seizures on amine metabolism in the rat brain. *Arch Gen Psychiatr* **29**:397–401, 1973.
139. Thierry AM, Blanc G, Glowinski J: Effect of stress on the disposition of catecholamines localized in various intraneuronal storage forms in the brain stem of the rat. *J Neurochem* **18**:449–461, 1971.
140. Hinesley RK, Norton JA, Aprison MH: Serotonin, norepinephrine and 3-4 dihydroxyphenylethylamine in rat brain parts following electroconvulsive shock. *J Psychiatr Res* **6**:143–152, 1968.
141. Ladisich W, Steinhauff N, Matussek N: Chronic administration of electroconvulsive shock and norepinephrine metabolism in the rat brain. *Psychopharmacologia* **15**:296–304, 1969.
142. Baldessarini RJ, Lipinski JF, Chace KV: Effects of amantadine hydrochloride on catecholamine metabolism in the brain of the rat. *Biochem Pharmacol* **21**:77–87, 1972.
143. Bliss EL, Thatcher W, Ailion J: Relationship of stress to brain serotonin and 5-hydroxyindoleacetic acid. *J Psychiatr Res* **9**:71–80, 1972.
144. Thierry AM, Javoy F, Glowinski J, Kety SS: Effects of stress on the metabolism of norepinephrine, dopamine and serotonin in the central nervous system of the rat. I. Modifications of norepinephrine turnover. *J Pharmacol Exp Therapeut* **163**:163–171, 1968.
145. Zigmond MJ, Harvey JA: Resistance to central norepinephrine depletion and decreased mortality in rats chronically exposed to electric foot shock. *J Neuro-Visc Rel* **31**:373–381, 1970.
146. Musacchio J, Julou L, Kety SS, Glowinski J: Effect of electroconvulsive shock on rat brain tyrosine hydroxylase. *Proc Nat Acad Sci* **63**:1117–1119, 1969.
147. Gravenstein JS, Anton AH, Wiener SM, Tetlow AG: Catecholamine and cardiovascular response to electroconvulsion therapy in man. *Br J Anaesth* **37**:833–839, 1965.
148. Messiha FS, Turek I: Electroconvulsive therapy: Effect on catecholamine excretion by psychiatric patients. *Res Commun Chem Pathol Pharmacol* **1**:535–546, 1970.
149. Schildkraut JJ, Draskoczy P: Effects of ECT on catecholamine metabolism: basic and clinical studies, in *Psychobiology of Convulsive Therapy.* Edited by Fink M, Kety S, McGaugh J, Washington, V.H. Winston & Sons, in press.
150. Maas JW, Landia DH: In vivo studies of metabolism of norepinephrine in central nervous system. *J Pharmacol Exp Therapeut* **163**:147–162, 1968.
151. Mandell AJ, Segal DS: The psychobiology of dopamine and the methylated indoleamines with particular reference to psychiatry, in *Biological Psychiatry.* Edited by Mendels J, New York, Wiley, 1973, Chap. 5, pp. 89–112.
152. Billiet M, Bernard P, Delaunois A, De Schaepdryver A: *Arch Int Pharmacodyn* **186**:179, 1970.
153. Engel J, Hanson LCF, Roos BE, Strombergsson LE: Effect of electroshock on dopamine metabolism in rat brain. *Psychopharmacologia* **13**:140–144, 1968.
154. Cooper AJ, Moir ATB, Guldberg HC: The effect of electroconvulsive shock on the cerebral metabolism of dopamine and 5-hydroxytryptamine. *J Pharm Pharmacol* **20**:729–730, 1968.
155. Garattini S, Kato R, Lamesta L, Valzelli L: Electroshock, brain serotonin and barbiturate narcosis. *Experientia* **16**:156–157, 1960.
156. Essman WB: Changes in ECS-induced retrograde amnesia with DBMC:

Behavioral and biochemical correlates of brain serotonin antagonism. *Physiol Beh* **3**:527–531, 1968.

157. Bonnycastle DD, Giarman NJ, Paasonen MK: Anti-convulsant compounds and 5-hydroxytryptamine in rat brain. *Br J Pharmacol Chemother* **12**:228–231, 1967.
158. Bertaccini G: Effect of convulsant treatment on the 5-hydroxytryptamine content of brain and other tissues of the rat. *J Neurochem* **4**:217–222, 1959.
159. Tagliamonte A and others: Increase of brain tryptophan by electroconvulsive shock in rats. *J Neurochem* **19**:1509–1512, 1972.
160. Shields PJ: Effects of electroconvulsive shock on the metabolism of 5-hydroxytryptamine in the rat brain. *J Pharm Pharmacol* **24**:919–921, 1972.
161. Feighner JP, King LJ, Schuckit MA, Croughan J, Briscoe W: Hormonal potentiation of imipramine and ECT in primary depression. *Am J Psychiatr* **128**:1230–1238, 1972.
162. Rosenblatt S, Chanley JD, Sobotka H, Kaufman MR: Interrelationships between electroshock, the blood-brain barrier, and catecholamines. *J Neurochem* **5**:172–176, 1960.
163. Nordin G, Ottosson JO, Roose BE: Influence of convulsive therapy on 5-hydroxyindoleacetic acid and homovanillic acid in cerebrospinal fluid in endogenous depression. *Psychopharmocolgia (Berl.)* **20**:315–320, 1971.
164. Ashcroft GW, Crawford TBB, Eccleston D, Sharman DF, MacDougall EJ, Stanton TB, Binns JK. *Lancet* **2**:1049–1052, 1966.
165. Denker SJ and others: Acid monamine metabolites of CSF in mental depression and mania. *J Neurochem* **13**:1545–1548, 1966.
166. Robinson, DS, Nies A, Davis JN, Bunney WE, Davis JM, Colburn RW, Bourne HR, Shaw DM, Coppen AJ: Ageing, monamines and monoamine-oxidase levels. *Lancet* **1**:290–291, 1972.
167. Pryor GT, Otis LS, Scott MK, Colwell JJ: Duration of chronic electroshock treatment in relation to brain weight, brain chemistry, and behavior. *J Comp Physiol Psychol* **63**:236, 1967.
168. Pryor GT, Otis LS: Brain biochemical and behavioral effects of 1, 2, 4 or 8 weeks' electroshock treatment. *Life Sci* **8**:387–399, 1969.
169. Pryor GT, Peache S, Scott MK: Effect of electroconvulsive shock on avoidance conditioning and brain monoamineoxidase activity. *Physiol Beh* **9**:623–638, 1972b.
170. Pryor GT, Otis LS: Persisting effects of chronic electroshock seizures on brain and behavior in two strains of rats. *Physiol Beh* **5**:1053–1055, 1970.
171. Pryor GT, Scott MK, Peache S: Increased monoamine oxidase activity following repeated electroshock seizures. *J Neurochem* **19**:891–893, 1972.
172. Lapin IP, Oxenkrug GF: Intensification of the central serotoninergic processes as a possible determinant of the thymoleptic effect. *Lancet* **1**:132–136, 1969.
173. Janowsky DS, Davis JM, El-Yousef MK, Sekerke HJ: A cholinergic-adrenergic hypothesis of mania and depression. *Lancet* **2**:632–635, 1972.
174. Janowsky DS, Khaled El-Yousef M, Davis JM, Sekerke HJ: Parasympathetic suppression of manic symptoms by physostigmine. *Arch Gen Psychiatr* **28**:542, 1973.
175. Essman WB: Neurochemical changes in ECS and ECT. *Sem Psychiatr* **4**:67–79, 1972.
176. Sachar EG, Hellman L, Gallagher TF, Fukushima DK: Endocrinology of depression, cortisal production in depressions, in *Psychobiology of Depressive Illness.* Edited by Williams TA, Katz MM, Schield GA Jr, Department HEW Publication (HFM) 70-9053, Washington DC, 1973, pp. 221–228.

177. Ito K, Hoshimura I, Yamashita T, Moroji, Endo M: *Folia Psychiatr Neurol Jap* **18**:287, 1964.
178. Ryan RJ, Swanson DW, Faiman C, Mayberry WE, Spadoni AJ: Effects of convulsive electroshock on serum concentrations of follicle stimulating hormone, luteinizing hormone, thyroid stimulating hormone and growth hormone in man. *J Clin Endocrin Metab* **30**:51–58, 1970.
179. Thorell JI, Adielsson G: Antidepressive effects of electroconvulsive therapy and thyrotrophin-releasing hormone. *Lancet* **819**:43, 1973.
180. Bonavita V, Piccoli F: Brain nucleotides and excitatory processes, in *Chemistry and Brain Development.* Edited by Paolett R, Davison AN, New York, Plenum Press, 1971.
181. Coppen A, Shaw DM: The distribution of electrolytes and water in patients after taking lithium carbonate. *Lancet* **2**:805, 1967.
182. Russell GFM: Body weight and balance of water, sodium and potassium in depressed patients given electro-convulsive therapy. *Clin Sci* **19**:327, 1960.
183. Gibbons JL: Total body sodium and potassium in depressive patients. *Clin Sci* **19**:133, 1960.
184. Platman SR, Fieve RR, Pierson RN: Effect of mood and lithium carbonate on total body potassium. *Arch Gen Psychiatr* **22**:297, 1970.
185. Coppen A, Shaw DM, Costain R: Mineral metabolism in mania. *Br Med J* **1**:71, 1966.
186. Flach FF: Calcium metabolism in states of depression. *Br J Psychiatr* **110**:588, 1964.
187. Faragalla FF, Flach FF: Studies of mineral metabolism in mental depression. I. The effects of imipramine and electric convulsive therapy on calcium balance and kinetics. *J Nerv Ment Dis* **151**:120–129, 1970.
188. Carney NW, Sheffield BF, Sebastian J: Serum magnesium, diagnosis, ECT and season. *Br J Psychiatr* **122**:427–429, 1973.
189. Cohen HB, Duncan RF, Dement WC: Sleep: The effect of electroconvulsive shock in cats deprived of REM sleep. *Science* **156**:1646–1648, 1967.
190. Cohen HB, Dement WC: Sleep: Suppression of rapid eye movement phase in the cat after electroconvulsive shock. *Science* **154**:396–398, 1966.
191. Kaelbling R, Koski EG, Hartwig CD: Reduction of rapid-eye-movement sleep after electroconvulsions: An experiment in cats on the mode of action of electroconvulsive treatment. *J Psychol Res* **6**:153–157, 1968.
192. Freemon FR: *Sleep Research. A Critical Review.* Springfield, Charles C Thomas, 1972.
193. Zarcone V, Gulevich G, Dement W: Sleep and electroconvulsive therapy. *Arch Gen Psychiatr* **16**:567–573, 1967.
194. Oswald I: Human brain protein, drugs & dreams. *Nature* **223**:893–897, 1969.
195. Van de Castle RL, Hawkins DR: The effect of electroconvulsive therapy on sleep patterns of depressed patients. *Psychophysiology* **6**:234, 1969.
196. Hendels J, Hawkins DR: The psychopathology and psychophysiology of sleep, in *Biological Psychiatry.* Edited by Mendels J, New York, Wiley, 1973, Chap. 13, p. 297.
197. Green WJ, Stajdahar PP: The effect of ECT on the sleep-dream cycle in a psychotic depression. *J Nerv Ment Dis* **143**:123–134, 1966.
198. Hauri P, Hawkins DR: Phasic REM, depression and the relationship between sleeping and waking. *Arch Gen Psychiatr* **25**:56–63, 1971.
199. Freeman W: Psychosurgery, in *American Handbook of Psychiatry.* Edited by Arieti S, New York, Basic Books, 1959, Chap. 76, pp. 1521–1540.

200. Holdan JMC, Hofstatter L: Prefrontal lobotomy: stepping-stone or pitfall? *Am J Psychiatr* **127**:5, 1970.
201. Livingston K: Neurosurgical aspects of primary affective disorders, in *Neurological Surgery.* Edited by Youmans JWB, New York, Saunders Co, 1973, Vol. 3, pp. 1881–1900.
202. Laitinen LV: Stereotactic lesions in the knee of the corpus callosum in the treatment of emotional disorders. *Lancet* **1**:472–475, 1972.
203. Knight G: Stereotactic surgery for the relief of suicidal and severe depression and intractable psychoneurosis. *Postgrad Med J* **45**:1–13, 1969.
204. Greenblatt M: Psychosurgery, in *Comprehensive Textbook of Psychiatry.* Edited by Freedman M, Baltimore, Williams & Wilkins Co, 1967, Section 35.8, pp. 1291–1295.
205. Bailey HR, Dowling JL, Swanton CH, Davies E: Studies in depression. 1. Cingulotractomy in the treatment of severe affective illness. *Med J Aust* **3**:8–12, January 1971.
206. Corkill G, Ratcliff E, Simpson CR: Leucotomy in the 1970's. *Med J Aust* **1**:442–443, 1973.
207. Kelly D, Walter CJS, Mitchell-Heggs N, Sargant W: Modified leucotomy assessed clinically, physiologically and psychologically at six weeks and eighteen months. *Br J Psychiatr* **120**:19–29, 1972.
208. Walter CJS, Mitchell-Heggs N, Sargant W: Modified narcosis, ECT and antidepressant drugs: A review of technique and immediate outcome. *Br J Psychiatr* **120**:651–662, 1972.
209. Stengel E: A follow-up investigation of 330 cases treated by prefrontal leucotomy. *J Ment Sci* **96**:633, 1950.
210. Post F, Linford-Rees WL, Schurr PH: An evaluation of bimedial leucotomy. *Br J Psychiatr* **114**:1223, 1968.

Sixteen

Sleep Changes and Affective Illness

Joseph Mendels, M.D.
Doris A. Chernik, Ph.D.

After many years of research we are still unable to answer the basic question, "Why do we sleep?" Until this question is answered we will remain uncertain about the answers to such fundamental questions as "How many hours should I sleep?" or "Why couldn't I sleep last night?" While there is a general consensus about the fact that most adults require about 7 hours sleep per night, some individuals maintain normal health and well-being on very small amounts of sleep, amounts that most people would regard as extremely pathological. For example, one study reports that two people slept for only 3 hours a night over long periods of time with no indication of mental or physical ill health. Sleep laboratory studies verified their claim (1). These extreme cases highlight the peril of attempting to prescribe a standard amount of sleep for everyone.

It is clear that psychiatrically disturbed individuals often complain of difficulty with sleep. This seems most likely to occur with depressed patients, who frequently complain of shortened, broken sleep, difficulty in falling asleep, a tendency to waken early in the morning, and being unduly tired in the morning.

Surprisingly, when the sleep of depressed patients is studied by objective criteria in the laboratory, their sleep is often not as disturbed as their subjective experiences and reports suggest. Indeed, there is evidence that the majority of people with sleep difficulty (not only depressives) will report a greater reduction in the *quantity* of their sleep than is actually found in the course of objective study. However, there may be important *qualitative* changes in their sleep.

In the sleep laboratory we usually find that the depressed patient sleeps for 5, 6, or even 7 hours a night. Yet he feels tired in the morning. He complains that he has not slept at all (or very little) during the night. Is he deliberately exaggerating? Probably not. Even though the depressed patient may actually obtain more sleep time than he realizes, the patterning (quality) of his sleep is markedly different from that of normal subjects (2–18). It may be that this change in the quality, rather than in the quantity, of sleep causes the patient to complain about his sleep. Clearly the solution is not simply to help him to sleep *more*.

Sleep Stages

In the sleep laboratory, a record of the night's sleep is obtained by recording the electroencephalogram (EEG), the electromyogram (EMG—a record of electrical activity in skeletal muscle, usually the submental muscles), and the electrooculogram (EOG—a recording of eye movement electrical potential). This allows the night's sleep to be divided into a number of stages.

On becoming drowsy, the first change is likely to be a reduction in the muscle potential (EMG) and a slight increase in amplitude of the alpha rhythm (8 to 12 cps) in the EEG. This is interrupted by periods of relatively low voltage activity in the EEG associated with slow lateral movements of the eyeball (Figure 1). This is known as stage 1, the lightest stage of sleep. It represents approximately 5% of a normal person's sleep, but may constitute as much as 15% of the sleep of a depressed person.

The normal young adult leaves stage 1 very soon after its onset and moves into the deeper stages of sleep. Stage 2 is heralded by the appearance in the EEG of spindles, the frequency of which is slightly faster than alpha waves (Figure 2). Stage 2 constitutes nearly 50% of the total sleep time of a normal young adult. Stages 3 and 4 sleep are characterized by the presence of delta waves (0.5 to 2.0 cps) (see Figure 3) and account for 20 to 25% of a young adult's sleep. During delta wave sleep there is a reduced response to external stimuli (it is, therefore, sometimes called deep sleep), while stages 1 and 2 are closer to the response capacities of waking.

In addition to these four stages of sleep, which collectively are called non-REM sleep, periodic intervals of sleep are characterized by the presence of rapid eye movements—REM sleep—during which most dreaming occurs (19). REM sleep appears to be a distinct physiological state, different from the other stages of sleep. The EEG is characterized by low voltage, fast activity, similar to stage 1. The important differences from stage 1 sleep are the significant reduction (and at times total absence) of muscle tension, as measured by the EMG, and the accompanying rapid eye movements (Figure 4). REM sleep accounts for 20 to 25% of an average night's sleep in the young adult. During REM sleep many physiological functions show an increased level of activity, often of an extremely erratic nature. It is a state of physiological activation or arousal. In contrast to this, delta wave sleep most closely approximates the popular concept of rest.

The Cyclic Nature of Sleep

These five stages of sleep (stages 1, 2, 3, 4, and 1 REM) usually relate to each other in a cyclic pattern through the night. Each cycle usually begins with stages 1 or 2, followed by stages 3 and 4. After the initial 60 to 90 minutes of

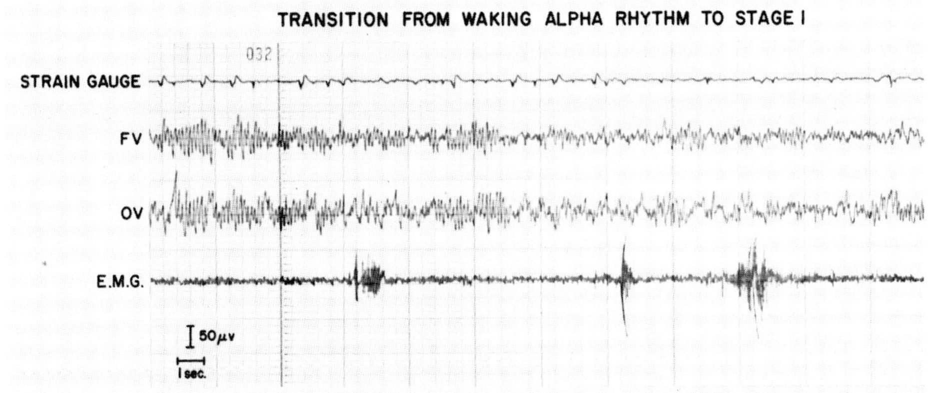

Figure 1. During relaxed wakefulness the EEG is composed of sinusodal alpha activity (8 to 10 cps) and low voltage activity of mixed frequency, accompanied by eye movements and high muscle tone. As the subject falls asleep, his EEG gives way to a stage 1 pattern of relatively low voltage and of mixed frequency.

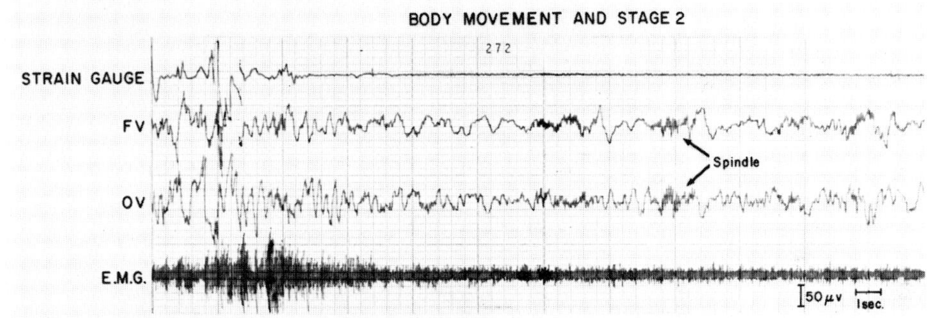

Figure 2. Stage 2 is characterized by 12 to 14 cps sleep spindles, similar in shape to alpha waves but higher in frequency, together with K complexes superimposed on a background of relatively low voltage, mixed frequency electroencephalographic activity.

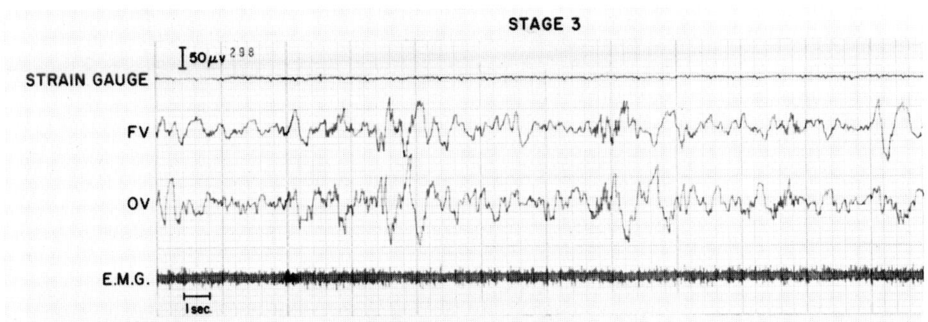

Figure 3. Stages 3 and 4 are defined by high voltage, slow waves of 1 to 2 cps; when more than half the record consists of this slow-wave activity, it is classified as stage 4, while lesser amounts (but greater than 20%) are classified as stage 3.

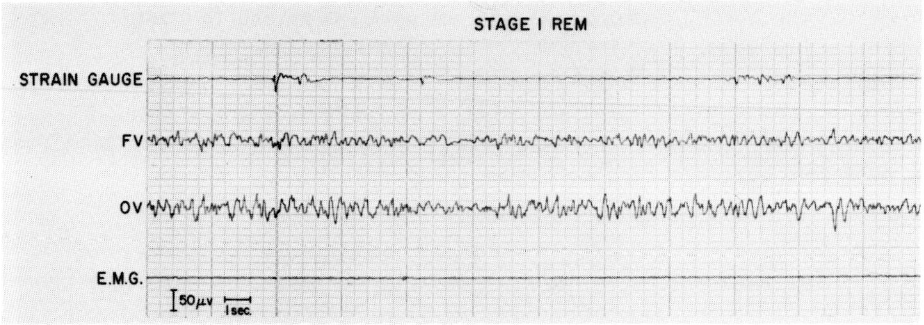

Figure 4. Stage 1 REM sleep shows an electroencephalographic pattern similar to that of stage 1 but is accompanied by episodic rapid eye movements and low amplitude EMG.

sleep each night, there is a shift from stage 4 to a lighter stage of sleep (probably stage 2), muscle tension decreases, and there is a brief period of REM sleep. Stage 2 follows this first REM period, and the cycle begins all over again. There are three to five such cycles during a typical night, with the end of each cycle marked by REM sleep.

The periods of REM sleep tend to lengthen while the periods of delta wave sleep shorten as the night progresses so that, in general, most of the delta wave sleep occurs during the first half of the night while most REM sleep occurs during the second half of the night (Figure 5).

Rapid Eye Movement Sleep

Several investigators have suggested that REM sleep is a necessary stage of semialertness, providing a sentinel function (20, 21). This postulate arose as it became known that the subject responds rapidly to meaningful stimuli which are presented during REM sleep, but is unresponsive when nonmeaningful stimuli are presented. During REM sleep a system is able to categorize incoming signals as "important" or "unimportant." With the former, activating mechanisms are invoked and arousal follows. With the latter, sleep is not interrupted (22–24). For example, Oswald and his colleagues conducted an experiment in which they tape recorded their subjects' names. They played these tapes in both the forward position and in reverse while the subjects were

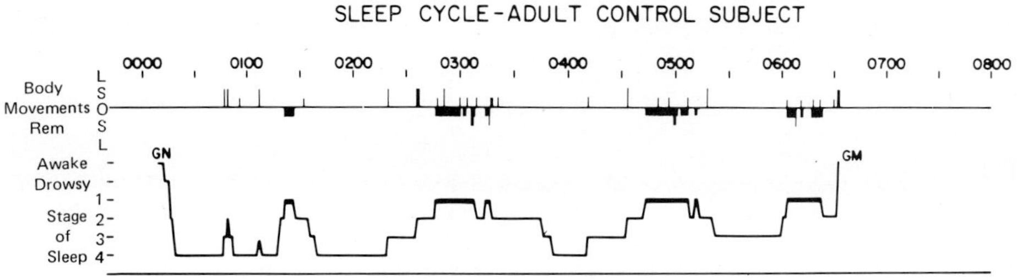

Figure 5. Sleep cycle—adult control subject.

asleep. They did not respond when their names were played in reverse, that is, a nonmeaningful stimulus, during both stage 4 and REM sleep. However, when their names were presented in their correct form, the subjects responded during REM sleep but not during delta wave sleep; this phenomenon suggests that during the former state a sifting process occurs which allows recognition of an appropriate response while meaningless stimuli are ignored.

It has been well established that if a person is deprived of REM sleep, he will develop increasing pressure to achieve it, with increased amounts of REM sleep (REM rebound) when the deprivation is stopped (25–30). This apparent "pressure" to achieve REM sleep is compatible with the view that REM sleep (or dreaming) is a "required" state and performs some needed function.

These studies have focused attention on REM sleep to the relative exclusion of the other stages of sleep. However, an early study of total sleep deprivation by Berger and Oswald (26) suggested that stage 4 may be even more important than REM sleep. They deprived subjects of all sleep for 4 days and nights. When they were then allowed to sleep, they found that recovery of delta wave sleep occurred *before* REM sleep. Delta wave sleep was significantly increased over baseline nights on the first recovery night, while REM rebound was delayed until the next night, suggesting that the need for delta wave sleep takes precedence over the need for REM sleep. There is also the normal occurrence of delta wave sleep at the beginning of the night with most of REM sleep taking place in the second half of the night.

Thus both REM and delta wave sleep appear to be physiologically required states, with the latter taking some priority over the former.

Sleep in Depression

Diaz-Guerrero and his colleagues were the first investigators to study the sleep EEG pattern of depressed patients (31). They studied the sleep of manic-depressive (bipolar) patients during the depressed phase and found that their patients had difficulty in falling asleep and had frequent awakenings during the night. They often woke early in the morning, had more frequent fluctuations from one level of sleep to another, and had lighter sleep than control subjects. No attempt was made to differentiate between the stages of sleep.

During the past decade there have been a number of additional and more extensive studies of the sleep of depressed patients (2–5, 7–18, 32) in which the sleep record was divided into stages. In summary, depressed patients are awake longer, and spend more time in the lighter stages of sleep (especially stage 1) and less, if any, time in stages 3 and 4 (delta wave sleep). The reduction in delta wave sleep is one of the most striking and consistent findings. Depressed patients take longer to fall asleep, wake more frequently during the night, have more body movements while asleep, and tend to wake somewhat earlier in the morning. They also have an unusual admixture of wave forms in the EEG record. Figure 6 illustrates, in a schematic fashion, the all-night sleep pattern of a patient during a period of severe depression (night 4) and his sleep on night 52, 3 weeks after discharge from the hospital.

Depressed patients may have abnormal amounts of REM sleep, although the

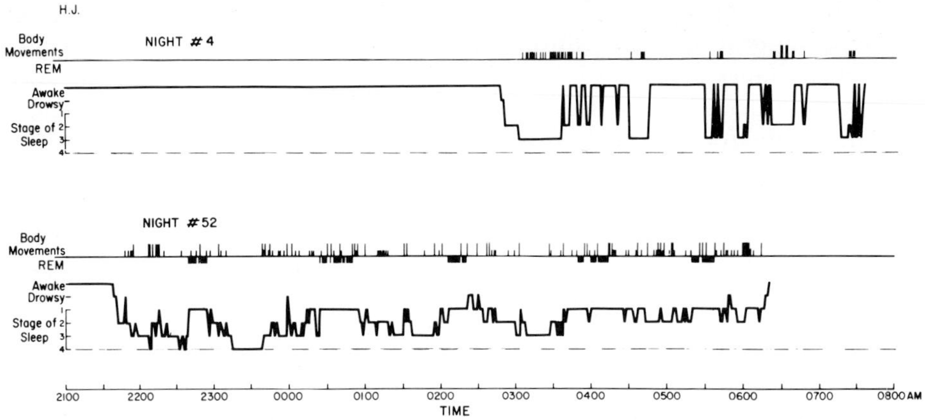

Figure 6. The all-night sleep pattern of patient HJ during the period of severe depression (night 4) and his sleep on night 52, 3 weeks after discharge from the hospital. There is a considerable increase in actual sleep, REM, and stage 4 sleep with clinical improvement.

data about this are contradictory. Some investigators have reported abnormally low levels of REM sleep (8–10, 12, 17, 18, 33). Others find relatively normal amounts of REM sleep in depression (2, 3, 34). Still others report some elevation in REM sleep in depression (4, 14, 32, 35, 36). It is clear that REM sleep is very variable both within subjects (from one night to the next) and across subjects. This variability may partially explain the inconsistencies among the various studies.

On the basis of initial short-term sleep studies (usually 3 or 4 nights in the laboratory), we had reported that REM sleep was reduced in depressed patients as a group (9, 10, 12). In more recent studies (14, 32), where we were able to monitor the sleep of our patients for much longer periods of time and under more controlled conditions, we have found that many of them have normal or even elevated amounts of REM sleep.

Recently, we studied 19 moderately or severely depressed hospitalized male patients (9 unipolar and 10 bipolar depressives) for up to 40 consecutive nights each (excluding adaptation nights) for a total of 209 study nights. All of the patients were without any drugs or alcohol for a minimum of 2 weeks prior and during the study, with the exception of one bipolar patient who had a single dose of a hypnotic 8 days before the study. Many of the patients had been drug-free for over 30 days prior to the study. They were studied on a special ward established for this type of research, which allowed for a minimum of disruption and enabled the patients to be monitored from their own beds. Eight control subjects (ages 37 to 67 years, mean of 47.9 years) were studied for comparison. Table 1 shows the amount of REM sleep (number of minutes per night and time in REM sleep expressed as a percentage of the actual sleep period) for each patient. Eighteen of the nineteen patients had normal or elevated amounts of REM sleep, and one subject had a large reduction in REM sleep, averaging only 13.6% ± 2.4 during 6 consecutive nights. In contrast, another patient had markedly elevated levels of REM sleep, averaging 45.6%

Table 1 Percentage of REM Sleep in Unipolar and Bipolar Depressed Male Patients

Unipolar		Age	Minutes Actual Sleep	% REM Sleep
GB		37	355.5 ± 43.8	25.0 ± 4.8
DP		40	336.8 ± 60.2	30.3 ± 3.4
WH		45	336.5 ± 17.8	45.6 ± 5.9
SO		45	387.5 ± 44.2	26.5 ± 1.1
OH		46	318.9 ± 66.5	27.7 ± 6.2
FH		48	348.8 ± 49.9	25.9 ± 3.5
GG		53	395.9 ± 47.2	23.6 ± 5.2
GS		60	389.3 ± 55.7	26.9 ± 7.7
RC		44	398.0 ± 42.0	22.4 ± 1.9
	Mean	46.4 ± 6.8	363.0 ± 30.0	28.2 ± 6.9
Bipolar I				
RM		37	423.6 ± 50.8	29.3 ± 2.4
WS		46	402.4 ± 33.9	23.9 ± 3.0
WC		47	424.9 ± 34.2	25.9 ± 3.7
JH		48	384.4 ± 20.6	23.3 ± 5.8
JD		55	384.3 ± 55.7	26.9 ± 7.7
	Mean	46.6 ± 6.4	403.9 ± 20.0	25.9 ± 2.4
Bipolar II				
JL		43	386.3 ± 31.6	26.2 ± 3.9
WO		64	323.0 ± 41.5	13.6 ± 2.4
WS		57	321.1 ± 44.0	18.4 ± 4.3
JG		61	384.8 ± 53.8	25.5 ± 3.4
JM		49	347.6 ± 21.8	29.3 ± 3.3
	Mean	54.8 ± 8.7	352.6 ± 31.9	22.6 ± 6.4

± 5.9 during 7 consecutive nights. The findings from these two patients clearly demonstrate the limited value of reporting average values for groups of patients without paying appropriate attention to this variability.

Since the finding of increased REM sleep in depression differs from our earlier findings (5, 7, 9) as well as from reports from other laboratories (8, 16–18, 33), we questioned whether the higher amounts of REM sleep found in this new group of patients might be due to a delayed rebound from prior medication. While most of the patients in this study had been drug-free for a minimum of 14 days, it is known that there is a delayed rebound from various antidepressant medications, with a peak effect occurring between the 11th and the 13th day after drug withdrawal (37). Thus the elevation in REM sleep which we found in some patients might represent a compensatory increase due to a previous drug-induced suppression. Many of the drugs used in the treatment of depressed patients suppress REM sleep. These include tricyclic antidepressants (38) and monoamine oxidase inhibitors (39), and also some of the hypnotics which are frequently prescribed for these patients (40). All drugs were discontinued prior to the sleep laboratory studies, and it is possible that we were measuring the subsequent rebound elevation in REM sleep. It is obviously important to determine whether this might have affected our findings.

Therefore, we analyzed the sleep records of six patients who had been drug-free for at least 2 months. These patients were studied for a total of 84 sleep nights, and an average of 29.1% or 108.1 minutes of REM sleep per night. It ranged from an individual mean of 25.8% or 96.5 minutes to 32.1% or 124.3 minutes per night. These values are similar to those for the entire group of 19 patients. Therefore, it seems that the elevation in REM sleep which we now find in depressed patients is not due to a delayed rebound from drug withdrawal.

The earlier findings of an apparent reduction in REM sleep in depression may be due to an insufficient interval between the discontinuation of medications (usually tricyclics and/or barbiturates) and initiation of the sleep study. Many of the patients were studied a day or two after the drugs were stopped, at a time when they may have still been exerting a REM suppressant effect.

Another important factor may have been an insufficient number of nights in the laboratory. There are major fluctuations in the amount of REM sleep from night to night among our patients (Figure 7); for example, patient FM had 133 minutes of REM sleep on night 2 in the laboratory, 68 minutes on night 3, 142 minutes on night 4, and 119 minutes on night 5. These fluctuations are not unusual. Thus if the sleep of these patients is not studied for a sufficient number of consecutive nights, the results obtained will depend on which particular night is studied and may be misleading.

Preliminary studies suggest that fluctuations in REM sleep may be related to the variations in the patients' psychopathology (41–44). Hauri and Hawkins (42) reported an inverse correlation between the percentage of phasic REM (to calculate this, the entire period of REM sleep is divided into 30-second epochs and the number of these epochs which contain at least one eye movement is then counted; this number is then expressed as a percentage of the total number of 30-second segments of REM sleep) and day-to-day changes in severity of the depression. As the depression improved they found an increase in the amount of REM sleep and in the percentage of phasic REM. The greater the percentage of phasic REM sleep a patient showed during a given night, the less his depression. This study is complicated by the fact that nearly half of the patients were receiving drugs known to affect REM sleep, so that additional data is needed to confirm this claim.

The variability in the sleep of individual patients could also be due to such factors as differences in severity of the depression, age, psychotic or neurotic features, varying adaptation to the experimental situation, different stages of the illness, or different subtypes of depression. We have begun to examine the possible contribution of some of the factors to this variability.

Age

Depressed patients who were over 50 years of age had more wakefulness than younger patients and only about one-fourth as much stage 4 sleep. It should be

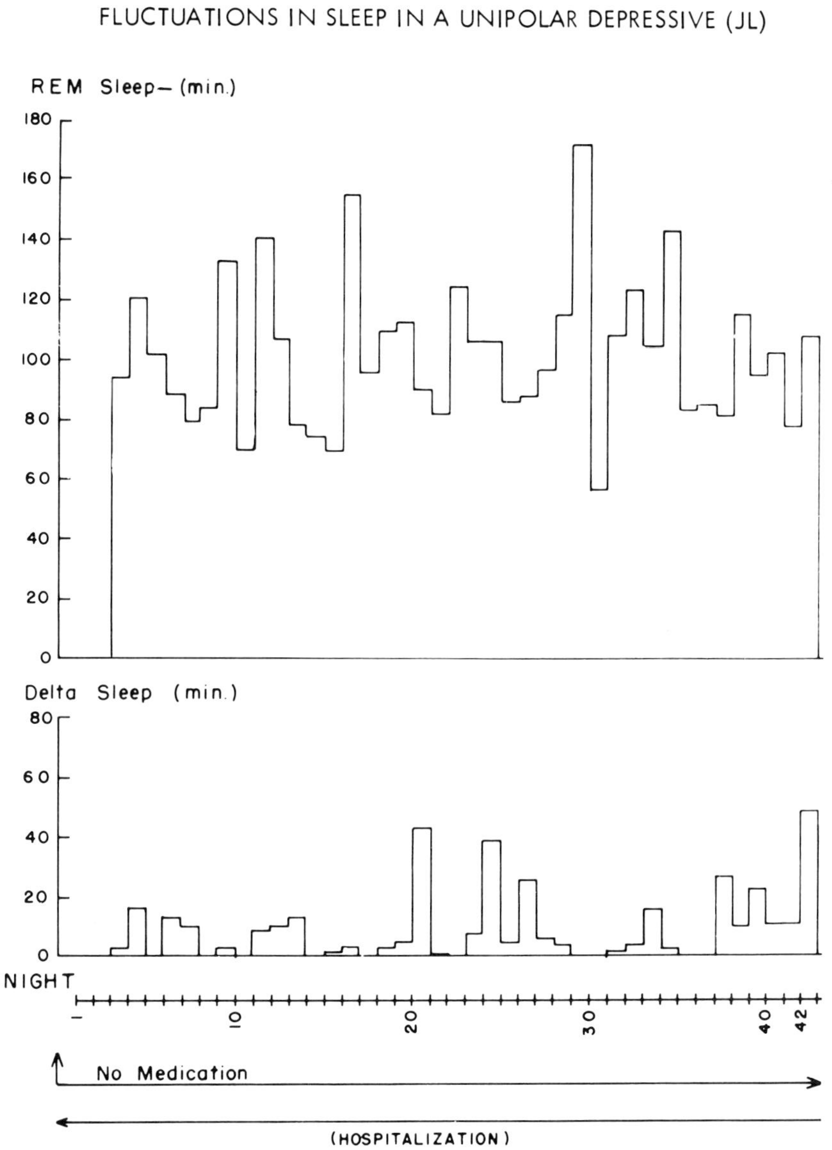

Figure 7. Fluctuations in sleep in a unipolar depressive.

noted that older people in general have less stage 4 sleep then younger people. There did not appear to be any effect of age on the amount of REM sleep (12).

Severity of the Depression

In an initial evaluation we found no significant association between changes in sleep pattern and severity of psychopathology as reflected by scores on the Beck Depression Inventory, although there was a trend toward more wakefulness and less delta and REM sleep in the more severely ill (12).

Psychotic-Neurotic Features

Psychotic depressives (determined by the presence of delusions) had significantly more time awake, more time in stage 1, less time in REM sleep, and a great deal less in stage 4 (an average of less than 1 minute per night) than neurotic depressives (12). Other investigators (17, 45) have obtained similar results, reporting somewhat greater sleep curtailment and sleep disturbance among psychotic depressives as compared with neurotic patients. The reduction of delta wave sleep is particularly marked in the psychotic patients. It has been suggested that this phase of sleep is partially mediated by serotonin (30, 46). We have also found a lower level of 5-hydroxyindoleacetic acid in the lumbar spinal fluid of psychotic depressives, compared with neurotic depressives (47), raising the possibility of some association between psychosis (in depressed patients) and an alteration in serotonin turnover (48).

Bipolar-Unipolar Classification

We have analyzed the sleep of our patients after dividing them into three diagnostic groups.*

1. *Bipolar I.* Patients studied while depressed who *have* a history of a prior hospitalization for mania. (These are equivalent to manic-depressives.)
2. *Bipolar II.* Patients studied while depressed with a history *suggestive* of hypomania or mania but who were not hospitalized for this. This group includes those with previous drug-induced manic or hypomanic episodes.
3. *Unipolar.* History of recurrent depression only.

The sleep characteristics for these three groups of patients are summarized in Table 2. The Bipolar I patients had less sleep disturbance than the other two groups, with more actual sleep time, less wakefulness, less early morning wakening, and a little more delta wave sleep. It should be noted that individual values overlap a great deal, and it would be premature to draw any conclusions about these differences. Some investigators have suggested that bipolar depressives actually have an increase in sleep time or hypersomnia, and that this might differentiate bipolar from unipolar patients (50, 51). This will need to be evaluated in further studies.

Follow-Up Sleep Studies

In an initial short-term follow-up study of the sleep of depressed patients, we were able to study the sleep of 13 patients, a mean of 47.1 (15 to 69) days after their first period in the laboratory. This was soon after admission to hospital when they were moderately or severely depressed (10). The patients were sufficiently improved to leave the hospital at the time of the follow-up study. We found that actual sleep time, REM sleep time, and early morning wakefulness had returned to control values. However, these patients continued

*These three groups correspond with the classification system proposed by Dunner and others (49). Bipolar II patients are equivalent to their group of "unclassified" patients.

Table 2 Sleep Patterns of Unipolar and Bipolar Depressives

	Depressed			Controls	
	5 Bipolar I	5 Bipolar II	9 Unipolar	14 Psychiatric Controls	8 Older Controls
Minutes of					
Actual sleep	404.0 ± 14.9	357.3 ± 31.7	359.8 ± 18.7	358.4 ± 45.4	358.2 ± 42.8
Wakefulness	45.1 ± 18.6	116.5 ± 47.1	63.9 ± 32.6	71.7 ± 26.5	49.9 ± 53.6
Latency to sleep onset	23.4 ± 14.7	18.6 ± 8.6	26.2 ± 19.8	30.5 ± 25.6	11.7 ± 13.7
Latency to REM sleep	38.1 ± 14.3	44.0 ± 7.1	45.6 ± 17.7	55.7 ± 24.6	73.5 ± 39.4
Early morning awakening (awake before 6 A.M.)	5.6 ± 8.7	11.0 ± 9.5	26.1 ± 46.8	12.6 ± 19.4	12.5 ± 21.1
Percentage (of actual sleep)					
REM sleep	27.4 ± 4.0	22.9 ± 6.0	27.1 ± 6.6	26.0 ± 5.8	22.8 ± 7.0
Delta wave sleep (stages 3, 4)	4.7 ± 5.1	0.5 ± 1.1	3.9 ± 4.7	1.7 ± 2.7	8.9 ± 6.8
Phasic Activity					
REM epochs with eye movements (number of)	77.2 ± 6.5	59.3 ± 22.4	71.3 ± 18.8	59.6 ± 14.2	44.4 ± 25.6
Phasic REM (% REM sleep with eye movements)	70.7 ± 7.8	72.8 ± 14.9	73.0 ± 9.9	64.5 ± 11.3	52.6 ± 18.2

to have significantly less stage 4 sleep, take longer to fall asleep, and spend more time awake during the night in comparison with the control subjects. It should be noted that these patients had received a variety of treatments (and in some instances were still under treatment) including tricyclic antidepressants, electroconvulsive therapy, barbiturates, and other sedatives, all of which may have affected their sleep pattern at the time of the follow-up study (52).

Figure 6 is a schematic presentation of the sleep of one depressed patient on admission to hospital contrasted with his sleep 48 nights later after successful treatment with electroconvulsive therapy.

In a long-term follow-up program, we have now studied 14 former patients who had initially been hospitalized with a diagnosis of unipolar depression (53). We included only those former patients who had returned to a premorbid level of functioning for at least 6 months and had not received any psychoactive drugs for at least 2 months prior to the follow-up study. Each former patient was individually matched by sex and age ($\mp$4 years) with a control subject. Total sleep time was very similar in the two groups. The former patients averaged 391.8 minutes of sleep compared with a mean of 393.4 minutes for the control subjects. However, the formerly depressed patients spent significantly more time in bed ($P = <0.02$), due, in large part, to the greater amount of time it took them to fall asleep. They also had significantly more stage 1 sleep ($P = <0.01$) and significantly less delta wave sleep ($P = <0.02$) than the control subjects. REM sleep was very similar in the two groups. Night-by-night variability was much higher for the formerly depressed group than for the controls.

We have also compared the pretreatment baseline sleep of four drug-free depressed patients on admission to the hospital with their sleep after discharge from the hospital. They were studied at three-month intervals for up to 15 months after being discharged from the hospital. Clinical improvement and discharge from the hospital were associated with changes in several parameters of sleep. There was a significant decrease in the minutes of REM sleep and a significant increase in the percentage of delta wave sleep. In both instances, values tended toward normal levels (54). Other features of their sleep are shown in Table 3.

These studies show that although there is an improvement in the sleep of depressed patients with clinical improvement, the sleep of *some* depressed patients may continue to be significantly different from that found in control subjects.

This finding of a persistent abnormality in the sleep of some recovered depressed patients is compatible with our hypothesis that there is a persistent abnormality in aspects of neurophysiological and biochemical functioning in some depressed patients after clinical recovery (55, 56). There is mounting clinical evidence that, for many patients, depression is not an acute, self-limiting disorder but a relatively chronic condition. For example, we have found that a high percentage of depressed patients are rehospitalized within 2 years (in preparation). An additional number require continuous or recurrent outpatient treatment. A number of biological abnormalities have been shown to persist after clinical recovery in *some* depressed patients (57).

Table 3 Sleep of Four Depressed Patients (Drug Free) Compared with Their Sleep after Discharge from the Hospital (Drug Free)

	Treatment (Hospitalized) (32 Nights)		After Discharge (20 Nights)		
	Mean	S.D.	Mean	S.D.	t
Minutes of					
Actual sleep	359.8	25.1	304.1	40.9	2.170
Wakefulness	48.2	18.5	53.2	43.4	0.229
REM	105.7	11.3	82.5	5.4	3.362[a]
Delta (stages 3, 4)	12.6	13.3	17.8	12.8	1.674
Movement time	5.2	5.4	3.8	2.3	0.463
Percentage of actual sleep					
Stage 1	10.5	4.0	10.5	5.3	0.013
Stage 2	57.2	2.2	55.1	11.2	0.366
REM	29.2	2.3	27.8	4.5	0.689
Delta (stages 3, 4)	3.2	3.8	6.3	5.3	3.130[a]
Other parameters					
Sleep latency (minutes to first spindle)	29.3	17.6	27.1	20.1	0.226
REM latency (minutes to first REM period)	44.6	12.7	49.4	20.8	0.612
Sleep cycle (minutes)	93.5	5.4	96.6	16.5	0.357
Actual sleep (% of TSP)	87.3	3.9	84.3	11.6	0.557
Early morning awakening (minutes awake before 6:00 A.M.)	49.1	67.5	47.2	60.9	0.042

[a] $P = 0.05$, two-tailed *t* test.

Sleep Patterns and Relapse

We have preliminary evidence that the appearance of abnormal features in the sleep of former depressed patients during follow-up studies may indicate an imminent clinical relapse. In the course of our quarterly follow-up of the sleep of 10 former patients (four were drug-free; six were receiving lithium carbonate therapy), there were significant changes in the sleep of four of these people. Three of the four had a clinical relapse shortly thereafter. The change in sleep preceded the clinical change by 2 to 8 weeks. The three people who relapsed had a prior reduction in REM sleep ranging from 15 to 30%. There was also a change in delta wave sleep prior to clinical relapse. However, these changes were not consistent. Two of the three former patients had a marked reduction in delta wave sleep (64% and 90% reduction respectively), whereas the third had a threefold increase in delta wave sleep. Figure 8 illustrates the changes in one of these patients.

If a disturbance in sleep consistently precedes the emergence of symptoms, this would constitute the first evidence for neurophysiological changes *prior* to

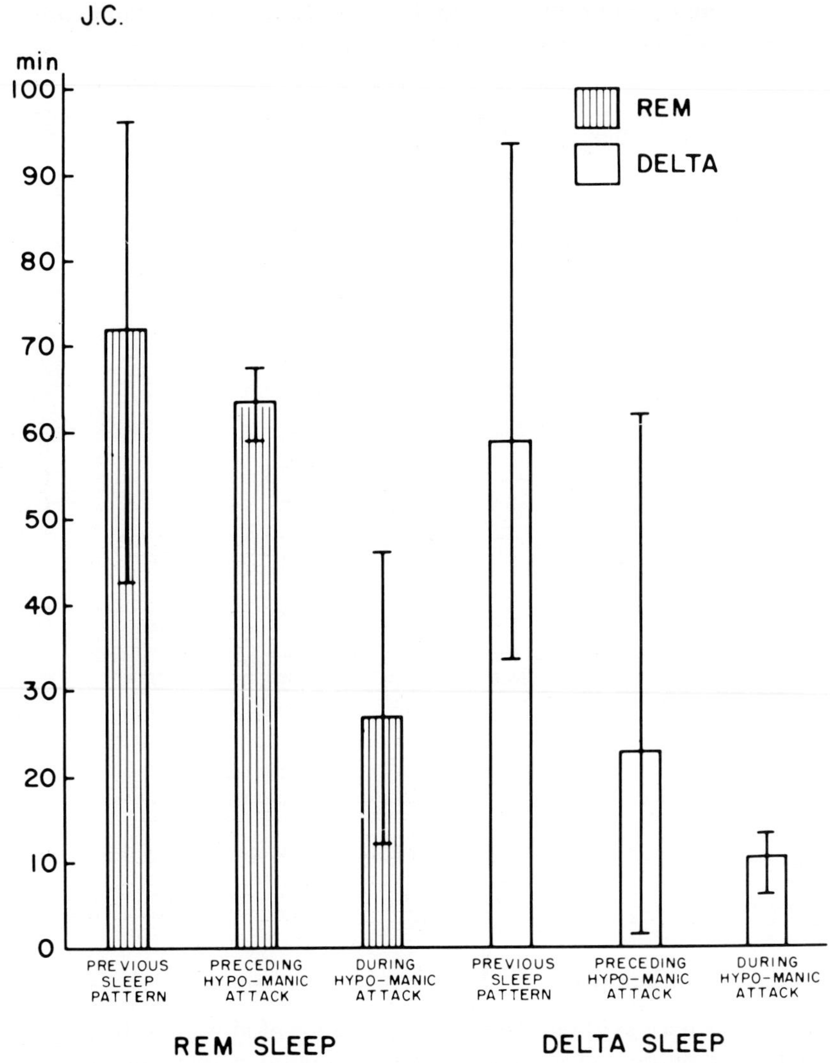

Figure 8. Change in mean levels of REM and delta wave sleep prior to and during a hypomanic attack.

clinical evidence of depression. If future studies were to support this finding, we would be in a position to predict future relapses and to plan clinical intervention. Furthermore, it would be important to try to "normalize" the sleep pattern in these patients to determine whether a recurrence of the illness could be prevented.

The Effects of Antidepressant Drugs on Sleep

The tricyclic antidepressants (amitriptyline, imipramine, desipramine, chlorimipramine, and doxepin) generally produce a significant reduction in REM sleep in both normal subjects (38, 39, 58–61) and depressed patients (62–65). In our study (62) we found a 78% decrease in REM sleep during the first week of administration of 150 to 250 mg/24-hour imipramine to hospitalized depressed patients. REM sleep was nearly abolished during the first few days of drug administration in four of the patients. Thereafter, there was some increase in REM sleep. A trend analysis indicated a significant linear trend for percentage REM sleep across drug nights ($f = 6.812$; $P = <0.05$), suggesting that REM sleep tends to increase with time toward baseline levels in the presence of continued imipramine administration. While the effect of imipramine on REM sleep was attenuated over time, REM time was still significantly reduced during the third week of drug administration (Table 4).

Other parameters of sleep may also be adversely affected, although the evidence is not as consistent across studies. Some investigators have noted some increases in delta wave sleep with relatively small doses of desipramine (61, 65), and amitriptyline (59), to normal subjects, and of imipramine to depressed patients (8). We have found some decrease in delta wave sleep with imipramine, as have Durrigl and others (63) and Ritvo and others (60). Dunleavy and others (66) found an increase in intrasleep restlessness produced by 75 mg of imipramine, desipramine, and chlorimipramine which did *not* diminish with time.

It has been suggested that the therapeutic effects of the antidepressant drugs may be related to the changes produced in sleep (65). Some investigators have specifically suggested that the antidepressant effect of the monoamine oxidase inhibitors is directly associated with their capacity to reduce REM sleep (39, 67–69). Oswald and his colleagues (39, 67, 68) administered 60, 75, or 90 mg of phenelzine to 22 depressed patients and reported that the change in mood was related in time to drug-induced abolition of REM sleep. Similar findings were suggested by Wyatt and others (69). Their patients showed relatively little clinical improvement with treatment until REM sleep was abolished.

A different approach to the problem has been adopted by Vogel and his colleagues (34). They studied the pretreatment sleep of 24 severely depressed patients (minimal Hamilton Depression Score of 25) for 6 to 10 nights, after which the patients were randomly assigned to experimental (REM deprived or control) groups. The patients who were to be REM deprived were awakened at the onset of each REM period for 6 consecutive nights or until they reached 30 awakenings in a single night, whichever came first. They then had one night of uninterrupted sleep, after which the same procedures were repeated. There were several such sequences. Control patients were awakened the same number of times as the experimental group, but always during NREM sleep. During the study period, patients were evaluated for depression using the Hamilton Depression Score and the Global Scale, by raters "blind" as to whether patients were experimental or control subjects. The patients who were deprived of REM sleep showed an improvement in their symptomatology, whereas control subjects remained unchanged. Vogel and others concluded that increased pressure for REM sleep associated with REM deprivation relieves the symptom of depression and may be the mechanism of action of the major antidepressant drugs. Recently it has been claimed that total sleep deprivation for one night is highly effective in alleviating depression (70). Further studies are required to fully evaluate these claims.

Table 4 Effects of Imipramine on Sleep

	(Mean Values ± Standard Deviation)		
	Baseline Sleep	First Week of Drug	Third Week of Drug
Minutes of			
Actual sleep	381.0 ± 26.3	368.0 ± 71.6	366.8 ± 44.7
Wakefulness	78.0 ± 34.9	94.7 ± 55.6	75.8 ± 14.4
REM	100.3 ± 19.7	22.7 ± 18.7[b]	46.6 ± 8.1[b]
Delta (stages 3, 4)	13.8 ± 26.9	7.2 ± 12.8	5.9 ± 8.2
Movement time	3.5 ± 0.7	2.2 ± 1.7	2.8 ± 1.7
Percentage of actual sleep			
Stage 1	11.7 ± 3.6	24.4 ± 12.6	14.3 ± 4.6
Stage 2	58.0 ± 6.1	68.3 ± 14.5	70.2 ± 6.1[a]
REM	26.3 ± 4.4	5.6 ± 3.6[c]	12.4 ± 1.0[c]
Delta (stages 3, 4)	3.8 ± 7.5	2.3 ± 4.3	1.9 ± 2.8
Other parameters (minutes)			
Latency to sleep onset (to first spindle)	29.5 ± 13.1	30.9 ± 20.0	27.6 ± 8.7
Latency to REM (to first REM period)	38.4 ± 17.2	196.7 ± 118.9[a]	165.5 ± 53.5[b]
Sleep cycles	94.6 ± 3.8	195.3 ± 98.2	165.1 ± 43.6[a]

[a] $P = 0.05$.
[b] $P = 0.01$.
[c] $P = 0.001$, two-tailed t test. The P value, represented by a difference in relation to baseline sleep.

The Effects of Lithium Carbonate on Sleep

Lithium is being increasingly used in the treatment of acute manic episodes, in the prophylaxis of recurrent depression and mania, and, more controversially, in the treatment of selected depressed patients (71–73). Lithium appears to normalize the sleep pattern of depressed patients by increasing both total sleep time and delta wave sleep and slightly decreasing the relatively elevated amounts of REM sleep. With the decrease in REM produced by lithium, the percent of REM remained within normal range, unlike the lowering effect produced by tricyclic drugs and monoamine oxidase inhibitors (74–77). The relationship appears to be dose related, as there is a significant positive correlation between plasma lithium levels and delta wave sleep and a significant negative correlation between plasma lithium and REM sleep (75).

These effects extend into remission although there may be some alteration over time. We compared the sleep of eight recovered depressed patients who continued to take lithium after discharge from the hospital with the sleep of 19 hospitalized untreated depressed patients and 12 age-matched control subjects. The outpatients who were receiving lithium had significantly more delta wave sleep ($P = <0.05$), an increased latency to the first REM period of the night ($P = <0.02$), and significant decreases in wakefulness, percentage stage 1, and REM sleep ($P = <0.05$) than the hospitalized patients. All of the changes which occurred in the lithium outpatients were in the direction of the control subjects. There was no significant difference between the lithium outpatients and control subjects on any one of 13 sleep measures. Figure 9 provides a comparison between mean values of delta wave and REM sleep for individual lithium outpatients and control subjects. It remains to be determined whether the improvement in sleep is linked with prophylactic effects of lithium carbonate.

Sleep Studies of Manic Patients

Only a small number of manic or hypomanic patients have been studied in the sleep laboratory (4, 78, 79). While their sleep may be severely disturbed, this is not always the case. Thus one manic patient we studied averaged only 105 minutes of sleep per night during 7 consecutive nights of sleep recording (Figure 10). In contrast, several other hypomanic and manic patients studied in our laboratory had relatively normal amounts of sleep (Table 5). It is noteworthy that these patients had a relatively normal mean percentage REM sleep even when their actual sleep time was very reduced. It is noteworthy that there are many similarities in the sleep changes seen in the manic patients and the depressed patients. This is reflected in a comparison of the sleep of a manic and an agitated depressed patient outlined in Table 6. We have elsewhere discussed the need to reevaluate the relationship between depression and mania and pointed out the relatively large number of physiological, biochemical, or behavioral features which these two syndromes share (47, 55–57).

In summary, the changes in the sleep of depressed patients, while marked, are extremely variable, both between subjects and in the same person from

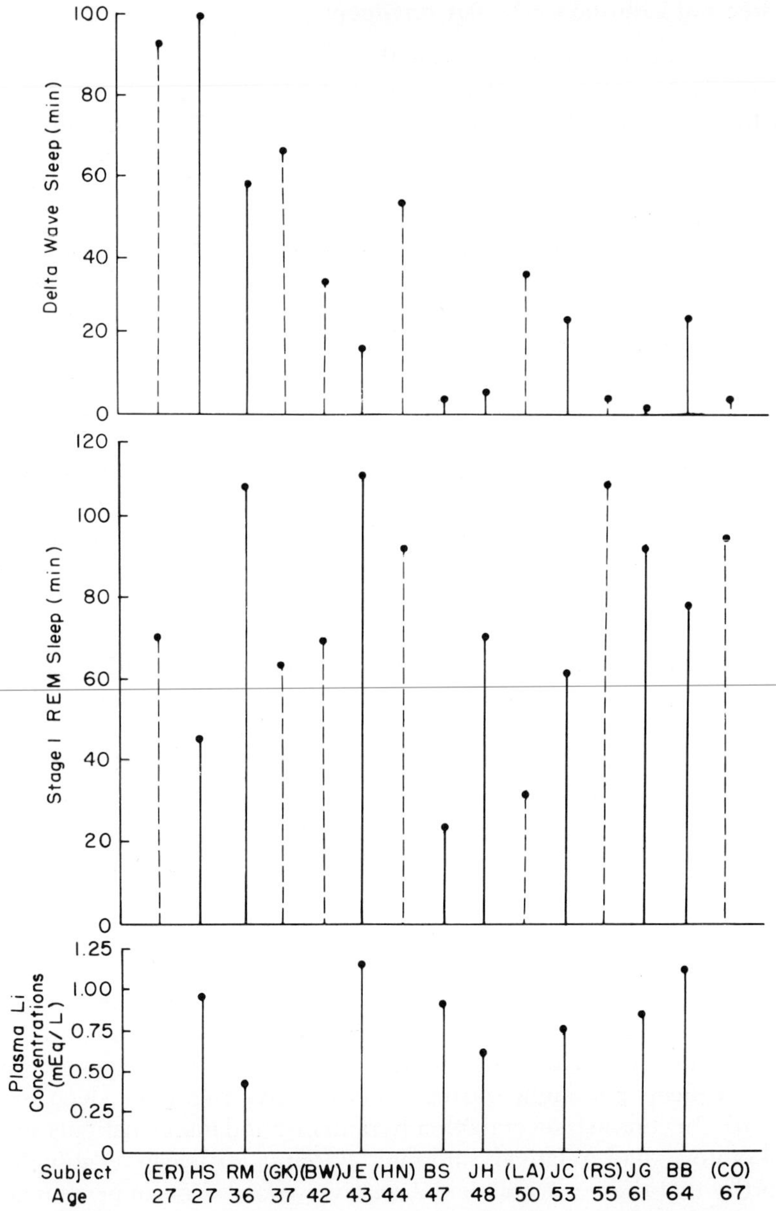

Figure 9. The mean minutes of delta wave sleep (stages 3 and 4) and stage 1 REM sleep during the last recording period (3 to 5 recording nights) for 8 lithium outpatients compared with similarly aged control subjects. The initials of the control subjects are given in parentheses ( ). The last recording period represents 7 to 35 months of lithium administration. HS had received 25 months of lithium therapy; RM, 20 months; JE, 19 months; BS, 31 months; JH, 7 months; JC, 16 months; JG, 7 months; BB, 35 months.

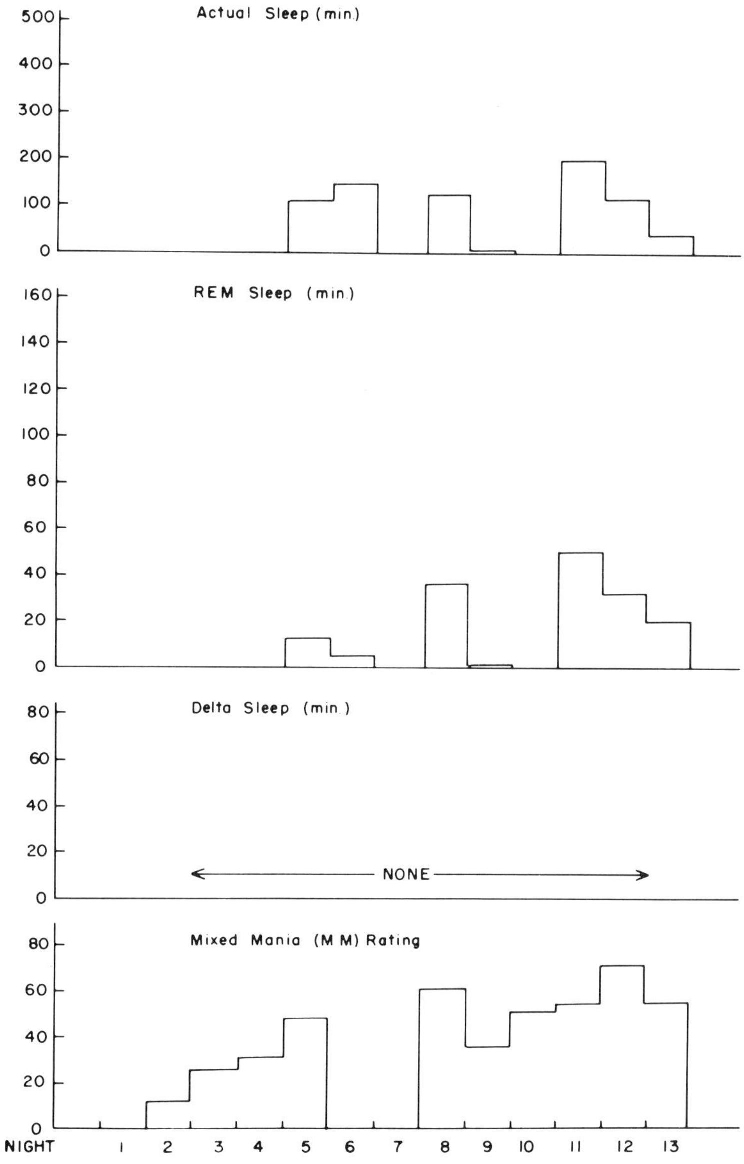

SLEEP OF A MANIC (AR) DRUG FREE

Figure 10. Sleep of manic (AR) while drug free. *Note:* Sleep recordings were not possible on nights 7 and 10.

night to night. This is not surprising in view of the fact that the clinical syndrome of depression is a heterogeneous state, and most parameters which have been studied, whether psychological or biological, do vary considerably.

Among the more striking changes are the reduction in slow wave sleep, the fragmentation of the normal night's sleep patterns, and the variable disruption of REM sleep with some evidence of an increased pressure to achieve this stage of sleep.

Table 5 The Sleep of Manic Patients (Drug Free) Compared to Eight Older Controls

	Manics				Hypomanic				8 Controls	
	S_1 (37 years) 7 Nights		S_2 (51 years) 3 Nights		S_3 (46 years) 4 Nights		S_4 (36 years) 10 Nights		(47.9 years) 26 Nights	
	Mean	S.D.	Mean	S.D.	Mean	S.D.	Mean	S.D.	Mean	S.D.
Minutes of										
Actual sleep	105.4 ±	67.0[c]	376.7 ±	65.5	373.6 ±	35.0	378.6 ±	30.7	358.2 ±	42.8
Wakefulness	100.1 ±	103.7	25.0 ±	38.1	61.1 ±	30.6	23.2 ±	21.6	49.9 ±	53.6
Delta (stages 3, 4)	0.0 ±	0.0[c]	34.7 ±	10.0	2.6 ±	1.3[a]	53.2 ±	21.7	35.1 ±	28.9
Stage 1 REM sleep	26.4 ±	16.9[c]	85.2 ±	14.9	80.1 ±	12.7	124.2 ±	18.7[c]	82.0 ±	28.4
Movement time	3.3 ±	2.9	8.7 ±	2.5[b]	6.9 ±	3.1[a]	10.0 ±	5.3[c]	3.0 ±	2.8
Percentage of actual sleep										
Stage 1	3.3 ±	4.9	16.7 ±	0.9	7.1 ±	2.9	1.4 ±	0.9[b]	9.1 ±	7.3
Stage 2	70.5 ±	17.9	63.3 ±	1.2	70.8 ±	1.2[b]	50.8 ±	7.4[a]	58.3 ±	8.2
Delta (stages 3, 4)	0.0 ±	0.0[b]	9.0 ±	1.6	0.7 ±	0.3[a]	13.9 ±	5.2	9.6 ±	7.6
Stage 1 REM sleep	25.4 ±	17.3	22.4 ±	0.7	21.4 ±	2.5	32.9 ±	4.6[c]	22.8 ±	7.0
Other sleep measures										
Latency to REM (minutes from stage 2)	32.4 ±	33.1[a]	20.3 ±	33.5[a]	60.4 ±	13.9	74.0 ±	25.3	74.4 ±	38.8
Latency to sleep onset (stage 2)	52.0 ±	49.4[b]	8.2 ±	10.8	5.8 ±	2.7	20.8 ±	14.3	17.8 ±	19.8
Early morning awakening (minutes awake prior to 6:00 A.M.)	181.1 ±	75.7[c]	0.5 ±	9.0	0.0 ±	0.0	2.7 ±	8.5	10.8 ±	21.2
Sleep cycle										
Length	56.5 ±	24.7[c]	76.2 ±	11.4	69.8 ±	8.5[b]	93.5 ±	9.1	90.3 ±	13.8
Number	2.0 ±	0.9[c]	4.6 ±	0.6[a]	5.3 ±	0.9[b]	3.8 ±	0.4	3.4 ±	0.8
Actual sleep/total sleep period (%)	53.2 ±	38.2[a]	91.4 ±	10.3	84.6 ±	7.2	94.1 ±	5.1	87.0 ±	38.8

Note: Phasic integrated activity (PIP) was not recorded on all study nights. *a*, *b*, *c* indicate significant difference between subject and older controls at $p = <0.05$, 0.01, and 0.001 levels of significance, two-tailed *t* test, independent measures.

Table 6 Comparison of the Sleep of the Manic Patient with the Sleep of an Agitated, Psychotic Depressed Patient (Drug Free)

	Manic S_1 (7 Nights)		Depressed S_2 (4 Nights)		
	Mean	S.D.	Mean	S.D.	t
Minutes of					
Actual sleep	105.4	67.0	196.0	113.3	1.695
Wakefulness	100.1	103.7	142.0	104.5	0.643
REM	26.4	16.9	71.8	49.3	2.130
Delta (stages 3, 4)	0.0	0.0	0.4	0.5	2.024
Movement time	3.3	2.9	8.3	4.2	2.248
Percentage of actual sleep					
Stage 1	3.3	4.9	14.7	7.4	2.962[a]
Stage 2	70.5	17.9	47.9	11.6	2.211
REM	25.4	17.3	32.0	15.5	0.614
Delta (stages 3, 4)	0.0	0.0	0.5	0.4	3.162[a]
Other Parameters					
Sleep latency (minutes to first spindle)	52.0	49.4	14.3	11.1	1.473
REM latency (minutes to first REM period)	32.4	33.1	49.3	42.7	0.708
Sleep cycle (minutes)	56.5	24.7	56.7	20.7	0.013
Actual sleep (% of TSP)	53.2	38.2	52.6	26.0	0.028
Early morning awakening (minutes awake before 6:00 A.M.)	181.1	75.7	24.1	20.2	3.980[b]

[a]$P = <0.05$; [b]$P = <0.01$; two-tailed t test; independent measures.

Most drugs which alter mood also affect sleep. To date, only lithium appears to have the effect of "normalizing" sleep in depressed patients. The significance of this awaits further evaluation.

Finally, some interesting similarities in the sleep changes of manic and depressed patients, together with other evidence, point to the need to reevaluate the relationship between depression and mania.

Acknowledgment

Preparation of this manuscript and some of the work summarized herein was supported by NIMH grants 1 RO1 MH17551-03, MH-06633, and by Research Funds from the Veterans Administration.

References

1. Jones HS, Oswald I: Two cases of healthy insomnia. *Electroencephalogr Clin Neurophysiol* **24**:378–380, 1968.

2. Green WJ, Stajduhar PP: The effect of ECT on the sleep-dream cycle in a psychotic depression. *J Nerv Ment Dis* **143**:123–134, 1966.
3. Gresham S, Agnew H, Williams R: The sleep of depressed patients: An EEG and eye movement study. *Arch Gen Psychiatr* **12**:503–507, 1965.
4. Hartmann E: Longitudinal studies of sleep and dream patterns in manic-depressive patients. *Arch Gen Psychiatr* **19**:312–329, 1968b.
5. Hawkins DR, Mendels J: Sleep disturbance in depressive syndromes. *Am J Psychiatr* **123**:682–690, 1966.
6. Hawkins DR, Mendels J: The psychopathology and psychophysiology of sleep, in *Biological Psychiatry.* Edited by Mendels J, New York, Wiley, 1973, pp. 297–330.
7. Hawkins DR, Mendels J, Scott J, and others: The psychophysiology of sleep in psychotic depression: A longitudinal study. *Psychosom Med* **29**:329–344, 1967.
8. Lowry FH, Clegborn JM, McClure DJ: Sleep patterns in depression: Longitudinal study of six patients and brief review of literature. *J Nerv Ment Dis* **153**:10–26, 1971.
9. Mendels J, Hawkins DR: Sleep and depression: A controlled EEG study. *Arch Gen Psychiatr* **16**:344–354, 1967a.
10. Mendels J, Hawkins DR: Sleep and depression. A follow-up study. *Arch Gen Psychiatr* **16**:536–542, 1967b.
11. Mendels J, Hawkins DR: Studies of psychophysiology of sleep in depression. *Ment Hyg* **51**:501–510, 1967c.
12. Mendels J, Hawkins DR: Sleep and depression: Further considerations. *Arch Gen Psychiatr* **19**:445–452, 1968.
13. Mendels J, Hawkins DR: Sleep and depression: IV. Longitudinal studies. *J Nerv Ment Dis* **153**:251–272, 1971b.
14. Mendels J, Hawkins DR: Sleep studies in depression, in *Recent Advances in the Psychobiology of the Depressive Illnesses.* Edited by Williams TA, Katz MM, Shields JA, Washington, DC, United States Government Printing Office, 1972, pp. 147–170.
15. Oswald I, Berger RJ, Jarmillo RA, and others: Melancholia and barbiturates: Controlled EEG, body and eye movement study of sleep. *Br J Psychiatr* **109**:66–78, 1963.
16. Snyder F: Electrographic studies of sleep in depression, in *Computers and Electronic Devices in Psychiatry.* Edited by Kline NS, Laske E, New York, Grune & Stratton, 1968, pp. 272–303.
17. Snyder F: Sleep disturbance in relation to acute psychosis, in *Sleep: Physiology and Pathology.* Edited by Kales A, Philadelphia, JB Lippincott Co, 1969b, pp. 170–182.
18. Zung WWK, Wilson WP, Dodson WE: Effect of depressive disorders on sleep EEG responses. *Arch Gen Psychiatr* **10**:439–445, 1964.
19. Dement WC, Kleitman N: Cyclic variations in EEG during sleep and their relation to eye movements, body motility and dreaming. *Electroencephalogr Clin Neurophysiol* **9**:673–690, 1957.
20. Snyder F: Toward an evolutionary theory of dreaming. *Am J Psychiatr* **123**:121–136, 1966.
21. Snyder F: Sleep and REM as biological enigmas, in *Physiology and Pathology.* Edited by Kales A, Philadelphia, JB Lippincott Co, 1969a, pp. 266–280.
22. Koella WP: *Sleep: Its Nature and Physiological Organization.* Springfield, Charles C Thomas, 1967.
23. Oswald I, Taylor AM, Treisman M: Discriminative responses to stimulation during human sleep. *Brain* **83**:440–453, 1960.

24. Williams HL, Morlock HC Jr, Morlock JV: Instrumental behavior during sleep. *Psychophysiology* **2**:208–216, 1966.
25. Agnew HW, Webb WB, Williams RL: Comparison of stage 4 and 1—REM sleep deprivation. *Percept Mot Skills* **24**:851–858, 1967.
26. Berger RJ, Oswald I: Effects of sleep deprivation on behaviour, subsequent sleep and dreaming. *J Ment Sci* **108**:457–465, 1962.
27. Dement WC: Effect of dream deprivation. *Science* **131**:1705–1707, 1960.
28. Dement WC: Recent studies on the biological role of rapid eye movement sleep. *Am J Psychiatr* **122**:404–408, 1965.
29. Hartmann E: *The Biology of Dreaming.* Springfield, Charles C. Thomas, 1967.
30. Jouvet M: Paradoxical sleep: A study of its nature and mechanisms, in *Sleep Mechanism: Progress in Brain Research.* Edited by Akert K, Bally C, Schade JP, New York, Elsevier, 1965, Vol. 18, pp. 20–62.
31. Diaz-Guerrero R, Gottlieb JS, Knott JR: The sleep of patients with manic-depressive psychosis, depressive type: An electroencephalographic study. *Psychosom Med* **8**:399–404, 1946.
32. Mendels J, Chernik DA: REM sleep and depression, in *Sleep Research.* Edited by Chase MH, Stern WC, Walter PL, Los Angeles, Brain Information Service, Brain Research Institute, 1972, Vol. 1, p. 141 (abstract).
33. Vogel GW, Traub AC, Ben-Horin P, and others: REM deprivation: II. The effects on depressed patients. *Arch Gen Psychiatr* **18**:301-312, 1968.
34. Vogel GW, Thompson FC Jr, Thurmond A, and others: The effect of REM deprivation on depression. *Psychosom Med* **14**:104–107, 1973.
35. Hartmann E, Verdone P, Snyder F: Longitudinal studies on sleep and dreaming patterns in psychiatric patients. *J Nerv Ment Dis* **142**:117–126, 1966.
36. Hartmann E: Mania, depression and sleep, in *Sleep Physiology and Pathology.* Edited by Kales A, Philadelphia, JB Lippincott Co, 1969, pp. 183–191.
37. Lewis SA, Oswald I: Overdose of tricyclic antidepressants and deductions concerning their cerebral action. *Br J Psychiatr* **115**:1403–1410, 1969.
38. Hartmann E: The effect of four drugs on sleep patterns in man. *Psychopharmacologia* **12**:346–353, 1968a.
39. Dunleavy DLF: Monoamine oxidase inhibitors, sleep and mood, in *The Nature of Sleep.* Edited by Jovanovic UJ, Stuttgart, Gustav Fischer Verlag, 1973, pp. 288–290.
40. Kales A, Malmstrom EJ, Kee HK, and others: Effects of hypnotics on sleep patterns, dreaming, and mood state: Laboratory and home studies. *Biol Psychiatr* **1**:235–241, 1969.
41. Bunney WE Jr, Goodwin FK, Murphy DL: The "switch process" in manic-depressive illness: II. Relationship to catecholamines, REM sleep and drugs. *Arch Gen Psychiatr* **27**:304–309, 1972.
42. Hauri P, Hawkins DR: Phasic REM, depression, and the relationship between sleeping and waking. *Arch Gen Psychiatr* **25**:56–63, 1971.
43. Kupfer DJ, Foster FG: Interval between onset of sleep and rapid-eye-movement sleep as an indicator of depression. *Lancet* **1**:684–686, 1972.
44. Snyder F: NIH studies of EEG sleep in affective illness, in *Recent Advances in the Psychobiology of the Depressive Illnesses.* Edited by Williams TA, Katz MM, Shields JA, Washington, DC, United States Government Printing Office, 1972, pp.171–192.
45. Hauri P, Hawkins DR: Individual differences in the sleep of depression, in *The Nature of Sleep.* Edited by Jovanovic UJ, Stuttgart, Gustav Fischer Verlag, 1973, pp. 193–197.

46. Wyatt RJ: The serotonin-catecholamine-dream bicycle: A clinical study. *Biol Psychiatr* **5**:33–64, 1972.
47. Mendels J, Frazer A, Fitzgerald RG, and others: Biogenic amine metabolites in cerebrospinal fluid of depressed and manic patients. *Science* **175**:1380–1382, 1972.
48. Mendels J: Lithium and depression, in *Lithium: Its Role in Psychiatric Research and Treatment.* Edited by Gershon S, Shopsin B, New York, Raven Press, 1973a, pp. 253–267.
49. Dunner DL, Goodwin FK, Gershon ES, and others: Excretion of 17-OHCS in unipolar and bipolar depressed patients. *Arch Gen Psychiatr* **26**:360–363, 1972.
50. Detre T, Himmelhoch J, Swartzberg M: Hypersomnia and manic-depressive disease. *Am J Psychiatr* **128**:1303–1305, 1972.
51. Kupfer DJ, Himmelhoch JM, Swartzberg M, and others: Hypersomnia in manic-depressive disease (a preliminary report). *Dis Nerv Syst* **33**:720–724, 1972.
52. Mendels J, Van de Castle RL, Hawkins DR: Electroconvulsive therapy and sleep, in *Psychobiology of Convulsive Therapy.* Edited by Fink M, Kety S, McGaugh J, Washington, DC, VH Winston and Sons, 1974, pp. 41–46.
53. Hauri P, Chernik DA, Hawkins D, and others: Sleep of depressed patients in remission. *Proceedings: 81st Annual Convention American Psychological Association,* 1973, pp.447–448.
54. Mendels J, Chernik DA: Psychophysiological studies of sleep of depressed patients: An overview, in *Annual Conference on Current Concerns in Clinical Psychology.* Edited by Fowles CD, to be published, 1974.
55. Whybrow PC, Mendels J: Toward a biology of depression: Some suggestions from neurophysiology. *Am J Psychiatr* **125**:1491–1500, 1969.
56. Mendels J: *Concepts of Depression.* New York, Wiley, 1970.
57. Mendels J: Biological aspects of affective illness, in *American Handbook of Psychiatry.* Edited by Arieti S, New York, Basic Books, 1974, pp. 448–479.
58. Brezinova V, Oswald I, Dunleavy DLF, and others: Chronic studies of tricyclic drugs, in *The Nature of Sleep.* Edited by Jovanovic UJ, Stuttgart, Gustav Fischer Verlag, 1973, pp. 87–89.
59. Hartmann E, Cravens J, Auchincloss S, and others: Long term drug effects on human sleep: Reserpine, amitriptyline, chlorpromazine, chloral hydrate, chlordiazepoxide and placebo, in *Sleep Research.* Edited by Chase MH, Stern WC, Walter PL, Los Angeles, Brain Information Service, Brain Research Institute, 1972, Vol. 1, pp. 52 (abstract).
60. Ritvo ER, Ornitz EM, LaFranchi S, and others: Effects of imipramine on the sleep-dream cycle: An EEG study in boys. *Electroencephalogr Clin Neurophysiol* **22**:465–468, 1967.
61. Zung WWK: Antidepressant drugs and sleep. *J Exp Med Surg* **27**:124–137, 1969a.
62. Chernik DA, Mendels J, Schless A: The chronic effects of imipramine on REM sleep and REM-associated events. Paper presented at the Annual Meeting of the Association for the Psychophysiological Study of Sleep, San Diego, May 3–6, 1973.
63. Durrigl V, Rogina V, Stojanovic V, and others: Sleep of depressed patients under the influence of antidepressive drugs—A study of two substances, in *The Nature of Sleep.* Edited by Jovanovic UJ, Stuttgart, Gustav Fischer Verlag, 1973, pp. 203–208.
64. Toyoda J: The effects of chlorpromazine and imipramine on the human nocturnal sleep electroencephalogram. *Folia Psychiatr Neurol Jap* **18**:198–221, 1964.
65. Zung WWK: Effect of antidepressant drugs on sleeping and dreaming: III. On the depressed patient. *Biol Psychiatr* **1**:283–287, 1969b.

66. Dunleavy DLF, Brezinova IA, Maclean AW, and others: Changes during weeks in effects of tricyclic drugs on the human sleeping brain. *Br J Psychiatr* **120**:663–672, 1972.
67. Akindele MO, Evans JI, Oswald I: Mono-amine oxidase inhibitors, sleep and mood. *Electroencephalogr Clin Neurophysiol* **29**:27–56, 1970.
68. Dunleavy DLF, Oswald I: Phenelzine, mood response, and sleep. *Arch Gen Psychiatr* **28**:353–356, 1973.
69. Wyatt RJ, Fram DH, Kupfer DJ, and others: Total prolonged drug-induced REM sleep suppression in anxious-depressed patients. *Arch Gen Psychiatr* **24**:145–155, 1971.
70. Pflug B, Tolle R: Disturbance of the 24-hour rhythm in endogenous depression, and the treatment of endogenous depression by sleep deprivation. *Int Pharmacopsychiatr* **6**:187–196, 1971.
71. Mendels J, Secunda SK: *Lithium and Medicine.* New York, Gordon & Breach, 1972.
72. Mendels J: The heterogeneity of depression. *Psychopharmacol Bull* **9**:62–64, 1973b.
73. Schou M: Lithium in psychiatric therapy and prophylaxis. *J Psychiatr Res* **6**:67–95, 1968.
74. Chernik DA, Cochrane C, Mendels J: The effects of lithium carbonate on sleep. *J Psychiatr Res,* **10**:133-146, 1974.
75. Chernik DA, Mendels J: Longitudinal study of the effects of lithium carbonate on the sleep of hospitalized depressed patients. *Biol Psychiatr,* in press, 1974.
76. Kupfer DJ, Wyatt RJ, Greenspan K, and others: Lithium carbonate and sleep in affective illness. *Arch Gen Psychiatr* **23**:35–40, 1970.
77. Mendels J, Chernik DA: The effect of lithium carbonate on the sleep of depressed patients. *Int Pharmacopsychiatr* **8**:184–192, 1973.
78. Chernik DA, Mendels J: The sleep of the manic, in *Sleep Research.* Edited by Chase MH, Stern WC, Walter PL, Los Angeles, Brain Information Service, Brain Research Institute, 1972, Vol. 1, pp. 131 (abstract).
79. Mendels J, Hawkins DR: Longitudinal sleep study in hypomania. *Arch Gen Psychiatr* **25**:274–277, 1971a.

Seventeen

Genetic Studies of Affective Disorders

Remi Cadoret, M. D.
George Winokur, M.D.

In genetics it has been often observed that extremely common conditions often prove to be heterogeneous with several different genetic causes. This seems to be true of affective disorder, which is an extremely common psychiatric condition as judged from studies of population prevalence. For example, Helgason reported a life expectancy for affective disorder of 5.2% for men and 8.3% for women in an Icelandic population (1). Some idea of the diversity and heterogeneity in affective disorders may be had from considering the various terms used in describing different kinds of depression in the past such as neurotic, psychotic depression, agitated depression, menopausal or involutional depression, exogenous depression, and endogenous depression. Although the bases of these classifications are varied and involve in some instances considerations of etiology and in others description of the course of illness or time of onset in life, they nevertheless reflect the considerable heterogeneity present in affective disorder.

Recent progress in genetic and family studies of affective disorder has mainly occurred as a result of the recognition of this heterogeneity . Older and classical studies of manic-depressive disease and involutional melancholia show that affective disorder tended to run in families: Given an individual with an affective disorder the increased incidence of affective disorder in relatives was higher than in the general population; and furthermore, in such families other psychiatric conditions such as schizophrenia usually were not increased (2, 3). These studies, of course, did not separate the effects of heredity from environmental factors. Accordingly the other classical approach to attempt to control environmental factors was used: It is possible to estimate the genetic component of inheritance more exactly in twin studies by comparing the incidence of affective disorder in co-twins of monozygotic and dizygotic pairs. Over the years a number of studies have been reported and summarized in reviews (4, 5). Generally, monozygotic pairs have been found to have a higher concordance rate for affective disorder than dizygotic pairs. This has been true when the control of same sexed dizygotic pairs has been used. For example, Price, in reporting concordance for manic-depressive psychosis in seven twin investigations, summarized the findings as follows: 68% of the monozygotic pairs were concordant for affective disorder in contrast to only 23% of the same sexed dizygotic pairs (4). Thus there is evidence from twin studies for a genetic component in affective disorders. However, because of limitations in the twin investigation method, this line of evidence cannot be considered absolute proof for a genetic component. More direct evidence of a genetic component is much more difficult to obtain for affective disorders. At the present time there are no studies of children reared apart from their parents, an approach which has netted positive results in schizophrenia and antisocial personality (6, 7). However, there are genetic methods of demonstrating a genetic etiology. One of these is the use of linkage, in which known genetic markers are used to follow other traits. When these other traits are located on the same chromosome and a short distance from the marker gene so that crossover does not occur too often, it is possible to follow the trait through several generations or study it in sibships, and from its correlation with the marker gene to demonstrate a genetic etiology. This approach has recently been used in one kind of affective disorder: bipolar or manic-depressive illness. This brings us back again to the question of heterogeneity, since it is quite likely that if affective disorder is heterogeneous there may be a number of separate and distinct and different genetic mechanisms contributing to each of the conditions, and so a necessary step in elucidating genetic mechanisms would involve starting with homogeneous groups.

Clinical studies of patients and their families led Karl Leonhard to propose two kinds of affective disorder: a monopolar and a bipolar (8). By monopolar he meant illnesses characterized by a swing of mood in only one direction. Bipolar illnesses, in contrast, were characterized by swings of mood from one extreme to the other, varying from depression to mania. In bipolar illness not only could different episodes be characterized by a single extreme mood swing (manic one episode, depressive the next), but also within the course of one single episode it was possible to note both these extremes of mood. In studying the families of monopolar and bipolar patients, Leonhard found that there was a higher incidence of psychosis in families of bipolar patients than of monopolar. Time and geography have contributed to changes of the concept of monopolar and bipolar. In North America and the United Kingdom the term unipolar has been widely used in place of monopolar. Bipolar has come to mean an affective disorder in which mania occurs. Unipolar to some investigators has meant individuals with three or more depressive episodes (9); to others, it has meant individuals with one or more episodes of depression *without* mania (10). Despite these differences in definition which seem to be minor in nature, and do not do violence to Leonhard's original concept, there have been a number of replications of the finding that a higher number of bipolar families are positive for psychosis (usually affective disorder). Table 1

Table 1 Incidence of Psychosis in One or More Relatives of Unipolar and Bipolar Probands

	Bipolar Probands		Unipolar Probands	
Source of Data (Ref. no.)	Number of Probands	Percentage of Affected Families	Number of Probands	Percentage of Affected Families
11	201	29.9	324	19.4
12	51	68.6	89	40.5
8	238	39.9	288	25.7
13	84	61.9	78	52.5
14	89	52.0	100	26.0
15	19	53.0[a]	139	26.0

[a]Represents number of families with primary affective disorder.

(8, 11–15) shows the results of a number of such investigations. Further studies of individual relatives of these patients have shown an increased risk for affective illness in both parents and sibs of bipolar probands compared to unipolar (16). These findings argue for heterogeneity not only on clinical grounds but also on genetic grounds. Further evidence for genetic heterogeneity between bipolar and unipolar illness was found in a different approach by Winokur and Clayton (17). These investigators studied a group of 426 probands diagnosed as having a primary affective disorder; that is, an illness defined as a depressive or manic syndrome which occurred without a previous history of another psychiatric illness. From this heterogeneous group of affective disorders (some individuals were manic, others depressed) they separated 112 probands who had a two-generation history of affective disorder suggestive of a dominant gene transmission (that is, a parent or child was also affected). They compared this group of 112 probands with another group of 129 patients who had no parent or child with affective disorder. They found one remarkable clinical difference between the probands in these two family groups: In the two-generation positive family history 14% of the probands were manic at the time of admission compared to only 3% of the negative family history group—statistically a very highly significant difference. This is further evidence that patients with mania have a pattern of inheritance different from that of patients without mania. Again, as with Leonhard's and other studies, it appeared that more bipolar relatives were ill with affective disorder. Thus these data are consistent with at least two groups of affective disorder: a bipolar one characterized by patients with mania (and depression) and an increased family risk of psychosis or affective disorder, and a unipolar one characterized by depressive illness and less family risk of psychosis. Further genetic evidence for a division of affective disorders into unipolar and bipolar types comes from the studies of Angst and of Perris (18). These two independently conducted family studies reported that the incidence of bipolar illness among relatives of bipolar probands was much higher than among relatives of unipolar probands. A still different line of evidence using a classical approach to genetics has netted further evidence of a unipolar-bipolar genetic difference. Zerbin-Rudin reported a series of twins gathered from a study of case reports in literature (5). The results of this study are shown in Table 2, where it can be seen that not only is there a high concordance rate overall for monozygotic twins compared to dizygotic, but there is a high correlation between the illness of one twin and that of the other as regards type, whether unipolar or bipolar. Additional evidence for unipolar-bipolar family differences comes from studies of Leonhard and others where incidence of different personality or temperament types are found to vary from unipolar to bipolar families (19). Bipolar families are described as having more family members with hypomanic personality traits in contrast to unipolar families where depressive personality traits are more prevalent.

Studies on the mode of inheritance have also contributed evidence that unipolar and bipolar illnesses are different. The pattern of inheritance of affective disorder in families of bipolar probands has been shown to be different in a number of important respects from the pattern of inheritance shown in unipolar families. Summarizing data from a number of independent family studies, Cadoret (20) reported the differences shown in Table 3. There are two important points of difference between the unipolar and bipolar patterns of inheritance. The most notable is the pattern shown by children of female probands. The children of bipolar females show an equal incidence of affective disorder between sons and daughters (Table 3, last column, bottom two rows). This contrasts with the marked and significant difference in incidence of affective disorder between sons and daughters of female unipolar probands (Table 3, second column, last two lines). The other important and distinguishing point of difference is the relative dearth of sick father-son pairs (Table 3, column 3, first two lines) in bipolar families. This contrasts with the equal incidence of illness in parents in the unipolar families (first column, lines 1 and 2). Thus in a number of family studies consistently *different patterns* of inheritance are found, in addition to the overall pattern of greater risk for illness in bipolar families which is also evident from Table 3. More direct evidence is available that shows that the inheritance in at least some

Table 2 Concordance of Affective Disorder in Twins (After Zerbin-Rudin, 1968)

	M-Z Twins	D-Z Twins
Both unipolar depressive	22	8
Both bipolar	21	0
One bipolar and one unipolar	7	5
Incompletely concordant or discordant	33	43
Total	83	56

Table 3 Morbid Risk for Affective Disorder in Relatives of Unipolar and Bipolar Probands[a]

	Unipolar		Bipolar	
	Proband Male	Proband Female	Proband Male	Proband Female
Mother	12.2	16.9	26.6	23.3
Father	14.2	11.8	6.8	17.1
Sister	11.7	13.1	18.0	23.4
Brother	15.8	7.4	28.9	6.7
Daughter	8.8	25.5	14.8	23.7
Son	6.6	8.8	15.4	22.9

[a]Data found in Ref. 20.

bipolar families may involve a sex-linked dominant gene. This line of evidence has involved two approaches. In one, four studies show that two traits known to be carried on the X-chromosome, the Xg^a antigen, and red-green color blindness, have assorted with a diathesis for bipolar illness. A summary of these studies is shown in Table 4 in the first four lines. This constitutes fairly direct evidence that in at least some manic-depressive families the diathesis for illness is transmitted on the X-chromosome, apparently as a dominant gene. The other approach to sex-linkage involves studies of father-son pairs. Obviously if a trait is transmitted as an X-linked dominant, there should be no chance for a son to receive the diathesis for illness from his father. At present a number of reports are incompatible with a strictly X-linked transmission in that father-son pairs where both are ill have been found in bipolar families. These studies are shown in the last four lines of Table 4 and the major findings summarized there. However, several series have reported no ill father-son pairs in rather extensive collections of family pedigrees (25, 30). Thus the results seem divided regarding this point. One possible explanation of these inconsistent findings is that in some of the series a diathesis of illness could have come from the maternal side. However, in at least two of the series, those of Von Greiff (26) and Green (29), the maternal side of the family tree was investigated, and ill father-son combinations were still found in families where there did not seem to be a history of illness on the maternal side. We are therefore left with the possibility of further heterogeneity in bipolar affective disorder: one group of families in which the illness may be transmitted as an X-linked dominant and another group of families in which the transmission is different and may involve an autosomal gene or genes.

One other family study finding leads us into the area of evidence for heterogeneity in unipolar depressive families. In the survey of published data on unipolar and bipolar family studies reported by Cadoret (20), differences in risk were broken down by age of onset of illness in the probands for both unipolar and bipolar groups. The only consistent difference to emerge from this breakdown by age was that unipolar families showed higher risk for affective disorder if the proband became ill under the age of 40 than those

Table 4 Evidence For and Against X-Linkage of Bipolar Illness

Study (Ref. No.)		Results Compatible with X-Linked Transmission
21	Red-green color-blindness	In two extensive families, highly significant association of carrier state and color-blindness
22	Xg^a	In three families, 10 children were compatible with sex-linked transmission, one against—a significant difference
23	Xg^a	Seven families studied. Significant association between blood type and illness
24	Red-green color-blindness	Nine families; close linkage found for proton and deuton and illness
25	Analysis of parent-child pairs—both disordered	In 55 families, *no* ill father-son pairs
		Results Incompatible with X-Linked Transmission
26	Analysis of parent-child pairs, both affectively disordered	In 16 male bipolar patients, four had affectively disordered fathers with *no* evidence of affective disturbance on maternal side
27	Analysis of parent-child pairs, both affectively disordered	Seven father-male proband pairs reported where both were ill
28	Analysis of parent-child pairs, both affectively disordered	In 23 bipolar male patients, four had affectively disordered fathers. Possibility for illness on maternal side
29	Analysis of parent-child pairs, both affectively disordered	In 35 bipolar families, four cases of father-son illness. No evidence of affective illness on maternal side

families where the proband became ill over the age of 40. Similar differences related to age were sought in bipolar families but no consistent difference emerged. This finding suggests that unipolar affective disorder may itself be heterogeneous. Further studies of unipolar depressive probands by Winokur and co-workers have confirmed these major findings (31). In a study of 100 unipolar depressions and their families, younger onset probands had more affectively ill first degree relatives, as shown in Table 5. In addition to confirming the difference in risk for affective disorder in relatives of early and late onset probands, the data showed a number of additional points suggesting heterogeneity within the unipolar affective disease category. The kinds of psychiatric conditions found among relatives of early onset probands showed an increase in both sociopathy and alcoholism when compared with relatives of late onset probands. This is shown in the second and third lines of Table 5. Furthermore, sociopathy and especially alcoholism seem to be characteristic of the male relatives. Indeed, the relative lack of depressive illness among the male relatives of early onset probands appears to be compensated for largely by increased risks for these individuals for alcoholism or sociopathy (see line 4 of Table 5). In addition to the differences already noted of more affective disorders in families of early onset and late onset probands and the higher incidence of alcoholism and sociopathy in relatives of early onset probands, there are two additional features of importance in Table 5. The first additional difference of importance is that male probands of late onset appear to have equal numbers of male and female relatives with affective disorder (line 1, columns 3 and 4, 19% versus 12%) in contrast to all of the other groups which show a preponderance of affectively ill female relatives (see remainder of line 1 of Table 5). The group with the largest difference in this contrast appears to be early onset female probands, where a highly significant difference was found between incidence of affective disorder between male and female relatives (see Table 5, columns 5 and 6, line 1, 9% versus 29%). These findings which we have just recounted have been looked for in additional data collected before and since the series described above. In five additional series these results described above have been essentially confirmed (10, 15, 32–34). These series comprise over 1250 probands and their families collected under a variety of circumstances and conditions. Despite the variety of the series the following results have been confirmed: (1) There is more affective disorder in families of early onset than late onset probands (six out of six series showed this difference). (2) There is more alcoholism in male relatives of early onset than late onset probands (six out of six series showed this difference consistently). In most of the other series, little or no information was available about sociopathy so that we are unable to make statements about this condition being a characteristic of early onset probands. (3) The risk for affective disorder in male relatives of late onset male probands is equal to or more than that for female relatives (five out of six series showed this type of difference). (4) The risk for affective disorder in female relatives of early onset female probands is greater than the risk in corresponding male relatives (five out of six series were consistent with the direction of this difference). The consistency of these results argues for heterogeneity in unipolar affective disorder. Winokur (10) has proposed on the basis of these findings that unipolar affective disorder be

Table 5 Risks for Depression, Alcoholism, and Sociopathy in Primary Relatives of 100 Depressive Probands Separated by Sex and Age of Onset (All Sources Data)[a]

	Male Probands[b] Early Onset ($n = 14$)		Male Probands[b] Late Onset ($n = 17$)		Female Probands[b] Early Onset ($n = 40$)		Female Probands[b] Late Onset ($n = 29$)	
	Male Relatives	Female Relatives	Male Relatives	Female Relatives	Male Relatives	Female Relatives	Male Relatives	Female Relatives
Risk for depression	(2/13) 16%	(5/14) 37%	(10/53) 19%	(5/43) 12%	(5/56) 9%	(16/55) 29%	(5/82) 6%	(16/87) 19%
Risk for sociopathy	(1/19) 5%	(0/23) —	(0/62) —	(0/51) —	(8/86) 9%	(3/83) 4%	(0/97) —	(0/102) —
Risk for alcoholism	(3/16) 19%	(1/17) 6%	(1/61) 2%	(0/48) —	(7/72) 10%	(1/66) 2%	(3/93) 3%	(1/94) 1%
Risk for alcoholism or sociopathy	24%	6%	2%	—	19%	6%	3%	1%
Total risk for alcoholism, sociopathy, or depression	40%	43%	21%	12%	28%	34%	9%	20%

[a]Data from Ref. 31.
[b]Within the parenthesis, the numerator of the fraction is the number of family members ill and the denominator is the number at risk. This fraction refers to the morbid risk percentage below.

divided into two kinds of illness—the first, an early onset type in which females suffer predominantly from depression and males from alcoholism. The second group is the late onset depression typified by late onset males where apparently there is little alcoholism in families, a lower overall risk of affective disorder, and equal numbers of male and female relatives affected with affective disorder. This latter group suggests a different type of genetic transmission or even a condition with predominantly environmental etiology, such as organic factors which might reflect aging. Unfortunately, at the present time there are no linkage studies of unipolar affective disorder so that direct proof of a genetic element is lacking. However, we can conclude from the family studies that unipolar affective disorder is likely a heterogeneous condition made up of at least the two subgroups mentioned above. The mode of transmission would appear to be different from that of bipolar. Unipolar and bipolar affective disorders between them account for a large number of the depressions seen in everyday practice. However, on the basis of social antecedents or presence of other psychiatric conditions it is possible to delineate clinically other affective disorders. These have been characterized by Robins and his co-workers (35) as: (1) grief reaction, which may be considered the prototype of reactive depression and (2) secondary depression; that is, a depressive syndrome which in many cases is indistinguishable from unipolar or bipolar depression and which occurs during the course of another pre-existing psychiatric illness such as organic brain syndrome, schizophrenia, anxiety, obsessional neuroses, and so on (35, 36). To date there are few family studies of individuals with grief reaction or secondary depression. One follow-up study of people who had recently lost a spouse showed that there was no difference in incidence of depression in family members and individuals who suffered such a reaction compared to individuals who did not suffer a grief reaction following loss of a close individual (37). One study of secondary depression in alcoholics showed that individuals who became depressed during the course of their alcoholism had no higher incidence in their family of affective disorder than did alcoholics who did not become depressed (38). Thus the role of familial affective disorder in grief reaction and secondary depression is not at all clear. While there is evidence for a definite genetic element in some of the primary conditions such as schizophrenia, antisocial personality, and alcoholism which precede the depression (6, 7, 39), we cannot state whether further genetic diathesis is important in the secondary depression in such individuals.

In summary, familial and other genetic studies have definitely shown that affective disorder can be subdivided into several categories. Most of the evidence supports the validity of division of primary affective disorders into unipolar and bipolar groups. The unipolar group would appear to be a heterogeneous one, and there is some evidence that the bipolar may be heterogeneous in the sense of having several different mechanisms of genetic transmission. Because the genetic information is not as precise as in some diseases, such as Huntington's chorea or color blindness, it is not possible to apply refined methods of probability to assess risks in relatives for purposes of genetic counseling. In both unipolar and bipolar illness, the published risk of illness in children of probands and among other family members is open to considerable methodologic criticism in that underdetermination or underreporting of affective illness is undoubtedly present in most of the published studies and must be taken into account if these risks are to be used as crude guidelines of risks for offspring or other relatives of patient probands. However, it is possible to make some practical use of the familial and genetic information given in this chapter. Division of probands into unipolar and bipolar and early onset and late onset in the case of unipolar patients can lead to certain useful predictions regarding not only the likelihood of affective disorder in relatives, but also risks for other kinds of clinically important conditions occurring in relatives. For example, the knowledge that bipolar probands are extremely likely to have relatives who themselves are bipolar is extremely useful in dealing with illnesses in family members. Prediction of other kinds of illness such as alcoholism or sociopathy in families with early onset unipolar depressive probands can be of considerable clinical value in helping understand the patient and his environment, which may be disturbed by the presence of other psychiatrically ill relatives. Knowledge of the type of familial transmission should certainly be of use to family practitioners and internists who frequently deal with entire families, since families or individuals who are at particularly high risk for some rather important and disabling psychiatric problems such as alcoholism and affective disorder can be pinpointed using this information. For crude purposes of clinical prediction the figures used in Table 5 represent a reasonable approximation of valid risks since relatives in this study were interviewed and therefore little illness in families was overlooked.

References

1. Helgason R: The frequency of depressive states in Iceland as compared with the other Scandinavian countries, in *Depression.* Edited by Kristiansen ES, *Acta Psychiatr Scand,* **162**, Munksgaard, Copenhagen, 1961.
2. Slater E, Cowie V: Affective psychoses, in *The Genetics of Affective Disorders.* London, Oxford University Press, 1971.
3. Zerbin-Rudin E: Manisch-depressive psychosen. Involutions psychosen, in *Humangenetic.* Edited by Becher PE, Bd. V/2, Thieme Verlag, Stuttgart, 1967.
4. Price J: The genetics of depressive behavior, in *Recent Developments in Affective Disorders.* Edited by Coppen A, Walk A, *Br J Psychiatr,* Special Publication 2, 1968.
5. Zerbin-Rudin E: Zur genetik der depressiven Erkrankungen, in *Das Depressive Syndrome.* Edited by Hippius H, Selbach H, Berlin, International Symposium, 1968.
6. Heston LL: Psychiatric disorders in foster-home-reared children of schizophrenic mothers. *Br J Psychiatr* **112**:819–825, 1966.
7. Schulsinger F: Psychopathy: Heredity and environment. *Int J Ment Health* **1**:190–206, 1972.
8. Leonhard K: *Aufteilung der Endogenen Psychosen.* Berlin, Akademie Verlag, 1966.
9. Perris C: A study of bipolar (manic-depressive) and unipolar recurrent depressive psychoses. *Acta Psychiatr Scand, Suppl* **194**:1966
10. Winokur G: The types of affective disorder. *J Nerv Ment Dis* **156**:82–96, 1973.

11. Neele E: *Die Phasischen Psychosen Nach Ihrem Erscheinungs und Erbbild.* Leipzig, Barth, 1949.
12. Kinkelin M: Verlauf und Prognose des Manisch-depressiven Irreseins. *Schweiz Arch Neurol Psychiatr* **73:**100–146, 1954.
13. Asano N: Study of manic-depressive psychosis, in *Clinical Genetics in Psychiatry.* Edited by Mitsuda H, Tokyo, Igaku Shoin, 1967.
14. Dorzab J, Baker M, Cadoret RJ, and others: Depressive disease: Familial psychiatric illness. *Am J Psychiatr* **127:**1128–1133, 1971.
15. Woodruff R, Guze S, Clayton P: Unipolar and bipolar primary affective disorder. *Br J Psychiatr* **119:**33–38, 1971.
16. Cadoret RJ, Winokur G: Genetic principles in the classification of affective illnesses. *Int J Ment Health* **1:**159–175, 1972.
17. Winokur G, Clayton P: Family history studies: I. Two types of affective disorders separated according to genetic and clinical factors, in *Recent Advances in Biological Psychiatry.* Edited by Wortis J, New York, Plenum, 1967.
18. Angst J, Perris C: The nosology of endogenous depression. Comparison of the results of two studies. *Int J Ment Health* **1:**145–158, 1972.
19. Cadoret RJ: Family differences in illness and personality in affective disorder, in *Life History Research in Psychopathology.* Edited by Roff M, Robins L, Pollack M, University of Minnesota Press, 1972.
20. Cadoret RJ, Winokur G, Clayton P: Family history studies: VII. Manic-depressive disease versus depressive disease. *Br J Psychiatr* **116:**625–635, 1970.
21. Reich T, Winokur G: Family history studies: V. The genetics of mania. *Am J Psychiatr* **125:**1358-1369, 1969.
22. Winokur G, Tanna VL: Possible role of x-linked dominant factor in manic-depressive disease. *Dis Nerv Syst* **30:**89–93, 1969.
23. Mendlewicz J, Fleiss J, Fieve RR: X-linked dominant transmission in manic-depressive illness (linkage studies with the Xg^a blood group). Paper presented at 63rd annual meeting, American Psychopathological Association, New York, 1973.
24. Fieve RR, Mendlewicz J, Rainer JD, and others: A dominant x-linked factor in manic-depressive illness: Studies with color blindness. Paper presented at 63rd annual meeting, American Psychopathological Association, New York, 1973.
25. Taylor M, Abrams R: Manic states. A genetic study of early and late onset affective disorders. *Arch Gen Psychiatr* **28:**656–658, 1973.
26. Von Greiff H, McHugh PR, Stokes P: The familial history in sixteen males with bipolar manic-depressive disorder. Paper presented at 63rd annual meeting, American Psychopathological Association, New York, 1973.
27. Perris C: Genetic transmission of depressive psychoses. *Acta Psychiatr Scand, Suppl* **203:**45–52, 1968.
28. Dunner D, Gershon E, Goodwin FK: Heritable factors in the severity of affective illness. Paper read at 123rd annual meeting APA, San Francisco, California, 1970.
29. Green R, Goetze V, Whybrow PC, and others: X-linked transmission of manic-depressive illness. In letters to the editor *JAMA* **223:**1289, 1973.
30. Winokur G, Clayton P, Reich T: *Manic Depressive Disease.* St. Louis, Mosby, 1970.
31. Winokur G, Cadoret RJ, Dorzab J, and others: Depressive disease: A genetic study. *Arch Gen Psychiatr* **24:**135–144, 1971.
32. Marten S, Cadoret RJ, Winokur G, and others: Unipolar depression: A family history study. *Biol Psychiatr* **4:**205–213, 1972.
33. Winokur G: Diagnostic and genetic aspects of affective illness. *Psychiatr Ann,* February, 1973.
34. Winokur G, Morrison J, Clancy J, and others: The Iowa 500: Familial and clinical findings favor two kinds of depressive illness. *Comp Psychiatr* **14:**99–107, 1973.

35. Robins E, Guze SB: Classification of affective disorders: The primary-secondary, the endogenous-reactive, and the neurotic-psychotic concepts, in *Recent Advances in the Psychobiology of the Depressive Illnesses: Proceedings of a Workshop Sponsored by NIMH.* Edited by Katz MM, Shield J Jr, United States Government Printing Office, Washington, DC, 1972.
36. Winokur G: Family history studies: VIII. Secondary depression is alive and well, and. . . . *Dis Nerv Syst* **33**:94–99, 1972.
37. Clayton P, Halikas J, Maurice W, and others: Anticipatory grief and widowhood. *Br J Psychiatr* **122**:47–51, 1973.
38. Cadoret RJ, Winokur G: Depression in alcoholism. *Ann NY Acad Sci,* **223**:34–39, 1974.
39. Goodwin DW, Schulsinger F, Hermansen L, and others: Alcohol problems in adoptees raised apart from alcoholic biological parents. *Arch Gen Psychiatr* **28**:238–243, 1973.

Eighteen

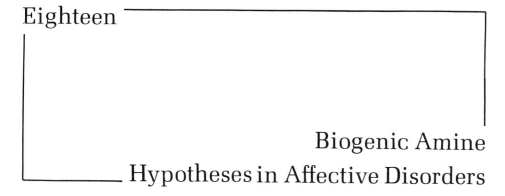

Biogenic Amine Hypotheses in Affective Disorders

Ross J. Baldessarini, M.D.

One of the most widely discussed current ideas concerning a biological basis of the affective disorders is that the metabolism of biogenic amines may be disturbed in these conditions. Several slightly different hypotheses have derived from the theory that biologically active monoamines, known to affect smooth muscle and other peripheral tissues, function in the central nervous system as neurotransmitters at chemical synapses, or otherwise as neurohumors modulating the bioelectrical activity of central neurons which are involved in the regulation of mood and behavior. The amines usually discussed in this context are the catecholamines, dopamine and norepinephrine; and the indoleamine, 5-hydroxytryptamine or serotonin; as well as the quarternary amine, acetylcholine. In their simplest form, the hypotheses would suggest that depression is associated with altered availability of one or another of these amines at functionally important sites referred to as "receptors," and conversely, that mania is associated with an alteration opposite to that present in depression.

The general idea that affective illness might be due to a derangement of the metabolic chemistry of the patient is at least as old as classical antiquity, since the Hippocratic tradition included the notion that melancholia represented a disorder of behavior and feeling associated with an excess of a humor, black bile. With the rise of modern scientific medicine, such ideas have persisted and expanded. Several features of affective illnesses are usually cited as supporting a biological hypothesis. These include the association of somatic symptoms with depression (disturbances of sleep, appetite, gastrointestinal function, sex drive, and sensation) and the diurnal pattern of depression, as well as the frequent association of depression with medical illness, including disorders of the adrenals and other endocrine glands as well as other metabolic diseases.

Furthermore, the growing impression that there may be a familial-genetic aspect of the major affective disorders also supports the existence of a biological component in their etiology. Finally, the apparent lack of association with obvious external "stress factors" in the initiation of many serious depressions or elations—their "endogenicity"—supports the suggestion that they might arise from a dysfunction of the internal milieu.

In addition to these general features of affective disorders suggestive of a biological etiology, the development of effective organic therapies for the disorders with the rise of modern psychopharmacology in recent decades has given more substantial and specific support to hypotheses relating affective disturbances to disorders of neurotransmitter function. In the following discussion, the topics to be reviewed include pertinent aspects of the history of the development of neuropsychopharmacology, the basic biology of central neurohumoral synaptic transmission and its relationship to behavior, and the pharmacology of the treatments useful for mania and depression, followed by a discussion of metabolic studies in patients which bear upon the amine hypotheses.

As early as 1785, Oliver used camphor to treat mania in London, 150 years prior to its use by von Meduna to induce seizures. In 1917 Wagner-Jauregg introduced malaria fever therapy for general paresis as the first specific organic therapy of a neuropsychiatric illness. There were also attempts in Europe in the early decades of this century to use opiates or the recently introduced barbiturates to induce prolonged narcosis for psychiatric disorders, including depression. However, perhaps the most influential development in this century which suggested that a physical treatment could have specific and profound effects on major endogenous or idiopathic psychiatric illnesses was the introduction of the "shock" therapies: first insulin coma, described by Sakel in 1933; then seizures chemically induced by camphor; later pentylenetetrazole introduced by von Meduna in 1934-35; followed soon thereafter by the use of electric shock by Cerletti and Bini in 1937 to 1938. Most of these treatments are now only of historical interest. Although the popularity of electroconvulsive therapies (ECT) has also waned somewhat following the advent of antidepressant drug therapies, modern ECT remains the most effective and a very safe form of treatment of severe depressive illness.

Although Cade of Australia is sometimes overlooked, he should be given historical credit for developing the first effective and specific chemical treatment of a major affective disorder and with opening the modern era of psychopharmacology with the introduction of lithium salts to psychiatric practice in 1949 for the treatment of mania. At about the same time, crude extracts of the Indian snake root (*Rauwolfia serpentina*) were being accepted into the armamentarium of Western medicine, and in 1952 Müller isolated a Rauwolfia alkaloid, reserpine. In the early 1950s it was appreciated that reserpine and its congeners were not only effective antihypertensive agents, but were also useful antipsychotic drugs and were used for a while in competition with phenothiazines in the management of mania and other acute psychoses. Chlorpromazine was developed in 1951 by Charpentier and introduced to clinical medicine soon thereafter (1952) by Laborit and by Delay and Deniker in France. The antipsychotic phenothiazines were soon found to be more useful than reserpine for mania as well as the schizophrenias, and although reserpine has become little more than a laboratory curiosity due to its limited effectiveness and serious side effects, its actions have had an enormous impact on the development of biogenic amine hypotheses for the affective disorders. Thus reserpine has been and continues to be associated with depressive reactions in patients receiving it for hypertension, and it provokes behavioral "depression" in laboratory animals. In 1955 to 1957, Shore and Brodie at the National Institutes of Health in the United States and Carlsson in Sweden found that reserpine and related compounds produce a profound depletion of dopamine, norepinephrine, and serotonin in peripheral tissues and in the brain, thus drawing attention to a relationship between monoamines and behavior.

Until the 1950s there was no effective and specific drug treatment for depression. Cocaine had been known since the late nineteenth century as a stimulant and euphoriant drug, and was the subject of considerable experimentation by Freud, and the amphetamines had been used in medicine since the 1930s. Nevertheless, these and other stimulants are not useful for the treatment of severe depressions. In 1951, iproniazid, a congener of the antituberculous drug isoniazid, was noted to elevate mood in medical patients, and in 1956 Crane reported the successful use of iproniazid in the treatment of depression. In the early 1950s Zeller and later Udenfriend noted the ability of hydrazine compounds such as isoniazid to inhibit the enzyme monoamine oxidase (MAO) which had been described earlier by Blaschko as a major means of inactivating biogenic amines in the tissues of many species. The hepatotoxicity of iproniazid led to its replacement by other hydrazine compounds and several nonhydrazines, all of which had the ability to inhibit MAO and to elevate depressed mood clinically, thus adding to the general impression that there might be an association between amine metabolism and mood disorders. In 1957 Kuhn introduced imipramine, originally developed as a structural analogue of the phenothiazines with hoped-for antipsychotic effects, as a clinically effective antidepressant drug. In 1961, Axelrod and his associates in their studies of amine metabolism pointed out the ability of imipramine to block the uptake of catecholamines into sympathetically innervated tissues. These observations have led to the theory that reuptake into the sympathetic nerve endings following release is a major means of physiologically inactivating catecholamines at the synapse, and that imipramine, and related tricyclic antidepressants, block this function and thus increase availability of catecholamines at the synapse.

Thus by 1957 psychiatry had available at least three kinds of drugs which were effective in mania (lithium salts, reserpine, and the phenothiazines) and two types of antidepressants (the MAO-inhibitors and the tricyclic agents such as imipramine). In addition, it was realized that reserpine and other related amine-depleting agents, as well as the methylated analogues of amino acid precursors of the catecholamines (such as α-methyl-dopa), were sometimes associated with a depressive syndrome in patients receiving the drugs for hypertension. Interestingly, each of these psychiatrically useful therapeutic discoveries occurred by serendipity or lucky accident without the benefit of the now current theories of their effects on the metabolism of central neurotransmitters, and certainly without the benefit of an amine hypothesis of the affective disorders. Clearly, by the late 1950s the time was ripe for specific formulations of such amine hypotheses, which started to appear (1) and to affect clinical metabolic experimentation (2, 3) by 1959, although Weil-Malherbe had begun to study the metabolism of catecholamines and serotonin in the body fluids of psychiatric patients several years earlier (4, 5). Since that time, specific hypotheses have been presented and discussed repeatedly. In this country, particularly by the influence of what might be called the "NIH school" in the field of catecholamine metabolism, the catecholamines and particularly norepinephrine have been emphasized, while many European investigators have been very interested in the indoleamines, particularly serotonin. These hypotheses arose in an era of biochemical optimism of the 1950s and 1960s which accompanied the enormous strides in basic and applied biochemistry, including the description of several genetically determined inborn errors of metabolism, and the impressive empirical successes of the psychopharmaceutical industry. The various amine hypotheses have often been called heuristic, and it is clear that they have kept many investigators busy and have led to the generation of many scientific papers. Sadly, to date they have not led to a coherent basic biological theory of abnormal human behavior, nor have they led to the rational development of more powerful or safer therapies than those available nearly 20 years ago through the benefits of empiricism and simple good luck.

Basic Neurobiology of Central Synaptic Neurotransmission

Why have pharmacologists directed so much effort and attention to the synapse as a likely site of action of drugs used in psychiatry and as a likely site of abnormality in psychiatric illness? There are at least two reasons. First, it is likely that the synapse represents a particularly vulnerable point of neuronal function where relatively selective and specific metabolic derangements or drug mechanisms might occur. In contrast, based on comparison with known instances of organic brain dysfunction, it seems likely that a disturbance of the metabolism of neurons affecting, for example, energy production, impulse conduction, or the structure of the cell or its myelin sheath would lead to a rather generalized dysfunction such as coma or dementia, or might produce a visible histologic neuropathology, none of which occurs in depression or mania. Second, the development of modern neuropharmacology has been heavily influenced by concepts and methods developed for the more classical pharmacology of the peripheral autonomic nervous system that have been very fruitfully applied to studies of the actions of psychopharmaca on the central nervous system (CNS).

The experimentation of most neuropharmacologists has dealt primarily with the metabolism and neurophysiological and behavioral effects of putative central neurotransmitters. For a biologically active small molecule to attain the distinction of "probable neurotransmitter," it must meet several criteria. The substance and enzymes and precursors necessary for its synthesis must be present in neurons at a presynaptic location. The substance must be released by nerve impulses or a reasonable imitation of physiological stimuli. There must be mechanisms available for the inactivation of the transmitter following its release, and its application to postsynaptic cells should reproduce the permeability changes or functional alterations known to occur during natural transmission. Finally, the effects of drugs on the action of the physiologically released or experimentally applied putative neurotransmitter should be similar. Based on their well-established roles in the periphery, norepinephrine and acetylcholine have long been considered likely candidates as mediators of chemical synaptic transmission in the CNS, but more recently several other candidates have also been considered (6). These neurohumors are nearly all aromatic monoamines or aliphatic amino acids such as the excitants glutamic acid and aspartic acid or the depressants glycine and γ-aminobutyric acid (GABA), plus the quarternary aliphatic amine, acetylcholine, the aromatic diamine, histamine, and less well-understood small polypeptides, including "substance P"; fatty acids called prostaglandins may also be involved in the regulation of synaptic function. There are also other amines present in brain tissue, the function of which is obscure; these include several phenylalkylamines such as phenethylamine, tyramine, and octopamine, and one or more indoleamines related to tryptamine, in addition to serotonin. This broad range of candidate neurohumors suggests that it is premature to focus too narrowly upon the catecholamines or serotonin as the only substances of interest in behavioral physiology and dysfunction. Nevertheless, since the current hypotheses regarding the affective illnesses have emphasized the catecholamines and indoleamines, the following discussion deals with them almost exclusively.

The presence of an adrenergic substance in extracts of mammalian brain was discovered by von Euler in 1946, and the regional distribution of norepinephrine in the brain was described in 1953 by Vogt and found to be dissimilar to the distribution of blood vessels, which suggests that catecholamines might arise in neurons intrinsic to the brain. The highest levels of norepinephrine are found in the brainstem and diencephalon, while dopamine, its immediate precursor, occurs independently in cells which do not form norepinephrine, particularly in the neostriatum and portions of the limbic system. In addition, serotonin occurs with a wide distribution, arising from cell bodies localized mainly in the midline raphe nuclei of the midbrain. Biochemical assays of these amines have usually relied on their ability to form fluorescent derivatives, and this property has been very successfully utilized in the development of histofluorescence techniques in Sweden which have permitted the direct visualization of amine-containing perikarya, axons, and nerve terminals. The terminals resemble closely the diffuse networks of fine terminal arborizations with varicosities seen histologically in peripheral sympathetically innervated tissues. These techniques have permitted the mapping of amine-containing pathways in the mammalian CNS, resulting in such schemes as illustrated in Figure 1. Other approaches to histologic localization of amine-containing neurons are also being developed. They include the identification of presynaptic terminals with dense-core vesicles by electron microscopy, and the use of fluorescence-producing labeled antibodies to specific enzymes (such as dopamine-β-hydroxylase) contained in aminergic

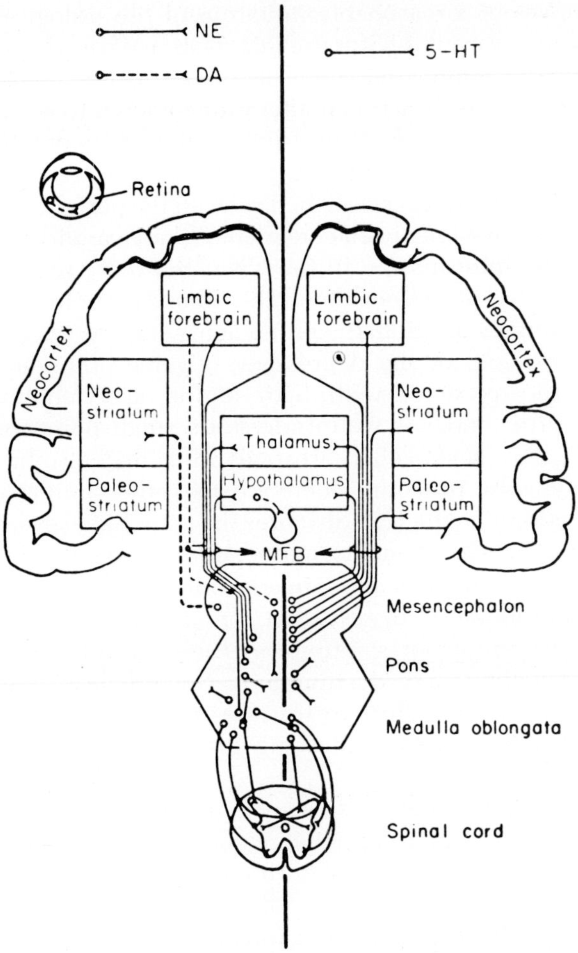

Figure 1. Distribution of monoamine-containing neurons in the mammalian central nervous system based on histofluorescence microscopy. The amines are NE: norepinephrine; DA: dopamine; and 5HT: serotonin; MFB: median forebrain bundle. (Reproduced with permission of the authors and publisher from Ref. 7.)

neurons. The results of such histologic studies lead to the conclusion that amine-containing systems arise from relatively few cell bodies, although their terminals are very widespread, rather diffuse, and apparently well suited to establishing relationships among primitive deeper structures commonly implicated in the central control of visceral and affective functions.

The intracellular localization of aromatic amines has been investigated by centrifugal fractionation techniques. A fraction rich in structures which appear to be "pinched-off" nerve endings has been studied extensively. These "synaptosomes" are enclosed by the cell membrane, which sometimes contains thickenings and other synaptic specializations; the interior of the synaptosomes includes vesicles, mitochondria, and neural cytoplasm. Catecholamines and serotonin have been localized to this fraction with their appropriate synthesizing enzymes, and the nerve endings can take up and store exogenous radioactively labeled amines and precursors. Storage probably occurs in the presynaptic vesicles where monoamines appear to be held in a membrane-enclosed site in the form of a complex with ATP, Mg^{2+}, and specific soluble protein molecules, which in the case of catecholamine-containing cells include the enzyme dopamine-β-hydroxylase and several acidic proteins called chromogranins, all of which are released with the neurotransmitter during synaptic transmission, at least with peripheral sympathetic neurons.

Both the catecholamines and serotonin are synthesized by a similar initial step of ring-hydroxylation which is the most critical, rate-limiting step in their synthesis (Figures 2 and 3). These enzymes are localized to specific neurons, and their presence determines the localization of specific amines. Next the hydroxylated amino acid precursors (L-dopa and 5-hydroxytryptophan for catecholamines and serotonin, respectively) are quickly decarboxylated by an abundant, highly active, and rather ubiquitous enzyme, "L-aromatic amino acid decarboxylase." There is presently some controversy as to whether this is in fact one enzyme or separate and distinct decarboxylases for catecholamine and indoleamine cells. Only in norepinephrine-producing cells is there

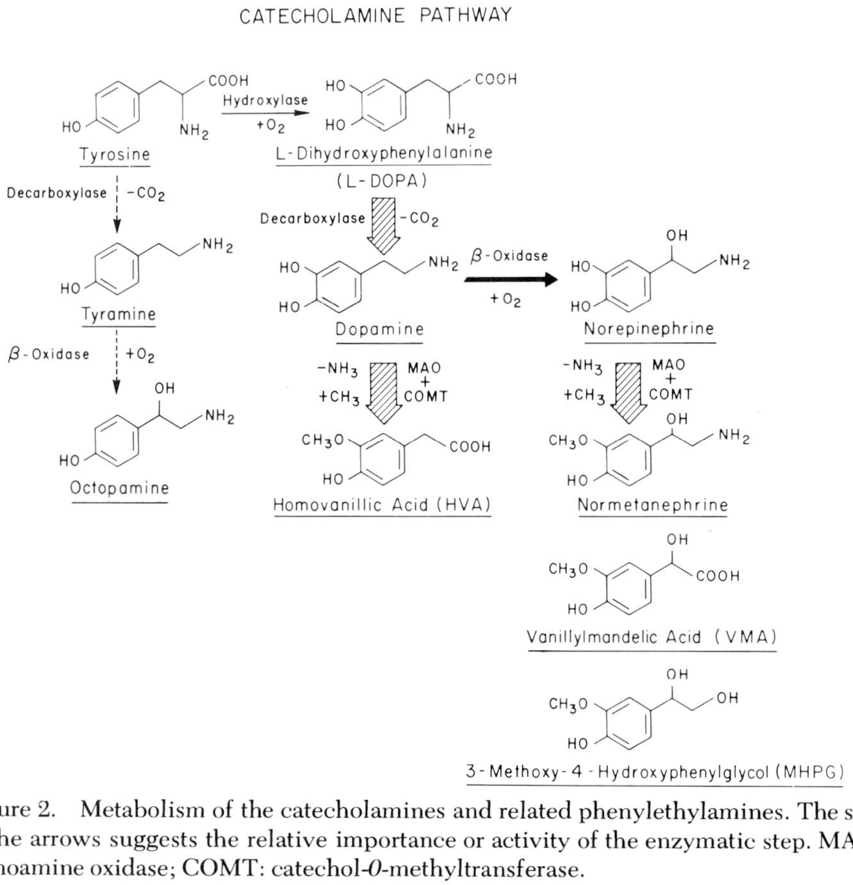

Figure 2. Metabolism of the catecholamines and related phenylethylamines. The size of the arrows suggests the relative importance or activity of the enzymatic step. MAO: monoamine oxidase; COMT: catechol-*O*-methyltransferase.

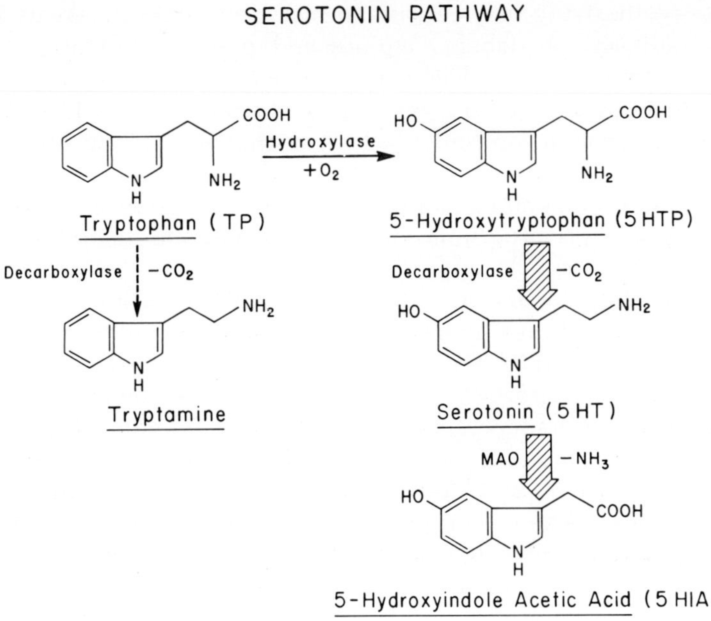

Figure 3. Metabolism of serotonin and tryptamine. Several other indoleamine compounds probably also occur in the brain and are also metabolized by monoamine-oxidase (MAO).

another hydroxylating enzyme, dopamine-β-hydroxylase, which adds the final hydroxyl group to the side chain of dopamine. "Tyrosine hydroxylase," for which both tyrosine and phenylalanine now are known to be substrates in the presence of the physiologic pteridine cofactor, has been studied intensively and appears to be an important site of regulation of catecholamine synthesis. For example, catechol compounds seem to exert a moment-to-moment end-product inhibitory influence on tyrosine hydroxylase which varies with local concentrations of catechols in a poorly defined "pool," possibly cytoplasmic, in the vicinity of the enzyme. Catechols appear to compete with the pteridine cofactor (which may be tetrahydrobiopterin) for binding to the hydroxylase molecule to exert this "negative feedback" effect. The short-term regulation of the activity of tyrosine hydroxylase is probably of considerable importance, since changes in the intracellular levels of catechols can occur through changes in the activity of the neurons which modify the release of neurotransmitter, and since the levels can be influenced by a variety of drugs. Another regulatory mechanism has also been proposed for the dopamine neurons of the nigrostriatal pathway (Figure 1), in which a feedback influence on the cell bodies in the midbrain may be modulated by changes in the availability of dopamine to its receptors at the striatal terminals. Thus increased availability seems to lead to a decreased firing rate of nigral cells and to decreased synthesis of dopamine in the striatal terminals, and vice versa. The feedback might be mediated by descending striatonigral circuits containing γ-aminobutyric acid (GABA). It is likely that this neurophysiologic regulation of catecholamine synthesis again ultimately depends on the amount of end product (dopamine) in a site close to tyrosine hydroxylase. Long-term regulation of catecholamine synthesis is apparently also possible through changes in the rate of synthesis or destruction of the crucial synthetic enzymes, since increased synthesis of tyrosine hydroxylase and dopamine-β-hydroxylase can be "induced" in response to sustained demands for neurotransmitter, or to stress, or possibly to steroid hormones or exposure to drugs which decrease the availability of the neurotransmitter to its receptors. Dopamine-β-hydroxylase in the CNS has recently received increased attention because of improved methods for its assay, and it appears to be a second important point of limitation of the synthesis of norepinephrine. There are endogenous inhibitors of this enzyme, but their possible physiologic significance as regulatory substances is uncertain.

The regulation of indoleamine synthesis is much less well understood. Short-term regulation of tryptophan-hydroxylation by end-product inhibition might occur in serotonin neurons, although this point is controversial. On the other hand, catechols can inhibit tryptophan hydroxylase, apparently by competing with a pteridine cofactor for the enzyme, but it is not certain whether catecholamine neurons might thus exert an important physiologic control on the synthesis of indoleamines. An important feature of tryptophan hydroxylase is that unlike tyrosine hydroxylase, it does not seem to be "saturated" with its substrate at physiological concentrations of tryptophan, so that changes in the availability of tryptophan can alter the rate of synthesis of 5-hydroxy-indoleamines, and more strikingly, can alter the rate of formation of the major metabolite 5-hydroxyindoleacetic acid (5 HIAA) by the action of MAO. The latter observation suggests that the rate of synthesis of serotonin may normally be in excess of intraneuronal storage capacity and in excess of the amounts required for functional needs, leading to a sustained "spillover" of excess amine onto MAO. This process would tend to maintain the available levels of transmitter, for example, in a presynaptic vesicular compartment, ready for use.

An important criterion for the consideration of an amine as a possible neurotransmitter is its release by stimulation or depolarization of the preterminal axons (Figure 4). In the CNS, however, it is virtually impossible to obtain experimental conditions comparable to an isolated perfused organ with stimulation of a single nerve, as used in classical demonstrations of the release of norepinephrine and acetylcholine in the periphery. Nevertheless, several attempts have been made to observe the release of transmitter amines from the intact brain, or from pieces of brain tissue *in vitro*. Usually these have involved the collection of fluid bathing the tissue under small cups placed on the cortex or on deeper structures following the removal of cortex, or by perfusing discrete areas of the brain with small invasive cannulae, or by perfusing the cerebral ventricles, or by superfusing brain slices exposed to electrical fields or ionic changes in small chambers. In these ways, spontaneous and stimulation-evoked efflux of several putative transmitters has been studied, and there have been attempts to correlate release with the stimulation of specific pathways in the CNS. Release of monoamines has been shown to be Ca^{2+}-dependent and to be inhibited by a variety of drugs. Several new concepts concerning transmitter release have begun to emerge from neuropharmacologic studies.

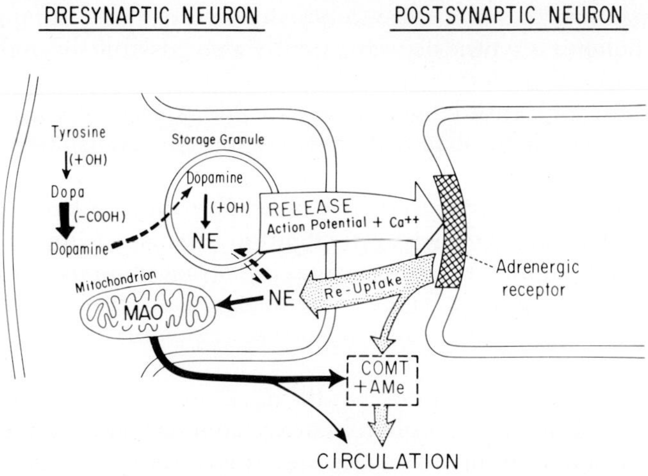

Figure 4. Metabolism and function of a typical monoamine-operated synapse. Very similar events occur at dopamine- or serotonin-containing nerve-terminals. NE: norepinephrine; MAO: monoamineoxidase; COMT: catechol-*0*-methyl-transferase; AMe: S-adenosylmethionine. (Reproduced with permission of the authors and publishers, with slight modification, from Ref. 8, 9.)

For example, postsynaptic tissues may secrete "intrasynaptic hormones," possibly including the prostaglandins, which appear to have an inhibitory influence on the presynaptic release process. Furthermore, it has been proposed that "presynaptic receptors" of the neurotransmitter amines may exist and may have important regulatory functions, possibly including influences on transmitter synthesis, and very likely including the inhibition of further release of the transmitter. Thus in addition to synthesis, release too may be a highly regulated and complex physiologic process, with its regulation tending to terminate the transmission sequence and to conserve transmitter molecules.

With the exception of acetylcholine, powerful transport processes ("reuptake") exist to reaccumulate released transmitter molecules and may represent the most important mechanism for inactivation and conservation of the released transmitter (Figure 4). The phenomenon procedes extremely quickly and utilizes transport mechanisms with high affinities for low concentrations of amines or certain amino acids. These transport systems seem to be specific for the appropriate molecules at a given type of nerve terminal. While vigorous and rapid enzymatic hydrolysis of acetylcholine by acetylcholinesterase seems to be the major means of inactivation of released acetylcholine, enzymatic mechanisms in the vicinity of the postsynaptic receptor do not seem to be so important for the rapid inactivation of released aromatic amines. The known catabolic pathways for amines include oxidative deamination by MAO located within intraneuronal mitochondria and elsewhere, and 3-*0*-methylation of catecholamines by catechol-*0*-methyl-transferase (COMT), utilizing *S*-adenosylmethionine as methyl donor (Figures 2, 3, and 4). The main function of these enzymatic processes appears to be to "mop up" excess quantities of the amines which are not stored or reutilized for transmission, and inhibition of the enzymes can result in increased levels of amines. The major metabolites produced by these enzymes include 5HIAA in the case of serotonin, and deaminated and methylated metabolites of the catecholamines: homovanillic acid (HVA) from dopamine and relatively large quantities of 3-methoxy-4-hydroxy-phenylethyleneglycol (MHPG) as well vanillylmandelic acid (VMA) and normetanephrine from norepinephrine. The production of large quantities of MHPG appears to be a unique aspect of the metabolism of norepinephrine in the CNS, and that derived from CNS may account for a sizeable proportion of the MHPG and its conjugated derivatives (mainly MHPG-sulfate) in the urine (perhaps as much as 50% in primates). The formation of so much glycol in the brain is probably due to the tendency for aldehydes which are formed directly by MAO to be reduced rather than oxidized further to acids, and a reductase specific for aromatic aldehydes has recently been characterized in brain tissue. The removal of acidic deaminated products from the CNS appears to involve a transport process which includes the transfer of aromatic acids such as 5HIAA and HVA from the cerebrospinal fluid (CSF) to the blood, probably at the choroid plexus. This process is known to be inhibited by drugs such as probenecid which also inhibit the renal tubular excretion and reabsorption of acidic substances. The transport of alcohols such as MHPG is much less important, and it is hardly affected by probenecid. Furthermore, it is not clear that the CSF is a quantitatively important route of exit for any deaminated metabolite; it is probably only a minor route for 5HIAA (10), and certainly of negligible importance for most amines.

The metabolism and turnover of amines in the brain has been studied with labeled precursors of high specific radioactivity, or the injection of labeled amines directly into the CSF to circumvent the blood-brain barrier to many amines. This approach has been particularly useful for studying the metabolism of norepinephrine, since the uptake and storage of exogenous norepinephrine are relatively vigorous and specific. The usefulness of labeled dopamine and serotonin as tracers is more limited, since their accumulation is much less specific. The turnover of amines has been estimated in several ways: by the rate of disappearance of exogenous labeled amines themselves or the change of specific radioactivity of amines after injection of their labeled precursor amino acids, or by the rate of disappearance of endogenous amines after inhibition of their synthesis. Both the catecholamines and serotonin disappear in a complex multiphasic way suggestive of rapid synthesis and utilization in some pools and of less metabolic activity in larger pools, probably representing stored neurotransmitter. The overall turnover of serotonin appears to be faster than that of the catecholamines (minutes versus hours), although at least one portion of the catecholamines probably also turns over rapidly and may be very important functionally. While the estimation of turnover has had some vogue in pharmacological investigations recently, and while it may be somewhat more sophisticated than the measurement of static levels of amines, its interpretation is difficult, since it is the resultant of many variables and because overall turnover poorly represents the rate of synthesis and utilization of small active pools of neurotransmitter. One other striking but poorly understood aspect of the metabolism of central monoamines is that their levels have wide diurnal variations. This phenomenon is often not adequately considered in clinical metabolic studies.

Further support for the possible role of monoamines as central neurotransmitters has been gained by the iontophoretic application of the substances by micropipette to a small area while simultaneously recording electrical responses of a subjacent neuron through another micropipette. Unfortunately, most surveys of the effects of such highly active substances have found variable depolarizing or hyperpolarizing effects with the same amine, or that an amine produced effects in many areas with little correlation to its endogenous distribution. Such investigations must be understood as *pharmacological* studies of potent hormones which may or may not be applied to their physiological postsynaptic sites of action. Recent iontophoretic studies have attempted to correlate such pharmacological responses with the findings of regional neurochemistry in systems which are relatively well characterized histologically and electrophysiologically. This multidisciplinary approach has been applied with particular success to the description of inhibitory influences on the cerebellar Purkinje cells mediated by norepinephrine-containing fibers arising from the locus ceruleus of the brainstem (11).

The postsynaptic effects of a neurotransmitter are believed to be mediated by specific "recognition molecules" or so-called "receptors"—a pharmacologic concept that assumes that a specific chemical interaction occurs between a drug or hormone and specific sites in a tissue. The receptors for neurotransmitters are usually conceived of as macromolecules within or upon the postsynaptic cell membrane (Figure 4). Attempts have been made to identify and to isolate receptor molecules for neurotransmitters, and these have usually involved the use of radioactively labeled agonists or antagonists of the transmitter molecule to bind to and thus mark the receptor sites prior to their biochemical isolation. This approach is limited by the specificity of the binding that is obtained, and is usually more successful with large and complex molecules rather than the monoamines themselves. These small molecules have a high probability of binding to many macromolecules in addition to the receptor, including enzymes or other proteins involved in their transport, metabolism, and storage; other nonspecific physicochemical interactions based on electrical polarity and lipid solubility also occur. Although the availability of specific and potent macromolecular toxins which bind to cholinergic receptors has begun to permit their isolation in the CNS, and while there is evidence that proteins which interact with catechol compounds can be isolated from the heart, there has been no success yet in isolating or chemically identifying specific receptors of the aromatic amines in the mammalian brain.

The postsynaptic actions of neurotransmitters are poorly understood at a functional biochemical level: It is not known, for example, how a biogenic amine alters the postsynaptic membrane chemically to change its state of polarization. Recently, the nucleotide adenosine-3',5'-cyclic-monophosphate (cyclic-AMP), considered an important substance for the mediation of effects of many hormones in peripheral tissues, has been found to be affected by several putative neurotransmitters. It is known that adenylcyclase, the enzyme that converts adenosine triphosphate (ATP) to cyclic-AMP, and a phosphodiesterase that inactivates cyclic-AMP, as well as cyclic-AMP-dependent protein kinases that are capable of altering the activity and conformation of several proteins and enzymes by adding phosphate moieties, are all present in the brain. Adenylcyclase activity in the brain is the highest of any mammalian tissue, and the synthesis of cyclic-AMP can be stimulated by norepinephrine or dopamine in suitable preparations of brain tissue. Furthermore, it has recently been reported that the selective destruction of central catecholamine-containing neurons by a drug (6-hydroxydopamine) which is selectively taken up by catecholamine cells leads to increased sensitivity of adenylcyclase activity in the cerebral cortex to norepinephrine (12). This change is presumably indicative of the phenomenon of "postdenervation supersensitivity" previously reported to follow the section of cholinergic nerves to skeletal muscle, or of adrenergic nerves to the heart, as indicated by increased contractile or bioelectrical responses to given doses of infused acetylcholine or norepinephrine. It is also known that iontophoretically applied cyclic-AMP mimics the effects of norepinephrine applied to the Purkinje cells, and that drugs (such as theophylline) that inhibit the destruction of cyclic-AMP by phosphodiesterase potentiate the effects of the catecholamines (11). These findings suggest that adenylcyclase may occur in close association with receptors of the neurotransmitters in the CNS. The usual model for the role of cyclic-AMP is that a hormone or neurotransmitter interacts with a target cell as by binding with a specific membrane protein or other macromolecule, leading to the activation of adenylcyclase and hence increased formation of cyclic-AMP. The cyclic-AMP then acts as a "second messenger" by leading to the modification of an important series of reactions in the receptive cell, often by stimulating the activity of protein kinases and culminating in an important postsynaptic functional change in a crucial enzyme or perhaps in a structural protein modulating ionic fluxes across the cell membrane in the case of the neurotransmitter hormones.

Behavioral Actions of Central Amines

There have been many attempts to define functional roles for the aromatic amines in the CNS, and a good deal of this effort has been stimulated by the hypothetical relationships between amine metabolism and psychiatric and neurological illnesses and their treatment. It must be stated at the outset that the results of behavioral and physiological studies to date do not come together into a coherent and consistent scheme, although many interesting theories and implications are evolving.

An early approach to the evaluation of the effects of amines was to introduce them directly into the CSF or brain tissue, or to inject the amines systematically in immature animals with a poorly developed blood-brain barrier (13). Most often such injections of catecholamines or serotonin have produced sedation, sleep, depressed electroencephalographic activity, and changes in body temperature. Less often, excitatory effects have been noted, and typically, effects have varied greatly with the dose administered. These studies are hard to interpret, since the biogenic amines in question have potent *pharmacological* effects that may not reflect their physiological activities because of delivery of nonphysiological doses to the wrong sites.

In recent years, quantitative and objective measures of evaluating behavior have been applied to the study of central amines. For example, it has been noted that drugs that interfere with the availability of the catecholamines can lead to decreases in spontaneous locomotion or exploratory behavior, or locomotion provoked by electrical shocks or stimulant drugs, as well as to decreases in various conditioned responses in laboratory animals. One model which has attracted a great deal of interest is the phenomenon of self-stimulation through electrodes implanted in the diencephalon, particularly the lateral hypothalamus, or in certain portions of the limbic system. This model is of interest because of its evident similarities to spontaneous appetitive and rewarded behaviors. The regions studied include the median forebrain bundle and structures close to it in which there are major ascending tracts of amine-producing neurons (Figure 1). Such behavior is usually decreased by drugs which decrease the availability of catecholamines and increased by drugs, such as amphetamine, which may increase their availability to physiological receptors, but the relative importance of dopamine tracts and ascending norepinephrine systems is still unclear; drugs which interfere with the synthesis of serotonin seem to have much less effect on the rate of self-stimulation. In other behaviors the importance of dopamine tracts is more clearly demonstrated. These include the syndrome of stereotyped sniffing and gnawing behaviors which are provoked in many species by amphetamines, and which appear to require the integrity of dopamine circuits in the nigrostriatal pathway and perhaps portions of the limbic system. Furthermore, rotational behavior induced by unilateral lesions of the midbrain substantia nigra or the nigrostriatal pathway also seems to be due to a resulting imbalance of the function of dopamine terminals in the caudate nucleus. The behaviors related to the function of the limbic system, basal ganglia, and diencephalon, including self-stimulation and the amphetamine syndrome, tend to be very stereotyped, repetitious, and "compulsive." These qualities, coupled with the pharmacological observations that suggest that the behaviors can be enhanced by drugs which increase the availability of catecholamines (including stimulants and antidepressants) and suppressed by drugs which decrease the availability of catecholamines (notably, most of the antipsychotic and antimanic agents except reserpine), have led to speculations about their possible relationships to a variety of psychiatric disorders, including schizophrenia as well as the affective illnesses.

Several studies suggest that the catecholamines and the indoleamines might be involved in neural systems which in a very general way are mutually antagonistic or tend toward opposite kinds of behaviors. The general idea is that serotonin might be involved in behavior-inhibiting systems while the catecholamines, and particularly norepinephrine, tend to facilitate or enhance many behaviors, while their deficiency leads to motor inertia, apathy, and decreased drive rather than frank sedation (5). Increased availability of serotonin often results in sedation and diminished responsiveness to stimulation at lower levels, although high levels may lead to toxic delirium. Decreased levels of serotonin, as are produced by inhibition of its synthesis, may not be associated with obvious changes in behavior, but there is often evidence of excitation, decreased habituation to stimuli, increased ability to respond in a conflicting approach-avoidance situation, increased sexual or aggressive behavior, and lowered seizure threshold and pain threshold (14, 15). The imaginative general concept that the catecholamines subserve an "ergotrophic" or sympathetic-arousal system and that serotonin subserves a "trophotropic" or parasympathetic-quieting system of the diencephalon as proposed by Hess was formulated by Brodie and Shore in the 1950s (5, 14).

States of consciousness have been associated with changes in amine metabolism repeatedly (14, 15), and the findings in this field are generally consistent with the Brodie and Shore hypothesis. For example, lesions of the raphe nuclei lead to decreased levels of serotonin in the forebrain and have been reported to produce generalized insomnia in animals, while stimulation here can induce sedation, probably decreased activation of thalamic relay centers by peripheral stimuli, and electrocorticographic changes associated with sleep. In contrast, lesions of norepinephrine-containing nuclei of the brainstem or inhibition of catecholamine synthesis tend to diminish paradoxical or rapid-eye-movement (REM) sleep selectively. The results of a variety of pharmacological experiments which are not easy to interpret suggest that drugs that interfere with the availability of serotonin can inhibit sleep and hibernation, while increased availability of this amine, as by the administration of its precursor amino acids, can in some circumstances increase the incidence of sleep, and particularly slow wave sleep. Unfortunately, several of the observations concerning the relationship of aromatic amines and the regulation of consciousness are inconsistent, methodologically unsound, or otherwise in need of cautious interpretation at the present time.

A large number of reports suggest that the exposure of animals or man to noxious, unpleasant, or otherwise stressful situations can lead acutely to the release and even depletion of amines and complex changes of their metabolites in the brain or urine, and later to increased rates of turnover, presumably reflecting increased rates of synthesis and utilization. There is even evidence that tyrosine hydroxylase levels will increase following prolonged exposure to presumably stressful stimuli or situations. Nevertheless, it is unclear how relatively crude forms of physical abuse to which animals have been exposed in such experiments might relate to human psychological stress or to major psychiatric illnesses. Furthermore, the fact that a very broad range of physical, pharmacological, and even "psychological" or situational stresses can lead to complex changes in the turnover of biogenic amines in central and peripheral tissues, depending on the duration and degree of stress, suggests that great caution should be exercised in the interpretation of correlations between changes in amine metabolism and major psychiatric illnesses, with their inevitable nonspecific stresses.

Other studies, which are in many ways similar to the "stress" experiments, suggest a possible relationship between defensive or aggressive behavior and amine metabolism. For example, displays of "sham rage" can be provoked by stimulation of the amygdala or following lesions of the brain. Such interventions tend to decrease the levels of catecholamines in the brainstem, and the behavior is respectively enhanced or inhibited by drugs which increase or decrease the availability of catecholamines at the synapse. Also, aggressive behavior among crowded rodents can be similarly increased or decreased by pharmacological alterations of the availability of catecholamines and serotonin, and the "muricidal" (mouse-killing) behavior of certain rats has been reported to correlate with decreased levels of serotonin in the brain. One difficulty for the interpretations of such experiments is that the changes in amine metabolism may be *secondary* to changes in neuronal activity associated with a change in behavior, rather than a cause of the behavioral alteration.

Another physiologically important and rapidly evolving hypothesis is that amines, and particularly catecholamines, modify the activity of hypothalamic neurons which secrete pituitary trophic-hormone-releasing factors. For example, the increased or decreased availability of dopamine and norepinephrine following pharmacological manipulations has led to correspondingly increased or decreased release of antidiuretic hormone, luteinizing hormone, and growth hormone. There is also evidence of a reciprocal relationship between norepinephrine and the secretion of adrenocorticotrophic hormone, so that decreased availability of the amine might be associated with increased adrenal cortical stimulation (14).

There is also evidence that norepinephrine may be involved in the initiation and maintenance of eating behaviors mediated by the hypothalamus. Thus injection of minute quantities of this amine into the hypothalamus can induce eating in a sated rat, and this effect is potentiated or blocked by drugs that either increase or decrease the availability of norepinephrine to its receptors, respectively. Nevertheless, the regulation of food intake is a complex and poorly understood function which is unlikely to be simply switched on or off by the availability of a single neurotransmitter. Amine metabolism has also been implicated in other homeostatic and autonomic functions of the diencephalon and brainstem, including temperature regulation and the control of respiratory and cardiovascular functions.

In general, it seems probable that many important functions of the brainstem and diencephalon subserving crucial autonomic and homeostatic mechanisms are partially regulated by neurons which synthesize and secrete monoamine neurotransmitters. It is clear that the very diffuse and widespread distribution of terminals arising from the cell bodies of serotonin- and norepinephrine-containing neurons is well suited to their serving rather generalized functions having a relatively leisurely time course. Such functions might include levels of arousal or consciousness, the tonic regulation of autonomic functions and their phasic responses to challenge and stress, and possibly mood or affect, either as a discrete function or as a condition of arousal and autonomic function; other functions might include the regulation of muscular tone and posture through the extrapyramidal motor system, and quite possibly, the regulation of timing and rhythm of other functions. In contrast, it seems very unlikely that the monoaminergic systems would be involved in very precise, rapidly changing functions subserving sensation or the central control of the phasic contraction of skeletal muscles. It is also unlikely that monoamine systems, arising from a mere few thousands of cell bodies, can account for a large proportion of the total millions of neurons and billions of synaptic connections in the brain. Nevertheless, in relation to the basic biology of behavior and psychiatric illness, it does seem that aminergic systems are particularly likely to be involved, if only secondarily or incidentally, in the disturbances of mood, drive, initiative, sleep, and diurnal rhythmicity as well as sexual and feeding behavior, and hypothalamic-adrenal function which are characteristic of the major affective disorders.

The Neuropsychopharmacology of the Biogenic Amines

The clinical and experimental effects of drugs which alter mood and behavior have provided an extremely influential source of support for hypotheses about the metabolism of amines in psychiatric disorders (16–18). While none of the drugs to be considered has only single action, it is helpful to bring some order to the discussion by considering the main actions of drugs as falling into one of several categories. These categories are based on the sites of relative vulnerability of the metabolism of neurotransmitters to the actions of toxic substances and include synthesis, storage, uptake and release, postsynaptic effects, and catabolism (Table 1, Figure 4).

One means of attempting to alter the synthesis of the amines is to provide supraphysiological amounts of their precursors. Since tyrosine hydroxylase activity is severely rate-limiting for the synthesis of catecholamines, it is not possible to increase their synthesis by the administration of even huge quantities of phenylalanine or tyrosine; on the contrary, it is likely that the normally minor pathway of direct decarboxylation of phenylalanine or tyrosine (Figure 2) would lead to the accumulation of aromatic amines which might act as "false transmitters" and so interfere with the availability of the catecholamines. While these aromatic amino acids have little effect on behavior, a small fraction of a dose of L-dopa can enter the brain to be decarboxylated locally to dopamine, and can produce behavioral effects which might be described as excitatory or alerting, particularly if dopa is given in high doses, or with drugs which prevent its peripheral metabolism by decarboxylation or *0*-methylation, or prevent the destruction by MAO of the amines produced. Since dopamine-β-hydroxylase is a second bottleneck in the synthesis of norepinephrine, it is not surprising that L-dopa has little ability to increase levels of norepinephrine; in fact, it can lead to the displacement of norepinephrine and even of serotonin from their neuronal storage sites, probably by a "false-transmitter" mechanism involving the accumulation of dopamine in inappropriate sites. While L-dopa has been very useful in alleviating the bradykinesia and rigidity of Parkinson's disease, it has not been useful for the clinical management of depressions, although it does seem to be able to produce motoric and even affective arousal in some patients with depressive retardation, and it may facilitate the switch from depression to mania in some bipolar manic-depressive patients (19–21). Interestingly, its use in treating Parkinson's disease sometimes results in mood elevation, possibly as a nonspecific effect of increased motility and freedom, but perhaps as a more direct central effect. On the other hand, it has led to a large number of untoward psychiatric side effects, including depressions as well as states of psychotic agitation. The mechanisms underlying these reactions are obscure, but they might be responses to excessive arousal or a psychotomimetic action

Table 1 Effects of drugs on the metabolism of amines in the CNS[a]

Type of drug	Drug	Actions	Behavioral Effects
Precursors	*L-dopa*	DA increased	Antiparkinsonian, dyskinetic, psychotogenic
	Tryptophan *5-HTP*	5-HT increased	Sedative usually, antimanic?
Inhibitors of synthesis	*α-Me-p-Tyrosine* (AMPT)	Blocks tyrosine hydroxylase, lowers CA levels	Sedative, antihypertensive
	α-Me-dopa (Aldomet)	Blocks decarboxylase	Sedative, antihypertensive, depressant
	Disulfiram (Antabuse)	Blocks β-hydroxylase, lowers NE	Little effect, some depression, some excitement on withdrawal
	p-Cl-Phenylalanine (PCPA)	Blocks tryptophan hydroxylase, lowers 5-HT	Aggression, hypersexuality, insomnia
Decrease retention	*α-Me-dopa*	False transmitter replaces endogenous CA	Sedative, antihypertensive, depressant
	Reserpine (tetrabenazine)	Blocks storage in vesicles, lowers amine levels	Sedative, depressant
Alter membrane crossing	*Amphetamines*	Increase release, decrease reuptake (some MAO-inhibition)	Stimulant, anorexic, psychotogenic
	Cocaine	Decreases reuptake	Stimulant, euphoriant
	Tricyclic antidepressants (e.g., imipramine)	Mainly block reuptake (some MAO-inhibition)	Antidepressant
	Lithium salts	Decrease release and storage (also block adenyl cyclase?)	Antimanic, mood-stabilizing
Block receptors	*Neuroleptics* (e.g., phenothiazines, butyrophenones)	Mainly CA-receptor-blockade	Antimanic, neuroleptic, antipsychotic, sedative
	Methysergide	Mainly indoleamine-receptor-blockade	Antimanic?
Inhibitors of catabolism	*MAO-inhibitors*	Block MAO, increase amine levels	Antidepressant, euphoriant
	Polyphenols (e.g., butyl-gallate)	Block COMT	Little effect or toxic

[a]Abbreviations and symbols used: DA: dopamine; NE: norepinephrine; CA: catecholamine; 5HT: serotonin; 5HTP: 5-hydroxytryptophan; Me: methyl; MAO: monoamineoxidase; COMT: catechol-*O*-methyltransferase.

by "amphetamine-like" effects of amines produced from L-dopa, followed by a depletion of norepinephrine by a "false-transmitter" action of these amines; it is also possible, though less likely, that dopamine could inhibit tyrosine hydroxylase and that dopa could interfere with the transport of tyrosine. The release and subsequent depletion of serotonin might also play a role in the psychotomimetic and depressant actions of L-dopa. Furthermore, the rather widespread abnormalities in the brains of Parkinson patients may make them particularly susceptible to these toxic effects of L-dopa. Theoretically, dihydroxyphenylserine can be directly decarboxylated to form norepinephrine, but in practice even large doses of this unusual amino acid have had relatively little effect on norepinephrine levels or on behavior.

Precursors of the indoleamines have also been given in enormous quantities to animals and to human subjects (5, 20). Generally, tryptophan has produced sedative effects, and 5-hydroxy-tryptophan has produced either little effect, or changes in the direction of sedation, although large doses can produce agitation or seizures, particularly on withdrawal. Furthermore, these amino acids are much less effective than L-dopa in reversing the sedative, behavior-depressant syndrome induced by reserpine or other amine-depleting agents. The reported studies of clinical effects of the indole-amino acids in affective disorders remain in conflict, although several are deficient in experimental design, including the lack of placebo control groups (20, 22), and the impression left by several recent controlled studies that the indoleamine precursors have little if any clinically beneficial effect in severe depression (20), although there is at least one report of an antimanic effect (15).

There are now fairly specific inhibitors of the rate-limiting enzymes involved in amine biosynthesis in the brain. For example, α-methyl-*p*-tyrosine inhibits tyrosine hydroxylase and produces sedative and hypotensive effects, although it is a relatively impotent drug in man. Its congener, α-methyl-dopa, seems to act mainly by competitively blocking dopa-decarboxylase and yielding the "false-transmitter" amines, α-methylated dopamine and norepinephrine (Table 1), resulting in the depletion of catecholamines. Both drugs have been associated with the production of depressive effects in man, or with the worsening of depression and lessening of mania in the case of α-methyl-*p*-tyrosine. The latter drug can also induce a "behavioral model of depression" and social withdrawal (or sedation) in certain primates (23). In both animals and man α-methyl-*p*-tyrosine can block the stimulation and euphoria induced by amphetamine (24). The best known inhibitor of dopamine-β-hydroxylase, disulfiram, a copper-chelating agent, is toxic to several other enzymes as well, so that its effects are difficult to interpret. While it has little effect on animal behavior, it has been reported to produce occasional psychiatric side effects in alcoholics receiving it chronically or in psychotic patients receiving it experimentally: These effects are usually toxic deliria and agitation, but sometimes include reactions described as depressive, and occasionally states of elation or agitation have been noted on the withdrawal of this drug. There are now much more potent and specific inhibitors of dopamine-β-hydroxylase, such as fusaric acid, which is being tested experimentally as an antihypertensive agent in Japan; it is not yet known whether it can induce depression or suppress mania, as it might be expected to do. The most specific (though not completely so) drugs available for the inhibition of tryptophan hydroxylase include *p*-chloro-phenylalanine and several halogenated amphetamine derivatives. Inhibition of the synthesis of serotonin in animals usually leads to states of *hyper*-responsiveness and aggression, and possibly increased "sexual" behavior and insomnia, but certainly not behavior that resembles the clinical depression associated with manic-depressive illness. In some species of monkeys, *p*-chloro-phenylalanine has little effect, and in others it produces effects similar to the behavioral and social "depression" induced by α-methyl-*p*-tyrosine; nevertheless, the reactions to both drugs may represent behavioral responses to "sickness" rather than serving as models of depression (15). The main clinical experience with *p*-chloro-phenylalanine has been in the management of the carcinoid syndrome, and depression does not seem to be a likely outcome of either the disease itself or its treatment, although some patients and normal subjects receiving the drug have become tense, irritable, and more susceptible to pain, or developed headache and malaise and something like "depression," or became paranoid and hallucinatory (15, 20).

Drugs that are known to decrease the ability of nerve endings to retain monoamines in vesicular or granular intracellular storage sites include the Rauwolfia alkaloids and the synthetic polycyclic compounds (benzoquinolizines), such as tetrabenazine. These depleting agents are well known to produce a behavior-depressing syndrome of sedation in animals which has served for many years as a "laboratory model of depression," and they have been associated with clinical depressions, as have most of the amine-depleting antihypertensive drugs which have central effects as well as peripheral effects on sympathetic nerve terminals (α-methyl-dopa, but not guanethidine, for example). The model is usually said to be further supported, since L-dopa (but not tryptophan or 5-hydroxytryptophan), amphetamine, and MAO-inhibitors can reverse the reserpine syndrome in animals, and L-dopa can even reverse reserpine sedation in man (16). The problems with this "model" are that some of the drugs which counter it are not antidepressants in patients and that the behavioral syndrome in animals more closely resembles sedation than depression, and even in man, many of the reports of so-called depression probably represent sedation and lethargy or even cases of organic brain syndrome (16, 25). Furthermore, the clinical reactions are difficult to interpret, since many of the antihypertensive drugs are more likely to produce frank depressions (not mere sedative effects) in presumably susceptible patients with past histories of depression, suggesting a biological or psychological predisposition; many of these patients are inclined to use "obsessional and activity defenses" and may be particularly vulnerable to drugs which induce persistent lethargy and decreased drive. It does seem to be true that antidepressant drugs are helpful for these antihypertensive depressions. Another problem for the "amine-depletion model" is that reserpine was actually used to treat some cases of depression in the 1950s, with some success evident with agitated psychotic patients or when used in combination with MAO-inhibitors (16). Furthermore, the timing of many reserpine depressions is such that they may occur weeks or months following profound depletion of amines, again suggesting that they require a susceptible "host," and that amine depletion *per se* in an otherwise healthy patient is not a sufficient cause for depression. Also, reserpine leads to an apparent "cholinergic dominance" in addition to antiadrenergic effects, as manifest, for example, in the frequent production of diarrhea, and an increase in cholinergic function itself may be associated with sedative or depressant effects (26). In short, antihypertensive "depression" is far from an adequate model of clinical depressive illness.

Several important drugs are now generally believed to alter the ability of amines to cross the cell membrane, either by release or by reuptake processes. These include the classical stimulants, cocaine and amphetamine, which are potent inhibitors of reuptake of catecholamines, and to a lesser extent, indoleamines. In addition, amphetamine may have modest MAO-inhibiting properties, and it, or more likely one of its hydroxylated metabolites, may displace or "release" catecholamines at the synapse (8). Unfortunately for the amine hypotheses, neither drug is a particularly useful antidepressant for major endogenous depressions, although stimulant drugs are still occasionally said to have some empirical usefulness in mild reactive or neurotic depressive states. While tricyclic drugs of the imipramine type are the currently most popular form of treatment for depressive illnesses, their efficacy is often exaggerated. While nearly all controlled studies report that they produce antidepressant effects, in most studies the improvement rates are only about 10 to 20% better than with placebo, and sometimes even less. The tricyclic antidepressant drugs of the imipramine type have powerful effects on the reuptake of catecholamines. Although it is still not certain whether this is their main mode of action, it is certainly one important effect; there may also be some mild inhibition of MAO, and these drugs are also anticholinergic. Effects on amine-uptake are supported with clinical studies of transport of amines into blood platelets and of changes in the pattern of excretion of catecholamine metabolites. The original compounds, imipramine and amitriptyline, have effects on indoleamine transport as well as catecholamine-uptake, but their *N*-desmethylated analogues appear to have more selective effects on norepinephrine transport; and halogenated derivatives appear to be more specific for serotonin-uptake: All are at least moderately effective antidepressants by controlled clinical investigations. One chronic difficulty for the explanation of their clinical effectiveness in terms of uptake inhibition is that antidepressant clinical effects are seen days to weeks after the effect on uptake has begun to occur, while early effects often include sedation. The saturation of tissue pools with drug might take time, but there are few convincing data to support this hypothesis as an explanation of the time-course of antidepressant action. While one might hope to find that other changes in amine metabolism, such as increased synthesis and turnover, occur after more prolonged exposure to the drugs, it has been reported that an apparently adaptive *decrease* of synthesis of norepinephrine can occur after chronic treatment with tricyclic agents (27). Alternatively, there might be other adaptational mechanisms at work which involve receptor sensitivity. Furthermore, "nonbiological" aspects of the psychological adaptation to change may require weeks to evolve in the patient. Another problem for monoamine hypotheses is that the anticholinergic effect of tricyclic antidepressants may also be important in their antidepressant actions (26). In further support of this view it has also been noted that the cholinomimetic agent physostigmine (a reversible cholinesterase inhibitor) can enter the brain and can exert antimanic effects; however, it can also counteract the psychotogenic action of stimulants in schizophrenic patients. While these observations may reflect an important and specific cholinergic effect in psychosis, they may also result from nonspecific sedative-like central depressant actions.

Another drug substance that may exert important effects on "membrane crossings" is the lithium ion. Its mechanism of action is not fully understood, but it is clear that it can decrease the release of catecholamines and serotonin from brain slices at concentrations which are close to those encountered clinically. In addition, lithium may alter the intraneuronal storage of amines, leading to their leakage into the cytoplasm and their greater availability to mitochondrial MAO for deamination. These effects would appear to be consistent with an amine hypothesis for the antimanic effects of lithium salts, in that they would tend to decrease the availability of the biogenic amines to their synaptic receptors. Recently, there has also been some indication that lithium might inhibit the responsiveness of receptors to stimulation by amines, as reflected in the decreased activation of adenylcyclase. On the other hand, the possibility that lithium salts may also exert a tonic mood-stabilizing effect to prevent the recurrence of both depressive and manic exacerbations of bipolar affective illnesses or even help monopolar depressive illness itself (28) is less readily explicable in terms of amine metabolism. Another metal ion, rubidium, is very similar to potassium and can release amines by membrane-depolarization, and it has been suggested as a potential antidepressant; it is also known that cesium, another metal ion which resembles potassium, can block monoamine-uptake and can exert central stimulant actions in animals.

Other drugs that appear to have important effects on postsynaptic receptors of amines, and particularly the catecholamines, are the antipsychotic neuroleptic drugs, the phenothiazines, thioxanthenes, and butyrophenones, all of which are useful in the management of acute manic episodes. On the other hand, these drugs produce many other metabolic effects, including the blockade of catecholamine release at higher doses, possibly by a "local anesthetic" effect, and an increase in catecholamine turnover, as well as a variety of effects not related to amine metabolism or to mood. Furthermore, their use is generally not associated with the induction of depression, although they might hasten the switch from mania to depression in some very sensitive manic-depressive patients (19). Furthermore, the neuroleptic-antipsychotic drugs are not specific for mania, and are very useful in schizophrenia, possibly in other atypical acute psychoses, and in a variety of neuropsychiatric disorders with dyskinesia and dystonia as prominent features. Other sympathetic blocking agents of the more classical alpha- (e.g., phenoxybenzamine) or beta-receptors (e.g., propranolol) also have central depressant or sedative actions, and propranolol may even have some antipsychotic effect in mania (but also in schizophrenia), although none of these appears to be capable of inducing frank clinical depressions.

Among drugs which alter the metabolism of biogenic amines, the most important are the MAO-inhibitors, the first effective antidepressants. They clearly increase the availability of both catecholamines and serotonin, and decrease urinary excretion of their deaminated metabolites. However, they also increase the availability of other amines, some of which might accumulate as relatively inactive or "false" transmitters to produce the *hypo*tensive effects that often occur with these drugs, or that can also act acutely as indirectly sympathomimetic amines to displace or "release" norepinephrine at sympathetic terminals to produce *hyper*tension. A very potent MAO-inhibitor, tranylcypromine, is a structural analogue of amphetamine and appears to have powerful reuptake-inhibiting amphetamine-like effects as well. The hydrazine MAO-inhibitors are relatively toxic substances and can poison a variety of enzymes, to complicate the understanding of their action. As with the tricyclic compounds, the antidepressant effects of MAO-inhibitors occur much later than their effects on deamination, and this delay is unexplained. Another major route of metabolism of the catecholamines is 3-*0*-methylation. Most methyltransferase inhibitors are either impotent or toxic, but one recently used clinically with psychiatric patients, butyl-gallate, seems to have little behavioral effect. There are as yet no drugs available that interfere with sulfation reactions, which may be important in the inactivation of indoleamines in the CNS and in the final conjugation of MHPG and other metabolites.

An important form of treatment of depressions that is usually discussed with the pharmacotherapies is ECT. Convulsive seizures are known experimentally and clinically to be associated with the acute release of catecholamines and serotonin, and a series of electroconvulsions can increase the synthesis and turnover of norepinephrine and serotonin in the rat brain. However, it now appears that the effects on norepinephrine metabolism are small and short-lived and that the effects on serotonin can be ascribed to nonspecific stress factors alone (29). Nevertheless, the latter conclusions are based on studies of otherwise normal laboratory animals, and it is still conceivable that even these small and transient effects could be of clinical importance if amine metabolism were initially subnormal and if the seizures tended to return function toward normal. However, that hypothesis is not well supported by clinical metabolic studies of ECT. There have been remarkably few studies of the effects of ECT *per se* on the metabolism of amines in patients, and many recent studies which include ECT are complicated by the inclusion of antidepressant drugs in the treatment regime and by comparisons of patients before and after clinical improvement. In the 1950s there were reports of the release of catecholamines into the blood and urine soon after ECT (5), corresponding with the striking physiological display of peripheral sympathetic discharge, particularly in ECT unmodified with anesthetics and muscle-relaxants. More recent clinical studies have led to the impression that modified ECT is associated with much less release of catecholamines from the sympathetic nerves and adrenals (30), although the antidepressant effects are not lost, which suggests that the convulsions exert an antidepressant effect not obviously associated with amine release and that release may be largely an effect of "stress." Studies of the effect of ECT on amine metabolites in the cerebrospinal fluid are rare, but also fail to support a correlation between ECT and changes in the metabolism of catecholamines or serotonin (31).

Clinical Studies of Amine Metabolism

There have been many reports of changes in the metabolism of biogenic amines in affective disorders. Since the antidepressant drugs have their least equivocal effects in the more serious depressions, variously described as major, endogenous, manic-depressive, or psychotic, most metabolic studies have concentrated on hospitalized patients with serious illnesses. However, there is considerable clinical heterogeneity among even the severe depressive and manic disorders (18, 19), and diagnostic categories vary considerably among different countries and even in different centers within this country. These differences have contributed to considerable confusion in this field. It is fair to characterize the clinical studies of metabolism in affective disorders as suggestive and tantalizing, but filled with confusing and contradictory data.

Since the early work of Ström-Olsen and Weil-Malherbe in the 1950s (32) there have been many other reports (5, 16, 18, 24, 33) of a general tendency for norepinephrine itself to be excreted in increased amounts during episodes of mania, and in decreased amounts in depression. While there are some hints that these changes may represent absolute increases or decreases in comparison to controls, that kind of intergroup comparison has not been easy because of variability between subjects as well as within the same subject over time. Thus the clearest results have come from longitudinal studies of individual patients at several phases of their illness. Increases of norepinephrine and epinephrine have been found in plasma as well as urine in some severely disturbed patients who were not manic, but were suffering from psychotic depressions, often with agitation, or even in cases of psychotic turmoil of a schizophrenic type. Much of the increased excretion can be accounted for by changes in motor activity or posture, in addition to the stresses of agitation and psychological disorganization. Thus the increases of catecholamine excretion reported to occur in psychoses do not correlate specifically with mania and might largely be due to nonspecific autonomic and adrenomedullary responses to turmoil and stress, or to changes in overall "psychomotor" activity. Among the urinary metabolites of the catecholamines, normetanephrine is often increased in the urine in mania, or with agitated depression, or with recovery from retarded depression, although even these generalizations are not true in all cases. Also VMA (vanillylmandelic acid, Figure 2) may be excreted in increased amounts in mania, although it is not clear to what extent this change might be due to increased overall physical activity (34).

A major problem for attempts to correlate blood or urinary concentrations of metabolites with mental status is that it is very difficult to learn from them about the metabolism of the brain, which is presumed to be the important site of metabolic abnormalities hypothesized to occur in mental illnesses. The blood-brain barrier to many amines retards the escape of the catecholamines, normetanephrine and serotonin; most of the circulating and excreted norepinephrine probably arises from peripheral sympathetic nerve endings, particularly in small blood vessels, and from the adrenal medulla, or in the case of serotonin, from the gut and other peripheral organs. Furthermore, serotonin metabolism is particularly sensitive to dietary intake of tryptophan or of preformed serotonin itself. Thus rates of excretion of amines and their metabolites might reflect in a general way the activity of the peripheral metabolism, but correlations with brain metabolism, although poorly worked out quantitatively, are likely to be obscure. Recently, there has been a great deal of interest in the metabolite MHPG (3-methoxy-4-hydroxy-phenylethyleneglycol, Figure 2) as one substance derived from the metabolism of catecholamines, the urinary excretion of which might relatively uniquely reflect metabolism in the CNS (24, 35–38). While the brain's contribution to urinary MHPG might be as low as 20 to 30% in most laboratory animals, it might reach 50% in primates. Thus the use of MHPG in clinical studies of CNS metabolism of norepinephrine represents a considerable step forward. Another improvement that has accompanied the study of MHPG is the use of much more powerful techniques for the assay of amine metabolites, including gas chromatography, which is much more sensitive and specific than previous chromatographic methods.

Generally, the urinary excretion of MHPG appears to follow mood changes in a direction consistent with a catecholamine hypothesis of their regulation: The excretion is often, but not always, decreased in depression, particularly in some bipolar patients, and often increased in mania. It has even been noted that MHPG excretion can be *decreased* in agitated depressed patients while the excretion of norepinephrine and normetanephrine is elevated (24), and that urinary MHPG changes can precede mood changes (35). These provocative findings suggest that central norepinephrine metabolism might be correlated in a unique way with mood, although they require confirmation and replication. Other evidence that is less supportive of such a norepinephrine hypothesis includes the observations that MHPG excretion can rise as a response to stress, with increased motor activity, and even by *simulating* the verbal and motoric expressions of mania (34). Since at least half of the urinary MHPG is apparently derived from the metabolism of norepinephrine in peripheral tissues, it is not surprising that such nonspecific changes should occur. Other studies do not confirm the association of increased or decreased MHPG-excretion with mania or depression, respectively (37, 38). Furthermore, there is a disagreement concerning the effects of amphetamine intoxication and withdrawal on the excretion of MHPG: After chronic abuse of amphetamine, the rise and then fall of MHPG followed the shift in mood from high to low (24), but this did not occur with acute administration of the drug (39). Another area of disagreement is that when MHPG has been used to predict the response to treatment with antidepressant drugs, the quite opposite suggestions have arisen that response is likely to be better if the initial rate of excretion of MHPG is low, but responsive to amphetamine (36), or high (24), and furthermore that MHPG may either increase (36) or decrease (37) with tricyclic antidepressants. These discrepancies may be due to local differences in diagnostic categorization or timing of the urine sampling, and the failure to find differences may at least partly be due to problems of scatter of data and regression-to-the-mean in instances when comparisons were made across groups of dissimilar individuals, particularly (and paradoxically) if the size of the groups was large. Nevertheless, one conclusion that such discrepancies and controversies support is that a single metabolite value in a given patient is highly unlikely to have clinical usefulness in predicting the response to treatment.

The excretion of other substances related to the metabolism of biogenic amines may also be altered in affective disorders. For example, there is some indication that the excretion of simple aromatic amines such as phenethylamine (40) or tryptamine (13) might be increased in mania and/or decreased in depression. Assessment of the metabolism of aromatic amino acids in the affective disorders has also been attempted and has resulted in conflicting findings (24). In studies of serotonin (13, 15, 33, 41–44) the greatest attention has been paid to its major metabolite, 5HIAA (5-hydroxy-indoleacetic acid, Figure 3). Ström-Olsen and Weil-Malherbe noted as early as the 1950s that urinary 5HIAA tended to rise in mania and fall in depression, especially retarded depression (32). Later reports suggested that 5HIAA excretion might vary among depressed patients in a systematic way, with consistent decreases in retarded depression and increases with agitation (43), and again raise the question of specificity for "depression" versus the state of overall psychomotor activation. There have also been some replicated findings that the clinical responsiveness to MAO-inhibitors might correlate with the depth of depression of initial urinary 5HIAA levels (43). One problem for nearly all of the clinical studies of the metabolism of the serotonin in depression and mania is that the urinary changes tend to be small, and really within normal limits in comparison with large series of normal subjects.

One approach to the metabolism of biogenic amines in the CNS has been to assay concentrations of metabolites in the cerebrospinal fluid (CSF). In some recent studies, probenecid has also been introduced in an attempt to block the removal of acid metabolites from the CSF to the blood so as to permit estimates of the rate of rise of these metabolites, and hence of amine turnover. There are many problems associated with this approach, including the practical clinical difficulties of obtaining CSF samples, nearly always by lumbar puncture. There are also fundamental questions of how to interpret changes of CSF metabolites. Their source and their quantitative relationships to brain metabolism are still poorly understood. Neither the amines themselves nor VMA occur in the CSF in usefully measurable quantities, although MHPG, HVA, and 5HIAA can be detected by sensitive methods. It does now seem, however, that a considerable proportion of the 5HIAA recovered from the lumbar subarachnoid space is derived from the metabolism of serotonin in the spinal cord and not the brain, and some of the HVA (homovanillic acid, Figure 2) may arise from the capillaries of the CNS and not from dopamine-containing neurons alone. The 5HIAA that does appear may bear little relationship even to spinal cord function, as it has been estimated that less than 10% of the 5HIAA produced in the CNS and removed in the venous blood passes through the CSF at all (10); it is unclear how much of the other deaminated metabolites passes through the CSF. The picture that is emerging is that the CSF compartment is not simply intermediary between the intravascular fluid compartment and the brain tissue, but that the three compartments relate to each other in a complex triangular manner. When probenecid is introduced into such studies, some gains may be made in approaching the dynamics of amine metabolism rather than relying on static levels of metabolites. Nevertheless, this gain is made at the cost of inconvenience and added risk to the patient by requiring multiple lumbar punctures, and it may be impractical to try to follow an individual over time, meaning the sacrifice of an important advantage in research strategy. The use of the probenecid technique in "control" subjects is open to even more serious ethical questions. Another methodological cost is the introduction of a number of new variables, including the distribution of probenecid and the individual's response to it as well as the unknown changes in the turnover of the amines wrought by such a perturbation. There is already some indication that probenecid may itself increase tryptophan entry into the CNS, and hence possibly increase the synthesis of serotonin (45). Another limitation of the probenecid technique is that it seems to be most useful for the acid metabolites, but not for the alcohol MHPG, a most interesting metabolite, the removal of which is little altered by probenecid. This has left HVA and 5HIAA as the compounds most intensively studied with probenecid.

The study of MHPG concentrations in the CSF has been a promising approach, but so far the results are inconsistent and include reports of no change or an increase in mania, and either no change or a decrease in depression (24, 38, 46). Even these changes may not be independent of general psychomotor activity, since the simulation of "mania" or simply activity itself can elevate CSF levels of MHPG, as well as of other deaminated metabolites (HVA and 5HIAA) (24, 34). Resting levels of the latter acid metabolites of dopamine (HVA) and serotonin (5HIAA) have been reported to be decreased or more or less unchanged in depression or in patients following depressions, and variously, increased, decreased, or unchanged in mania (15, 24, 38, 47), and furthermore, to be unresponsive to ECT (24, 31). Furthermore, the rate of rise or accumulation of HVA after probenecid has been reported to be up, down, or unchanged in both depression and mania (24). With 5HIAA the situation is equally confusing: decreased or unchanged in most depressed patients, although even elevated in some involutional and elderly cases, and in mania, up, down, or unchanged; the addition of probenecid has led to the fairly consistent and replicable finding that 5HIAA accumulation is decreased in depression, although in other studies there were only small changes or even no difference from controls, and there were variable changes with treatment (24, 47, 48). It also appears that neurotic depressions may be associated with decreases of the accumulation of 5HIAA in the CSF following probenecid at least as great as in severe endogenous depressions, and that CSF probenecid levels may themselves decrease with depression (48), to complicate the interpretation of the findings even further.

Other approaches to the correlation of amine metabolism with affective disorders have included a small number of attempts to assay biogenic amines and their metabolites directly in the brains of successful suicides, in comparison usually with victims of "accidents" or other causes of sudden death (16, 24, 49), no doubt including some persons with preterminal emotional disturbances. This type of experiment appears to represent the only example of the attempt to approach the metabolism of the brain directly in affective disorders. Concentrations of catecholamines have consistently been unchanged, while serotonin and 5HIAA were either unchanged or moderately decreased. The problems and limitations of such studies are many. In cases of suicide or other sudden deaths, the mental status and past history are often unknown, and the occurrence of suicide itself does not prove that a depressive disorder was present; many suicides are schizophrenic, for example. It is also very difficult to define, much less to select, an appropriate comparison group for suicides considering variables of age, time of day, time of recovery of the tissue, dietary, metabolic, and other variables that preceded death, as well as the probability that some accidental deaths represented suicides. One example of the kind of problem that can arise is that most of the instances of decreased brain levels of 5HIAA following suicide have occurred after overdoses of barbiturates, and so may not reflect an abnormality of serotonin metabolism specifically associated with depression.

The probable function of amine-secreting neurons in the hypothalamus, of regulating cells which secrete releasing factors for the pituitary trophins, may permit another more indirect method of estimating the functional status of these CNS neurons. Although it is possible to measure the levels and the effects of many trophic hormones, one that may be particularly promising is ACTH, since there is a tendency for secretion of adrenocorticosteroids to be elevated in depressed patients, and not necessarily as a nonspecific result of stress, psychotic turmoil, or agitation. This abnormality includes elements of alteration of diurnal rhythm of adrenal function and a failure for dexamethasone to suppress ACTH release. Part or all of these apparent changes in pituitary function could be due to a deficient suppression of ACTH release because of deficient function of central catecholaminergic neurons.

A different approach to the study of amine metabolism has been to evaluate the activity of the enzymes involved in their metabolism. The enzymes involved in the synthesis of amines have been studied only very indirectly by estimating rates of turnover, as, for example, by estimating the rate of rise of CSF metabolites following blockade of their removal with probenecid. Only slightly less indirectly, the rate of formation of tryptamine has been estimated following the administration of exogenous tryptophan, and has been reported to be decreased or unchanged (24, 43). There has been at least one attempt to estimate MAO activity *in vivo* by the rate of appearance of labeled 5HIAA in urine after the ingestion of radioactive serotonin, and no change was found in depression (43). Recently, there has been more attention given to the assay of enzyme activities in components of the blood *in vitro*. This approach has been possible for dopamine-β-hydroxylase, MAO, and COMT (catechol-*O*-methyltransferase). Studies of the activity of dopamine-β-hydroxylase in serum in a variety of psychiatric disorders have found no differences from normal (50). MAO has been reported to be *increased* in activity in the serum and in blood platelets in a heterogeneous group of endogenously depressed patients, while other studies have reported that this activity is *decreased* in some types of depressed patients, particularly those with monopolar endogenous depressions. Also, in bipolar or manic-depressive depressed patients, the activities were only equivocally greater than in controls, and the activity did not change with clinical status; decreased MAO activity may also occur in some schizophrenics and their twins (16, 24, 51). It has also been reported that bipolar depressed patients excrete more amines relative to deaminated metabolites of infused tritiated norepinephrine in comparison to monopolar and normal subjects (52)—a finding consistent with decreased MAO activity in bipolar patients. These various findings would thus appear to be mutually contradictory. The differences can only partly be due to the mixture of subtypes of endogenous depression associated with the finding of increased MAO activity in platelets. Other factors are known to be associated with variations of MAO activity. For example, the activity may be somewhat higher in females; it may increase with age in human plasma, platelets, and even in brain tissue; and it may be decreased by estrogens, perhaps partly explaining a reported rise of MAO activity in postmenopausal females. There are also confirmed reports that the activity of COMT in the red blood cell is decreased in some depressed patients, particularly those who are female and unipolar in type (53). The possible significance of these findings, if they are valid, is uncertain. It seems improbable that small changes in the activity of ubiquitous scavenger enzymes which are probably present in superabundance could contribute greatly to the etiology or pathophysiology of severe depressive illnesses. A more likely importance of such enzyme studies is that they might provide metabolic indices of unique biological features of certain subclasses of patients, or might serve as "genetic markers" of an idiosyncracy associated with affective illnesses by inheritance, though not necessarily associated with their cause.

One imaginative idea concerning the metabolism of indoleamines in the affective disorders has started from the observations which suggest that the availability of tryptophan may to a degree regulate the rate of synthesis of serotonin, that most of the metabolism of tryptophan passes by way of hepatic tryptophan pyrrolase—an enzyme which splits the indole ring and leads to the production of kynurenine, xanthurenic acid, and other related metabolites—and that pyrrolase is an induceable enzyme. Since the secretion of corticosteroids is often increased in affective disorder (though not necessarily specifically), it is conceivable that the steroids might lead to decreased availability of tryptophan for the synthesis of indoleamines. Evidence for this hypothesis included the observation that administration of steroids can decrease the levels of serotonin and 5HIAA in animal brains, and that this effect is blocked by allopurinol, a drug which inhibits pyrrolase *in vitro*. Although this hypothesis remains a topic of active interest in Europe and the USSR, it is unlikely to be valid for the following reasons (15, 20, 24, 37, 43). First, while there is some equivocal evidence that kynurenine and xanthurenic acid are excreted in higher-than-normal amounts in depression, in some studies the excretion of kynurenine bore no relationship to the clinical status of the patients, and in others there was either no difference from a comparison group or even an increase. Also, the induction of pyrrolase is unlikely to produce a physiologically significant increase in the rate of metabolism of tryptophan through the kynurenine pathway of the intact liver, and the effect of allopurinol on pyrrolase *in vivo* is at best equivocal; furthermore, allopurinol might be expected to have antidepressant effects, but it does not. There is also some evidence that tryptophan hydroxylase might be induceable by steroids, and this change should exert a much more powerful effect on the rate of serotonin synthesis than would follow modest changes in precursor availability. Furthermore, there is no compelling reason to accept a "stress hypothesis," which is implicit in the pyrrolase idea, for any affective illness, and particularly the endogenous depressions. Even if the importance of stress were accepted, an increase of steroids can occur in many psychiatric and medical conditions which are not necessarily associated with depression. The mechanism of the effect of steroids on rat brain serotonin remains unexplained, but in any event it appears to be transient and no longer evident after several days of treatment.

An extremely important aspect of neurotransmitter function which has hardly been approached experimentally is the status of receptor sensitivity in the affective disorders, though it has often been discussed (13, 16, 41, 43). One type of observation that may be relevant to receptors is that drugs which are believed to block central catecholamine receptors, and particularly the antipsychotic butyrophenones, have been associated with some depressive reactions, and more clearly with rather sudden shifts from mania into depression in patients with bipolar affective disease (19). Other blockers of more traditional alpha- or beta-adrenergic receptors are less clearly associated with depressive side effects, although they can produce sedative effects. These observations tend to support in a very indirect way the hypothesis that alteration of the interaction of catecholamines with their receptors might be associated with a shift in mood and activity. For a while, it appeared that a similar concept might be supportable for the indoleamines when it appeared that blocking agents of their receptors, including methysergide and cinnanserin, might be effective antimanic agents; this suggestion has not been supported by subsequent controlled clinical trials, and these drugs may even make mania worse (20, 24, 41). More direct attempts to investigate receptor function have been rare. There have been consistent reports of increased excretion of cyclic-AMP in the urine during mania or at least at its onset, and it may also be decreased in depression, while it is reported not to change in recurrent catatonia. In spite of these findings, it is difficult to make simple connections between the excretion of cyclic-AMP and the function of receptors of amines in the brain, since this nucleotide has been associated with a large number of hormonal effects in many tissues, since its urinary excretion increases with exercise, and since its levels in the CSF do not appear to change with depression or mania (19). There is also some evidence that physiological responses to infusions of norepinephrine may be subnormal in depression, suggesting that receptors may be insensitive (54). There has also been some speculation that the reported ability of triiodothyronine or of thyroid-stimulating hormone to increase the clinical efficacy of tricyclic antidepressants might be related to the ability of thyroid hormone to increase the sensitivity of catecholamine receptors; whether the putative clinical effect of thyrotropin releasing factor as an antidepressant is similarly mediated is unknown (22, 37, 55). Intriguing but paradoxical reports of antimanic effects of amphetamine have also been interpreted in terms of changes in receptor function (41).

Discussion and Conclusions

The preceding review of the basic biology, pharmacology, and clinical aspects of the metabolism of biogenic amines in the nervous system and their possible relationship to the affective disorders suggests several points for discussion. These fall into the categories of basic biological, biopsychological, and clinical psychiatric considerations. An important point is that there may have been a tendency to focus too narrowly on the catecholamines and serotonin in the past. Since it is likely that there are many neurotransmitters, including other amines and amino acids, these substances should also be considered in future hypotheses. Much of the interest in the catecholamines and indoleamines has evolved through the application of similar attractive unifying concepts and reliable experimental methods to both preclinical and clinical studies which have been mutually supportive, but which may have reinforced the retention of a somewhat constricted and simplistic set of hypotheses.

One very broad criticism of the amine hypotheses is that they have often not taken into account the physiology of central neurotransmitters. This may have been due to the relatively primitive state of knowledge of the function of central neurotransmitters, which has lagged behind developments in the biochemical pharmacology of central synapses, although this situation is changing. The development of the "indoleamine hypotheses" may represent one example of the failure to consider what is known physiologically. These have generally followed the lead of the "catecholamine hypotheses" in assuming that a deficiency of serotonin equals depression and that an excess equals mania. Such a simple view seems no longer to be tenable in light of considerations of the functional role of the indoleamines in the CNS discussed earlier; in fact, it might make more sense to consider the converse hypothesis—that *too much* serotonin may have something to do with some depressions.

A second criticism derives from the previous discussion of the metabolic regulation of aminergic synapses in the brain. Initially, amine hypotheses and even experiments were based on the grossly simplistic notion that too much amine did one thing, and that too little did the opposite; "much" and "little" were taken to mean concentration or "level" of a substance as measured chemically. One of the earliest observations contradicting that idea was that reserpinized animals are still responsive to behavioral stimulation by amphetamine, suggesting that depletion of an amine with reserpine may remove large stores of transmitter amines not directly involved in synaptic function. In recent years the concept has evolved that most, if not all, amine-containing nerve terminals have multiple "pools" of transmitter, that only a small portion of the total is essential for function, and that the rest is held in storage, possibly in the presynaptic vesicles and granules. Animal experimentation has made an important step forward in considering the dynamics rather than the "statics" of amines in the brain, but even the attempt to correlate "turnover" with function or with the action of a drug is fraught with difficulty, because overall turnover is heavily biased toward measuring metabolism in the relatively large storage pools rather than in the presumptive small functional pools of neurotransmitter.

A similar consideration which is often overlooked is that synapses are highly regulated, complex, dynamic functional systems. The degree of complexity and the physiological importance of the multiple means of regulation are only beginning to be appreciated. A few of the regulatory features of synaptic metabolism include precursor availability, the activity and concentrations of rate-limiting synthetic enzymes, the availability of their cofactors, the short-term and long-term responsiveness of transmitter synthesis to functional demands, the involvement of local and more distant feedback loops built into the neuronal circuitry, and the role of presynaptic receptors and local hormones in modulating the rate of release of transmitter. It is also likely that regulation occurs between neurons as well as within a neuron, and that the transmitters can affect the availability of other transmitters and their synthesizing enzymes in cells with which a given neuron has synaptic relationships. One other complicating feature of central amine-containing neurons is that their morphology is not irrevocably fixed; for example, the portion of an axon proximal to a lesion can grow and sprout, leading to a paradoxical excess of terminals and an *increase* in neurotransmitter in some areas. The importance of all these regulatory features is that synaptic transmission must be considered a marvelously plastic and adaptive function which is not simply turned on or off, and which is protected by a series of redundant homeostatic mechanisms. Unfortunately, most of the hypotheses about neurotransmission in psychiatric illness have assumed that the synapses are vulnerable and brittle and that their dysfunction should be easy to detect, overlooking the fact that synapses respond to perturbation by compensatory changes which tend to reestablish physiologic equilibrium. In an attempt to circumvent these various complications, there has been some consideration of the idea that the important aspect of transmitter function is the amount of transmitter that reaches and interacts with a receptor, but even this approach falls short at our complete ignorance of the function of the "effectors" which are moved by the interaction of transmitter and receptor.

Another aspect of the complexity of neurotransmitters and synaptic function is that normal behavior seems to require a well-orchestrated balance of the function of many component parts of the CNS, each involving different transmitters. A useful, if oversimplified, generalization is that in the CNS, as in the peripheral autonomic nervous system, there seem to be at least two fundamental types of function which can be called sympathetic or ergotrophic, and parasympathetic or trophotropic. The neurotransmitters which subserve these functions in the periphery are the catecholamines and acetylcholine, respectively. In the CNS, it also appears that catecholamines are involved with functions that might be described as activation, alertness, and appetitive or consummatory activity, while acetylcholine and serotonin seem to subserve quieting, behavior-inhibiting functions. Thus depression and mania need not represent simply the loss of one type of function, but might rather represent a change in balance between generally opposing tendencies—for example, a shift toward decreased catecholaminergic function in depression and the opposite in mania.

There has been considerable debate about how well each of the monoamines fits the hypothesis that it is uniquely deficient in depression and excessively active in mania. In favor of both hypotheses, it is usually pointed out that reserpine may lead to depression in susceptible patients and to a reduction of activity in animals while depleting both classes of monoamines. On the other hand, other antihypertensive drugs which more specifically antagonize the catecholamines have been associated with sedation, depression, and antimanic effects. Furthermore, precursors of the catecholamines, but not of the indoleamines, can reverse the sedation produced by reserpine in animals and man. The effects of the MAO-inhibitors in depression and in preventing the inactivation of most monoamines help both hypotheses about equally, although it may be possible to develop more selective MAO-inhibitors. The clinical effects of the precursor indoleamino acids are either minimal or controversial, although they might have some antimanic effect, and can have a sedative effect under some circumstances; L-dopa has stimulant properties, even though it is no more useful in treating serious depressions than amphetamine or other stimulants. On the whole, the effects of precursors support the conclusion that catecholamines favor stimulation and that serotonin favors sedation. Similarly, the relatively specific inhibition of tyrosine hydroxylase produces sedation or behavioral depression and can suppress mania, while the somewhat less specific inhibition of tryptophan hydroxylase on the whole tends to produce behavioral activation and hyper-responsiveness. While the original tricyclic antidepressants prevent the inactivation of both catecholamines and serotonin, the fact that the desmethylated drugs are more selective for norepinephrine favors a catecholamine hypothesis. The effects of lithium are generally supportive of an amine hypothesis, but do not support one amine exclusively. The metabolic effects of ECT suggest that seizures can release catecholamines and serotonin acutely, but that effects of repeated seizures are likely to be nonspecific in the case of serotonin, and small and of short duration in the case of norepinephrine. Perhaps the most important support for a single-amine hypothesis are the physiologic and behavioral effects of the catecholamines and indoleamines, and again, the evidence clearly favors the catecholamines. On balance, the behavioral and pharmacological data support a catecholamine hypothesis much more consistently than an indoleamine hypothesis. An alternative position would be that an indoleamine deficiency might help to explain some features of depressive illness, such as the insomnia and possibly some aspects of agitation, while a deficiency of catecholamines would perhaps better explain decreased drive, pleasure, enthusiasm, and appetite for food and sex, particularly in retarded depressions. Since both amines undergo important diurnal variations, a deficiency of either one might underlie the diurnal pattern of depressive symptoms. Acetylcholine could also be added as another variable which might be increased in retarded depressions and decreased in mania and other states of psychotic agitation.

Although the preceding arguments are the common ones presented in discussions of catecholamine *versus* indoleamine hypotheses, there are many limitations and problems associated with them. All of the amine hypotheses seem to presume that mania and depression represent opposite poles along a single mood scale, although manic-depressive illness is much more complicated than that, and there are at least several clinical types of both endogenous depressions and manias. The current amine hypotheses do not readily account for this kind of clinical variability, and instead tend to view manic-depressive illness as a one-dimensional problem of too little or too much of something in the brain.

Another fundamental problem is that the arguments based on the metabolic or behavioral actions of drugs require gross oversimplification and selective inattention to many aspects of preclinical and clinical pharmacology. For example, none of the drugs does only one thing chemically or clinically, as is sometimes implied. Furthermore, much of what is known about the actions of drugs is strongly biased because so much attention has been given to an overly restricted range of clinically relevant theories, perhaps partly based on a desire to provide social justification for the pursuit of basic science. The investigation of drugs has usually been done with doses and schedules that are very different from the clinical situation: Doses tend to be huge, and long-term experiments are almost never done, largely because it is more difficult and expensive to do so. Even though many of the behavioral effects of the drugs in normal laboratory animals treated in this way are not similar to the clinical effects, the corresponding metabolic effects observed under the same conditions are usually accepted uncritically. Since it often happens that metabolic effects after repeated administration are opposite or at least dissimilar to those observed after a single dose of a drug, it is possible to be badly misled by short-term experiments.

The behavioral effects of drugs in the experimental situation are often very different from the effects observed clinically. An outstanding example of this phenomenon is that large acute doses of most antidepressants tend to produce sedation in normal laboratory animals, and it has been very difficult to devise reliable laboratory tests to screen potential new antidepressant drugs. Another problem is that most of the so-called animal models of affective illness are really more nearly models of sedation or stimulation; thus it is very tricky to make comparisons between human disease and animal models or to make predictions about human clinical responses based on animal behavior. Clinically too some marked peculiarities of the effects of drug substances are difficult to reconcile with the current amine hypotheses. For example, the idea that psychiatric complications of antihypertensive drugs are a good "clinical model" of spontaneous depressions is increasingly difficult to accept as they may represent individual responses to sedative effects, and since it is difficult to produce clinical depression in a normal person with an antihypertensive drug. Furthermore, the division of somatic therapies into antidepressant and antimanic has certain inconsistencies. It is clear that the most effective antimanic agents are highly nonspecific; they are useful in many psychotic and nonpsychotic conditions, and they are even useful in the management of some agitated depressions. Less easily evaluated are the occasional reports that several forms of treatment have antimanic effects which are at variance with the amine hypotheses: For example, amphetamine, tricyclic antidepressants, and ECT have all at one time or another been used to treat manic patients, evidently with some success. Finally, a persistent difficulty for the current hypotheses is the slowness of clinical action of both the MAO-inhibitors and the tricyclic antidepressants, while their much-discussed metabolic effects occur quickly. Another theoretical and practical problem of the available antidepressants is that in my opinion they appear to be unsatisfactory drugs, the efficacy of which is sometimes barely demonstrable.

In reviewing the clinical metabolic studies in this field, one is forced to conclude that it is a tribute to the persuasiveness and attractiveness of current pharmacological theories concerning the biogenic amines that they have persisted in spite of conflicting and inconsistent clinical findings. Even the most cautious conclusions based on the clinical literature are hard to propose without fear of contradiction. Nevertheless, they would seem to include the following: Many amines seem to be released from peripheral tissues and made more available to general metabolism and urinary excretion during states of excitement or agitation, regardless of the diagnostic label applied (mania or agitated depression); conversely, in retarded depressive states, the opposite tends to occur. Comparable events may also occur in the brain, although this point is still unclear. Since similar changes may also be associated with other psychiatric illnesses or even "stress," their specificity to affective illness is questionable. There is almost no evidence to suggest that these changes are primary and thus perhaps etiologically important in initiating the severe endogenous affective disorders, although the recent hint that changes in the rate of excretion of MHPG in the urine may slightly precede the clinical change in mood and behavior (35) is very interesting in this regard. While the changes might be only peripheral or incidental, it is not unlikely that changes in the metabolism of the monoamines are one part of the pathophysiology of the affective disorders, and that can be true without any implication about etiology or "cause." Thus the increased understanding of the physiology of central neurotransmission should help greatly to make sense of the clinical pathophysiology of depression and mania, as it has already helped to evolve theories concerning the actions of several forms of physical treatment that really do something for the affective illnesses and which have clear effects on the metabolism of biogenic amines in the brain. Even if alterations in amine metabolism have nothing to do with the cause of the illnesses, but modifying this metabolism with drugs or other treatments has therapeutic value, then an understanding of the biogenic amines would indeed still be worthwhile.

The confusing state of affairs in the clinical literature on amine metabolism has led to a tendency to seek finer subdivisions of the diagnostic categories, in search of some coherence in the psychological and metabolic correlations, or some ability to make predictions about clinical outcome. While this attempt has some merit, it may be premature. There is certainly a growing impression that there are several sorts of depression and mania. Depressions at least divide into serious ones and lesser ones, and the concept of "endogenicity" seems to be useful. Within the severe endogenous depressions, it does seem that some are agitated and that some are retarded, and that the latter are quite characteristic of bipolar case histories. Even the manias might be subdivided into two or more types: an elated or grandiose type, an angry-paranoid type, and even a "depressed" or dysphoric type. While the latter categories sound paradoxical, it is clear that many patients manifest manic speech and activity while maintaining a distinctly noneuphoric mood. There are genetic data to support some of these subdivisions, and attempts are being made to find metabolic or clinical pharmacologic correlations with them. Unfortunately, there is as yet no universal agreement about how to categorize the affective disorders, and there are few independent means of arriving at a single scheme. One could attempt to evolve an hypothesis based on the metabolism of the catecholamines, serotonin and acetylcholine, with sufficient variables so as to fit any diagnostic system. On the other hand, it would be unfortunate if a basically attractive hypothesis were to be weakened by the premature accretion of excessive complications and embellishments before the basic idea is established on a firm foundation.

Have there been any practical gains in the clinical areas of this field? It is clear that there have been enormous improvements in the laboratory techniques and analytical methods applied to both the basic and clinical study of amine metabolism. There has also been important progress in the design of clinical studies, with attention now routinely paid to the objective evaluation of behavior and mood, the use of control groups and placebo conditions, and the attempt to avoid or control as many spurious environmental and biological variables as possible. On the other hand, many hoped-for gains have not been forthcoming. For example, regardless of whether the currently available metabolic findings suggest interesting generalizations about groups of patients, it is not yet possible to base clinical decisions or predictions about a major affective illness on any known measure of amine metabolism. Another unhappy realization is that the amine hypotheses have not yet led to the prediction and rational development of a therapy which is better or safer than those essentially known two decades ago.

For the future, it seems highly likely that a more rational understanding of the pathophysiology of the affective illnesses will include an appreciation of the function of the biogenic amine neurotransmitters of the central nervous system. Even if one of the current hypotheses is correct, and the strongest seems to be that a deficiency of central catecholamines is an important aspect of the occurence of retarded depression, we would still be left with the riddle of what makes that so!

Acknowledgment

Partially supported by U.S. Public Health Service (NIMH) Grant MH-16674 and U.S.P.H.S. (NIMH) Career Development Award, Type II, MH-74370.

References

1. Jacobsen E: The theoretical basis of the chemotherapy of depression, in *Depression: Proceedings of the Symposium at Cambridge, September 1959.* Edited by Davies EB, New York, Cambridge University Press, 1964, p. 208.
2. Everett GM, Toman JEP: Mode of action of Rauwolfia alkaloids and motor activity, in *Biological Psychiatry.* Edited by Masserman JH, New York, Grune & Stratton, 1959, pp. 75–81.
3. Pare CMB, Sandler M: A clinical and biochemical study of a trial of iproniazid in the treatment of depression. *J Neurol Neurosurg Psychiatr* **22**:247–251, 1959.
4. Weil-Malherbe H: The concentration of adrenaline in human plasma and its relation to mental activity. *J Ment Sci* **101**:733–755, 1955.
5. Weil-Malherbe H: The biochemistry of the functional psychoses. *Adv Enzymol* **29**:479–553, 1967.
6. Baldessarini RJ, Karobath M: Biochemical physiology of central synapses. *Ann Rev Physiol* **35**:273–304, 1973.
7. Andén NE, Dahlström A, Fuxe K, and others: Ascending neurons to the telencephalon and diencephalon. *Acta Physiol Scand* **67**:313–326, 1966.
8. Baldessarini RJ: Pharmacology of the amphetamines. *Pediatrics* **49**:694–701, 1972.

9. Mountcastle VB, Baldessarini RJ: Synaptic transmission, in *Medical Physiology*. Edited by Mountcastle VB, CV Mosby Co, St. Louis, ed. 13, Chap. 57, 1974, pp. 182–223.
10. Meek JL, Neff NH: Is cerebrospinal fluid the major avenue for the removal of 5-hydroxyindoleacetic acid from the brain? *Neuropharmacology* **12**:497–499, 1973.
11. Hoffer BJ, Siggins GR, Oliver AP, and others: Activation of the pathway from locus ceruleus to rat cerebellar Purkinje neurons: Pharmacological evidence of noradrenergic central inhibition. *J Pharmacol Exp Ther* **184**:553–569, 1973.
12. Kalisker A, Rutledge CO, Perkins JP: Effect of nerve degeneration by 6-hydroxy-dopamine on catecholamine-stimulated adenosine 3',5'-monophosphate formation in rat cerebral cortex. *Mol Pharmacol*, **9**:619–629, 1973.
13. Dewhurst WG: Amines and abnormal mood. *Proc Roy Soc Med* **62**:32–37, 1969.
14. Baldessarini RJ: Biogenic amines and behavior. *Ann Rev Med* **23**:343–354, 1972.
15. Barchas J, Usdin E (eds): *Serotonin and Behavior*. New York, Academic Press, 1973, 642 pp.
16. Davis JM: Theories of biological etiology of affective disorders, in *International Review of Neurobiology*. Edited by Pfeiffer CC, Smythies JR, New York, Academic Press, 1970, Vol. 12, pp. 145–175.
17. Glowinski J, Baldessarini RJ: Metabolism of norepinephrine in the central nervous system. *Pharmacol Rev* **18**:1201–1238, 1966.
18. Schildkraut JJ: *Neuropsychopharmacology and the Affective Disorders*. Boston, Little, Brown, 1970, 111 pp.
19. Bunney WE Jr, Goodwin FK, Murphy DL: The "switch process" in manic-depressive illness. *Arch Gen Psychiatr* **27**:295–317, 1972.
20. Carroll BJ: Monoamine precursors in the treatment of depression. *Clin Pharmacol Ther* **12**:743–761, 1971.
21. Goodwin FK, Murphy DL, Brodie HKH, and others: L-Dopa, catecholamines and behavior: A clinical and biochemical study in depressed patients. *Biol Psychiatr* **2**:341–366, 1970.
22. Coppen A, Whybrow PC, Noguera R, and others: The comparative antidepressant value of L-tryptophan and imipramine with and without attempted potentiation by liothyronine. *Arch Gen Psychiatr* **26**:234–241, 1972.
23. Redmond DE Jr, Maas JW, Kling A, and others: Social behavior of monkeys selectively depleted of monoamines. *Science* **174**:428–430, 1971.
24. Schildkraut JJ: Neuropsychopharmacology of the affective disorders. *Ann Rev Pharmacol* **13**:427–454, 1973.
25. Goodwin JK, Ebert MH, Bunney WE Jr: Mental effects of reserpine in man: A review, in *Psychiatric Complications of Medical Drugs*. Edited by Shader R, New York, Raven Press, 1972, pp. 73–101.
26. Janowsky DS, El-Yousef MK, Davis JM, and others: Parasympathetic suppression of manic symptoms by physostigmine. *Arch Gen Psychiatr* **28**:542–547, 1973.
27. Roffler-Tarlov S, Schildkraut JJ, Draskoczy PR: Effects of acute and chronic administration of desmethylimipramine on the content of norepinephrine and other monoamines in the rat brain. *Biochem Pharmacol* **22**:2923–2926, 1973.
28. Goodwin FK, Murphy DL, Dunner DL, and others: Lithium response in unipolar versus bipolar depression. *Am J Psychiatr* **129**:44–47, 1972.
29. Ebert M, Baldessarini RJ, Lipinsky JF, and others: Effects of electroconvulsive seizures on amine metabolism in the rat brain. *Arch Gen Psychiatr* **29**:397–401, 1973.
30. Messiha FS, Turek I: Electroconvulsive therapy: Effect on catecholamine

excretion by psychiatric patients. *Res Comm Chem Path Pharmacol* **1**:535–546, 1970.

31. Nordin G, Ottoson J-O, Roos B-E: Influence of convulsive therapy on 5-hydroxyindoleacetic acid and homovanillic acid in cerebrospinal fluid in endogenous depression. *Psychopharmacologia (Berl)* **20**:315–320, 1971.
32. Ström-Olsen R, Weil-Malherbe H: Humoral changes in manic-depressive psychosis with particular reference to the excretion of catechol amines in urine. *J Ment Sci* **104**:696–704, 1958.
33. Matussek N: Biochemie der Depression. *J Neural Transmission* **33**:223–234, 1972.
34. Post RM, Kotin J, Goodwin EK, and others: Psychomotor activity and cerebrospinal fluid amine metabolites in affective illness. *Am J Psychiatr* **130**:67–72, 1973.
35. Jones FK, Maas JW, Dekirmenjian H, and others: Urinary catecholamine metabolites during behavioral changes in a patient with manic-depressive cycles. *Science* **179**:300–302, 1973.
36. Maas JW, Fawcett JA, Dekirmenjian H: Catecholamine metabolism, depressive illness, and drug response. *Arch Gen Psychiatr* **26**:246–262, 1972.
37. Schildkraut JJ (ed): Symposium on biochemical and pharmacological aspects of affective disorders. *J Psychiatr Res* **9**:163–270, 1972.
38. Shopsin B, Wilk S, Sathananthan G, and others: Catecholamines and affective disorders revised: A critical assessment. *J Nerv Ment Dis* **158**:369–383, 1974.
39. Angrist B, Shopsin B, Gershon S, and others: Metabolites of monoamines in urine and cerebrospinal fluid, after large dose amphetamine administration. *Psychopharmacologia (Berl)* **26**:1–9, 1972.
40. Mosnaim AD, Inwang EE, Sugarman JH, and others: Ultraviolet spectrophotometric determination of 2-phenylethylamine in biological samples and its possible correlation with depression. *Biol Psychiatr* **6**:235–257, 1973.
41. Ashcroft G, Eccleston D, Murray L, and others: Modified amine hypothesis for the aetiology of affective illness. *Lancet (London)* **2**:573–577, 1972.
42. Glassman A: Indoleamines and affective disorders. *Psa Med* **31**:107–114, 1969.
43. Himwich HE: Indoleamines and the depressions, in *Biochemistry, Schizophrenias and Affective Illnesses.* Edited by Himwich HE, Baltimore, Williams & Wilkins, 1970, pp. 230–282.
44. Van Praag HM: Indoleamines and the central nervous system. *Psychiatr Neurol Neurochirurg* **73**:9–36, 1970.
45. Tagliamonte A, Tagliamonte P, Gessa R, and others: Increase of brain tryptophan by probenecid. *Riv Farmacol Ter* **11**:207–213, 1971.
46. Post RM, Gordon EK, Goodwin FK, and others: Central norepinephrine metabolism in affective illness: MHPG in the cerebrospinal fluid. *Science* **179**:1002–1003, 1973.
47. Bowers MB Jr: Cerebrospinal fluid 5-hydroxyindoleacetic acid (5HIAA) and homovanillic acid (HVA) following probenecid in unipolar depressives treated with amitriptyline. *Psychopharmacologia (Berl)* **23**:26–33, 1972.
48. Van Praag HM, Korf J, Schut D: Cerebral monoamines and depression. *Arch Gen Psychiatr* **28**:827–831, 1973.
49. Bourne HR, Bunney WE Jr, Colburn RW, and others: Noradrenaline, 5-hydroxytryptamine and 5-hydroxyindoleacetic acid in hindbrain of suicidal patients. *Lancet* **2**:805–808, 1968.
50. Shopsin B, Freedman LS, Goldstein M, and others: Serum dopamine-β-hydroxylase (DBH) activity and affective states. *Psychopharmacologia (Berl)* **27**:11–16, 1972.

51. Murphy DL, Weiss R: Reduced monoamine oxidase activity in blood platelets from bipolar depressed patients. *Am J Psychiatr* **128:**1351–1357, 1972.
52. Rosenblatt S, Chanley JD, Leighton WP: Temporal changes in the distribution of urinary tritiated metabolites in affective disorders. *J Psychiatr Res* **6:**321–333, 1969.
53. Dunner DL, Cohn DK, Gershon ES, and others: Differential catechol-*0*-methyl-transferase activity in unipolar and bipolar affective illness. *Arch Gen Psychiatr* **26:**364–366, 1972.
54. Prange AJ Jr, McCurdy RL, Cochrane CM: The systolic blood pressure response of depressed patients to infused norepinephrine. *J Psychiatr Res* **5:**1–13, 1967.
55. Wilson IC, Prange AJ Jr, McClane JK, and others: Thyroid-hormone enhancement of imipramine in nonretarded depressions. *New Eng J Med* **282:**1063–1067, 1970.

Nineteen

Mineral Metabolism

Farouk F. Faragalla, D.Sc.

Little more than half a century ago, Allers (1) investigated water and electrolytes in affective disorders and found that only a small proportion of depressed patients were dehydrated. It is possible that later studies on electrolytes in affective disorders have been stimulated by the introduction of flame photometry for estimating sodium and potassium. The relatively recent observation of Schottstaedt and associates (2) that periods of depression in normal people were accompanied by a decreased urinary excretion of sodium, and the significance of sodium in regulating brain excitability as described by Woodbury and Esplin (3) have given further impetus to studies on mineral metabolism in emotional depression. The relevance of mineral metabolism to depressive illness was also strengthened by the introduction of the ionic theory of neural activity in the early 1950s, which proposes that excitation produces a local increased permeability which allows sodium to flow inward and potassium outward. Calcium has been postulated to interact with certain neural membrane molecules and thus impose constraints upon the ionic movements of Na^+ and K^+. The neurophysiological issues of the ionic theory have been discussed by Katz (4). On the basis of the ionic theory of neural activity it is theoretically possible that changes in sodium, potassium, or calcium concentration on either side of the neuronal membrane could affect their function and might therefore account for some of the symptomatology of functional psychoses.

In this chapter I describe the studies that have dealt with the metabolism of sodium, potassium, calcium, and magnesium in depressed patients.

Sodium Metabolism

Under this heading both sodium and water metabolism are discussed. Several investigators have reported that various types of mental illness and transient emotional disturbances are associated with retention of sodium and water, but in these studies the intake of sodium and water was seldom accurately known. Klein (5) described this finding in the depressive phase of periodic psychoses, and Rowntree and Kay (6) found it in recurrent schizophrenia, whereas Ström-Olsen and Weil-Malherbe (7) observed the reverse in the manic-depressive psychoses. Schottstaedt and others (2) claimed that they had detected, during transient depressive moods in normal subjects, retention of sodium and water sufficient to cause considerable increase in body weight. In accurately controlled investigations, Trolle (8) showed that the recovery from depression was associated in some patients with an increase, and in other patients with a decrease, in water excretion. In cases of periodic catatonia Gjessing (9) described a small retention of sodium and water during the ill phase when there occurred a paradoxical loss of weight. Crammer (10, 11) had stated that gross changes in weight may precede the mental variations in cyclical psychoses and had suggested that these weight changes are determined by alterations in water and sodium balance.

Russell (12) studied the weight and the balance of sodium and water before, during, and after electric convulsive therapy (ECT) in depressed patients kept on a strictly controlled intake of food and fluids. He found that the electrically induced convulsions were followed by a significant retention of sodium and water during the next 24 hours. These transient changes, however, occurred even after patients were subjected only to procedures preliminary to ECT. It is probable, therefore, that the sodium and water retention was related to the emotional reaction to ECT rather than the convulsions themselves. The therapeutic effect of ECT was not dependent on the occurrence of such sodium and water retention.

The recovery from depression did not alter the trend in body weight present during the illness so long as the caloric intake was kept constant. Russell (12) also found no significant change in the balance of sodium, water, and potassium following recovery.

The availability of radioactive isotopes of sodium made it possible to measure another dimension of sodium metabolism, which is the exchangeable body sodium. The determination of the latter is based on the principle of the isotope dilution technique which has been discussed in detail by Coppen (13) and Veall and Vetter (14). For the determination of the 24-hour exchangeable sodium, a known amount of ^{22}Na or ^{24}Na is administered and its excretion is monitored for 24 hours. At that time a blood sample is collected for determination of the concentration of serum sodium and radioactive sodium. The specific activity of serum sodium is then derived by dividing the concentration of radioactive serum sodium by the concentration of serum sodium. The exchangeable sodium can then be calculated as follows:

$$\frac{\textit{radioactive sodium administered} - \textit{radioactive sodium excreted}}{\textit{specific activity of serum sodium}}$$

Gibbons (15) was the first to apply the isotope dilution technique to measure exchangeable sodium in depression. He examined the 24-hour exchangeable sodium in a group of 24 adult patients suffering from severe depression. Estimations were carried out initially just after admission when all the patients were depressed and later, after several weeks, when 16 of the patients had recovered. Eight of the patients who had failed to respond to treatment were also retested. Gibbons found that the 24-hour exchangeable sodium decreased significantly on the average by 9% (209 mEq) after recovery; the patients who did not recover showed no significant alteration in exchangeable sodium. Alterations in the diet did not appear to produce these results since 10 patients who were kept on a constant intake of sodium showed the same changes as the rest of the patients. One explanation of Gibbon's finding is that during depression patients retain sodium and during recovery they excrete more sodium so that the total body sodium decreases. However, such an explanation would be in apparent contradiction to the findings of Russell (12), whose balance studies showed no significant change in sodium balance during recovery from depression. In a series of 12 depressed patients Coppen, Shaw, and Mangoni (16) were unable to confirm Gibbon's findings as they observed no statistical difference in the exchangeable sodium before and after recovery. This led these authors to hypothesize that in depression there may be no change in total body sodium, but that during depression there may be redistribution of sodium within the body between the extracellular and the intracellular spaces. To test this hypothesis, Coppen and Shaw (17) investigated the electrolyte distribution between the cells and extracellular fluid in 23 depressed patients by utilizing multiple isotope dilution techniques. Total body water (TBW) was estimated by tritiated water, and extracellular water (ECW) was measured by ^{82}Br and exchangeable sodium by ^{24}Na. The extracellular sodium may be derived from the ECW and sodium concentration in the serum. The difference between the exchangeable sodium and the extracellular sodium is the residual sodium (i.e., the intracellular sodium and exchangeable bone sodium). After recovery from depression there was a significant increase of 1.2L/TBW which was paralleled by a rise of 1.2 kg of body weight. ECW also increased significantly by 0.5L, and the intracellular water showed a similar but less consistent rise. Similar changes in ECW had been previously reported by Altschule and Tillotson (18) and Dawson, Hullin, and Crocket (19). The total exchangeable sodium fell with recovery and the extracellular sodium rose slightly, but neither change was significant. When the exchangeable sodium was expressed on body weight basis the decrease became statistically significant. Coppen and Shaw (17) also found that after recovery there was a highly significant decrease of residual sodium. This alteration in the distribution of sodium was reflected in the ratio extracellular sodium/residual sodium which was 4.3 during depression and 9.9 after recovery. Since estimate of the residual sodium is derived after estimation of the ECW, the ^{82}Br method used for determining the latter needs some comment. While ^{82}Br generally yields a reliable measure of ECW, errors might be introduced because of changes in gastrointestinal function upon recovery from depression, since the ratio of Br^- to Cl^- in gastric fluid is considerably higher than this ratio in the serum. However, the finding that an elevated residual sodium in depression might be reflective of an elevated intracellular sodium is a provocative one. Unfortunately, it is not possible to estimate whether the increase in residual sodium represents an increase in intracellular sodium or bone sodium or both. On the assumption that the changes in residual sodium may reflect changes in intracellular sodium, Coppen and Shaw (17) hypothesized that small changes in electrolyte gradients across membrane of certain neurons in the CNS might be crucial determinants of depressive illness. Electrophysiological evidence of abnormal function of pathways in the nervous system in depression has been obtained by the study of evoked cortical potentials (20).

Using a whole body counter, Baer and colleagues (21) reported that during depression there was significantly greater tendency to retain ^{22}Na than during periods when the patients were less depressed or recovered. This result seems to be consistent with an increase in 24-hour exchangeable sodium in depression as described by Gibbons (15) and Coppen (13).

In summary, then, it seems that upon recovery from endogenous depression there is a decrease in 24-hour exchangeable sodium. Some believe that such a change should be accompanied by negative sodium balance during recovery. However, so far this has not been demonstrated. The finding that residual sodium (which is intracellular sodium and a small amount of exchangeable bone sodium) was increased by nearly 50% during the depressive illness and returned to normal after recovery as described by Coppen and Shaw (17) is of special interest and awaits to be corroborated. The finding concerning changes in residual sodium during depression suggests that in depression there is a redistribution of sodium between the cells and the extracellular fluid.

The movement of sodium between cells and ECW cannot be studied easily in man, but its transfer between blood and CSF can be measured. Coppen (22) found that in depressed subjects the rate of entry of ^{24}Na in the CSF (expressed as the percentage of ^{24}Na activity in lumbar CSF compared to plasma after 1 hour) was about 2% as compared to 4% in normal subjects. In recovered depressed patients the rate of ^{24}Na entry in the CSF becomes normal. Coppen had produced evidence to suggest that the lower rate of entry of sodium in depression was due to a decrease in permeability to sodium rather than a vascular change in the CNS. Fotherby and others (23) found that exercise significantly increased the calculated transfer rate of ^{24}Na and suggested that decreased physical activity in depressed patients could account for the differences in sodium transfer rate. He was unable to confirm a lower transfer rate of sodium in depressed patients when compared to schizophrenic patients. However, these authors observed that the transfer rates of sodium in several very depressed patients were much lower than in other patients. The mechanism by which sodium handling is altered in depression is not completely known. Baer and colleagues (21) found that changes in depression ratings, sodium retention, and 17-hydroxycorticosteroid excretion paralleled each other, suggesting that the level of adrenal cortical activity is related to the sodium retention in depression. Direct measurements of aldosterone excretion in depression have been reported to be within normal limits (24).

Maas (25) has attempted to relate the available biochemical findings regarding steroid hormones and electrolytes to possible catecholamine deficiency in depressive illness. He suggested that the increased adrenocortical steroid secretion observed in depression would be expected to be associated with retention of sodium which could lead to accelerated uptake of noradrenaline in the neuron, and thus lead to a decreased rate of synthesis of catecholamine.

Potassium Metabolism

Russell (12) conducted balance studies of sodium and water as well as potassium in depressed patients before and after ECT and was unable to show any change in total potassium upon recovery from depression. The 24-hour exchangeable potassium in depressed patients was measured by Gibbons (15), who failed to demonstrate any difference in the exchangeable potassium after recovery. Shaw and Coppen (26) determined total body potassium in depressed patients by whole body counting, which measures the radioactivity of the naturally occurring isotope of potassium ^{40}K. Furthermore, they used ^{82}Br and tritium to estimate ECW and total body water. Their results indicated that in depression there was a relative deficiency of total body potassium and a low intracellular potassium concentration when compared to values obtained on normal subjects. It was found that these patients showed a relatively increased ICW (intracellular water) and decreased ECW. These abnormalities showed no change with clinical recovery. One limitation of the Shaw and Coppen (26) investigation was that the data for normal subjects were obtained from other laboratories. Accordingly, Shaw and Coppen's findings concerning potassium abnormalities in depression must be corroborated before being accepted.

Bunney (27) found an increase in total body potassium accompanying clinical improvement in depression. These changes were associated with decreases in the urinary content of 17-OHCS. These results, if corroborated, complement the findings of decreased 24-hour exchangeable sodium and strengthen the hypothesis that changes in both sodium and potassium metabolism in depression are related to alterations in adrenal steroid secretion rates.

Shaw and associates (28) have reported on postmortem study of brain electrolytes in suicide patients and compared these values to the brain electrolyte concentration in a group of patients who died of natural causes. The brain samples from suicide patients showed an increase in brain water and a significant decrease in sodium, when the latter is expressed as mEq/100 g fat-free weight, but no significant change in potassium concentration. On the basis of these results and on the findings that the concentrations of sodium and potassium in the cerebrospinal fluid (and therefore of the whole extracellular phase) are within normal limits in depression, these authors deduced that in depression brain extracellular space may be contracted and intracellular space may be enlarged, resulting in a reduction of the intracellular potassium concentration.

Calcium and Magnesium

Neurophysiological studies have indicated that calcium plays an important role in nerve transmission. Presently, it is well known that the excitation process can be modified by changes in the external concentration of calcium ions in the media bathing nerve axons or nerve ganglia. Brink (29) postulates that the major role of calcium ions in the neural process is to impose constraints upon the ionic movements of sodium and potassium. The mechanism by which calcium ions bring about the permeability changes is not well understood. One possibility is that calcium ions combine with molecules of the membrane to increase its stability, and another possibility is that calcium ions combine with molecules (receptor sites) required for sodium or potassium transport. Several workers have investigated one aspect or another concerning calcium metabolism in emotional depression. Harris and Beauchemin (30) found that Ca^{2+}/Mg^{2+} ratio in CSF is abnormally high in depression because of low Mg^{2+} concentration. The normal CSF for Ca^{2+}/Mg^{2+} ratio is 1.6 as compared to 2 to 3.4 in depressed patients. Eiduson and associates (31) have shown that ECT did not have any effect on CSF calcium concentrations. These authors observed that the pretreatment CSF calcium levels were higher in the unimproved group when compared with CSF levels in the improved group. Gour and Chaudhry (32) noted that transient hypercalcemia occurs immediately after ECT and that such hypercalcemia was followed by a gradual fall in serum calcium, even reaching levels less than the initial values. Coirault and associates (33) found that under the influence of ECT or imipramine there is a decrease in total blood calcium; however, ionized calcium as well as urinary calcium increased. These authors formulated the concept that depression is improved as soon as calcium is excreted. Flach and associates (34) and Flach (35) were unable to corroborate Coirault's results and, as a matter of fact, found the opposite. In 70% (14 out of 20 patients) ECT was associated with a 15 to 20% decrease in urinary calcium excretion, and in 18 out of 32 patients (about 56%) treated with imipramine there was a decrease in urinary calcium. Depressed and paranoid patients who recovered showed a significant decrease in urinary calcium excretion during recovery, whereas neurotics and patients who did not recover did not show this change. Faragalla and Flach (36) applied both calcium balance and kinetic techniques (using ^{47}Ca) to explore the possible mechanisms which might bring about a decrease in urinary calcium after treatment with ECT or imipramine. In essence, calcium kinetic studies were carried out by intravenous injection of ^{47}Ca. On the first day of injection, blood samples were drawn at 0.5, 1, 3, 6, 12, 18, and 24 hours. Thereafter blood samples were drawn every 24 hours for 9 days. Twenty-four-hour urine collection and the stool excreted for 10 days after injection as well as serum were analyzed for calcium and the radioactivity. The serum calcium specific activity curve was constructed and resolved into its exponential components. The coefficients and rate constants of the final two compartments which gave the best fit for the observed serum specific activity curve were used in deriving the pool and its turnover. Bone formation rate was calculated as the difference between calcium pool turnover and the sum of urinary and endogenous fecal calcium. The bone resorption rate was derived as the difference between bone formation and calcium balance. In three out of four patients treated with imipramine, improved calcium retention was noted and was due to increased net calcium absorption, and to decreased urinary calcium excretion. Kinetic studies showed that imipramine treatment was associated with increased bone formation rate. The mechanism whereby imipramine stimulates the rate of bone formation is unknown and deserves further investigation. In four patients receiving ECT, improved calcium retention was also noted and was due to increased calcium absorption from the intestine and to decreased urinary calcium excretion. In all patients receiving ECT there was marked reduction in the bone resorption rate.

The serum calcium concentration in these patients was within the normal range before and after treatment. However, treatment was associated with a significant decrease in serum calcium concentration in three out of four patients receiving either imipramine or ECT.

On the basis of these data Faragalla and Flach (37) postulated the following hypothesis: Emotional depression is associated with relatively high extracellular calcium concentration which could be decreased by ECT or imipramine treatment. The increased extracellular calcium concentration in depression may be due to decreased bone formation or to increased bone resorption. It is possible that bone response is affected by neurohumoral or neurogenic factors which in turn are influenced by emotions. This hypothesis seems to fit Coppen's (13) finding in depression concerning the marked increase in residual sodium which probably represents an increase in intracellular sodium. The latter inference is compatible with our hypothesis, since it is possible that intracellular sodium accumulation could be affected by increased extracellular calcium. Evidence from *in vitro* experiments has indicated that lowering of external calcium concentrations appears to facilitate sodium movement out of the cells of cerebral cortex slices. It is also a speculative possibility that the decrease in serum calcium concentration observed after treatment in most patients may lead to decreased release of biogenic amines from the brain, thus alleviating depression. Support for this notion comes from the work of Douglas and Rubin (38), who demonstrated that the concentration of calcium in the solution perfusing the adrenal glands influences the release of catecholamines. The possible use of the hormone thyrocalcitonin, which is known to lower serum calcium, as a therapeutic agent in depressive illness can serve as one route to further test our hypothesis.

To find out whether the decreased urinary calcium associated with ECT or imipramine treatment was accompanied by other metabolic changes, Flach and Faragalla (39) studied the urinary excretion of calcium, phosphorus, magnesium, sodium, and potassium before and after treatment in 14 depressed patients. These authors found that ECT or imipramine therapy was associated with shifts in electrolyte excretion which varied among the patients studied. The common denominator in these shifts was the observable decrease in urinary calcium which was preceded or accompanied by change in one or another of the measured electrolytes such as phosphates, magnesium, sodium, and potassium.

Flach and Faragalla pointed out that these urinary findings reflect overall metabolic changes in the body, including the nervous system if it is similarly affected. However, if these metabolic changes do not take place in the nervous system itself the possibility still remains that metabolic changes occurring in other parts of the body may have an influence on the function of the nervous system. Thus it is possible to speculate that the metabolic shifts in mineral metabolism associated with ECT or imipramine may have beneficial effects in the process of recovering from depression. However, direct evidence for such a notion does not exist at the present time.

Cade (40) reported significant elevations in plasma magnesium concentration in depressed patients before and after recovery, and also in schizophrenia. Frizel, Coppen, and Marks (41) found that total plasma magnesium was lower in depressed patients and increased with recovery from the depression. The latter finding is just the opposite of Cade's observation in depressed patients, and further work is needed to clarify this controversy.

References

1. Allers R: Ergebnisse Stoffwechselpathologischer Untersuchungen bei Pschosen: III. das Manisch-Depressive Irresein. *Z Ges Neurol Psychiatr* **9**:585, 1914.
2. Schottstaedt WW, Grace WJ, Wolff HG: Life situations, behavior, attitudes, emotions and renal excretion of fluid and electrolytes: I–V. *J Psychosom Res* **1**:75, 147, 203, 287, 292, 1956.
3. Woodbury DM, Esplin DW: Neuropharmacology and neurochemistry of anti-convulsant drugs. *Res Pub Assoc Nerv Ment Dis* **37**:24, 1959.
4. Katz B: *Nerve, Muscle and Synapse.* London, McGraw-Hill, 1966.
5. Klein R: Clinical and biochemical investigations in a manic-depressive with short cycles. *J Ment Sci* **96**:293, 1950.
6. Rowntree DW, Kay WW: Clinical, biochemical and physiological studies in cases of recurrent schizophrenia. *J Ment Sci* **98**:100, 1952.
7. Ström-Olsen R, Weil-Malherbe H: Humoral changes in manic-depressive psychosis with particular reference to the excretion of catecholamines in urine. *J Ment Sci* **104**:696, 1958.
8. Trolle C: Studies of water excretion in recovery from manic-depressive psychosis (depressive phase). *Acta Psychiatr Kbh* **20**:235, 1945.
9. Gjessing R: Beitrage sur somatologie der periodischen katatonie: VII. *Arch Psychiatr Nervenkr* **191**:247, 1953.
10. Crammer JL: Rapid weight-changes in mental patients. *Lancet* **2**:259, 1957.
11. Crammer JL: Water and sodium in two psychotics. *Lancet* **1**:1122, 1959.
12. Russell GFM: Body weight and balance of water, sodium and potassium in depressed patients given electroconvulsive therapy. *Clin Sci* **19**:327, 1960.
13. Coppen A: Mineral metabolism in affective disorders. *Br J Psychiatr* **111**:1133, 1965.
14. Veall N, Vetter H: *Radio-Isotope Techniques in Clinical Research and Diagnosis.* London, Butterworths, 1958.
15. Gibbons JL: Total body sodium and potassium in depressive illness. *Clin Sci* **19**:133, 1960.
16. Coppen A, Shaw DM, Mangoni A: Total exchangeable sodium in depressive illness. *Br Med J* **2**:295, 1962.
17. Coppen A, Shaw DM: Mineral metabolism in melancholia. *Br Med J* **2**:1439, 1963.
18. Altschule MD, Tillotson KJ: Effects of electroconvulsive therapy on water metabolism in psychotic patients. *Am J Psychiatr* **105**:829, 1949.
19. Dawson J, Hullin RP, Crocket BM: Metabolic variations in manic depressive psychosis. *J Ment Sci* **102**:168, 1956.
20. Shagass C, Schwartz M: Somatosensory cerebral evoked responses in psychotic depression. *Br J Psychiatr* **111**:799, 1966.

21. Baer L, Durell J, Bunney WE, and others: Sodium-22 retention and 17-hydroxy-corticosteroid excretion in affective disorders: A preliminary report. *J Psychiatr Res* **6**:289, 1969.
22. Coppen A: Abnormality of the blood-cerebrospinal-fluid barrier of patients suffering from a depressive illness. *J Neurol Neurosurg Psychiatr* **23**:156, 1960.
23. Fotherby K, Ashcroft GW, Affleck JW, and others: Studies on sodium transfer and 5-hydroxy indoles in depressive illness. *J Neurol Neurosurg Psychiatr* **26**:71, 1962.
24. Murphy DL, Goodwin FK, Bunney WE Jr: Aldosterone and sodium response to lithium administration in man. *Lancet* **2**:458, 1969.
25. Maas JW: Adrenocortical steroid hormones, electrolytes and the disposition of the catecholamine with particular reference to depressive states. *J Psychiatr Res* **9**:227, 1972.
26. Shaw DM, Coppen A: Potassium and water distribution in depression. *Br J Psychiatr* **112**:269, 1966.
27. Bunney WE, Murphy DL: Cited by Durell J, Baer L, Green R: Electrolytes and psychoses, in *Biochemistry, Schizophrenias and Affective Illnesses.* Edited by Himwich HE, Baltimore, Williams & Wilkins Co, 1970.
28. Shaw DM, Frizel D, Camps FE, and others: Brain electrolytes in depressive and alcoholic suicides. *Br J Psychiatr* **115**:69, 1969.
29. Brink F: Role of calcium ions in neural processes. *Pharmacol Rev* **6**:234, 1954.
30. Harris WH, Beauchemin JA: Cerebrospinal fluid calcium, magnesium and their ratio in psychosis of organic and functional origin. *Yale J Biol Med* **29**:117, 1959.
31. Eiduson S, Brill NO, Crumpton E: The effect of electro-convulsive therapy on spinal fluid constituents. *J Ment Sci* **106**:692, 1960.
32. Gour KN, Chaudhry NM: Study of calcium metabolism in electroconvulsive therapy (E.C.T.) in certain mental diseases. *J Ment Sci* **103**:275, 1957.
33. Coirault R, Desclos-de-la-Fonchais S, Ramel R, and others: Les variations du calcium sanguin ionisé et du calcium urinaire 24 heures au cours de la sismotherapie et des traitments chimiotherapiques à action anxiolytique. (Imipramine et Nialamid) *Med Exper* **1**:178, 1959.
34. Flach FF, Liang E, Stokes PE: The effects of electric convulsive treatments on nitrogen, calcium, and phosphórus metabolism in psychiatric patients. *J Ment Sci* **106**:638, 1960.
35. Flach FF: Calcium metabolism in states of depression. *Br J Psychiatr* **110**:588, 1964.
36. Faragalla FF, Flach FF: Studies in mineral metabolism in mental depression: II. The effects of imipramine and electric convulsive therapy on calcium balance and kinetics. *J Nerv Ment Dis* **151**:120, 1970.
37. Faragalla FF, Flach FF: Calcium metabolism in emotional depression. *Proc Am Psychiatr Assoc* **125**:18, 1969.
38. Douglas WW, Rubin RP:The mechanism of catecholamine release from the adrenal medulla and the role of calcium in stimulus-secretion coupling. *J Physiol* (London) **167**:288, 1963.
39. Flach FF, Faragalla FF: Studies in mineral metabolism in mental depression: I. The effects of Imipramine and electric convulsive therapy on the excretion of various urinary metabolites in depressed patients. *Br J Psychiatr* **116**:438, 1970.
40. Cade JFL: A significant elevation of plasma magnesium levels in schizophrenia and depressive states. *Med J Aust* **1**:195, 1964.
41. Frizel D, Coppen A, Marks V: Plasma magnesium and calcium. *Br J Psychiatr* **115**:1375, 1969.

Twenty

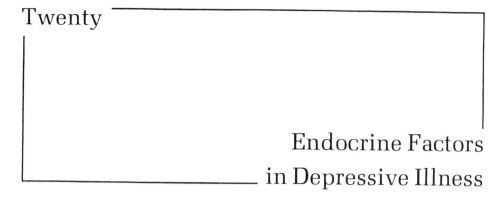

Endocrine Factors in Depressive Illness

Edward J. Sachar, M.D.

The interrelationship between depressive states and hormonal disturbance is complex. Many endocrine illnesses are associated with symptom syndromes very similar to the endogenous depressions, while many endogenous depressive illnesses also appear to be associated with abnormalities in neuroendocrine function. Investigation of the brain mechanisms involved in these psychoendocrine associations may further the understanding of the nature of psychobiological dysfunction in the depressive illnesses.

Depressive States Associated with Endocrinopathies

For the psychobiologist there are special problems in evaluating reports of depressions occurring in association with endocrine disease. Before concluding that a depressive illness has been specifically induced by hormonal influences on the central nervous system, other factors must be considered: *(a)* Is the psychobiological state a true depressive syndrome, or an appropriate affective response to being ill? *(b)* Are such symptoms as fatigue, anorexia, weakness, and malaise part of a depressive syndrome, or are they primarily symptoms of somatic debilitation? *(c)* If the patient is experiencing a depressive syndrome, is it primarily produced by hormonal effects on brain, or is it a secondary effect of electrolyte imbalance or other metabolic disturbances associated with the endocrinopathy; or is it a depression brought on by the nonspecific stress of illness in a person prone to affective disorder? *(d)* Can depression be induced in a nonendocrine patient by exogenous administration of the hormone, for example, for therapy?

To answer these questions properly, psychiatric studies of endocrine patients should be conducted with the same rigorous standards that have been brought to recent psychopharmacological research. These should include: *(a)* comprehensive standardized psychiatric assessment scales; *(b)* control groups matched for age, severity of illness, and other relevant factors; *(c)* careful description of associated medical complications; *(d)* assessment of previous psychiatric history; and *(e)* follow-up evaluation of the effects of correcting the hormonal disturbance.

Unfortunately, with very few exceptions, the older literature describing psychiatric complications of endocrine disorders is deficient in many of these areas, and most of the earlier observations should now be replicated with improved techniques and designs.

Even with these qualifications, however, it appears certain that a markedly increased incidence of significant depressive syndromes, very similar to the naturally occurring psychiatric conditions, is associated with several endocrinopathies, especially Cushing's syndrome, hyperparathyroidism, and during the premenstrual phase of the female cycle (1–3). In addition, depressive states are very common in Addison's disease and hypothyroidism (1–5), although in both conditions it is harder to separate the affective features from the somatic debilitation and from organic mental syndromes. In all these diseases, of course, many psychiatric disturbances are noted besides depression, and sometimes several types of psychopathology may be mixed or may succeed each other.

In hyperparathyroidism the mental changes are not directly hormonally induced. They are directly correlated with the degree of hypercalcemia, while parathyroid hormone itself has no effect (6). Between calcium concentrations of 10 and 15 mg%, depressive symptoms are primarily seen, and above 15 mg% symptoms of organic mental disturbance with paranoid trends become increasingly prominent (6). Renal dialysis immediately reverses the mental symptomatology while leaving the concentration of parathyroid hormone unchanged (6). It is interesting to speculate on the possible mechanism by which hypercalcemia can induce depressive states; Axelrod has recently reported that calcium ion promotes the discharge and depletion of noradrenalin and its biosynthetic enzyme, dopamine-beta-hydroxylase, from nerve granules (7).

Direct hormonal influences on brain do appear to be responsible for most of the depression seen in Cushing's syndrome. The symptoms range from depressive overreactions to stresses, to profound depressed mood with hopelessness, self-reproach, suicidal thoughts, and depressive delusions (2). Manic reactions also occur in Cushing's syndrome, although much less so than depression. They range from a sense of increased energy and stimulation to full manic syndromes with grandiose delusions, overactivity, and inappropriate impulsivity.

Corticosteroid therapy is associated with much the same range of mental disturbances—but in contrast to Cushing's syndrome, hypomanic and manic responses are, curiously, much more common than depression (8). In trying to account for the differences, it is worth keeping in mind that Cushing's syndrome includes three different hormonal conditions. In about one-fourth of the cases, there is a corticosteroid secreting tumor of the adrenal cortex, with secondary suppression of ACTH. In other cases there is a pituitary tumor, with hypersecretion of both ACTH and corticosteroids. In chronic hypothalamic Cushing's disease, however, corticosteroids are hypersecreted, but ACTH secretion is normal. In all of these conditions a variety of adrenal steroids are hypersecreted. In exogenous steroid therapy, however, one administers a specific synthetic steroid, which suppresses endogenous ACTH secretion as well as secretion of endogenous corticosteroids. One must consider, then, the possibility that ACTH itself may be psychoactive, which may account for the greater incidence of depression, and lesser incidence of mania in Cushing's syndrome than in steroid therapy; indeed, ACTH does have effects on operant behavior in rats, which are due to direct action on the brain and independent of its endocrine properties (9). One also must consider the possibility that different adrenal corticosteroids may have differing effects on brain (as has already been shown for cortisol and desoxycorticosterone); they may vary, then, in their "depressogenic" properties.

What effects do alterations in ACTH and corticosteroid secretion have on brain that might account for the affective psychopathology? The myriad effects of these hormones on a variety of neurochemical, metabolic, and neurophysiological systems have recently been reviewed (10). Of possible special relevance are effects on brain catecholamine and serotonin metabolism.

Cortisol has been shown to increase the reuptake of NA by rat brain tissue (11); presumably this would increase the catabolism of NA by mitochondrial monoamine oxidase, and eventually lead to its functional depletion. However, *chronic* administration of cortisol does not apparently deplete rat brains of total NA or serotonin content, nor does adrenalectomy (10). Cortisol does appear to prevent the increase in brain serotonin associated with tryptophan loads (10).

There also are effects of both ACTH and cortisol on the enzymes involved in the synthesis of catecholamines (CA) and indoleamines. Regarding the enzymes involved in serotonin synthesis, adrenalectomy decreases tryptophan hydroxylase activity and synthesis in the rat brain; this activity is partly restored by corticosteroids (12). Regarding enzymes involved in CA synthesis, hypophysectomy decreases both dopamine-beta-hydroxylase and tyrosine hydroxylase activity in the adrenal medulla; corticosteroids do not restore this activity, but ACTH does, indicating a specific role of ACTH in CA metabolism (13). Cortisol induces PNMT activity in the adrenal medulla, thus promoting the synthesis of adrenalin from NA; the enzyme has been recently found in brain, its significance unknown. In sum, however, there are no reports suggesting dramatic effects of corticosteroids or ACTH on biogenic amine metabolism (10), but the papers in this area are relatively few, and many do not use the recently developed sophisticated techniques for studying turnover rates.

The premenstrual depressions represent another fascinating area for psychoendocrine study. One does not ordinarily consider the menstrual cycle an endocrine disorder, of course, but the fact remains that for many women it is associated with considerable psychological and somatic disability, and in this sense at least, premenstrual tension can be regarded as the most common of endocrinological ailments. Several recent careful studies of normal women (14, 15) have confirmed that the psychological state tends to fluctuate with the cycle, with feelings of well-being reaching a high, and dysphoric affect a low, at the time of ovulation in midcycle. From then until the menses, dysphoric affect, particularly depression, increases, reaching its height in the immediate premenstrual phase. For a small but significant subgroup of women, the depressive experience, although transient, reaches clinical proportions. Moos and his colleagues (16) have identified several types of syndromes within the group, and it is noteworthy that the depressive experience can be separated from the discomfort of distention and bloating associated with fluid retention. Rees has also shown that diuretic treatment of the fluid problem is not effective in relieving the depressive elements of the syndrome (17). However, others have recently suggested that renin, angiotensin, and aldosterone may be involved (18).

Is hormonal regulation in the women who are subject to premenstrual depression in any way abnormal? Research on this point is ongoing, but so far there is no clear evidence for it. Can the syndrome be reproduced by administration of sex hormones? Again, the answer is yes—depression is a significant complication of oral contraceptive treatment (15, 19).

The premenstrual aspect of the disturbance would suggest that progesterone might be a "depressogenic" hormone, although there is no evidence yet that mood changes correlate closely with changes in plasma progesterone concentrations. Several reports of the psychological effects of oral contraceptives have seemed to implicate progesterone. Grant and Pryse-Davies (19) showed that the contraceptives with a high progestogen to estrogen ratio were more likely to induce depression. Comparison of the psychological effects of fixed combination versus sequential contraceptives has shown that the sequential type, in which estrogens are replaced by progestogen in the latter part of the month, reproduces the U-shaped curve of dysphoric affect seen in the normal cycle, while the combination type obliterates the curve (15). It should be noted, however, that synthetic progestogens differ significantly in their biological actions from endogenous progesterone, and in some respects are more like androgens.

How might estrogens and progesterone affect the brain to produce psychological effects? There are a few reports suggesting influences on catecholaminergic and serotoninergic systems. Grant and Pryse-Davies reported an increase in uterine MAO activity associated with the progestational phase of the cycle, and correlated such increases associated with oral contraceptives to their progestogen content (19). If similar changes occur in the brain, the effect could be to deplete the brain of monoamines by increasing catabolism. Estrogens also have an effect on brain catecholamines. Their administration decreases catecholamine turnover in the hypothalamus, while ovarectomy increases CA turnover; these changes are probably related to the role of catecholamines in regulating secretion of LH-releasing factor (20).

Finally, a few comments on depression in hypothyroidism. Lethargy, apathy, and depressed mood are part of the typical picture of hypothyroidism. In an exceptional study, involving the use of comprehensive psychiatric rating scales and psychological testing, Whybrow and others (5) demonstrated the presence of not only organic intellectual impairment of varying degree in all cases of myxedema, but also significant depressive syndromes. The depressions seemed to be more than an affective response to illness and to impaired mental functioning. (There was, however, no control group of patients with organic mental syndrome from other causes.) Thyroid hormone corrected the affective state and improved the cognitive impairment, but some residual organic deficit was noted.

In terms of effects on neurochemical systems possibly relevant to depression, hypothyroidism appears to desensitize receptors to catecholamines (21). In hypothyroid animals there is a concomitant marked increase in brain catecholamine turnover (23) which is consistent with the theory that receptor insensitivity leads to a compensatory increase in discharge and synthesis. Conversely, administration of excessive thyroid hormone decreases brain catecholamine turnover. It may be relevant that, while thyroid hormone of itself does not alleviate endogenous depressions, small doses of triiodothyronine do potentiate the therapeutic effectiveness of antidepressant drugs. It is not known whether this effect is central, or whether it is mediated by altering drug metabolism or transport. The hypothalamic hormone thyrotropin releasing hormone (TRH) also appears, of itself, to exert a moderate, transient antidepressant action in depressed patients (24). (These observations are discussed more fully below.)

There is clinical evidence, then, that certain hormones possess significant psychotropic properties in man. Moreover, it appears that alterations in the exposure of the brain to these hormones, through endocrine disease or exogenous administration, can produce psychopathological states which closely resemble the depressive illnesses, and in the instance of corticosteroids, mania as well. However, the clinical phenomena and their correlations with endocrine dysfunction need to be reevaluated and reconsidered by more modern techniques and more sophisticated experimental designs. Furthermore, there is evidence that these hormones may influence the same neurochemical systems which are currently believed to play a role in the naturally occurring psychoses, and which are under intense scrutiny by psychopharmacologists. It would seem, then, that this area is a prime one for a major psychobiological research effort, offering real promise for the integration of psychopharmacological and psychoendocrine investigations.

Altered Endocrine Function in Primary Affective Disorders

An important aspect of the depressive syndrome is a group of symptoms which strongly suggest disturbances in hypothalamic and limbic system functions: decreased appetite, autonomic dysfunction (dry mouth, constipation, sweating), decreased libido, decreased aggressive drive, sleep disturbance, and diurnal variation in symptom intensity.

Neuroendocrine regulation is another major hypothalamic function, and if the hypothalamus is involved in the pathophysiology of depression, it would not be surprising to find evidence of hormonal disturbance in depressive illness.

Furthermore, there is considerable evidence that brain biogenic amines play an important role in modulating secretion of the hypothalamic releasing hormones which regulate anterior pituitary function. If there are abnormalities in brain monoamine metabolism in affective disorders as has been hypothesized, they might well be reflected in neuroendocrine changes.

It is not yet possible to measure in plasma directly the hypothalamic hormones themselves, although many have been isolated and several have been purified. Their secretory rate may be estimated, however, by measuring the secretion of their target pituitary hormones; recent advances in radioimmunoassay techniques have made it possible to measure nearly all the pituitary hormones in small amounts of serum or plasma. ACTH secretion is regulated by corticotropin releasing hormone (CRH), growth hormone (GH), by a growth hormone releasing factor (GHRF), and by a growth hormone inhibiting factor (somatostatin), prolactin by prolactin inhibiting factor (PIF), thyrotropin by thyrotropin releasing hormone (TRH), and luteinizing hormone (LH) by luteinizing hormone releasing factor (LHRF). We briefly review some of the studies of these hormones in affective disorders.

ACTH and Cortisol

Because plasma ACTH has been difficult to assay, nearly all studies in depressed patients have been of cortisol secretion. Indeed, cortisol has been the most extensively studied of all hormone systems in affective disorders, with scores of reports over the past two decades from research centers throughout the world, and discussions in numerous review papers (25–30). Yet the data have been rather contradictory and hard to interpret. In part, this is because of differences in endocrine assessment techniques, ranging from measurements of single samples of plasma cortisol, to 24-hour urinary excretion of 17-hydroxy corticosteroids, to measurement of cortisol production rate by isotope dilution techniques, to studies of the detailed 24-hour pattern of plasma cortisol concentration.

It has been established, however, that a subgroup of depressed patients are hypersecretors of cortisol, but the clinical characteristics of this subgroup remain unclear. A major problem in interpretation is the fact that emotional distress typically is associated with increased ACTH and cortisol secretion in animals and man (31), and it is often difficult to tell how much of the increased cortisol production in depressed patients is due to nonspecific stress factors, such as the anxiety associated with hospital admission, or with being ill (26, 32). Even after patients have adapted to hospitalization, however, some continue to manifest increased cortisol production well beyond the range usually seen in normals responding to stress. The cortisol elevations are of the same magnitude as those seen in nondepressed psychotic patients during periods of severe emotional turmoil (30, 33, 34).

The hypersecreting depressed patients generally come from the group rated clinically severely ill; but many severely ill depressed patients are not hypersecretors. The specific clinical characteristics which appear most closely to correlate with increased cortisol production are active suicidal impulses (35), severe anxiety (36), and acute psychotic decompensation with or without depressive stupor (33). Apathetic depressed patients without these features generally do not have marked hypersecretion (36), although there are significant exceptions. After treatment and clinical recovery, cortisol secretion returns toward normal.

There have also been numerous studies of possible disturbances in the 24-hour pattern of plasma cortisol secretion in depressed patients (which also have been reviewed elsewhere) (26, 29, 37). Most of these studies were conducted, however, before the complex nature of the normal 24-hour secretory pattern had been demonstrated, and the earlier data, based on infrequent blood sampling, now are seen to have limited validity. (Nevertheless, elevated evening plasma cortisol concentrations were rather consistently noted.)

Normally, cortisol (and, it appears, ACTH) is secreted episodically in a series of bursts throughout the day, synchronized with the sleep-wake cycle, rather than in a smooth continuous outflow, and a sampling schedule of at least every 20 minutes (through a cannula) is required to outline the pattern adequately (38). In the normal subject who sleeps from midnight to 8 *A.M.* and who spends the day relatively isolated, cortisol secretion virtually ceases for the six hours between 8 *P.M.* and 2 *A.M.* Subsequently there occurs a series of seven to nine short secretory episodes, the largest occurring between 5 and 9 *A.M.* The timing of the daytime secretory bursts may be partially influenced by meals and activity, as well as, of course, episodes of anxiety (39).

One recent study of six hypersecreting depressed patients which involved sampling every 20 minutes around the clock demonstrated significant disturbances in the 24-hour cortisol patterns (37). Throughout both day and night, plasma cortisol concentration was markedly elevated both at the beginning and end of secretory episodes, and cortisol was actively secreted in the late evening and early morning hours, when normally secretion is minimal. Compared to normals, the patients while ill had more secretory episodes, more cortisol secreted per episode, more time spent in active secretion, and more cortisol secreted per minutes of active secretion. After treatment the secretory pattern returned to normal, especially in patients making complete clinical recoveries. Biological half-life of cortisol in plasma remained relatively constant and normal throughout.

The cortisol hypersecretion during some depressive illnesses almost certainly reflects hypersecretion of ACTH, and therefore, in all probability, hyperactivity of the hypothalamic neuroendocrine centers secreting CRH. The question remains whether this disturbed pattern of secretion is a nonspecific response to emotional distress, or whether both the emotional distress and neuroendocrine disturbance reflect central limbic system dysfunction in depressive illness (25). The fact that in the 24-hour study cited the cortisol elevations were not confined to the waking hours, but extended through sleep periods as well, suggests that the hypersecretion is not exclusively a function of waking, consciously experienced anxiety. Furthermore, as mentioned previously, some apparently apathetic, unanxious patients also hypersecrete cortisol. It appears doubtful, then, that all hyperadrenalcorticism in depressed patients can be related to the stress response alone.

Evidence for a dysfunction of the normal inhibitory neuroendocrine mechanisms in depressive illness can be seen in reports that some depressed patients fail to manifest suppression of cortisol secretion following dexamethasone administration (40, 41). Dexamethasone is a potent synthetic corticosteroid which normally suppresses endogenous ACTH secretion, presumably by acting on CNS receptors which are involved in feedback regulation of CRH release. However, in two other investigations, all depressed patients showed normal cortisol suppression after dexamethasone (30, 42). The apparent discrepancies in these findings may be due to the infrequent sampling of plasma cortisol in all these studies, with consequent inadequate assessment of the impact of dexamethasone on the secretory pattern. An evaluation of the effects of dexamethasone on the detailed 24-hour secretory pattern of cortisol in depressed patients would be useful.

Cortisol secretion in mania has also been studied intensively, but the findings are confusing. In some reports, but not all, cortisol secretion was greater during depressive than manic periods in the same patients (43). Furthermore, it has been reported that corticosteroid excretion is generally less in bipolar depression than in unipolar depression of comparable severity (44). Hypomania in one group of patients was not associated with increased cortisol production when compared to recovery periods in the same subjects (43). During a subsequent period of acute mania, however, one of these same patients manifested marked hypersecretion of cortisol with a 24-hour secretory pattern very similar to that seen in hypersecreting depressed patients (45). These endocrine inconsistencies in the same patients underscore the difficulty of developing a unified neuroendocrine theory of depression and mania at this time, and emphasize the problem of separating the hormonal effects of arousal from those of affective illness per se.

The role of brain biogenic amines in regulation of CRH, ACTH, and cortisol secretion is obviously highly relevant, but the nature of this regulation is still obscure. The hypothalamic regulation of the circadian cortisol secretory pattern, of the adrenocortical response to stress, and of "baseline" cortisol secretion may be mediated by different neurotransmitters. Furthermore, a given neurotransmitter may have different neuroendocrine actions in different parts of the limbic system. In addition, some neuropharmacologic agents exert actions acutely which are not sustained after chronic administration. There also appear to be differences between animal and human responses. The current status of research in this complex area has recently been reviewed (46, 47).

Suffice it to say here that there is good evidence that a brain noradrenergic system normally inhibits tonically the secretion of ACTH and cortisol, and that pharmacologic depletion of brain noradrenalin is associated with a marked increase in ACTH and cortisol secretion (47). It is also clear, however, that this noradrenergic system is not the only brain regulator of CRH and ACTH secretion; serotonin and acetylcholine also play a role, and in some specific areas of the brain, noradrenalin implants appear to stimulate ACTH secretion. Nevertheless, it is conceivable that the hypothesized functional depletion of noradrenalin in depression could involve the inhibitory system for CRH, resulting in the hypersecretion of cortisol seen in many depressed patients.

Thyroid

Those indices of thyroid function which have been studied in depressed patients have revealed no significant abnormalities. In one investigation, plasma concentration of PBI and triiodothyronine (T3) and the thyroid uptake of radioactive iodine were within normal limits, and did not change after recovery (48). Ankle reflex time was similarly within normal limits, although patients with faster ankle reflex times tended to respond better to imipramine.

On the other hand, as described before, T3 has been shown in several studies to potentiate the antidepressant action of imipramine and amitriptyline in depressed women (49, 50), although it is not known whether this effect is due to an effect of T3 on the CNS. Two recent reports have indicated that TRH (thyrotropin releasing hormone) administered in a single intravenous dose temporarily alleviates depressive symptomatology in unipolar depressed patients (24, 51). The mechanism of this action of TRH in depression is completely obscure, although it is probably a direct effect of TRH on the brain. It is not yet known whether TRH is effective as a clinical treatment; similar transient clinical improvement can be produced, for example, by dextroamphetamine in some depressed patients (52). There is also some very preliminary evidence that the pituitary TSH response to TRH may be blunted in depressed patients compared to normals.

A critical question would seem to be the endogenous secretion of TRH in depressed patients; this problem will have to await a radioimmunoassay for plasma TRH. TRH release is regulated by brain catecholamines; NE stimulates TRH release from hypothalamic tissue *in vitro* and *in vivo,* while NE depletion inhibits TRH secretion (53).

Growth Hormone

In the adult, GH release physiologically occurs in response to a falling blood sugar, certain amino acids, exercise, stress, and during slow wave sleep (54). The neurotransmitter regulation of these various responses is unclear, except for the hypoglycemic response, for which there is good evidence for catecholamine mediation. Both reserpine and phentolamine inhibit the GH response to hypoglycemia in man.

Pharmacological manipulations of brain catecholaminergic activity will affect GH secretion (54). Thus L-dopa administration will stimulate GH secretion in man, a response which is inhibited by phentolamine. Amphetamine also stimulates GH secretion. In baboons, norepinephrine infused intraventricularly or into the ventromedial nucleus of the hypothalamus produces a GH response. Parenteral administration of apomorphine in man also stimulates GH secretion.

It can be seen, then, that catecholamine systems are involved in GH secretion, and particularly in the responses to hypoglycemia and L-dopa. However, whether these latter responses are mediated by dopamine, noradrenalin, or both is not yet determined.

At any rate, it is obviously relevant to study GH responses in depressed patients. Four recent reports indicate diminished GH responses to hypoglycemia in unipolar depressed patients, as compared to age-matched normal subjects (55–58); these data support the hypothesis that hypothalamic catecholaminergic activity is diminished in unipolar depressive illness. However, the GH responses, in general, do not change following clinical recovery from depression. This may indicate an enduring neurochemical defect associated with vulnerability to affective illness (or, of course, some artifactual variable which has no relation to depression).

Studies of GH response to L-dopa ingestion initially seemed also to indicate diminished responses in unipolar depressed patients, compared to age-matched normal controls. However, subsequent studies have shown that the GH response to L-dopa declines not only with age, but also with the female menopause; when postmenopausal depressed and normal women are compared, differences are no longer apparent in the GH responses to L-dopa (59). On the other hand, in response to hypoglycemia, unipolar depressed postmenopausal women do have significantly diminished GH responses compared to normal postmenopausal women (59). One might speculate that the L-dopa and hypoglycemic GH responses are mediated by different catecholamine pathways, the former perhaps dopaminergic, the latter perhaps noradrenergic; alternatively, one might see the hypoglycemic response as calling on endogenous brain catecholamines, while the L-dopa response involves conversion of exogenous catecholamine precursor.

Systematic studies of the GH responses during sleep or during arginine infusion in depressed patients have yet to be reported. These data would be of considerable interest, since these responses appear to be mediated by noncatecholaminergic systems (54).

Prolactin

Prolactin secretion typically increases in man in response to stress, in association with sleep and nursing, and after estrogen administration (60). Prolactin secretion is regulated by PIF, prolactin inhibiting factor, which in turn is responsive to brain dopamine activity (61). Thus chlorpromazine, which blocks dopamine receptors, stimulates prolactin secretion, presumably due to a fall in PIF secretion (62). L-dopa, on the other hand, suppresses prolactin secretion, presumably by increasing brain dopamine and stimulating PIF secretion (62). Intraventricular dopamine similarly suppresses prolactin secretion (61).

In one series of normals, unipolar, and bipolar depressed patients, baseline prolactin concentrations were found to be somewhat higher in the depressed patients (58); this may reflect the increased emotional stress in the depressed patients. However, nearly all subjects, both normal and depressed, showed normal prolactin suppression in response to L-dopa. There is, then, no evidence as yet that prolactin responses are abnormal in affective disorders, but this is an area that has just opened for research.

Sex Hormones

The decreased libido characteristic of depressive illness has led to speculation that sex hormones may be affected in depression. Occasionally, depressive illness is associated with amenorrhea, although this is not common. The release of LH (which stimulates testosterone and estrogen secretion) appears to be influenced by brain catecholamines, but the manner in which this occurs appears quite complex, and no consistent formulation can be derived from the literature at this time (63–66). LH secretion normally increases after gonadectomy, which eliminates the feedback inhibition by estrogens; blockade of brain catecholamine synthesis inhibits this LH response to gonadectomy in animals (67).

There is as yet no substantial body of evidence that sex hormones are secreted abnormally in depressive illness. One study reported no change in plasma LH concentration from illness to recovery in postmenopausal depressed women (68). In another study, plasma and urinary testosterone levels were within normal limits in a group of depressed middle-aged and elderly men, and there was no change in levels after recovery (69). This was true even of the men who manifested considerable emotional distress and increased cortisol production during illness, which is somewhat surprising since both monkeys and normal young men under stress, who manifest increased corticosteroid output, typically show reduced plasma and urinary testosterone (70, 71).

LH secretion normally increases dramatically after menopause in women, probably because estradiol, which normally inhibits LH secretion, is no longer secreted in any significant amount. This postmenopausal LH response is analagous, then, to the LH response to gonadectomy, which is catecholamine regulated. In a recent study comparing plasma LH concentrations in unipolar primary depressed postmenopausal women and normal postmenopausal women, it was found that plasma LH in the depressed group was significantly less than in the normal group (59). If replicated on a larger sample, these data could be consistent with the hypothesis of diminished hypothalamic catecholamine reserves in women prone to depressive illness.

In summary, then, neuroendocrine function in patients with affective disorders does appear to be abnormal in several areas. The strongest evidence is for disturbances in the regulation of ACTH and growth hormone secretion, and possibly in LH responses as well. These abnormalities are consistent with recent hypotheses about altered brain biogenic amine activity in the affective disorders, but only future research will provide the necessary documentation for the specificity to depressive illness of these hormonal disturbances, and further clarification of the underlying brain mechanisms.

References

1. Michael RP, Gibbons JL: Interrelationships between the endocrine system and neuropsychiatry, in *International Review of Neurobiology.* Edited by Pfeiffer CC, Smythies JR, New York, Academic Press, 1963, Vol. 54.
2. Smith CK, Barish J, Correa J, Williams RH: Psychiatric disturbance in endocrinologic disease. *Psa Med* **34**:69–86, 1972.
3. Sachar EJ: Psychiatric disturbances associated with endocrine disorders, in *American Handbook of Psychiatry.* Edited by Reiser M, New York, Basic Books, in press, Vol. 4.
4. Cleghorn RA: Psychological changes in Addison's disease. *J Clin Endocrinol* **13**:1291–1293, 1953.
5. Whybrow PC, Prange AJ, Treadway CR: Mental changes accompanying thyroid gland dysfunction. *Arch Gen Psychiatr* **20**:48–63, 1969.
6. Pederson KO: Hypercalcemia in Addison's disease. *Acta Med Scand* **181**:691, 1967.

7. Axelrod J: Brain monoamines and endocrine function. Presented to Fourth International Congress of Endocrinology. Washington, DC, June 20, 1972.
8. Nelson JB, Drivsholm A, Fischer F, Brochner-Mortensen K: Long term treatment with corticosteroids in rheumatoid arthritis. *Acta Med Scand* **173:**177–183, 1963.
9. De Wied D, Witter A, Lande S: Anterior pituitary peptides and avoidance acquisition of hypophysectomized rats, in *Progress in Brain Research.* Edited by De Wied D, Weijnen JAWM, Amsterdam, Elsevier Press, 1969, Vol. 32, pp. 213–220.
10. Woodbury DM: Biochemical effects of adrenocortical steroids on the central nervous system, in *Handbook of Neurochemistry.* Edited by Lajtha A, New York, Plenum Press, 1972, Vol. 7. .
11. Maas JW: Adrenocortical steroid hormones, electrolytes, and the disposition of the catecholamines with particular reference to depressive states. *J Psychiatr Res* **9:**227–241, 1972.
12. Azmitia EC, McEwen B: Corticosterone regulation of tryptophan hydroxylase in midbrain of rat. *Science* **166:**1274–1276, 1969.
13. Weinshilbaum R, Axelrod J: Dopamine beta hydroxylase activity in the rat after hypophysectomy. *Endocrinology* **87:**894, 1970.
14. Moos R, Kopell B, Melges F, Yalom I, Lunde R, Hamburg D: Fluctuations in symptoms and moods during the menstrual cycle. *J Psychosom Res* **13:**37–44, 1969.
15. Paige KE: Effects of oral contraceptives on affective fluctuations associated with the menstrual cycle. *Psychosom Med* **33:**515–537, 1972.
16. Moos R: Typology of menstrual cycle syndrome. *Am J Obstet Gynecol* **103:**390–402, 1969.
17. Rees L: The premenstrual tension syndrome and its treatment. *Br Med J* **1:**1014–1016, 1953.
18. Janowsky DS, Berens SC, Davis JM: Correlations between mood, weight, and electrolytes during the menstrual cycle: A renin-angiotensin-aldosterone hypothesis of premenstrual tension. *Psychosom Med* **35:**143–154, 1973.
19. Grant C, Pryse-Davies J: Effects of oral contraceptives on depressive mood changes and on endometrial monoamine oxidase and phosphates. *Br Med J* **28:**777–780, 1968.
20. Coppola JA: Brain catecholamines and gonadotropin secretion, in *Frontiers in Neuroendocrinology.* Edited by Martini L, Ganong WF, New York, Oxford University Press, 1971, pp. 129–143.
21. Waldstein SS: Thyroid catecholamine interrelationships. *Ann Rev Med* **17:**123–132, 1966.
22. Lipton M, Prange A, Dairman W, Udenfriend S: Increased rate of noradrenalin biosynthesis in hypothyroid rats. *Fed Proc* **27:**399, 1968.
23. Prange A, Meek J, Lipton M: Catecholamines: Diminished rate of synthesis in rat brain and heart after thyroxine pretreatment. *Life Sci* **9:**901–907, 1970.
24. Prange A, Wilson I, Lara P, Alltop L, Breese GR: Effects of thyrotrophin releasing hormone in depression. *Lancet* **1:**999–1002, 1972.
25. Rubin RT, Mandell AJ: Adrenal cortical activity in pathological emotional states. *Am J Psychiatr* **123:**387–400, 1966.
26. Sachar EJ: Corticosteroids in depressive illness: I. A reevaluation of control issues and the literature. *Arch Gen Psychiatr* **17:**544–553, 1967.
27. Fawcett JA, Bunney WE: Pituitary adrenal function and depression. *Arch Gen Psychiatr* **16:**517–535, 1967.
28. Gibbons JL: Steroid metabolism in schizophrenia, depression and mania, in *Biochemistry, Schizophrenia and Affective Illness.* Edited by Himwich HE, Baltimore, Williams & Wilkins Co, 1970, pp. 308–332.

29. Carroll BJ: Plasma cortisol levels in depression, in *Depressive Illness: Some Research Studies.* Edited by Davies B, Carroll BJ, Mowbray RM, Springfield, Charles C Thomas, 1972, pp. 69–86.
30. Carpenter WT, Bunney WE: Adrenal cortical activity in depressive illness. *Am J Psychiatr* **128**:31–40, 1971.
31. Mason J: A review of psychoendocrine research on the pituitary adrenal system. *Psychosom Med* **30**:576–607, 1968.
32. Sachar EJ: Corticosteroids in depressive illness: II. A longitudinal psychoendocrine study. *Arch Gen Psychiatr* **17**:554–567, 1967.
33. Bunney WE, Mason JM, Roatch J, Hamburg DA: A psychoendocrine study of severe psychotic depressive crises. *Am J Psychiatr* **122**:72–80, 1965.
34. Sachar EJ, Kanter S, Buie D, Engel R, Mehlman R: Psychoendocrinology of ego disintegration. *Am J Psychiatr* **126**:1067–1078, 1970.
35. Bunney WE, Fawcett JA, Davis JM, Gifford S: Further evaluation of urinary 17–hydroxycorticosteroids in suicidal patients. *Arch Gen Psychiatr* **21**:138–150, 1969.
36. Sachar EJ, Hellman L, Fukushima DK, Gallagher TF: Cortisol production in depressive illness. *Arch Gen Psychiatr* **23**:289–298, 1970.
37. Sachar EJ, Hellman L, Roffwarg HP, Halpern FS, Fukushima DK, Gallagher TF: Disrupted 24-hour patterns of cortisol secretion in psychotic depression. *Arch Gen Psychiatr* **28**:19–24, 1973.
38. Weitzman ED, Fukushima DK, Nogeire C, Roffwarg HP, Gallagher TF, Hellman L: Twenty-four hour pattern of the episodic secretion of cortisol in normal subjects. *J Clin Endocrinol Met* **33**:14–22, 1971.
39. Krieger DT, Allen W, Rizzo F, Krieger HP: Characterization of the normal temporal pattern of plasma corticosteroid levels. *J Clin Endocrinol Met* **32**:266–284, 1971.
40. Stokes PE: Studies on the control of adrenocortical function in depression, in *Recent Advances in the Psychobiology of Depressive Illnesses.* Edited by Williams TA, Katz MM, Shield JA, U.S. DHEW Publication 70–9053, 1972, pp. 199-220.
41. Carroll BJ: Control of plasma cortisol levels in depression: Studies with the dexamethasone suppression test, in *Depressive Illness: Some Research Studies.* Edited by Davies B, Carroll BJ, Mowbray RM, Springfield, Charles C Thomas, 1972, pp. 87–148.
42. Shopsin B, Gershon S: Plasma cortisol response to dexamethasone suppression in depressed and control patients. *Arch Gen Psychiatr* **24**:322–326.
43. Sachar EJ, Hellman L, Fukushima DK, Gallagher TF: Cortisol production in mania. *Arch Gen Psychiatr* **26**:137–139, 1972.
44. Dunner DL, Goodwin FK, Gershon ES, Murphy DL, Bunney WE: Excretion of 17-OHCS in unipolar and bipolar depressed patients. *Arch Gen Psychiatr* **26**:360–363, 1972.
45. Sachar EJ, Roffwarg HP, Gallagher TF, Hellman L: Twenty-four hour plasma cortisol pattern in an acutely manic patient. To be published.
46. Carroll BJ: The hypothalamic pituitary adrenal axis: Functions, control mechanisms and methods of study, in *Depressive Illness: Some Research Studies.* Edited by Davies B, Carroll BJ, Mowbray RM, Springfield, Charles C Thomas, 1972, pp. 23–68.
47. Van Loon GR: Brain catecholamines and ACTH secretion, in *Frontiers in Neuroendocrinology.* Edited by Ganong FW, Martini L, New York, Oxford University Press, 1973, pp. 209–247.
48. Whybrow PC, Coppen A, Prange AJ, Noguera R, Bailey JE: Thyroid function and the response to liothyronine in depression. *Arch Gen Psychiatr* **26**:242–245, 1972.

49. Whybrow PC, Noguera R, Maggs R, Prange AJ: Comparative antidepressant value of L-tryptophan and imipramine with and without attempted potentiation by liothyronine. *Arch Gen Psychiatr* **26**: 234–241, 1972.
50. Wheatley D: Potentiation of amitryptyline by thyroid hormone. *Arch Gen Psychiatr* **26**:229–233, 1972.
51. Kastin AJ, Ehrensing RH, Schalch DS, Anderson MS: Thyrotrophin releasing hormone in depression. *Lancet* **2**:740–742, 1972.
52. Fawcett J, Siomopoulos V: Dextroamphetamine response as a possible predictor of improvement with tricyclic therapy in depression. *Arch Gen Psychiatr* **25**:247–255, 1971.
53. Reichlin S: Hypothalamic pituitary function, in *Endocrinology.* Edited by Scow RO, New York, Elsevier, 1973, pp. 1–16.
54. Martin J: Neural regulation of growth hormone secretion. *NEJM* **288**:1384–1393, 1973.
55. Sachar EJ, Finkelstein J, Hellman L: Growth hormone responses in depressive illness: Response to insulin tolerance test. *Arch Gen Psychiatr* **24**:263–269, 1971.
56. Mueller PS, Heninger GR, McDonald PK: Studies on glucose utilization and insulin sensitivity in affective disorders, in *Recent Advances in the Psychobiology of the Depressive Illnesses.* Edited by Williams TA, Katz MM, Shield JA, U.S. DHEW Publication 70–9053, 1972, pp. 235–245.
57. Carroll BU: Studies with hypothalamic-pituitary-adrenal stimulation tests in depression, in *Depressive Illness: Some Research Studies.* Edited by Davies B, Carroll BJ, Mowbray RM, Springfield, Charles C Thomas, 1972, pp. 149–201.
58. Sachar EJ, Frantz AG, Altman N, Sassin J: Growth hormone and prolactin in unipolar and bipolar depressed patients: Responses to hypoglycemia and L-dopa. *Am J Psychiatr* **130**:1362–1367, 1973.
59. Sachar EJ, Altman N, Gruen P, Halpern FS, Sassin J: Plasma growth hormone and LH in postmenopausal depressed women. Presented to the American Psychosomatic Society, Philadelphia, Pa, March 30, 1974.
60. Frantz AG, Kleinberg DL, Noel GL: Studies on prolactin in man. *Rec Prog Horm Res* **28**:527–573, 1972.
61. Meites J, Lu KH, Wuttke W, and others: Recent studies on function and control of prolactin secretion in rats. *Rec Prog Horm Res* **28**:471–526, 1972.
62. Kleinberg DL, Noel GL, Frantz AG: Chlorpromazine stimulation and L-dopa suppression of plasma prolactin in man. *J Clin Endocrinol Met* **33**:873–876, 1971.
63. Kamberi IA: Biogenic amines and neurohumoral control of gonadotropin and prolactin secretion, in *Endocrinology.* Edited by Scow RO, New York, American Elsevier, 1973, pp. 112–119.
64. Kordon C: Effect of drugs acting on brain monoamines and the control of gonadotropin secretion. *Ibid.*, pp. 120–124.
65. Hokfelt T, Fuxe K, Ajika K, Lofstrom A: Central catecholamine neurons and gonadotropin secretion, in *Endocrinology.* Edited by Scow RO, New York, American Elsevier, 1973, pp. 138–143.
66. Lebovitz HE, Boyd AE, Feldman JM: Endocrine effects of dopamine and L-dopa. *Ibid.*, pp. 150–155.
67. Ojeda SR, McCann SM: Evidence for participation of a catecholaminergic mechanism in the post castration rise in plasma gonadotropins. *Neuroendocrinology* **12**:295–315, 1973.
68. Sachar EJ, Schalch DS, Reichlin S, Platman SS: Plasma gonadotropins in depressive illness: A preliminary report, in *Recent Advances in the Psychobiology of Depressive Illnesses.* Edited by Williams TA, Katz MM, Shield JA, U.S. DHEW Publication 70–9053, 1972, pp. 229–234.

69. Sachar EJ, Halpern FS, Rosenfeld RS, Gallagher TF, Hellman L: Plasma and urinary testosterone levels in depressed men. *Arch Gen Psychiatr* **28**:15–18, 1973.
70. Kreuz LE, Rose RM, Jennings JR: Suppression of plasma testosterone levels and psychological stress. *Arch Gen Psychiatr* **26**:479–482, 1972.
71. Rose RM, Bernstein IS, Holaday JW: Plasma testosterone, dominance rank, and aggressive behavior in a group of male rhesus monkeys. *Nature* **231**:366–368, 1971.

Author Index

Subject Index